TOPIC	AUTHOR	ABBREVIATED TITLE	KAL... (PAGES)	
Cooperative Learning	Johnson & Johnson	*Making Cooperative Learning Work*	194–201	5
Curriculum	Hirsch	*The Core Knowledge Curriculum*	143–147	5, 9
	Popham	*Curriculum Matters*	113–117	5, 7, 11, 12
	Glasser	*The Quality School Curriculum*	128–133	2, 5
	Nord	*The Relevance of Religion to the Curriculum*	138–142	5, 8, 12
	Peddiwell	*The Saber-Tooth Curriculum*	118–122	5
Diversity	Glenn	*The Challenge of Diversity and Choice*	322–327	3, 4, 5, 10, 12
Ethics of Teaching	Strike	*The Ethics of Teaching*	243–246	8, 9
Finance	Miles	*Putting Money Where It Matters*	290–294	11
Gender Issues	Gurian & Stevens	*With Boys and Girls in Mind*	342–347	3, 4, 8
Harassment	San Antonio & Salzfass	*How We Treat One Another in School*	42–47	3, 4, 8
Inclusion	Villa & Thousand	*Making Inclusive Education Work*	336–341	3
	Kauffman, McGee, and Brigham	*Enabling or Disabling?*	328–335	3
Instruction	Tomlinson	*Mapping a Route Toward Differentiated Instruction*	202–207	5
	Johnson & Johnson	*Making Cooperative Learning Work*	194–201	5
	Moran, Kornhaber, & Gardner	*Orchestrating Multiple Intelligences*	188–193	3
Law and the Teacher	McDaniel	*The Teacher's Ten Commandments*	247–257	8
Multicultural Education	Banks, et al.	*Diversity Within Unity*	315–321	3, 5, 10, 12
	Ravitch	*A Considered Opinion*	312–314	3, 5, 10, 12

Kaleidoscope

Kaleidoscope

Contemporary and Classic Readings in Education

KEVIN RYAN
Boston University

JAMES M. COOPER
University of Virginia

twelfth
EDITION

WADSWORTH
CENGAGE Learning

AUSTRALIA · BRAZIL · JAPAN · KOREA · MEXICO · SINGAPORE · SPAIN · UNITED KINGDOM · UNITED STATES

WADSWORTH
CENGAGE Learning™

Kaleidoscope

Contemporary and Classic Readings in Education

KEVIN RYAN | JAMES M. COOPER

Acquisitions Editor: Christopher Shortt

Senior Development Editor: Lisa Mafrici

Assistant Editor: Caitlin Cox

Editorial Assistant: Linda Stewart

Associate Media Editor: Ashley Cronin

Marketing Manager: Kara Kindstrom Parsons

Marketing Communications Manager: Martha Pfeiffer

Content Project Manager: Tanya Nigh

Creative Director: Rob Hugel

Art Director: Maria Epes

Print Buyer: Linda Hsu

Rights Acquisitions Account Manager, Text: Katie Huha

Rights Acquisitions Account Manager, Image:
   Amanda Groszko

Production Service: S4Carlisle Publishing Services

Text Designer: Marsha Cohen

Copy Editor: Chris Feldman

Cover Designer: Ellen Pettengell

Compositor: S4Carlisle Publishing Services

For product information and technology assistance, contact us at Cengage Learning Customer & Sales Support, 1-800-354-9706.

For permission to use material from this text or product, submit all requests online at www.cengage.com/permissions.

Further permissions questions can be e-mailed to permissionrequest@cengage.com.

Library of Congress Control Number: 2009923269

ISBN-13: 978-1-4266-4933-2
ISBN-10: 1-4266-4933-9

Wadsworth
10 Davis Drive
Belmont, CA 94002-3098
USA

Cengage Learning is a leading provider of customized learning solutions with office locations around the globe, including Singapore, the United Kingdom, Australia, Mexico, Brazil, and Japan. Locate your local office at www.cengage.com/international.

Cengage Learning products are represented in Canada by Nelson Education, Ltd.

To learn more about Wadsworth, visit **www.cengage.com/wadsworth**

Purchase any of our products at your local college store or at our preferred online store www.ichapters.com.

Printed in Canada
1 2 3 4 5 6 7 12 11 10 09

PART 4

Curriculum and Standards   112

PART 5

Instruction   154

After we finished putting together this collection of educational articles, we went in search of a title. Our intention for the book was to offer educators an anthology rich in ways to conceive of teaching and learning. Our primary focus was on the quality of the individual entries, but we especially wanted to engage readers in a wide array of (often competing) points of view. As we struggled for a title, we remembered a favorite childhood toy: the kaleidoscope. This cylindrical instrument contains loose bits of colored glass between two flat plates and two mirrors. When the cylinder is shaken or rotated, it causes the bits of glass to be reflected in an endless variety of patterns. Somehow, the image of a kaleidoscope captured our goal for this book.

Our Endless Variety of Patterns

Kaleidoscope is intended for use either as a supplemental book of readings to accompany any "Introduction to Education," "Foundations of Education," or "Issues in Education" textbook, or as a core textbook itself.

The book's wide range of sources and writers—from classic writers like John Dewey and Carl Rogers to contemporary authors like Diane Ravitch, Elliot Eisner, Linda Darling-Hammond, and Alfie Kohn—makes it highly flexible and responsive to a broad variety of course needs. The text's mixture of topic areas includes students and teachers; schools and instruction; curriculum and standards; foundations, philosophy, and reform; educational technology; and diversity and social issues.

The material we have selected for *Kaleidoscope* is not technical and can be understood, we believe, by people without extensive professional backgrounds in education. The articles are relatively brief and come from classroom teachers, educational researchers, journalists, and educational reformers. Some selections are summaries of research. Some are classic writings by noted educators. Some are descriptions of educational problems and proposed solutions. And, we hasten to add, we agree with the perspectives of some articles and do not agree with others. Our aim is to present a wide variety of philosophical and social science positions to reflect the varied voices heard in education today.

Endless Variety of Patterns: The Parts

Kaleidoscope is divided into nine parts. Part 1 concentrates on teachers, with articles ranging from personal reports by teachers to an article about what constitutes great teaching. Part 2 contains selections about students, dealing with topics from the changing nature of childhood in the United States to student cheating. Part 3 looks at schools, specifically the characteristics of good schools and ways to improve them. Part 4 examines curriculum issues (a mainstay of past editions of *Kaleidoscope*) and deals with the classic question: "What is most worth knowing?" Part 4 also continues to focus on what we believe is the major curricular issue facing today's educators: content standards and their accompanying high-stakes testing and assessment. The effects of the movement to increase students' academic achievement are reflected in a number of articles in other sections. Part 5 focuses on instruction and includes selections on cooperative learning, classroom management, constructivist learning, differentiated instruction, and multiple intelligences. Part 6 contains articles on the foundations of education that discuss the historical, philosophical, psychological, and legal roots of contemporary education. Part 7 contains articles on contemporary educational reform efforts in the United States, focusing on several different avenues toward reform, including the No Child Left Behind Act. Part 8 examines various aspects of how educational technology is affecting—or is likely to affect—teaching and learning. Finally, Part 9 focuses on various social issues affecting education in the United States today, with particular attention to ethnic and linguistic diversity as well as gender issues and special education inclusion efforts.

New Bits of Colored Glass: Features of the New Edition

We have completely revised and updated the twelfth edition in response to extensive surveying of the market. As a result, you will see the following improvements.

1. We have organized the text, beginning with the new subtitle, "Contemporary and

Classic Readings in Education," around *contemporary* **and** *classic* **writings from a variety of authors.** Articles marked with special *"Education Classic"* icons provide readers with a foundation in some of the ideas that have stood the test of time and shifts in educational priorities over many years. As we explain in the postnotes for these articles, they were chosen because the article's author has been highly influential, the author is well known, or the article addresses an enduring idea or controversy in American education.

2. We have reduced the number of readings from seventy to around fifty-five to allow room for additional pedagogical features to enhance each article. Given that almost 50 percent of the selections are new to this edition, *Kaleidoscope* covers current topics such as multicultural education, standards-based education, professional development of teachers, teacher reflection, technology, classroom management, brain research, inclusion, school reform, gender issues, student cheating, and curriculum reform. The website includes additional articles that no longer appear in the text.

3. We have added *new* **video cases.** Approximately half of the articles are now followed by recommended video cases from the Cengage Learning collection. These video cases bring the articles to life! They are opportunities to see subjects and issues raised by the articles worked by actual practicing teachers. We also provide several questions concerning each video case, helping the reader to focus on important aspects of the video case.

4. We have added a *new* **Appendix, "Tips for Teaching: Educator's Resource Guide."** This thirteen-page multi-part special feature will assist your students in making classroom observations and participating in classroom discussions. Written in a student-centered fashion, it provides valuable information on issues related to classroom observation and data-gathering techniques. It also offers study tips both in the Appendix itself and by including relevant lists of websites for both students and educators.

Special Learning Features of the Book

To facilitate understanding of the selections in this book, the twelfth edition of *Kaleidoscope* includes a number of especially helpful features.

- Each of the nine major sections is introduced by a **section-opening overview** to place the readings into a broader context.

- At the beginning of each article, we have introduced a **FOCUS Question** to guide the reader as to the most important point or issue to think about as he or she reads the article.

  - A brief **biographical sketch of each author** appears at the beginning of each article. So, too, is a designation as to whether the article is a contemporary work or an educational classic.

- **Key terms** are introduced at the beginning of each article, providing students valuable additions to their educational vocabularies and reminding them that a glossary of these terms is included at the end of the book. Students can test their knowledge of key terms with the interactive glossary flashcards on the companion website.

- The end of each reading features a **postnote**, several **discussion questions**, and, *new* to this edition, relevant **websites** and **award-winning video cases**.

  - **Postnotes** comment on the issues raised by the article.

  - **Discussion questions** prompt readers to do some additional thinking about the major points made in the article.

  - **Websites** point to further information on issues raised by the articles.

  - **Video cases** offer opportunities to see subjects and issues raised by the articles worked by actual practicing teachers.

- True to our "kaleidoscopic plan" we do not want readers to be captive of a single point of view. Therefore, in some of the articles, we point readers to **"For Another Perspective"** articles on the website that offer a different perspective than the article in the text.

- The **Glossary** of key terms at the end of the book is especially useful to those students taking their first course in education or those using this book as a primary text. A detailed subject index also appears at the end of the book.

- The **Article Review Form,** found at the end of the book, will help you to analyze and discuss the articles in the text.

- The **Correlating Table,** arranged alphabetically by topic, relates each *Kaleidoscope* selection to specific chapters in *Those Who Can, Teach,* twelfth edition, by Kevin Ryan and James M. Cooper. We hope this chart will serve as a handy cross-reference for users of this book. This chart is printed on the inside covers of the text for easy reference.

Accompanying Website Resource

A premium website for instructors and students accompanies the text. This edition's website is enhanced with Cengage Learning **video cases**—four- to six-minute video clips filmed in actual classrooms and accompanied by teacher interviews, classroom "artifacts," and viewing questions—that bring the topics in this text to life. In addition, the website offers nine articles from previous editions of *Kaleidoscope.* Glossary flashcards and an article review form are also included. Finally, an **Education Portfolio Building Tutorial,** an interactive tool that helps preservice teachers learn about the portfolio building process, is also included. Go to **www.cengage.com/login** to register your access code.

Acknowledgments

We are especially grateful to a number of reviewers and survey respondents for their excellent recommendations and suggestions, most notably: Peter Bastardo, Rutgers University; Sally R. Beisser, Drake University; Christine Belongia, Genesee Community College; Jeannine Boutte, University of New Orleans; Donna Brent, Skidmore College; Timothy M. Briles, Georgian Court University; C. M. Bunch, Hannibal LaGrange College; Patricia Clanton, Southern Arkansas University; John F. Covaleskie, University of Oklahoma; Cheri Crowl, Georgian Court University; Georges E. Fouron, Stony Brook University; Claire Gallagher, Georgian Court University; Alan W. Garrett, Eastern New Mexico University; Judy Hassen, Pacific Lutheran University; Christie Herbert, Landmark College; Carol Kennett, Trinity International University; Kelly Ann Kolodny, Framingham State College; David LaVere, Clemson University; David Locascio, Longwood University; Patricia K. Lowry, Jacksonville State University; Christopher Maglio, Truman State University; Joseph Mannion, Concordia University; Chuck McCombie, Lynchburg College; Charlotte Mendoza, Colorado College; Lourdes Mitchel, Seton Hall University; Michelle Morris, Northwestern State University; Steve Oates, Northern Michigan University; Robert Oprandy, University of the Pacific; Paul T. Parkison, University of Southern Indiana; Nancy B. Powers, Longwood University; Jonathan Silverman, Saint Michael's College; Miriam J. Singer, Fairleigh Dickinson University; Dale Spector, San Diego State University; Cathleen Stutz, Assumption College; Phil Tate, Boston University; Catherine C. Wasson, Belhaven College; Cynthia W. Wilkins, Belhaven College; Patricia Wojtowicz, Raritan Valley Community College; Susan Skinner Wyatt, Eastfield College.

In addition, we would like to offer a special note of thanks to the many users of this book who have been kind enough to share with us their impressions of it and their suggestions for how we might improve it in subsequent editions. We hope this tradition will continue as you send us your comments via the Cengage Learning website at **www.cengage.com/contact.**

Kevin Ryan and James M. Cooper

Teachers

Being a teacher today has special drawbacks. It is difficult to be a teacher in an age that mocks idealism. It is also difficult to be a teacher without the traditional authority and respect that once came with the title. Being a teacher in a time of permissive childrearing causes special strains, given that many students and some parents are filled with anti-authoritarian attitudes. It is punishing to work at an occupation that is not keeping up economically. It is painful to be part of a profession that is continually asked to solve deep social problems, do the essential job of educating children, and then is regularly criticized for its failings. A good case can be made for discouragement among teachers…even for self-pity.

This negativism, or at least acknowledgment of the negative, obscures the fact that teaching is one of the truly great professions. These passing conditions overlook the greatness that resides in the teacher's work. These current conditions are coming under increased scrutiny as the public and our leaders realize the need for a world class teaching force. Change is coming.

Even amid the difficulties just cited, teachers are buoyed up by a deep conviction. While many adults struggle with the work-life question, "Am I engaged in significant work?" teachers have the luxury of always knowing that they are engaged in crucial, life-shaping work.

1

Reflection Is at the Heart of Practice

Simon Hole and Grace Hall McEntee

Simon Hole is a fourth-grade teacher at Narragansett Elementary School in Narragansett, Rhode Island. **Grace Hall McEntee** is co-founder of Educators Writing for Change. Together they have written *At the Heart of Teaching: A Guide to Reflective Practice* (Teachers College Press, 2003). Ms. McEntee may be reached at Box 301, Prudence Island, RI 02872 (e-mail: Gmcente\@aol.com).

"Reflection Is at the Heart of Practice" by Simon Hole and Grace Hall McEntee, *Educational Leadership,* May 1999, pp. 34–37. Used with permission. The Association for Supervision and Curriculum Development is a worldwide community of educators advocating sound policies and sharing best practices to achieve the success of each learner. To learn more, visit ASCD at **www.ascd.org.**

F|O|C|U|S QUESTION

What is one habit that separates ordinary teachers from constantly improving teachers?

KEY TERM
Guided reflection protocol

The life force of teaching practice is thinking and wondering. We carry home those moments of the day that touch us, and we question decisions made. During these times of reflection, we realize when something needs to change.

A protocol, or guide, enables teachers to refine the process of reflection, alone or with colleagues. The Guided Reflection Protocol is useful for teachers who choose to reflect alone. The Critical Incidents Protocol, which we developed through our work with the Annenberg Institute for School Reform at Brown University, is used for shared reflection. The steps for each protocol are similar; both include writing.

Guided Reflection Protocol

The first step in guided reflection is to collect possible episodes for reflection. In his book *Critical Incidents in Teaching: Developing Professional Judgment* (1993), David Tripp encourages us to think about ordinary events, which often have much to tell us about the underlying trends, motives, and structures of our practice. Simon's story, "The Geese and the Blinds," exemplifies this use of an ordinary event.

STEP ONE: WHAT HAPPENED?

> Wednesday, September 24, 9:30 A.M. I stand to one side of the classroom, taking the morning attendance. One student glances out the window and sees a dozen Canada geese grazing on the playground. Hopping from his seat, he calls out as he heads to the window for a better view. Within moments, six students cluster around the window. Others start from their seats to join them. I call for attention and ask them to return to their desks. When none of the students respond, I walk to the window and lower the blinds.

Answering the question What happened? is more difficult than it sounds. We all have a tendency to jump into an interpretive or a judgmental mode, but it is important to begin by simply telling the story. Writing down what happened—without analysis or judgment—aids in creating a brief narrative. Only then are we ready to move to the second step.

Guided Reflection Protocol (For Individual Reflection)

1. *Collect stories.* Some educators find that keeping a set of index cards or a steno book close at hand provides a way to jot down stories as they occur. Others prefer to wait until the end of the day and write in a journal.

2. *What happened?* Choose a story that strikes you as particularly interesting. Write it succinctly.

3. *Why did it happen?* Fill in enough of the context to give the story meaning. Answer the question in a way that makes sense to you.

4. *What might it mean?* Recognizing that there is no one answer is an important step. Explore possible meanings rather than determine the meaning.

5. *What are the implications for practice?* Consider how your practice might change given any new understandings that have emerged from the earlier steps.

STEP TWO: WHY DID IT HAPPEN?

Attempting to understand why an event happened the way it did is the beginning of reflection. We must search the context within which the event occurred for explanations. Simon reflects:

> It's not hard to imagine why the students reacted to the geese as they did. As 9-year-olds, they are incredibly curious about their world. Explaining my reaction is more difficult. Even as I was lowering the blinds, I was kicking myself. Here was a natural opportunity to explore the students' interests. Had I stood at the window with them for five minutes, asking questions to see what they knew about geese, or even just listening to them, I'd be telling a story about seizing the moment or taking advantage of a learning opportunity. I knew that even as I lowered the blinds. So, why?

Searching deeper, we may find that a specific event serves as an example of a more general category of events. We need to consider the underlying structures within the school that may be a part of the event and examine deeply held values. As we search, we often find more questions than answers.

> Two key things stand out concerning that morning. First, the schedule. On Wednesdays, students leave the room at 10:00 A.M. and do not return until 15 minutes before lunch. I would be out of the classroom all afternoon attending a meeting, and so this half hour was all the time I would have with my students.
>
> Second, this is the most challenging class I've had in 22 years of teaching. The first three weeks of school had been a constant struggle as I tried strategy after strategy to hold their attention long enough to have a discussion,

give directions, or conduct a lesson. The hectic schedule and the need to prepare the class for a substitute added to the difficulty I've had "controlling" the class, so I closed the blinds.

There's something satisfying about answering the question Why did it happen? Reflection often stops here. If the goal is to become a reflective practitioner, however, we need to look more deeply. The search for meaning is step three.

STEP THREE: WHAT MIGHT IT MEAN?

Assigning meaning to the ordinary episodes that make up our days can feel like overkill. Is there really meaning behind all those events? Wouldn't it be more productive to wait for something extraordinary to happen, an event marked with a sign: "Pay attention! Something important is happening." Guided reflection is a way to find the meaning within the mundane. Split-second decision making is a crucial aspect of teaching. Given the daily madness of life in a classroom, considering all the options and consequences is difficult. Often, it is only through reflection that we even recognize that we had a choice, that we could have done something differently.

> Like a football quarterback, I often make bad decisions because of pressure. Unlike a quarterback, I don't have an offensive line to blame for letting the pressure get to me. While it would be nice to believe that I could somehow make the pressure go away, the fact is that it will always be with me. Being a teacher means learning to live within that pressure, learning from the decisions I make and learning to make better decisions.

Our growing awareness of how all events carry some meaning is not a new concept. In *Experience and Education* (1938), John Dewey wrote about experience and its relationship to learning and teaching: "Every experience affects for better or worse the attitudes which help decide the quality of further experience" (p. 37). He believed that teachers must be aware of the "possibilities inherent in ordinary experience" (p. 89), that the "business of the educator [is] to see in what direction an experience is heading" (p. 38). Rediscovering this concept through the examination of ordinary events creates a fresh awareness of its meaning.

The search for meaning is an integral part of being human. But understanding by itself doesn't create changes in classroom practice. The last phase of guided reflection is more action oriented and involves holding our practice to the light of those new understandings.

STEP FOUR: WHAT ARE THE IMPLICATIONS FOR MY PRACTICE?

Simon continues:

> My reaction to the pressure this year has been to resort to methods of control. I seem to be forever pulling down the blinds. I'm thinking about how I might better deal with the pressure.
>
> But there is something else that needs attention. Where is the pressure coming from? I'm sensing from administration and parents that they feel I should be doing things differently. I've gotten subtle and overt messages that I need to pay more attention to "covering" the curriculum, that I should be finding a more equal balance between process and product.
>
> Maybe they're right. What I've been doing hasn't exactly been a spectacular success. But I think that what is causing the lowering of the blinds stems from my not trusting enough in the process. Controlling the class in a fairly traditional sense isn't going to work in the long run. Establishing a process that allows the class to control itself will help keep the blinds up.

Cultivating deep reflection through the use of a guiding protocol is an entry into rethinking and changing practice. Alone, each of us can proceed step-by-step through the examination of a particular event. Through the process, we gain new insights into the implications of ordinary events, as Simon did when he analyzed "The Geese and the Blinds."

Whereas Guided Reflection is for use by individuals, the Critical Incidents Protocol is used with colleagues. The goal is the same: to get to the heart of our practice, the place that pumps the lifeblood into our teaching, where we reflect, gain insight, and change what we do with our students. In addition, the Critical Incidents Protocol encourages the establishment of collegial relationships.

Critical Incidents Protocol

Schools are social places. Although too often educators think and act alone, in most schools colleagues do share daily events. Stories told in teachers' lounges are a potential source of rich insight into issues of teaching and learning and can open doors to professional dialogue.

Telling stories has the potential for changing individual practice and the culture of our schools. The Critical Incidents Protocol allows practitioners to share stories in a way that is useful to their own thinking and to that of the group.

Three to five colleagues meet for the purpose of exploring a "critical incident." For 10 minutes, all write a brief account of an incident. Participants should know

---

Critical Incidents Protocol (For Shared Reflection)

1. *Write stories.* Each group member writes briefly in response to the question: What happened? (10 minutes)

2. *Choose a story.* The group decides which story to use. (5 minutes)

3. *What happened?* The presenter reads the written account of what happened and sets it within the context of professional goals. (10 minutes)

4. *Why did it happen?* Colleagues ask clarifying questions. (5 minutes)

5. *What might it mean?* The group raises questions about the incident in the context of the presenter's work. They discuss it as professional, caring colleagues while the presenter listens. (15 minutes)

6. *What are the implications for practice?* The presenter responds, then the group engages in conversation about the implications for the presenter's practice and for the participants' own practice. A useful question at this stage might be, "What new insights occurred?" (15 minutes)

7. *Debrief the process.* The group talks about what just happened. How did the process work? (10 minutes)

---

that the sharing of their writing will be for the purpose of getting feedback on what happened rather than on the quality of the writing itself.

Next, the group decides which story to use with the protocol. The presenter for the session then reads the story while the group listens carefully to understand the incident and the context. Colleagues ask clarifying questions about what happened or why the incident occurred, then they discuss what the incident might mean in terms of the presenter's practice. During this time, the presenter listens and takes notes. The presenter then responds, and the participants discuss the implications for their own practice. To conclude, one member leads a conversation about what happened during the session, how well the process worked, and how the group might change the process.

The sharing of individual stories raises issues in the fresh air of collegial support. If open dialogue is not already part of a school's culture, however, colleagues may feel insecure about beginning. To gain confidence, they may choose to run through the protocol first with a story that is not theirs. For this purpose, Grace offers a story about an incident in the writing lab from her practice as a high school English teacher.

STEP ONE: WHAT HAPPENED?

We went into the computer lab to work on essay drafts. TJ, Neptune, Ronny, and Mick sat as a foursome. Their sitting together had not worked last time. On their single printer an obscene message had appeared. All four had denied writing it.

The next day Ronny, Neptune, and Mick had already sat together. Just as TJ was about to take his seat, I asked him if he would mind sitting over at the next bay of computers. He exploded. "You think I'm the cause of the problem, don't you?"

Actually I did think he might be, but I wasn't at all certain. "No," I said, "but I do want you to sit over here for today." He got red in the face, plunked down in the chair near the three other boys, and refused to move.

I motioned for him to come with me. Out in the hall, I said to him quietly, "The bottom line is that all of you need to get your work done." Out of control, body shaking, TJ angrily spewed out, "You always pick on me. Those guys...You..." I could hardly hear his words, so fascinated was I with his intense emotion and his whole-body animation.

Contrary to my ordinary response to students who yell, I felt perfectly calm. I knew I needed to wait. Out of the corner of my eye, I saw two male teachers rise out of their chairs in the hallway about 25 feet away. They obviously thought that I, a woman of small stature, needed protection. But I did not look at them. I looked at TJ and waited.

When he had expended his wrathful energy, I said softly, "You know, TJ, you are a natural-born leader." I waited. Breathed in and out. "You did not choose to be a leader; it was thrust upon you. But there you are. People follow you. So you have a tremendous responsibility, to lead in a positive and productive way. Do you understand what I am saying?"

Like an exhalation after a long in-breath, his body visibly relaxed. He looked down at me and nodded his head. Then he held out his hand to me and said, "I'm sorry."

Back in the room, he picked up his stuff and, without a word, moved to the next bay of computers.

STEP TWO: USING THE CRITICAL INCIDENTS PROTOCOL

At first you'll think that you need more information than this, but we think that you have enough here. One member of the group will take the role of Grace. Your "Grace" can answer clarifying questions about what happened or why it happened in whatever way he or she sees fit. Work through the protocol to figure out what the incident might mean in terms of "Grace's" practice. Finally, discuss what implications the incident in the writing lab might have for her practice and for your own as reflective educators. Then, try an event of your own.

We think that you will find that whether the group uses your story or someone else's, building reflective practice together is a sure way to get to the heart of teaching and learning.

REFERENCES

Dewey, J. (1938). *Experience and education.* New York: Macmillan.

Tripp, D. (1993). *Critical incidents in teaching: Developing professional judgment.* New York: Routledge.

POSTNOTE

Teachers often note that they don't have enough time to do all the things that they either need or want to do. The day just doesn't seem to have enough hours. When time is precious, making the time to reflect on one's teaching seems extravagant. After all, there are so many more pressing items. However, if teachers are asked if they want to improve their teaching, it's hard to imagine one saying, "No." The authors of this article make the case that teacher reflection is the key component for improving our teaching. And, if you think about it, improving

your teaching without seriously reflecting on it is virtually impossible.

Reflective teaching involves the process of examination and evaluation in which you develop the habits of inquiry and reflection. By describing two structured ways of reflecting, one individually and one with colleagues, the authors give us useful protocols for conducting a reflective process. The use of journal writing, observation instruments, simulations, and videotaping can also help you examine teaching, learning, and the contexts in which they occur. Comparing your perspectives with those of fellow students, professors, and school personnel will broaden your interpretations and give you new insights. As you reflect on your experiences, you will come to distrust simple answers and explanations. Nuances and subtleties will start to become clear, and situations that once seemed simple will reveal their complexities. Moral and ethical issues are likely to be encountered and thought about. By practicing reflective teaching, you will grow and develop the attitudes and skills to become a life-long student of teaching—you will become an effective, professional teacher.

Discussion Questions

1. What do you see as the primary benefits of reflecting on your teaching? What concerns do you have about it?
2. What case do the authors make for reflecting on ordinary, as opposed to special, events? Do you agree?
3. Are you more likely to use an individual or a cooperative form of reflection? Why?

RELATED WEBSITE RESOURCES AND VIDEO CASES

 Web Resources:

Becoming a Reflective Practitioner. Available at:

**http://www.education.umd.edu/teacher_education/
sthandbook/reflection.html.**

This site, which is part of a larger, more comprehensive site, is sponsored by the University of Maryland's College of Education and treats several key issues and methodologies for improving teaching.

Demonstrating Capacity for Reflective Practice: The Reflective Practitioner. Available at:

**http://www.lcsc.edu/education/teacherprep/
standards/rp.shtml.**

Focused on a number of issues, the Division of Education of Lewis-Clark State College maintains this site for its students and the profession in general.

Video Case:

Mentoring First Year Teachers: Keys to Professional Success

In this video case, you will see a new teacher, Dania Diaz, working with a mentor teacher, Abdi Ali. First, Dania lays out her expectations to students for an upcoming lesson. Then we watch Dania raise a question in a faculty meeting about plagiarism. Related to the theme of this article, notice how Dania is developing the habit of reflecting on her practice. As you watch the clip, reflect upon the following questions:

1. Dania keeps a "reflective journal." Do you think it would be useful for her to regularly share her journal with her mentor, Abdi?
2. Having viewed Dania's interaction with her mentor, how comfortable do you believe you would be "opening up" your teaching to a mentor teacher?

The Great Teacher Question: Beyond Competencies

2

Edward R. Ducharme

Edward R. Ducharme, a former teacher and teacher educator, is now a writer and consultant living in Brewster, Massachusetts.

"The Great Teacher Question: Beyond Competencies" by Edward R. Ducharme, *Journal of Human Behavior and Learning*, Vol. 7, No. 2, 1991. Reprinted by permission of the author.

F|O|C|U|S| QUESTION

How can the teacher qualities mentioned by the author be learned?

KEY TERMS

Aesthetic
At-homeness
Teacher competencies

I begin this essay by defining a great teacher as one who influences others in positive ways so that their lives are forever altered, and then asking a question I have asked groups many times. How many teachers fitting that description have you had in your lifetime? It is rare for anyone to claim more than five in a lifetime; the usual answer is one or two.

I ask this question of groups whose members have at least master's degrees, often doctorates. They have experienced anywhere from eighty to one hundred or more teachers in their lifetimes and usually describe no more than 2% of them as great. Those voting are among the ones who stayed in school considerably longer than most people do; one wonders how many great teachers those dropping out in the 9th or 10th grade experience in their lifetimes. My little experiment, repeated many times over the years, suggests that the number of great teachers is very limited. They should be cherished and treasured because they are so rare; we should do all that we can to develop more of them.

This paper is purely speculative; no data corrupt it; no references or citations burden it. It began as I sat with a colleague at a meeting in 1987 in Washington; we were listening to a speaker drone on about the competencies teachers need. I asked my friend: "How would you like to write a paper about qualities great teachers have that do not lend themselves to competency measurements?" The proposed shared writing exercise did not get much beyond our talking about it the next couple of times we saw each other, but I have continued to speculate on these qualities as I have read, taught, studied, talked with others, and relived my own learning experiences.

The remarks result from years of being with teachers, students, and schools; of three decades of being a teacher; of five decades of being a learner. There is no science in the remarks, no cool, objective look at teaching. These are personal reflections and observations to provoke, to get some of us thinking beyond numbers, test scores, attendance rates, and demographics, to reflect on the notion of the Great Teacher.

I am weary of competencies even though I recognize the need for specific indicators that teachers possess certain skills and knowledge. I believe, however, that good teacher preparation programs do more than a reasonable job on these and are doing better and better. Three conditions lead me to believe that most future graduates of teacher education programs will be competent. First, the overall quality of teacher candidates is improving; second, there is a great deal more known about helping to develop people to the point where they are competent; third, the level of the education professoriate has improved dramatically. Thus, I think that *most* preparation programs will be graduating competent teachers. We should begin to worry about what lies beyond competency.

My interests extend beyond competencies to qualities that I see from time to time as I visit classrooms. Few teachers possess even several of the qualities I will describe—no great teacher lacks all of them. In the remainder of this paper, I will name and describe the qualities and show what these qualities might look like in prospective teachers.

1. Penchant for and Skill in Relating One Thing with Another with Another and with Another

John Donne, the 17th century English poet and cleric, once wrote "The new science calls all into doubt." He was referring to the Copernican contention that the earth is not the center of the universe, that humankind may not be the cynosure of divine interest, countering beliefs that the old Ptolemaic system of earthcenteredness had fostered.

Donne saw relationships among things not readily apparent to many others. He recognized a new truth cancelled another belief, one that had affected attitudes and actions among his fellow Christians for a long time, and would have a dramatic effect. He knew that if something held eternally true were suddenly shown to be false, conclusively false, then other things would be questioned; nothing would be steadfast.

Many of us do not see the implications and relationships among seemingly unrelated events, people, places, works of art, scientific principles. Some great teachers have the ability to see these relationships and, equally important, help others see them. Donne saw them. His collected sermons evidence the intellectual force of great teachers.

I once took a course in which John Steinbeck's *The Sea of Cortez* and *The Grapes of Wrath* were among the readings. *The Sea of Cortez* is Steinbeck's ruminations on the vast complexity and interrelatedness of life under the water; *The Grapes of Wrath,* his ruminations on the complexities of life on land, on what happens when a natural disaster combines with human ineptness and lack of concern, one for the other. The professor used a word not much in vogue in those ancient days: ecology. He defined it as the "interrelatedness of all living things." He raised questions about the relationships of these issues to the problems of New York City and its schools, as we sat in class in Memorial Lounge at Teachers College, Columbia.

E. D. Hirsch, in *Cultural Literacy: What Every American Needs to Know,* has a series of provocative listings under each letter of the alphabet. His point is that in order to grasp the meanings of words on pages, readers must know things not part of the page. Hirsch's book contains pages of items. Under the letter C, he lists caste, cool one's heels, *Crime and Punishment,* coral reef, and czar. One would "know" such things by studying sociology, language, literature, biology, and history or, perhaps equally often, simply by living for a period of time and reading newspapers, watching movies, and so forth. Hirsch's point is that when one hears a sentence like "He runs his business as though he were the czar," one would think of autocratic, harsh rule, tyranny, Russia, lack of human rights. Some might think of how the word is sometimes spelled tsar and wonder why. Others might think of the song about the czar/tsar from *Fiddler on the Roof,* while a few would think the person incapable of pronouncing the word tsar. Hirsch has in mind one kind of "relating one field to another": that which occurs when one sees a known reference and makes the associative leap.

Edna St. Vincent Millay, in her poem on Euclid's geometry, also drew associations from seemingly unrelated things. She saw the design and texture in poetry related to the design and texture of a geometric theorem. The quality described here is the same quality that Donne and Steinbeck manifested: seeing the interrelatedness of things.

What does that quality look like in prospective teachers? Sometimes it is the person who sees the connections between sociological and educational themes; sometimes, the person who wants to introduce students to the variety of language by teaching them about snowflakes and the vast number of words Eskimos have for them; sometimes, the person who understands mathematics through music, in fact, it may be the person who says mathematics is a kind of music or that music is a kind of mathematics.

2. Lack of Fondness for Closure or, Put Another Way, Fondness for Questions over Answers

Many of us are constantly on the lookout for answers to questions. For example, we might give a great deal to know the answer to the two-part question: What makes a great teacher and how do we produce one? Of course, the answer to the first part of the question depends on who is answering it. For someone in need of specific guidance at some point in life, the great teacher may be the one pointing the way to a different kind of existence, the one making the individual feel strong. To another person, confident about life, the great teacher may be the one raising questions, challenging, making the person wonder about certitudes once held dearly.

I teach Leadership and the Creative Imagination, a course designed as a humanities experience for doctoral students in educational administration. In the course, students read twelve novels and plays, discuss them effectively, and write about them in ways related to the leadership theory literature, their own experience, and the works themselves. In the fall semester of 1987, I had what has become a redundant experience. A student in the course stopped me in the hall after class one night in November. She said that she had taken the course because her advisor had said it would be a good experience for her. And, said she, she had truly enjoyed the early readings and the discussions. But now she found the readings troubling; they were causing her to question things she does, ways she relates to people, habits of thinking. She said that she was losing a sense of assuredness of what life was all about. The books, she said, just kept raising questions. "When do we get answers?" she asked.

We talked for a while, and I reminded her of a point I had made repeatedly during the first couple of classes: there are two kinds of books, answer books and question books. Writers of answer books raise provocative questions and then provide comfortable, assuring answers. Then there are the writers who raise the provocative issues—"Thou know'st 'tis common,—all that lives must die, passing through nature into eternity," (if you get the source of that, Hirsch will like you)—and then frustrate the reader looking for facile answers by showing that the realization in the statement prompts questions: Why must all that lives die? What does it mean to pass through nature into eternity? What or when is eternity? Are we supposed to know that all that lives must die?

The predisposition to raise questions is present in all of us to varying degrees. In young, prospective teachers, the predisposition takes on various shades and hues. They ask questions like: Why do some children learn more slowly than others? Tell me, why is that, whatever that may be, a better way to do it? But how do I know they learned it? In more mature prospective teachers coming back for a fifth year and certification, it might look different: Why is this more meaningful than that? Why should we teach this instead of that? Why does my experience teach me that this is wrong? What happens next? How do I know if this is right or wrong?

Persons with fondness for questions over answers recognize that most "answers" to complex questions are but tentative, that today's answers provoke tomorrow's uneasiness. As prospective teachers, they show a disrespect for finite answers to questions about human development, the limits of knowledge, the ways of knowing, the ways of doing. They itch to know even though they have begun to believe that they can never really know, that there is always another word to be said on every subject of consequence. Often, to answer-oriented teacher educators, these students are seen as hindrances instead of prospective great teachers. In truth, they stand the chance of provoking in their future students the quest to explore, to question, to imagine, to be comfortable with the discomfort of never "really knowing," of lifelong pursuit of knowledge.

3. Growing Knowledge, Understanding, and Commitment to Some Aspect of Human Endeavor; for Example, Science, Literature, Mathematics, or Blizzards

In the last several years, the point that teachers must know something before they can teach it has been made ad nauseam. We have admonitions from the Carnegie Forum to the Holmes Group to Secretary Bennett to the person on the street to all the teachers in the field who prepared with BS degrees in education all belaboring the obvious need for knowledge, albeit with a slightly different twist than the argument had the first twenty times around: teachers must have a bachelor's degree in an academic major before being admitted to a teacher preparation program.

But we all know that to know is not enough. Merely holding a bachelor of arts does not answer the question of the relationship between teacher and knowledge. What answers the question?

Teachers are rightfully and powerfully connected with knowledge when, even early in their learning careers, they begin to make metaphors to explain their existence, their issues and dilemmas, their joys and sorrows, from the knowledge they are acquiring. I speak not of that jaded notion of students being excited by what they are learning. I get excited watching a baseball game, but it doesn't have much meaning for me the next day. I mean something including and transcending excitement. Great teachers are driven by the power, beauty, force, logic, illogic, color, vitality, relatedness, uniqueness of what they know and love. They make metaphors from it to explain the world; they are forever trying to understand the thing itself, always falling a bit short yet still urging others on. They are the teachers who make learners think what is being taught has value and meaning and may actually touch individual lives.

This quality shows itself in a variety of ways in prospective teachers. Often, it is hidden because that which captures the imagination and interest of a student may not be part of the course, may have no way of being known. I have never forgotten a young woman in a class I taught fifteen years ago. She was a freshman in one of those horrible introduction to education courses. For the last assignment, each student in the class had to teach something to the class. This young woman, who had spoken, but rarely and only when challenged during the semester, asked if the class might go to the student lounge when her turn came. I agreed; we went as a group. There was a piano in the room and she proceeded to play a piece by Chopin and explain to the class why it was an important piece of music. I suspected—and subsequent discussions with her bore out my thought—that this young woman saw the world through music, that she could explain almost anything better if she could use music as the metaphor, the carrier of her thoughts.

Most of us do not have students in our classes capable of playing a piece by Chopin, but we all have students who understand the world through a medium different from what the rest of the group may be using. Experience has taught many young people to hide this quality because it is not honored in classrooms.

4. A Sense of the Aesthetic

The development of the aesthetic domain in young people is critical to their growth and development; it is a fundamental right. The ability to grasp the beautiful makes us human; to deny that to young people is to deny their humanity. Great teachers often have an acutely developed sense of the aesthetic; they are unafraid to show their fondness for beauty in front of young people; they do so in such a manner as to make the young people themselves value beauty and their own perceptions of it.

For many young people, the world is a harsh and barren place, devoid of beauty. But in every generation, there are those who emerge spiritually changed from their schooling experiences, eager to face what is at times a hostile world. The changes are sometimes the result of a teacher with a sense of the aesthetic, one able to see beyond the everydayness and blandness of institutional life.

In a world stultified by the commercial definitions of beauty, individuals preparing to teach with this embryonic sense of the aesthetic are rare. Our own jadedness and mass-produced tastes make it difficult for us

to recognize this quality in students. What does it look like? In its evolutionary phases, it might be an impulse to make the secondary methods classroom more attractive; it might be a choice of book covers; it might be in the selection of course materials for young people; it might be in the habits of an individual. I'm uncertain as to its many forms, but I am quite certain that when we see it we should treasure its existence and support its development.

5. Willingness to Assume Risks

There are teachers who say the right things, prescribe the right books, associate with the right people, but never take risks on behalf of others, beliefs, and ideas, never do more than verbalize. They are hollow shams.

The quality of risk-taking of great teachers is subtle, not necessarily that which puts people on picket lines, at the barricades, although it might be. The quality is critical to teacher modeling, for great teachers go beyond the statement of principles and ideas, beyond the endorsement of the importance of friendships, as they move students from the consideration of abstract principles to the actualization of deeds.

The 1960s and 1970s were filled with risk-taking teachers. While neither praising nor disparaging these obvious examples, I urge other instances for consideration inasmuch as the "opportunity" for collective risk-taking is a rare occurrence in the lives of most of us. While it was not easy to be a risk-taker then, it wasn't very lonely either. Other instances, some more prosaic, abound: teachers in certain parts of the country who persist in teaching evolution despite pressure to desist, teachers who assign controversial books despite adverse criticism, teachers who teach the Civil War and the Vietnam War without partisanship or chauvinism. These quiet acts of risk-taking occur daily in schools and universities; they instruct students of the importance of ideas joined with actions.

I recall my high school art teacher who took abuse from the principal because she demanded the right for her students to use the gymnasium to prepare for a dance. He rebuked and embarrassed her in front of the students for "daring to question [my] authority." His act prompted some of us to go to the superintendent to complain about him; we got the gym. But we also each had a private interview with the principal in which he shared his scorn and derision for us for having "gone over [my] head to the superintendent." We learned that acting on principles is sometimes risky, that we had to support a teacher who took risks for us, that actions have consequences, that a "good" act like defending a brave teacher can lead to punishment. But her risk-taking led us to risk-taking on behalf of another person and the resolution of a mild injustice.

Detecting this quality in the young is difficult. The young often appear cause-driven and it is hard to distinguish when students are merely following a popular, low-risk cause and when they are standing for something involving personal decisions and risk. We might see it in its evolutionary form in some quite simple instances. Many teacher educators suffer the indignity of seeing their ideas and principles distorted by the wisdom of the workplace, of having their students grow disenchanted with what they have been taught as they encounter the world of the school: "We'll knock that Ivory Tower stuff out of you here. This is the *real* world." Of course, we all know some of it should be knocked out, but much of it should remain. It is a rare student who during practical, internship, and early years of teaching remains steadfast to such principles as: all student answers, honestly given, merit serious consideration; or worksheets are rarely good instructional materials. It is risky for young pre-professionals and beginning professionals to dispute the wisdom of the workplace and maintain fidelity to earlier acquired principles. Perhaps in these seemingly small matters lies the quality to be writ large during the full career.

6. At-Homeness in the World

Great teachers live effectively in what often seems a perverse world. Acutely aware of life's unevenness, the disparities in the distribution of the world's goods, talents, and resources, they cry out for justice in their own special ways while continuing to live with a sense of equanimity and contribute to the world. They demonstrate that life is to be lived as fully as one can despite problems and issues. They show that one can be a sensitive human being caring about and doing things about the problems and issues, and, at the same time, live a life of personal fulfillment. They are not overwhelmed by the insolubility of things on the grand scale, for they are able to make sense of things on the personal level.

I once had a professor for a course in Victorian poetry. In addition to his academic accomplishments, the professor was a fine gardener, each year producing a beautifully crafted flower garden, filled with design and beauty.

We were reading "In Memoriam," the part in which Tennyson refers to nature, red in tooth and claw. All of a sudden, the professor talked about how, that morning, while eating his breakfast, he had watched his cat stalk a robin, catch it, and devour part of it. He related the incident, of course, to the poem. (Clearly he had the

quality alluded to earlier, the sense on inter-relatedness of things.) I am uncertain what I learned about "In Memoriam" that morning, but I know I learned that this man who earlier in the semester had pointed out the delicate beauty of some of Tennyson's lyrics had integrated death into his life while remaining sensitive to beauty, to love. It was partly through him that I began to see that the parts of life I did not like were not to be ignored nor to be paralyzed about. All this in the death of a bird? No, all this in a powerful teacher's reaction to the death of a bird in the midst of life.

And what does at-homeness in the world look like in prospective teachers? I am quite uncertain, very tentative about this one. Perhaps it shows itself in a combination of things like joy in life one day and despair over life the next as the young slowly come to grips with the enigmas of life, its vicissitudes and sorrows. The young are often studies in extremes as they make order of life, of their lives. As a consequence, one sees a few students with vast energy both to live life and to anguish over its difficulties. But one cannot arrive at the point of my professor with his lovely garden and dead robin simultaneously entertained in his head without a sense of the joyful and the tragic in life, without a constant attempt to deal with the wholeness that is life, without a sense of being at home in the world.

All prospective teachers have touches of each of these qualities which should be supported and nurtured so that their presence is ever more manifest in classrooms. But a few students have some of these qualities writ large. Buttressed by programs that guarantee competency in instructional skills, these individuals have the potential to become great teachers themselves, to be the teachers who take the students beyond knowledge acquisition and skill development to questioning, to wondering, to striving. We must, first, find these prospective teachers, help them grow and develop, treasure them, and give them to the young people of America, each one of whom deserves several great teachers during thirteen years of public schooling.

And what has all this to do with the preparation of teachers? Surely, preparing teachers to be competent in providing basic instruction to as many students as possible is enough of a major task. Clearly, the raising of reading scores, of math achievement levels, of writing skills, of thinking processes are significant accomplishments. Of course, all these things must be accomplished, and teacher preparation programs around the country are getting better and better at these matters.

But we must have more; we must have an increase in the presence of greatness in the schools, in the universities. Love for a teacher's kindness, gratitude for skills acquired, fondness for teachers—these are critically important. But equally important is the possibility that students will encounter greatness, greatness that transcends the everydayness of anyplace, that invites, cajoles, pushes, drags, drives, brings students into the possibilities that questions mean more than answers; that knowledge is interrelated; that there is joy to be had from beauty; that knowledge can affect people to the cores of their being; that ideas find their worth in actions; that life is full of potential in a sometimes perverse world.

POSTNOTE

Ducharme's article is provocative in its challenge to go beyond mere competence and instead reach for greatness in our teaching. The characteristics that he suggests embody greatness in teaching and are difficult to challenge because they ring true. They also are formidable if we want to become teachers who possess these characteristics.

In an effort to ensure that prospective teachers will be "safe to practice," many teacher educators focus their instruction on the knowledge and skills (competencies) new teachers will need to function effectively in classrooms. It may be a rare instance where the focus of teacher education is on what it will take to become a *great* teacher, not merely a *competent* one.

Discussion Questions

1. Is a particular kind of teacher preparation needed to produce great, rather than just competent, teachers? Or does a prospective teacher need to earn competence before greatness can be achieved? Explain your answers.
2. Think of the great teachers you have had. Did they possess the characteristics Ducharme describes? Briefly discuss what made these teachers great.
3. Can you think of any other characteristics that great teachers possess that were not identified by Ducharme? If so, what are they?

RELATED WEBSITE RESOURCES

 Web Resources:

The National Board of Professional Teaching Standards. Available at:

http://www.nbpts.org.

This organization has, for over two decades, led the fight both to define excellence in teaching and recognize excellent teachers.

3

The Power of Personal Relationships

Thomas S. Mawhinney and Laura L. Sagan

Thomas S. Mawhinney is an associate professor at Touro College in New York. He is a former high school principal, an education consultant, a teacher trainer, and the president of Leading for Learning, Inc., Poughkeepsie, NY. **Laura L. Sagan** is the social studies coordinator for the Mohonasen Central School District, Rotterdam, NY; a part-time teacher trainer; and a former middle school principal.

"The Power of Personal Relationships" by Thomas S. Mawhinney and Laura L. Sagan, *Phi Delta Kappan* 88, no. 6, February 2007, pp. 460–464. Reprinted with permission of the authors.

| F | O | C | U | S | QUESTION

What does a teacher need to do to establish the proper personal relationship with students?

KEY TERMS

Differentiation (differentiated instruction)
Empathetic listening
Fight-or-flight response
Pedagogic caring

Donta stayed after class a few minutes to ask her teacher for help. As she hurried to get to her next class on time her boyfriend cornered her and questioned her about a rumor he had heard involving Donta and her best friend. She could not get away. She was torn because she had been late for this class several times before and did not want to disappoint her teacher again.

When Donta finally got to her class, she was obviously nervous. Her teacher simply said, "Donta, how nice to see you. Come on in and take a seat." Donta smiled and felt relieved. She loved this class because the teacher made her feel important. "Why couldn't all teachers treat kids this way?" she thought.

Donta had just experienced the power of personal-relationship building. Her teacher could have demanded a pass, interrogated her in front of the class, greeted her with a sarcastic remark, or embarrassed her in some other way. Instead, she made her feel welcome. Donta was in a frame of mind ready to learn.

There are many children who make up their minds on the first day of class whether they are going to succeed or fail—sometimes consciously and sometimes not. How can this be, one might ask? Simply put, the initial student/teacher encounter often determines how well or poorly a child will perform throughout the school year. Likewise, a positive teacher/student relationship creates the classroom atmosphere necessary to maximize a student's mental state of readiness.

Picture the teacher who, in an attempt to establish control from the beginning, spends the first day describing classroom rules and routines and emphasizes what will happen if they are not followed. Coercive classrooms are not conducive to learning, yet many teachers continue to believe that a dominating relationship such as that between a parent and child ensures student compliance. How often have instructional leaders advised the first-year teacher to be tough in the beginning and loosen up later—that one can never do it in reverse? Well, after that first day of toughness, many students have "downshifted" into a fight-or-flight mode. In doing so they have bypassed much of their capacity for higher-order thinking or creative thought, and it is hard to learn when your bodily functions are focused on survival. We now understand that higher-level thinking is more likely to occur in the brain of a student who is emotionally secure than in the brain of a student who is scared, upset, anxious, or stressed.

Researchers continue to report that the teacher has a significant impact on student achievement. Based on an extensive analysis of research, Robert and Jana Marzano claim that "the quality of teacher-student relationships is the keystone for all other aspects of classroom management."[1] As former secondary school principals, we feel that personal-relationship building is one of the most important skills a teacher can possess and continue to refine. In this article, we intend to describe the many dimensions of this skill.

Personal-Relationship Building

We first encountered the term "personal-relationship building" as the title of the shortest chapter in *The Skillful Teacher,* by Jon Saphier and Robert Gower.[2] The authors classify this skill under the broader category of motivation and supply a two-part definition: "the variety of ways teachers have of contacting students' personal worlds and the traits of teachers that seem to engender affection and regard in a relationship."[3]

We will use this framework in an attempt to paint a clear picture of this powerful tool in a teacher's pedagogical "bag of tricks." We do not expect even great teachers to have all the skills and characteristics we will describe. Adding one or two to one's repertoire each year will put the self-renewing teacher on a path to canonization.

Ways of Contacting Students' Personal Worlds

A beginning teacher gets only one chance to make a first impression. As we noted above, despite the advice commonly given to new teachers to be tough in the beginning, one does not want to scare off the marginal students or those students who need a caring and nurturing environment to survive and prosper. Teachers can create such an environment by consciously engaging in particular practices and behaviors.

KNOWING YOUR STUDENTS AND ALLOWING THEM TO KNOW YOU

Differentiating instruction—planning varied lessons according to students' interests—is an important skill. Therefore we recommend that teachers spend the first few days of the school year or new semester getting to know their students by using interest surveys or other activities to discover the ways in which each one of them is unique.

We also support those teachers who allow their students to know them. Teachers who offer their students "genuineness and self-disclosure"[4] reveal "aspects of themselves that allow [the] image of authority figure to be tempered by images of teacher-as-a-real-person."[5]

Steven Wolk believes that "teachers need to allow students to see them as complete people with emotions, opinions, and lives outside of school. A good way for a teacher to get students to treat him or her as a human being is to act like one."[6]

Two of our most beloved teachers are women who, when faced with child-care problems, bring their young children to school for short periods of time. Whenever this happens, secondary and middle school students flock to them. While some schools frown on teachers using the workplace as a backup day-care facility, we find that the practice allows students to get a peek at the other side of a teacher's life. Not only does it improve relationships, it forms a long-lasting bond between the students and the teacher's own children.

REESTABLISHING CONTACT AND HIGH EXPECTATIONS

Reestablishing contact with a student with whom one has had a negative interaction is one of the most difficult things a teacher can do. Yet if that student is ever to feel a sense of belonging again, the teacher must somehow have a positive interaction with the student around some other issue. No apology is needed, but the message that the negative incident is in the past and that it is time to move on must be clear. How often have you heard students claim that they are doing poorly in a class because the teacher "hates" them? We believe that students have an innate sense that adults hold grudges and it is not clear to them when an incident of misbehavior has been forgotten. Therefore, we feel that teachers—and schools, for that matter—need to consciously apply techniques to bring closure to discipline problems, so that students understand that "everyone makes mistakes. You need to learn from it, and move on."

There is an abundance of research on the academic benefits of high expectations for students. High expectations are a crucial ingredient in personal-relationship building. In our years of administrative experience, we have seen the damage that low expectations can do even before a student walks through the classroom door for the first time. We fought in our respective schools for heterogeneous grouping, yet many days we were butting up against a wall of long-held teacher beliefs in the efficiency of sorting and separating students. We encountered one teacher who had special education students coloring rather than participating in a writing assignment with the rest of the class. You can imagine how demeaned those children felt. We will leave it at this: a student—especially a young person who has experienced the negative effects of low expectations over time—can sense when a teacher has high expectations for all students.

ACTIVE AND EMPATHETIC LISTENING

Active listening not only helps build personal relationships but is a powerful teaching strategy as well. James Stronge places this practice under the more general category of caring.[7] We feel that it deserves special mention, having observed its effect on student participation in the classroom as well as the expressions on the faces of those students who are the recipients of this potent form of attention from the teacher.

Active listening serves to:

- reaffirm to the speaker the content of his or her remark;
- confirm to the students that they have been heard in a nonjudgmental way;
- restate or infer the feeling state of the speaker; and, most important,
- send a message to the students that their comments or responses are important to the teacher.[8]

You can imagine the look on an insecure student's face when the teacher refers to an answer he or she gave earlier in the class—"as Jimmy said at the beginning of class, one of the main causes of the Civil War was...." Even using students' names when repeating or rephrasing a comment is a powerful teaching and personal-relationship-building move. We cannot encourage teachers enough to use active listening in their classrooms.

INVOLVEMENT

For more than 30 years, first as teachers and then as administrators, we have enjoyed being involved with students, whether chaperoning a dance, overseeing a field trip, or watching a school sporting or other extracurricular event. School staff members who appear at activities taking place outside the normal school day are those with whom students most easily connect. Many veteran teachers feel that they have paid their dues with respect to this aspect of school life and pass on such duties to their younger colleagues. Yet we find that students appreciate the fact that *any* teacher attends an event or chaperones an activity. We ourselves showed up at so many events that students began to ask why we were not at every activity—too much of a good thing, perhaps?

Teacher Traits That Engender Affection and Regard

In addition to using particular practices, teachers who successfully build personal relationships with students exhibit certain attitudes and qualities.

RESPECT, COURTESY, AND FAIRNESS

One of the most respected teachers that we have observed was a traditional, veteran teacher. Year after year, students would affirm that he was one of the best teachers they had ever had. In his classroom, you had to pay particular attention to understand why. He was courteous, always saying please and thank you. He frequently gave students one last chance to increase their grades on a quiz or exam. He insisted that those who did not do well see him for help. He never got mad or raised his voice. He used humor but was never sarcastic. He was loyal to the absent, never speaking of other students in front of their peers or with his fellow teachers. He disciplined students privately; he never did so publicly. He is our "poster child" for the category of respect, courtesy, and fairness.

We believe that these basic human qualities are often lost in secondary schools. As adults, we bring to school scripts that we learned, not from teacher training, but from our experiences as parents and as children being parented. Under pressure, we often revert to these scripts. Take the example of a teacher we overheard when one of her students walked out of her class in anger. The teacher followed the student into the hall, asking, "Who do you think you are?" How is the student supposed to answer that question?

Respect, courtesy, and fairness cover a wide variety of teacher behaviors. A teacher can demonstrate respect by:

- using students' interests in class activities,
- allowing students to express ideas without criticism,
- correcting errors without putdowns,
- balancing corrective feedback with recognition of strengths,
- displaying student products, and
- using specific praise.[9]

According to students, fairness on the part of the teacher includes:

- treating students as people,
- refraining from ridicule and from creating situations that cause students to lose the respect of their peers,
- being consistent and giving students opportunities to have input into the classroom, and
- providing opportunities for all students to participate and succeed.[10]

A teacher displays courtesy by:

- smiling often,
- being polite,

- not interrupting,
- exhibiting simple kindnesses such as picking up a dropped item or holding a door, and
- greeting students when they arrive and wishing them well when they leave.

Caring and Understanding

Caring too much can be dangerous for teachers. We all have heard stories of teachers who have blurred the line between their professional and personal lives. It is possible to develop unhealthy relationships that are damaging to both the teacher and the child. Yet not caring can be equally debilitating. How often do youths who drop out of school complain that no one cares about them or even cares if they exist? We believe that the right kind of caring is the secret to developing students' motivation to achieve.

Nancy Hoffman asserts, "There is a great deal to be done to make the caring work of teachers less elusive, to name it among our expectations, to study how it works, and to reward it as a substantial component of excellence in teaching."[11] While teachers cannot possibly involve themselves completely in the lives of all their students, they can exhibit a burning interest in student achievement by using effective praise and by showing an almost parental pride in exceptional student work. Hoffman uses the term "pedagogic caring," which she defines as a passion for learning that emanates from the teacher. It is easy to gauge the level of this type of caring by observing the display of student work in and around a teacher's room or office.

We think Peter Senge sums it up well: "When people genuinely care, they are actively committed. They are doing what they truly want to do. They are full of energy and enthusiasm. They persevere, even in the face of frustration and setbacks, because what they are doing is what they must do. It is their work."[12]

When we speak of "understanding" on the part of teachers, we are referring primarily to empathy, defined as "the ability to vicariously feel what another person is feeling, to understand and connect where that person is."[13] We agree with Arnold Goldstein that this capacity to understand/empathize is positively associated with a broad range of prosocial behaviors, such as cooperation, sociability, and interpersonal competence, and negatively associated with aggressive behavior.[14] It is so important for the teacher to know that each of her students is walking through the door with a myriad of social experiences from neglect to overindulgence. "While we do not advocate for the lessening of standards or expectations for students who may not be having a good day, we do think that getting inside a child's head and empathizing with what is there will go a long way toward fostering the kinds of relationships that promote higher achievement.

Humor

According to Rita Dunn, students who are global processors—those who see the big picture and learn better through anecdotes—need humor to function more effectively.[15] Roland Barth states that his personal vision of a great school is one that is characterized by humor, and we concur.[16] But teachers need to be aware that there is a fine line between appropriate and inappropriate humor. Poking fun at someone in an attempt to win students' favor is inappropriate. The ability to see humor in situations, and to laugh at oneself is key. Appropriate humor makes people smile, it creates warmth in a classroom, it relaxes students, and it reverses the "fight-or-flight" response that many troubled students take with them into every class they enter.

Love of Children

It would seem obvious that all teachers must possess this quality to work in education. Unfortunately, we have encountered teachers and other staff members who leave us scratching our heads, wondering how and why these individuals ever chose—and were hired—to work with children. There are adults in our schools who do not like "other people's children" and do not like being around them. We absolutely have to prevent these individuals from entering the profession, or, if we mistakenly hire them, we must have the courage to weed them out.

Risking Closeness

Andy Hargreaves refers to the "emotional geographies of teaching"—the patterns of closeness and distance that shape the emotions we experience.[17] In his discussion of professional distance, he observes, "School teaching has become an occupation with a feminine caring ethic that is trapped within a rationalized and bureaucratic structure." This is the problem for educators working in politically sensitive environments. Teachers and administrators are often directed to distance themselves from children in order to avoid the risks of personal relationships. As Hargreaves notes, "The dilemma for teachers is that although they are supposed to care for their students, they are expected to do so in a clinical and detached way—to mask their emotions."[18] We know there is validity in establishing closeness, yet there are land mines all about the countryside. We can be safe and sterile or take a chance and create a warm, loving community of learners.

We wrote this article because we deeply believe in the concept of personal-relationship building. We wanted to add to the knowledge base regarding this valuable skill and to describe it in a way that makes it real—something you can see and feel, something that is coachable, and, above all, something that plays a key role in the teaching act. There used to be a myth that good teachers are born, not made, and that there is nothing one can do to help the unfortunate who do not have this natural ability. We disagree and believe that "being skillful means you can do something that can be seen; it means different levels of skill may be displayed by different individuals; and it means, above all, that you can learn how to do it and continue to improve at it."[19]

NOTES

1. Robert J. Marzano and Jana S. Marzano, "The Key to Classroom Management," *Educational Leadership,* September 2003, p. 6.
2. Jon Saphier and Robert Gower, *The Skillful Teacher: Building Your Teaching Skills,* 5th ed. (Acton, Mass.: Research for Better Teaching, 1997).
3. Ibid, p. 345.
4. Richard P. Dufour and Robert E. Eaker, *Fulfilling the Promise of Excellence: A Practitioner's Guide to School Improvement* (Westbury, N.Y.: J. L. Wilkerson, 1987), p. 144.
5. Saphier and Gower, p. 348.
6. Steven Wolk, "Hearts and Minds: Classroom Relationships and Learning Interact," *Educational Leadership,* September 2003, p. 18.
7. James H. Stronge, *Qualities of Effective Teachers* (Alexandria, Va.: Association for Supervision and Curriculum Development, 2002).
8. Saphier and Gower, op. cit.
9. Ibid.
10. Stronge, op. cit.
11. Nancy Hoffman, "Toughness and Caring," *Education Week,* 28 March 2001, p. 42.
12. Peter M. Senge, *The Fifth Discipline* (New York: Doubleday, 1990), p. 148.
13. David A. Levine, *Teaching Empathy: A Social Skills Resource* (Accord, N.Y.: Blue Heron Press, 2000), p. 13.
14. Arnold P. Goldstein, *The Prepare Curriculum: Teaching Prosocial Competencies* (Champaign, Ill.: Research Press, 1999).
15. Rita S. Dunn, "The Dunn and Dunn Learning-Style Model and Its Theoretical Cornerstone," in Rita S. Dunn and Shirley A. Griggs, eds., *Synthesis of the Dunn and Dunn Learning-Style Model Research: Who, What, When, Where, and So What?* (Jamaica, N.Y.: St. John's University, 2003).
16. Roland S. Barth, "A Personal Vision of a Good School," *Phi Delta Kappan,* March 1990, pp. 512–16.
17. Andy Hargreaves, "Emotional Geographies of Teaching," *Teachers College Record,* vol. 103, 2000, pp. 1056–80.
18. Ibid., p. 1069.
19. Saphier and Gower, p. 3.

POSTNOTE

This article, written by two experienced administrators, makes several useful and practical points. It summarizes in vivid fashion important research on teacher-student relationships. In addition, it catalogs many attitudes and behaviors, such as teacher sarcasm and aloofness, that build barriers between teachers and their students. As such, the article can serve as a "teacher's self-evaluation" tool. That said, we do, however, raise one caveat.

One of the besetting mistakes of new teachers is in this area of teacher-student relationships. Further, much of the struggle and uncertainty of the first year of teaching is finding and becoming comfortable with a productive social distance. A "productive" social distance is one that "produces" good results: students learn and feel good about themselves; and teachers achieve their learning goals and feel good about themselves. However, one very human flaw often gets in the way of beginning teachers.

Instead of looking for the signs that their students are learning, they are looking for signs that their students *like* them. They are [often unknowingly] seeking love rather than respect. As the song says, they are "lookin' for love in all the wrong places." Settle for respect, and good relationships will most likely follow.

Discussion Questions

1. What are the advantages and disadvantages of spending initial class time establishing rules and procedures?
2. Which method of "contacting students' personal world" do you admire most?
3. The authors speak of the dangers of involving oneself too closely in the personal lives of students. What are your views on this issue? In your own school experience, did you observe problematic examples of this?

RELATED WEBSITE RESOURCES AND VIDEO CASES

 Web Resources:

Questia's Teacher-Student Relationship site. Available at:

**http://www.questia.com/library/education/
teacher-student-relationship.jsp.**

This site is a treasure trove of books and articles on teacher-student relationships and many, many related topics.

The Value of Student-Teacher Relationships. Available at:

http://www.ucgstp.org/lit/vt/ym03/relationships.htm.

This religiously oriented website opens with a useful article and then links to other sources.

Video Case:

Secondary Classroom Management: Basic Strategies

In this clip, James Turner, an American History teacher, discusses personal classroom management strategies, which are also demonstrated in the clips of his teaching. As you watch the clips and study the artifacts in the case, reflect on the following questions:

1. How does the teacher in this video case handle teacher-student relationships?
2. Does the teacher remaining calm and firm in the face of violations of classroom rules help or hinder the situation?

For Another Perspective:

Claudia Graziano, *Lessons of a First-Year Teacher*

www.cengage.com/login

4

Why New Teachers Leave...

Leslie Baldacci

Leslie Baldacci was a Teach For America teacher in the Chicago Public Schools from 1999 to 2005. She is currently a reporter for the *Chicago Sun-Times*.
Reprinted with permission from the Summer 2006 issue of *American Educator*, the quarterly journal of the American Federation of Teachers, AFL-CIO; originally from *Inside Mrs. B's Classroom: Courage, Hope, and Learning on Chicago's South Side.* Copyright © 2004 by The McGraw-Hill Companies, Inc. Reprinted by permission of The McGraw-Hill Companies, Inc.

F|O|C|U|S QUESTION

What should a first year teacher expect?

My classroom was just one deck chair on the Titanic. The kids ran wild. They swore, fought, refused to work. At assemblies they booed the principal. The only punishment was suspension, and that wasn't so terrible. As one of my students, Cortez, put it "At least it's better than having to come up here."

This was seventh and eighth grade in a poverty-level, urban school on the South Side of Chicago. Our classes were bursting at the seams with 35, 36, and 37 kids apiece. Tough kids, many of them raising themselves in tough circumstances. There was barely room to walk around the classrooms for all the desks. When the kids were in the room, there was no room left. The noise and heat levels were like a steel mill.

I understand the teacher shortage and why one-third of new teachers quit after three years and nearly half bail out after five years. I believe my experience was more typical than extraordinary.

What was not typical about my experience was my background. As a newspaperwoman for 25 years, I had reported on Chicago's education crises long before the city's "school reform" effort started in the late 1980s. By 1999, Chicago's schools had improved their finances, halted a disastrous cycle of teacher strikes, fixed crumbling buildings, and put up new ones. Student test scores were beginning to improve. Yet, Mayor Daley worried about sustaining the momentum. He asked, "How do you know that we set the foundation and it's not going to fall back?"

I believed the answer lay in the front-line troops, teachers. So, after being accepted to the alternative certification program called Teachers For Chicago, I turned in my press credentials to become a teacher. The program would pay for my master's degree, minimize the requirements for entering graduate school, and put me in a classroom immediately as a teacher, with a mentor looking over my shoulder and working with me daily. I would earn $24,000 a year.

* * *

My school had two buildings—a beautiful old yellow brick school, built like a fortress in 1925, and another from the 1970s, a poured-concrete prefab shell three stories high. Built as a temporary solution to overcrowding, it had long ago outlived its intended lifespan. Over time, the windows had become a cloudy opaque, impossible to see in or out.

I walked in a side door, past a security guard who did not question me, and introduced myself to the ladies in the office as "the new Teachers For Chicago intern."

"Hello!" they said, friendly and smiling.

They paged the principal, who came right away and took me into his office to chat. He looked weary. His eyes were bloodshot. Above his desk, tufts of pink insulation poked through a hole where ceiling tiles were missing. Other tiles were water-stained.

When I asked the principal for copies of the books I'd be using when school started in eight weeks, he sighed heavily and folded his hands on his desk. It wasn't that simple, he said. He wasn't sure what grade I'd be teaching. He was still working on his organizational lineup for fall. He assured me that my Teachers For Chicago mentor would be in touch and help me with the details of getting set up.

In late July, when I stopped by the school again, the principal emerged from behind closed doors to level his bloodshot eyes at me and tell me he still wasn't sure what grade I was going to get, but it would definitely be fifth grade or higher. Two more teachers had quit, I later learned, and he had requested four additional Teachers For Chicago interns to fill the many empty spots on his organizational chart. The school's first experience with the nine-year-old internship program would place interns in eight of his classrooms. The poor man looked beleaguered. Running a school with 900 kids, 89 percent from poverty-level homes, had to be tough. Student achievement was low: At third grade, 86 percent of the student body was below grade level standards in reading and 79 percent was below grade level in math. On top of that, experienced teachers were bailing out right and left.

It was precisely the setting I wanted. The optimist in me, by virtue of a scant six weeks of education training, thought, "What if this turns out to be a turning point for the school? What if all these new people coming in with their energy and ideas make a difference?"

"I'm counting on you," he told me. I pledged my allegiance with a handshake.

"Put me where you need me," I told him. I sent up a simple prayer, "Thy will be done."

About two weeks before school started I finally heard from my mentor; I would be teaching seventh grade in Room 118.

Room 118 was painted seafoam green, which didn't look nearly as putrid with the dark woodwork as the pink in the library across the hall. The ceilings were so high the room echoed. My desk had four drawers; my chair was broken. The cupboards were full of junk I would never use, coated with years of dust. There were 40 desks, which seemed excessive.

All the maps and the AV screen were pulled down. What was behind them? I clomped and creaked over the wood floors to the far corner of the room and tried to roll up the AV screen. A huge chunk of blackboard, ancient, heavy slate, jagged and lethal, lunged forward behind the screen, threatening to slash right through it. Behind the slate was exposed brick, internal walls, vintage 1925. Behind the maps were unsightly chalk boards ruined by years of wear and subsequent efforts to cover them with contact paper and other sticky stuff. What a mess.

* * *

I had never seen kids act like that in a classroom with an adult present. Throughout the first week, they talked incessantly. They shouted to be heard over the talking. They didn't do their work. They got up out of their seats without permission and wandered around, touching and bothering each other on their way. They shouted out questions and comments, including, "This is stupid." Any little ripple set off a chain reaction. Someone passed gas and everyone leapt from his seat fanning the air and jumping around. They threw things. They hit. I had broken up two fist fights already. They yelled out the window to their gang-banger friends and relatives, who gathered outside at dismissal time. They swore like sailors. I felt like the old woman who lived in the shoe; I had so many children I didn't know what to do. In addition to the 35 students in my homeroom, more than 100 other students, seventh- and eighth-graders, called me their English teacher.

And where was my backup? What were the consequences? Everyone I sent to the office bounced right back in. There was no detention. There had been no suspensions, even for fighting. I was beginning to think "alternative" schools for poorly behaved students were a myth made up by the board of education. Was my school an alternative school and no one told me about it?

All good questions, but ones I could not resolve. These were issues I needed to discuss with an experienced hand, but I had not seen much of my mentor. I felt like a prisoner in solitary confinement, thrown into a cell and forgotten. I was lucky to get to the bathroom in the course of a day.

* * *

A five-week reorganization brought new levels of angst. I had never heard of such a thing. My children had always had the same teacher from the first day of school to the last. There were no switcheroos unless someone had a baby or got sick. But apparently a principal has a right to shake things up through the fifth week of school. He can move teachers around and fine-tune the operation if things aren't going well. This, it seems, is an annual event at some schools.

That is how my colleague Astrid got switched from seventh-grade social studies to a sixth-grade, self-contained classroom and how Mr. Diaz joined the seventh- and eighth-grade team. Jennifer, an intern with a third-grade class, got switched to second grade.

Astrid was devastated at leaving her seventh-graders and starting over with a sixth-grade class. New faces, new books, new routines. And she had to teach every subject! Her seventh-graders gave her a farewell party. They took a collection and raised $13.00. Donna went to Sam's Club and bought a cake decorated with "Movin' On Up!" Astrid's new classroom was on the second floor.

When one intern explained to her third-graders that they were getting a new teacher, a student asked, "Why are you giving us up?" The enormity of the question caused the first-year teacher to lose her composure. She started to cry. Then the kids all started bawling. They spent the rest of the day watching a video. "We couldn't do anything else," she said. "We were wrecked."

Besides disrupting children's classroom situations, no one seemed to have given any thought to which children should or shouldn't be together. Most of the kids had been together since they were tiny. They had history together. Yet no teachers seemed to have been asked for insight on the group dynamic. At my children's public school, teachers met at the end of the school year to make their lists with an eye toward who worked well with whom and who needed to be separated.

Then again, at a school like mine with a 40 percent mobility rate, who knew who would be back? Year to year, five weeks into the year, changes came.

* * *

My students were ignorant of geography. They didn't know the states; they had vague ideas of continents. I decided to craft a research project around travel so they'd get some geography along with language arts. The project was planning their dream trip. I went to a couple of travel agents and grabbed every glossy brochure I could get my hands on.

They had to decide where they wanted to go and how far it was from Chicago. They had to determine the cost, pack a suitcase, and write an itinerary of sightseeing and other activities specific to their destination. They had to find out the currency, the language, what different foods they might eat, and what were good souvenirs to buy. They had to convert currency and account for time zones.

Destinations included Mexico, Jamaica, Africa, Wyoming, Florida, California, and England. The dream trip project, with its cross-curricular integrations of math and social studies, came in handy when, two days before first-quarter report card pick-up, our principal informed Mr. Diaz and me that our worst fear had been realized: The seventh and eighth grades would no longer be departmentalized. No more changing classes. Each of us would teach all subjects to our homerooms. Starting that day.

Apparently, he had decided this some weeks before. He had informed the eighth-grade teachers the week before. "I should have told you, too. My fault. Apologies," he said curtly before turning on his heel and walking away.

We were in shock. Suddenly, we were on the hook for lesson plans in all subjects, coming up to speed on the curriculum, and teaching the lessons. But that was only a week-by-week crisis. The deeper crisis was whether or not we were up to the task of teaching our students in all subjects. Seventh-grade standardized test scores determine a child's high school options. What if my ineptitude kept someone from getting into an accelerated program or a better high school? I'd become comfortable with language arts. This new responsibility was daunting.

When my graduate school advisor came to observe just a few days later, she was so upset that she called for the mentor and the principal. "This is a joke," she informed them. She reminded the mentor that her job was to spend an hour each day in each intern's room, co-teaching and modeling for us how to teach. The mentor replied that she was the "disciplinarian."

"You're the mentor," my advisor told her. "If you can't do that job, maybe someone else should. And maybe if this school can't give these interns the support they need, Teachers For Chicago doesn't belong in this school."

I prayed they wouldn't pull us out. There were so many things I had learned already but much I still needed to find out. Why weren't there any television sets or VCRs? Why were there so few books in the library? Why didn't the upper grades get time in the computer lab? Were chronic, truly dangerous kids ever sent to alternative schools?

The bottom line was, I couldn't leave the class. The upset of the reorganization made me realize how desperately they needed continuity. There had to be some value in coming back day after day, trying hard, doing my best, even if my best was woefully inadequate. Those were the only terms under which I could ask the same from them.

After my advisor left, the principal and mentor returned to my room.

"Where's your fire escape plan?" asked my mentor.

"Hanging right there, by the door," I said, pointing to the pink sheets. The children watched, rapt.

"Where's your schedule?"

"Nichelle, please put up the map at the back of the room. The schedule is behind it."

"Where's your grading scale?"

"Bulletin board, lower right corner."

"Where's your time distribution chart?"

"I don't know what that is."

"You should have it posted in the classroom," she said. "Have it on my desk at eight o'clock tomorrow morning."

They turned and left.

* * *

Near the end of the school year, the principal informed me that I would be teaching second grade the following year. I assured him I would do my best.

I walked back to my classroom with conflicting emotions. We had filled out wish lists and I had asked for seventh grade again, feeling I could do better now that I knew the pitfalls. My second choice was sixth grade, my third choice fourth. Being sent to second grade, clearly not what I desired, looked like a punishment. Had I been such a dismal failure with my seventh-graders, self-contained in the largest classroom in the school with all of our personalities and problems? Surely someone else would have been a better teacher for them than I was. Was it criminal to leave them with me all year? Would I be equally as dismal with second-graders? My eyes were watery with tears.

* * *

While the whole group of interns was exhausted, as the oldest I may have been feeling it more than the others. And the fatigue was not just physical. It was mental as well. I was drained more every day by the limits of poverty, the unprofessional manner in which our school was run, the criticism, the nitpicking, the zero encouragement or respect. No one ever told you when you did a good job. It was like no other job situation I had ever experienced.

Toward the end of my second year of teaching, I did a mental count of the teacher interns who had come through the doors and who had left. By my tally, 16 interns came on board in my two years. All but five left in one circumstance or another. I had to find a more supportive school where I was viewed as competent and dedicated.

I made only one effort to find another job. I wrote to a principal who had come up to me after a speech I gave to the Annenberg Foundation a year before, a woman with a short blond Afro and fantastic jewelry who told me, "When you're done with your internship, call me. I like your attitude." Her school was known throughout the city as an exciting school that works for kids.

She called me soon after she received my letter to set up an interview. When I returned her call at 5:40 P.M., she answered the office phone herself. I was not surprised. By then, I understood the extraordinary dedication it took to be a strong school leader.

I set my sights on this school and this leader.

With bags under my eyes, wearing a ridiculous flowered dress and a jean jacket, I went for my interview at the new school. The day happened to be the day of the annual school carnival. I arrived as students were being dismissed. I couldn't believe how many children's names the principal knew. As the students left the building, they were walking, not running. Most were quiet, but if they were talking, it was in normal conversational tones, not screaming. At least 20 kids said to their principal as they left, "Thanks for the carnival."

The principal, vice principal, and I talked for nearly two hours. About teaching children. About testing. About assessment. About curriculum integration. About teams of teachers working collaboratively. The school, with corridors that looked like a museum of African art, had three bands, sports teams, afterschool dance and art programs, an entrepreneurship initiative and video club and book clubs, among other programs. We talked about a school paper and what they would like to see on a fifth-grade reading list.

I realized that I was poised on the brink of an excellent opportunity to see in action the kind of leadership that made this school stand out among 700 elementary schools in our city. I very much wanted to be part of an organization working hard, plowing forward. The faculty was dedicated, innovative, bright. Initiative was applauded. Everyone wore many hats. There were responsibilities to serve on committees, to formulate policies and philosophies. It was a unique team, constantly evolving, positive.

"I'm going to do something strange and forgo the secret conference with the vice principal and listen to my heart," the principal said. "I'm going to offer you the job right now."

I accepted the position on the spot, with sincere gratitude and humility.

POSTNOTE

Like the first year in many occupations (medicine, sales, the law), teaching often has a taxing break-in period. It is complicated by the fact that new teachers are shocked by the strangeness of something that is quite familiar: being in school. The issue, and the problem, is that new teachers are in an entirely different role. Being on "the other side of the desk" can be a world away. One of the most difficult aspects of the work for many new teachers is being "in charge." They know about school. They know their subjects. They know what their students should be doing. They don't, however, know how to get them to do it. They have not had much experience being the boss or "the responsible person." Neither have they had much experience with directing others or with what the military would call giving orders. Necessity, however, is still the mother of invention, and most new teachers adapt in time.

Ms. Baldacci's experience, however, was particularly challenging. With minimal training and little support, she was assigned to an extremely difficult teaching situation. It would be dangerous to generalize from Ms. Baldacci's experiences, as many beginning teachers make the transition to teacher with success and joy.

Discussion Questions

1. As a student, what memorable experiences did you have with new teachers? Describe them.
2. If and when you become a new teacher, what do you believe will be your most vulnerable areas?
3. What can you learn from this teacher's experience that may mitigate problems of your first year of teaching?

RELATED WEBSITE RESOURCES AND VIDEO CASES

 ## Web Resources:

Teachers First. Available at:

http://www.teachersfirst.com.

This website is a treasure trove of information, good ideas, lesson plans, and even humor. It is well organized and easy to search for the topic or need of choice.

 ## Video Case:

Teaching as a Profession: Collaboration with Colleagues

In this video case, you will hear teachers talk about the importance and the "how-to" of collaborating with colleagues. You will also see a formal collaborative work group in action. As you watch the clips and study the artifacts in the case, reflect upon the following questions:

1. How do the teachers' definitions of collaboration fit with your understanding of the concept?
2. Does the idea of the type of collaboration exhibited in this video case appeal to you? Why or why not?

For Another Perspective:

Claudia Graziano, *Lessons of a First-Year Teacher*

www.cengage.com/login

5

. . . And Why New Teachers Stay

Susan Moore Johnson

Susan Moore Johnson is a professor of teaching and learning at the Harvard University graduate School of Education. Professor Johnson is a former high school teacher and administrator.

Adapted from Susan Moore Johnson, *Finders and Keepers: Helping New Teachers Survive and Thrive in Our Schools.* Copyright © 2004 by Jossey-Bass. Reprinted in the Summer 2006 issue of *American Educator*, the quarterly journal of the American Federation of Teachers, AFL-CIO. Reproduced with permission of John Wiley & Sons, Inc.

| F | O | C | U | S | QUESTION

What keeps new teachers in the profession?

Esther spent nine years as an engineer designing flight simulators for Navy pilots before she considered teaching. She loved her job for its intellectual challenge, the collegial nature of her workplace, and the variety of tasks and responsibilities it offered. But she resigned when her first child was born because she did not think the demands of the job were compatible with raising a family. Her substantial salary had allowed Esther and her husband to build savings that would support them for several years on a single wage. However, after six years, their savings were low, prompting Esther to decide to work part-time as a substitute teacher in her children's school where she already served as a volunteer.

Gradually, Esther began to think about becoming a teacher. People had always said that she was good at explaining things, and she had enjoyed her work as a substitute. Also, teaching would make it possible for her to be home with her children after school and during vacations. But the decision was not easy. A beginning teacher's salary would be at least $30,000 less than she could earn if she returned to work as an engineer.

Nonetheless, Esther began to investigate education programs that would lead to a teaching license. Then, in spring 1999, the Massachusetts Department of Education announced the Massachusetts Signing Bonus Program (MSBP), which offered outstanding candidates $20,000 to participate in an intensive summer training institute and then teach in the state's public schools for at least four years. Massachusetts legislators intended the program to recruit talented individuals who traditionally would not have considered teaching, particularly in high-need subject areas, such as math, science, or special education, and in schools serving low-income populations (Fowler, 2001, 2003).

Esther found the bonus and its selectivity appealing, but she was most attracted by the fast-track alternative preparation program that state officials created to move bonus recipients quickly into the classroom. A seven-week institute, which included student teaching in a summer school, would enable Esther to have her own classroom of students by September. Given the length and expense of traditional teacher education programs, she found this very attractive and applied. She recalled, "It got me in at least a full year, if not more, earlier than I would have [entered]."

Soon after Esther learned that she had received the bonus, she was encouraged to apply for a job working on the space shuttle, a job she would have pursued if a suitable job had been available for her husband nearby. But this did not work out, so Esther completed the summer institute for MSBP teachers, and accepted a position teaching ninth-grade math in an urban, vocational high school. Given the shortage of mathematics and science teachers, particularly in urban areas, Esther was just the sort of skilled, unconventional candidate Massachusetts reformers had hoped to recruit. With idealism and enthusiasm, she hoped to draw on her experience as an engineer to help her students enjoy learning math.

But after her first year, Esther left for a more affluent school in the suburbs. What happened? And what happens across the nation to the 50 percent of new teachers who quit teaching all together within five years?

* * *

As Esther and her counterparts began teaching in 1999, public educators and policymakers across the country were preparing in earnest for a predicted teacher shortage. At the start of the new century, about 30 percent—approximately one million—of the nation's public school teachers were over 50 years old (NCES, 2002) and expected to retire by 2010. At the same time, increasing birth and immigration rates and, in some states, class-size reductions further expanded the need for new teachers. Experts projected that public schools would have to hire 2.2 million teachers during the first decade of the new century (Hussar, 1999).

This enormous hiring challenge is exacerbated by the very high turnover rates of new teachers. Nationally, approximately 15 percent of new teachers leave teaching within the first year, 30 percent within three years, and 40 to 50 percent within five years (Ingersoll, 2002; Smith and Ingersoll, 2003). To make matters worse, each year, 15 percent of new teachers change schools (Smith and Ingersoll, 2003).

The cost of this turnover is staggering: The Alliance for Excellent Education (2005) estimates the cost of teachers leaving their schools to be $4.9 billion per year. Of course, the greatest cost is not so easily quantified; it's the price paid in student learning. Researchers have consistently found that first-year teachers are dramatically less effective than their more experienced colleagues (Hanushek et al., 2004).

How can the constant turnover be reduced so our classrooms can be stably staffed? We can only answer the question by understanding the motivations, priorities, and experiences of the next generation of teachers. To do just that, in 1999, we began a four-year study of 50 first- and second-year Massachusetts

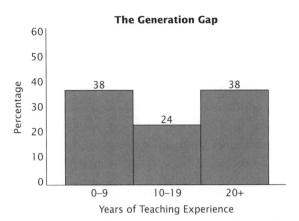

The Generation Gap

Source: *National Education Association*, Status of the American Public School Teacher, 2000–2001, Table 6. "Years of Full-time Teaching Experience, 1961–2001."

A large proportion of the teachers hired in the 1960s and 1970s made teaching a lifelong career; subsequently, student enrollment declined in the 1980s. As a result, the profile of today's national teaching force is increasingly U-shaped, with one peak of educators about to retire, another peak beginning to teach, and a valley in between.

teachers, including Esther,* who had entered teaching via various paths: traditional teacher education programs, the Massachusetts Signing Bonus Program, and charter schools (which, at that time, could hire teachers without state licenses). As we selected participants, we ensured that our sample included variation by race, gender, ethnicity, and career stage.

In our interviews and follow-up surveys, we sought to understand why they had chosen to teach, how they prepared, what their career plans were, what they encountered in their jobs, and why they ultimately chose to stay in their schools, switch schools, or leave the profession altogether.** In a nutshell, what we found was this: This next generation of teachers approaches teaching somewhat tentatively; they will only stay in the classroom if they feel successful and they are most likely to feel successful if they've received support in their jobs—specific, ongoing help from colleagues, administrators, and mentors—and been able to work in conditions that enable good teaching.

---

*Pseudonyms are used throughout this article to protect the teachers who participated in our research.

**Although the focus of this article is our longitudinal study of 50 teachers, we have conducted many related studies, including a four-state survey of 486 randomly selected first- and second-year teachers that was designed to generate broader, more generalizable findings.

In this article, we'll look at three aspects of our research that bring us to this conclusion: First, we'll consider the labor context in which these new teachers find themselves—and which makes them, like others in their generation, so much more open to changing jobs. Second, we'll look at the types of problems that thwart new teachers' classroom success, and then return to Esther to discover why she didn't feel successful in her vocational high school. Finally, we'll see that whether or not new teachers stay is strongly shaped by the amount of help they receive. Recognizing that success is possible, a sidebar (p. 20) looks at the case of Fred to understand how a strong induction experience, combined with a strong professional, collegial environment, can help teachers succeed—and in doing so, also lead them to stay a while.

I. The Next Generation Is Open to Job-Switching

The next generation of teachers makes career decisions in a labor context strikingly different from 40 years ago, and the interests and options of today's prospective teachers are unlike those of any teachers who preceded them. Until the mid-1960s, teaching was the primary career option for large numbers of well-educated women and people of color, for whom other professions were formally or informally off limits. That is no longer true. Individuals who consider teaching today have many more career options than the retiring generation—many of them with much higher salaries and better working conditions than teaching. In addition, today's new teachers are encountering unprecedented demands: The public now expects schools to teach all students so that they meet high standards—rich and poor, immigrant and native-born, white and minority, special needs and mainstream—and to take on new functions beyond the traditional scope of schools' responsibility. Teachers bear the burden of society's newer, higher expectations for schools (Hargreaves, 2003).

Let's briefly examine three significant ways in which the next generation of teachers differs from the retiring generation: the stage in their career in which they enter teaching, the routes they take to the classroom, and the number of years they expect to spend teaching (Peske, Liu, Johnson, Kauffman, and Kardos, 2001).

ENTERING TEACHING AT DIFFERENT CAREER STAGES
Many of today's new teachers are entering teaching midcareer (far more than ever before), most having worked for a substantial period of time in another

field. In our carefully selected sample of 50 Massachusetts first- and second-year teachers, 52 percent entered teaching as a first career, at an average age of 24, whereas 48 percent entered at midcareer, at an average age of 36. Although the number of midcareer entrants in our sample may seem high, subsequent random samples of first- and second-year teachers in seven states revealed that our sample was fairly representative; we found a range of midcareer entrants from 28 percent in Michigan to 47 percent in California (Kardos, 2001, 2003; Kauffman, 2004; Liu, 2001, 2003).

Many of the first-career entrants are similar to the reciting generation in that they always wanted to teach and never seriously considered any other careers: "I feel like I always just knew," explained one. "It sounds corny, but I was born wanting to teach," echoed another. They believed that teaching would be socially valuable and personally rewarding work, yet recognized that the work was neither high-paying nor high-status.

The 24 midcareer entrants in our study came to teaching later, believing that it offered more meaningful work than did their previous employment. As a group, these midcareer entrants brought with them a familiarity with large and small organizations, for-profit and non-profit enterprises, entrepreneurial and bureaucratic settings. Some had worked for multiple supervisors, whereas others had been supervisors themselves. Some had experienced well-defined, useful, and ongoing on-the-job training; some had devised such training for other employees. Thus, midcareer entrants often enter their new school expecting a workplace that was better equipped, more flexible, and more committed to their success than the one they found. They were often dismayed when they found that their new workplaces were dreary or dilapidated, that they had scant access to telephones or the time to use them, that basic resources such as paper were in short supply, and that they had to use precious time to do routine, clerical tasks.

TAKING MULTIPLE ROUTES TO THE CLASSROOM
Thirty-two of the 50 new teachers we studied entered teaching by traditional routes, pursuing undergraduate and graduate programs that included at least one academic year of coursework, supervised student teaching for six weeks to 10 months, and, ultimately, certification. In general, they appreciated that their programs offered valuable information about pedagogy and opportunities to practice their craft under the supervision of an experienced veteran during the school year.

Eighteen teachers in our study entered through an alternate route—five via charter schools and 13 via the Massachusetts Signing Bonus Program (MSBP). The teachers who went to work in charter schools completed no teacher preparation program. The MSBP participants completed a seven-week, summer preparation program operated by the state, including a short stint of student teaching in summer school. Nine of these 13 had entered the MSBP with no prior teacher preparation; three others had previously completed certification requirements in traditional master's programs before joining the program, and one had completed all but the student teaching requirement in an undergraduate teacher preparation program. In general, the nontraditional entrants counted more on the value of innate teaching ability and professional experience than on the content of education courses or a student teaching experience. The alternative route was particularly appealing for the midcareer entrants who otherwise would have had to forego a year's pay while completing a traditional program.

COMMITTING FOR A WHILE, NOT A LIFETIME

In contrast to their veteran colleagues who will retire from a lifelong career in the classroom, many new teachers in our sample approached teaching tentatively, conditionally, or as one of several careers they expected to have. Although some expected to remain in the field of education long-term, surprisingly few envisioned remaining exclusively in the classroom long-term. Even the first-career entrants, who 30 years ago would probably have approached teaching as a long-term endeavor, were surprisingly tentative about a career limited to classroom teaching. In fact, only four of the 26 first-career entrants said that they planned to remain classroom teachers until they retire. Likewise, even though they had fewer working years left, only six of the 24 midcareer teachers intended to stay in the classroom full time for the rest of their careers.

Many of the teachers—11 first-careers and 13 midcareers—stated explicitly that they did not intend to stay for the rest of their careers. One respondent, a former software developer, explained, "I'm a career changer. I figured, Why not explore a new field?" Another, a recent college graduate, planned to enroll in medical school after teaching for two years. He said, "I knew I wanted to go to medical school. I knew I did not want to go right after college, and so I decided, What can I do that won't pay too badly and that will make me feel like I'm doing something interesting and important?" Though these teachers made only a short-term commitment, they were not at all casual about what they hoped to achieve in the classroom. They intended to pour themselves into the job, giving it all they had, but only for a few years.

II. What New Teachers Want— and Often Aren't Getting

Given the career options and lack of long-term commitment to teaching that characterize the next generation of teachers, schools and districts that hope to hold on to new teachers will have to pay close attention to what these teachers say they want: support. The new teachers in our study described in considerable detail the internal workings of their schools, explaining the ways in which those schools succeeded or failed in supporting learning (of both the teachers and the students). Their accounts make it clear that the support they seek isn't just a matter of wanting their jobs to be easier—it's a matter of making their jobs doable, and giving them a chance to experience the success with their students that is teaching's primary reward.

Threaded through the new teachers' stories were accounts of inattentive or abusive principals, inappropriate or unfair assignments, inadequate supplies, ad hoc approaches to discipline, insufficient time with other teachers, and insufficient opportunities to grow—each of which we briefly discuss below. New teachers who worked in schools lacking these basic supports were demoralized and often felt ineffective with their students. They typically were the ones who left teaching.

PROBLEMS WITH PRINCIPALS

These new teachers' accounts reinforce the finding of repeated research studies that the principal is central in shaping how, and how well, a school works (Murphy, 2002). Teachers we studied spoke intently about how their principals related to them personally and professionally. They wanted administrators to be present, positive, and actively engaged in the instructional life of the school. Often, the principals failed to meet these teachers' expectations. Most were said to succeed in some things but fall short in others. A surprising number were, in these teachers' views, ineffectual, demoralizing, or even destructive.

Teachers frequently said that the principal was preoccupied and did not make time for them. Carolyn, who worked in a large, urban elementary school where 70 percent of the students qualified for free- or reduced-price lunch, found her principal "a little gruff," and said she was disappointed to see her keep such a distance from the staff: "She has bulletins that she sends out. It's really her main form of communication with us." As a result, Carolyn explained, "there is a sense of the administration being higher and separate from the teachers." Carolyn looked to her principal for direction, but said that she often took problems out of

Carolyn's hands with a brusque "I'll take care of it," rather than recommending how she might respond. Like other new teachers, Carolyn wanted to learn from her principal: "So a lot of time, I'll have to keep probing her [by asking], 'In another scenario, how would I handle this…?' or 'What are the consequences [for the student] that the school has for this?'"

PROBLEMS WITH TEACHING ASSIGNMENTS

In the typical professional setting, it is common to give inexperienced staff less responsibility combined with fairly intensive oversight by a veteran—but not in teaching. No teacher in our study had a reduced teaching assignment. Bernie's high school load in the history department was typical: "I have two honors classes and three of what they have labeled as 'open' classes [for low-achieving students]. Open classes also have special ed kids.…Five classes, five times a week: The kids have seven periods. I have one free period a day. Otherwise, I'm on hall duty, or bathroom duty, or what have you." Bernie, whose time as a corporate lawyer had been billed by the minute, was dismayed to find that his time as a teacher was used to "make sure that nobody smokes in the boys' room."

Not only was Bernie's assignment not reduced, but he, like many in our study, actually had a more difficult assignment than his more experienced colleagues. "I have the highest class size of any open [lower track] class. All the other open classes in the school, I found out this week, are all like 10 kids. Mine are 30 and 25." Moreover, Bernie had no classroom or desk to call his own and moved from room-to-room during the day as an itinerant instructor. Throughout the study, teachers described assignments that, although technically comparable to those of their colleagues (the same number of students, the same number of classes), were actually far more challenging. Their loads included a preponderance of low-level classes, grade-levels in which students would take the state exam, split grades, or assignments that required traveling from classroom-to-classroom or school-to-school.

PROBLEMS WITH SUPPLIES AND EQUIPMENT

There was wide variation in the equipment and supplies provided to the new teachers, with predictable differences between urban and suburban schools (although some teachers in urban schools said that they had all they needed). Like many who came from other careers, Esther was stunned at how ill-equipped her school was, particularly compared to the suburban school where she had done substitute teaching. She recalled a time when there was no paper available and "the secretary

was taking out her secret stash." Likewise, Bernie said it was "just ridiculous" that he was allotted three reams of paper per quarter. With no classroom of his own, Bernie had to rely on photocopied handouts rather than blackboards in order to convey important information to students. Three reams of paper didn't last long: "I go through that probably in…a week and a half, two weeks." He said only somewhat wryly, "Some of the most useful tips I've gotten from veteran teachers have to do with font size and making sure I copy on both sides of paper.…" Bernie, like many others, complained that the photocopiers in his school never worked. He observed, "In the business world, they would have a photocopy center where you could either do it yourself, or have somebody on staff [do it]."

PROBLEMS WITH STUDENT BEHAVIOR

There is no more immediate and worrisome challenge for new teachers than establishing and maintaining order in their classroom. Some new teachers worked in schools that deliberately focused everyone's efforts on instruction and systematically discouraged disruption and distraction; they supported instruction respectfully with a calm and purposeful environment. Far more often, however, teachers talked about coping on their own, without the benefit of a schoolwide approach to discipline that was endorsed and upheld by teachers and administrators alike. Many teachers complained about school administrators who failed to follow through on discipline. Often, new teachers reported being reluctant to ask for help from school administrators, believing that their requests would evoke disapproval. For example, Bernie was not confident he could rely on administrators for support: "I'm not sure that they back people up. I've heard stories that have made me really nervous about teachers being called to the mat…for something as simple as removing a kid from the classroom because they're disruptive."

PROBLEMS WITH SCHEDULING TIME TO COLLABORATE

How their time was scheduled was very important to the new teachers, particularly whether their preparation periods—usually one per day—were coordinated with those of other teachers who taught the same subject or students. New teachers praised schools that deliberately arranged their schedules so that they could plan classes or review students' progress together.

Secondary schools that featured project-based learning, interdisciplinary classes, or team-based instruction often arranged time for teachers to collaborate. But in more traditional secondary schools, preparation periods often seemed haphazardly assigned, more likely the byproduct of a computerized scheduling program than the result of deliberate planning. Bernie was dismayed that teachers—particularly new ones—did not have the benefit of their peers' knowledge and advice. He thought that the teachers in his school would have worked more closely together if their assignments had made that possible.

At the elementary level, teachers were even less likely to have coordinated planning or grade-level meeting time. Keisha, who worked in a school where 83 percent of the students were below grade level in reading, wished that there were opportunities to observe other teachers in their classrooms, "but we don't have that type of release time. Our [paraprofessionals] are hung up doing whatever. We can't get subs." However, Victoria said that in her suburban school, time was reserved for weekly grade-level meetings to "just go over what's happening."

PROBLEMS WITH PROFESSIONAL GROWTH OPPORTUNITIES

Focused though they were on developing classroom competence, the new teachers nonetheless continued to assess what a career in teaching could offer them over time. Many of these teachers hoped to eventually take on a new role that would allow them to continue, at least part-time, as classroom teachers. They did not want to exit the classroom entirely and become a principal or district administrator, but they also did not want to be confined to the classroom. They believed that a hybrid role might combat boredom and burnout while offering new challenges and rewards that would keep them engaged in teaching over the long term.

Some new teachers liked the professional advancement inherent in a career ladder. As novices, they saw that such positions could offer a formal conduit through which experts could pass on teaching expertise—and they looked forward to taking on roles as expert teachers in the future. Mary, who had done crisis work with adults for six years before becoming a teacher, explained, "My sense is that there are a lot of people coming in and then leaving, with very little connection between the new people and the experienced people. Then you get experienced people…who want to share their experience, but don't really know how.…There would be a value in passing along their experience and knowledge." Without such roles, Mary said, "I don't think people will stay."

Despite considerable interest in differentiated roles, with the exception of the well-established position of department head, few could point to examples of the kind of role they had in mind. One new teacher bemoaned this situation: "You're either a teacher or you're a coach or you're a principal, and I don't like that idea at all."

* * *

All new teachers believed that schools could either facilitate or impede good teaching. When the basics like supplies and a schoolwide discipline plan were combined with an administration that offered useful feedback and scheduled time for teachers to collaborate, new teachers were very likely to stay in their schools. Unfortunately, such schools were not the norm. Nonetheless, even when the new teachers were only reasonably hopeful that they could become effective with their students, they were still likely to stay. However, those who thought that their school's lack of support interfered with successful teaching often moved on—either to another school or another career. The table below provides the bare facts on the numbers of new teachers who stayed, switched schools, or left teaching after the first year of our study and after the fourth year. The new teachers are broken down by first-career vs. midcareer entrants to highlight one interesting trend: Midcareer entrants were more likely to switch schools right away. Since they had already changed jobs at least once when they entered teaching, they knew that work sites could vary tremendously. They did not regard the problems they encountered as inevitable, so they quickly looked for a place where they could give teaching another chance.

Esther did just that.

Who Stayed? Who Moved? Who Left? First-career vs. Midcareer Entrants after the First Year of Our Study and after the Fourth Year

	After 1 year		After 4 years	
	First-Career Entrants	Midcareer Entrants	First-Career Entrants	Midcareer Entrants
Stayed in the school where they started	21	13	8	9
Moved to another school	1	7	8	8
Left public school teaching	4	4	10	7

ESTHER STRUGGLES—AND MOVES ON

Esther, a MSBP participant and former engineer, was dropped into teaching math at an urban vocational high school with virtually no explanation or advice. She summarized the guidance she had: "Here are your keys, here's your room, good luck." Entering a complex vocational school with only summer preservice training behind her, Esther was bewildered and overwhelmed. A sudden and solo entry not only stymies new teachers, it shortchanges students. Success in a new assignment requires much more than having a set of keys and knowing where the classroom is.

During the first two weeks, Esther thought about quitting every day. She could not figure out how to get her students to listen to her. In December of that first year, she reported, "They won't sit still; their rudeness; their total disrespect for each other, for the teacher, their language, everything. They can't speak to you; they only yell...I have never seen anything like it."

Esther received little help in teaching students from the teachers and administrators in her school. She said her ineffectual principal—whom her colleagues openly mocked in the teachers' room—did not seem to like her, and other teachers kept their doors closed before and after school. Aside from another new teacher with whom she shared ideas and one veteran who offered informal advice when they saw each other during hall duty, she felt she was on her own in learning to reach her students.

Esther was assigned a mentor, but she was a special education teacher who knew little about the math that Esther was teaching: "I've spoken to this lady twice, maybe for five minutes....She's very nice and stuff, but she kind of goes by and kind of gives me a worried look [and says], 'How's it going?' I say, 'OK.' And then, that's it." But Esther had hoped for curricular and instructional support from someone who knew how to teach math. One person she logically looked to for help was the math department head. However, the department head explained that she could not step in as Esther's mentor because she was responsible for evaluating her, and she could only observe her class for the purpose of formal review. Learning to teach was hard enough; learning to teach on her own, with students whose disengagement and behavior so surprised her, was overwhelming.

Feeling exhausted and defeated in the spring of her first year, she decided to look elsewhere for work. "It was too hard emotionally. There was nothing I could do.... I think I would have tried it another year because there were kids there that were very nice, but the administration was not...supportive." Esther found a job teaching math at a more affluent high school near her home in the suburbs. As she left the vocational high school she was surprised and touched by the students' reactions. "It was funny. When I quit the last day of school last year...when I told the kids I wasn't coming back, they said, 'Why are you leaving us? What did we do to you?' I am thinking, 'What did you do to me? What did you call me?'"

At her new high school, Esther found supportive colleagues and administrators. She recalled, "I had a director who...said 'What can I do for you? Come to me with your questions.'" Moreover, Esther benefited from her department's deliberate introduction to the math curriculum: "At the beginning of the year, we sat down, and they told us what chapters to teach. You know, 'This is what we do. This is the order we do it.'"

She also achieved a much greater sense of success. She recalled that at the end of the year at her new school, "I had several students say 'You have to keep teaching. You did a good job.'" The positive feedback heartened her—teaching students was a key reason she had switched careers in the first place.

Esther regarded her decision to leave her urban vocational school with some regret, wishing she had found a way to succeed with her students there. But her decision is not unusual. Recent work by researchers studying teacher turnover in Texas and New York (Hanushek, Kain, and Rivkin, 2001; Lankford, Loeb, and Wyckoff, 2002) reveals that teachers consistently move to schools with "higher achieving, non-minority, non-low-income students" (Hanushek et al., 2001, p.12). In fact, large, urban schools that serve low-income students have nearly twice the annual teacher turnover as large, suburban schools that serve fewer low-income students (19 percent versus 11 percent) (Ingersoll, 2006).

Why? Working conditions are key. Recently, a survey of 3,336 teachers in California, Wisconsin, and New York was conducted to learn how working conditions differed in low-income versus affluent communities (Carroll, Fulton, Abercrombie, and Yoon, 2004). Researchers found that schools serving large numbers of low-income students and children of color were reported to have a much higher incidence of inadequate physical facilities than other schools; evidence of vermin (cockroaches, mice, and rats) in the school buildings; dirty, closed, or inoperative student bathrooms; inadequate textbooks and materials for students to use in class or to take home; inadequate computers and limited Internet access; inadequate science equipment and materials; and higher personal expenditures by teachers to compensate for insufficient classroom materials and supplies.

Another reason why teachers move to more affluent schools is that learning to teach is difficult, complex work. New teachers need support and guidance in order to achieve success. But we have found that support is often hardest to come by in low-income urban and rural schools, which very often have few institutional resources and low levels of student achievement. Our work shows that more affluent schools tend to provide more support to help new teachers succeed.

III. Support Breeds Success and Stability

When we examined teachers' reasons for staying in their school, transferring to another school, or leaving public school teaching entirely, we realized there were three distinct kinds of schools—and only one of them was doing a good job supporting, and holding on to, new teachers. The key was in the schools' professional culture. The first kind of school had a mix of veterans and novices, but teachers worked in isolation instead of learning from one another. The second kind had a teaching staff comprised almost entirely of novices who were bound by their enthusiasm, but lacking skill. The third kind had veterans and novices who were encouraged to work together, sharing expertise and fresh ideas. In our sample of 50 new Massachusetts teachers, 17 began their careers in schools that fostered such collaborations—and 82 percent of them stayed in those schools after the first year of our study. In contrast, just 57 percent of the 21 teachers who began their careers in schools where teachers worked in isolation stayed, as did just 67 percent of the 12 who began in schools filled with novices. Just what does a school where teachers collaborate look like? Fred's experience, described in the sidebar (p. 20), provides an excellent example.

* * *

New teachers yearn for professional colleagues who can help them acclimate to their school's unique culture, help them solve the complicated, daily dilemmas of classroom teaching, and guide their ongoing learning. When the 50 teachers in our study chose teaching, they envisioned the stimulating classroom they hoped to create and the buzz of their students engaged in learning. In the ideal, they also hoped for colleagues and administrators who would be committed to student learning and would help them, as new teachers, achieve success with their students.

Regardless of the quality or duration of new teacher's preservice preparation, novice teachers must continue to learn long after they enter the classroom.

They continue to improve their skills and adjust their strategies for delivering engaging lessons. They learn about the philosophy of their school and what administrators, colleagues, and parents expect of them. They learn about the students, their families, and the community. They learn to keep order in their classroom, better manage their time, and differentiate instruction in response to students' needs. They become better at involving parents more effectively, fostering student responsibility, and assessing student progress. They learn to create curriculum, integrate technology into their teaching, and better prepare students for standardized tests. Leaving new teachers on their own to address these complex and dynamic challenges is both unreasonable and unnecessary, particularly since they are surrounded by colleagues doing similar work.

By building a career ladder for classroom teachers, schools can deliver what the new teachers in our study want—both a supportive work environment while they are new and opportunities to grow once they have more experience. With career ladders that formalize roles such as mentors, master teachers, curriculum developers, or professional development planners, schools can be organized so that novices have a well-integrated support system with plenty of colleagues to turn to, and veterans have options that will challenge them without removing them from the classroom completely. Ideally, school districts and teacher unions will collaborate to create these career ladders and help schools become supportive workplaces that foster new teachers' success. Our study demonstrated that such schools—schools like Fred's—have dramatically less attrition among new teachers. That's good for the schools' bottom line and great for students' academic achievement.

Fred Plans to Stay "Forever"

Fred began his teaching career at a small, urban secondary school. He was deeply committed to his students' success and to the continuing development of his school. When we first met Fred, his school included grades seven, eight, and nine, and school leaders planned to add one grade every year through grade 12. Though it is a neighborhood public school, drawing its students from the low-income community that immediately surrounds it, it is also a professional development school, the result of a unique partnership between a local university and the city school district. The faculty includes both highly experienced teachers and newer teachers. Most of the newer teachers have traditional teacher preparation, master's degrees, and internship experience at the school.

To Fred, his school is about high expectations, collaboration, and ongoing teacher learning, all in the service of high student achievement. As he explained, "the expectations are so clear...we're gearing these kids to college, that that's our ultimate goal: to get the kids ready for college." The expectations are high for student and teacher performance, but neither is left alone to achieve the mission.

Given that these students had varying levels of academic skills and primarily came from low-income neighborhoods, every aspect of the school had to focus on academic success—even the approach to managing student behavior. Both the faculty and the administration, Fred said, "treat every problem, no matter how minute, as a significant disciplinary issue. And because of that, we don't have the typical problems that other schools do. I mean, problems that other schools would laugh at in terms of discipline are dealt with pretty harshly here. But I think that has created an atmosphere that is conducive to good discipline." In the school's three-year history, there had been no fights among students. "And that's pretty remarkable when you think that it's seventh-, eighth-, and ninth-graders." He credited the principal with setting the standard: "Things are dealt with immediately by the principal. She's got a good relationship with the kids. They know not to disappoint her."

But the principal wasn't just the disciplinarian. She founded the professional development school and was deeply involved in making it work. Fred said, "She's an innovator. She's an example....She's constantly looking for new ideas and new ways of solving old problems, which is unique....No problem is too large [for her] and...you don't have to guess where she stands on the issues." But at the same time, "She's very good at telling us what kind of job we do and how she appreciates it....She's willing to put her confidence in the hands of the professionals that are teachers here." He explained, "That type of freedom and confidence creates a good feeling amongst the faculty."

According to Fred, the fact that the faculty included a mix of new and experienced teachers "promotes the best type of situation for faculty." He described the interaction among novice and veteran teachers this way: "So we have a nice blend of veteran teachers who have been in the system for a long time and know the art of teaching. Then we also have a nice core of... young teachers like myself with less than five years of teaching experience. And that creates a really good atmosphere. So I think the young teachers learn from the veteran teachers. And I think the veteran teachers get sparked a little bit from the young teachers coming in, you know, a new, fresh attitude. So it's mutually enriching in that sense."

It is important to note that there is nothing inherently beneficial about simply having a mix of novices and veterans within the same school. What is exceptional at Fred's school is that teachers of varying experience levels interact regularly, both formally and informally. Fred described a typical situation: "If I have a question or if I had something happen in class that perplexed me that I didn't know how to deal with, then I go down to [Sue] or [Tom] and say, 'I'm having trouble, how do I deal with this?'"

Fred said the school's culture emphasizes "teachers as learners," and it is expected that teachers will learn when they work together. The teachers had 90 minutes four times each week for preparation and collaborative work. Learning to teach is an ongoing process; a teacher masters the art by practicing, over time. Thus, administrators and teacher leaders at Fred's school realized that it serves their school well to recognize that new teachers grow in skill and expertise day-to-day and year-to-year: "There's an expectation that you would mature as a teacher and develop new strategies in various arenas that you may not have had in your bag of tricks to begin with."

Fred also explained that his fellow teachers feel and act as if they are collectively responsible for the school, the students, and each other: "We're all in the same game here together." He explained that he believed it is his "responsibility, as it is everybody else's, to share in the burden" of achieving the school's mission. In speaking of his duty to all of the students in the school he said, "I'm not primarily a social studies teacher here; I'm a teacher here primarily."

After just a few years of teaching in this supportive environment, Fred was ready to start venturing beyond the traditional role of a classroom teacher. He became the de facto head of the social studies department: "The principal has kind of put me in charge of making sure that the social studies curriculum is being covered." He also supervised two student teachers, which he especially enjoyed: "It worked great. I love it. Their ideas keep me fresh. And I think I lend a little bit of experience to them. And it's mutually enriching, you know." Fred looked forward to being able to take on even more in the years ahead; his school had specialized roles for master teachers who serve as staff developers and work with intern teachers. Fred observed that such positions were "enriching" both for the individuals holding them and for the people they assisted.

Clearly, those in Fred's school believe that teachers hold knowledge and power, and that students are best served when teachers assist each other and share responsibility for their students' learning as well as their own. Mentoring is organized to benefit both the novice and the experienced teachers, and the administration ensures that structures are in place to further facilitate teacher interaction and reinforce interdependence. Fred said he hoped to remain in his school "forever." But he made it clear that, were it not for his school, he might have left teaching: "If I weren't at this school, I wouldn't be a teacher. I really don't think I would be." It was his appreciation for his school that reinforced his commitment: "I plan on making it a career. So, 20, 30 years."

—S.M.J.

REFERENCES

Alliance for Excellent Education (2005). "Teacher attrition: A costly loss to the nation and states," *Issue Brief.* Washington, D.C.: Alliance for Excellent Education.

Carroll, T. G., Fulton, K., Abercrombie, K., and Yoon, I. (2004). *Fifty Years After Brown v. Board of Education: A Two-Tiered Education System.* Washington, D.C.: National Commission on Teaching and America's Future.

Fowler, R.C. (2001). *An analysis of recruitment, preparation, attrition, and placement of the Massachusetts Signing Bonus teachers.* Unpublished manuscript.

Fowler, R.C. (2003, April 22). "The Massachusetts Signing Bonus Program for New Teachers: A model of teacher preparation worth copying?" *Education Policy Analysis Archives, 11*(13). Available: **http://epaa.asu.edu/epaa/vlln13/** [2003. July 15].

Hanushek, E.A., Kain, J.F., and Rivkin, S.G. (2001). *Why public schools lose teachers* (Working Paper 8599). Cambridge, Mass.: National Bureau of Economic Research.

Hanushek, E.A., Kain, J.F., O'Brien, D.M., and Rivkin, S.G. (2004). "The market for teacher quality." Paper prepared for American Economic Association Meetings, Philadelphia, January 6–8, 2005.

Hargreaves, A. (2003). *Teaching in the knowledge society: Education in the age of insecurity.* New York: Teachers College Press.

Hussar, W.J. (1999). *Predicting the need for newly hired teachers in the United States to 2008–09.* Washington, D.C.: National Center for Education Statistics, U.S. Department of Education.

Ingersoll, R. (2002). "The teacher shortage: A case of wrong diagnosis and wrong prescription." *NASSP Bulletin, 86,* 16–31.

Ingersoll, R.M. (2006). "The Teacher Shortage: A case of wrong diagnosis and wrong prescription." Presentation acquired via personal communication, May 2006.

Kardos, S.M. (2001). *New teachers in New Jersey schools and the professional cultures they experience: A pilot study.* Unpublished Special Qualifying Paper, Harvard University Graduate School of Education, Cambridge.

Kardos, S.M. (2003). *Integrated professional culture: Exploring new teachers' experiences in four states.* Paper presented at the American Educational Research Association, Chicago, Ill.

Kauffman, D. (2004). *Second-year teachers' experiences with curriculum materials: A three-state survey.* Cambridge, Mass.: Harvard University Graduate School of Education.

Lankford, H., Loeb, S., and Wyckoff, J. (2002). "Teacher sorting and the plight of urban schools: A descriptive analysis." *Educational Evaluation and Policy Analysis, 24*(1), 37–62.

Liu, E. (2001). *New teachers' experiences of hiring.* Unpublished Special Qualifying Paper, Harvard University Graduate School of Education, Cambridge, Mass.

Liu, E. (2003). *New teachers' experiences of hiring: Preliminary findings from a four-state study.* Paper presented at the American Educational Research Association, Chicago, Ill.

Murphy, J. (Ed.) (2002). *The educational leadership challenge: Redefining leadership for the 21st century.* Chicago, Ill.: University of Chicago Press.

NCES (2002). *Schools and Staffing Survey, 1999–2000: Overview of the Data for Public, Private, Public Charter, and Bureau of Indian Affairs Elementary and Secondary Schools,* by Kerry J. Gruber, Susan D. Wiley, Stephen P. Broughman, Gregory A. Strizek, and Marisa Burian-Fitzgerald. Washington, D.C.: U.S. Department of Education.

Peske, H.G., Liu, E., Johnson, S.M., Kauffman, D., and Kardos, S.M. (2001). "Counting on colleagues: New teachers encounter the professional cultures of their schools." *Educational Administration Quarterly, 37*(2), 250–290.

Peske, H.G., Liu, E., Johnson, S.M., Kauffman, D., and Kardos, S.M. (2001). "The next generation of teachers: Changing conceptions of a career in teaching." *Phi Delta Kappan, 83*(4), 304–311.

Smith, T. and Ingersoll, R. (2003). "The wrong solution to the teacher shortage." *Educational Leadership, 60*(8), 30–33.

Smith, T. and Ingersoll, R. (2003, April). *Reducing teacher turnover: What are the components of effective induction?* Paper presented at the American Educational Research Association, Chicago, Ill.

POSTNOTE

This article, a companion piece to the previous article by Leslie Baldacci, looks at the same issues of new teacher initiation. However, while identifying many of the same problems, such as inept or unsupportive principals and assignments to the more difficult classrooms, this article stresses the positive. In particular, Professor Johnson identifies a crucial factor: the existence of special support for new teachers. Having a mentor who can interpret what is going on in the school culture or help you get your hands on textbooks and materials can make all the difference for a new teacher.

The author also points out that approximately fifty percent of new teachers have left the field after five years. While this is distressing and, as she points out, socially quite expensive, the figure is in line with general first job figures. Most young people do, indeed, change their first jobs, typically moving into another line of work. In this regard, teaching is not an exception to the rule. It should be noted, though, that the daily experience of teaching—that is, of being "in charge" of groups, of planning lessons, of delivering them, of making mid-course adjustments, and of evaluating results—is quite valuable. New teachers, unlike many of their college peers, are given a great deal of responsibility right away. This is experience they can use in many walks of life.

Discussion Questions

1. What were the new teacher's problems and how did she eventually solve them?
2. What were the teacher's sources of distress and support in her first two assignments?
3. What does the author suggest you look for in your first teaching assignment?

RELATED WEBSITE RESOURCES AND VIDEO CASES

 Web Resources:

Teachers First. Available at:

http://www.teachersfirst.com.

This website, cited in the previous article, is a valuable resource of information, good ideas, lesson plans, and even humor. It is well organized and easy to search for the topic or need of choice.

 **Video Case:**

Collaboration with School Specialists: An Elementary School Lesson

Older, Career-changing teachers, in particular, may not be familiar with the range of school specialists which are available to classroom teachers in many schools. In this video, you will see one specialist, a school-based Literacy Coordinator, Caitlin McArdle, help classroom teacher, Brian LoBue. Brian has questions about the effectiveness of the reading comprehension strategies he is teaching one child. Through conversation and observation, Caitlin helps Brian answer his questions. As you watch the clips and study the artifacts in the case reflect upon the following questions:

1. A new teacher might be shy about asking for help. Why do you think a new teacher may feel this away? What could a new teacher do to overcome such feelings?
2. Caitlin suggests that teaching is a journey in which there is always something new to learn. How might collaboration with someone like Caitlin make your journey as a teacher all the richer?

For Another Perspective:

Claudia Graziano, *Lessons of a First-Year Teacher*

www.cengage.com/login

Teachers as Transformative Intellectuals

6

Henry Giroux

Henry Giroux currently holds the Global Television Network Chair in English and Cultural Studies at McMasters University in Ontario, Canada. A former social studies teacher, Giroux has, for thirty years, been a leading theorist for, and advocate of, critical pedagogy, the school of educational thinking which attempts to stimulate students' critical consciousness. In this classic 1985 essay, Giroux challenged teachers to escape the chains of the status quo and embrace the true liberatory mission of education. © *National Council for the Social Studies.* Reprinted by permission.

The call for educational reform has gained the status of a recurring national event, much like the annual Boston Marathon. There have been more than 30 national reports since the beginning of the 20th century, and more than 300 task forces have been developed by the various states to discover how public schools can improve educational quality in the United States.[1] But unlike many past educational reform movements, the present call for educational change presents *both* a threat and challenge to public school teachers that appears unprecedented in our nation's history. The threat comes in the form of a series of educational reforms that display little confidence in the ability of public school teachers to provide intellectual and moral leadership for our nation's youth. For instance, many of the recommendations that have emerged in the current debate either ignore the role teachers play in preparing learners to be active and critical citizens, or they suggest reforms that ignore the intelligence, judgment and experience that teachers might offer in such a debate. Where teachers do enter the debate, they are the object of educational reforms that reduce them to the status of high-level technicians carrying out dictates and objectives decided by "experts" far removed from the everyday realities of classroom life.[2] The message appears to be that teachers do not count when it comes to critically examining the nature and process of educational reform.

The political and ideological climate does not look favorable for teachers at the moment. But it does offer them the challenge to join in a public debate with their critics as well as the opportunity to engage in a much-needed self-critique regarding the nature and purpose of teacher preparation, inservice

Should a teacher be an intellectual or an educational technician?

KEY TERMS

Deskilled teachers
Disempowerment
Reflective practitioner
Teacher-proof curriculum
Transformative intellectual

---

[1] K. Patricia Cross, "The Rising Tide of School Reform Reports," *Phi Delta Kappan, 66*:3 (November 1984), p. 167.

[2] For a more detailed critique of the reforms, see my book with Stanley Aronowitz, *Education Under Siege* (South Hadley, MA: Bergin and Garvey Publishers, 1985); also see the incisive comments on the impositional nature of the various reports in Charles A. Tesconi, Jr., "Additive Reforms and the Retreat from Purpose," *Educational Studies* 15:1 (Spring 1984), pp. 1–11; Terrence E. Deal, "Searching for the Wizard: The Quest for Excellence in Education," *Issues in Education* 2:1 (Summer 1984), pp. 56–67; Svi Shapiro, "Choosing Our Educational Legacy: Disempowerment or Emancipation?" *Issues in Education* 2:1 (Summer 1984), pp. 11–22.

teacher programs and the dominant forms of classroom teaching. Similarly, the debate provides teachers with the opportunity to organize collectively so as to struggle to improve the conditions under which they work and to demonstrate to the public the central role that teachers must play in any viable attempt to reform the public schools.

In order for teachers and others to engage in such a debate, it is necessary that a theoretical perspective be developed that redefines the nature of the educational crisis while simultaneously providing the basis for an alternative view of teacher training and work. In short, recognizing that the current crisis in education largely has to do with the developing trend towards the disempowerment of teachers at all levels of education is a necessary theoretical precondition in order for teachers to organize effectively and establish a collective voice in the current debate. Moreover, such a recognition will have to come to grips not only with a growing loss of power among teachers around the basic conditions of their work, but also with a changing public perception of their role as reflective practitioners.

I want to make a small theoretical contribution to this debate and the challenge it calls forth by examining two major problems that need to be addressed in the interest of improving the quality of "teacher work," which includes all the clerical tasks and extra assignments as well as classroom instruction. First, I think it is imperative to examine the ideological and material forces that have contributed to what I want to call the proletarianization of teacher work; that is, the tendency to reduce teachers to the status of specialized technicians within the school bureaucracy, whose function then becomes one of managing and implementing curricula programs rather than developing or critically appropriating curricula to fit specific pedagogical concerns. Second, there is a need to defend schools as institutions essential to maintaining and developing a critical democracy and also to defending teachers as transformative intellectuals who combine scholarly reflection and practice in the service of educating students to be thoughtful, active citizens. In the remainder of this essay, I will develop these points and conclude by examining their implications for providing an alternative view of teacher work.

Toward a Devaluing and Deskilling of Teacher Work

One of the major threats facing prospective and existing teachers within the public schools is the increasing development of instrumental ideologies that emphasize a technocratic approach to both teacher preparation and classroom pedagogy. At the core of the current emphasis on instrumental and pragmatic factors in school life are a number of important pedagogical assumptions. These include: a call for the separation of conception from execution; the standardization of school knowledge in the interest of managing and controlling it; and the devaluation of critical, intellectual work on the part of teachers and students for the primacy of practical considerations.[3]

This type of instrumental rationality finds one of its strongest expressions historically in the training of prospective teachers. That teacher training programs in the United States have long been dominated by a behavioristic orientation and emphasis on mastering subject areas and methods of teaching is well documented.[4] The implications of this approach, made clear by Zeichner, are worth repeating:

> Underlying this orientation to teacher education is a metaphor of "production," a view of teaching as an "applied science" and a view of the teacher as primarily an "executor" of the laws and principles of effective teaching. Prospective teachers may or may not proceed through the curriculum at their own pace and may participate in varied or standardized learning activities, but that which they are to master is limited in scope (e.g., to a body of professional content knowledge and teaching skills) and is fully determined in advance by others often on the basis of research on teacher effectiveness. The prospective teacher is viewed primarily as a passive recipient of this professional knowledge and plays little part in determining the substance and direction of his or her preparation program.[5]

The problems with this approach are evident in John Dewey's argument that teacher training programs that emphasize only technical expertise do a disservice both

---

[3]For an exceptional commentary on the need to educate teachers to be intellectuals, see John Dewey, "The Relation of Theory to Practice," in John Dewey, *The Middle Works, 1899–1924*, edited by Jo Ann Boydston (Carbondale, Southern Illinois University Press, 1977), [originally published in 1904]. See also, Israel Scheffler, "University Scholarship and the Education of Teachers," *Teachers College Record,* 70:1 (1968), pp. 1–12; Henry A. Giroux, *Ideology, Culture, and the Process of Schooling* (Philadelphia: Temple University Press, 1981).

[4]See for instance, Herbert Kliebard, "The Question of Teacher Education," in D. McCarty (ed.), *New Perspectives on Teacher Education* (San Francisco: Jossey-Bass, 1973).

[5]Kenneth M. Zeichner. "Alternative Paradigms on Teacher Education," *Journal of Teacher Education* 34:3 (May–June 1983), p. 4.

to the nature of teaching and to their students.[6] Instead of learning to reflect upon the principles that structure classroom life and practice, prospective teachers are taught methodologies that appear to deny the very need for critical thinking. The point is that teacher education programs often lose sight of the need to educate students to examine the underlying nature of school problems. Further, these programs need to substitute for the language of management and efficiency a critical analysis of the less obvious conditions that structure the ideological and material practices of schooling.

Instead of learning to raise questions about the principles underlying different classroom methods, research techniques and theories of education, students are often preoccupied with learning the "how to," with "what works," or with mastering the best way to teach a *given* body of knowledge. For example, the mandatory field-practice seminars often consist of students sharing with each other the techniques they have used in managing and controlling classroom discipline, organizing a day's activities and learning how to work within specific time tables. Examining one such program, Jesse Goodman raises some important questions about the incapacitating silences it embodies. He writes:

> There was no questioning of feelings, assumptions, or definitions in this discussion. For example, the "need" for external rewards and punishments to "make kids learn" was taken for granted; the educational and ethical implications were not addressed. There was no display of concern for stimulating or nurturing a child's intrinsic desire to learn. Definitions of *good kids* as "quiet kids," *workbook work* as "reading," *on-task time* as "learning," and *getting through the material on time* as "the goal of teaching"— all went unchallenged. Feelings of pressure and possible guilt about not keeping to time schedules also went unexplored. The real concern in this discussion was that everyone "shared."[7]

Technocratic and instrumental rationalities are also at work within the teaching field itself, and they play an increasing role in reducing teacher autonomy with respect to the development and planning of curricula and the judging and implementation of classroom instruction. This is most evident in the proliferation of what has been called "teacher-proof" curriculum packages.[8] The underlying rationale in many of these packages reserves for teachers the role of simply carrying out predetermined content and instructional procedures. The method and aim of such packages is to legitimate what I call management pedagogies. That is, knowledge is broken down into discrete parts, standardized for easier management and consumption, and measured through predefined forms of assessment. Curricula approaches of this sort are management pedagogies because the central questions regarding learning are reduced to the problem of management, i.e., "how to allocate resources (teachers, students and materials) to produce the maximum number of certified . . . students within a designated time."[9] The underlying theoretical assumption that guides this type of pedagogy is that the behavior of teachers needs to be controlled and made consistent and predictable across different schools and student populations.

What is clear in this approach is that it organizes school life around curricular, instructional and evaluation experts who do the thinking while teachers are reduced to doing the implementing. The effect is not only to deskill teachers, to remove them from the processes of deliberation and reflection, but also to routinize the nature of learning and classroom pedagogy. Needless to say, the principles underlying management pedagogies are at odds with the premise that teachers should be actively involved in producing curricula materials suited to the cultural and social contexts in which they teach. More specifically, the narrowing of curricula choices to a back-to-basics format, and the introduction of lock-step, time-on-task pedagogies operate from the theoretically erroneous assumption that *all* students can learn from the same materials, classroom instructional techniques and modes of evaluation. The notion that students come from different histories and embody different experiences, linguistic practices, cultures and talents is strategically ignored within the logic and accountability of management pedagogy theory.

Teachers as Transformative Intellectuals

In what follows, I want to argue that one way to rethink and restructure the nature of teacher work is to view teachers as transformative intellectuals. The category of intellectual is helpful in a number of ways. First, it provides a theoretical basis for examining teacher work as a form of intellectual labor, as opposed to defining

---

[6]Dewey, op. cit.

[7]Jesse Goodman, "Reflection and Teacher Education: A Case Study and Theoretical Analysis," *Interchange* 15:3 (1984), p. 15.

[8]Michael Apple, *Education and Power* (Boston: Routledge & Kegan Paul, Ltd., 1982).

[9]Patrick Shannon, "Mastery Learning in Reading and the Control of Teachers and Students," *Language Arts* 61:5 (September 1984), p. 488.

it in purely instrumental or technical terms. Second, it clarifies the kinds of ideological and practical conditions necessary for teachers to function as intellectuals. Third, it helps to make clear the role teachers play in producing and legitimating various political, economic and social interests through the pedagogies they endorse and utilize.

By viewing teachers as intellectuals, we can illuminate the important idea that all human activity involves some form of thinking. In other words, no activity, regardless of how routinized it might become, can be abstracted from the functioning of the mind in some capacity. This is a crucial issue, because by arguing that the use of the mind is a general part of all human activity we dignify the human capacity for integrating thinking and practice, and in doing so highlight the core of what it means to view teachers as reflective practitioners. Within this discourse, teachers can be seen not merely as "performers professionally equipped to realize effectively any goals that may be set for them. Rather [they should] be viewed as free men and women with a special dedication to the values of the intellect and the enhancement of the critical powers of the young."[10]

Viewing teachers as intellectuals also provides a strong theoretical critique of technocratic and instrumental ideologies underlying an educational theory that separates the conceptualization, planning and design of curricula from the processes of implementation and execution. It is important to stress that teachers must take active responsibility for raising serious questions about what they teach, how they are to teach, and what the larger goals are for which they are striving. This means that they must take a responsible role in shaping the purposes and conditions of schooling. Such a task is impossible within a division of labor in which teachers have little influence over the ideological and economic conditions of their work. This point has a normative and political dimension that seems especially relevant for teachers. If we believe that the role of teaching cannot be reduced to merely training in the practical skills, but involves, instead, the education of a class of intellectuals vital to the development of a free society, then the category of intellectual becomes a way of linking the purpose of teacher education, public schooling and inservice training to the very principles necessary for developing a democratic order and society.

I have argued that by viewing teachers as intellectuals those persons concerned with education can begin to rethink and reform the traditions and conditions that have prevented schools and teachers from assuming their full potential as active, reflective scholars and practitioners. It is imperative that I qualify this point and extend it further. I believe that it is important not only to view teachers as intellectuals, but also to contextualize in political and normative terms the concrete social functions that teachers perform. In this way, we can be more specific about the different relations that teachers have both to their work and to the dominant society.

A fundamental starting point for interrogating the social function of teachers as intellectuals is to view schools as economic, cultural and social sites that are inextricably tied to the issues of power and control. This means that schools do more than pass on in an objective fashion a common set of values and knowledge. On the contrary, schools are places that represent forms of knowledge, language practices, social relations and values that are representative of a particular selection and exclusion from the wider culture. As such, schools serve to introduce and legitimate *particular* forms of social life. Rather than being objective institutions removed from the dynamics of politics and power, schools actually are contested spheres that embody and express a struggle over what forms of authority, types of knowledge, forms of moral regulation and versions of the past and future should be legitimated and transmitted to students. This struggle is most visible in the demands, for example, of right-wing religious groups currently trying to institute school prayer, remove certain books from the school library, and include certain forms of religious teachings in the science curricula. Of course, different demands are made by feminists, ecologists, minorities and other interest groups who believe that the schools should teach women's studies, courses on the environment, or black history. In short, schools are not neutral sites, and teachers cannot assume the posture of being neutral either.

In the broadest sense, teachers as intellectuals have to be seen in terms of the ideological and political interests that structure the nature of the discourse, classroom social relations and values that they legitimate in their teaching. With this perspective in mind, I want to conclude that teachers should become transformative intellectuals if they are to subscribe to a view of pedagogy that believes in educating students to be active, critical citizens.

Central to the category of transformative intellectual is the necessity of making the pedagogical more political and the political more pedagogical. Making the pedagogical more political means inserting schooling directly into the political sphere by arguing that

---

[10]Israel Scheffler, op. cit., p. 11.

schooling represents both a struggle to define meaning and a struggle over power relations. Within this perspective, critical reflection and action become part of a fundamental social project to help students develop a deep and abiding faith in the struggle to overcome economic, political and social injustices, and to further humanize themselves as part of this struggle. In this case, knowledge and power are inextricably linked to the presupposition that to choose life, to recognize the necessity of improving its democratic and qualitative character for all people, is to understand the preconditions necessary to struggle for it.

Making the political more pedagogical means utilizing forms of pedagogy that embody political interests that are emancipatory in nature; that is, using forms of pedagogy that treat students as critical agents; make knowledge problematic; utilize critical and affirming dialogue; and make the case for struggling for a qualitatively better world for all people. In part, this suggests that transformative intellectuals take seriously the need to give students an active voice in their learning experiences. It also means developing a critical vernacular that is attentive to problems experienced at the level of everyday life, particularly as they are related to pedagogical experiences connected to classroom practice. As such, the pedagogical starting point for such intellectuals is not the isolated student but individuals and groups in their various cultural, class, racial, historical and gender settings, along with the particularity of their diverse problems, hopes and dreams.

Transformative intellectuals need to develop a discourse that unites the language of critique with the language of possibility, so that social educators recognize that they can make changes. In doing so, they must speak out against economic, political and social injustices both within and outside of schools. At the same time, they must work to create the conditions that give students the opportunity to become citizens who have the knowledge and courage to struggle in order to make despair unconvincing and hope practical. As difficult as this task may seem to social educators, it is a struggle worth waging. To do otherwise is to deny social educators the opportunity to assume the role of transformative intellectuals.

POSTNOTE

This classic article was written almost a quarter of a century ago, at the dawn of what has been called the School Reform Movement. Its author, Henry Giroux, has been instrumental in bringing the educational thought of the Brazilian educator, Paulo Freire [1921–1995], and adapting it to the North American scene. In this essay, Giroux prophetically predicted many of the negative consequences of the national effort to reform our schools. Among his major points is the "deskilling" and "disempowerment" of teachers, as well as moving more and more of their classroom decision-making power further and further away to curriculum specialists, purchased curriculum packages, and state departments of education. Increasingly, teachers have become what Giroux calls "educational technicians," following the directions of others.

Giroux has made survival suggestions to counter this altering of the teacher's role. He was, in fact, one of the first to hold up the ideal of teachers as reflective practitioners. That is, professionals who have the habit of stepping back from their day-to-day teaching and who attempt to gain an objective view of their work, putting it into a larger social and intellectual frame.

It is curious that while Giroux was challenging teachers to play a strong role in the direction of education and, in effect, to claim their birthright as educators, the teaching profession moved in a different direction. During the 1970s and 1980s, teachers built two strong professional associations, the NEA and the AFT. They gained power and earned a place at the seat of educational decision making. The power of teachers has more often been turned to the political arena and to bread-and-butter, trade-union issues than to freeing teachers to be "transformative intellectuals" and captains of their own classrooms.

Discussion Questions

1. How is a "transformative intellectual" different from an everyday intellectual?
2. What are Giroux's primary criticisms of American schooling?
3. Which of Giroux's criticisms do you believe are most evident in today's schools?

RELATED WEBSITE RESOURCES

 Web Resources:

Henry A. Giroux. Available at:

http://www.henryagiroux.com/index.html.

This site is dedicated to the writings and work of Giroux and has several useful links for a greater understanding of critical pedagogy.

Paulo Freire Institute. Available at:

http://www.paulofreireinstitute.org/.

The PFI, housed at the University of California at Los Angeles, is one of several centers of thought about critical pedagogy.

Students

Teaching is one of life's most complex activities. So much is involved: knowledge, attitudes, values, and skills to be learned; the process of instruction; and the management of the learning environment. To teach well, to be an effective educator, demands so much of our attention that an essential element in the teaching-learning process may be lost: the student.

The entire purpose of teaching is to make positive change in students. They are the main event, but sometimes teachers lose focus. We become so involved in the knowledge to be conveyed or in the process of instruction that we often lose sight of our students. We need to remind ourselves continually that the entire enterprise of education fails if the student is ill served. In addition, we need to remind ourselves constantly that each student has a different set of needs, preferences, and goals.

One thing that should help us stay attuned to the student is the fact that modern life regularly requires us all to become students. No longer is the term *student* reserved for a relatively few young people receiving formal education. With the explosion of education in the last quarter century, people continually move in and out of student status. A knowledge-based and information-oriented society such as ours requires continuous education. Whether it is acquiring computer literacy or learning how to run cooperative learning groups, we all return to being students from time to time. Having to struggle with new information or trying to master a new skill may be the best thing we can do to improve our teaching.

7

How We Treat One Another in School

Donna M. San Antonio and Elizabeth A. Salzfass

Donna M. San Antonio is director of the Appalachian Mountain Teen Project, Wolfeboro, New Hampshire, and lecturer on education, Harvard Graduate School of Education, Cambridge, Massachusetts. **Elizabeth A. Salzfass** is program and evaluation coordinator for Responsive Advocacy for Life and Learning in Youth (RALLY), and community service learning coordinator with Peace Games, Boston, Massachusetts.

"How We Treat One Another in School" by Donna M. San Antonio and Elizabeth A. Salzfass, *Educational Leadership* 64, no. 8, May 2007, pp. 32–38. Used with permission.

F|O|C|U|S| QUESTION

Why do so many students experience the effects of bullying?

KEY TERM

Cyberbullying

When rising middle school students are asked to name their biggest worry about going to a new school, they most often answer, "That I will not have any friends" or "That people will make fun of me" (San Antonio, 2004). The prospect of being friendless or getting teased looms large for many students at this age and can profoundly affect their sense of affiliation with school. Students tell us with heartbreaking regularity of the pain and anger they feel when their peers do not see them, include them, or care about them. At the extreme, some students not only are treated with indifference but also become targets of bullying.

Devastating Effects

Olweus (1993) defines bullying as verbal, physical, or psychological abuse or teasing accompanied by real or perceived imbalance of power. Bullying most often focuses on qualities that students (and the broader society) perceive to be different from the established norm, such as expected genderspecific behavior for boys and girls, dress and physical appearance, and manner of speaking. Bullying is connected to diversity, and reducing bullying means taking steps to make the community and the school safe for diversity of all kinds.

Research indicates that bullying—with its accompanying fear, loss of self-efficacy, anger, and hurt—negatively affects the school environment and can greatly diminish students' ability to engage actively in learning (Hoover & Oliver, 1996). Being bullied has been linked with high rates of school absence (Fried & Fried, 1996); dropping out of school (Weinhold & Weinhold, 1998); and low self-esteem, anxiety, and depression (Banks, 1997). A U.S. Department of Education study (1998) found that students who had experienced sustained threats and verbal and physical peer aggression carried out two-thirds of school shootings.

Some researchers and practitioners believe that the impact of bullying is as devastating and life changing as that of other forms of trauma, such as physical abuse. The effects of bullying may linger long into the victims' adulthood (Kaltiala-Heino, Rimpelae, Rantanen, & Rimpelae, 2000). Recent research has documented increased levels of depression and anxiety in adults who had been bullied in their youth (Gladstone, Parker, & Malhi, 2006).

Because of the documented harmful effects of bullying—as well as other forms of social isolation—on school climate and student achievement, educators are taking this problem seriously. Many schools have explored the benefits of implementing schoolwide programs to promote social and emotional learning, prevent bullying, and nurture positive peer relationships. A survey of middle school students that we recently conducted in three schools provides information on bullying behavior that can inform such programs.

A Middle School Survey on Bullying

To measure students' experience with physical, verbal, and relational[1] bullying, we administered surveys in spring 2006 to 211 7th and 8th grade students in three K–8 schools in New England. The three schools differ significantly by race, socioeconomic status, and urbanicity. Rural School,[2] located in a small town, serves a student population that is socioeconomically diverse but is 94 percent white; 25 percent of the students are eligible for free or reduced-price lunch. Big City School is located in a low-income urban neighborhood and serves primarily Latino (65 percent) and black (33 percent) students; 93 percent are eligible for free or reduced-price lunch. Small City School has a socioeconomically and ethnically diverse student body composed of 40 percent white, 36 percent black, 11 percent Latino, and 10 percent Asian students; 30 percent of the students are eligible for free or reduced-price lunch.

We surveyed nearly all the students in each grade, with the exception of 8th graders at Rural School, where we were able to survey only half of the class. The surveys included multiple-choice and open-ended questions. Respondents were evenly split between boys and girls. Most of our findings were consistent with what other research has found and what middle grades teachers know about bullying in the adolescent years. Some of our most significant findings follow.

Extent of Bullying

Most students (76.5 percent) felt safe most of the time. However, students at Big City School reported feeling safe much less often than did their peers at the other two schools (65 percent, compared with 83 percent at Small City School and 81 percent at Rural School). They also feared bullying more, even though students at Rural School reported seeing it occur more often. We believe this reflects the greater incidence of community violence to which Big City School students are exposed.

Rural School was the only school in which a majority of students (about 2 in 3) said that bullying was a serious problem. Many of the respondents from Rural School spoke about the difference between physical and emotional safety. As one 7th grade girl said, "I feel safe physically but my emotions take a blow here."

In terms of grade level, bullying was more common for 7th graders than for 8th graders at the three schools we surveyed, with two notable exceptions: Verbal bullying affected 8th grade girls more than any other subgroup at Small City School, and physical violence affected 8th grade boys and girls more than 7th graders at Big City School.

Finally, across schools, boys and girls experienced physical and verbal bullying to a similar extent, but girls experienced more relational bullying than boys did. Girls at all three schools worried more often than boys that if they did or said something wrong, their friends would gang up on them and decide not to be their friends. This problem appeared to be most dire for girls at Rural School: A full 72 percent of them reported suffering relational bullying either "every once in a while," "often," or "every day," compared with 58 percent of girls at Big City School and 48 percent at Small City School. This finding raises the question of the effect of socioeconomic status and cultural background on the bullying phenomenon. The almost entirely white population of girls at the school with the widest gap between wealthy and poor students was the group most at risk of relational aggression.

Boys were more likely to admit to bullying other students than girls were (which may have something to do with the way bullying is traditionally defined), but no significant gender difference was expressed overall when we asked students whether boys or girls bullied other students more. We also found that boys bullied both boys and girls, whereas girls typically only bullied other girls. We were troubled by girls' graphic narrative responses that demonstrated that boys often bullied girls with demeaning comments about the girls' appearance and demands for sexual interactions, particularly oral sex.

Location of Bullying

In all three schools, bullying happened most frequently in the hallways. When asked how to mitigate bullying at their school, many students suggested putting more adult supervisors in the hallways between classes. The second most common place in which bullying occurred differed across the three schools. At Big City School, bullying tended to happen in the bathrooms, where there was generally no adult supervision. At Small City School and Rural School, bullying happened on the playground and in the cafeteria, both places where adults were on duty.

Reasons Students Are Bullied

Students at all three schools perceived that "being overweight" and "not dressing right" were the most common reasons an individual might be bullied. At Small City School and Rural School, the second most common reason stated was being perceived as gay, which suggests rigid behavior expectations for boys and girls. Many students commented that someone might be a target for bullying if they look or act "different" or "weird."

Students' Reactions to Bullying

The most common strategies students reported using when confronted by bullies were walking away, saying mean things back, hitting back, or telling the bully to stop. The least common strategy was telling an adult at the school. Hitting back was a particularly popular response to bullying at Big City and Small City Schools, particularly among the boys. Given steadily increasing numbers of violent deaths over the last few years in many urban communities, we believe that this finding highlights the importance that urban youth put on maintaining a tough appearance to survive, as well as a perceived lack of options for nonviolent conflict resolution.

Student reactions to bullying also differed according to gender. More boys than girls believed that they had the right to use violence to protect themselves from physical violence or someone hurting their feelings or reputations. Girls reported being more likely to help a victim of bullying than boys did and more often said that bullying is wrong.

Inadequate Adult Response

Most students said they were not confident that adults could protect them from being bullied. Students at Rural School had more faith that their teachers could stop the bullying when they were told about it than did students at the other two schools. However, students in this school agreed with their urban peers that teachers did not seem to notice bullying and did not take it seriously enough. Most students said they wanted teachers to be more aware of all types of bullying and to intervene more often. These findings are consistent with past research in which students reported that most bullying goes undetected by school staff (Skiba & Fontanini, 2000).

When we talk with students in a variety of settings, they have many thoughts about how adults can help to make school safer and stop bullying. They frequently answer with statements like these: "Watch out for us and don't ignore us." "Pay attention." "Just ask us what's wrong." "Talk to the students who have been bullied to see how to stop it." "Start caring more." "Believe us." "Punish the bullies." "Do something instead of nothing." One thing seems certain: Most students want adults to see what is going on in their world and respond to bullying in caring, effective, and firm ways.

What Schools Can Do

The following recommendations for a schoolwide approach to bullying prevention are derived from our review of the literature, our survey findings, and a report generated by Northwest Regional Educational Laboratory (Railsback & Brewster, 2001). All sources agree that schoolwide strategies must complement classroom curriculum. Schools should not frame the issue of how students and educators treat one another as an issue of behavior. Instead, they should opt for a more comprehensive set of goals that address social and moral development, school and classroom climate, teacher training, school policies, and community values, along with student behavior.

CONDUCT AN ASSESSMENT

The first step toward creating an effective schoolwide antibullying program is identifying where, when, and how students experience bullying at a particular school. As our study demonstrated, different types of bullying occur with different frequency and magnitude among different populations in different school settings; therefore, a one-size-fits-all approach is not an appropriate solution. Schoolwide bullying intervention programs are more purposeful and relevant when they are informed by students' views. We strongly recommend using a participatory action research approach that involves students in framing a problem statement; constructing a survey; summarizing, analyzing, and reporting the results; and generating ideas for how staff and students can respond to the issues uncovered by the survey.

CREATE A COMMITTEE TO FOCUS ON SCHOOL RELATIONSHIPS

A committee involving students, parents, and community members along with school staff should focus on schoolwide relationships, not only on student bullying. This committee will assist the school in generating developmentally and culturally sound prevention and intervention ideas.

IMPLEMENT AN ANTIBULLYING POLICY

When asked what teachers could do to stop bullying, many of the students we surveyed said that teachers should be stricter with bullies. An effective policy should be developed through collaboration among students, teachers, parents, and administrators.

Pepler and Craig (2000) say that a whole-school policy is the foundation of antibullying interventions, and they recommend that a policy include the following: a schoolwide commitment to address bullying; a statement of rights and responsibilities for all members of the school community; a definition of bullying, including types and dynamics; the process for identifying and reporting bullying; expected ways for students and staff to respond to bullying; strategies that will be implemented; and a way to assess the effectiveness of antibullying efforts.

TRAIN ALL SCHOOL EMPLOYEES

Bullying can be subtle and hard to detect, making it challenging for adults to intervene effectively. To stop bullying, school staff (including custodians, clerical staff, bus drivers, and lunchroom staff) must first have an opportunity to discuss the various ways and locations in which bullying occurs. From there, they can develop structures for communicating across roles within a school district and decide on an appropriate unified response. Considering that the majority of students in our study did not believe they could count on adults to protect them from being bullied, ongoing training and communication in this area is key. For students to develop positive attitudes toward school, they need to know that all staff members are committed to making it a safe and friendly environment.

HELP THE BULLIED AND THE BULLIES

Another step in implementing a schoolwide antibullying program involves providing resources for those most affected by bullying. Many of the students we surveyed who had experienced bullying said that they wanted adults to listen to their stories. Some schools have had success with facilitating groups in which students address issues directly with their peers. The PALS program at Rocky Mountain Middle School in Idaho trains teachers to facilitate these groups, which increase communication and social skills and give stigmatized students a chance to experience a positive interpersonal connection with others and with the school.

Some students who are highly involved in bullying (either as perpetrators or victims) will need one-to-one support. It is important to involve parents and provide referrals for mentoring or counseling. Journaling with a teacher or counselor who reads and replies to concerns and issues may help particularly reticent students. Connecting students to after-school and summer programs will enable them to socialize with their peers outside of the school and form new friendships.

When children have been treated unfairly or violently in their primary relationships, it can be difficult for them to understand why they and their peers should be treated with respect. Nakkula and Selman (1991) describe an effective intervention called *pair counseling* as a way for two children who have difficult peer relationships to come together with the help of a counselor to negotiate differences and learn how to be a friend.

RECOGNIZE AND NAME ALL FORMS OF BULLYING

Be aware of the relationships among students and of shifts in cliques and friendships as much as possible. Look for subtle signs of relational aggression that may occur between students, such as whispering, spreading rumors, and exclusion. Let students know that comments and actions against any racial, ethnic, or social group will not be tolerated. Be prepared to explain your ethical position to your students. The students we surveyed suggested that teachers ask students what would benefit them and help students generate realistic and effective ideas. On this topic, one 7th grade girl wrote,

> Teachers do everything, I think, in their power, but if they would just listen to the person who says they're being bullied, instead of just saying "stay away from them" or "ignore it" maybe we would see some change.

RECLAIM GOODNESS

School classrooms and corridors contain a full spectrum of behavior, from countless everyday small acts of kindness to serious acts of aggression. In our effort to mitigate negative student behavior, a commonly overlooked but essential aspect of creating emotionally and socially safe environments is noticing, acknowledging, and actively drawing out acts of kindness. Schools are places of tremendous courage, generosity, and thoughtfulness. Some students risk their own social standing by being kind to an "unpopular" classmate. Some students talk with others who appear lonely and try to offer friendship; they speak up when they see injustice because, in the words of one student, they "don't think it is right to judge people by how they dress." In past research (San Antonio, 2004) and in the survey we describe here, students frequently spoke with admiration about teachers who actively intervened against stereotyping and teasing based on gender, social class, race, and learning needs. Naming and reclaiming goodness in the school community is an important step toward reducing bullying.

INTEGRATE SOCIAL-EMOTIONAL EDUCATION INTO THE CURRICULUM

An effective curriculum for social, emotional, and ethical learning addresses bullying as a social and moral development issue. Activities in such a program focus on self-understanding, understanding of others, appreciation for diversity, and responsibility to the community. By encouraging empathy, respect, and acceptance and giving students tools for communicating their feelings and confronting conflict positively, an effective social-emotional learning curriculum will likely improve school climate and culture beyond just the mitigation of bullying. (See Choosing a Social-Emotional Learning Curriculum.)

Choosing a Social-Emotional Learning Curriculum

Look for a curriculum that

- Becomes part of a schoolwide and communitywide discussion (with parents) about values, beliefs about how to treat one another, and policies that reflect these values.
- Poses developmentally and culturally appropriate social dilemmas or discussion.
- Challenges the idea that aggression and bullying are inevitable and expected behavior. Demonstrates how people can resolve tensions and disagreements without losing face by giving detailed examples of people who responded to violence in an actively nonviolent manner.
- Encourages students to express their feelings and experiences concerning bullying and enables students to generate realistic and credible ways to stay safe.
- Supports critical analysis of the issues and rejects explanations of behavior based on sterotypes (such as the idea that boys will use physical violence and girls will use relational violence).
- Helps children and teens become critical consumers of popular culture.
- Addresses all types of bullying.
- Discusses how bullying reflects broader societal injustice.
- Gives ideas for what the adults in the school can do as part of a whole-school effort.

Beware of any curriculum that

- Ignores such issues as injustice, stereotype and imbalance of power regarding gender, race, social class, and sexual orientation.
- Focuses on the victim's behavior as the reason for being a target of bullying.
- Focuses on student behavior without addressing schoolwide climate.
- Emphasizes having students tell the teacher about the bullying and ignoring bullying assaults.
- Focuses on either bullying only or victimization only.
- Portrays victims or bullies as unpopular misfits.
- Promotes simplistic or trendy solutions (for example, "boys will be boys").
- Promotes good solutions, such as peer mediation, but does not provide clear guidelines for when these strategies should and should not be used.
- Lacks evidence-based, population-specific suggestions for design, implementation, training, and evaluation.

Educators Set the Tone

As a primary social environment for young people, classrooms and schools are uniquely good places to learn how to treat others and how to tell others the way we want them to treat us. Dozens of times a day, people in schools negotiate interpersonal exchanges with others from diverse backgrounds, making schools a premier learning environment for social, emotional, and ethical learning. Nel Noddings (2002) has long held that a key purpose of schooling is to educate moral people:

> An emphasis on social relationships in classrooms, students' interest in the subject matter to be studied and the connections between classroom life and that of the larger world provides the foundation of our attempts to produce moral people. As educators we must make it possible and desirable for students to be good. (p. 85)

Of course, students behave in aggressive or submissive ways for a variety of reasons that are not always easy to discern or manage. Some students may posture aggressively because they face violent behavior at home or in their neighborhoods, some have problems reading social cues or controlling their impulses, and some are simply scared. But in our work with schools, we have found that when educators take students' concerns seriously, teach them alternative ways to communicate their needs assertively but not violently, and provide adult guidance, vigilance, safety, good role models, and support, students are more likely to interact positively with their peers.

The findings from the survey we conducted among middle grade students support the concept that educators *can* influence the social and emotional climate of schools. Students' written comments on the survey make it clear that they value fairness, respectful communication, and adults who make them feel physically and emotionally safe and cared for. By implementing an effective social-emotional learning curriculum and addressing the systemic factors that determine school climate, we can create schools where bullying is rare and where all students are ready to learn.

REFERENCES

Banks, R. (1997). *Bullying in schools*. Champaign, IL: ERIC Clearinghouse on Elementary and Early Childhood Education. (ERIC No. ED407154)

Crick, N. R., & Bigbee, M. A. (1998). Relational and overt forms of peer victimization: A multi-informant approach. *Journal of Consulting and Clinical Psychology, 66*, 337–347.

Fried, S., & Fried, P. (1996). *Bullies and victims: Helping your child survive the schoolyard battlefield*. New York: M. Evans and Company.

Gladstone, G., Parker, G. B., & Malhi, G. S. (2006). Do bullied children become anxious and depressed adults? A cross-sectional investigation of the correlates of bullying and anxious depression. *Journal of Nervous and Mental Disease, 194*(3), 201–208.

Hoover, J. H., & Oliver, R. (1996). *The bullying prevention handbook: A guide for principals, teachers, and counselors*. Bloomington, IN: National Educational Service.

Kaltiala-Heino, R., Rimpelae, M., Rantanen, P., & Rimpelae, A. (2000). Bullying at school: An indicator of adolescents at risk for mental disorders. *Journal of Adolescence, 23*(6), 661–674.

Nakkula, M., & Selman, B. (1991). How people "treat" each other: Pair therapy as a context for the development of interpersonal ethics. In W. M. Kurtines & J. Gewirtz (Eds.), *Handbook of moral behavior and development* (Vol. 3, pp. 179–210). Hillsdale, NJ: Erlbaum.

Noddings, N. (2002). *Educating moral people: A caring alternative to character education*. New York: Teachers College Press.

Olweus, D. (1993). *Bullying at school: What we know and what we can do*. Malden, MA: Blackwell.

Pepler, D. J., & Craig, W. (2000). *Making a difference in bullying* (Report #60). Toronto, Ontario: La Marsh Centre for Research on Violence and Conflict Resolution.

Railsback, J., & Brewster, C. (2001). *Schoolwide prevention of bullying*. Portland, OR: Northwest Regional Education Laboratory. Available: **www.nwrel.org/request/dec01**

San Antonio, D. M. (2004). *Adolescent lives in transition: How social class influences adjustment to middle school*. Albany: State University of New York Press.

Skiba, N., & Fontanini, A. (2000). *Fast facts: Bullying prevention*. Bloomington, IN: Phi Delta Kappa International. Available: **www.pdkintl.org/newsroom/newsletters/fastfacts/ffl2.pdf**

U.S. Department of Education. (1998). *Preventing bullying: A manual for schools and communities*. Washington, DC: Author.

Weinhold, B. K., & Weinhold, J. B. (1998). Conflict resolution: The partnership way in schools. *Counseling and Human Development, 30*(7), 1–2.

ENDNOTES

1. *Physical bullying* includes hitting, kicking, or otherwise physically attacking the victim, as well as taking or damaging the victim's possessions. *Verbal bullying* includes name-calling, aggressive teasing, or making insulting comments designed to humiliate the victim. *Relational bullying* includes any behavior that intimidates and hurts the victim by harming or threatening to harm relationships or feelings of friendship and belonging (Crick & Bigbee, 1998). *Cyberbullying* involves the use of information and communication technologies, such as e-mail, cell phone and pager text messages, instant messaging, and Web sites to deliberately harm others (**www.cyberbullying.org**).

2. To preserve confidentiality, schools are identified by community type rather than by name.

POSTNOTE

Although bullying has probably existed ever since schools were created, the issue has generated considerable discussion of late. Reports of children skipping school or even committing suicide because they fear being bullied occur commonly in both professional literature and news coverage. A relatively new form of bullying, *cyberbullying,* is of growing concern. Cyberbullying refers to bullying through information and communication technologies, such as mobile phone text messages, e-mail messages, Internet chat rooms, and social networking websites such as MySpace or Facebook. Recent surveys show that fully one-third of teenagers have had mean, threatening, or embarrassing things said about them online. Ten percent of teenagers were threatened online with physical harm. The results of such cyberbullying can cause shame, embarrassment, depression, anger, withdrawal, and even lead to suicide.

As the article indicates, by developing a heightened awareness of bullying and its negative consequences, teachers can take actions to make the school environment more hospitable and inviting for all students.

Discussion Questions

1. Have you or any of your friends experienced firsthand the effects of bullying? If so, how did you cope with it?
2. If you, as a teacher, witnessed one child picking on another one, how would you handle the situation? What would you do?
3. What kind of information or skills do you believe you still need to be effective in preventing bullying? How will you get that information or develop those skills?

RELATED WEBSITE RESOURCES AND VIDEO CASES

 ## Web Resources:

Connect for Kids. Available at:

http://www.connectforkids.org/node/614.

This website provides a list of various resources useful in preventing bullying.

Video Case:

Social and Emotional Development: The Influence of Peer Groups

Although not dealing directly with the issue of bullying, this video case examines the issue of peer pressure. A sixth-grade teacher, Voncille Ross, has students use drama to better understand real-life situations, the choices they can make, and the potential consequences of those choices. As you watch the clips and study the artifacts in the case, reflect upon the following questions.

1. What insights did you gain from listening to students discuss peer pressure? How might these insights influence your teaching?
2. In the bonus segment, "A Real Story About Bullying," the teacher describes two students who are bullied for reading books during lunch period. The students say that while they are comfortable with being smart, they still want to fit in with everyone else and not stand out. How can you help students realize that they can be strong academically and still fit in socially?

8

Cheating in Middle and High School

Paris S. Strom and Robert D. Strom

Paris S. Strom is associate professor, Educational Foundations, Leadership and Technology, Auburn University, Auburn, Alabama. **Robert D. Strom** is professor, Psychology in Education, Arizona State University, Tempe, Arizona.

"Cheating in Middle and High School" by Paris S. Strom and Robert D. Strom, *The Educational Forum* 71, Winter 2007, pp. 104–116. Reprinted by permission of the publisher, Taylor and Francis, **www.informaworld.com.**

Abstract

Many parents believe that growing up now presents more complicated challenges for adolescents than in the past (Sclafani 2004). Teenagers need to develop certain attributes so that they are able to cope with the predictable difficulties they will face as they grow older (Peterson and Seligman 2004). A national sample of 1,600 parents with students in middle school and high school was surveyed about the relative importance of teaching 11 values relating to character development (Farkas et al. 2002). The value ranked highest, chosen by 91 percent of the parents as absolutely essential to teach their children, was "to be honest and truthful."

One method to assess parent performance, in their own estimate, is to compare the percentage identifying a particular goal as essential with the percentage stating they have succeeded in teaching that attribute to children. The results revealed a large gap of 36 percentage points between the 91 percent of parents who declared that honesty and truthfulness are fundamental lessons and the 55 percent reporting that their instruction had been successful. These findings indicate that, even for those values that parents regard as indispensable, significant differences exist between their intentions and what they have been able to accomplish.

Prevalence of Dishonesty

Teachers and students also are appropriate sources to assess whether lessons about honesty and truthfulness have been learned. A nationwide survey of 36,000 secondary students found that 60 percent admitted to cheating on tests and assignments (Josephson Institute of Ethics 2006). Some might assume that teens who cheat are characterized by marginal abilities causing them to resort to dishonesty as the only way to keep pace with more intelligent classmates. However, when 3,000 students chosen for scholastic recognition in the prestigious *Who's Who among American High School Students* were asked about their experiences, 80 percent acknowledged cheating on teacher-made and state tests (Lathrop and Foss 2005). The high proportion of these academic achievers who engaged in deception reflects a 10 percent increase since the question was initially presented to honor students 20 years ago. Among the adolescent leaders who acknowledged that they had cheated on tests and assignments,

95 percent said that they were never caught and consider themselves to be morally responsible individuals.

Cheating is not a phase of development characterizing middle school and high school students alone. Evidence abounds that dishonesty is ubiquitous in colleges and universities (Cizek 2003; Johnson 2004; Lipson 2004). The University of Michigan convened a national meeting of scholars to address the growing national concern about originality, imitation, and plagiarism in such diverse fields as journalism, the arts, and science (Lipson, Biagioli, and Vicinus 2005). The Center for Academic Integrity, located at Duke University, represents 250 colleges that are collaborating to find ways of restoring ethical behavior in higher education (McCabe and Pavela 2004). The members of this consortium are developing principles to define the conditions of integrity that should be expected of students and building strategies to help faculty members influence students to adopt honesty as an essential element of lifestyle.

Cheating in school also is becoming an international concern. For example, 900 college students in China were surveyed about their involvement in dishonest testing practices (*The Epoch Times* 2005). The results indicated that 83 percent had cheated. Frustration over cheating in later adolescence prompted Peking University, the country's most prestigious institution, to announce that starting in 2006 students caught plagiarizing would be expelled from the school (Dan 2005). A government committee has been debating a policy for dealing with cheaters for several years, and recently submitted its recommendations for a Chinese National Examination Law to the central cabinet of legislators for review. The proposed penalties for cheating in college would include jail sentences of up to seven years (Dongdong 2005). Widespread cheating among middle school, high school, and college students also has been reported in Australia, England, India, Japan, Korea, Spain, and Scotland (Callahan 2004).

Cheating can influence admission to higher education, favoring dishonest students while placing peers who are honest at a disadvantage. The Educational Testing Service (ETS), in Princeton, New Jersey, was concerned that scores on the Graduate Record Exam (GRE®), administered to more than 500,000 prospective graduate students each year, not be compromised. ETS first became aware that it had security problems in 2002 when a number of Chinese, Taiwanese, and South Korean students boosted their verbal scores by memorizing questions and answers that previous test takers had posted on the Web. Radical changes were made to the October 2006 version of the GRE to protect the integrity of test results (ETS 2005).

Similarly, the Graduate Management Admissions Test (GMAT), taken by students in nearly 100 countries, is considered an essential criterion for decisions on business school applicants. According to officials in McLean, Virginia (Ludwig and Silverstein 2006), the GMAT will not be altered because it requires students to respond to an individually tailored series of questions designed to gauge mathematics and verbal ability levels. However, because of incidents where individuals have taken the test for others, the GMAT now is requiring that each respondent provide a fingerprint when checking in and each time entering the examination room. That unique fingerprint, along with a digital photograph and signature, become a permanent part of a test taker's record.

Unfortunately, cheating in schools doesn't stop with students. In this current environment of high-stakes testing, faculty members' and administrators' salaries and career paths increasingly are tied to students' academic performance. Some teachers and principals have been fired for providing test answers to students, prompting changes in responses by students while they are being tested, altering answers after the tests are completed and before they are submitted to school district officials for processing, and providing students more time to complete examinations than is permitted by test directions (Axtman 2005).

The extent to which educators are willing to go to fabricate student achievement is illustrated by a case that received great attention in Long Island, New York. A student taking the 2005 Regents' annual high-stakes test was caught with blue writing on his hand that matched all of the correct responses. The source of answers was quickly traced to the student's father, an assistant principal who was responsible for state examinations in a nearby school district (Lambert 2005). Public outrage over this type of illegal activity is prompting new initiatives and policies to protect the evaluation process. In Ohio, teachers are obliged to sign a code of conduct and warned that inappropriate monitoring of examinations could lead to the revocation of their license. Kentucky administers six different versions of its state tests to frustrate the practice of teaching students answers that might be easier known by faculty members if only a single version of the measure existed (Callahan 2004).

Dishonesty is not unique to students and educational professionals. It also is widespread among adults in the workplace and presents similar challenges involving integrity, trust, and giving credit where credit is due (Evans and Wolf 2005; Maciariello 2005). One estimate is that the unauthorized copying and distribution of software alone costs businesses $12 billion a year (Schwartz 2001).

Motivation for Cheating

Why do students from all age groups and achievement levels participate in cheating? One line of speculation is that dishonesty in school is merely a reflection of the broader erosion of ethical behavior which has become commonplace in societies that tend to support self-centeredness over concern for others (Sommers and Satel 2005). Another observation is that concern about high-stakes testing is a cause for deception, particularly by students having difficulty meeting minimal competency skills required for high school graduation (Callahan 2004). Other observers contend that teachers are partially responsible because they ignore evidence of character failure and choose not to hold students accountable (Peterson and Seligman 2004). Educators agree that a growing number of parents seem obsessed with wanting their children to perform better than classmates, regardless of the steps taken to get the desired results (Baker and LeTendre 2005; Nichols and Good 2004).

One way of accurately determining why students cheat is to poll them. Polling, more than any other education reform, could show students that faculty members and the adult community are interested in their points of view and want to understand them. Toward this goal, the authors designed and field tested a number of polls for adolescents that are administered on the Internet (Strom and Strom 2005; 2006).

One of these polls addresses cheating in school and includes items regarding observed prevalence in classes, reactions to deception by classmates, punishment for test abuse and plagiarism, and teacher use of software to detect cheating. Students are asked to identify situations that constitute cheating, conditions that might legitimize dishonest behavior, characteristics of cheaters, frequency of involvement in cheating, and motives for misconduct. This sample item reflects student motivation and justification.

> The main reasons that peers in my classes gave for cheating are:
>
> - I need good grades to get into college.
> - There is not enough time to do the work.
> - Everyone else is cheating.
> - This course is not important to me.
> - Other.

Most adolescents agreed that the identified options reflected prominent reasons for cheating. For the "other" option, students often mentioned "lack of access to free competent tutoring" and "adults teach this kind of behavior by example."

Every school district should have policies and procedures on cheating so that faculty members can respond to incidents without being subjected to duress. Whereas 80 percent of the students responding to the *Who's Who among American High School Students* survey admitted cheating on tests, a separate survey administered to their parents found 63 percent felt certain that their child would not cheat in any circumstance (Lathrop and Foss 2005). Perhaps those parents believed that teaching the distinction between right and wrong is sufficient without also helping adolescents link this understanding with a sense of responsibility to behave honestly and truthfully at school.

A familiar outcome is that educators feel vulnerable to threats of lawsuits by parents when their child is accused of cheating. Many teachers worry that they may erroneously accuse a student of cheating and then have to suffer dreadful consequences. Indeed, 70 percent of educators agree that concern about parent reaction discourages them from identifying and punishing cheaters (Whitley and Keith-Spiegel 2002). A disappointing and unintended outcome is student awareness that misconduct seldom produces punishment and, therefore, poses a low risk.

Technology and Test Monitoring

Teachers are advised to be vigilant when administering tests. A perennial form of student dishonesty involves referral to messages that have been written on parts of their body, clothing, or belongings kept nearby. A common practice has been to remind test takers not to glance at the papers of others during a test.

Emergence of technological devices has spawned new and more sophisticated approaches to deceptive conduct. Students with handhelds or cell phones can "beam" or call data silently from across a classroom or, with a cell phone, from anywhere off campus. During a test such tools frequently are hidden under the table or in baggy pockets. Both devices could be equipped with text messaging, instant messaging, e-mail, and a camera or video recorder that makes capture or transmission of answers a relatively easy task. Cell phones could have a hands-free function allowing users to listen to sound files (e.g., prerecorded class notes). Applying the same method of sound files, others make use of music-playing devices such as iPods®. The listening piece connected to a cell phone or some music-playing device could be concealed beneath a student's long hair that covers ears from the teacher's view (Cizek 2003).

Some teachers appropriately permit use of personal data assistants (PDAs) and graphing calculators during tests because those tools offer helpful functions for solving problems. However, educators must be aware that whenever a device displays data on the screen, it also might have a minimized screen containing cheat data that can be accessed for a few seconds and then entirely hidden (minimized) with just the press of a key. In a similar way, screen protectors include decorative patterned holograms intended to allow only the user to observe the screen and prevent viewing by onlookers from other angles. If a teacher permits calculators or PDAs, certain ground rules should be understood. Technology contributes to learning and assessment, but devices must be applied in responsible and ethical ways.

When the same course has multiple sections, tests typically are scheduled on different days and times. This practice allows students to buy questions from someone who already has completed the examination. In such cases, buyer and seller are both engaged in cheating. A more daring risk involves paying a person to take a test for someone else.

In an effort to help educators identify cheaters, Fremer and Mulkey (2004), experts within the emerging field of test fraud and piracy, put together a list of the "ten most wanted test cheaters." They have given each of these test-taking thieves a name and a description of his or her underhanded efforts.

To help thwart cheating, the identity of all students in an examination should be verified, and, the test for all sections of a course should be scheduled on the same day and at the same time. In addition, teachers should modify course tests each semester to lessen the likelihood of cheating by students able to access the previous answer keys. Administration of multiple versions of a test, with items appearing in different sequence, proves frustrating to anyone who tries to borrow answers by peering over the shoulder of another student. Changing the seating location of students is also beneficial during testing because students are less likely to copy from classmates whose record of achievement is unknown. When a teacher leaves the room or permits students to do so during an examination, the chances for cheating increase. No student should be out of a teacher's sight while taking a test (Johnson 2003). Giving periodic open book examinations and allowing students to bring notes can increase their familiarity with the course content, improve their review process, and reduce the incidence of cheating.

Though some considerations described here may seem unduly cautious, collectively these steps do much to prevent dishonesty and support the integrity of a test environment. Students take academic honesty more seriously when they see their teacher make an effort to ensure fair and honest conditions for assessment. Barbara Davis (2002) at the University of California in Berkeley provided helpful tips about preventing cheating, scoring, and returning test results; handling fraudulent excuses to postpone an examination; turning in late assignments; missing classes, and clarifying expectations for course performance.

Delaware, North Carolina, South Carolina, and Texas are among the growing number of states contracting with Caveon, the nation's first test security company that monitors annual assessments for the No Child Left Behind Act. This company has developed a process called "data forensics" that searches for unusual response patterns, such as students getting difficult questions correct while missing easy questions, abnormally high pass rates for one classroom or school, and tests where incorrect answers have been erased and replaced with correct ones. The service includes protection of existing instruments from fraudulent practices, erecting barriers to prevent unauthorized access to copyright materials, and applying sophisticated statistical and Web patrolling tools that track cheaters and hold them accountable by providing evidence to school administrators (Foster 2003).

Ethics and the Internet

In 2000, Congress passed the Children's Internet Protection Act requiring public schools and libraries to install filters that minimize student exposure to objectionable materials like pornography. Another feature of the same legislation included guarantees to safeguard copyrighted materials of authors and artists whose music and ideas are available on the Internet

However, a national rush to ensure that all age groups have an opportunity to be online has overlooked the essential training necessary to support ethical behavior on the Internet. Today, a rapidly growing population of young computer pirates choose to bootleg music and misrepresent themselves as authors of assignments and projects without identifying original sources.

When students lack training regarding ethical practices for searching the Internet, they may suppose it is all right to present the words and views of another person as their own thinking. Web sites such as **www .schoolsucks.com** warehouse term papers that students can access without cost. Also, sources such as **www .termpaper.com** have costs associated with them. That particular site is a data bank of 20,000 on-file papers for purchase from $20 to $35. Another general site is **http://academictermpapers.com,** which offers 30,000 ready-made research papers at $7–$120 per page and even more expensive pricing for the preparation of custom papers designed to fit the unique needs of a client.

Plagiarism on the Internet is a monumental problem that educators in middle school, high school, and college are struggling to confront (Axtman 2005). However, cyber law proposals that define offenses and penalties have begun to emerge as agenda that, in the future, could be determined in the courts rather than by teachers and school administrators. Ronald Standler (2000), a copyright attorney, has an informative essay about plagiarism that illustrates the wide range of issues involved along with results of court cases at **www .rbs2.com/plag.htm.**

Parents share responsibility for helping their daughters and sons realize that, similar to visiting the library, looking up a topic on the Web is only the initial step in conducting research. Copying materials from books, journals, or sources on the Internet and portraying these products as one's own invention is dishonest and defined as cheating. Deceptive practices by students have been reported as moving downward to earlier grades because of growing access to the Internet. The Center for Academic Integrity (McCabe and Pavela 2004) surveyed middle schools throughout the nation and found that 73 percent of seventh graders and 66 percent of sixth graders admitted to regularly borrowing materials without giving credit to their sources. The practice of cut-and-paste plagiarism is widespread, with students acting as though whatever they find on the Internet can be submitted as their own work.

Prevention of Plagiarism

Teachers want their students to practice search skills on the Internet, but are plagued by the increasing level of plagiarism. To encourage originality and prevent students from taking credit for the writing of other people, school districts are turning to a service that quickly can identify academic work that is plagiarized. This service, which detects whenever more than eight words are used in a paper without identifying the original source, can serve as evidence to confront misbehaving students and parents. This prevention resource, already applied by public schools in many states and the authors of this manuscript with their college students, can be found at **www.turnitin.com.** On a typical day, 30,000 papers are submitted to the service for checking. More than 30 percent of those documents include plagiarism. The cost of this service can be substantial, however. For a high school of 1,400 students, the software license for one year and related materials, including digital portfolios, amounts to $5,200. Bruce Leland (2002), a professor at Western Illinois University, provided suggestions for teachers on how to deal with plagiarism and what to

tell students about ethical expectations at **www.wiu .edu/users/mfbhl/wiu/plagiarism.htm.**

Adolescents rarely are asked to evaluate the merit of assignments their teachers give them, but one conversation with a student about the work he is asked to do put the onus for plagiarism and other forms of cheating back on educators. Jamal, a sophomore from Montgomery, Alabama, suggested that focusing only on the inappropriate motives of students is misleading. Jamal suggested, "Maybe a bigger problem is that teachers require students to memorize instead of teaching them how to think. You can cheat if all you are going to be tested on are facts, but it is much harder to cheat when you are asked to attack or defend a particular position and actually write an essay."

Jamal's outlook may not reflect the consensus of classmates. Nevertheless, his view that teachers could minimize cheating by developing more challenging tasks, which are less vulnerable to cheating, is gaining support. Assignments that motivate students to learn by doing, that encourage reciprocal learning in cooperative groups, that support self-directedness, and that foster original thinking are essential shifts in teaching that will allow students to become actively involved in construction of their own knowledge. Traditionally, teachers have prepared primarily for the direct instruction to be presented in class and spent little effort on developing assignments that permit students to learn on their own.

These suggestions regarding assignments can help teachers reduce the likelihood of dishonest behavior by students.

1. The purpose of every project should be clear, identify anticipated benefits, and invite dialogue regarding methods, resources, and the types of products that are acceptable for submission.
2. Relevance for the students should be established. The connection between curriculum and real life is confirmed when students can get credit for interaction with other generations or cultures whose experience goes beyond the perspective that is offered by the teacher and text.
3. Encourage students to express their feelings and describe the processes used to reach their conclusions. These presentations are more interesting to write and more satisfying to read (Johnson 2004).
4. Emphasize higher-order thinking and creative behavior. Instead of reporting only knowledge, student participation should involve practice with higher-level abilities identified in "A Revision of Bloom's Taxonomy: An Overview" (Krathwohl 2002).
5. Go beyond the customary scope for problem solving. Students frequently are presented questions

to which the teacher already knows the answers or could readily find them. Generating alternative solutions and then making choices is often the key to overcoming challenges in life (de Bono 1999).

6. Encourage varied types of information gathering. Submissions might include a hard copy of located Web data accompanied by the same information summarized and interpreted in a student's own words, results drawn from polls or interviews, and descriptions of steps in an experiment.

7. Identify the criteria that will be used for evaluating the quality of performance. When students know in advance the criteria by which their work will be judged, they can concentrate on the work without being anxious and reporting at the end "I wasn't sure if this is what you wanted."

8. Allow students to reflect, revise, and improve their final product. Having access to suggestions from classmates who have read their work and being expected to revise their product supports perseverance and teaches students how to accept constructive criticism.

9. Consider the use of oral critique. This method allows students to make their views known verbally, permits classmates to practice offering helpful criticism, enables teachers to call for clarification when points are unclear, and eliminates the use of technology tools for deception.

Student Integrity and Maturity

Legalistic syllabi and tough policies alone are unreliable ways to prevent cheating. Instructional efforts are needed as well. Students are able to understand that honesty is an important indicator of developing maturity. Indeed, maturity cannot materialize without a sense of obligation to treat other people fairly. Adolescents can benefit from periodic discussions about the need to maintain integrity across all sectors of life. They also can be informed of seldom-considered damaging effects of cheating, such as gaps in knowledge and skills that can adversely impact later success when the foundation of knowledge necessary to understand processes in higher-level courses has not been acquired.

Academic dishonesty results in another significant long-term disadvantage. The moral compass students need to guide personal conduct in class and outside of school can be thrown off-course. This message is effectively portrayed in *The Emperors Club* (2002), a film starring Kevin Cline. As a teacher and assistant principal at St. Benedict's High School for Boys, he motivates students to choose a moral purpose for their lives in addition to selecting occupational goals. The story illustrates how great teachers can have a profound influence on students and how cheating during the teenage years can become a lifelong habit. An interactive Web site for this film, **www.theemperorsclub.com,** includes an interesting quiz on how to define morality.

Educators cannot provide all the guidance students require to adopt honesty as a lifestyle. Some parents tell daughters and sons that cheating is a fact of life in the world of work, which has forced them to cheat to succeed. When parents condone dishonesty and deception as normative and defensible, educators have far more difficulty countering the message that the prevalence of cheating makes the practice acceptable (Carter 2005). Schools could provide workshops for parents that focus on the range of cheating issues adolescents face and offer agenda questions for discussions at home about honesty, integrity, trust, and maturity. In this way, mothers and fathers would be enlisted to sustain efforts that nurture these valuable attributes in their children. Successful academic performance rooted in honesty enables students to take pride in work that is their own and to make known when tutoring is needed to improve learning (McCabe and Pavela 2004). Ultimately, the success of individual students depends on the positive values they adopt and the level of maturity they are able to attain. These aspects of healthy development warrant greater attention in a society that aspires to provide world leadership.

Conclusion

Adolescents offer many reasons for cheating at school. The most common explanations are: "I didn't have time to do the work," "This course is not important to me," "Everyone else is cheating," and "I have to get good grades." Motivating teachers to address the problem could begin by considering relevant questions in faculty meetings. What can schools do to turn things around before the nation becomes one of adults who got where they are by cheating? What can educators do to become better models of ethical conduct? How can parents help their children embrace honesty? What can be done to ensure that moral development is part of the curriculum to support student development? What are the effects when students present other people's ideas without giving credit to the source? How do students respond to a poll about the incidence of cheating and the ways faculty deals with this issue? How do we feel about honest students being denied educational opportunities because others gain unfair advantage using deceptive practices? Do we believe that honesty could become a norm in secondary education? What efforts have we made to obtain input from students through their organizations and focus groups? Should we concentrate only on the detection of cheating or also strive to raise the standard of student morality at this school?

Teenagers are in the process of formulating lifelong attitudes about social justice and determining their expectations for personal conduct. They have much to gain from reflective discussions regarding how honesty and dishonesty impact the well-being of individuals, families, businesses, and communities. Discussions should take place as appropriate in all subjects of the curriculum. The promotion of integrity requires high priority. Parents must become partners with teachers. Schools should reinforce the continued guidance from parents and provide them with questions on ethical lessons for home discussion. Skeptics may doubt whether schools or parents can affect honesty later than early childhood. However, most of the public has faith in the power of education at any age to equip students with competencies they need to become successful. Secondary schools could provide curricula that illustrate how honesty serves as the sole basis for survival of trust, equality, fair treatment, and maturity. The curricula also should emphasize how motivation to learn, effort to persevere, and recognition of achievement that is earned can be influenced by ethics. When students receive such an orientation and respond by adopting integrity as their lifestyle, the beneficiaries are everyone in society.

REFERENCES

Axtman, K. 2005. When tests' cheaters are the teachers. *The Christian Science Monitor,* January 11. Available at: **www.csmonitor.com/2005/0111/p01s03-ussc.html.**

Baker, D. P., and G. K. LeTendre. 2005. *National differences, global similarities: World culture and future of schooling.* Stanford, CA: Stanford University Press.

Callahan, D. 2004. *The cheating culture: Why more Americans are doing wrong to get ahead.* New York: Harcourt.

Carter, J. 2005. *Our endangered values: America's moral crisis.* New York: Simon & Schuster.

Cizek, G. J. 2003. *Detecting and preventing classroom cheating: Promoting integrity in assessment.* Thousand Oaks, CA: Sage.

Dan, L. 2005. Essay plagiarists to be kicked out of school. *China Daily,* December 14. Available at: **www.chinadaily.com.cn/english/doc/2005-12/14/content_503398.htm.**

Davis, B. G. 2002. *Tools for teaching: Preventing academic dishonesty.* Berkeley: University of California. Available at: **http://teaching.berkeley.edu/bgd/prevent.html.**

de Bono, E. 1999. *Six thinking hats.* New York: Little, Brown and Company.

Dongdong, S. 2005. Exam cheaters may face 7 years in jail. *China Daily,* September 14. Available at: **http://en1.chinabroadcast.cn/2238/2005-9-14/148@271735.htm.**

Educational Testing Service. 2005. Revised GRE general test to premiere in October 2006. Princeton, NJ: ETS. Available at: **www.rxpgnews.com/careers/article_2690.shtml**.

The Emperors Club, 109 min., Universal Studios, 2002.

The Epoch Times. 2005. 83% of college students in China cheat on exams. September 8. Available at: **www.theepochtimes.com/news/5-9-8/32106.html.**

Evans, P., and B. Wolf. 2005. Collaboration rules. *Harvard Business Review,* July–Aug: 1–10.

Farkas, S., J. Johnson, A. Duffett, L. Wilson, and J. Vine. 2002. *A lot easier said than done: Parents talk about raising children in today's America.* New York: State Farm Companies Foundation and Public Agenda.

Foster, D. 2003. The growing problem of cheating. *Caveon Test Security Bulletin* 1(4): 1. Draper, UT: Caveon, LLC. Available at: **www.caveon.com/Caveon_TSB_10-03.pdf.**

Fremer, J., and J. Mulkey. 2004. The ten most wanted test cheaters. Draper, UT: Caveon, LLC. Available at: **www.caveon.com /10_Most_Wanted.pdf.**

Johnson, D. 2004. Keeping kids engaged fights plagiarism too. *Education Digest* 69(9): 16–21.

Johnson, V. E. 2003. *Grade inflation: A crisis in college education.* New York: Springer.

Josephson Institute of Ethics. 2006. *2006 Josephson Institute report card on the ethics of American youth.* Los Angeles, CA: Josephson Institute of Ethics.

Krathwohl, D. R. 2002. A revision of Bloom's taxonomy: An overview. *Theory Into Practice* 41(4): 216–18.

Lambert, B. 2005. L.I. school official helped son cheat on test, investigators say. *The New York Times,* June 28.

Lathrop, A., and K. Foss. 2005. *Guiding students from cheating and plagiarism to honesty and integrity: Strategies for change.* Englewood, CO: Libraries Unlimited.

Leland, B. 2002. *Plagiarism and the Web.* Macomb, IL: Western Illinois University. Available at: **www.wiu.edu/users/mfbhl/wiu/plagiarism.htm.**

Lipson, C. 2004. *Doing honest work in college. How to prepare citations, avoid plagiarism, and advance academic success.* Chicago, IL: University of Chicago Press.

Lipson, C., M. Biagioli, and M. Vicinus. 2005. A plague of plagiarism? *Michigan Today* 37(1). Available at: **www.umich.edu/news/MT/05/Fall05/story.html?plagiarism2.**

Ludwig, B., and S. Silverstein. 2006. GMAT expands reach, further strengthens test security measures. McLean, VA: Graduate Management Admission Council. Available at: **www.gmac.com/gmac/NewsCenter/PressReleases/GMATExpandSReachFurtherStrengthensTestSecurityMeasures.htm.**

Maciariello, J. A. 2005. Peter F. Drucker on a functioning society. *Leader to Leader* 37(summer): 26–34. Available at: **www.pfdf.org/leaderbooks/121/summer2005/maciariello.html.**

McCabe, D. L., and G. Pavela. 2004. Ten [updated] principles of academic integrity. *Change* 36(3): 10–15.

Nichols, S. L., and T. L. Good. 2004. *America's teenagers— Myths and realities: Media images, schooling, and the social costs of careless indifference.* Mahwah, NJ: Lawrence Erlbaum.

Peterson, C., and M. E. P. Seligman. 2004. *Character strengths and virtues: A handbook and classification.* New York: Oxford University Press and the American Psychological Association.

Schwartz, J. 2001. Trying to keep young Internet users from a life of piracy. *The New York Times,* December 25.

Sclafani, J. 2004. *The educated parent: Recent trends in raising children.* Westport, CT: Greenwood.

Sommers, C. H., and S. Satel. 2005. *One nation under therapy: How the helping culture is eroding self-reliance.* New York: St. Martin's Press.

Standler, R. B. 2000. Plagiarism in colleges in USA. Concord, NH: R. B. Standler. Available at: **www.rbs2.com/plag.htm.**

Strom, P., and R. Strom. 2005. Cyberbullying by adolescents: A preliminary assessment. *The Educational Forum* 70(1): 21–36.

Strom, P., and R. Strom. 2006. Polling adolescents to improve learning. Paper presented at the Conference of the American Association of Behavioral and Social Sciences, February 17, Las Vegas, NV.

Whitley, B. E., Jr., and P. Keith-Spiegel. 2002. *Academic dishonesty: An educator's guide.* Mahwah, NJ: Lawrence Erlbaum.

POSTNOTE

Most new teachers want to trust their students, but they are also keenly aware that cheating is commonplace in schools. What to do? As the authors of this article outline, knowing why students cheat may provide insight into steps to alleviate the problem. For instance, "not having enough time to do the work" is a common reason students give for cheating. Knowing this, educators might want to examine whether the school's or teacher's policies on homework assignments are reasonable since burdensome policies might contribute to student cheating. Also, being aware of the various methods students use to cheat can assist teachers in preventing opportunities to cheat.

Teachers can also discuss with students who are planning to attend college that many colleges and universities— Stanford, University of Virginia, and Randolph College, to name a few—have honor codes against cheating, lying, and stealing. Cheating in high school may become a hard-to-break habit when attending such universities, which could result in severe penalties, including dismissal. Cheating might also become habit forming in other endeavors, such as business or sports. It may not be easy to restrict cheating to school work, but be honest in business dealings.

Discussion Questions

1. Have you witnessed cheating in school? Why do you think the student(s) did it?
2. Were you surprised by the extent of cheating reported by the authors? Why or why not?
3. What do you think are the most effective steps you can take to curb cheating by your students?

RELATED WEBSITE RESOURCES

 Web Resources:

Plagiarism and the Web. Available at:

http://www.wiu.edu/users/mfbhl/wiu/plagiarism.htm.

This website, created by Professor Bruce Leland at Western Illinois University, is designed to help teachers deal with plagiarism.

The Perils and Promises of Praise

9

Carol Dweck

Carol S. Dweck is the Lewis and Virginia Eaton Professor of Psychology at Stanford University.

"The Perils and Promises of Praise" by Carol S. Dweck, *Educational Leadership* 65, no. 2, October 2007, pp. 34–39. Used with permission.

F O C U S QUESTION

What are the different effects of teacher praise on student motivation and learning?

KEY TERMS

Fixed mind-set
Growth mind-set

We often hear these days that we've produced a generation of young people who can't get through the day without an award. They expect success because they're special, not because they've worked hard.

Is this true? Have we inadvertently done something to hold back our students?

I think educators commonly hold two beliefs that do just that. Many believe that (1) praising students' intelligence builds their confidence and motivation to learn, and (2) students' inherent intelligence is the major cause of their achievement in school. Our research has shown that the first belief is false and that the second can be harmful—even for the most competent students.

As a psychologist, I have studied student motivation for more than 35 years. My graduate students and I have looked at thousands of children, asking why some enjoy learning, even when it's hard, and why they are resilient in the face of obstacles. We have learned a great deal. Research shows us how to praise students in ways that yield motivation and resilience. In addition, specific interventions can reverse a student's slide into failure during the vulnerable period of adolescence.

Fixed or Malleable?

Praise is intricately connected to how students view their intelligence. Some students believe that their intellectual ability is a fixed trait. They have a certain amount of intelligence, and that's that. Students with this fixed mind-set become excessively concerned with how smart they are, seeking tasks that will prove their intelligence and avoiding ones that might not (Dweck, 1999, 2006). The desire to learn takes a backseat.

Other students believe that their intellectual ability is something they can develop through effort and education. They don't necessarily believe that anyone can become an Einstein or a Mozart, but they do understand that even Einstein and Mozart had to put in years of effort to become who they were. When students believe that they can develop their intelligence, they focus on doing just that. Not worrying about how smart they will appear, they take on challenges and stick to them (Dweck, 1999, 2006).

More and more research in psychology and neuroscience supports the growth mind-set. We are discovering that the brain has more plasticity over time than we ever imagined (Doidge, 2007); that fundamental aspects of intelligence can be enhanced through learning (Sternberg, 2005); and that dedication and persistence in the face of obstacles are key ingredients in outstanding achievement (Ericsson, Charness, Feltovich, & Hoffman, 2006).

Alfred Binet (1909/1973), the inventor of the IQ test, had a strong growth mind-set. He believed that education could transform the basic capacity to learn. Far from intending to measure fixed intelligence, he meant his test to be a tool for identifying students who were not profiting from the public school curriculum so that other courses of study could be devised to foster their intellectual growth.

The Two Faces of Effort

The fixed and growth mind-sets create two different psychological worlds. In the fixed mind-set, students care first and foremost about how they'll be judged: smart or not smart. Repeatedly, students with this mind-set reject opportunities to learn if they might make mistakes (Hong, Chiu, Dweck, Lin, & Wan, 1999; Mueller & Dweck, 1998). When they do make mistakes or reveal deficiencies, rather than correct them, they try to hide them (Nussbaum & Dweck, 2007).

They are also afraid of effort because effort makes them feel dumb. They believe that if you have the ability, you shouldn't need effort (Blackwell, Trzesniewski, & Dweck, 2007), that ability should bring success all by itself. This is one of the worst beliefs that students can hold. It can cause many bright students to stop working in school when the curriculum becomes challenging.

Finally, students in the fixed mind-set don't recover well from setbacks. When they hit a setback in school, they *decrease* their efforts and consider cheating (Blackwell et al., 2007). The idea of fixed intelligence does not offer them viable ways to improve.

Let's get inside the head of a student with a fixed mind-set as he sits in his classroom, confronted with algebra for the first time. Up until then, he has breezed through math. Even when he barely paid attention in class and skimped on his homework, he always got *A*s. But this is different. It's hard. The student feels anxious and thinks, "What if I'm not as good at math as I thought? What if other kids understand it and I don't?" At some level, he realizes that he has two choices: try hard, or turn off. His interest in math begins to wane, and his attention wanders. He tells himself, "Who cares about this stuff? It's for nerds. I could do it if I wanted to, but it's so boring. You don't see CEOs and sports stars solving for *x* and *y*."

By contrast, in the growth mind-set, students care about learning. When they make a mistake or exhibit a deficiency, they correct it (Blackwell et al., 2007; Nussbaum & Dweck, 2007). For them, effort is a *positive* thing: It ignites their intelligence and causes it to grow. In the face of failure, these students escalate their efforts and look for new learning strategies.

Let's look at another student—one who has a growth mind-set—having her first encounter with algebra. She finds it new, hard, and confusing, unlike anything else she has ever learned. But she's determined to understand it. She listens to everything the teacher says, asks the teacher questions after class, and takes her textbook home and reads the chapter over twice. As she begins to get it, she feels exhilarated. A new world of math opens up for her.

It is not surprising, then, that when we have followed students over challenging school transitions or courses, we find that those with growth mind-sets outperform their classmates with fixed mind-sets—even when they entered with equal skills and knowledge. A growth mind-set fosters the growth of ability over time (Blackwell et al., 2007; Mangels, Butterfield, Lamb, Good, & Dweck, 2006; see also Grant & Dweck, 2003).

The Effects of Praise

Many educators have hoped to maximize students' confidence in their abilities, their enjoyment of learning, and their ability to thrive in school by praising their intelligence. We've studied the effects of this kind of praise in children as young as 4 years old and as old as adolescence, in students in inner-city and rural settings, and in students of different ethnicities—and we've consistently found the same thing (Cimpian, Arce, Markman, & Dweck, 2007; Kamins & Dweck, 1999; Mueller & Dweck, 1998): Praising students' intelligence gives them a short burst of pride, followed by a long string of negative consequences.

In many of our studies (see Mueller & Dweck, 1998), 5th grade students worked on a task, and after the first set of problems, the teacher praised some of them for their intelligence ("You must be smart at these problems") and others for their effort ("You must have worked hard at these problems"). We then assessed the students' mind-sets. In one study, we asked students to agree or disagree with mind-set statements, such as, "Your intelligence is something basic about you that you can't really change." Students praised for intelligence agreed with statements like these more than students praised for effort did. In another study, we asked students to define intelligence. Students praised for intelligence made significantly more references to innate, fixed capacity, whereas the students praised for effort made more references to skills, knowledge, and areas they could change through effort and learning. Thus, we found that praise for intelligence tended to put students in a fixed mind-set (intelligence is fixed, and you have it), whereas praise for effort tended to put them in a growth mind-set (you're developing these skills because you're working hard).

We then offered students a chance to work on either a challenging task that they could learn from or an easy one that ensured error-free performance. Most of those praised for intelligence wanted the easy task, whereas most of those praised for effort wanted the challenging task and the opportunity to learn.

Next, the students worked on some challenging problems. As a group, students who had been praised for their intelligence *lost* their confidence in their ability and their enjoyment of the task as soon as they began to struggle with the problem. If success meant they were smart, then struggling meant they were not. The whole point of intelligence praise is to boost confidence and motivation, but both were gone in a flash. Only the effort-praised kids remained, on the whole, confident and eager.

When the problems were made somewhat easier again, students praised for intelligence did poorly, having lost their confidence and motivation. As a group, they did worse than they had done initially on these same types of problems. The students praised for effort showed excellent performance and continued to improve.

Finally, when asked to report their scores (anonymously), almost 40 percent of the intelligence-praised students lied. Apparently, their egos were so wrapped up in their performance that they couldn't admit mistakes. Only about 10 percent of the effort-praised students saw fit to falsify their results.

Praising students for their intelligence, then, hands them not motivation and resilience but a fixed mind-set with all its vulnerability. In contrast, effort or "process" praise (praise for engagement, perseverance, strategies, improvement, and the like) fosters hardy motivation. It tells students what they've done to be successful and what they need to do to be successful again in the future. Process praise sounds like this:

- You really studied for your English test, and your improvement shows it. You read the material over several times, outlined it, and tested yourself on it. That really worked!
- I like the way you tried all kinds of strategies on that math problem until you finally got it.
- It was a long, hard assignment, but you stuck to it and got it done. You stayed at your desk, kept up your concentration, and kept working. That's great!

- I like that you took on that challenging project for your science class. It will take a lot of work—doing the research, designing the machine, buying the parts, and building it. You're going to learn a lot of great things.

What about a student who gets an *A* without trying? I would say, "All right, that was too easy for you. Let's do something more challenging that you can learn from." We don't want to make something done quickly and easily the basis for our admiration.

What about a student who works hard and *doesn't* do well? I would say, "I liked the effort you put in. Let's work together some more and figure out what you don't understand." Process praise keeps students focused, not on something called ability that they may or may not have and that magically creates success or failure, but on processes they can all engage in to learn.

Motivated to Learn

Finding that a growth mind-set creates motivation and resilience—and leads to higher achievement—we sought to develop an intervention that would teach this mind-set to students. We decided to aim our intervention at students who were making the transition to 7th grade because this is a time of great vulnerability. School often gets more difficult in 7th grade, grading becomes more stringent, and the environment becomes more impersonal. Many students take stock of themselves and their intellectual abilities at this time and decide whether they want to be involved with school. Not surprisingly, it is often a time of disengagement and plunging achievement.

We performed our intervention in a New York City junior high school in which many students were struggling with the transition and were showing plummeting grades. If students learned a growth mind-set, we reasoned, they might be able to meet this challenge with increased, rather than decreased, effort. We therefore developed an eight-session workshop in which both the control group and the growth-mind-set group learned study skills, time management techniques, and memory strategies (Blackwell et al., 2007). However, in the growth-mind-set intervention, students also learned about their brains and what they could do to make their intelligence grow.

They learned that the brain is like a muscle—the more they exercise it, the stronger it becomes. They learned that every time they try hard and learn something new, their brain forms new connections that, over time, make them smarter. They learned that intellectual development is not the natural unfolding of intelligence, but rather the formation of new connections brought about through effort and learning.

Students were riveted by this information. The idea that their intellectual growth was largely in their hands fascinated them. In fact, even the most disruptive students suddenly sat still and took notice, with the most unruly boy of the lot looking up at us and saying, "You mean I don't have to be dumb?"

Indeed, the growth-mind-set message appeared to unleash students' motivation. Although both groups had experienced a steep decline in their math grades during their first months of junior high, those receiving the growth-mind-set intervention showed a significant rebound. Their math grades improved. Those in the control group, despite their excellent study skills intervention, continued their decline.

What's more, the teachers—who were unaware that the intervention workshops differed—singled out three times as many students in the growth-mindset intervention as showing marked changes in motivation. These students had a heightened desire to work hard and learn. One striking example was the boy who thought he was dumb. Before this experience, he had never put in any extra effort and often didn't turn his homework in on time. As a result of the training, he worked for hours one evening to finish an assignment early so that his teacher could review it and give him a chance to revise it. He earned a *B+* on the assignment (he had been getting *C*s and lower previously).

Other researchers have obtained similar findings with a growth-mind-set intervention. Working with junior high school students, Good, Aronson, and Inzlicht (2003) found an increase in math and English achievement test scores; working with college students, Aronson, Fried, and Good (2002) found an increase in students' valuing of academics, their enjoyment of schoolwork, and their grade point averages.

To facilitate delivery of the growth-mind-set workshop to students, we developed an interactive computer-based version of the intervention called *Brainology*. Students work through six modules, learning about the brain, visiting virtual brain labs, doing virtual brain experiments, seeing how the brain changes with learning, and learning how they can make their brains work better and grow smarter.

We tested our initial version in 20 New York City schools, with encouraging results. Almost all students (anonymously polled) reported changes in their study habits and motivation to learn resulting directly from their learning of the growth mind-set. One student noted that as a result of the animation she had seen about the brain, she could actually "picture the neurons growing bigger as they make more connections."

One student referred to the value of effort: "If you do not give up and you keep studying, you can find your way through."

Adolescents often see school as a place where they perform for teachers who then judge them. The growth mind-set changes that perspective and makes school a place where students vigorously engage in learning for their own benefit.

Going Forward

Our research shows that educators cannot hand students confidence on a silver platter by praising their intelligence. Instead, we can help them gain the tools they need to maintain their confidence in learning by keeping them focused on the *process* of achievement.

Maybe we have produced a generation of students who are more dependent, fragile, and entitled than previous generations. If so, it's time for us to adopt a growth mind-set and learn from our mistakes. It's time to deliver interventions that will truly boost students' motivation, resilience, and learning.

REFERENCES

Aronson, J., Fried, C., & Good, C. (2002). Reducing the effects of stereotype threat on African American college students by shaping theories of intelligence. *Journal of Experimental Social Psychology, 38,* 113–125.

Binet, A. (1909/1973). *Les idées modernes sur les enfants* [Modern ideas on children]. Paris: Flamarion. (Original work published 1909)

Blackwell, L., Trzesniewski, K., & Dweck, C. S. (2007). Implicit theories of intelligence predict achievement across an adolescent transition: A longitudinal study and an Intervention. *Child Development, 78,* 246–263.

Cimpian, A., Arce, H., Markman, E. M., & Dweck, C. S. (2007). Subtle linguistic cues impact children's motivation. *Psychological Science, 18,* 314–316.

Doidge, N. (2007). *The brain that changes Itself: Stories of personal triumph from the frontiers of brain science.* New York: Viking.

Dweck, C. S. (1999). *Self-theories: Their role in motivation, personality and development.* Philadelphia: Taylor and Francis/Psychology Press.

Dweck, C. S. (2006). *Mindset: The new psychology of success.* New York: Random House.

Ericsson, K. A., Charness, N., Feltovich, P. J., & Hoffman, R. R. (Eds.). (2006). *The Cambridge handbook of expertise and expert performance.* New York: Cambridge University Press.

Good, C., Aronson, J., & Inzlicht, M. (2003). Improving adolescents' standardized test performance: An intervention to reduce the effects of stereotype threat. *Journal of Applied Developmental Psychology, 24,* 645–662.

Grant, H., & Dweck, C. S. (2003). Clarifying achievement goals and their impact. *Journal of Personality and Social Psychology, 85,* 541–553.

Hong, Y. Y., Chiu, C., Dweck, C. S., Lin, D., & Wan, W. (1999). Implicit theories, attributions, and coping: A meaning system approach. *Journal of Personality and Social Psychology, 77,* 588–599.

Kamins, M., & Dweck, C. S. (1999). Person vs. process praise and criticism: Implications for contingent self-worth and coping. *Developmental Psychology, 35,* 835–847.

Mangels, J. A., Butterfield, B., Lamb, J., Good, C. D., & Dweck, C. S. (2006). Why do beliefs about intelligence influence learning success? A social-cognitive-

neuroscience model. *Social, Cognitive, and Affective Neuroscience, 1,* 75–86.

Mueller, C. M., & Dweck, C. S. (1998). Intelligence praise can undermine motivation and performance. *Journal of Personality and Social Psychology, 75,* 33–52.

Nussbaum, A. D., & Dweck, C. S. (2007). Defensiveness vs. remediation: Self-theories and modes of self-esteem maintenance. *Personality and Social Psychology Bulletin.*

Sternberg, R. (2005). Intelligence, competence, and expertise. In A. Elliot & C. S. Dweck (Eds.), *The handbook of competence and motivation* (pp. 15–30). New York: Guilford Press.

POSTNOTE

Most of us probably grew up thinking that praise was a good thing to receive. However, research by Carol Dweck and others shows praise to be a more complicated issue. Depending on a student's mind-set, praising students for being smart can actually be harmful in developing their confidence and motivation to learn. Seeing intellect as a fixed entity—either you're smart or you're not—can cause students to decline opportunities to learn if there is a chance they might fail. Students who view their intelligence as something that can grow and develop seek opportunities to learn and meet new challenges. Rather than praising students for their intelligence, teachers should encourage students to try hard and to learn something new, even if they don't succeed right away. In this way, students can develop their intelligence through effort and learning.

Discussion Questions

1. Were there any findings in this article that surprised you? If so, what were they?
2. Which mind-set, growth or fixed, do you think you have? Why do you think this?
3. How might you incorporate the findings of this research into your own classroom?

RELATED WEBSITE RESOURCES

 ### Web Resources:

Po Bronson, "How Not to Talk to Your Kids," *New Yorker Magazine* (February 12, 2007). Available at:

http://nymag.com/news/features/27840/.

A good summary of some of Carol Dweck's research, as seen applied to a particular child.

Jennifer Henderlong and Mark R. Lepper, "The Effects of Praise on Children's Intrinsic Motivation: A Review and Synthesis," *Psychological Bulletin* 2002, Vol. 128, No. 5, 774–795. Available at:

http://academic.reed.edu/motivation/docs/ PraiseReview.pdf.

An excellent review of the effects of praise on children.

10

How to Create Discipline Problems

M. Mark Wasicsko and Steven M. Ross

M. Mark Wasicsko is currently professor and Bank of Kentucky Endowed Chair in Educational Leadership at Northern Kentucky University. **Steven M. Ross** is executive director at The Center for Research in Educational Policy (CREP) and is a professor of Educational Psychology and Research at The University of Memphis.

"How to Create Discipline Problems" by M. Mark Wasicisko and Steven M. Ross, *The Clearing House,* May/June 1994. Reprinted with permission of the Helen Dwight Reid Educational Foundation. Published by Heldref Publications, 1319 Eighteenth St, NW, Washington, DC 20036-1802. Copyright © 1994.

F|O|C|U|S QUESTION

What is the classroom philosophy inherent in the authors' suggestions?

KEY TERMS

Discipline problems
Teacher expectations

Creating classroom discipline problems is easy. By following the ten simple rules listed you should be able to substantially improve your skill at this popular teacher pastime.

1. ***Expect the worst from kids.*** This will keep you on guard at all times.
2. ***Never tell students what is expected of them.*** Kids need to learn to figure things out for themselves.
3. ***Punish and criticize kids often.*** This better prepares them for real life.
4. ***Punish the whole class when one student misbehaves.*** All the other students were probably doing the same thing or at least thinking about doing it.
5. ***Never give students privileges.*** It makes students soft and they will just abuse privileges anyway.
6. ***Punish every misbehavior you see.*** If you don't, the students will take over.
7. ***Threaten and warn kids often.*** "If you aren't good, I'll keep you after school for the rest of your life."
8. ***Use the same punishment for every student.*** If it works for one it will work for all.
9. ***Use school work as punishment.*** "Okay, smarty, answer all the questions in the book for homework!"
10. ***Maintain personal distance from students.*** Familiarity breeds contempt, you know.

We doubt that teachers would deliberately follow any of these rules, but punishments are frequently dealt out without much thought about their effects. In this article we suggest that many discipline problems are caused and sustained by teachers who inadvertently use self-defeating discipline strategies. There are, we believe, several simple, concrete methods to reduce classroom discipline problems.

Expect the Best from Kids

That teachers' expectations play an important role in determining student behavior has long been known. One author remembers two teachers who, at first glance, appeared similar. Both were very strict, gave mountains of homework, and kept students busy from the first moment they entered the classroom. However, they differed in their expectations for students. One seemed to say, "I know I am hard on you, but it is because I know you can do the work." She was effective and was loved by students. The other conveyed her negative expectations, "If I don't keep these kids busy they will stab me in the back." Students did everything they could to live up to each teacher's expectations. Thus, by conveying negative attitudes toward students, many teachers create their own discipline problems.

A first step in reducing discipline problems is to demonstrate positive expectations toward students. This is relatively easy to do for "good" students but probably more necessary for the others. If you were lucky, you probably had a teacher or two who believed you were able and worthy, and expected you to be capable even when you presented evidence to the contrary. You probably looked up to these teachers and did whatever you could to please them (and possibly even became a teacher yourself as a result). Now is the time to return the favor. Expect the best from *each* of your students. Assume that *every* child, if given the chance, will act properly. And, most important, if students don't meet your expectations, *don't give up!* Some students will require much attention before they will begin to respond.

Make the Implicit Explicit

Many teachers increase the likelihood of discipline problems by not making their expectations about proper behavior clear and explicit. For example, how many times have you heard yourself saying, "Now class, BEHAVE!"? You assume everyone knows what you mean by "behave." This assumption may not be reasonable. On the playground, for example, proper behavior means running, jumping, throwing things (preferably balls, not rocks), and cooperating with other students. Classroom teachers have different notions about proper behavior, but in few cases do teachers spell out their expectations carefully. Sad to say, most students must learn the meaning of "behave" by the process of elimination: "Don't look out the window. . . . Don't put hands on fellow students. . . . Don't put feet on the desk . . . don't . . . don't . . . don't. . . ."

A preferred approach would be to present rules for *proper* conduct on the front end (and try to phrase them positively: "Students should . . ."). The teacher (or the class) could prepare a poster on which rules are listed. In that way, rules are clear, explicit, and ever present in the classroom. If you want to increase the likelihood that rules will be followed, have students help make the rules. Research shows that when students feel responsible for rules, they make greater efforts to live by them.

Rewards, Yes! Punishments, No!

A major factor in creating classroom discipline problems is the overuse of punishments as an answer to misbehavior. While most teachers would agree with this statement, recent research indicates that punishments outweigh rewards by at least 10 to 1 in the typical classroom. The types of punishments identified include such old favorites as The Trip to the Office and "Write a million times, 'I will not. . . .'" But punishments also include the almost unconscious (but frequent) responses made for minor infractions: the "evil eye" stare of disapproval and the countless pleas to "Face front," "Stop talking," "Sit down!" and so on.

Punishments (both major and minor) have at least four consequences that frequently lead to increased classroom disruption: 1) Punishment brings attention to those who misbehave. We all know the adage, "The squeaky wheel gets greased." Good behavior frequently leaves a student nameless and unnoticed, but bad behavior can bring the undivided attention of the teacher before an audience of classmates! 2) Punishment has negative side effects such as aggression, depression, anxiety, or embarrassment. At the least, when a child is punished he feels worse about himself, about you and your class, or about school in general. He may even try to reduce the negative side effects by taking it out on another child or on school equipment. 3) Punishment only temporarily suppresses bad behavior. The teacher who rules with an iron ruler can have students who never misbehave in her presence, but who misbehave the moment she leaves the room or turns her back. 4) Punishment disrupts the continuity of your lessons and reduces the time spent on productive learning. These facts, and because punishments are usually not premeditated (and frequently do not address the real problems of misbehavior such as boredom, frustration, or physical discomfort), usually work to increase classroom discipline problems rather than to reduce them.

In view of these factors, the preferred approach is to use rewards. Rewards bring attention to *good* behaviors: "Thank you for being prepared." Rewards provide an appropriate model for other students, and make students feel positive about themselves, about you, and about your class. Also, reinforcing positive behaviors reduces the inclination toward misbehavior and enhances the flow of your lesson. You stay on task, get more student participation, and accentuate the correct responses.

Let the Punishment Fit the Crime

When rewards are inappropriate, many teachers create discipline problems by using short-sighted or ineffective punishments. The classic example is the "whole class punishment." "Okay, I said if anyone talked there would be no recess, so we stay in today!" This approach frustrates students (especially the ones who were behaving properly) and causes more misbehavior.

Research indicates that punishments are most effective when they are the natural consequences of the behavior. For example, if a child breaks a window, it makes sense to punish him with clean-up responsibilities and by making him pay for damage. Having him write 1,000 times, "I will not break the window," or having him do extra math problems (!) does little to help him see the relationship between actions and consequences.

In reality, this is one of the hardest suggestions to follow. In many cases, the "natural consequences" are obscure ("Okay, Steve, you hurt Carlton's feelings by calling him fat. For your punishment, you will make him feel better."). So, finding an appropriate punishment is often difficult. We suggest that after racking your brain, you consult with the offenders. They may be able to come up with a consequence that at least appears to them to be a fit punishment. In any case, nothing is lost for trying.

If You Must Punish, Remove Privileges

In the event that there are no natural consequences that can serve as punishments, the next best approach is to withdraw privileges. This type of punishment fits in well with the actual conditions in our society. In "real life" (located somewhere outside the school walls) privileges and responsibilities go hand in hand. People who do not act responsibly quickly lose freedoms and privileges. Classrooms provide a great opportunity to teach this lesson, but there is one catch: *There must be privileges to withdraw!* Many privileges already exist in classrooms and many more should be created. For example, students who finish their work neatly and on time can play an educational game, do an extra credit math sheet, work on homework, or earn points toward fun activities and free time. The possibilities are limitless. The important point, however, is that those who break the rules lose out on the privileges.

"Ignor"ance Is Bliss

One of the most effective ways to create troubles is to reward the very behaviors you want to eliminate. Many teachers do this inadvertently by giving attention to misbehaviors. For example, while one author was observing a kindergarten class, a child uttered an expletive after dropping a box of toys. The teachers quickly surrounded him and excitedly exclaimed, "That's nasty! Shame! Shame! Don't ever say that nasty word again!" All the while the other kids looked on with studied interest. So by lunch time, many of the other students were chanting, ". . . (expletive deleted) . . ." and the teachers were in a frenzy! Teachers create similar problems by bringing attention to note passing, gum chewing, and countless other minor transgressions. Such problems can usually be avoided by ignoring minor misbehaviors and, at a later time, talking to the student individually. Some minor misbehavior is probably being committed by at least one student during every second you teach! Your choice is to spend your time trying to correct (and bring attention to) each one *or* to go about the business of teaching.

Consistency Is the Best Policy

Another good way to create discipline problems is to be inconsistent with rules, assignments, and punishments. For example, one author's daughter was given 750 math problems to complete over the Christmas holidays. She spent many hours (which she would rather have spent playing with friends) completing the task. As it turned out, no one else completed the assignment, so the teacher extended the deadline by another week. In this case, the teacher was teaching students that it is all right to skip assignments. When events like this recur, the teacher loses credibility and students are taught to procrastinate, which they may continue to do throughout their lives.

Inconsistent punishment has a similar effect. By warning and rewarning students, teachers actually cultivate misbehavior. "The next time you do that, you're going to the office!" Five minutes pass and then, "I'm warning you, one more time and you are gone!" And later, "This is your last warning!" And finally, "Okay, I have had it with you, go stand in the hall!" In this instance, a student has learned that a punishment buys him/her a number of chances to misbehave (she/he might as well use them all), and that the actual punishment will be less severe than the promised one (not a bad deal).

To avoid the pitfalls of inconsistency, mean what you say, and, when you say it, follow through.

Know Each Student Well

Discipline problems can frequently be caused by punishing students we intended to reward and vice versa.

When a student is told to clean up the classroom after school, is that a reward or punishment? It's hard to tell. As we all know, "One person's pleasure is another's poison."

One author remembers the difficulty he had with reading in the fourth grade. It made him so anxious that he would become sick just before reading period in the hope that he would be sent to the clinic, home, or anywhere other than to "the circle." One day, after helping the teacher straighten out the room before school, the teacher thanked him with, "Mark, you've been so helpful, you can be the first to read today." The author made sure he was never "helpful" enough to be so severely punished again.

The opposite happens just as often. For example, there are many class clowns who delight in such "punishments" as standing in the corner, leaving the room, or being called to the blackboard. The same author recalls having to stand in the school courtyard for punishment. He missed math, social studies, and English, and by the end of the day had entertained many classmates with tales of his escapades.

The key to reducing discipline problems is to know your students well; know what is rewarding and what is punishing for each.

Use School Work as Rewards

One of the worst sins a teacher can commit is to use school work as punishments. There is something sadly humorous about the language arts teacher who punishes students with, "Write 1,000 times, I will not . . ." or the math teacher who assigns 100 problems as punishment. In cases like these we are actually punishing students with that which we want them to use and enjoy! Teachers can actually reduce discipline problems (and increase learning) by using their subjects as rewards. This is done in subtle and sometimes indirect ways, through making lessons meaningful, practical, and fun. If you are teaching about fractions, bring in pies and cakes and see how fast those kids can learn the difference between ½, ¼, and ⅛. Reading teachers should allow free reading as a reward for good behavior. Math teachers can give extra credit math sheets (points to be added to the next test) when regular assignments are completed. The possibilities are endless and the results will be less misbehavior and a greater appreciation for both teacher and subject.

Treat Students with Love and Respect

The final suggestion for reducing discipline problems is to treat students kindly. It is no secret that people tend to respond with the same kind of treatment that they are given. If students are treated in a cold or impersonal manner, they are less likely to care if they cause you grief. If they are treated with warmth and respect they will want to treat you well in return. One of the best ways to show you care (and thus reduce discipline problems) is to surprise kids. After they have worked particularly hard, give them a treat. "You kids have worked so hard you may have 30 minutes extra recess." Or have a party one day for no good reason at all. Kids will come to think, "This school stuff isn't so bad after all!" Be careful to keep the surprises unexpected. If kids come to expect them, surprises lose their effectiveness. Recently, one author heard a student pay a teacher the highest tribute. He said, "She is more than just a teacher; she is our friend." Not surprisingly, this teacher is known for having few major discipline problems.

Final Thoughts

When talking about reducing discipline problems, we need to be careful not to suggest that they can or should be totally eliminated. When children are enthusiastic about learning, involved in what they are doing, and allowed to express themselves creatively, "discipline problems" are apt to occur. Albert Einstein is one of numerous examples of highly successful people who were labeled discipline problems in school. It was said of Einstein that he was "the boy who knew not merely which monkey wrench to throw in the works, but also how best to throw it." This led to his expulsion from school because his "presence in the class is disruptive and affects the other students." For dictators and tyrants, robot-like obedience is a major goal. For teachers, however, a much more critical objective is to help a classroom full of students reach their maximum potential as individuals.

The theme of this article has been that many teachers create their own discipline problems. Just as we teach the way we were taught, we tend to discipline with the same ineffectual methods that were used on us. By becoming aware of this and by following the simple suggestions presented above, learning and teaching can become more rewarding for all involved.

POSTNOTE

A friend of ours, Ernie Lundquist, claims that as a student he actually saw a sign on his principal's door that read, "The beatings will continue until the morale improves." While over the years Ernie has not proved to be a particularly reliable source in these matters, his reported sign-sighting underlines the point that student misbehavior often brings out the very worst in educators. In dealing with disruptive, misbehaving students, we who are supposed to stand for the use of intelligence, compassion, and imagination all too often demonstrate stupidity, insensitivity, and a complete lack of imagination.

The authors of this essay take the problem and turn it inside out, suggesting how we can create discipline problems for ourselves. But the real answer they offer us, and one the teacher frequently forgets in the heat of dealing with a discipline problem, is to *be creative!* We expect creativity from our students. Why not show a little in dealing with our discipline problems?

Discussion Questions

1. Which of the authors' "ten simple rules" have you seen demonstrated most frequently in our schools?
2. What do you believe is the central message of this article?
3. What, in your judgment, are the three most practical suggestions offered by the authors? Why?

RELATED WEBSITE RESOURCES AND VIDEO CASES

 Web Resources:

Education World. Available at:

> **http://educationworld.com/a_cur/archives/
> classmanagement.shtml.**

This website includes a database of teacher resources related to classroom management.

⏩ ▶ ⏪ *Video Case:*

Classroom Management: Handling a Student with Behavior Problems

In this video you will see how two teachers, working with a student-support coach, design strategies and interventions to cope with particular students' disruptive behavior. As you watch the clips and study the artifacts in the case, reflect upon the following questions:

1. What concerns about your own ability to work with students who have emotional or behavioral problems did this video raise? How can you prepare yourself to deal with these kinds of problems?
2. What do you see as the strongest points of the strategies and interventions that Ellen Henry, the student-support coach, suggests?

At Risk for Abuse: A Teacher's Guide for Recognizing and Reporting Child Neglect and Abuse

11

Dennis L. Cates, Marc A. Markell, and Sherrie Bettenhausen

At the time this article was written, **Dennis L. Cates** was an assistant professor in Programs in Special Education at the University of South Carolina in Columbia. **Marc A. Markell** is currently a professor in the Department of Special Education at St. Cloud State University in St. Cloud, Minnesota. **Sherrie Bettenhausen** died in August 2003. At the time this article was written, she was a professor in the Special Education Department of the University of Charleston.

Dennis L. Cates, Marc A. Markell, and Sherrie Bettenhausen, "At Risk for Abuse: A Teacher's Guide for Recognizing and Reporting Child Neglect and Abuse," *Preventing School Failure*, Vol. 39, No. 2, Winter 1995. Reprinted by permission of the authors.

|F|O|C|U|S| QUESTION

Child abuse is becoming increasingly common in our society. What exactly are the classroom teacher's responsibilities?

KEY TERM

Behavioral indicators
Child abuse
Physical indicators of child abuse

In 1992, 2.9 million children were reported as suspected victims of abuse or neglect, an increase of 8% from 1991 (Children, Youth, & Families Department [CYFD], 1993). [Editor's note: In 2006, 3.6 million incidents of child abuse or neglect were reported, and 905,000 of these reported cases were sustained ("Child Maltreatment 2006," U.S. Department of Health and Human Services, Administration for Children & Families. Available at: **http://www.acf.hhs.gov/programs/cb/pubs/cm06/chapter3.htm#subjects.**] The exact number of children who are abused is, of course, difficult to determine because many cases of abuse go unreported and the definition of abuse varies from state to state (Winters Communication, Inc. [WCI], 1988). Not only does the definition of abuse differ among states, but professionals also define abuse in different ways (Pagelow, 1984). An additional reason for the difficulty in determining an accurate rate is that there may be a failure to recognize and report child abuse among professionals. Giovannoni (1989) stated that the failure to uncover child abuse and neglect is generally a result of three factors: (a) failure to detect injury caused by abuse, particularly when parents use different medical treatment facilities each time or do not seek medical treatment; (b) failure to recognize the indicators of abuse and neglect, especially for middle- and upper-income families; and (c) failure to report the case to the appropriate agency when injury is detected and recognized as abuse or neglect.

Although exact numbers for children who are abused are not available, it is known that an alarming number of children are abused each year. These children are in our classrooms throughout the United States.

Child abuse can lead to the development of a full range of problems in children, from poor academic performance and socialization to a variety of physical and cognitive disabilities. Because children are required to attend school, teachers and other educators are faced with the responsibility of maintaining a protective and vigilant posture in relation to their students' well-being.

Studies have shown that children with disabilities are at greater risk for abuse and neglect than are nondisabled children (Ammerman, Lubetsky, Hersen, & Van Hasselt, 1988). Meier and Sloan (1984) suggested that "most certifiably abused children have been identified as suffering from various developmental handicaps" (p. 247). They further stated that "it is seldom clear whether or not the handicapping conditions are a result of inflicted trauma or, because of a misreading of the child's abilities by parents, such disappointing delays precipitate further abuse" (pp. 247–248). Blacher (1984) suggested that children with disabilities are more likely to supply the "trigger mechanism" for abuse or neglect. It has further been indicated that parents who abuse often describe their children as being backward, hyperactive, continually crying, or difficult to control.

The premise that a disability, developmental delay, or problem adjusting to the school environment may be directly linked to an abusive home environment requires that educators must be especially vigilant in dealing with those children who are at risk for the development of educational disabilities or poor school performance. Because many children will not report abuse directly, teachers need to be aware of specific behavioral and physical indicators that may indicate that abuse has occurred (Parent Advocacy for Educational Rights [PACER], 1989). The purpose of this article is to provide teachers with potential indicators of abuse, guidelines in dealing with child abuse in at-risk children, and information related to their legal responsibilities in reporting suspected child abuse.

Definitions and Extent of the Problem

The Child Abuse Prevention and Treatment Act of 1974 defines child abuse and neglect as follows:

> the physical or mental injury, sexual abuse or exploitation, negligent treatment, or maltreatment of a child under the age of eighteen, or the age specified by the child protection law of the state in question, by a person who is responsible for the child welfare under the circumstances which indicate that the child's health or welfare is harmed or threatened thereby. (42 U.S.C. § 5102)

Maltreatment of a child can be further described in terms of neglect and physical, verbal, emotional, and sexual abuse.

Neglect typically involves a failure on the part of a parent, guardian, or other responsible party to provide for the child's basic needs, such as food, shelter, medical care, educational opportunities, or protection and supervision. Further, neglect is associated with abandonment and inadequate supervision (Campbell, 1992).

Verbal abuse may involve excessive acts of derision, taunting, teasing, and mocking. Verbal abuse also involves the frequent humiliation of the child as well as a heavy reliance on yelling to convey feelings. Physical abuse can involve shaking, beating, or burning.

Emotional abuse is a pattern of behavior that takes place over an extended period of time, characterized by intimidating, belittling, and otherwise damaging interactions that affect a child's emotional development (PACER, 1989). It may be related to an intent to withhold attention or a failure to provide adequate supervision, or relatively normal living experiences. Sensory deprivation and long periods of confinement are also related to emotional abuse. Emotional abuse is very difficult to define or categorize.

Sexual abuse of children is also referred to as child sexual abuse and child molesting. It is typically defined in terms of the criminal laws of a state and involves intent to commit sexual acts with minors or to sexually exploit children for personal gratification (Campbell, 1992). Sexual intercourse need not take place and, in fact, is rare in prepubertal children. Sexual abuse involves coercion, deceit, and manipulation to achieve power over the child (PACER, 1989).

In Table 1, we provide possible physical and behavioral indicators of neglect and physical, emotional, and sexual abuse. A child who persistently shows several of these characteristics *may* be experiencing the symptoms of abuse or neglect.

It is important to note that the physical and behavioral indicators of neglect and emotional, sexual, and physical abuse *suggest* or *indicate* that abuse *may* have taken place. They *do not prove* that abuse has occurred and may be indicators of other situations happening in the child's life. Additionally, educators need to be cognizant of the fact that children who are motorically delayed or impaired may be prone to accidents and as a result have bruises, scrapes, cuts, or other minor injuries. This may also be true of children with severely limited vision. Children with diagnosed medical conditions may develop symptoms that result in a change of demeanor or physical appearance. It is important that teachers who serve these children become familiar with the child's condition and be well acquainted with the child's family. Frequent meetings, by telephone and in person, will assist the teacher in keeping up to date with changing medical conditions and aid in monitoring changes in family life patterns.

A teacher who is equipped with knowledge of the symptoms of child abuse and neglect and the characteristics of the child and the family will be able to better determine whether an at-risk learner or child with a disability is a victim of abuse.

Legal Obligations

Children who are at risk for developmental delays are at greater risk for child abuse than children who are not. Teachers who work with these students should, therefore, be aware of their responsibilities relative to child abuse and neglect.

TABLE 1

Physical and Behavioral Indicators of Possible Neglect and Abuse

Physical Indicators	Behavioral Indicators
EMOTIONAL ABUSE AND NEGLECT	
• Height and weight significantly below age level	• Begging or stealing food
• Inappropriate clothing for weather, scaly skin	• Constant fatigue
• Poor hygiene, lice, body odor	• Poor school attendance
• Child left unsupervised or abandoned	• Chronic hunger
• Lack of safe and sanitary shelter	• Dull, apathetic appearance
• Unattended medical or dental needs	• Running away from home
• Developmental lags	• Child reports that no one cares for/looks after him/her
• Habit disorders	• Sudden onset of behavioral extremes (conduct problems, depression)
PHYSICAL ABUSE	
• Frequent injuries such as cuts, bruises, or burns	• Poor school attandance
• Wearing long sleeves in warm weather	• Refusing to change clothes for physical education
• Pain despite lack of evident injury	• Finding reasons to stay at school and not go home
• Inability to perform motor skills because of injured hands	• Frequent complaints of harsh treatments by parents
• Difficulty walking or sitting	• Fear of adults
SEXUAL ABUSE	
• Bedwetting or soiling	• Unusual, sophisticated sexual behavior/knowledge
• Stained or bloody underclothing	• Sudden onset of behavioral extremes
• Venereal disease	• Poor school attendance
• Blood or purulent discharge from genital or anal area	• Finding reasons to stay at school and not go home
• Difficulty walking or sitting	
• Excessive fears, clinging	

Child abuse cannot be legally ignored by school officials. Teachers and administrators are required by law in all 50 states to report suspected child abuse (Fossey, 1993; Trudell & Whatley, 1988). In most jurisdictions, it is a criminal offense for a person to fail to report abuse when he or she is required by law to do so (Fossey, 1993). Therefore, failure to act may result in the filing of criminal charges or civil suits. The courts have also ruled against teachers for delaying their actions (McCarthy & Cambron-McCabe, 1992). The possibility of criminal or civil proceedings may give many teachers pause and result in undue anxiety or overreaction to the problem. Educators must, therefore, become aware of their legal and administrative responsibilities.

The state laws governing the reporting of child abuse generally require teachers, doctors, school counselors, nurses, dentists, and police, to name a few, to report suspected child abuse to those human services agencies responsible for child welfare. Generally, teachers are required only to have a reasonable suspicion that child abuse has occurred before they are required to report it. Reasonable suspicion suggests that one is relieved of the responsibility of researching a case or of having specific facts related to the incidence of abuse. Given teachers' training in child behavior and their daily contact with children, they are in a position to recognize unusual circumstances. Exercising prudence in reporting suspected abuse will generally protect the teacher from criminal or civil action. Persons who report abuse and neglect *in good faith* to the appropriate state agency are immune from civil liability (Fossey, 1993). Laws vary from state to state in this regard, however.

Reporting laws in all states give final authority to investigate abuse charges to agencies other than the schools (Fossey, 1993). The advantage of reporting suspected abuse to agencies other than the school lies in the fact that the burden of gathering facts does not rest with the school. These agencies can research each case objectively and determine the need for action. Teachers may report child abuse to law enforcement officials; however, most states require them to report to local service agencies such as children's protective services, child abuse hotlines, local welfare departments, local social service agencies, public health authorities, school social workers, nurses, or counselors. In extreme cases, teachers may be required to report cases to hospital emergency rooms. Questions often arise, however, about the procedures for reporting abuse.

Should teachers report suspected abuse directly to the appropriate human service agency or to their building principal or immediate supervisor? These questions may be difficult to answer if specific policies and procedures have not been outlined. If no policy exists, and a teacher reports suspected abuse to the principal, and the principal fails or refuses to report the case to the proper authorities, both teacher and principal may be subject to legal action. In such a case, a teacher may be held responsible depending upon specific circumstances involved.

A specific policy or procedure for reporting abuse should protect the teacher from legal liability if those procedures are followed. A policy requiring a teacher to report to the principal or school counselor relieves the teacher of the need to second-guess the system. Teachers are encouraged to familiarize themselves with existing law as well as district policies related to child abuse. If policies do not exist or are not clear, teachers should work through their professional organizations to help promote institutionalization of such policies.

McCarthy and Cambron-McCabe (1992) suggest that low levels of reporting by teachers may be related to the lack of clearly defined administrative policy. Additionally, they recommend the development of in-service programs to acquaint teachers with their legal responsibilities as well as the signs of abuse.

Even though specific laws may require the person suspecting abuse to report specific information, the following suggestions from PACER (1989), CYFD (1992), and WCI (1988) should answer many questions a teacher may have concerning the reporting of suspected abuse.

1. ***To whom should I report suspected child abuse?*** If the teacher suspects that a child has been abused, she or he must report the suspected abuse to the local social service agency, the local police, or the local county sheriff's department. Reporting the suspected abuse to another teacher or the school principal may not be enough to fulfill the requirements of mandatory reporting.
2. ***Should I tell the parents or alleged abuser of my suspicion of child abuse?*** The teacher should not disclose the suspicion of abuse or neglect of a child to either the parents, the caregiver, or the alleged perpetrators. The teacher should report the suspected abuse to the local social service agency, the local police, or the county sheriff's department.
3. ***What should I report?*** The teacher should report the following information (if known):
   • identifying information about the child (name, age, grade, address, and names of parents)
   • name of the person responsible for the abuse
   • where the alleged abuse took place
   • description of the child, any relevant statements made by the child, and any observations made
   • how long ago the incident described took place
   • the reporter's name, address, and phone number
   • if the child has a disability, any information that may be helpful to the officials (i.e., if the child has difficulty with communication, uses a hearing aid, has mental retardation, emotional, or behavioral difficulties, or has a learning disability that indicates special needs)

Summary

To ensure that accurate information is reported to the appropriate human service agency, teachers who serve children at risk for the development of educational problems must be prudent in their efforts to know their children and their families well. Parents who abuse or neglect their children often exhibit characteristics that may be heightened or triggered during family crises. This is of critical importance to teachers of children at risk for developing educational problems because of the additional stress that often results from the child's presence. Parents who abuse or neglect their child may exhibit low self-esteem or appear to be isolated from the community. They typically fail to appear for parent–teacher conferences and are often defensive when questioned about their child. Their child's injuries are often blamed on others or unsatisfactorily explained. The child may relate stories of abuse or unusual behavior by his or her parents. Limited parenting skills may be a result of lack of education, experience, or maturity. Parents may lack patience and be overly demanding of a child who, because of developmental difficulties, is unable to meet their demands in a timely manner. Often, parents who abuse their children were abused themselves.

In determining whether a child is subject to abuse or neglect, the teacher should make note of consistent behaviors or physical evidence, being aware that one incident may not be evidence of child abuse. An isolated incident should be recorded for future reference but should not necessarily be reported immediately. This will depend, of course, on the severity of the injury or the effect on the child's behavior. Knowing the parents well will certainly aid in making a decision relative to reporting of abuse and neglect.

Recognizing abuse and reporting it to the appropriate agency is expected of all teachers and administrators. The experienced teacher makes the extra effort to gather information about the family, to become well acquainted with the parents, and to monitor all of his or her students' physical and behavioral conditions. Teachers must know their students if they intend to effectively deal with child abuse and neglect.

In addition to understanding the procedures for reporting abuse and neglect, teachers may also contribute to improved parent–student relations by participating in the development of parenting education programs or in setting up a more flexible schedule for parent conferences. Efforts should be made to help parents see the advances and improvements made by their children. As parents develop a more realistic view of their child's abilities and potential, they may become more patient and understanding of their child's actions. Teachers should preface a note home with a friendly telephone call or an informal letter discussing the child's overall performance in school. Given a situation in which abuse is present, a teacher's first note home detailing a disciplinary action may precipitate undue punishment. One key to reduced child abuse is improved parent–teacher communication. Teachers cannot afford to wait for the parent to initiate contact. Open lines of communication must be established and supported by the school's administration.

Children at risk for the development of educational problems are at greater risk for abuse and neglect than those children who develop normally. Teachers who serve these children must be aware of this and be able to recognize the warning signs. They must also have a complete understanding of the legal and administrative procedures for reporting abuse. Most important, they must know their students and work to establish effective parent–teacher communication. To stem the tide of abuse and neglect among disabled and at-risk children, teachers must be vigilant, understanding, observant, prudent, and effective record keepers.

Acknowledgment

We wish to thank Dr. J. David Smith and Dr. Mitchell L. Yell for their editorial assistance in the preparation of this manuscript.

REFERENCES

Ammerman, R., Lubetsky, M., Hersen, M., & Van Hasselt, V. (1988). Maltreatment of children and adolescents with multiple handicaps: Five case examples. *Journal of the Multihandicapped Person, 1,* 129–139.

Blacher, J. (1984). A dynamic perspective on the impact of a severely handicapped child on the family. In J. Blacher (Ed.), *Severely handicapped young children and their families: Research in review* (pp. 3–50). New York: Academic Press.

Campbell, R. (1992). Child abuse and neglect. In L. Bullock (Ed.), *Exceptionalities in children and youth* (pp. 470–475). Boston: Allyn and Bacon.

Child Abuse Prevention and Treatment Act of 1974, 42 U.S.C. § 5101 et. seq.

Children, Youth, and Families Department (CYFD). (1993). *Stop child abuse/neglect: Prevention and reporting kit.* Available from Children, Youth and Families Department, Social Services Division, Child Abuse Prevention Unit, 300 San Mateo NE, Suite 802, Albuquerque, NM 87108-1516.

Fossey, R. (1993). Child abuse investigations in the public school: A practical guide for school administrators. *Education Law Reporter.* St. Paul, MN: West.

Giovannoni, J. (1989). Definitional issues in child maltreatment. In D. Cicchitti & V. Carlson (Eds.), *Child maltreatment: Theory and research on the causes and consequences of child abuse and neglect* (pp. 48–50). New York: Cambridge University Press.

McCarthy, M., & Cambron-McCabe, N. (1992). *Public school law: Teachers' and students' rights.* Boston: Allyn and Bacon.

Meier, J., & Sloan, M. (1984). The severely handicapped and child abuse. In J. Blacher (Ed.), *Severely handicapped young children and their families: Research in review* (pp. 247–272). New York: Academic Press.

Pagelow, M. D. (1984). *Family violence.* New York: Praeger Publishing.

Parent Advocacy for Educational Rights (PACER). (1989). *Let's prevent abuse: An informational guide for educators.*

Available from PACER Center, Inc., 4826 Chicago Avenue South, Minneapolis, Minnesota 55407-1055.

Trudell, B., & Whatley, M. H. (1988). School sexual abuse prevention: Unintended consequences and dilemmas. *Child Abuse and Neglect, 12,* 103–113.

Winters Communication, Inc. (WCI). (1988). *Child abuse and its prevention.* Available from Winters Communication, Inc., 1007 Samy Drive, Tampa, Florida 33613.

POSTNOTE

The abuse (or, more accurately stated, the torture) of a helpless child by an adult is one of those crimes that truly cries out for attention. The effects of abuse usually spill over into a child's school life and can make him or her impervious to the best schooling. Recently, greater attention has been given to child abuse in the hope of alerting teachers and other youth workers to the problem and of sensitizing adults to its long-term harm.

Discussion Questions

1. Describe a case of child abuse you know of personally or through media accounts. What was the outcome of the case for all parties involved?

2. What legal responsibilities do teachers have in your state for reporting child abuse? Do they have any legal protection (such as anonymity) once they have reported a case? How comfortable are you with the possibility of meeting these responsibilities?

3. What services are available in your area for children who have been abused? Consider child protection or welfare services as well as law enforcement agencies at the state, county, and city levels.

RELATED WEBSITE RESOURCES

 Web Resources:

Children's Bureau, Administration for Children & Families, U.S. Department of Health and Human Services. Available at:

http://www.acf.hhs.gov/programs/cb.

This website provides statistics, research, programs, and many other resources on children, including information on child abuse and neglect.

Schools

Schools and schooling in the United States have been under intense scrutiny and considerable criticism in recent years. Disappointing test scores, disciplinary problems, violence, and a lack of clear direction are all points of tension. In the past few years, there has been a shift in what educators, legislators, and critics say schools must do to address these and other problems. There is a sense that schools have drifted away from their most important purpose—that is, to prepare students academically and intellectually for the future. Schools have lost sight, some say, of a sense of excellence.

Some of the following selections consider this emphasis, whereas others pose alternative solutions. The topics include school culture, the size of schools, demographic trends affecting schools, school safety, and bringing parents to school.

12

What Makes a Good School?

Joan Lipsitz and Teri West

Joan Lipsitz is co-founder of the National Forum to Accelerate Middle-Grades Reform as well as the Schools to Watch Initiative and currently serves as a senior fellow at MDC, Inc. **Teri West** is the senior program officer at the Academy for Educational Development.

Joan Lipsitz and Teri West, "What Makes a Good School? Identifying Excellent Middle Schools," *Phi Delta Kappan*, September 2006, pp. 57–66. Reprinted by permission of the authors.

F|O|C|U|S QUESTION

What should you look for if you are trying to identify a high performance school?

KEY TERMS

Developmentally responsive
High performing school
Socially equitable

Excellent schools have a sense of purpose that drives every facet of practice and decision making. But what are the critical priorities that fuel that sense of purpose? The National Forum to Accelerate Middle-Grades Reform is a group of educators who believe that young adolescents are capable of learning and achieving at high levels and who are dedicated to improving schools for middle-grades students across the country. Believing that there is nothing as practical as a vision, the first step taken by the members of the forum was to develop a vision statement that would both answer the question posed above and express our shared convictions about school excellence. Through this process, we identified three interlocking priorities that are critical to the sense of purpose that permeates all aspects of successful schools. Briefly, high-performing schools with middle grades are:

- academically excellent—they challenge all of their students to use their minds well;
- developmentally responsive—they are sensitive to the unique developmental challenges of early adolescence and respectful of students' needs and interests; and
- socially equitable, democratic, and fair—they provide every student with high-quality teachers, resources, learning opportunities, and supports and make positive options available to all students.

The forum also concluded that in order to pursue these priorities, high-performing schools must be learning organizations that establish norms, structures, and organizational arrangements that will support and sustain their trajectory toward excellence.

There isn't anything in the forum's work that is exclusive to the middle grades; we believe our vision applies to all schools teaching all grade levels. However, the forum was created to advocate for dramatically improved schools for young adolescents, and, therefore, our emphasis is on the middle grades.

After developing and adopting our vision statement by unanimous consent, we all celebrated—but only briefly. We recognized that for our work to be practical, the forum would need to turn the vision statement into specific criteria for evaluating schools. We needed to develop an instrument that identified the qualities to examine and the questions to ask when assessing a middle-grades school. Could we come up with a set of criteria that would be as useful to a team of classroom teachers as it would be to a group of community members on a school governance committee, or to citizens advocating for school improvement, or to individual parents seeking a good school for their children? And would this set of criteria help the forum identify high-performing schools that others could visit and learn from?

The forum identified a set of criteria on which to evaluate each of the three priorities for high-performing middle-grades schools. The priorities and their criteria are complementary and interdependent. So, for example, an academically excellent school is one in which all students are learning to use their minds well in challenging classrooms where the curriculum, instruction, and assessments are responsive to children's developmental needs. The truly high-performing school sits at the intersection of academic excellence, developmental responsiveness, and social equity.

It is extremely difficult to find schools that excel in all three areas, as the forum discovered in 1999 when it launched its Schools to Watch (STW) program to identify, recognize, and learn from exemplary schools. Since the vision was developed, STW has become a national movement in middle-level education. Fourteen states have recognized 87 STWs, and new states and schools are being added each year. Far more important, the forum's Schools to Watch have become models from which many other schools can learn to "get it right."

In the pages that follow, we describe a selection of the criteria for each of our three priorities for excellent schools. We offer this selection to give readers examples of our approach to assessing schools and to share specific bits and pieces from our observations of four schools. We also describe a sampling of criteria for evaluating a school's organizational structures and processes.[1] Our purpose in presenting the forum's construct of high performance is both to shape the way that readers think about school excellence and to give them explicit guidelines for action when they answer the question "Is this a good school?"

Academic Excellence

CRITERIA

At high-performing schools, curriculum, instruction, and assessment are aligned with high standards, and all students are expected to meet or exceed those standards. These schools provide a coherent vision of what students should know and be able to do. They use instructional strategies that include a variety of challenging and engaging activities that are clearly related to the concepts and skills being taught.

When talking to teachers in an academically excellent school, it quickly becomes clear that they hold high expectations for all of their students and insist that all of their students can master the curriculum. Teachers at such schools say things like, "We don't let up on the students," "We want everyone to achieve," and "We are a no-excuses school." Likewise, the principal expects a great deal from all the teachers at the school, holding them responsible for improving the quality of student work over time.

The curriculum at high-performing schools follows a coherent plan that builds systematically on instruction from earlier grades—what students learn is neither haphazard nor random. When we ask teachers at such schools how they decide what to teach, they report spending a great deal of their planning time working individually or with their colleagues to incorporate the best of professional and state standards in their content-area lessons. Vibrant displays of student work in the halls reflect students' care in meeting those standards. In one school held accountable by high-stakes testing, teachers insist that, because the state test is based on state and national standards, preparing students for the state test is not "teaching to the test" but rather "teaching to the standards." When we ask these teachers what accounts for the rising test scores in such unusual schools, they talk about highly focused and energetic teaching.

When we ask students what they are learning, they not only express their enthusiasm but also can describe the content and purpose of the lesson. For instance, students in a language arts class said they were learning how to analyze a short story and predict its outcome. They were able to recognize that the lesson called for inference and "higher-order thinking skills." In other words, the students were aware of how they were thinking, and, though they did not know it, they were learning about metacognition.

We ask students how they know if they are doing a good job. In some cases, the students are aware of and understand the performance standards because their teachers have told them what they are expected to master before starting a major activity. In some classes, students help develop the rubrics for judging the quality of their work. In one interdisciplinary classroom that integrates art, math, and science, we observed students preparing a group presentation on empathy. When asked how they would be assessed, the students reported that they and their teacher had designed a grading rubric. These rubrics are often posted on the classroom walls, or the students are given a copy to keep in their notebooks. In all cases, the rubrics are explicit and make sense to the students—the criteria for good work are not a mystery.

When we ask students if they have opportunities to investigate and solve problems that interest them, they like to talk about the projects they have designed. For instance, in a seventh-grade math lab, each student was to choose an area in which to become proficient. The students were given a choice of topics drawn from the state's learning goals for seventh-graders, including bar graphs, fractions, perimeter, the Pythagorean theorem, and volume. The students' task was to study their chosen topic and then teach it to their classmates using a PowerPoint presentation of their own design. The goal was for all students to master a set of mathematical concepts while, at the same time, learning a useful application of technology. The students in this class were deeply engaged in becoming proficient in their chosen areas.

When evaluating schools on these criteria, ask yourself:

- Do I see zest for learning among both the teachers and the students?
- Are students expected to meet high academic standards? How are these standards communicated?
- Can students explain what they are doing in their classes and why it is important?
- How is the school's curriculum selected? Who is involved in the process, and what guidelines do they use? Do teachers know why they are teaching what they are teaching?
- Does the school's assessment program support its vision for curriculum and instruction?

CRITERIA

The school provides opportunities for teachers and other instructional staff to plan for, select, and engage in professional development that is aligned with nationally recognized standards. They have regular opportunities to work with their colleagues to deepen their knowledge and improve their practice. They collaborate in making decisions about substantive and challenging curriculum and effective instructional methods.

When the forum members visit schools, we ask teachers and administrators to define professional development in the context of their school. Invariably, they first tell us what it is not. As one principal says, "It does not occur once in the summer and go away. It keeps coming back and back and back." They also stress that professional development takes place during team meetings, in which teachers meet to discuss their practice and how to improve it. During such meetings, the teachers plan and reflect together about ways to deepen instruction in individual content areas or in interdisciplinary units. To teachers in high-performing schools, professional development is an integral part of everyday life in the school. Professional development also occurs in divisional meetings, in which teachers come together to analyze student progress. In some schools, professional development occurs as a result of teachers' individual growth plans. One principal said, "I think we grow more across the year through nudges, conversations, and lesson planning than we ever do on professional development days."

In one school, one of the teams constructed the year's curriculum around interdisciplinary units. The team members decided what topics they would explore and then designed and developed the unit together using district standards. While we were visiting this school, the team was in the process of developing a unit on inventions. One of the teachers shared materials and resources from an inventions convention she had just attended. The teachers on the team were excited about planning this unit, and they shared ideas freely and gave one another feedback without fear of judgment. They were honest with one another when an idea didn't seem right or if they felt it might create a problem.

In the social studies and language arts segments of the unit, the students were asked to explore the legal issues around inventions, to learn the difference between a copyright and a patent, and to investigate the history of inventions in the United States. In the math and science segments, students were challenged to design and build their own inventions in small groups of two or three. The teachers had brainstormed about the kinds of reading and writing students would do in this unit. They wanted their students to design inventions for real-world problems or needs. The unit was to culminate with the students presenting their work to the school and community at their own invention convention.

When the forum visits schools, we ask teachers what help they have received in aligning their curriculum with state and national standards. In one school, the mathematics curriculum is driven by the state's learning goals, which, according to one of the mathematics teachers, encourage a balance of skill building and application. All the mathematics teachers at this school worked together closely to align the curriculum with the state standards. After aligning the curriculum, the teachers then piloted three textbooks but were not satisfied with any. After discussing what worked well and what didn't, they finally decided to use a combination of teacher-developed curriculum units, a pre-algebra textbook, and Connected Math, which offers a range of hands-on activities.

The teachers at this school had administrative support during this intensive planning period from the school's learning coordinator, who facilitated their conversations. They now meet each grading quarter with the coordinator and the principal to review where they are and to make further decisions. In addition, the teachers meet regularly to refine their curriculum.

When evaluating a school on these criteria, ask yourself:

- Does the principal support professional development opportunities for teachers and staff members?
- How does the school's professional development plan help increase teachers' knowledge and skills?
- Does the professional development challenge teachers' current beliefs and assumptions?
- Does it provide classroom support and coaching?
- How is professional development related to the school's improvement plan?

Developmental Responsiveness

CRITERION

The school provides access to comprehensive services that foster healthy physical, social, emotional, and intellectual development.

In *high-performing schools,* the adults work together to provide a web of emotional and social support for the students, not just in the services the school provides but in the attitudes and relationships the adults establish with students. When visiting schools, we ask students where they go if they are having a problem. In almost all of the schools, students mention the names of one or two teachers with whom they have a good relationship. We can see signs of these relationships when we walk through the halls and sit in classrooms. Students have smiles on their faces and laugh with their teachers and their friends. During the change of classes at one school, a teacher who is clearly one of the favorites is surrounded by a half-dozen students, all wanting to share something about themselves or their families.

The affection and genuine caring between the students and faculty at this school is expressed in the way one principal puts her arm around a student to reprimand him about shouting a profanity in the hall. It is also expressed in the way students affectionately refer to members of the staff as "Mom" and to the school as a "second home." In one School to Watch, the principal collected money from teachers and parents in order to buy presents for the students who were living in the local youth home during the winter holidays. She spent one night and more than $1,000 on gifts for these children. The teachers and administrators in these schools care about the details of their students' lives.

Understanding that the faculty and staff do not have the capacity to attend to all of their students' needs, one school seeks out partnerships with a local agency that can provide social services and programs to students with demonstrated need. The agency provides guidance; a creative arts program; individual, family, group, and crisis counseling; support for the schools parent involvement program; and classroom and faculty support services. The agency works only with schools that are committed to the partnership and able to make a financial contribution, albeit a small one. At this particular school, the partnership with the agency is written into the School Improvement Plan, and faculty members are identified to work with agency staff. Together, the teachers and agency staff members review the criteria for the partnership and then develop the kinds of programs and services that are most needed in the school.

Another school responded to its teen pregnancy rate by investing in a program designed to give young adolescents a sense of what being the primary caretaker for an infant is like. While the program is designed to help students make intelligent physical and emotional choices, the ultimate goal is to prevent teen pregnancy.

The school invested in 23 baby simulators, and every student is required take a simulator home for at least one weekend during his or her two years at the school. These lifelike dolls are computer programmed to look, weigh, and behave like three-month-old infants. They need to be fed, picked up, held, and cuddled. They cry when they are hungry or need affection, when their diapers need changing, or when their head is not supported correctly. Sometimes they cry inconsolably for no apparent reason. The only way to stop the baby from crying is to turn a key a certain way to respond to the baby's particular need. The keys are locked onto students' wrists so they cannot give their 24-hour-a-day responsibility to anyone else. Sometimes, particularly during the night, parents want to help, but that would break the rules. The parents report how the weight of parenthood starts descending upon their children as the weekend progresses. The youth service agency worker says that most students are eager to take the baby home with them, but they are even more eager to bring it back. The students are sadder, wiser, and much more tired.

Another issue that the forum looks at when evaluating schools on this criterion is how they address conflicts between students. In most schools, when a conflict between two students escalates, a fight breaks out, and students are suspended. And time out of the classroom is not time well spent. At each of the schools we visited, there was some form of peer mediation in which students learn to address and solve problems before they escalate. In this way, the schools help foster students' social and emotional development. At one school, 20 students are selected by their peers and trained to be peer mediators. They are required to take a six-hour training program that focuses on rules and standards for mediation, leadership, and being accountable for what occurs in sessions. This school, which averages one peer mediation session per day, has seen a dramatic reduction in the number of discipline referrals to the principal's office. At another school, the eighth-grade student conflict managers developed a presentation about the school's peer mediation program for the seventh-graders in order to identify and begin to train the peer mediators for the following year.

When evaluating a school on this criterion, ask yourself:

- Where can students go when they are having a problem?
- Does every student in the school feel there is an adult he or she trusts and can turn to?
- How do the adults in the building relate to the students? Is there evidence of strong and respectful relationships between adults and students? Is there a feeling of warmth and genuine caring between teachers and their students? Are students smiling and laughing?
- What does respecting students' needs and interests mean to the faculty, staff, and administration? How does this fit into the school's overall mission? Do the school's programs and practices reflect this understanding?
- What programs, services, and support systems are in place to address students' needs?
- Does the school have a network of health care providers, counselors, education and job training specialists, and other providers that is available to serve students and families? Does the school publicize this network well? Do students and families feel comfortable using these services?

CRITERION

The school develops alliances with families to enhance and support the well-being of students. It regards families as partners in their children's education, keeping them informed, involving them in their children's learning, and including them in decision making.

When we visit schools, we hear over and over again that when children get to middle school, parents tend to "drop out" of school involvement. This happens just when young adolescents are beginning to seek greater autonomy from their parents and to crave acceptance from their peers. But parent involvement in the middle grades is crucial to student success. Therefore, schools must do more than invite parents into the school; they must reach out into their communities and make parents feel needed and welcomed. They also must help parents see the value to their children of being active in the middle school. High-performing schools create structures and systems to facilitate parent involvement. We ask principals what the school does to make parents feel that they are an integral part of the school.

In one school with a student population of around 570, about 70 parents are actively involved under the leadership of a volunteer coordinator. Parents at this school donated over 5,000 academic hours in one year as part of the parent volunteer program. This level of parental activity does not happen by chance. A parent volunteer coordinator is trained by the district's central office for the position; in turn, the coordinator trains the school volunteers. Parents fill out applications to volunteer, indicating their available hours. The parent volunteer coordinator calls the parents, who must be fingerprinted, have criminal background checks, and get a TB skin test prior to volunteering. The parent volunteers take part in an orientation session, in which they receive training in areas as diverse as student confidentiality and running the copying machines. Most important, the parents become an integral part of the school's aspirations for student development and achievement. A father at this school summed up parent involvement this way: "At this school the child is in the center of a circle, and everyone is around that child to reach out and help him or her mature and learn."

We ask parents what they think is the key to increasing parent involvement, and they often mention the responsiveness of staff members and the welcoming environment of the school. Many parents we speak with say that it means a lot to them when the principal greets them by name when they walk in the school door. These details are important to parents and communicate to them that they are valued members of the school. One parent said, "Parents are accepted as full partners in the school. We are welcomed with open arms."

Parents also appreciate that the school shares information with them. At one school, parents can call into an information-on-demand system. Using a PIN number, they have immediate access to their child's academic, attendance, and discipline records. A homework hotline gives parents access to their child's homework assignments on any given night. At another school, parents can access their child's homework assignments through the school's website. Some teachers communicate with parents via e-mail during the course of the day. If a problem comes up or if there is something positive the teachers want to share with parents, they can do so immediately and at their convenience. In these various ways, schools help parents gain access to information and be more involved in their children's education.

When evaluating a school on this criterion, ask yourself:

- Are there many parents in the school? Do they have lunch with the students and talk to the teachers and counselors?
- Is there a family center in the school, and do parents run it?
- What communication systems does the school have to make sure that every family is contacted at least once a month?
- Does the principal know many family members by name?
- What does the school do to ensure that parents and family members play meaningful roles, for instance, on the school council and school committees?

Social Equity

Criteria

Faculty and administrators expect high-quality work from all students and are committed to helping each student produce it. Evidence of this commitment includes tutoring, mentoring, offering special adaptations, and other supports. All students have equal access to valued knowledge in all classes and school activities.

When the forum visits schools, we are especially interested in how accessible academic and extracurricular programs are to students with disabilities. Inclusion for students with special needs means more than simply including them in the same classes as regular students. It often means adapting curriculum, instruction, and assessment to their special needs. For a socially equitable school, ensuring that all students have access to academic and extracurricular programs, having high expectations for all students, and providing the support to help them meet those expectations are paramount.

When evaluating a school, we ask the teachers and principal about the kinds of support they provide for students with disabilities and special needs. At one school, students with diagnosed learning and behavioral disabilities are included in classes that are co-taught by regular teachers and special education teachers. In this school, students with learning disabilities and their teachers are not relegated to an out-of-the-way room; they are an integral part of the school community. The special education teachers are equal partners in the design and delivery of classroom instruction. They collaborate with subject-matter teachers in designing instructional units and share the responsibility of teaching classes. The special education teachers are consulted by many teachers in the school and are valued for their knowledge about teaching students with learning disabilities.

In another school, students with severe cognitive or behavioral disabilities cannot be included in regular academic classes. Nonetheless, these students participate in school life to the greatest extent possible and are held accountable for their work. Their teacher believes it is important for these students to be expected to accomplish a great deal in their self-contained class. So, for example, when this teacher reads his students a story, they know they are going to be assessed on it the next day.

Another thing that we look at when evaluating schools is how they support those students who are at risk academically. In an otherwise heterogeneously grouped school we visited, the principal had instituted a program called "Academic Connections" to help students achieve the required standards and beyond. In this program, students are divided into three groups according to their achievement test scores and are provided with instruction specifically geared to their skill levels. Another school offers two after-school programs that provide additional instructional time to students who are not meeting academic standards. The student/teacher ratio in the after-school classes is low—about 12 students per teacher—in order to allow for more individualized instruction. The participating teachers meet with one another to determine which students will receive additional tutorial time based on the students' needs. At yet another school, the resource room is open to all students for additional tutorials in reading and math. While some students are assigned to the reading and math resource tutorials, all students have the option to drop in voluntarily.

Principals and teachers at socially equitable schools foster an atmosphere of inclusion by ensuring that all students have access to the richest and most challenging programs—programs that are usually available to only some students. Many schools across the country have mandated special programs for their highest-achieving students. One principal who believes that all her students should have access to the enriched learning opportunities offered in these programs is in the process of ensuring that all her teachers become certified in instruction for the gifted and talented. So far, 50% of her faculty has earned this certification. This principal also allows any student who has the motivation, the will, and parental permission to do so to take an advanced class in math or language arts.

When evaluating a school on these criteria, ask yourself:

- Is there evidence that all students are being held accountable to high standards? Are students with disabilities and limited English proficiency held to those same standards?
- Do students have access to supports and programs to help them meet or exceed the standards?
- Do teachers work together to identify the students who need additional support? Do teachers share their knowledge and expertise with one another about the best ways to provide support to struggling students?
- Are special education teachers, extracurricular teachers, and others who deliver services to students seen as equal partners in the education of all students? Are their special skills and expertise valued in the school?
- Is there evidence of tracking or low-level classes with watered-down curricula in the school? Are students grouped by skill level for the purposes of instruction?
- If the school has a mandated program for the gifted and talented, how are students selected for this program? How do students and teachers who are not participating benefit from the program?

CRITERION

The school's suspension rate is low, and students from specific demographic groups are not disproportionately represented among the suspended.

Each school's suspension rate became a critical factor in our evaluation—actually rising to the level of "deal breaker" in deciding whether to designate a school an STW. This is because we believe that when a school has a high suspension rate or suspends students from particular groups at a grossly higher rate than others and has no plan for addressing these problems, it is a sign that the school does not have the same expectations for all students.

Suspended students miss valuable classroom time, and the time they spend in in-school suspension is generally a waste. Therefore, a crucial factor in our evaluations of schools is what students are required to do during suspensions. Are they expected to complete the work they are missing in their classes? Do their teachers visit them to keep them up-to-date on assignments? If the students need counseling in order to get back on track, do they receive it from a school counselor or social worker? Is the school aware of the obstacles and barriers the students may be facing outside of school, and do school personnel intervene to help these students get assistance or counseling? While in order to ensure students' safety all schools must have a discipline code that establishes clear consequences for students who break rules, the way a school understands and tries to change patterns of suspension ultimately reflects its beliefs about social equity.

One school we visited disaggregated its suspension data manually by race, socioeconomic status, and gender because its district did not have the technological capacity to provide this service. As a result of their data analysis, which identified unacceptably high suspension rates, the staff members of this school zeroed in on reducing the amount of instructional time missed. Staff members tracked the amount of time that passed from the moment a student was referred to the administration for disciplinary action until a decision about consequences was made. As a result of this exercise, students no longer waste instructional time sitting in the office waiting for administrative disposition. In addition, the school registers student demographic information for each referral (e.g., gender, race, free/reduced-priced-lunch status, length of time in the school), the name of the student's teacher, and other categories of information. Administrators share this information at faculty meetings, and the staff discusses why the referral happened and what to do about it. Through this process the principal and her staff also found a positive correlation between discipline referrals and reading failure. They instituted a schoolwide reading program to address problems in reading and, consequently, to help reduce the school's suspension rate. This kind of data gathering and school-wide effort bears dramatic results: in just one year this school reduced its suspension rate by one-third.

When evaluating a school on this criterion, ask yourself:

- What is the school's suspension rate, and are particular groups of students disproportionately represented among the suspended?
- Do key people in the school know its suspension rates?
- What are students required to do during in-school suspension?
- Does the school examine data related to suspension rates? What does it do with the data?
- If the school's suspension rates are high, particularly among a racial or ethnic group, what are the principal and the faculty doing to lower these rates?

Organizational Structures and Processes

In order for schools to be academically excellent, developmentally responsive, and socially equitable, there must be appropriate structures and processes in place. When evaluating schools, the forum looks at whether these structural factors are in place to allow the school to excel.

CRITERION

Someone in the school has the responsibility and authority to oversee the school improvement enterprise and move it forward. This person or group has the knowledge and the ability to conduct the daily coordination, strategic planning, and communication needed to improve a school.

There is just no getting around it, to become excellent a school must have a risk-taking, visionary, practical leader. One of the STW principals likes to quote Joel Barker: "A leader is a person you would follow to a place you wouldn't go to by yourself."[2]

When evaluating a school, we ask the principal what he or she finds lacking in the school. We then ask the action question: What steps will you take to address the problem? Invariably, the principal has a plan on the drawing boards. In one school, for instance, the principal believes her students are being shortchanged technologically. Her action plan includes:

- *Studying.* She and her teachers will look at outstanding programs across the state.
- *Training.* She will draw on the expertise of the district's curriculum director, who is a proponent of instructional technology. The director has a train-the-trainers process that the principal would like to adopt in her school so that the teachers can teach one another.

- *Monitoring.* She will require her teachers to report how their specific plans to use technology will improve instruction and increase student performance.

We ask principals about their sources of inspiration. Excellent school leaders can answer this question articulately. For instance, one principal, who is an ardent proponent of school-based decision making, was influenced by John Goodlad's school renewal plan. This principal organized her school staff into Goodlad's five cadres: planning, curriculum and instruction, communication, school climate, and staff development. (She later added a technology cadre.) Each cadre chooses by consensus co-leaders who constitute the "campus advisory team," which is the school's shared-decision-making committee. This is not process for the sake of process; the purpose is to create a structure and climate for school improvement. All staff members must serve on the cadres so that, as the principal says, everyone is "part of the solution. No one can sit back and whine."

When we ask principals what their goals were when they first came to their schools, they have no trouble rattling them off. One principal's three major goals were to strengthen the school's academics, improve the learning environment, and increase parent participation. Over the course of her first year at the school, this principal met with her staff to turn these goals into manageable objectives for their school improvement plan. She wanted staff members both to see the big picture and to be able to focus on what was doable. In her second year, she and the staff developed specific goals in all three areas, which have driven the school ever since.

We ask principals to tell us very specific anecdotes that illustrate their leadership styles. Here is one such story, in which the principal's leadership combines strategic thinking, inclusiveness, and humor. At the outset of her administration, this principal took the building itself under her wing as part of an effort to get an unruly school back under control. While the building needed repairs—even the water fountains were broken—the custodial staff argued that the students would destroy anything they fixed. The principal disagreed and, in order to quickly accomplish a visual change—what she calls "the image of discipline"—she had the school facilities fixed and cleaned.

From the beginning of her principalship, she wove the contributions of community partners into the school's goals. To encourage teachers to help keep the building clean by getting their hands dirty picking things up from the floors, the principal got Target, a new school partner, to contribute 100 bottles of hand cleaner, which she dispensed to a surprised staff during a faculty meeting.

We also ask principals to list the top three to five things they would do if moving to another school. This is one of the principal's favorite questions, because it challenges them to evaluate their work to date and fantasize about starting over. One principal came up with the following:

1. Communicate a vision for student success very early on, continually articulate the vision throughout the year, and have a plan for realizing it. Staff members need to see very early on how high the bar is raised, what the expectations are, and what needs to be done to get there.

2. Look at how the school collects data, in which areas, and how the data are used for planning. What guides schoolwide initiatives? It is extremely important to collect data, formally and informally, to support the school's goals. There is no other way to be able to assess accurately the school's strengths and weaknesses.

3. Look at how each schoolwide initiative is tied into the school improvement plan. It is easy to get off track quickly. Before you know it, there is so much going on in the school that things can quickly become disconnected.

4. Continually encourage the staff in the great things they are already doing and give them the latitude and flexibility to try something new and different.

5. Open the school and its classrooms to external critical friends. We constantly talk about the need for accountability as well as the need for continuous school improvement. What a great way to achieve both by having professionals in the field with specific expertise come into the school to observe our teaching practices in the classroom and review our supports for students and provide feedback.

When evaluating a school on this criterion, ask yourself:

- Does the school look like what it wants to be?
- Does it have a single, thorough, credible plan for reaching its vision?
- Does everyone know what the plan is? Do they respect it? Do they endorse it enthusiastically? Can they articulate it?
- Is the plan a healthy stretch for faculty and students?

CRITERIA

The school holds itself accountable for its students' success rather than blaming others for its shortcomings. The school collects, analyzes, and uses data as a basis for making decisions, including school-generated evaluation data that it uses to identify areas for more extensive and intensive improvement. The school delineates benchmarks and insists upon evidence and results. The school intentionally and explicitly reconsiders its vision and practices when data call them into question.

We ask high-performing schools how they know if they are meeting their behavioral and academic goals. Their answers invariably have to do with "sleuthing their data." The data the administration and staff collect and analyze serve as the basis for decisions about areas needing more focused attention and changes in practice. Data provide evidence of need, improvement, and success or failure.

One school collects student work, sometimes monthly and sometimes biweekly, as evidence of whether its school improvement plan is leading to higher student achievement. The school has developed what it calls a "crate system." All teachers submit a crate of examples of high-, medium-, and low-level student work along with lesson plans that they propose to help improve their students' knowledge and skills. A curriculum committee meets monthly to evaluate the content of the crates. The information from this evaluation is compiled into what the school calls a "Vital Signs Report."

In addition, at least once every nine weeks, "content leaders" facilitate a content-area meeting—a time for all teachers of the same subject matter to evaluate student work and student progress. Information from this "impact check," along with the "vital signs report," is forwarded to the school's decision-making council, where schoolwide decisions affecting continuous improvement are made. Teachers' data collection improves their day-to-day instructional practice; it also ties the school's governance structure to the school's achievement goals.

We ask schools what they do when their data analysis tells them they are not meeting their goals. We have observed a school that uses staff development days to go over students' state test data by subject area. Test data have become one of several lenses for understanding the strengths and weaknesses of every student and teacher and for setting improvement strategies. Together, the principal and the teachers study state data, objective by objective, and then take action. For instance, when only 53% of the school's students were skilled in summarization, teachers focused on that objective schoolwide. In this school, analysis of test data makes the test serve the school's instructional goals.

Data analysis is not a dry affair in these schools. One principal has studied patterns of teacher absences to learn which times of the year absences are greatest and to devise morale-building strategies for those times. Running the numbers helps her meet the needs of the adults in her school so that her teachers are energized to work with their students.

When evaluating a school on these criteria, ask yourself:

- What tools and processes does the school use to set high standards for progress?
- Does the school continually collect and use data to seek evidence that it is meeting its goals?
- Does the school avoid blaming others for its shortfalls?
- Are there examples of ways that the school changed its approach in response to an examination of its data?

Conclusion

Using a construct for assessing schools concentrates the mind on their mission, accomplishments, and failures. But using evaluation criteria as part of a rigid checklist can lead to looking at the parts disconnected from the whole—or the soul—of the school. The ethos of the school—its personality, its environment, its spirit—is every bit as important as its particular practices and

structures. High-performing schools are places where adults and children live, grow, and learn well. These schools are driven by a sense of purpose about children's intellectual, ethical, social, and physical development. These schools are also vibrant adult learning communities. The intellectual ante is high, and a can-do spirit pervades the school, from the janitors and cafeteria workers to the parents, students, teachers, and administrators. The work ethic is palpable. Relationships between adults and students are relaxed, demanding, and caring. The corridors and cafeteria are noisy but peaceable, the adults are energetic and enthusiastic, and the students are attentive and expressive. These schools are a part of, not apart from, their communities. One leaves these schools with a renewed sense of hopefulness about the power of the teaching/learning contract between adults and students.

It is a joy to visit these schools. You may not be able to quantify "joy," but look for it within both the school and yourself. It is the most important criterion of all.

NOTES

1. The full set of criteria for each priority and for assessing the organizational structure of a school can be viewed at the forum's website, **www.schoolstowatch.org.**
2. Joel Barker, *Paradigms* (New York: HarperCollins, 1992).

POSTNOTE

The authors of this comprehensive article are reporting on their research on middle schools. However, as they acknowledge, the various criteria and factors related to high-performing schools they identify also have relevance to elementary and high schools. As such, the article provides a rich bank of questions that educators can use as they reflect on their own school or as school observers.

The question, "Which of the three divisions, elementary, middle, or high school, is most important?" is difficult to determine. Various "blue ribbon" educational reports and the views of individual experts do not provide a clear consensus. However, the middle school years, particularly in the early years, appear to be a time when many students "disengage" from the educational mission. They become frustrated with the academic work, distracted by outside concerns, or both. While they continue to show up for school, academic knowledge and skills are hardly on their priority list. This often casual and "below-the-radar" choice they make has a profound impact on their futures.

As the authors note, a high-performing school is not one that simply caters to eager and cooperative students. Rather, the teachers and administrators in such a school go after the potentially "lost sheep." They make special efforts to keep these vulnerable students engaged and moving forward.

Discussion Questions

1. The authors identify three priorities of high-performing schools. What are they? In your view, what is their order of importance, and why?
2. Toward the end of the article, the authors report on five questions a principal (or any educator) might ask about a school to which he or she might move. What are they?
3. What does the term *sleuthing the data* mean and how might it be used to improve the performance of a school?

RELATED WEBSITE RESOURCES

 Web Resources:

ASCD Community Blog, Crashing the School Gates. Available at:

http://ascd.typepad.com/blog/2008/09/ crashing-the-sc.html.

This blog deals with a myriad of fresh ideas related to school improvement and educational reform.

The National Forum to Accelerate Middle-Grade Reform. Available at:

http://www.mgforum.org/Improvingschools/ Improveschools.asp.

This organization, which one of the authors has been associated with, maintains a school improvement website which addresses many of the issues raised by this article.

A Tale of Two Schools

Larry Cuban

Larry Cuban is an emeritus professor of education at Stanford University, Stanford, California. Prior to university teaching, Cuban had a rich career as a teacher, trainer of Peace Corps volunteers, principal, and school superintendent. His major con-

tributions to the field include his studies of urban education and his historical perspectives on school curricula.

"A Tale of Two Schools" by Larry Cuban, *Education Week*, Vol. 17, No. 20, January 28, 1998. Reprinted by permission of the author.

F | O | C | U | S QUESTION

Can schools with seemingly divergent philosophies of education nevertheless prepare their students to be good citizens in a democracy?

KEY TERMS

Good school
Progressive school
Traditional school

For this entire century, there has been conflict among educators, public officials, researchers, and parents over whether traditionalist or progressive ways of teaching reading, math, science, and other subjects are best. Nowhere has this unrelenting search for the one best way of teaching a subject or skill been more obvious than in the search for "good" schools. Progressives and traditionalists each have scorn for those who argue that there are many versions of "good" schools. Partisan debates have consumed policymakers, parents, practitioners, and researchers, blocking consideration of the unadorned fact that there is more than one kind of "good" school.

What follows is a verbal collage of two elementary schools I know well. School A is a quiet, orderly school where the teacher's authority is openly honored by both students and parents. The principal and faculty seek out students' and parental advice when making schoolwide decisions. The professional staff sets high academic standards, establishes school rules that respect differences among students, and demands regular study habits from the culturally diverse population. Drill and practice are parts of each teacher's daily lesson. Report cards with letter grades are sent home every nine weeks. A banner in the school says: "Free Monday through Friday: Knowledge—Bring Your Own Container." These snippets describe what many would call a "traditional" school.

School B prizes freedom for students and teachers to pursue their interests. Most classrooms are multiage (6- to 9-year-olds and 7- to 11-year-olds). Every teacher encourages student-initiated projects and trusts children to make the right choices. In this school, there are no spelling bees; no accelerated reading program; no letter or numerical grades. Instead, there is a year-end narrative in which a teacher describes the personal growth of each student. Students take only those standardized tests required by the state. A banner in the classroom reads: "Children need a place to run! explore! a world to discover." This brief description describes what many would call a "progressive" school.

I will argue that both Schools A and B are "good" schools. What parents, teachers, and students at each school value about knowledge, teaching, learning, and freedom differs. Yet both public schools have been in existence for 25 years. Parents have chosen to send their children to the schools. Both schools have staffs that volunteered to work there. And both schools enjoy unalloyed support: Annual surveys of parent and student opinion have registered praise for each school; each school has had a waiting list of parents who wish to enroll their sons and daughters; teacher turnovers at each school have been virtually nil.

Moreover, by most student-outcome measures, both schools have compiled enviable records. In academic achievement, measured by standardized tests, School A was in the top 10 schools in the entire state. School B was in the upper quartile of the state's schools.

These schools differ dramatically from one another in how teachers organize their classrooms, view learning, and teach the curriculum. Can both of them be "good"? The answer is yes.

What makes these schools "good"? They have stable staffs committed to core beliefs about what is best for students and the community, parents with beliefs that mirror those of the staffs, competent people working together, and time to make it all happen. Whether one was traditional or progressive was irrelevant. The century-long war of words over traditional vs. progressive schooling is a cul-de-sac, a dead end argument that needs to be retired once and for all.

What partisans of each fail to recognize is that this pendulum-like swing between traditional and progressive schooling is really a deeper political conflict over what role schools should play in society. Should schools in a democracy primarily concentrate on making citizens who fulfill their civic duties? Should schools focus on efficiently preparing students with skills credentials to get jobs and maintain a healthy economy? Honor individual excellence yet treat everyone equally? Or should schools do everything they can to develop the personal and social capabilities of each and every child? For almost two centuries of tax-supported public schooling in the United States, all of these goals have been viewed as both important and achievable.

The war of words between progressives and traditionalists has been a proxy for this political struggle over goals. Progressive vs. traditionalist battles over discipline in schools, national tests, tracking students by their performance, and school uniforms mask a more fundamental tension in this country over which goals for public schools should have priority.

The problem lies not in knowing how to make schools better. Many parents and educators already know what they want and possess the requisite knowledge and skills to get it. Schools A and B are examples of that knowledge in action. The problem is determining what goals public schools should pursue, given the many goals that are desired and inescapable limits on time, money, and people.

Determining priorities among school goals is a political process of making choices that involves policymakers, school officials, taxpayers, and parents. Deciding what is important and how much should be allocated to it is at the heart of the process. Political parties, lobbies, and citizen groups vie for voters' attention. Both bickering and deliberation arise from the process. Making a school "good" is not a technical problem that can be solved by experts or scientific investigation into traditional or progressive approaches. It is a struggle over values that are worked out in elections for public office, tax referendums, and open debate in civic meetings, newspapers, and TV talk shows. Yet these simple distinctions between the political and the technical, between goals for schools and the crucial importance of the democratic process determining which goals should be primary, seem to have been lost in squabbles over whether progressive or traditional schools are better.

And that is why I began with my descriptions of the two schools. They represent a way out of this futile struggle over which kind of schooling is better than the other. I argue that both these schools are "good."

One is clearly traditional in its concentration on passing on to children the best knowledge, skills, and values in society. The other is progressive in its focus on students' personal and social development. Each serves different goals, each honors different values. Yet—and this is the important point that I wish to drive home—these seemingly different goals are not inconsistent. They derive from a deeply embedded, but seldom noticed, common framework of what parents and taxpayers want their public schools to achieve.

What is different, on the surface, are the relative weights that each "good" school gives to these goals, how they go about putting into practice what they seek, and the words that they use to describe what they do. The common framework I refer to is the core duty of tax-supported public schools in a democracy to pass on to the next generation democratic attitudes, values, and behaviors. Too often we take for granted the linkage between the schools that we have and the kind of civic life that we want for ourselves and our children. What do I mean by democratic attitudes, values, and behaviors? A few examples may help:

- Open-mindedness to different opinions and a willingness to listen to such opinions.
- Respect for values that differ from one's own.
- Treating individuals decently and fairly, regardless of background.
- A commitment to talk through problems, reason, deliberate, and struggle toward openly arrived-at compromises.

I doubt whether partisans for traditional and progressive schools, such as former U.S. Secretary of Education William J. Bennett, educator Deborah Meier, and academics like Howard Gardner and E. D. Hirsch, Jr., would find this list unimportant.

Tax-supported public schools in this country were not established 150 years ago to get jobs for graduates. They were not established to replace the family or church. They were established to make sure that children grew into literate adults who respected authority, could make reasoned judgments, accept differences of opinions, and fulfill their civic duties to participate in the political life of their communities. Over time, of course, as conditions changed, other responsibilities were added to the charter of public schools. But the core duty of schools, teachers, and administrators—past and present—has been to turn students into citizens who can independently reason through difficult decisions, defend what they have decided, and honor the rule of law. Our traditional and progressive schools each have been working on these paramount and essential tasks.

Consider such democratic values as individual freedom and respect for authority. In School A, students have freedom in many activities, as long as they stay within the clear boundaries established by teachers on what students can do and what content they must learn. Staff members set rules for behavior and academic performance, but students and parents are consulted; students accept the limits easily, even enjoying the bounded freedom that such rules give them. School A's teachers and parents believe that students' self-discipline grows best by setting limits on freedom and learning what knowledge previous generations counted as important. From these will evolve students' respect for the rule of law and their growth into active citizens.

In School B, more emphasis is placed on children's individual freedom to create, diverge from the group, and work at their own pace. Students work on individually designed projects over the year. They respect teachers' authority but often ask why certain things have to be done. The teacher gives reasons and, on occasion, negotiates over what will be done and how it will be done. School B's teachers and parents believe that students' self-discipline, regard for authority, and future civic responsibility evolve out of an extended, but not total, freedom.

Thus, I would argue, both of these schools prize individual freedom and respect for authority, but they define each value differently in how they organize the school, view the curriculum, and engage in teaching. Neither value is ignored. Parents, teachers, and students accept the differences in how their schools put these values into practice. Moreover, each school, in its individual way, cultivates the deeper democratic attitudes of open-mindedness, respect for others' values, treating others decently, and making deliberate decisions.

Because no researcher could ever prove that one way of schooling is better than the other, what matters to me in judging whether schools are "good" is whether they are discharging their primary duty to help students think and act democratically. What we need to talk about openly in debates about schooling is not whether a traditional school is better or worse than a progressive one, but whether that school concentrates on instilling within children the virtues that a democratic society must have in each generation. Current talk about national goals is *not* about this core goal of schooling. It is about being first in the world in science and math achievement; it is about preparing students to use technology to get better jobs. Very little is said about the basic purpose of schooling except in occasional one-liners or a paragraph here and there in speeches by top public officials.

What are other criteria for judging goodness? I have already suggested parent, student, and teacher satisfaction as reasonable standards to use in determining how "good" a school is. I would go further and add: To what degree has a school achieved its own explicit goals? By this criterion, School A is a clear success. Parents and teachers want children to become literate, respectful of authority, and responsible. Although School B scores well on standardized tests, parents and teachers are less interested in test results. What School B wants most are students who can think on their own and work together easily with those who are different from themselves; students who, when faced with a problem, can tackle it from different vantage points and come up with solutions that are creative. Parents and teachers have plenty of stories about students' reaching these goals, but there are few existing tests or quantitative measures that capture these behaviors.

So, another standard to judge "goodness" in a school is to produce graduates who possess these democratic behaviors, values, and attitudes. This is, and always has been, the common, but often ignored, framework for our public schools. It has been lost in the battle of words and programs between public officials and educators who champion either traditional or progressive schools. A "good" school, I would argue, even in the face of the technological revolution and globalization of the U.S. economy in this century, is one that has students who display those virtues in different situations during their careers as students and afterwards as well.

My criteria, then, for determining good schools are as follows: Are parents, staff, and students satisfied with what occurs in the school? Is the school achieving the explicit goals it has set for itself? And, finally, are democratic behaviors, values, and attitudes evident in the students?

Why is it so hard to get past the idea that there is only one kind of "good" school? Varied notions of goodness have gotten mired in the endless and fruitless debate between traditionalists and progressives. The deeply buried but persistent impulse in the United States to create a "one best system," a solution for every problem, has kept progressives and traditionalists contesting which innovations are best for children, while ignoring that there are more ways than one to get "goodness" in schools.

Until Americans shed the view of a one best school for all, the squabbles over whether a traditional schooling is better than a progressive one will continue. Such a futile war of words ignores the fundamental purpose of public schooling as revitalizing democratic virtues in each generation and, most sadly, ignores the good schools that already exist.

POSTNOTE

We select this article as a Classic because of the profound importance of its message: a call to educators to rise above ideological squabbles and get on with the serious business of educational excellence.

What one defines as a "good" school depends on what one values, says Larry Cuban, which makes perfectly sound sense. A person's educational philosophy will determine how that person views schooling, teaching, and curriculum. Thus, many different types of good schools can—and do—exist.

Cuban's point argues for giving parents choices about the kinds of school that their children attend. By offering different kinds of schools that represent different educational philosophies and by allowing parents to select the school of their choice, school boards can better satisfy parents' educational preferences. In this way, more parents will be more committed to the school they have selected, as well as inclined to believe that their children attend good schools.

Discussion Questions

1. Of the two schools that Cuban describes in his article, would you prefer to teach in School A or School B? Why?
2. Describe the characteristics of the kind of school that you would consider to be "good."
3. Do you agree with Cuban's assertion that the common framework of public schools should be to "pass on to the next generation democratic attitudes, values, and behaviors"? Is there anything else that you would add to this common framework?

RELATED WEBSITE RESOURCES

 ### Web Resources:

American Philosophical Association (APA). Available at:

http://www.apaonline.org/.

This excellent website provides basic information and reference material on many branches and schools of philosophy.

The Society for Philosophical Inquiry (SPI). Available at:

www.philosopher.org.

SPI is a grassroots nonprofit organization devoted to supporting philosophical inquirers of all ages and walks of life. There are a number of ways to get involved, such as their Socrates Cafe program.

"As Though They Owned the Place": Small Schools as Membership Communities

CLASSIC

14

Deborah Meier

Deborah Meier is a senior scholar at New York University and the MacArthur Award-winning founder of Central Park East School in East Harlem, New York. Deborah Meier has spent more than thirty years working in public education as a teacher, principal, and writer. As reflected in this essay, her primary focus has been finding ways to make schools work. Her most recent book [with Theodore and Nancy Sizer] is *Keeping School: Letters to Families from Principals of Two Small Schools* (Beacon, 2005).

"'As Though They Owned the Place': Small Schools as Membership Communities" by Deborah Meier, *Phi Delta Kappan* 87, no. 9, May 2006, pp. 657–662. Reprinted by permission of the author.

F O C U S QUESTION

What have we lost by all this "bigness" in schooling?

Small schools were once the norm. When I was born, there were 200,000 school districts in North America. Schools generally averaged under a hundred students. Most people—above all in the vast majority of communities that had only one or two schools in the district—knew their schools and school board members well. Accountability was a thing very close to home and often highly contentious. If you were a member of a community, you had a say—however irritating it might be to your neighbors.

Today, there are fewer than 15,000 school districts serving nearly three times as many children, and most districts have relatively little say over matters that were once their primary responsibility. More and more decisions lie in hands far removed from communities, families, teachers, and kids.

This change has happened within my lifetime. The reasons have been many—including the greater importance of education itself in the future of both individuals and the nation and the struggle for equity and civil rights that reshaped school law with regard to race, gender, and the rights of the handicapped. The change went hand in hand with the diminishing of the role of local life in so many matters, as it has seemed more appropriate to handle more decisions on a state, regional, or national level. Whether all of these changes necessitated larger schools and larger school districts and whether some of the tradeoffs made were truly necessary are issues worth examining.

The pendulum has swung too far away from the face-to-face quality of old-time accountability ("vote the rascals out") and the potential for strong parent and community involvement that went more naturally with greater local voice. The question we face today is how to determine the value of small schools in redressing some of the negative consequences associated with large schools and districts without sacrificing the benefits that came along with them.

If a central, nonnegotiable function of public schooling in the U.S. is to strengthen our democracy, then we must examine all the issues that affect the ability of schools to do so, many of which are at the heart of why we need small schools. Students learn from us; the robustness of our school community, its capacity to exercise judgment on important matters, and its inclusiveness are all part of young people's education. Where else might kids learn about the tradeoffs, critical judgments, and responsibilities inherent in democratic life—including when and how to resist? If educating young people to make judgments based on credible evidence, reasoning, and collaboration with others is essential to our task, then we must create schools that have the intention of practicing these arts and the time to do so. In order to align the means with the ends, we must ask more probing questions about the ends we desire for our schools. If we seek only to improve scores on tests of standards determined by others, then educating students for democratic life is not necessary—and maybe small schools aren't either.

Some of the consequences of consolidating small schools into larger schools and districts have not only been bad for democracy but have also made all forms of serious intellectual rigor in schools more, not less, difficult to address. The kinds of relationships that can develop in a small school between students and their teachers and between teachers and the school's community turn out to be critical in determining what can be effectively demanded of its students.

While small schools can have a significant impact on the education of our kids, it is not ordained that small schools will achieve the ends we seek. We can have small schools that behave like big ones, or we can have small schools that take advantage of their size to improve the learning that goes on within them in terms of intellectual standards and the development of responsible citizens.

The official distribution of power within a school is always a difficult issue to discuss. But when we fail to do so, we tend to overlook that the unofficial powers often end up undermining the official ones. For example, kids and teachers have the power to sabotage and resist the best intentions of reformers. When a big school, especially if it is in a big district, decides to go small, it is often responding to a struggle over power. Control and accountability with regard to money, safety, personnel, and educational outcomes—far removed these days from the daily life of the school and its immediate constituents—will be more difficult to keep track of and monitor if we quadruple the number of schools. Too often, having more small schools becomes a nuisance instead of an asset and leads to new forms of resistance and new efforts to monitor and control. Are we prepared to tackle this problem?

Small schools are an idea that will work only if we are prepared to open up and examine the contents of other cans of worms. Is the district ready to reconsider where each of a wide range of decisions is made? How money is distributed? What the line of command is? We've had a history of fads that sputter out because we tend to simply pile one reform on top of another without looking carefully at the foundation. Let me share

what I call the "big five" issues that those considering a move to smaller schools would do well to consider.

1. *Acknowledge that there will be tradeoffs.* If we opt for small schools, we are making choices, accepting tradeoffs that big schools do not have to make. The big comprehensive high school can teach five foreign languages, even if no one really learns any of them. They can have honors tracks and semi-vocational tracks large enough so that each segment can feel like a school of its own, not a marginalized group. Large schools can afford orchestras, bands, a newspaper, and lots of other exciting stuff—even if only a small elite group of students actually experiences the wide range of electives and extracurricular activities. Each of these "extras" has a constituency ready to go to the mat for it.

Small schools force us to ask: What matters most? What are kids not getting in the larger educational world of media/TV/screen/etc. or from their busy families that is essential to the good health of the public sphere? What's altogether out of balance now without the intervention of schools? What aspects of being "well educated" must the school provide in order to create an appropriate balance? For example, schools can provide inter-generational relationships; thoughtful and long-standing personal ties; communication across otherwise alienated and separated communities of heart and mind; direct, authentic experience with the natural world; experience with books, with writing, with scientific tools and experimentation; the nuances of mathematics; civil debate and disagreement; experience with compromise; and on and on. None of these come to us naturally today, but they are all naturals for small schools. But at what price? And it is a price that must be considered so that it doesn't spark a backlash that we're unprepared for.

2. *Pay attention to genuine outcomes.* We should assess and graduate kids based on their real capacity to show us what they know and can do. Real-life projects, portfolios, auditions, exhibitions, oral defenses, and so on are natural demonstrations of solid academic work, well suited to small schools. In addition, building our assessment around long-term impacts is another obvious approach that has been neglected. But even if the roots of such practices predate standardized tests, we will need to sort out the proper balance between these types of assessment and the ones most communities are now accustomed to.

We must keep coming back to the basics. The power of smallness lies in the effectiveness of learning through the company one keeps—the oldest teaching method on earth. We know that most important adult occupations have historically been passed on in just this way.

We abandoned the apprenticeship model of learning at a price that we needn't have paid.

Smallness allows young people to learn again in the company of powerful adults. Learning to be a citizen, like learning math or science, is best accomplished by observing adults engaged in the same kinds of activity. Young people today have little experience seeing what makes adults powerful and effective. But even here the realities need to be monitored. How do we know that ownership of learning is being shared? Or that kids are interested in the adults (and vice versa)? Is there the same percentage of kids who are not noticed and fall through the cracks in a small school as in a big school, or are there fewer of them? In short, the forms of accountability need to be broadened to embrace the school's mission.

3. *Be sure important constituents are on board.* If not, go slower or offer choices. Even if you can "make 'em," it doesn't last.

Start only as many small schools as you have people to staff them and families to choose them. Avoid choices that divide haves from have-nots or the "gifted" from the "others." Otherwise, go for whatever is legal and exciting, even if it's just a group of adults who want to work together. Give those involved maximum autonomy, which is what will grease the wheels for otherwise reluctant faculty members and maybe even for families. People will tend to exploit their capacities to the fullest in the interests of proving that their own ideas work. Above all, give schools their own per-capita budgets, so that they can make choices that reflect their own priorities. And don't believe it when people say such changes won't cost any more. At least for starters, they will.

4. *Avoid false efficiencies.* Speaking of money, start counting what a small school costs not per student but per graduate. Remember, a new practice that drives up the dropout rate is anything but an efficient use of scarce dollars. Be sure that the methods you have for keeping track are consistent with your purposes.

5. *Reassure the recalcitrant.* Tell folks that over the next decade you expect to gradually increase the number of small schools and the range of choices—but only as people are persuaded to want them. There may always be room for one big school in a district with 25 small ones. Don't, I repeat, don't mandate smallness so that everyone must do it. Who knows? Let the old schools and the new schools speak for themselves. If I'm right about small schools, it will get easier and easier to persuade folks.

But even if you keep these big five principles in mind, going small still will not be easy. Here are some other hints for getting a change to small schools off on the right foot.

It takes time. How long? Three to five years, at least. And don't start with a whole school at once. Begin with one age group of 60 to 80 kids and three or four adults, with a plan to grow, year by year, into a school of 200 or so. Or start with a sixth and ninth grade and let the school grow over the years until it includes grades 6–12. Set a realistic time line for when you expect to have the start-up glitches fixed. It can easily take three to five years for you to grow a school to its full size, build communitywide understanding of its mission, and tweak it as needed. It will require a few more years to make sure a school's approach doesn't need more than tweaking. This is where external school reviews are so useful in giving the public some feedback.

The importance of continuity. Make sure a school has a plan to enroll kids for four or more years. Such grade spans as K–3, K–6, K–8, 4–8, 5–12, etc., can all work. It's in knowing kids year after year, and gaining in the process the trust of families and the understanding in the larger community, that big changes become possible—and successful. This continuity allows reforms to be sustained.

Be inclusive. Make sure each school has a plan that can handle both those students who make running a school easier and those who make it harder. It's okay to have a focus or theme, but not one that rules out kids who might be hard to teach. (Figuring out how to be sure every kid has real freedom of choice is the district's task.) From the start, think through what small schools can offer to the full range of kids and which kids, if any, might be better served separately. Be sure the funds for special needs go with the kids.

Physical space. Small schools waste space. Of necessity. So bear that in mind when planning. Make sure each small school has turf to call its own—including a bathroom and a way to get into and out of the building without bothering others. Make sure that the offices aren't all centralized; guidance staff and school heads need to be close to the action. If necessary, settle for science labs that are less fancy, so that each school has its own labs. Create spaces where different constituencies and different ages can interact—large faculty rooms where everyone has a desk or "central" offices with computers, copying machines, and phones in which principal, office manager, parents, teachers, and kids can congregate. This kind of use of space creates a sense of community and ownership.

Don't be missionaries. Make sure that new and fragile schools are not expected to carry the burden of convincing others—beyond their own community of kids and families—that they are doing good work. Those who are struggling to create a good small school can't be proselytizers for the small schools movement. That's the district's job. When the time seems ripe, arrange for visiting days, led by parents and kids as well as by staff members.

Keep lines of communication open. Be sure to build in ways for the new schools to interact with one another and with the schools not in the project. Arrogance can kill the whole program off. Beware the "one true way," and don't abandon the ones "left behind" in the traditional schools—or they'll get their revenge.

Keep lots of data. Keep a wide range of data—who signs on, who leaves and for what reason (kids and teachers), what the evidence is for student achievement, who gets in trouble. Pay attention to trends. Since longitudinal data on cohorts of kids are the only truly reliable data, build in a way to collect such data right from the start. And keeping in touch with families and kids who leave the school or who graduate is the best source of feedback a faculty and other families can get. Make sure it's in the district's plans to shoulder part of this burden of accounting for results.

Different data are needed for different audiences. For kids and their parents, data drawn from a sample of students won't do; this audience needs information about individual students. On the other hand, the larger, more anonymous public wants information on the overall performance of schools, so sample data are appropriate because they provide a richer and more accurate picture of student achievement across schools.

Accountability. The kind of data a school and district keep will determine the kind of accountability that can be pursued. Make sure that the form of accountability recognizes the special nature of these new schools. So be sure that standardized test scores are only part of, not the complete definition of, the school's standards. Make sure that the school says up front what it's aiming for and works out within a few years some ways to provide evidence of its success or failure. Schools should also report the means they are using to improve practice when faults and flaws are discovered.

School review can be a form of accountability. From the start, build in a process for reviewing school progress that's consistent with the reform itself. This means that you will need some form of school review that allows judges to get to know a school well enough to comment knowledgeably on its strengths and weaknesses and to have access to a wide range of evidence. Such a process is more costly than just printing out test scores, but it's the district's most critical task.

In Boston, the new, small Pilot schools are reviewed every four years by five educators from different fields and areas of expertise. They examine specified documents ahead of time and spend three days visiting a school. Then they prepare a document for the school's own board and for Boston's superintendent, who has ultimate authority. The process leads to one of three ratings: all's well; the school should be placed in a probationary status while certain specific issues are addressed; or the district should consider closing or reorganizing the school.

Professional development. No plan is any better than what's actually happening inside schools—first and foremost in classrooms, but also in all those shared spaces and the places where key actors interact and at meetings with families. Keep large-scale districtwide (or even buildingwide) professional development to a minimum—at least at first. Instead, give schools the time to build a community of adults as well as youngsters. That means providing time for staff to meet daily—even for a short rime. Also provide for more extended weekly gatherings and for less frequent prolonged "retreats." Since faculty stability is at the heart of building a school culture (and constantly recycling staff is costly and inefficient), having the funds required for internal professional development is key. Make sure professionals have a week to talk among themselves before the school year, as well as a week during the year and one afterward. This is a practice any summer camp thinks necessary, but many schools don't. Involve faculty members in the selection of their colleagues, as well as in observing and critiquing one another. Treat staff morale as central; it is not a luxury item.

The union. Don't start off by assuming that union leaders won't love this idea. In many places, unions have been the initiators of small school reform. As long as the development of small schools doesn't become a tactic for union busting or for undermining teachers' collective power, it can be viewed as a perfect tool for providing a strong professional base for teacher unions. Make sure to have an understanding with the union of what a living contract could be like—one that leaves most details to the school site and can be changed as conditions change. School staff members need to be able to shape aspects of the contract to match their school's design and governance style. Bring these issues down to the school level, where all parties can reach the best understanding of how strong unions lead to good teaching and learning.

Leadership. The success of small school reform depends on a different kind of school-based leadership, a kind more collegial than administrative. There are many different models of such leadership, but all require principals who think more like teachers than they do in big schools and teachers who think more like principals. There must be co-ownership of the reform. Teachers and principals must be eager to see what their colleagues are up to. Most would-be principals have never experienced such co-leadership and will need help in doing so. If we don't provide models, they may view such a style as "weak" leadership. They need to interact with colleagues in the same situation: handling the problems that come with being half colleague and half school head. We need new forms of training in leadership for small schools.

It's also important, as small schools are phased in, that one strong and respected member of the district-level team be there as a trusted ally and resource for the school-level leaders. Having a strong advocate in the central office is key to making sure folks feel they are being heard.

Parent involvement. If parents are to be our allies—which is possible when they know their children's teachers well—we need to tackle another can of worms. In the past, when we've decried the lack of parent involvement, we've mostly not meant it. Few schoolpeople really feel comfortable when a group of parents starts hanging around asking questions and wanting a voice in decisions. We want parents there when we need them, but we don't spend a lot of time imagining what it would require if we were to be there when they need us. We need a different view of time. How can we ensure that parents will have the time to attend to their children's school issues without losing their jobs? What would we need to put in place so that parents could reach us easily and comfortably with information about family emergencies or just to share their worries about their children? While some of the necessary changes will be at least partly beyond our control, they ought to be on our agenda. However, one thing within our control is reducing the number of adults parents must get to know well to one or two individuals over two, three, or more years.

Probably each school will find that what it needs is not more guidance counselors, but a wise family/school coordinator, trained to help allies with different kinds of tunnel vision to work well together. This position is not a throwaway to hand over to an active parent as a reward. It requires real skill and training. At best, it requires someone with experience as a family therapist and as a consultant and advisor to organizations.

Buildingwide issues. Finally, never let small details go unnoticed. One that sometimes gets overlooked when small schools share a building is: who's minding the physical plant?

A plethora of details will crop up daily as different autonomous schools with different styles share a building. How kids and adults who attend different schools in the same building relate to one another is important. It helps a lot if the students are not all of the same age, so wherever possible schools serving different age groups should be placed in the same building. Sometimes parents worry about this idea. Can young children be assigned to the same building as teenagers? Actually, in my experience, this almost always is mutually beneficial to both groups.

It helps if the heads of all the small schools in a building meet regularly to discuss shared issues, with someone responsible (perhaps on a rotating basis) for following up on decisions made. A plant manager will probably be needed to deal with the kitchen, security, and custodial issues. It also helps to figure out how to use shared spaces and to remember that any decision must be sufficiently flexible to allow for the kinds of lives that schools live—full of emergencies, unexpected crises, joyful celebrations, and more.

These fledgling new schools need to see one another as allies—even though at times they may bump into one another. They need to take pride in the "complex"—the site—as a whole and in all its parts. They need to appreciate their diversity, not their sameness. There are some practices that may help in this regard, such as common sports teams and after-school activities or shared fund-raisers to build a common photo lab, ceramics studio, or dance room.

Putting all of this down on paper scares me. I hope it doesn't scare readers. It's a lot to do at once. Fortunately, some of it will come naturally, while other aspects will bedevil you for years. And who knows which will prove to be which?

But this much I know: it will be exciting, and kids will thrive in the excitement of being part of a new venture. A colleague at a new small school in San Francisco complained to me recently, "The trouble is the kids walk around the school like they own it." And then after a pause she added, "And I suppose that's the good thing too. But it takes time to get used to it and get the balance right." Ditto for parents and, blessedly, for teachers too. And that's why it works.

The more complex, centralized, distanced, virtual, and diverse the larger world, the more important it is for young people, their parents, and their teachers to feel the power of their own ideas; to embrace their own capacity to influence and have an impact; to learn to hear, to listen, and to argue; to check out abstractions through metaphors that they have experienced together. It's the solid foundation they need in order to move into the larger world with confidence, "as though they owned the place."

POSTNOTE

Americans are an innovative and restless people. These characteristics are seen in the way we "do" education. We love our schools, but continually criticize them. We seem to be constantly in search of the "new new thing." One of the newest movements in American schooling is "smallness." Large high schools are being reconfigured into "schools within schools" with separate faculties and student bodies. Where once a community would build one big elementary school, now they will build three small schools. "Small" is in!

This article is a classic because the author's ideas were instrumental in challenging the educational status quo. Deborah Meier is one of the pioneers of this movement toward smaller schools. However, she is no one-sided cheerleader. Her reflections here, based on her own experience and having observed many new efforts to convert to smaller schools, provide balance and direction to teachers and administrators. Her title, "'As Though They Owned the Place': Small Schools as Membership Communities,"

captures the "two-edged" quality of many small schools: an environment of personal connectedness. One of the major criticisms of our large schools is that they breed impersonal relationships among teachers, students, administrators, and parents. The complaint is that the "connective tissue" among these groups is weak and thin. In small schools, however, people know one another and, in turn, are known. There is an environment of personal accountability and a shared sense of ownership. This places demands on all concerned, but the benefits are looking increasingly attractive.

Discussion Questions

1. What are the major educational advantages for students in small school settings?
2. What are the major advantages for teachers?
3. On the other hand, what is lost? Or rather, what are the advantages of large schools?

RELATED WEBSITE RESOURCES AND VIDEO CASES

 Web Resources:

Planning Resources for Teachers in Small High Schools. Available at:

http://www.smallschoolsproject.org.

The Small Schools Project, founded and funded by the Gates Foundation, has many resources on this site for educators to maximize the impact of small schools.

Small Schools Workshop. Available at:

http://www.smallschoolsworkshop.org.

This site has several links to subtopics, such as arguments for small schools, ways to increase students' achievement, and small school-related research.

⏩ ▶ ⏪ **Video Case:**

Social and Emotional Development: Understanding Adolescents

In this video case, you will see how Shania Martinez, a guidance counselor, helps a group of seventh-grade boys deal with the anger they feel in every day life. As you watch the clips and study the artifacts in the case, reflect upon the following questions:

1. What do you think of the ideas students generate in how to deal with frustration?
2. One student, Alan, advises teachers to really listen to their students. Can you recall any of your teachers who were particularly good listeners? Was their listening effective? In what ways?

Safety from the Inside Out: Rethinking Traditional Approaches

15

Alfie Kohn

Alfie Kohn, the author of the book *The Schools Our Children Deserve*, has been highly praised as a writer and speaker on education, human behavior, and social theory issues.

|F|O|C|U|S| QUESTION

Are guns and knives the only things that make schools unsafe for students?

KEY TERM
Zero-tolerance policies

For many people, the idea of safety in an educational context brings to mind the problem of school violence, and specifically the string of shootings at schools across the country in recent years. Let's begin, then, by noting that the coverage of those events has obscured several important facts:

- The real horror is that young people die, not where they die. To be sure, there's something deeply unsettling about the juxtaposition of the words "violence" and "schools." But keep in mind that the vast majority of young homicide victims are killed at home, on the streets, or somewhere else other than school. During one three-year period in the 1990s, for example, about eighty homicides took place on school grounds—while more than 8,000 children were killed elsewhere. This is important to keep in mind, both so that we recognize the full extent of the problem and so we don't exaggerate how dangerous schools really are.
- There is a tendency, upon hearing about stunning cases of school violence, to infer that adolescents are Public Enemy No. 1. But Mike Males, a sociologist, urges us to focus our attention on the "far more common phenomenon of adults killing kids." He points out that Americans blame teenagers too easily, and usually inaccurately, for what's wrong with our society.[1]
- When school violence does occur, low-income students of color are disproportionately likely to be the victims, Columbine and other notorious school-shooting incidents notwithstanding. If that fact is surprising, it may be because of the media's tacit assumption that any problem—crime, drugs, violence—is more newsworthy when white people in the suburbs are affected.

* * *

Yet another series of mistaken assumptions comes into play when educators and policymakers try to respond to violence—or to their fear of it. Questionable beliefs often lead to wrongheaded policies.

First, we Americans love to imagine that *technical fixes* will take care of complicated problems. (Remember the V-chip, which was supposed to be the solution to children's exposure to violent television programming?) Some people still cling to the hope that schools can be made safer if we just install enough surveillance cameras and metal detectors. In reality, though, it's simply not feasible to guard every doorway or monitor every screen. The number of cameras at one Washington, D.C., high school was recently doubled, from thirty-two to sixty-four, but the principal admitted that it's hard to keep guns "on the outside of the school unless we become armed camps, and I don't think anyone wants to send their child to an armed camp." His comments were reported in a newspaper article that was aptly headlined "Trust, Not Cameras, Called Best Prevention."[2]

Pedro Noguera, who teaches at New York University, put it this way: "Design and staffing of schools are driven by security concerns, but no thought is given to how these designs and atmospheres make students and [teachers] feel. If we use prisons as our models for safe schools—well, prisons are not safe places, right? Safety comes from human relations. I'd say we'd do much better to invest in counselors than armed guards."[3]

Second, when we do focus on the human element of violence prevention, we often assume that students just need to be taught the appropriate *skills*.[4] This model is so simple and familiar to us that we don't even think of it as a model at all. It seems a matter of common sense that if children don't pay attention to what someone else is saying, they would benefit from some remedial listening skills. If they fail to lend a hand to someone in distress, they need to hone their helping skills. If they're reluctant to stand up for themselves, they're candidates for assertiveness training. Thus, by analogy, if violence keeps breaking out, all we need to do is teach students the skills of conflict resolution.

Unfortunately, skills are not enough. Most kids already know how to listen, how to help, and how to assert themselves. The question is why they sometimes lack the *disposition* to act in these ways. It's much the same with efforts to raise academic achievement: a skills-based approach has its limits if we ignore the question of how interested students are in what they're being taught. Such efforts may even do more harm than good if an emphasis on teaching basic skills makes school downright unappealing. The same goes for literacy in particular: consider how many children know how to read, but don't. In short, what matters is not only whether people can learn, or act, in a particular way, but whether they have the inclination to do so.

Why, then, do we spend so much time teaching skills? For one thing, this implies that it's the students who need fixing. If something more complicated than a lack of know-how is involved, we might have to question our own practices and premises, which can be uncomfortable. Moreover, a focus on skills allows us to ignore the structural elements of a classroom (or school or family). If students hurt one another, it's easier for us to try to deal with each individual's actions than it is to ask which elements of the system might have contributed to the problem.

A skills-based approach is also compatible with behaviorism, whose influence over our schools—and, indeed, over all of American society—is difficult to overstate. Behaviorism dismisses anything that can't be reduced to a discrete set of observable and measurable behaviors. This dogma lies behind segmented instructional techniques, as well as many of the most popular approaches to character education, classroom management, and our practices with students who have special needs.

When we're preoccupied with behaviors, we're less likely to dig deep in order to understand the reasons, values, and motives that give rise to those behaviors. We end up embracing superficial responses, such as trying to improve the climate of a school by forcing students to dress alike. (Among other limitations of such a policy, our assumption seems to be that we can reduce aggression by borrowing an idea from the military.) But any time we talk about changing students' "behaviors," we run the risk of ignoring the students who are doing the behaving. We lose the human beings behind the actions. Thus, we may come to see students as computers that can be reprogrammed, or pets that can be retrained, or empty receptacles that can be refilled—all dangerously misleading metaphors. We offer behavioral instruction in more appropriate ways to express anger, but the violence continues because we haven't gotten anywhere near where the problem is.

* * *

It often doesn't work, then, to employ technical fixes or to teach skills. But there's a third response that isn't merely ineffective—it's actively counterproductive. I have in mind the policies that follow from assuming we can stamp out violence—or create safety—by *coercive means*. In her book *A Peaceable School*, Vicky Dill remarked that while it can be bad to have no plan for dealing with school violence, "it can be much worse to have a simplistic, authoritarian policy."[5]

A reliance on old-fashioned discipline, with threats of punishments for offenders, not only distracts us from dealing with the real causes of aggression, but in effect *models* bullying and power for students. Many school officials fail to understand that fact and end up throwing fuel on the fire by responding to signs of student distress with ever-harsher measures. Consistent with the tendency to ignore the structural causes of problems, they seem to think sheer force will make the bad stuff go away; if students are made to suffer for doing something wrong, they will see the error of their ways. When that proves ineffective, it's assumed that *more* punishment—along with tighter regulations and less trust—will do the trick.[6]

The shootings at Columbine provoked a general panic in which hundreds of students across the country were arrested, while "countless others were suspended or expelled for words or deeds perceived as menacing."[7] The fear here is understandable: administrators wondered whether their districts, too, might be incubating killers. But we need to understand the difference between *overreaction,* such as closing down a school to search for bombs after a student makes an offhand joke, and *destructive reactions,* such as coercive policies.

A particularly egregious example of the latter is the so-called "zero tolerance" approach, which is based on the premise that harsh punishment works better if it's meted out indiscriminately—indeed, in robotic fashion. It took a few years before this strategy began to attract critical attention in the media.[8] Research, meanwhile, has been accumulating to confirm that it makes no sense at all. One study discovered that students in schools with such a policy "actually report feeling less safe... than do students in schools with more moderate policies."[9] That subjective impression is supported by objective evidence: another analysis showed that "even after schools with zero tolerance policies had implemented them for more than four years, those schools were still less safe than schools without such policies."[10] Moreover, zero tolerance doesn't affect everyone equally: African-American and Latino students are more likely than their white counterparts to be targeted by this sort of punitive discipline.[11] As a society, we seem to have a lot more tolerance for the misbehavior of white children.

The finding that schools become less safe as a result of adopting zero-tolerance policies will sound paradoxical only to those readers who believe that threats and punishment can create safety. In reality, safety is put at risk by such an approach. A safe school environment is one where students are able to really know and trust—and be known and trusted by—adults.[12] Those bonds, however, are ruptured by a system that's about doing things *to* students who act inappropriately rather than working *with* them to solve problems. "The first casualty" of zero-tolerance policies "is the central, critical relationship between teacher and student, a relationship that is now being damaged or broken in favor of tough-sounding, impersonal, uniform procedures."[13]

Zero tolerance is bad enough, but the situation becomes even worse when the punishments in question are so harsh that students are turned into criminals. Across the country, the *New York Times* reported in early 2004, schools "are increasingly sending students into the juvenile justice systems for the sort of adolescent misbehavior that used to be handled by school administrators."[14] Apart from the devastating effects that turning children over to the police can have on

their lives, the school's climate is curdled because administrators send the message that a student who does something wrong may be taken away in handcuffs and, in effect, exiled from the community. Here we see the *reductio ad absurdum* of trying to improve schools by relying on threats and fear.

There are many explanations for this deeply disturbing trend, including the loss of school-based mental health services due to budget cuts. But Mark Soler of the Youth Law Center, a public interest group that protects at-risk children, observes that these days "zero tolerance is fed less by fear of crime and more by high-stakes testing. Principals want to get rid of kids they perceive as trouble" because doing so may improve their school's overall test results.[15] School safety is at risk, that is, not merely because some educators wrongly believe that stricter or more consistent application of punitive discipline will help, but because of the pressure to raise test scores.

What's more, that same pressure, which leads some people to regard students in trouble as disposable commodities, also has the effect of squeezing out efforts to help them avoid getting into trouble in the first place. Programs to promote conflict resolution and to address bullying and other sorts of violence are being eliminated because educators are themselves being bullied into focusing on standardized test results to the exclusion of everything else. Scott Poland, a school psychologist and expert in crisis intervention, writes: "School principals have told me that they would like to devote curriculum time to topics such as managing anger, violence prevention and learning to get along with others regardless of race and ethnicity, but... [they are] under tremendous pressure to raise academic scores on the state accountability test."[16]

Thus, argues Margaret McKenna, the president of Lesley University, "Some of the most important lessons of Columbine have been all but forgotten—left behind, so to speak, in no small measure because of... the No Child Left Behind Act. The law's narrow focus on yearly improvement in test scores has [made schools]... even less conducive to teachers' knowing their students well." To drive home the point that our priorities have become skewed, she observes that "the test scores at Columbine High were among the highest in Colorado."[17]

* * *

Even in cases where a student's actions pose a significant risk to the safety of others, an educator's first response should not be "Have we used sufficient force to stamp out this threat?" but "What have we done to address the underlying issues here? How can we transform our schools into places that meet students' needs so there is less chance that someone will be moved to lash out in fury?"

Here's another way to look at it: we need to stop talking primarily about creating peaceful schools, which is not a particularly ambitious or meaningful goal. Schools, after all, are completely peaceful at 3 A.M. Similarly, a classroom full of docile, unquestioning students may be peaceful, even if they aren't learning much of value, don't care much about one another, and would rather be someplace else. What we need to work for is the creation of schools that are *peaceable*— that is, committed to the value of peace and to helping students feel safe, in all senses of that word.[18]

Physical safety, the most obvious kind, has understandably been the priority, particularly where it seems to be in short supply. But intellectual and emotional safety matter, too—in their own right and also because they're related to physical safety. Bullying and other violent acts are less likely to happen in a school that feels like a caring community, a place where children experience a sense of connection to one another and to adults, a place where they come to think in the plural and feel a sense of belonging. That's the polar opposite of a school where kids are picked on for being different or uncool, to the point that they fear entering certain hallways or sections of the cafeteria. Caring school communities don't let that happen: they regard any evidence of nasty cliques or hurtful exclusion as serious problems to be addressed. They do everything possible so that no one fears being laughed at, picked on, or humiliated.

These efforts take place in individual classrooms and also as a matter of school policy. Proactive efforts to build community and resolve conflicts are important, but so too must educators focus on what gets in the way of safety and community. Thus, teachers not only hold class meetings on a regular basis so that students can participate in making decisions; they also use these meetings to address troubling things that may be going on. One teacher spoke up after a math lesson, for example, to talk with her students about

> something I *don't* like and I *don't* want to hear because it makes me feel bad, and if it makes me feel bad it probably makes someone else in here feel bad. It's these two words. (She writes "That's easy" on the chalkboard and draws a circle around the phrase.)... When I am struggling and trying so hard, [hearing that phrase] makes me feel kind of dumb or stupid. Because I am thinking, gosh, if it's so easy why am I having so much trouble with it?. . . And what's one of our rules in here? It's to be considerate of others and their feelings.[19]

Such an intervention may be motivated not only by a general commitment to ensuring that students don't feel bad, but also by a desire to promote high-quality learning. There are intellectual costs when students don't feel safe to take risks. A classroom where kids worry that their questions will be thought silly is a classroom where unself-conscious engagement with ideas is less likely to take place. (Of course, students often are unwilling to ask questions or acknowledge that they're struggling for fear of the reaction from the teacher, not just from their classmates.)

On a schoolwide level, intellectual and emotional safety require that students are freed from being rated and ranked, freed from public pressure to show how smart they are—or even worse, how much smarter they are than everyone else. Awards assemblies and honor rolls are very effective ways to destroy the sense of safety that supports a willingness to learn. Some schools that pride themselves on their commitment to high standards and achievement have created a climate that really isn't about learning at all—let alone about caring. Such places are more about results than about kids. Their students often feel as though they're in a pressure cooker, where some must fail in order that others can succeed. The message students get is that other people are potential obstacles to their own success.[20]

There is much more to be said, of course, about how and why to build community, to meet kids' needs, to create a culture of safety and caring.[21] The benefits of doing so are most pronounced in schools that have more low-income students,[22] yet such schools are often distinguished instead by punitive discipline and a climate of control. However, schools in affluent areas may also feel unsafe in various ways. Columbine High School was reportedly a place where bullying was common and a sharply stratified social structure was allowed to flourish, one in which athletes were deified. (Some of these sports stars taunted other students mercilessly "while school authorities looked the other way."[23]) In some suburban schools, the curriculum is chock full of rigorous advanced placement courses and the parking lot glitters with pricey SUVs, but one doesn't have to look hard to find students who are starving themselves, cutting themselves, or medicating themselves, as well as students who are taking out their frustrations on those who sit lower on the social food chain.

Even in a school free of weapons, children may feel unsafe and unhappy. And that's reason enough to rethink our assumptions, redesign our policies, and redouble our commitment to creating a different kind of educational culture.

NOTES

1. Mike Males, "Who's Really Killing Our Schoolkids?" *Los Angeles Times,* May 31, 1999. Also see other writings by Males, including his book *The Scapegoat Generation: America's War on Adolescents* (Monroe, Maine: Common Courage Press, 1996).

2. The article, by Debbi Wilgoren, appeared in the *Washington Post* on February 3, 2004: A-7.

3. Pedro A. Noguera, "School Safety Lessons Learned: Urban Districts Report Progress," *Education Week,* May 30, 2001: 15.

4. This section is adapted from my article "The Limits of Teaching Skills." *Reaching Today's Youth,* Summer 1997, which is available at **<www.alfiekohn.org/teaching/lts.htm>.**

5. Vicky Schreiber Dill, *A Peaceable School: Creating a Culture of Nonviolence* (Bloomington, Ind.: Phi Delta Kappa, 1997), 24. Also see Irwin A. Hyman and Pamela A. Snook, *Dangerous Schools* (San Francisco: Jossey-Bass, 1999), an excerpt from which appeared in the March 2000 issue *of Phi Delta Kappan.*

6. This section is adapted from my article "Constant Frustration and Occasional Violence: The Legacy of American High Schools," *American School Board Journal,* September 1999, which is available at **<www.alfiekohn.org/teaching/cfaov.htm>.** For more on the counterproductive effects of—and some alternatives to—punitive "consequences" and rewards, see my book *Beyond Discipline: From Compliance to Community* (Alexandria, Va.: Association for Supervision and Curriculum Development, 1996).

7. Caroline Hendrie, "In Schools, A Sigh of Relief as Tense Spring Draws to a Close," *Education Week,* June 23, 1999.

8. For example, see Dirk Johnson, "Schools' New Watchword: Zero Tolerance," *New York Times,* December 1, 1999; and Jesse Katz, "Taking Zero Tolerance to the Limit," *Los Angeles Times,* March 1, 1998.

9. This quotation is from Robert Blum of the University of Minnesota. The study, to which he contributed, was published in the *Journal of School Health* and summarized in Darcia Harris Bowman, "School 'Connectedness' Makes for Healthier Students, Study Suggests," *Education Week,* April 24, 2002: 16.

10. John H. Holloway, "The Dilemma of Zero Tolerance," *Educational Leadership,* December 2001/January 2002: 84. The analysis summarized here was published by the National Center for Education Statistics in 1998. Also see an excellent review of the effects of such policies in Russ Skiba and Reece Peterson, "The Dark Side of Zero Tolerance: Can Punishment Lead to Safe Schools?" *Pbi Delta Kappan,* January 1999: 372–76, 381–82.

11. A report by a civil rights group called The Advancement Project, based on an analysis of federal statistics, was described in Kenneth J. Cooper, "Group Finds Racial Disparity in Schools' 'Zero Tolerance,'" *Washington Post,* June 15, 2000.

12. For example, see Deborah Meier, *In Schools We Trust* (Boston: Beacon Press, 2002).

13. William Ayers and Bernadine Dohrn, "Have We Gone Overboard with Zero Tolerance?" *Chicago Tribune,* November 21, 1999.

14. Sara Rimer, "Unruly Students Facing Arrest, Not Detention," *New York Times,* January 4, 2004: A-l.

15. That explanation also makes sense to Augustina Reyes of the University of Houston: "If teachers are told, 'Your [test] scores go down, you lose your job,' all of a sudden your values shift very quickly. Teachers think, 'With bad kids in my class, I'll have lower achievement on my tests, so I'll use discretion and remove that kid.'" Both Reyes and Soler are quoted in Annette Fuentes, "Discipline and Punish," *The Nation,* December 15, 2003: 17–20.

16. "The Non-Hardware Side of School Safety," *NASP* [National Association of School Psychologists] *Communique* 28:6 (March 2000). Poland made the same point while testifying at a congressional hearing on school violence in March 1999—a month before the shootings at Columbine.

17. Margaret A. McKenna, "Lessons Left Behind," *Washington Post,* April 20, 2004: A-19.

18. The distinction between peaceful and peaceable was popularized by Bill Kreidler, who worked with Educators for Social Responsibility and wrote several books about conflict resolution. He died in 2000 at the unripe age of forty-eight.

19. Paul Cobb, Erna Yackel, and Terry Wood, "Young Children's Emotional Acts While Engaged in Mathematical Problem Solving." In *Affect and Mathematical Problem Solving: A New Perspective,* ed. D. B. McLeod and V. M. Adams (New York: Springer-Verlag, 1989), 130–31.

20. Our culture's uncritical acceptance of the ideology of competition is such that even people who acknowledge the damaging effects of an "excessive" emphasis on winning may continue to assert that competition *per se* is inevitable or productive. If this assertion is typically unaccompanied by evidence, that's probably because the available data support exactly the opposite position—namely, that a win/lose arrangement tends to hold us back from doing our best work and from optimal learning. I've reviewed some of that evidence in *No Contest: The Case Against Competition* (Boston: Houghton Mifflin, 1986).

21. See my article "Caring Kids: The Role of the Schools," *Phi Delta Kappan,* March 1991: 496–506 (available at **<www.alfiekohn.org/teaching/cktrots.htm>**); and chapter 7 ("The Classroom as Community") of *Beyond Discipline,* op. cit. Many other writers, of course, have also addressed this question.

22. Victor Battistich, Daniel Solomon, Dong-il Kim, Marilyn Watson, and Eric Schaps, "Schools as Communities, Poverty Levels of Student Populations, and Students' Attitudes, Motives, and Performance: A Multilevel Analysis," *American Education Research Journal* 32 (1995): 627–58.

23. Lorraine Adams and Dale Russakoff, "Dissecting Columbine's Cult of the Athlete," *Washington Post,* June 12, 1999: A-1.

POSTNOTE

One of the key advances in social planning in recent years is called the "law-of-unintended-consequences." Emerging from the physical and social sciences, this law looks at the unexpected effects of actions—often carefully and well thought-out actions—on conditions or people. For instance, well-meaning politicians raise the minimum wage and a hard pressed store owner has to raise his prices or fire some workers to meet the new payroll. A farmer buys a new high-powered fertilizer which improves his crops but poisons his water supply. The best of intentions is often not enough.

As this article points out schools, like other systems, often react in unanticipated ways when one important element is changed. A new sex education curriculum may appear to be comprehensive and answer all the questions on students' minds, but have the unintended consequence of causing great consternation among parents. Or, the teachers association may win a budget battle with the school board to dramatically increase salaries, only to discover that in order to meet the new teachers' salary budget, most of the new teachers have lost their jobs. The habit of thinking hard about the unintended consequences of innovations has not characterized many recent changes in our field. Perhaps it is time they do.

Discussion Questions

1. Which of the violence-related factors noted at the beginning of this article surprised you most?
2. What are the most prevalent forms of school violence that you have witnessed during your earlier school years?
3. Specifically, what positive suggestions does the author offer to lessen school violence?

RELATED WEBSITE RESOURCES AND VIDEO CASES

 Web Resources:

School Violence. Available at:

http://www.safeyouth.org/scripts/topics/school.asp.

This site, supported by the National Youth Violence Prevention Resource Center, has a massive amount of information and materials on an array of related issues.

School Violence: Causes, Effects, and Ideas to Combat School Violence. Available at:

http://712educators.about.com/od/schoolviolence/ School_Violence.htm.

This site has practical tips for teachers and parents on how to handle bullying and other problematic behaviors, plus numerous links to other useful resources.

 **Video Case:**

Social and Emotional Development: Understanding Adolescents

In this video case, you will see how Shania Martinez, a guidance counselor, helps a group of seventh-grade boys deal with the anger they feel in every day life. As you watch the clips and study the artifacts in the case, reflect upon the following questions:

1. What do you think of the ideas students generate in how to deal with frustration?
2. One student, Alan, advises teachers to really listen to their students. Can you recall any of your teachers who were particularly good listeners? Was their listening effective? In what ways?

16

Uncovering Academic Success

Karin Chenoweth

Karin Chenoweth, an experienced educational writer, currently writes for the Achievement Alliance. This article was adapted from her book, *"It's Being Done": Academic Success in Unexpected Schools* (Harvard University Press, 2007).

"Uncovering Academic Success" by Karin Chenoweth. Reprinted with permission from the Summer 2007 issue of *American Educator*, the quarterly journal of the American Federation of Teachers, AFL-CIO. This article is adapted from Karin Chenoweth's book, "'It's Being Done': Academic Success in Unexpected Schools," published by Harvard Education Press. For more information, please visit **www.hepg.org/hep/Book/65.**

|F|O|C|U|S| QUESTION

What are the keys, if any, to first class education in urban schools?

Can it be done? Can schools help all children learn to high levels, even poor children who typically enter school far behind their more privileged peers? Is it even possible?

As a longtime education reporter and columnist, I knew the answer was yes, but I knew it as an article of faith rather than actual knowledge. I had never actually seen such a school. I had seen glimmers of hope in the fifth-grade classroom of Linda Eberhart, where African-American boys and girls from a very poor section of Baltimore met state math standards at higher rates than any other school in the state. I had seen hope in the extraordinary kindergarten class of Lorraine Gandy, who could boast without fear of contradiction that in 30 years she had taught just about every one of her students to read. I had also seen hope in a couple of schools that were committed to educating every child. But a whole school where the average poor child and child of color could walk in from the neighborhood and be pretty sure he or she would learn to read and do math and otherwise succeed academically? That I had never seen.

But I would not let go of the notion that our public schools are places that offer all children the chance to become educated and where, if they work hard, they can gain access to all the opportunities our country has to offer. The folks at The Education Trust, a national education organization that for years has identified schools where poor children and children of color do better than their peers in other schools, would not give up on that notion either. The Education Trust had actually identified such schools through their data—but it had never explained what they do to have such dramatically different results from other schools. In late 2004, The Education Trust joined together with four other organizations—the Business Roundtable, the Citizens' Commission on Civil Rights, the National Center for Educational Accountability, and the National Council of La Raza—to form The Achievement Alliance, and they hired me to visit such schools and describe what they do.

To determine which schools to visit, analysts from The Education Trust and I pored over state data. We were looking for public, open-enrollment schools that had high percentages of students of poverty and students of color, had at least two years of data showing high levels of student achievement (or very rapid, sustained improvement), and had closed (or greatly narrowed) achievement gaps between various groups of students.

The two years I spent visiting schools were a revelation in a lot of ways. I began this project not knowing at all what I would find. For all I knew (and feared), I would find soul-deadening test-prep factories. Perhaps, I worried, I would find schools where the teachers and principals were worn to a frazzle, burnt-out and bitter with all the expectations that have been placed on their shoulders. Or, even worse, I would find schools where the teachers were automatons, robbed of all creativity.

I found none of that. Instead, I found dedicated, energetic, skilled professionals who care deeply that all their students have access to the kinds of knowledge and opportunities that most middle-class white children take for granted. That means they include art and music and physical fitness and field trips and science and history and all the things that some people say schools must cut in order to focus on the reading and math skills tested in state assessments. That doesn't mean that the people in the schools I have visited don't care deeply about reading and math or doing well on state assessments. But they, and their principals, know that it is a mistake to "narrow the curriculum" and "teach to the test"—two of the epithets floating around the education world.

And happily, I found teachers and principals who love their jobs. They work hard, and some work long hours. They may occasionally be tempted to move to schools where it might be easier to teach; but they stay on the job because, as one teacher said to me, "We're successful. And we're like family." Many are bolstered by the idea that they are engaged in important work—work that, if enough people paid attention, could improve the public schools and, to some extent, the nation itself. But, stunningly, their work has gone almost unnoticed.

Early on in this project, I was talking with a very thoughtful principal. I said that many people think schools cannot help children who are behind because of poverty and discrimination catch up to their more privileged peers. "They say it can't be done," I said. She replied simply, "It's being done." I spent the next two years proving her point and then stole her words as the title of the book I wrote profiling each of these schools.

Although all the schools I profiled for this project have large concentrations of students of color, students of poverty, or both, they are very different in just about every other way. They are big and small; integrated and racially isolated; high-tech and low-tech; urban, rural, and suburban. Some require uniforms; some do not. Some follow traditional school calendars; some follow year-round calendars. Some are in big districts; some are in small ones. Some have adopted pre-packaged school improvement designs; some have developed their own model of improvement. Some have beautiful facilities; some are in buildings that should have been torn down years ago. Some have successfully engaged their parents and communities; some have not.

Those are the characteristics that many say make the difference in school quality. And yet, despite those differences, all these schools either have very high rates of proficiency or impressive trajectories of improvement. So the question arises: Is there something deeper that these schools share? Is there something more than uniforms and school size and computers that makes the difference?

I have become convinced that there is no single factor that is at the core of a successful school. That is, there is no one structure that, if every school in the country were to adopt, would transform them into high-achieving schools. Schools are too complex for simple solutions. Over and over, the teachers and principals in these schools told me, "There is no magic bullet."

But there are some characteristics that they all share, and I was pondering how to try to convey them when I had an experience that brought into stark relief the things I wanted to highlight. I visited a school that on paper looked like another success story; it posted very high proficiency rates on state tests in a state with high standards. The students were all African American and almost all were poor, most lived in a nearby housing project. I was looking forward to another "beating the odds" story.

When I arrived at the school, the hallways were filled with children gathering for the start of school, but few looked as if they had anything to look forward to. When I got to the office, it was locked. I asked an adult where the principal was; she said, "She's not here yet," as though it were normal for the principal not to be there at the beginning of school. When the principal did show up, she was surprised I was there, even though I had called and e-mailed several times in the previous weeks to confirm my visit.

The principal showed me around the school. In many classrooms she opened the door onto quickly dampened noise. The teachers (there were several substitutes that day) looked up with relief. Quite a few said things like, "Oh, I'm glad you're here—the kids are really acting up." On those occasions the principal yelled at the disruptive students in front of their teachers, classmates, and me, a stranger taking notes. "What did you promise me?" she shouted at a young boy who looked absolutely miserable being humiliated in public. "You sat in that office and promised me and your mother something. What was it?" She yelled at teachers and even a parent in the same way. At no time did the principal say she wanted to introduce me to a teacher or a student or see classroom teaching. In fact, there was very little classroom instruction visible. The two exceptions were a kindergarten teacher who was enthusiastically leading her students in a song they were preparing for an end-of-the-year ceremony and a class where a poet had come in as part of a foundation grant to introduce older children to poetry. Finally, the principal stated the obvious: "Once the state tests are done, we don't do a lot of instruction—we're doing field trips and getting ready for the end of the year." The state tests are given in March and April, months before school lets out. What little she did say about instruction made it clear that it was focused almost entirely on what would appear on the state test, such as teaching students the specific words that the state tests use and teaching them to take notes on reading passages.

Some students had been left behind from a field trip that day either because they hadn't gotten their permission forms in on time or because they were being punished for poor behavior. They had been given an assignment to write about what job they would like in the future. Although the students were in seventh grade, none of their essays was longer than a paragraph, and none included many salient details. Two of the most ambitious of the students said that they would like to run a laundry and a hairbraiding and nail salon. The principal gave the students a lecture about how they should think about other possibilities, such as running a shaved ice booth or selling cold water on a hot day.

From all I had seen—the atmosphere of distrust, disrespect, and barely controlled chaos; little interest in instruction; and extremely low ambitions for the kids (a water stand!)—I concluded that the high scores the school posted had not been attained in a legitimate way. That conclusion was strengthened when the principal told me that teachers administering state tests were "under strict accountability to not allow students to turn in half-filled-out answer sheets, and they can't have any wild answers either." Though I tried to keep my face as deadpan as possible, I think the principal knew she had made a damaging admission: There are no legitimate ways to keep students from giving "wild answers" on a state test. In addition, the principal said she had some concerns this spring because the testing protocols had changed. I could barely wait to escape, and I caught an early flight home, depressed by what I had seen. Months later, my suspicions about the level of learning at the school were confirmed when that

spring's test results were published—fewer than 10 percent of the students had met state standards.

Seeing that school helped crystallize in my mind what I wanted to say about schools that are getting the job done. I did not hit on a magic bullet, far from it: I found that these schools shared about two dozen characteristics that—together—contributed to their success. I describe all of them in my book; here I present just a handful of those characteristics that seem most important. Much of what I saw in these impressive schools was extremely high-quality teaching. But I also saw leadership that supported such teaching, so I think it is essential for teachers and principals alike to carefully study these characteristics.

They have high expectations for their students. They assume that their students are able to meet high standards and believe their job is to help their students get there. They do not assume that their students are so crippled by poverty and discrimination that they cannot meet high standards. "It's not about feeling sorry for kids," says Barbara Adderley, principal of Stanton Elementary (see article, "Inside a Philadephia Success Story"), located in an economically devastated part of North Philadelphia. "It's about making sure that they understand what it is they're expected to do." They talk with their students about going to college or into high-level technical training. This is true for all the levels of schooling—elementary, middle, and high.

They use all the data they can get their hands on and embrace accountability, but they don't teach to the state tests. They want to know how their students are doing, and they know that classroom observation by teachers, though important, is fragmentary and doesn't allow overall patterns to be observed. State test data, district data, classroom test data, and any formative assessment data they can get their hands on are all eagerly studied. If the district doesn't provide the data in the form they need, they come up with their own ways of charting and displaying data. And, if another school nearby outperforms them, they are the first ones to try to figure out what that school did and incorporate it into their own practice.

All the schools make sure their students know what their state's tests look like in terms of the format, and they try to ensure that their students aren't surprised by the material or the kinds of questions that will be asked. But none of them spend a huge amount of time teaching their students what will be on the state tests or teaching them how to "bubble in" a scoring sheet. They teach a rich, coherent curriculum tied to state standards. They don't teach the test, particularly in those states where the tests are low-level reading and math tests. In the states where the tests are a bit more sophisticated and high-level, such as the Massachusetts MCAS and the New York Regents, the schools might spend more time teaching directly to what will be tested, but that is because those tests are more closely tied to a set of high standards.

They use school time wisely and add time for students, particularly those who are struggling. They establish classroom and school routines to ensure that endless amounts of time are not spent going to the bathroom, getting out and putting away books and materials, and going from one activity or class to another. School time is for instruction, and instruction is treated as something sacred. Most of the schools establish uninterrupted blocks of time for instruction so that classes aren't disrupted by bus announcements or by students being pulled out for speech therapy or counseling. Using time wisely doesn't mean that kids don't ever have fun or recess. It means that students are engaged in productive activities just about all the time.

Different schools add time in different ways. Some have before-and-after-school classes and summer school. Some have year-round calendars with intensive tutoring during the intersessions. They all figure out ways to get their children more time for instruction, and they do so with the same kinds of resources (often involving federal funds) that are available to many high-poverty schools and within the parameters of the teacher union contracts. Many also see that extra time as an opportunity for enrichment, and they offer interesting classes such as music, drama, and sign language.

They do not spend a lot of time disciplining students in the sense of punishing them. They do spend time disciplining children in the original sense of the word: leading them (think of the word disciple). They teach students how to act by noticing and encouraging kindness and consideration and they teach kids how to have good social and professional relationships by explicitly teaching them how to disagree with someone without getting upset and fighting. But their main method of discipline is to aim for high-quality instruction every moment, on the theory that busy and actively engaged students do not have time to misbehave. In those instances when behavior issues are deeper than boredom-induced mischief, teachers aren't left high and dry. These schools have additional interventions to use when needed, such as pairing disruptive students and their families with mentors or with outside social services.

They provide teachers with the time to meet, observe each other, and do serious professional development. Either the principal or an assistant principal spends a great deal of time building a schedule so that children have coherent instructional days and teachers have time to work together. The most common strategy in elementary and middle school is to schedule an entire grade to have "specials" (usually art, music, physical education, and sometimes science) at the same time so that the teachers can meet. Teachers review data, go over student work, develop lesson plans, and map curriculum. Teachers are also encouraged to seek out and observe colleagues who have perfected a particular lesson or who are trying something new and want feedback about whether it is clear and coherent.

The general theory among these schools is that if students are weak in a particular area, the teachers need to learn more about it. Professional development that does nothing to deepen teachers' content knowledge, understanding, or pedagogical skill is not typical in these schools. And, they realize that new teachers often don't know enough about classroom management, curriculum, assessment, reading instruction, or how to physically set up a classroom, so mentors are often provided to help induct new teachers into the profession.

Although the principals are important leaders, they are not the only leaders. Teachers and other administrators, and sometimes parents and community members as well, sit on committees that make important decisions for the school, such as hiring, curriculum, school policies and procedures, Title I spending, and much more. Trennis Harvey, assistant principal of Capitol View Elementary in Atlanta said, "Of course your leader has to make some decisions, but most decisions here are made by teams." In most cases, this is part of an explicit practice to institutionalize improvement so that it is not reliant on a single individual. These principals are consciously trying to build enduring structures that will outlast them.

These schools are achieving at higher levels and improving at faster rates than some in the education world think is possible. It would be reasonable to wonder if the teachers and principals are nearing nervous-breakdown level. Overwhelmingly, that's not what I found. Mind you, the schools are not easy places to work. But because the atmosphere is respectful and teachers' work is organized in a way that allows them to be successful and take leadership roles, they are nice places to work. As a result, they do not have the kind of turnover that many schools with similar demographics have.

After visiting all the schools profiled in this book, I began to feel as if the folks in these schools can be likened to the Wright brothers, who proved once and for all that manned flight was possible. In much the same way, the schools profiled in my book demonstrate that the job of educating all kids to high levels is possible. When you overcome drag and gravity with enough thrust and lift, you get flight; when you overcome poverty and discrimination with effective leadership, thoughtful instruction, careful organization, and what can only be recognized as the kind of pigheaded optimism displayed by the Wright brothers, you get learning—even in schools where many people wouldn't expect it.

POSTNOTE

There is much hand wringing and dismal talk about urban education and the schools serving our minority populations. Also, much of the research and reportage on urban schools provides chilling evidence of failing students and frustrated educators. Ms. Chenoweth's article, based on extensive "embedded" reporting, tells a different story. Urban schools may have severe challenges, but they are hardly hopeless. Her article again reminds us that focusing on the essentials of learning—that is, high expectations for students and focusing support on students-in-need—will bear results.

Among the excellent issues raised by this article is the attention given to the professional development of teachers. Few teachers themselves come from the troubled urban classrooms. Few have had adequate preparation for the problems and issues they encounter in these schools. Therefore, in-service training and opportunities to plan together are important ingredients in order for them to develop into effective teachers.

Although the author tells us, "there is no silver bullet," she offers us valuable insights into the puzzle of urban schools.

Discussion Questions

1. Of the several principles or characteristics of successful urban schools, which two do you think are most important? Why?
2. Based on this article, what is your disposition to teaching in schools serving the urban poor?
3. Are there other suggestions or ideas for improvement that could be added to the author's list? What are they?

RELATED WEBSITE RESOURCES

 ### Web Resources:

National Institute for Urban School Improvement. Available at:

http://urbanschools.org/.

This site is a deep and varied resource on many aspects of urban education compiled from free learning modules and informative articles.

FOCUS. Available at:

http://www.focus-dccharter.org/.

FOCUS, or Friends of Choice in Urban Schools, is a site primarily devoted to supporting educators interested in or involved in the charter school movement.

17

Why Some Parents Don't Come to School

Margaret Finders and Cynthia Lewis

Margaret Finders is director of the School of Education and associate dean of the University of Wisconsin–LaCrosse's College of Liberal Studies. **Cynthia Lewis** is on the faculty at Grinnell College, Grinnell, Iowa.

"Why Some Parents Don't Come to School" by Margaret Finders and Cynthia Lewis, *Educational Leadership*, May 1994. Used with permission. The Association for Supervision and Curriculum Development is a worldwide community of educators advocating sound policies and sharing best practices to achieve the success of each learner. To learn more, visit ASCD at **www.ascd.org.**

| F | O | C | U | S | QUESTION

Why is it that some parents just won't come to their children's schools?

KEY TERM

Institutional perspective

In our roles as teachers and as parents, we have been privy to the conversations of both teachers and parents. Until recently, however, we did not acknowledge that our view of parental involvement conflicts with the views of many parents. It was not until we began talking with parents in different communities that we were forced to examine our own deeply seated assumptions about parental involvement.

From talking with Latino parents and parents in two low-income Anglo neighborhoods, we have gained insights about why they feel disenfranchised from school settings. In order to include such parents in the educational conversation, we need to understand the barriers to their involvement from their vantage point, as that of outsiders. When asked, these parents had many suggestions that may help educators re-envision family involvement in the schools.

The Institutional Perspective

The institutional perspective holds that children who do not succeed in school have parents who do not get involved in school activities or support school goals at home. Recent research emphasizes the importance of parent involvement in promoting school success (Comer 1984, Lareau 1987). At the same time, lack of participation among parents of socially and culturally diverse students is also well documented (Clark 1983, Delgado-Gaitan 1991).

The model for family involvement, despite enormous changes in the reality of family structures, is that of a two-parent, economically self-sufficient nuclear family, with a working father and homemaker mother (David 1989). As educators, we talk about "the changing family," but the language we use has changed little. The institutional view of nonparticipating parents remains based on a deficit model. "Those who *need* to come, don't come," a teacher explains, revealing an assumption that one of the main reasons for involving parents is to remediate them. It is assumed that involved parents bring a body of knowledge about the purposes of schooling to match institutional knowledge. Unless they bring such knowledge to the school, they themselves are thought to need education in becoming legitimate participants.

Administrators, too, frustrated by lack of parental involvement, express their concern in terms of a deficit model. An administrator expresses his bewilderment:

> Our parent-teacher group is the foundation of our school programs. . . . This group (gestures to the all-Anglo, all-women group seated in the library) is the most important organization in the school. You know, I just don't understand why *those other parents* won't even show up.

Discussions about family involvement often center on what families lack and how educators can best teach parents to support instructional agendas at home (Mansbach 1993). To revise this limited model for interaction between home and school, we must look outside of the institutional perspective.

The Voices of "Those Other Parents"

We asked some of "those other parents" what they think about building positive home/school relations. In what follows, parents whose voices are rarely heard at school explain how the diverse contexts of their lives create tensions that interfere with positive home/school relations. For them, school experiences, economic and time constraints, and linguistic and cultural practices have produced a body of knowledge about school settings that frequently goes unacknowledged.

DIVERSE SCHOOL EXPERIENCES AMONG PARENTS

Educators often don't take into account how a parent's own school experiences may influence school relationships. Listen in as one father describes his son's school progress:

> They expect me to go to school so they can tell me my kid is stupid or crazy. They've been telling me that for three years, so why should I go and hear it again? They don't do anything. They just tell me my kid is bad.
>
> See, I've been there. I know. And it scares me. They called me a boy in trouble but I was a troubled boy. Nobody helped me because they liked it when I didn't show up. If I was gone for the semester, fine with them. I dropped out nine times. They wanted me gone.

This father's experiences created mistrust and prevent him from participating more fully in his son's education. Yet, we cannot say that he doesn't care about his son. On the contrary, his message is urgent.

For many parents, their own personal school experiences create obstacles to involvement. Parents who have dropped out of school do not feel confident in school settings. Needed to help support their families or care for siblings at home, these individuals' limited schooling makes it difficult for them to help their children with homework beyond the early primary level. For some, this situation is compounded by language barriers and lack of written literacy skills. One mother who attended school through 6th grade in Mexico, and whose first language is Spanish, comments about homework that "sometimes we can't help because it's too hard." Yet the norm in most schools is to send home schoolwork with little information for parents about how it should be completed.

DIVERSE ECONOMIC AND TIME CONSTRAINTS

Time constraints are a primary obstacle for parents whose work doesn't allow them the autonomy and flexibility characteristic of professional positions. Here, a mother expresses her frustrations:

> Teachers just don't understand that I can't come to school at just any old time. I think Judy told you that we don't have a car right now. . . . Andrew catches a different bus than Dawn. He gets here a half an hour before her, and then I have to make sure Judy is home because I got three kids in three different schools. And I feel like the teachers are under pressure, and they're turning it around and putting the pressure on me cause they want me to check up on Judy and I really can't.

Often, parents work at physically demanding jobs, with mothers expected to take care of child-care responsibilities as well as school-related issues. In one mother's words:

> What most people don't understand about the Hispanic community is that you come home and you take care of your husband and your family first. Then if there's time you can go out to your meetings.

Other parents work nights, making it impossible to attend evening programs and difficult to appear at daytime meetings that interfere with family obligations and sleep.

At times, parents' financial concerns present a major obstacle to participation in their child's school activities. One mother expresses frustration that she cannot send eight dollars to school so her daughter can have a yearbook to sign like the other girls.

> I do not understand why they assume that everybody has tons of money, and every time I turn around it's more money for this and more money for that. Where do they get the idea that we've got all this money?

This mother is torn between the pressures of stretching a tight budget and wanting her daughter to belong. As is the case for others, economic constraints prevent her child from full participation in the culture of the school. This lack of a sense of belonging creates many barriers for parents.

DIVERSE LINGUISTIC AND CULTURAL PRACTICES

Parents who don't speak fluent English often feel inadequate in school contexts. One parent explains that "an extreme language barrier" prevented her own mother from ever going to anything at the school. Cultural mismatches can occur as often as linguistic conflicts. One Latino educator explained that asking young children to translate for their parents during conferences grates against a cultural norm. Placing children in a position of equal status with adults creates dysfunction within the family hierarchy.

One mother poignantly expresses the cultural disconnect she feels when communicating with Anglo teachers and parents:

> [In] the Hispanic culture and the Anglo culture things are done different and you really don't know—am I doing the right thing? When they call me and say, "You bring the plates" [for class parties], do they think I can't do the cookies, too? You really don't know.

Voicing a set of values that conflicts with institutional constructions of the parent's role, a mother gives this culturally-based explanation for not attending her 12-year-old's school functions:

> It's her education, not mine. I've had to teach her to take care of herself. I work nights, so she's had to get up and get herself ready for school. I'm not going to be there all the time. She's gotta do it. She's a tough cookie. . . . She's almost an adult, and I get the impression that they want me to walk her through her work. And it's not that I don't care either. I really do. I think it's important, but I don't think it's my place.

This mother does not lack concern for her child. In her view, independence is essential for her daughter's success.

Whether it is for social, cultural, linguistic, or economic reasons, these parents' voices are rarely heard at school. Perhaps, as educators, we too readily categorize them as "those other parents" and fail to hear the concern that permeates such conversations. Because the experiences of these families vary greatly from our own, we operate on assumptions that interfere with our best intentions. What can be done to address the widening gap between parents who participate and those who don't?

Getting Involved: Suggestions from Parents

Parents have many suggestions for teachers and administrators about ways to promote active involvement. Their views, however, do not always match the role envisioned by educators. Possessing fewer economic resources and educational skills to participate in traditional ways (Lareau 1987), these parents operate at a disadvantage until they understand how schools are organized and how they can promote systemic change (Delgado-Gaitan 1991).

If we're truly interested in establishing a dialogue with the parents of all of our nation's students, however, we need to understand what parents think can be done. Here are some of their suggestions.

CLARIFY HOW PARENTS CAN HELP

Parents need to know exactly how they can help. Some are active in church and other community groups, but lack information about how to become more involved in their children's schooling. One Latina mother explains that most of the parents she knows think that school involvement means attending school parties.

As Concha Delgado-Gaitan (1991) points out ". . . the difference between parents who participate and those who do not is that those who do have recognized that they are a critical part of their children's education." Many of the parents we spoke to don't see themselves in this capacity.

ENCOURAGE PARENTS TO BE ASSERTIVE

Parents who do see themselves as needed participants feel strongly that they must provide their children with a positive view of their history and culture not usually presented at school.

Some emphasize the importance of speaking up for their children. Several, for instance, have argued for or against special education placement or retention for their children; others have discussed with teachers what they saw as inappropriate disciplinary procedures. In one parent's words:

> Sometimes kids are taken advantage of because their parents don't fight for them. I say to parents, if you don't fight for your child, no one's going to fight for them.

Although it may sound as if these parents are advocating adversarial positions, they are simply pleading for inclusion. Having spent much time on the teacher side of these conversations, we realize that teachers might see such talk as challenging their positions as professional decision makers. Yet, it is crucial that we expand the dialogue to include parent knowledge about school settings, even when that knowledge conflicts with our own.

DEVELOP TRUST

Parents affirm the importance of establishing trust. One mother attributes a particular teacher's good turnout for parent/teacher conferences to her ability to establish a "personal relationship" with parents. Another comments on her need to be reassured that the school is open, that it's OK to drop by "anytime you can."

In the opportunities we provide for involvement, we must regularly ask ourselves what messages we convey through our dress, gestures, and talk. In one study, for example, a teacher described her school's open house in a middle-class neighborhood as "a cocktail party without cocktails" (Lareau 1987). This is the sort of "party" that many parents wouldn't feel comfortable attending.

Fear was a recurrent theme among the parents we interviewed: fear of appearing foolish or being misunderstood, fear about their children's academic standing. One mother explained:

> Parents feel like the teachers are looking at you, and I know how they feel, because I feel like that here. There are certain things and places where I still feel uncomfortable, so I won't go, and I feel bad, and I think maybe it's just me.

This mother is relaying how it feels to be culturally, linguistically, and ethnically different. Her body of knowledge does not match the institutional knowledge of the school and she is therefore excluded from home/school conversations.

BUILD ON HOME EXPERIENCES

Our assumptions about the home environments of our students can either build or serve as links between home and school. An assumption that "these kids don't live in good environments" can destroy the very network we are trying to create. Too often we tell parents what we want them to do at home with no understanding of the rich social interaction that already occurs there (Keenan et al. 1993). One mother expresses her frustrations:

> Whenever I go to school, they want to tell me what to do at home. They want to tell me how to raise my kid. They never ask me what I think. They never ask me anything.

When we asked parents general questions about their home activities and how these activities might build on what happens at school, most thought there was no connection. They claimed not to engage in much reading and writing at home, although their specific answers to questions contradicted this belief. One mother talks about her time at home with her teenage daughter:

> My husband works nights and sometimes she sleeps with me. . . . We would lay down in bed and discuss the books she reads.

Many of the parents we spoke to mentioned Bible reading as a regular family event, yet they did not see this reading in relation to schoolwork. In one mother's words:

> I read the Bible to the children in Spanish, but when I see they're not understanding me, I stop (laughing). Then they go and look in the English Bible to find out what I said.

Although the Bible is not a text read at public schools, we can build on the literacy practices and social interactions that surround it. For instance, we can draw upon a student's ability to compare multiple versions of a text. We also can include among the texts we read legends, folktales, and mythology—literature that, like the Bible, is meant to teach us about our strengths and weaknesses as we strive to make our lives meaningful.

As teachers, of course, we marvel at the way in which such home interactions do, indeed, support our goals for learning at school; but we won't know about these practices unless we begin to form relationships with parents that allow them to share such knowledge.

USE PARENT EXPERTISE

Moll (1992) underscores the importance of empowering parents to contribute "*intellectually* to the development of lessons." He recommends assessing the "funds of knowledge" in the community, citing a teacher who discovered that many parents in the Latino community where she taught had expertise in the field of construction. Consequently, the class developed a unit on construction, which included reading, writing, speaking, and building, all with the help of responsive community experts—the children's parents.

Parents made similar suggestions—for example, cooking ethnic foods with students, sharing information about multicultural heritage, and bringing in role models from the community. Latino parents repeatedly emphasized that the presence of more teachers from their culture would benefit their children as role models and would help them in home/school interactions.

Parents also suggested extending literacy by writing pen pal letters with students or involving their older children in tutoring and letter writing with younger students. To help break down the barriers that language differences create, one parent suggested that bilingual and monolingual parents form partnerships to participate in school functions together.

An Invitation for Involvement

Too often, the social, economic, linguistic, and cultural practices of parents are represented as serious problems rather than valued knowledge. When we reexamine our assumptions about parental absence, we may find that our interpretations of parents who care may simply be parents who are like us, parents who feel comfortable in the teacher's domain.

Instead of operating on the assumption that absence translates into noncaring, we need to focus on ways to draw parents into the schools. If we make explicit the multiple ways we value the language, culture, and knowledge of the parents in our communities, parents may more readily accept our invitations.

REFERENCES

Clark, R. M. (1983). *Family Life and School Achievement: Why Poor Black Children Succeed or Fail.* Chicago: University of Chicago Press.

Comer, J. P. (1984). "Homeschool Relationships as They Affect the Academic Success of Children." *Education and Urban Society* 16: 323–337.

David, M. E. (1989). "Schooling and the Family." In *Critical Pedagogy, the State, and Cultural Struggle,* edited by H. Giroux and P. McLaren. Albany, N.Y.: State University of New York Press.

Delgado-Gaitan, C. (1991). "Involving Parents in the Schools: A Process of Empowerment." *American Journal of Education* 100: 20–46.

Keenan, J. W., J. Willett, and J. Solsken. (1993). "Constructing an Urban Village: School/Home Collaboration in a Multicultural Classroom." *Language Arts* 70: 204–214.

Lareau, A. (1987). "Social Class Differences in Family-School Relationships: The Importance of Cultural Capital." *Sociology of Education* 60: 73–85.

Mansbach, S. C. (February/March 1993). "We Must Put Family Literacy on the National Agenda." *Reading Today:* 37.

Moll, L. (1992). "Bilingual Classroom Studies and Community Analysis: Some Recent Trends." *Educational Researcher* 21: 20–24.

POSTNOTE

Much research supports the principle that children whose parents are active in their schools are more likely to succeed in school, whereas children whose parents are not involved are more apt to do poorly. Some parents are eager to work as partners with schools to be certain that their children are well prepared for the life and career choices they will make. Other parents are almost never involved with the school.

This article is useful to educators working at schools where parental involvement is less than what they hoped for. By understanding why some parents never show up at schools, educators can take steps to help overcome the parents' reluctance. Remember, teachers need parents to help them succeed.

Discussion Questions

1. List some of the main reasons Finders and Lewis give for parents not coming to school. Which of these reasons do you find compelling? Do any of the reasons surprise you?

2. Can you identify any additional reasons for parents to stay away from school, besides those given by the authors?

3. What strategies for involving parents in school have you seen employed, and how successful were they?

RELATED WEBSITE RESOURCES AND VIDEO CASES

 Web Resources:

How to Make Parent-Teacher Conferences Work for Your Child. Available at:

http://www.nea.org/parents/ptconf.html.

This National Education Association website is an excellent resource on many educational issues, including teacher-parent relations.

Building Successful Partnerships. Available at:

http://www.pta.org/local_leadership_ subprogram_1116958575937.html.

This website, supported by the parent-teacher association, provides helpful insights and information from the parents' perspective.

 *Video Case:*

Home-School Communications: The Parent-Teacher Conference

In this video case, you will meet teacher Jim St. Clair. His approach weaves actual examples of the child's work and his own observations into a discussion of the child's strengths and weaknesses. You will also see Jim listen and respond to a mother's concerns. As you watch the clips and study the artifacts in the case, reflect upon the following questions:

1. Why might a teacher ask family members what the student says about school when they are at home? What is the value in asking this?
2. What, if anything, would you do differently in parent-teacher conferences to reflect the age of students you teach and your own personal teaching style?

For Another Perspective:

James P. Comer, Parent Participation: Fad or Function?

www.cengage.com/login

Curriculum and Standards

The bedrock question of education is this: What knowledge is most worth knowing? This question goes right to the heart of individual and social priorities. As our world has become more and more drenched with information—information pouring out at us from many different media—the question of what is worth our limited time and attention has increased in importance. It is the quintessential curriculum question.

In recent years, however, policymakers and educators have attempted to improve our schools by establishing what should be learned through state-mandated curriculum standards and by enforcing those standards through regular testing. The federal No Child Left Behind Act of 2001 requires states to test students in reading and mathematics each year in grades 3 through 8. This effort has dramatically affected what is going on in today's classrooms.

The question of what is most worth knowing, however, begets others. What is the purpose of knowledge? To make a great deal of money? To become a wise person? To prepare oneself for important work? To contribute to the general good of society?

This difficult question becomes more and more complex, and swiftly takes us into the realm of values. Nevertheless, it is a question communities must regularly address in our decentralized education system. In struggling with curriculum issues, a community is really making a bet on the future needs of society and of the young people who will have to live in that society. Behind the choice of a new emphasis on foreign language instruction or on computer literacy is a social gamble, and the stakes are high. Offering students an inadequate curriculum is like sending troops into battle with popguns.

Curriculum Matters

W. James Popham

W. James Popham is professor emeritus in the UCLA Graduate School of Education and Information Studies. He is a former president of the American Educational Research Association and widely recognized as one of the nation's top evaluation and measurement experts. In 2000, he was recognized by *UCLA Today* as one of UCLA's top 20 professors of the 20th century.

F O C U S QUESTION

How has the No Child Left Behind Act affected the way state standards are taught in schools and the way assessments are employed?

KEY TERMS

Assessment

Coalesced content standard

Content standards

Derivative assessment framework

American educators use the word *curriculum* almost every day—and why not, since it describes the stuff we want our students to learn. What a curriculum contains, however, has historically had far less impact on instructional practice than is widely thought. But curriculum's modest influence on instruction has been dramatically transformed in the past few years, especially with respect to state-sanctioned curricula. These days, a state's curricular aims can have a decisive impact—either positive or negative—on the way students are taught.

Note that I am using the term *curriculum* in its traditional sense, namely, to describe the knowledge, skills, and (sometimes) feelings that educators want their students to acquire. In this time-honored definition, a curriculum represents educational *ends*. Educators hope, of course, that such ends will be attained as a consequence of instructional activities, which serve as the *means* of promoting the curricular ends.

In the past, the curricular things we wanted our students to learn were typically described as *goals* or *objectives*. These days, however, most educators tend to use the term *content standards* instead. But regardless of the label that's used, what's in a curriculum is supposed to describe the intended impact of an educational enterprise on the students being taught.

A Personal Perspective

My first serious brush with curriculum occurred some five decades ago, when I began teaching in eastern Oregon. Even way back then, Oregon had a state-approved curriculum syllabus, and I was given a copy of that thick text for my bookshelf. And that's where it stayed—right on that shelf. Other than glancing at the syllabus for an hour or so before the school year began to find out what goals the state decreed for the courses I was scheduled to teach, I never looked at it again.

What actually determined the content I taught in my classes was, almost totally, the textbooks I used. As a first-year teacher in a small high school, I had five different preparations. Accordingly, my frantic instructional planning revolved completely around the textbooks I'd been told to use for those five courses. To illustrate, I was required, by a principal who had never heard of "highly qualified teachers," to teach a course in geography even though I had never in my entire life taken a course in geography. Given my lack of geographic expertise, I truly cherished the large red geography text without which I could not have survived a class of 30 sophomores, most of whom did not truly care about the location of Khartoum or the subtleties of a Mercator map projection.

But I was not alone. All of the other teachers in my school paid little, if any, attention to the state curriculum syllabus. My faculty colleagues, too, decided on what they should teach according to what was treated in their textbooks. In retrospect, "alignment" in those days might have referred to whether a teacher's lesson plan meshed suitably with the textbook's upcoming chapter.

No Clarity, No Consequences

The trifling impact that official curriculum documents have on teachers' instructional practices can probably be attributed, at least in part, to the documents' excessive generality. If, for example, social studies teachers discover that their students are supposed to acquire "a meaningful understanding of how our nation's government functions," there is obviously so much latitude in this curricular aim that a wide range of instructional activities legitimately could be regarded as germane. The mushiness of many curricular aims certainly plays a role in reducing the impact of those aims on classroom instruction.

However, a more fundamental reason that our nation's curricula have had so little influence on instructional practice is that what was in a curriculum, even a state-sanctioned or district-sanctioned curriculum, rarely made any sort of difference to anyone.

Oh, certainly, there have been occasional instances when a particular body of content was thought to be appropriate or inappropriate for a state curriculum. You might recall, for instance, the recent flap in Kansas about the inclusion of evolution content in the state's science curriculum. And, when a state's textbooks are under consideration for adoption, those doing the adopting surely pay some attention to what's in the state's curriculum when they review contending textbooks. But, considering the full-blown panorama of American public education, what has been identified in official curriculum documents has typically had only a slight impact on what actually goes on in classrooms.

Then Came NCLB

But that situation came to a screeching halt on Jan. 8, 2002, when President Bush affixed his signature to the No Child Left Behind Act. This important reauthorization of a federal law, first enacted in 1965, substantially altered the relationship between curriculum and instruction in America.

That's because NCLB first tied *assessments* to a state's curriculum, then tied important decisions to students' performances on those curriculum-based assessments. If students failed to make sufficient progress in their *assessed* mastery of a state's curricular aims, then all sorts of sanctions and public embarrassment would follow for educators who were running the schools and districts where insufficient progress had been seen. Because NCLB required a state's annual assessments to be based on the state's official curriculum, and because those annual assessments could cause plenty of trouble, what was in the curriculum suddenly mattered.

Educators, of course, were eager to avoid NCLB sanctions (or NCLB-induced embarrassment) by having been identified as failing to make adequate yearly progress in students' test performances. Accordingly, educators became far more attentive to what would be covered in their state's NCLB tests. But a state's NCLB tests, as required by law, must be based on the state's official curriculum, as represented by a state's "challenging" content standards.

Let me quickly tie a ribbon around this logic chain:

1. A state's schools and districts can get battered by NCLB sanctions and/or public embarrassment if students don't score well enough on the state's annual NCLB tests;
2. But what's measured on those annual NCLB tests must be based on a state's official curriculum; and, therefore,
3. Teachers will be certain to try to boost NCLB test scores by devoting substantial instructional time to what's likely to be assessed by their state's curriculum-based NCLB tests.

So, for the first time in the history of American public schooling, a potent federal law has made curriculum truly count—big time.

The problem is that most state curricula, against a backdrop of these significant NCLB pressures to improve test scores, are actually *lowering* the quality of education in a state's schools. We need to understand why that is so. And we need to do something about it.

Too Many Targets

Here, in a nutshell, is what currently constitutes an NCLB-triggered, curriculum-caused calamity. The content standards now found in almost all of our states originally were devised by competent, well-intentioned individuals—but at a time when a state-approved curriculum was merely supposed to reflect worthwhile educational aspirations for a state's students.

Unfortunately, in most states' current collections of content standards, there are far too many curriculum aims to teach or to test in the time available for teaching or testing. Almost all states' content standards reflect a "wish-list" mentality; that is, the determiners of a state's content standards in, say, mathematics, have listed all the nifty mathematical skills and knowledge they *wish* the state's students would be able to master. But the result of these cover-the-waterfront curriculum exercises—carried out before NCLB's arrival made curriculum a potent factor in a state's accountability game—was invariably to lay out way too many curricular targets.

A state's educators, therefore, have been forced to deal with—or try to deal with—an excessive number of curricular targets. Too many curricular aims must be assessed by a given year's NCLB tests, so teachers are obliged to guess which ones actually will be tested in a given year. On probability grounds alone, of course, many teachers guess wrong and end up teaching things that aren't on the NCLB tests or not teaching things that are on the tests.

A related problem arises because teachers are unable to learn from the results of NCLB tests which of their instructional activities have or haven't worked. Because there are so many curricular aims, the ones that actually are measured on a given year's test can't be assessed with enough test items to supply any sort of sensible estimate about which curricular aims were or weren't well taught. A collection of too-general score reports simply doesn't provide teachers with the information they need to improve their instruction, for those reports do not let teachers know *which* curricular aims have or haven't been mastered by their students. And, lurking as the culprit in this instructionally meaningless score reporting is a state curriculum containing too many curricular aims in the first place.

Given this regrettable situation, it is any wonder that some NCLB-pressured teachers engage in rampant curricular reductionism, excising any content—even important content—if it seems unlikely to be tested. Is it any wonder that some teachers oblige their students to take part in endless, mind-numbing test-preparation sessions? Is it any wonder that some engage in such dishonest practices as supplying their students with advance copies of covertly copied items from the actual tests?

All of these bad outcomes could be reduced or eliminated if only more sensible NCLB tests were employed. But, as you have now seen, first we must grapple with the inappropriate curricular targets found in so many states. Unless a state's decision makers figure out a way to have their state's NCLB tests function as a force for instructional improvement, not instructional decline, too many students will suffer. That suffering can be traced directly to curricular aims that, though perhaps serviceable in a former time, just don't work today.

These days, because of NCLB, curriculum *does* make a difference. And these days, because of NCLB, we need to rethink whether our state curricula are suitable.

Three Options

The task before education policy makers is to reduce the number of eligible-to-be-assessed curricular aims so that (1) teachers are not overwhelmed by too many instructional targets and (2) a student's mastery of each curricular aim that's assessed can be determined with reasonable accuracy.

Teachers who can focus their instructional attention on a modest number of truly significant skills usually can get their students to master those skills—even if the skills are genuinely challenging. Accurate reports of students' mastery of each skill will let the students and their parents know which curricular aims have or haven't been mastered—and let teachers know which ones have or haven't been well taught.

Here are three potential ways of coping with this curricular crisis:

BRAND NEW CONTENT STANDARDS

The first option involves a start-from-scratch approach to identifying a state's curricular aims. Given a clean slate, and the recognition that a subject matter's most important curricular aims must be assessed by NCLB tests, a state's curriculum makers could attempt to come up with a markedly winnowed, more instructionally beneficial set of unarguably significant curricular aims.

COALESCED CONTENT STANDARDS

A second alternative would be for a state's curriculum officials to rework existing curricular aims so that the most important of them were subsumed under a smaller number of reconceptualized and measurable targets. Although, in many ways, this approach is similar to the first option, it might represent a modest repackaging of a state's extant curricular aims without a complete start-again approach to curriculum building.

DERIVATIVE ASSESSMENT FRAMEWORKS

The final option is to leave the state's current content standards untouched but derive from them a framework for NCLB assessment that focuses on a small number of reconceptualized, eligible-to-be-taught curricular targets. That way the state's curriculum-based NCLB tests would be likely to have a beneficial rather than a harmful impact on education. The skills and bodies of knowledge identified in an NCLB assessment framework would, of course, influence instructional practices and would need to be chosen with consummate care.

Proceeding Sensibly

Because the first two options are both likely to involve substantial time-consuming and resource-consuming activities, I believe option three is the most sensible way to proceed. Indeed, in many states the existing content standards have already been approved by a state school board or, sometimes, by the legislature itself—usually after substantial input from the state's educators and citizens. I prefer to leave those extant content standards as they are—untouched. If the content standards truly exert much of a positive influence on schooling (which I doubt), then that positive influence should continue. But if the content standards really aren't a positive factor (which I suspect), then letting them languish will be just fine.

However, because the law requires that a state's NCLB tests be clearly based on the state's content standards, it would be imperative to build a defensible case for federal officials that describes both the framework-derivation process and the relevant stakeholders involved. It is important that the state's NCLB assessment targets be *demonstrably* derivative from a state's existing curricular aims.

Let me illustrate, in the field of reading, how a defensible NCLB assessment framework might be derived from a state's existing curricular aims. Most states' content standards in reading contain a dozen or more specific reading skills, such as identifying a selection's main idea, isolating key details in a reading passage, and using context clues to infer the meaning of unfamiliar words. A markedly more comprehensive curricular aim in reading has recently been devised by Indiana University's Roger Farr. It is a sort of "super-skill" that effectively subsumes a great many more specific skills such as those just mentioned. Farr's super-skill requires students to be able to read different kinds of reading materials in order to accomplish any of the most common real-world purposes for which people read such materials.

Described as *purposeful reading*, this super-skill can be assessed via constructed-response items (for example, essay or short answer) or selected-response items (for example, multiple choice). From an instructional perspective, delightfully, a student's responses to such items are always evaluated by using a scoring guide whose key evaluative criteria can be taught directly to students. The criteria, always based on the reader's purpose as well as the type of material being read, focus on the *relevance, accuracy,* and *sufficiency* of a student's response. Thus, a powerful and teachable curricular aim can be derived from a flock of more specific skills that, therefore, can be regarded as "en route" or "enabling" skills for the more comprehensive super-skill that would be assessed via a state's NCLB tests.

Farr's *purposeful reading* is clearly analogous to the kinds of composition skills we routinely assess when we measure students' ability to write via writing-sample tests. In these tests, which have been in widespread use for over two decades in the United States, we call on students to display a super-skill, namely, being able to write an original composition (for example, a persuasive or narrative essay). Based on the student's essay, we are then able to gauge the student's ability to organize content, to use appropriate mechanics, and to display a number of other more specific subskills relevant to composition.

To derive an appropriate assessment framework from a state's collection of numerous existing curricular aims requires more than modest instructional and assessment acumen. The trick is to isolate a small number of aims that can be described to teachers, are genuinely teachable, and coalesce the most important of the state's existing curricular aims. That sort of activity, of course, demands loads of curricular artistry from those who are deriving the assessment framework. But this approach seems to be the most sensible way of dealing with our current NCLB-induced curricular crisis.

A Final Plea

The need to deal with our current state-approved curricular aims is, in my view, imperative. The longer we delay in coming up with educationally sound, curriculum-derived NCLB tests, the more children there will be who receive a less-than-lustrous education because their teachers are being driven by ill-conceived, curriculum-based NCLB assessments into shabby instructional practices.

Sure, I know many states have invested dollars galore in the creation of customized state-based tests that are supposedly "aligned" to their states' official curriculum. And, of course, it would be costly to move toward different tests. But those existing tests were developed at a time when a state's curriculum exercised little or no impact on classroom instruction. Those times have changed. And that's because, unless NCLB is seriously altered or disappears altogether, today's state curricula do make a difference. It's time to fix them.

POSTNOTE

W. James Popham sees a dysfunctional relationship between the No Child Left Behind (NCLB) Act and state standards and assessments. He argues that most state content standards are too encyclopedic. That is, they try to cover too much material, so much so that teachers have to guess which standards are likely to be tested and have to focus their instruction only on those standards, often eliminating instruction on other important content. He is also critical because teachers are unable to learn from the results of their assessments and cannot tell which of their instructional activities have or have not worked.

Popham's proposed solution is for states to take their content standards and choose a modest number among them to be tested for purposes of the NCLB Act, while also alerting educators and students as to those selected. In this manner, educators can focus on a reasonable number of content standards for assessment.

His solution is, we suspect, a compromise. He, and others, would probably prefer that the high-stakes testing imposed by the NCLB legislation be abandoned because the testing creates more problems than it purports to solve.

Discussion Questions

1. Do you agree with Popham's analysis of the misfit between state content standards and the requirements of NCLB? Why or why not?
2. What do you think should be done with students who fail the assessments of state standards? Should they be eligible to move on to the next grade or graduate from high school? Why or why not?
3. What is the strongest argument you can make in favor of high-stakes testing? What is the strongest argument you can make against it?

RELATED WEBSITE RESOURCES AND VIDEO CASES

 ### Web Resources:

Education World. Available at:

http://www.education-world.com.

This site contains links to state content standards and lesson plans.

U.S. Department of Education. Available at:

http://www.ed.gov/nclb/overview/intro/index.html.

This page on the U.S. Department of Education website contains an introduction to the No Child Left Behind Act.

 ### Video Case:

Foundations: Aligning Instruction with Federal Legislation

In this video case, you will view a roundtable discussion by educators of the Individuals with Disabilities Act (IDEA) and the No Child Left Behind (NCLB) legislation and how they affect their teaching. As you watch the clips and study the artifacts in the case, reflect upon the following questions:

1. What concerns did the teachers in the video case express regarding the effects of NCLB standardized testing on their teaching and on their students? Do you agree or disagree with these concerns?
2. What changes in NCLB would you make if you had the authority? What issues or concerns would these changes address?

19

The Saber-Tooth Curriculum

J. Abner Peddiwell

J. Abner Peddiwell is the pseudonym for Harold W. Benjamin, a professor of education who was a prominent figure in 20th-century education in the United States. He died in 1969.

|F|O|C|U|S| QUESTION

As you read this article, what subjects, if any, in the current school curriculum do you believe are outmoded and should be replaced?

The first great educational theorist and practitioner of whom my imagination has any record (began Dr. Peddiwell in his best professional tone) was a man of Chellean times whose full name was *New-Fist-Hammer-Maker* but whom, for convenience, I shall hereafter call *New-Fist*.

New-Fist was a doer, in spite of the fact that there was little in his environment with which to do anything very complex. You have undoubtedly heard of the pear-shaped, chipped-stone tool which archaeologists call the *coup-de-poing* or fist hammer. New-Fist gained his name and a considerable local prestige by producing one of these artifacts in less rough and more useful form than any previously known to his tribe. His hunting clubs were generally superior weapons, moreover, and his fire-using techniques were patterns of simplicity and precision. He knew how to do things his community needed to have done, and he had the energy and will to go ahead and do them. By virtue of these characteristics he was an educated man.

New-Fist was also a thinker. Then, as now, there were few lengths to which men would not go to avoid the labor and pain of thought. More readily than his fellows, New-Fist pushed himself beyond those lengths to the point where cerebration was inevitable. The same quality of intelligence which led him into the socially approved activity of producing a superior artifact also led him to engage in the socially disapproved practice of thinking. When other men gorged themselves on the proceeds of a successful hunt and vegetated in dull stupor for many hours thereafter, New-Fist ate a little less heartily, slept a little less stupidly, and arose a little earlier than his comrades to sit by the fire and think. He would stare moodily at the flickering flames and wonder about various parts of his environment until he finally got to the point where he became strongly dissatisfied with the accustomed ways of his tribe. He began to catch glimpses of ways in which life might be made better for himself, his family, and his group. By virtue of this development, he became a dangerous man.

This was the background that made this doer and thinker hit upon the concept of a conscious, systematic education. The immediate stimulus which put him directly into the practice of education came from watching his children at play. He saw these children at the cave entrance before the fire engaged in activity with bones and sticks and brightly colored pebbles. He noted that they seemed to have no purpose in their play beyond immediate pleasure in the activity itself. He compared their activity with that of the grown-up members of the tribe. The children played for fun; the adults worked for security and enrichment of their lives. The children dealt with bones, sticks, and pebbles; the adults dealt with food, shelter, and clothing. The children protected themselves from boredom; the adults protected themselves from danger.

"If I could only get these children to do the things that will give more and better food, shelter, clothing, and security," thought New-Fist, "I would be helping this tribe to have a better life. When the children became grown, they would have more meat to eat, more skins to keep them warm, better caves in which to sleep, and less danger from the striped death with the curving teeth that walks these trails at night."

Having set up an educational goal, New-Fist proceeded to construct a curriculum for reaching that goal. "What things must we tribesmen know how to do in order to live with full bellies, warm backs, and minds free from fear?" he asked himself.

To answer this question, he ran various activities over in his mind. "We have to catch fish with our bare hands in the pool far up the creek beyond that big bend," he said to himself. "We have to catch fish with our bare hands in the pool right at the bend. We have to catch them in the same way in the pool just this side of the bend. And so we catch them in the next pool and the next and the next. And we catch them with our bare hands."

Thus New-Fist discovered the first subject of the first curriculum—fish-grabbing-with-the-bare-hands.

"Also we club the little woolly horses," he continued with his analysis. "We club them along the bank of the creek where they come down to drink. We club them in the thickets where they lie down to sleep. We club them in the upland meadow where they graze. Wherever we find them we club them."

So woolly-horse-clubbing was seen to be the second main subject of the curriculum.

"And finally, we drive away the saber-tooth tigers with fire," New-Fist went on in his thinking. "We drive them from the mouth of our caves with fire. We drive them from our trail with burning branches. We wave firebrands to drive them from our drinking hole. Always we have to drive them away, and always we drive them with fire."

Thus was discovered the third subject—saber-tooth-tiger-scaring-with-fire.

Having developed a curriculum, New-Fist took his children with him as he went about his activities. He gave them an opportunity to practice these three subjects. The children liked to learn. It was more fun for them to engage in these purposeful activities than to play with colored stones just for the fun of it. They learned the new activities well, and so the educational system was a success.

As New-Fist's children grew older, it was plain to see that they had an advantage in good and safe living over other children who had never been educated systematically. Some of the more intelligent members of the tribe began to do as New-Fist had done, and the teaching of fish-grabbing, horse-clubbing, and tiger-scaring came more and more to be accepted as the heart of real education.

For a long time, however, there were certain more conservative members of the tribe who resisted the new, formal educational system on religious grounds. "The Great Mystery who speaks in thunder and moves in lightning," they announced impressively, "the Great Mystery who gives men life and takes it from them as he wills—if that Great Mystery had wanted children to practice fish-grabbing, horse-clubbing, and tiger-scaring before they were grown up, he would have taught them these activities himself by implanting in their natures instincts for fish-grabbing, horse-clubbing, and tiger-scaring. New-Fist is not only impious to attempt something the Great Mystery never intended to have done; he is also a damned fool for trying to change human nature."

Whereupon approximately half of these critics took up the solemn chant, "If you oppose the will of the Great Mystery, you must die," and the remainder sang derisively in unison, "You can't change human nature."

Being an educational statesman as well as an educational administrator and theorist, New-Fist replied politely to both arguments. To the more theologically minded, he said that, as a matter of fact, the Great Mystery had ordered this new work done, that he even did the work himself by causing children to want to learn, that children could not learn by themselves without divine aid, that they could not learn at all except through the power of the Great Mystery, and that nobody could really understand the will of the Great Mystery concerning fish, horses, and saber-tooth tigers unless he had been well grounded in three fundamental subjects of the New-Fist school. To the human-nature-cannot-be-changed shouters, New-Fist pointed out the fact that paleolithic culture had attained its high level by changes in human nature and that it seemed almost unpatriotic to deny the very process which had made the community great.

"I know you, my fellow tribesmen," the pioneer educator ended his argument gravely, "I know you as the humble and devoted servants of the Great Mystery. I know that you would not for one moment consciously oppose yourselves to his will. I know you as intelligent and loyal citizens of the great cave-realm, and I know that your pure and noble patriotism will not permit you to do anything which will block the development of that most cave-realmish of all our institutions—the paleolithic educational system. Now that you understand the true nature and purpose of this institution, I am serenely confident that there are no reasonable lengths to which you will not go in its defense and its support."

By this appeal the forces of conservatism were won over to the side of the new school, and in due time everybody who was anybody in the community knew that the heart of good education lay in the three subjects of fish-grabbing, horse-clubbing, and tiger-scaring. New-Fist and his contemporaries grew older and were gathered by the Great Mystery to the Land of the Sunset far down the creek. Other men followed their educational ways more and more, until at last all the children of the tribe were practiced systematically in the three fundamentals. Thus the tribe prospered and was happy in the possession of adequate meat, skins, and security.

It is to be supposed that all would have gone well forever with this good educational system if conditions of life in that community had remained forever the same. But conditions changed, and life which had once been so safe and happy in the cave-realm valley became insecure and disturbing.

A new ice age was approaching in that part of the world. A great glacier came down from the neighboring mountain range to the north. Year after year it crept closer and closer to the head-waters of the creek which ran through the tribe's valley, until at length it reached the stream and began to melt into the water. Dirt and gravel which the glacier had collected on its long journey were dropped into the creek. The water grew muddy. What had once been a crystal-clear stream in which one could see easily to the bottom was now a milky stream into which one could not see at all.

At once the life of the community was changed in one very important respect. It was no longer possible to catch fish with the bare hands. The fish could not be seen in the muddy water. For some years, moreover, the fish in the creek had been getting more timid, agile, and intelligent. The stupid, clumsy, brave fish, of which originally there had been a great many, had been caught with the bare hands for fish generation after fish generation, until only fish of superior intelligence and agility were left. These smart fish, hiding in the muddy water under the newly deposited glacial boulders, eluded the hands of the most expertly trained fish-grabbers. Those tribesmen who had studied advanced fish-grabbing in the secondary school could do no better than their less well-educated fellows who had

taken only an elementary course in the subject, and even the university graduates with majors in ichthyology were baffled by the problem. No matter how good a man's fish-grabbing education had been, he could not grab fish when he could not find fish to grab.

The melting waters of the approaching ice sheet also made the country wetter. The ground became marshy far back from the banks of the creek. The stupid woolly horses, standing only five or six hands high and running on four-toed front feet and three-toed hind feet, although admirable objects for clubbing, had one dangerous characteristic. They were ambitious. They all wanted to learn to run on their middle toes. They all had visions of becoming powerful and aggressive animals instead of little and timid ones. They dreamed of a far-distant day when some of their descendants would be sixteen hands high, weigh more than half a ton, and be able to pitch their would-be riders into the dirt. They knew they could never attain these goals in a wet, marshy country, so they all went east to the dry, open plains, far from the paleolithic hunting grounds. Their places were taken by little antelopes who came down with the ice sheet and were so shy and speedy and had so keen a scent for danger that no one could approach them closely enough to club them.

The best trained horse-clubbers of the tribe went out day after day and employed the most efficient techniques taught in the schools, but day after day they returned empty-handed. A horse-clubbing education of the highest type could get no results when there were no horses to club.

Finally, to complete the disruption of paleolithic life and education, the new dampness in the air gave the saber-tooth tigers pneumonia, a disease to which these animals were peculiarly susceptible and to which most of them succumbed. A few moth-eaten specimens crept south to the desert, it is true, but they were pitifully few and weak representatives of a once numerous and powerful race.

So there were no more tigers to scare in the paleolithic community, and the best tiger-scaring techniques became only academic exercises, good in themselves, perhaps, but not necessary for tribal security. Yet this danger to the people was lost only to be replaced by another and even greater danger, for with the advancing ice sheet came ferocious glacial bears which were not afraid of fire, which walked the trails by day as well as by night, and which could not be driven away by the most advanced methods developed in the tiger-scaring course of the schools.

The community was now in a very difficult situation. There was no fish or meat for food, no hides for clothing, and no security from the hairy death that walked the trails day and night. Adjustment to this difficulty had to be made at once if the tribe was not to become extinct.

Fortunately for the tribe, however, there were men in it of the old New-Fist breed, men who had the ability to do and the daring to think. One of them stood by the muddy stream, his stomach contracting with hunger pains, longing for some way to get a fish to eat. Again and again he had tried the old fish-grabbing technique that day, hoping desperately that at last it might work, but now in black despair he finally rejected all that he had learned in the schools and looked about him for some new way to get fish from that stream. There were stout but slender vines hanging from trees along the bank. He pulled them down and began to fasten them together more or less aimlessly. As he worked, the vision of what he might do to satisfy his hunger and that of his crying children back in the cave grew clearer. His black despair lightened a little. He worked more rapidly and intelligently. At last he had it—a net, a crude seine. He called a companion and explained the device. The two men took the net into the water, into pool after pool, and in one hour they caught more fish—intelligent fish in muddy water—than the whole tribe could have caught in a day under the best fish-grabbing conditions.

Another intelligent member of the tribe wandered hungrily through the woods where once the stupid little horses had abounded but where now only the elusive antelope could be seen. He had tried the horse-clubbing technique on the antelope until he was fully convinced of its futility. He knew that one would starve who relied on school learning to get him meat in those woods. Thus it was that he too, like the fishnet inventor, was finally impelled by hunger to new ways. He bent a strong, springy young tree over an antelope trail, hung a noosed vine therefrom, and fastened the whole device in so ingenious a fashion that the passing animal would release a trigger and be snared neatly when the tree jerked upright. By setting a line of these snares, he was able in one night to secure more meat and skins than a dozen horse-clubbers in the old days had secured in a week.

A third tribesman, determined to meet the problem of the ferocious bears, also forgot what he had been taught in school and began to think in direct and radical fashion. Finally, as a result of this thinking, he dug a deep pit in a bear trail, covered it with branches in such a way that a bear would walk on it unsuspectingly, fall through to the bottom, and remain trapped until the tribesmen could come up and despatch him with sticks and stones at their leisure. The inventor showed his friends how to dig and camouflage other pits until

all the trails around the community were furnished with them. Thus the tribe had even more security than before and in addition had the great additional store of meat and skins which they secured from the captured bears.

As the knowledge of these new inventions spread, all the members of the tribe were engaged in familiarizing themselves with the new ways of living. Men worked hard at making fish nets, setting antelope snares, and digging bear pits. The tribe was busy and prosperous.

There were a few thoughtful men who asked questions as they worked. Some of them even criticized the schools.

"These new activities of net-making and operating, snare-setting, and pit-digging are indispensable to modern existence," they said. "Why can't they be taught in school?"

The safe and sober majority had a quick reply to this naive question. "School!" they snorted derisively. "You aren't in school now. You are out here in the dirt working to preserve the life and happiness of the tribe. What have these practical activities got to do with schools? You're not saying lessons now. You'd better forget your lessons and your academic ideals of fish-grabbing, horse-clubbing, and tiger-scaring if you want to eat, keep warm, and have some measure of security from sudden death."

The radicals persisted a little in their questioning. "Fishnet-making and using, antelope-snare construction and operation, and bear-catching and killing," they pointed out, "require intelligence and skills—things we claim to develop in schools. They are also activities we need to know. Why can't the schools teach them?"

But most of the tribe, and particularly the wise old men who controlled the school, smiled indulgently at this suggestion. "That wouldn't be *education*," they said gently.

"But why wouldn't it be?" asked the radicals.

"Because it would be mere training," explained the old men patiently. "With all the intricate details of fish-grabbing, horse-clubbing, and tiger-scaring—the standard cultural subjects—the school curriculum is too crowded now. We can't add these fads and frills of net-making, antelope-snaring, and—of all things—bear-killing. Why, at the very thought, the body of the great New-Fist, founder of our paleolithic educational system, would turn over in its burial cairn. What we need to do is to give our young people a more thorough grounding in the fundamentals. Even the graduates of the secondary schools don't know the art of fish-grabbing in any complete sense nowadays, they swing their horse clubs awkwardly too, and as for the old science of tiger-scaring—well, even the teachers seem to lack the real flair for the subject which we oldsters got in our teens and never forgot."

"But, damn it," exploded one of the radicals, "how can any person with good sense be interested in such useless activities? What is the point of trying to catch fish with the bare hands when it just can't be done any more? How can a boy learn to club horses when there are no horses left to club? And why in hell should children try to scare tigers with fire when the tigers are dead and gone?"

"Don't be foolish," said the wise old men, smiling most kindly smiles. "We don't teach fish-grabbing to grab fish; we teach it to develop a generalized agility which can never be developed by mere training. We don't teach horse-clubbing to club horses; we teach it to develop a generalized strength in the learner which he can never get from so prosaic and specialized a thing as antelope-snare-setting. We don't teach tiger-scaring to scare tigers; we teach it for the purpose of giving that noble courage which carries over into all the affairs of life and which can never come from so base an activity as bear-killing."

All the radicals were silenced by this statement, all except the one who was most radical of all. He felt abashed, it is true, but he was so radical that he made one last protest.

"But—but anyway," he suggested, "you will have to admit that times have changed. Couldn't you please *try* these other, more up-to-date activities? Maybe they have *some* educational value after all?"

Even the man's fellow radicals felt that this was going a little too far.

The wise old men were indignant. Their kindly smiles faded. "If you had any education yourself," they said severely, "you would know that the essence of true education is timelessness. It is something that endures through changing conditions like a solid rock standing squarely and firmly in the middle of a raging torrent. You must know that there are some eternal verities, and the saber-tooth curriculum is one of them!"

POSTNOTE

The Saber-Tooth Curriculum is one of the greatest Classic curriculum articles ever written; its message is timeless. One might think it was written by a modern-day critic of the public school curriculum instead of someone writing in 1939. It is virtually impossible to read this selection without drawing parallels to courses and curricula that we have experienced. Fish-grabbing-with-the-bare-hands has not disappeared. It still exists today in many American schools, but it is called by a different name. And the same arguments used by the elders to defend the saber-tooth curriculum are used today to defend subjects that many say have outlived their right to remain in the curriculum. Why do they remain?

Discussion Questions

1. What is the main message of this excerpt from *The Saber-Tooth Curriculum?*

2. What subjects, if any, in the current school curriculum would you equate with fish-grabbing-with-the-bare-hands? Why?

3. What new subjects would you suggest adding to the school curriculum to avoid creating our own saber-tooth curriculum? Why?

20

Faulty Engineering

Chester E. Finn, Jr.

Chester E. Finn, Jr. is president of the Thomas B. Fordham Foundation, senior fellow at the Hoover Institution, and senior editor of *Education Next*.

Chester E. Finn, Jr., "Faulty Engineering," *Education Next*, Spring 2004, Vol. 4, No. 2. Reprinted by permission of Hoover Press.

| F | O | C | U | S | QUESTION

Does the diversity of values within American society render public schools ill-equipped to produce the engaged citizens our democracy requires?

KEY TERM
Liberal democracy

Every society creates mechanisms for teaching its young what they must know to become contributing citizens. Yet in a liberal democracy such as the United States, the proper ordering of those mechanisms is beset by paradox: if free citizens are to rule the state, does the state have a legitimate role in shaping their values and beliefs via its public schools, universities, and other institutions?

Because Americans insist that government is the creature of its citizens, we are loath to rely on state decisions and institutions to instruct our children in how to think, how to conduct themselves, and what to believe. After all, civic education may sound like a good idea in theory, but in practice public schools could even do harm in this realm. Some educators harbor worrisome values: moral relativism, atheism, doubts about the superiority of democracy, undue deference to the "*pluribus*" at the expense of the "*unum*," discomfort with patriotism, cynicism toward established cultural conventions and civic institutions. Transmitting those values to children will gradually erode the foundations of a free society. Perhaps society would be better off if its schools stuck to the three Rs and did a solid job in domains where they enjoy both competence and wide public support.

However, a free society is not self-maintaining. Its citizens must know something about democracy and about individual rights and responsibilities. They must also learn how to behave in a law-abiding way, respecting basic societal norms and values. Thus all educational institutions, especially primary and secondary schools, would seem to have an obligation to help transmit these core ideas, habits, and skills. Indeed, we fret when we learn of schools that *neglect* this role—the more so in a dangerous world where attacks on American values and institutions (and people) make it more important than ever to rear children who understand and prize those values.

One of the more effective debating points scored against voucher plans, for example, is the charge that "Klan schools," "witchcraft schools," and "fundamentalist madrasas" will qualify for public subsidy while imparting malign values to their pupils. Yet should government define which values are sound? And how is that different from an Orwellian regime of authoritarianism and theocracy? A fine dilemma indeed.

Standards and Civics

Our quandaries grow more vexing still as the standards movement transfers key decisions about the content of education from local neighborhoods and communities to distant policymakers in state and national capitals.

Under federal law, every state must now have state-wide standards in reading, math, and science, and nearly every state has also developed standards in social studies and other important areas of the school curriculum. Social studies standards typically focus not only on history, geography, economics, and government, but also on citizenship, social norms, and the like. Here, for example, is the opening of New Jersey's description of its "core curriculum content standards for social studies":

> Citizen participation in government is essential in forming this nation's democracy, and is vital in sustaining it. Social studies education promotes loyalty and love of country and it prepares students to participate intelligently in public affairs. Its component disciplines foster in students the knowledge and skills needed to make sense of current political and social issues. By studying history, geography, American government and politics, and other nations, students can learn to contribute to national, state, and local decisionmaking. They will also develop an understanding of the American constitutional system, an active awareness and commitment to the rights and responsibilities of citizenship, a tolerance for those with whom they disagree, and an understanding of the world beyond the borders of the United States.

A worthy aspiration indeed, yet one that is rarely attained. There is ample evidence to demonstrate that U.S. schools have failed even to impart basic information to children about their country's history and how its government and civil institutions work. For example, just 26 percent of U.S. high-school seniors attained the "proficient" level on the 1998 National Assessment of Educational Progress civics exam. Just 11 percent reached that level on the 2001 assessment of U.S. history. (Fifty-seven percent scored below the "basic" level on that assessment.)

If young people don't know that their state has two senators, don't understand the separation of powers, cannot explain the causes of the Civil War, and have difficulty distinguishing the New Deal from a poker game, what chance is there that they are acquiring—from the schools, anyway—"an active awareness and commitment to the rights and responsibilities of citizenship"? Is it not imperative for schools to establish a solid foundation of basic knowledge on which values, attitudes, and behaviors can securely rest?

Outside the Classroom

There's good news, too, but of a perverse sort: the very limits of schooling—both its ineffectiveness and the relatively small place it occupies in children's lives—leave ample room for other influences to work on youngsters' civic values and behavior. Parents, neighbors, churches, scouts, girls and boys clubs, the media—all play a significant role in sculpting children's understanding of the world around them. America has a vibrant civil society that does a decent job of forging good citizens even if the schools don't. That's why so many young Americans do obey the law (if not necessarily the speed limit), do volunteer, do help old people across the street, do serve valiantly in the military, and so forth.

But we also know that many young Americans don't vote, don't read the newspaper, don't serve their communities, and show dwindling interest in current affairs. Worse, there is the huge problem of young people whose lives are influenced mainly by gangs, street culture, hip hop, and the worst of movies and television. These young people lack good role models at home and have few ties to civil society.

Which brings the problem into clearer focus. Let me recap. First, we are ambivalent about the role of the schools in teaching citizenship. Second, U.S. schools don't do a very good job today, either on the cognitive side or on the attitudinal and behavioral side. Third, though nearly all children suffer from the schools' shortcomings on the cognitive side, many fare reasonably well when it comes to the behavioral aspects of citizenship, thanks to other healthy influences in their lives. Fourth, young people without such influences are doubly victimized by the schools' failings—because they have little with which to compensate, either in acquiring knowledge or in forging decent civic values.

The Pitfalls of Civics Education

Can this knot of problems be untangled and solved? Many are trying. Innumerable foundations, commissions, state initiatives, and federal programs are now seeking to renew civic education in American schools. But solutions run headlong into a series of barriers. Four of these seem especially troublesome.

- First, efforts to develop a civics curriculum are snagged by a basic truth about America: beyond a narrow core of shared beliefs (honesty, tolerance, obeying the law), Americans hold strong but often divergent views about the values they want their children to acquire and about the role of teachers and schools in inculcating those values. It may, therefore, be impossible for the publicly operated schools of a society that is so diverse to do a good job of forging citizens. Consider the challenge of deciding what experiences constitute "service learning" for high-school students in jurisdictions where this is now expected as part of a civics class or social studies curriculum. Does volunteering in one's church qualify? In an abortion clinic? Bringing coffee and donuts to grateful GIs at the nearby military base? Leading a protest against military action? When adults heatedly disagree about the value of such activities, how can a democracy's public schools decide on their proper role in the lives and education of the young?

Fierce watchdog groups constantly scrutinize the public schools for signs of religiosity. Activists pressure schools to redefine "civic education" in terms of influencing public policy and engaging in political activity—while giving short shrift to being a good parent, dependable neighbor, and conscientious member of the nongovernmental institutions that compose civil society. And everybody gangs up on textbooks, which are afflicted by hypersensitivity to the possibility of bias or controversy. This baleful influence comes from both the left and the right.

Hence much gets omitted from class materials and much of what remains has been sanitized to the point of banality. This has the effect of depriving schools and teachers of many of the stories, books, poems, plays, and legends from which children might best learn the difference between good and evil, right and wrong, hero and villain, patriot and traitor. Moreover, the fear of being criticized by pressure groups encourages curriculum writers and textbook publishers to make their instructional materials value-free from the outset.

- Second, within the field of civics education, a battle rages between those who believe that the schools' responsibility is mainly cognitive (imparting specific knowledge to children) and those who insist that youngsters' behavior and attitudes are what schools should work on. It's one thing to explain the role of voting in a democracy, for example, but quite another to help young people acquire the habit of voting or internalize a sense of obligation that they must vote. For many civic educators, these habits, beliefs, and dispositions matter more than "book learning." For example, a recent Carnegie Corporation report, *The Civic Mission of Schools,* offers four takes on "competent and responsible citizens." The first of these says such citizens are "informed and thoughtful," which can mesh with a cognitive view of the school's role. But the other three—"participate in their communities," "act politically," and "have moral and civic virtues"—are harder to instill through conventional books and teaching. They rekindle old debates about the propriety and competency of schools' intruding into people's beliefs and behaviors.

Recall that, in the 1980s, a number of states poked into students' values and behavior through what was termed "outcomes-based" education. This began innocently and earnestly, as a logical response to the era's focus on school results rather than simply inputs. As it spread to include pupil attitudes, actions, and ideologies, however, many people balked at what they saw as government imposing patterns of behavior and thought on children under the guise of mandatory academic standards. For example, the Minnesota state board of education proposed in 1991 that high-school graduation should hinge on students' contributing to "global communities" and the "economic well-being of society," understanding the "interdependency of people," and "working cooperatively in groups." Rightly or not, some parents and religious leaders held that these smacked of socialism and one-worldism, if not Marxism, and that the state had no business imposing such things on its young people. The upshot was that most jurisdictions pulled back to the more strictly cognitive domains.

- Third, there are the limits of schooling itself. Between birth and age 18, a typical young American spends just 14 percent of waking hours beneath the school roof. That's barely enough time to cover reading, writing, and arithmetic well, much less to offset the harmful influences that may be at work on children during the other 86 percent of their lives. In response, one may want the school day or year to lengthen, and many good schools, especially those serving disadvantaged students, have striven to enlarge their portion of children's lives. But the overwhelming majority of schools start at about 8 a.m. and end around 2 p.m. Moreover, they are in session for only half the days in the year. Nor do children go near a public school until the age of five or six. How large a share of responsibility for shaping tomorrow's citizens is it practical for those schools to shoulder?

- Fourth and finally, the civic and pedagogical values of many educators differ from those of many parents. Faithful to "progressive" traditions and postmodern beliefs, too many education school professors signal to future teachers that they should abjure firm distinctions between right and wrong. Nowhere is this more evident than in the social studies—the part of the curriculum that is commonly held responsible for civics education.

The man in the street probably supposes that social studies consist mainly of history and civics, leavened with some geography and economics. At the end of a well-taught K–12 social studies sequence, one would expect young people to know at least who Abraham Lincoln and Theodore Roosevelt were, why

World War II was fought, how to find Italy and Iraq on a map, and what "supply and demand" mean.

If that were so, school-based social studies would contribute to the forging of citizens, at least on the cognitive side. But that's not what animates the experts who rule this field. They are more concerned with imparting multiple "perspectives" to students, as described in a position paper of the National Council for the Social Studies (NCSS):

> Students should be helped to construct a personal perspective that enables them to explore emerging events and persistent or recurring issues, considering implications for self, family, and the whole national and world community. This perspective involves respect for differences of opinion and preference; of race, religion, and gender; of class and ethnicity; and of culture in general. This construction should be based on the realization that differences exist among individuals and the conviction that this diversity can be positive and socially enriching.

One may or may not find these to be valid goals for social studies, but it's reasonably safe to say that, as a framework for civics education in particular, they will stir dissent from American parents, voters, and taxpayers. Thus a clash is inevitable between what we can term the social studies view of civics and the popular view. Indeed, such a clash has been under way for decades. "During the 1930s," writes New York University scholar Diane Ravitch, "one national report after another insisted that social studies should replace chronological history and that young people should study immediate personal and social problems rather than the distant, irrelevant past."

Diversity in Civics Education

Can education reformers overcome these four barriers and place American schools on a sure-footed path to effective civics education? I think not, at least not through top-down reform strategies that emphasize uniform school practices, and certainly not as long as the real pressure for performance and accountability centers on reading and math.

There is, however, another possibility for strengthening civics education. It is to be found in the reform strategy known as school choice. Besides its other strengths, school choice sidesteps one of the big obstacles to better civic education: it accommodates the divergent views and priorities of ethnic and religious groups, parents, and educators, and allows them to tailor the approach to civics that they favor for their children rather than settling for awkward efforts at lowest-common-denominator consensus. Parents who decide that a

given school's approach is not right for their daughters and sons are free to make other selections.

The accompanying risk is balkanization: discordant approaches to civic education as one school emphasizes Athenian values while another stresses those of Sparta. In response, choice proponents cite evidence that private school students are more civically engaged than their public school peers. They remind us that government-operated schools are doomed to do a lackluster job in this area. And they note that, as long as states retain the authority to establish core academic standards for all public schools, they have the opportunity to mitigate curricular balkanization, even in such fractious fields as social studies.

Although certain forms of school choice (tax credits, some voucher programs) abjure state academic standards and tests, others (such as charter schools and public school choice) normally take them for granted. Hence if the state—or other cognizant authority—can get its civics standards right, can attach decent assessments to them, and can steel itself to insist that student performance in this field "counts," it will go a considerable distance toward infusing both standards-based and choice-based education reform with a decent possibility of making a difference in this field.

But those are enormous ifs. All the aforementioned obstacles in society and within the education profession impede any large political unit (such as a state) from attaining consensus about what should be in its civics standards—much less tying an enforcement regimen to them. Today's pressure to boost math and reading achievement makes it less likely that the requisite political energy and resources can be mustered on behalf of a field like civics. The fractures within social studies and the ambivalence of parents will tend to deter public officials from even trying very hard. Moreover, the aspects of civics that can be spelled out in academic standards and accurately assessed through statewide tests are almost entirely cognitive: well worth learning, to be sure, even a necessary precondition for successful adult life, but not exactly what people have in mind when they say that schools should forge "responsible citizens."

In the end, we may need to accept the fact that the school's—and the state's—role in this domain is simply limited: by its meager portion of children's lives, by its pedagogical weakness, by the absence of political and intellectual consensus, and by the modest capabilities of state standards and tests. We may do well to acknowledge that the solemn duty of readying young people for successful participation in adult society depends at least as much—and perhaps quite a lot more—on what happens to them when they are not in school.

POSTNOTE

From the birth of our nation forward, preparation in citizenship has been a goal of education. Our Founding Fathers, and the leaders who have followed them, realized that to sustain a liberal democracy people must both understand what that involves, but also be ready to live in accordance with its percepts. For our country to "work," we must both talk the talk *and* walk the walk.

Chester Finn, a leading educational policy expert, suggests that one of America's great achievements—an ethnically, religiously, and racially diverse society—is inhibiting public school teachers and administrators from effectively addressing the teaching of citizenship. The problem, according to Finn, is that the term *citizenship* contains conflicting behavioral and attitudinal referents. Are you a good citizen if you join an anti-war movement? Are you a good citizen if you join the Marines? In effect, *good citizenship* has become a loaded term.

One possible solution to this problem of citizenship is for the schools to focus more on teaching and instilling the core moral values upon which citizenship in a liberal democracy rests. For our nation to prosper and for individuals to develop their potentials, both need certain moral habits or virtues, such as the habit of taking responsibility, of being honest in dealing with one another, of knowing how to persevere in the face of difficulty, and, of course, knowing how to be tolerant of others. If students are educated in these values and others—such as fairness, kindness, and care for the less fortunate—they will, in effect, be able to transcend narrow disagreements of competing views of citizenship.

Discussion Questions

1. What are the author's key criticisms of public education?
2. What are the barriers to effectively teaching citizenship in our current public schools?
3. The author sees school choice as a means to more effectively teach citizenship. Do you agree? Why or why not?

RELATED WEBSITE RESOURCES AND VIDEO CASES

 ### Web Resources:

The Thomas Fordham Institute. Available at:

http://www.fordhaminstitute.org/template/index.cfm.

This educational policy center, whose president is the author of the previous article, has been a major voice in school reform efforts and various choice-related research efforts.

Citizenship Education. Available at:

http://www.citizenshipeducation.org/home.html.

This website is supported by a small family foundation. One of many such citizenship education efforts, this site provides teachers and students with excellent materials to engage in citizenship education.

Video Case:

Philosophical Foundations of American Education: Four Philosophies in Action

In this video, you will see how four different philosophical frameworks—progressivist, critical theory, perennialism, and essentialism—shape various teachers' practices in the classroom. As you watch the clips and study the artifacts in the case, reflect upon the following questions:

1. How do the philosophical frameworks and educational theories presented in these four videos help you examine your own emerging philosophical beliefs? What questions have these examples raised in your mind?
2. How would you compare and contrast the perennialist and progressive philosophies presented in these videos?

The Quality School Curriculum

William Glasser

William Glasser, MD, is a board-certified psychiatrist and founder and president of the William Glasser Institute, an international training organization devoted to teaching his ideas in countries across the world.

"The Quality School Curriculum" by William Glasser, *Phi Delta Kappan,* May 1992. Reprinted by permission of the author.

F O C U S QUESTION

What elements do you believe constitute a quality school curriculum?

Recently I had a chance to talk to the staff members of a high school who had been hard at work for six months trying to change their school into a Quality School. They believed that they were much less coercive than in the past, but they complained that many of their students were still not working hard and that a few continued to be disruptive. They admitted that things were better but asked me if maybe they should reinject a little coercion back into their classroom management in order to "stimulate" the students to work harder.

I assured them that the answer to their complaints was to use less, not more, coercion. At the same time, I realized that in their teaching they had not yet addressed a vital component of the Quality School, the curriculum. To complete the move from coercive boss-managing to noncoercive lead-managing,[1] they had to change the curriculum they were teaching.

This was made ever clearer to me during the break when I talked to a few teachers individually. They told me that they had already made many of the changes that I suggest below and that they were not having the problems with students that most of the staff members were having. Until almost all the teachers change their curriculum, I strongly believe that they will be unable to rid their classrooms of the coercion that causes too many of their students to continue to be their adversaries.

In Chapter 1 of *The Quality School,* I briefly cited the research of Linda McNeil of Rice University to support my claim that boss-management is destructive to the quality of the curriculum.[2] From feedback I have been receiving, it seems that the schools that are trying to become Quality Schools have not paid enough attention to this important point. I am partly at fault. When I wrote *The Quality School,* I did not realize how vital it is for teachers to make sure that they teach quality, and I did not explain sufficiently what this means. To correct this shortcoming, I want to expand on what I wrote in the book, and I strongly encourage staff members of all the schools that seek to move to quality to spend a great deal of time discussing this matter.

We must face the fact that a majority of students, even good ones, believe that much of the present academic curriculum is not worth the effort it takes to learn it. No matter how well the teachers manage them, if students do not find quality in what they are asked to do in their classes, they will not work hard enough to learn the material. The answer is not to try to make them work harder; the answer is to increase the quality of what we ask them to learn.

Faced with students who refuse to make much effort, even teachers who are trying to become lead-managers give a lot of low grades—a practice so traditional that they fail to perceive it as coercive. Then the students deal with their low grades by rebelling and working even less than before. The teachers, in turn, resent this attitude. They believe that, because they are making the effort to be less coercive, the students should be appreciative and work harder. The teachers fail to see that the students are not rebelling against them and their efforts to become lead-managers; they are rebelling against a curriculum that lacks quality. Therefore, if we want to create Quality Schools, we must stop *all* coercion, not just some, and one way to do this is to create a quality curriculum.

Before I describe a quality curriculum, let me use a simple nonschool example to try to explain what it is about the curriculum we have now that lacks quality. Suppose you get a job in a factory making both black shoes and brown shoes. You are well-managed and do quality work. But soon you become aware that all the brown shoes you make are sold for scrap; only the black shoes are going into retail stores. How long would you continue to work hard on the brown shoes? As you slack off, however, you are told that this is not acceptable and that you will lose pay or be fired if you don't buckle down and do just as good a job on the brown as on the black. You are told that what happens to the brown shoes is none of your business. Your job is to work hard. Wouldn't it be almost impossible to do as you are told?

As silly as the preceding example may seem, students in schools, even students in colleges and graduate schools, are asked to learn well enough to remember for important tests innumerable facts that both they and their teachers know are of no use except to pass the tests. I call this throwaway information because, after they do the work to learn it, that is just what students do with it. Dates and places in history, the names of parts of organisms and organs in biology, and formulas in mathematics and science are all examples of throwaway information.

Newspapers sometimes publish accounts of widespread cheating in schools and label it a symptom of the moral disintegration of our society. But what they call "cheating" turns out to be the ways that students have devised to avoid the work of memorizing throwaway knowledge. The honest students who are penalized are not pleased, but many students and faculty members and most of the informed public do not seem unduly upset about the "cheating." They are aware that there is no value to much of what students are asked to remember. I certainly do not condone cheating, but

I must stress that, as long as we have a curriculum that holds students responsible for throwaway information, there will be cheating—and few people will care.

Elsewhere I have suggested that this throwaway knowledge could also be called "nonsense."[3] While it is not nonsense to ask students to be aware of formulas, dates, and places and to know how to use them and where to find them if they need them, it becomes nonsense when we ask students to memorize this information and when we lower their grades if they fail to do so. Whether called throwaway knowledge or nonsense, this kind of memorized information can never be a part of the curriculum of a Quality School.

This means that in a Quality School there should never be test questions that call for the mere regurgitation of bare facts, such as those written in a book or stored in the memory of a computer. Students should never be asked to commit this portion of the curriculum to memory. All available information on what is being studied should always be on hand, not only during class but during all tests. No student should ever suffer academically because he or she forgot some fact or formula. The only useful way to test students' knowledge of facts, formulas, and other information is to ask not what the information is, but where, when, why, and how it is of use in the real world.

While a complete definition of quality is elusive, it certainly would include usefulness in the real world. And useful need not be restricted to practical or utilitarian. That which is useful can be aesthetically or spiritually useful or useful in some other way that is meaningful to the student—but it can never be nonsense.

In a Quality School, when questions of where, why, when, and how are asked on a test, they are never part of what is called an "objective" test, such as a multiple-choice, true/false, or short answer test. For example, if a multiple-choice test is used to ask where, why, when, and how, the student in a Quality School should not be restricted to a list of predetermined choices. There should always be a place for a student to write out a better answer if he or she believes that the available choices are less accurate than another alternative. For example, a multiple-choice test question in history might be: "George Washington is called 'the father of his country' for the following reasons: [four reasons would then be listed]. Which do you think is the best reason?" The student could choose one of the listed answers or write in another and explain why he or she thought it better than those listed.

In a Quality School questions as narrow as the preceding example would be rare, simply because of the constant effort to relate all that is taught to the lives of the students. Therefore, if a question asking where, when, why, and how certain information could be used were asked, it would always be followed by the further question: "How can you use this information in your life, now or in the future?"

However, such a follow-up question would never come out of the blue. The real-world value of the material to be learned would have been emphasized in lectures, in class discussions, in cooperative learning groups, and even in homework assignments that ask students to discuss with parents or other adults how what they learn in school might be useful outside of school. The purpose of such follow-up questions is to stress that the curriculum in a Quality School focuses on useful skills, not on information that has no use in the lives of those who are taught it. I define a *skill* as the ability to use knowledge. If we emphasized such skills in every academic subject, there would be no rebellion on the part of students. Students could earn equal credit on a test for explaining why what was taught was or was not of use to them. This would encourage them to think, not to parrot the ideas of others.

Continuing with the George Washington question, if a student in a Quality School said that Washington's refusal to be crowned king makes him a good candidate to be considered father of this republic, a teacher could ask that student how he or she could use this information in life now or later. The student might respond that he or she prefers to live in a republic and would not like to live in a country where a king made all the laws. A student's answer could be more complicated than this brief example, but what the student would have thought over would be how Washington's decision affects his or her life today.

Without memorizing any facts, students taught in this way could learn more history in a few weeks than they now learn in years. More important, they would learn to *like* history. Too many students tell me that they hate history, and I find this to be an educational disaster. I hope that what they are really saying is that they hate the history curriculum, not history.

Another important element in the curriculum of a Quality School is that the students be able to *demonstrate* how what they have learned can be used in their lives now or later. Almost all students would have no difficulty accepting that reading, writing, and arithmetic are useful skills, but in a Quality School they would be asked to demonstrate that they can use them. For example, students would not be asked to learn the multiplication tables as if this knowledge were separate from being able to use the tables in their lives.

To demonstrate the usefulness of knowing how to multiply, students would be given problems to solve and asked to show how multiplication helped in solving them. These problems might require the use of several different mathematical processes, and students could show how each process was used. Students would learn not only how to multiply but also when, where, and why to do so. Once students have demonstrated that they know *how* to multiply, the actual multiplication could be done on a small calculator or by referring to tables.

In a Quality School, once students have mastered a mathematical process they would be encouraged to use a calculator. To do math processes involving large numbers over and over is boring and nonessential. Today, most students spend a lot of time memorizing the times tables. They learn how to multiply, but fail to demonstrate when, where, and why to multiply. I will admit that the tables and the calculators do not teach students *how* to multiply, but they are what people in the real world use to find answers—a fact finally recognized by the Educational Testing Service, which now allows the use of calculators on the Scholastic Aptitude Test.

Teachers in a Quality School would teach the "how" by asking students to demonstrate that they can do calculations without a calculator. Students would be told that, as soon as they can demonstrate this ability by hand, they will be allowed to use a calculator. For most students, knowing that they will never be stuck working one long, boring problem after another would be more than enough incentive to get them to learn to calculate.

In a Quality School there would be a great deal of emphasis on the skill of writing and much less on the skill of reading. The reason for this is that anyone who can write well can read well, but many people who can read well can hardly write at all. From grade 1 on, students would be asked to write: first, words; then, sentences and paragraphs; and finally, articles, stories, and letters. An extremely good project is to have each middle school student write a book or keep a journal. Students who do so will leave middle school with an education—even if that is all that they have done.

To write a great deal by hand can be onerous, but using a computer makes the same process highly enjoyable. In a Quality School, all teachers would be encouraged to learn word-processing skills and to teach them to their students. Moreover, these skills should be used in all classes. Computers are more readily available in schools today than would seem to be the case, judging from their actual use. If they are not readily available, funds can be raised to buy the few that would be needed. If students were encouraged to write, we would see fewer students diagnosed as having language learning disabilities.

At Apollo High School,[4] where I consult, the seniors were asked if they would accept writing a good letter on a computer as a necessary requirement for graduation. They agreed, and almost all of them learned to do it. One way they demonstrated that their letters were good was by mailing them and receiving responses. They were thrilled by the answers, which we used as one criterion for satisfying the requirement. Clearly, demonstrating the use of what is learned in a real-life situation is one of the best ways to teach.

While demonstrating is the best way to show that something worthwhile has been learned, it is not always easy or even possible to do so. Thus there must be some tests. But, as I stated above, the tests in a Quality School would always show the acquisition of skills, never the acquisition of facts or information alone.

Let me use an example from science to explain what would be considered a good way to test in a Quality School. Science is mostly the discovery of how and why things work. But where and when they work can also be important. Too much science is taught as a simple listing of what works—e.g., these are the parts of a cell. Students all over America are busy memorizing the parts of a cell, usually by copying and then labeling a cell drawn in a textbook. The students are then tested to see if they can do this from memory—a wonderful example of throwaway information, taught by coercion. Teaching and testing in this way is worse than teaching no science at all, because many students learn to hate science as a result. Hating something as valuable as science is worse than simply not knowing it.

The students in a Quality School would be taught some basics about how a cell works, and they would be told that all living organisms are made up of cells. To show them that this is useful knowledge, the teacher might bring up the subject of cancer, explaining how a cancer cell fails to behave as normal cells do and so can kill the host in which it grows. All students know something about cancer, and all would consider this useful knowledge.

The subsequent test in a Quality School might ask students to describe the workings of a cell (or of some part of a cell) with their books open and available. They would then be asked how they could use this information in their lives and would be encouraged to describe the differences between a normal cell and a cancer cell. They would be taught that one way to use this information might be to avoid exposure to too much sunlight because excessive sunlight can turn normal skin cells into cancer cells. For most students, this information would be of use because all students have some fear of cancer.

Readers might feel some concern that what I am suggesting would not prepare students for standardized tests that mostly ask for throwaway information, such as the identification of the parts of a cell. My answer is that students would be better prepared—because, by learning to *explain* how and why something works, they are more likely to remember what they have learned. Even if less ground is covered, as is likely to be the case when we move from facts to skills, a little ground covered well is better preparation, even for nonsense tests, than a lot of ground covered poorly.

We should never forget that people, not curriculum, are the desired outcomes of schooling. What we want to develop are students who have the skills to become active contributors to society, who are enthusiastic about what they have learned, and who are aware of how learning can be of use to them in the future. The curriculum changes I have suggested above will certainly produce more students who fit this profile.

Will the students agree that these outcomes are desirable? If we accept control theory, the answer is obvious. When the outcomes the teachers want are in the quality worlds of their students, the students will accept them. In my experience skills will be accepted as quality in almost all cases; facts and information will rarely be accepted.

Assuming that skills are taught, the teacher must still explain clearly what will be asked on tests. Sample questions should be given to the students, and the use of all books, notes, and materials should be permitted. Even if a student copies the workings of a cell from a book at the time of the test, the student will still have to explain how this information can be used in life. If students can answer such questions, they can be said to know the material—whether or not they copied some of it.

Tests—especially optional retests for students who wish to improve their grades—can be taken at home and can include such items as, "Explain the workings of a cell to an adult at home, write down at least one question that was asked by that person, and explain how you answered it." All the facts would be available in the test; it is the skill to use them that would be tested. The main thing to understand here is that, after a school stops testing for facts and begins to test for skills, it will not be long before it is clear to everyone that skills are the outcomes that have value; facts and information have none.

In most schools, the teacher covers a body of material, and the students must guess what is going to appear on the test. Some teachers even test for material that they have not covered. In a Quality School this would not happen. There would be no limitation on input, and the teacher would not ask students to figure out which parts of this input will be on the test. There would be no hands raised asking the age-old question, Is this going to be on the test?

Since it is always skills that are tested for in a Quality School, it is very likely that the teacher would make the test available to the students before teaching the unit so that, as they went through the material in class, they would know that these are the skills that need to be learned. Students could also be asked to describe any other skill that they have learned from the study of the material. This is an example of the open-endedness that is always a part of testing and discussion in a Quality School. A number of questions would be implicit in all tests: What can you contribute? What is your opinion? What might I (the teacher) have missed? Can you give a better use or explanation?

Keep in mind that, in a Quality School, students and teachers would evaluate tests. Students who are dissatisfied with either their own or the teacher's evaluation could continue to work on the test and improve. Building on the thinking of W. Edwards Deming, the idea is to constantly improve usable skills. In a Quality School, this opportunity is always open.

As I look over what I have written, I see nothing that requires any teacher to change anything that he or she does. If what I suggest appeals to you, implement it at your own pace. Those of us in the Quality School movement believe in lead-management, so there is no coercion—no pressure on you to hurry. You might wish to begin by discussing any of these ideas with your students. In a Quality School students should be aware of everything that the teachers are trying to do. If it makes sense to them, as I think it will, they will help you to put it into practice.

NOTES

1. For a definition of boss-management and lead-management, see William Glasser, "The Quality School," *Phi Delta Kappan,* February 1990, p. 428.
2. William Glasser, *The Quality School: Managing Students Without Coercion* (New York: Harper & Row, 1990), Ch. 1.
3. See Supplementary Information Bulletin No. 5 of the Quality School Training Program. All of these bulletins are available from the Institute for Reality Therapy, 7301 Medical Center Dr., Suite 104, Canoga Park, CA 91307.
4. Apollo High School is a school for students who refuse to work in a regular high school. It enrolls about 240 students (9–12) and is part of the Simi Valley (Calif.) Unified School District.

POSTNOTE

William Glasser's training as a psychiatrist has enabled him to examine schools and their effects on children in ways that are unique and important, earning his article a place among our Classic selections. His *choice theory* represents an attempt to base schooling on different principles that satisfy students' needs for friendship, freedom, fun, and power. Glasser's philosophy has been implemented by many educators for whom his humanistic approach has great appeal.

Glasser asserts that a majority of students believe that much of the present academic curriculum is not worth the effort needed to learn it. To overcome this problem, Glasser suggests that the quality of what we ask students to learn must be increased. Some guiding principles of this quality curriculum include reducing the quantity of what students are asked to memorize, emphasizing the usefulness of knowledge and the development of useful skills (including writing skills), covering less material, and assessing performance.

Many of Glasser's ideas are compatible with the curriculum reform movement occurring in such fields as mathematics, science, and history. Asking students to construct their own knowledge, rather than memorize packaged knowledge, is clearly the direction in which these curriculum efforts are headed. However, many of the content standards being implemented by states, along with their associated assessments, seem to be emphasizing memorization of facts.

Discussion Questions

1. Do Glasser's ideas appeal to you? Why or why not? What problems, if any, do you see in implementing them?
2. What do you think about Glasser's notion of allowing open-book tests? Explain your position.
3. Glasser states that in looking over his ideas, he sees nothing that requires teachers to change what they do. Do you agree or disagree with his statement? Why?

RELATED WEBSITE RESOURCES

 Web Resources:

William Glasser Institute. Available at:

http://www.wglasser.com.

This website of the William Glasser Institute contains materials, training programs, and information on choice theory.

Teaching What We Hold to Be Sacred

John I. Goodlad

John Goodlad, professor emeritus at the University of Washington, is also president of the Institute for Educational Inquiry and a founder of the Center for Educational Renewal at the University of Washington. He was dean of the Graduate School of Education at UCLA for a number of years, and is known as one of America's advocates and experts on educational renewal.

"Teaching What We Hold to Be Sacred" by John I. Goodlad, *Educational Leadership,* December 2004, pp. 18–21. Used with permission. The Association for Supervision and Curriculum Development is a worldwide community of educators advocating sound policies and sharing best practices to achieve the success of each learner. To learn more, visit ASCD at **www.ascd.org.**

| F | O | C | U | S | QUESTION

What are some ways that schools can address social inequality to promote social justice?

KEY TERMS

Moral ecology
Social justice

On February 1, 1994, the U.S. Postal Service added a new postage stamp honoring Allison Davis to its Black Heritage Series. An important figure in psychology, social anthropology, and education for more than 40 years, Davis was the first person from the field of education to be elected to the American Academy of Arts and Sciences (Unicover, 2003).

In the 1940s, Davis became the first African American ever appointed to a tenured position at a major "white" university, the University of Chicago. His appointment was controversial. Ralph Tyler, chairman of the department of education, and Robert M. Hutchins, president of the university, overcame the opposition's pretext of lack of funds for hiring Davis by securing private funding to underwrite Davis's salary and related expenses for the first three years.

Even so, Davis did not gain access to the amenities that his colleagues took for granted. He unsuccessfully sought housing in the surrounding Hyde Park neighborhood. He was ineligible for membership in the university's Quadrangle Club until women, too, finally gained admittance in 1948. And he could not find living quarters and mixed-race meeting places when conducting field research in the South and the Southwest (Finder, in press).

Much of Davis's research centered on the effects of the color-caste system in U.S. society, particularly on the ways in which biases in standardized intelligence tests unfairly stigmatized poor and minority students. With colleague Robert Havighurst, Davis produced a series of papers arguing that the American social class system actually prevents the vast majority of children of the working classes, or of the slums, from learning any culture but that of their own groups (cited in University of Chicago, 2003).

Davis and Havighurst challenged the conventional wisdom of their day that claimed that social inequalities resulted from racial biological inferiority. They envisioned a day in which this misconception would be replaced by the knowledge that inequalities in achievement stemmed from environmental factors, such as widespread denial of educational and economic opportunities to people of color.

In the ensuing years, innumerable researchers and thinkers have confirmed Davis's message, including James B. Conant (1961), who documented the shameful differences between the relatively lavish provisions for schooling in the suburbs and the shamefully shabby provisions in the inner cities.

Unfortunately, the biological causation thesis as an explanation of social inequality has had a stubborn longevity. As Stephen J. Gould tells us in *The Mismeasure of Man* (1981), researchers (of a sort) have extended this thesis beyond race. Gould's account of the efforts to assign lower levels of intelligence to women because of their generally smaller craniums is eerily hilarious. He cites the French anthropologist Hervé, who savaged women and black men with one stroke in 1881: "Men of the black races have a brain scarcely heavier than that of white women" (p. 3). As Gould points out, attempts to rank people—whether by brain size or by an IQ test score—have consistently recorded "little more than social prejudice" (p. 28).

History demonstrates that people will find ingenious ways and develop elaborate constructs to create and harden categories of status and privilege among the diverse groups that constitute humankind. And they will produce a litany of justifications to convince the populace that these inequalities are natural and right.

One might argue that a more enlightened era has, in part, arrived. The end of legal racial segregation, improved access to higher education for minorities, and increased economic opportunities have improved individual lives. But the caste system is still entrenched in society; social prejudices and injustices remain.

Our Moral Ecology

Will humankind ever manage—or want—to do away with social inequality? The apparent inevitability and tenacity of caste as a way of life may make us feel hopeless about trying to eliminate this system. Why try to reform what exists? To quote the 19th century British politician, Lord Thomas Macaulay, "Reform, reform, don't speak to me of reform. We have enough problems already."

Nonetheless, the history of civilization reveals that in every era, some people, somewhere, have envisioned gaining freedom from the caste system. The themes of enlightenment have been argued from both the rational and the divine perspectives. The two perspectives have come together to form a central core of common principles. This evolving center, never static, takes on a kind of cultural sacredness, an abstract moral ecology. It provides, in Seymour Sarason's words, a "sense of interconnections among the individual, the collectivity, and ultimate purpose and meaning of human existence" (1986, p. 899).

In societies seeking to balance the private and public good, we might well consider what we commonly hold sacred. If our moral ecology encompasses equality and social justice, and if we want that moral ecology to guide our society, then equality and social justice must be taught—carefully taught.

Many people assign to our schools the task of nurturing these values in the populace. In its much lauded experiment, universal schooling, the United States set as a major purpose the enculturation of the young—specifically the children of immigrants—into a social and political democracy.

But when we place this responsibility entirely on schools, we forget that between the years of 6 and 18, young people spend approximately 55 percent of their time in activities other than school and sleep. We give little critical thought to the cacophony of teaching that now surrounds our young throughout the day, and nearly all of which is driven by economic ends rather than by the ideals of education that we espouse in the rhetoric of school and college graduation ceremonies.

Political scientist Benjamin Barber brings our attention sharply to the daunting task that schools undertake when they attempt to develop students' democratic character amid the ubiquitous culture that surrounds young people throughout the day:

> We honor ambition, we reward greed, we celebrate materialism, we worship acquisitiveness, we cherish success, and we commercialize the classroom—and then we bark at the young about the gentle art of the spirit. (1993, p. 42)

The Role of Schools

In spite of the obstacles, it would be the height of folly for our schools not to have as their central mission educating the young in the democratic ideals of humankind, the freedoms and responsibilities of a democratic society, and the civil and civic understandings and dispositions necessary to democratic citizenship. And yet here we are, hardening into place the caste categories linked to test scores, a practice that directly impedes such a mission. When polls ask people what they want of their schools, the people say over and over that the personal and social development of their children is just as important to them as vocational and academic development. As the accumulating body of knowledge about cognition clearly reveals, test scores do not correlate at all with the other attributes that people believe their schools should develop in students.

But not to worry. High test scores will get your offspring into a college or university if the money is available from family resources or scholarships. Forget those who dominate among the low scorers, such as low-income children whose late-in-the-year birthdays kept them out of kindergarten for most of an additional year, during which their families had no resources to send them to preschool. Funding for Head Start did not quite embrace their neighborhoods. And, oh yes, those children in the inner cities who had substitute teachers for every year of their schooling did not reach the upper levels of test scores, either. But let us keep the system, anyway—it offers special rewards for those who succeed and who then join the upper levels of the layers of power.

We need to pay increased attention to the commonalities that bind humankind. Our schools are not lacking in the rhetoric of "respecting diversity" and social studies texts extolling "understanding other people." What *other* people?

We all belong to one species—humankind. There is only one ongoing conversation—the human conversation, consisting of the work, play, parenting, conversing, and imagining in which we all engage and of the beliefs, hopes, and aspirations that we hold. To be sure, within those commonalities there is rich diversity—not only in the rainbow of colors to which the Reverend Jesse Jackson refers, but also in all human characteristics. The diversity in color, language, song, ceremony, religion, games, flora, and fauna that exists among us adds to the miracle of life. Why else do we travel to other parts of the world?

But if we begin with the concept of one humankind and then add the concept of diversity in addressing such democratic essentials as liberty and justice for all, we embark on a slippery slope. Some years ago, a critic attacked the late Ernest Boyer's book, *High School* (1983), and my book, *A Place Called School* (1984), on the grounds that we did not address special education. A specialist in the field defended us by pointing out that we *had* addressed special education—by advocating individualized education for all students.

A few years later, Thomas Lovitt and I were gently taken to task for our advocacy of integrating general and special education (Goodlad & Lovitt, 1993). Critics argued that the road to bringing attention—some of it now required by federal law—to students who require substantial deviations from the norms of schooling had been a rocky one. Many of the hard-won gains could be wiped out if schools eliminated special education as a separate service, even with the best intentions of providing for the individual differences and education needs of all children. We agreed with their assessment. Our agreement did not change our basic argument for the benefits of bringing general and special education together in classrooms, but it did caution us to emphasize that exceptional provisions are sometimes necessary to provide equal opportunity in education. The same perspective applies to our efforts to provide equal education opportunities to diverse students, no matter what type of diversity we mean.

Beyond Social Caste

The struggle for justice, equity, respect, and appreciation for human diversity has been long and often troubled. It continues to be so. The human race's proclivity for arranging its members in hierarchies of strongly maintained status and privilege is likely to continue as a malaise that can become cancerous.

The answer, we know, is education. But education, despite our honoring the concept, is not in itself good. We must intentionally and even passionately inject morality into education (Goodlad, 1999).

Winston Churchill said, "Democracy is the worst form of government except for all those others that have been tried." If we agree, we must do more than teach students only about the political structures of democracy. We must teach students the ideals of democracy and social equality and give our young people opportunities to practice those ideals in their daily lives, both in and out of school.

Unless we work simultaneously as a society to eliminate in our schools and society a caste system harboring and even fostering beliefs and practices that contradict these ideals, our hypocrisy will become transparent. We are all participants in the informal education that goes on outside of schools. The larger community must ensure a democracy that protects and supports the democratic education that needs to go on inside of schools. The clear purpose of schooling, then, becomes attending to all those educational matters that the larger community does not address, especially enculturating the young into satisfying, responsible citizens in a social and political democracy.

Once formal education inside of schools and informal education outside of schools, working together, make morally grounded democratic behavior routine—as John Dewey said it must become—such principles as justice, equity, and freedom for everyone will need no special advocacy. But when we parcel them out into the tiers of caste privilege, as we often do today, we endanger these precious principles.

REFERENCES

Barber, B. R. (1993, November). America skips school. *Harper's Magazine, 286*, 42.

Boyer, E. L. (1983). *High school.* New York: Harper & Row.

Conant, J. B. (1961). *Slums and suburbs: A commentary on schools in metropolitan areas.* New York: McGraw-Hill.

Finder, M. (in press). *Educating America: The extraordinary career of Ralph W. Tyler.* New York: Praeger.

Goodlad, J. I. (1984). *A place called school.* New York: McGraw-Hill.

Goodlad, J. I. (1999). Convergence. In R. Soder, J. I. Goodlad, & T. J. McMannon (Eds.), *Developing Democratic Character in the Young* (pp. 1–25). San Francisco: Jossey-Bass.

Goodlad, J. I., & Lovitt, T. C. (Eds.). (1993). *Integrating general and special education.* New York: Merrill.

Gould, S. J. (1981). *The mismeasure of man.* New York: W. W. Norton.

Sarason, S. B. (1986, August). And what is the public interest? *American Psychologist, 41,* 899.

Unicover. (2003). *U.S. proofcard: 29¢ Dr. Allison Davis: Black heritage series* [Online]. Available: **www.unicover.com/ EA4PAD1J.htm**

University of Chicago. (2003). *The University of Chicago faculty: A centennial view—Allison Davis/Education* [Online]. Available: **www.lib.uchicago.edu/ projects/centcat/centcats/fac/facch25_01.html**

POSTNOTE

John Goodlad is one of the elder statesmen of education. He has written on many different topics throughout his career, such as teacher education, curriculum, and instruction. On all of these topics, he focuses on the important, salient features and never becomes bogged down in details. In this article, he addresses one of the ultimate purposes of public schooling in a democratic society: ensuring that principles of equality and social justice are carefully taught.

With our current focus on content standards, high-stakes testing, and other accountability features, Goodlad reminds us that most parents want more from our schools than this emphasis on acquiring knowledge. They want their children to learn the freedoms and responsibilities of living in a democracy. Sometimes, we lose sight of this most important goal of schooling. As Socrates said, education has a dual responsibility: to make people smart and to make people good.

Discussion Questions

1. In your own schooling, did you receive specific instruction or lessons on social justice or civic responsibility? If so, can you describe them?
2. Can you think of any events that you observed in school that violated the concept of social justice and equality? Was anything done about them? If so, what?
3. If you were to design a school that focused strongly on civic responsibility, social justice, and equality, what would be some of its practices?

RELATED WEBSITE RESOURCES

 ### Web Resources:

Institute for Educational Inquiry. Available at:

http://www.ieiseattle.org/.

This site of the Institute for Educational Inquiry contains links to other affiliated organizations that promote educational efforts in a democracy.

23

The Relevance of Religion to the Curriculum

Warren A. Nord

Warren A. Nord works in the philosophy of the humanities, the philosophy of religion, the philosophy of education (especially moral education), and the relationship of religion and education.

"The Relevance of Religion to the Curriculum" by Warren A. Nord, *The School Administrator,* January 1999. Reprinted by permission of American Association of School Administrators.

F O C U S QUESTION

What, if anything, should public schools teach about religion?

For some time now, public school administrators have been on the front lines of our culture wars over religion and education—and I expect it would be music to their ears to hear that peace accords have been signed.

Unfortunately, the causes of war are deep-seated. Peace is not around the corner.

At the same time, however, it is also easy to overstate the extent of the hostilities. At least at the national level—but also in many communities across America—a large measure of common ground has been found. The leaders of most major national educational, religious and civil liberties organizations agree about the basic principles that should govern the role of religion and public schools. No doubt we don't agree about everything, but we agree about a lot.

For example, in 1988, a group of 17 major religious and educational organizations—the American Jewish Congress and the Islamic Society of North America, the National Association of Evangelicals and the National Council of Churches, the National Education Association and American Federation of Teachers, the National School Boards Association and AASA among them—endorsed a statement of principles that describes the importance of religion in the public school curriculum.

The statement, in part, says this: "Because religion plays significant roles in history and society, study about religion is essential to understanding both the nation and the world. Omission of facts about religion can give students the false impression that the religious life of humankind is insignificant or unimportant. Failure to understand even the basic symbols, practices and concepts of the various religions makes much of history, literature, art and contemporary life unintelligible."

A Profound Problem

As a result of this (and other "common ground" statements) it is no longer controversial to assert that the study of religion has a legitimate and important place in the public school curriculum.

Where in the curriculum? In practice, the study of religion has been relegated almost entirely to history texts and courses, for it is widely assumed that religion is irrelevant to every other subject in the curriculum—that is, to understanding the world here and now.

This is a deeply controversial assumption, however. A profoundly important educational problem lingers here, one that is almost completely ignored by educators.

Let me put it this way. Several ways exist for making sense of the world here and now. Many Americans accept one or another religious interpretation of reality; others accept one or another secular interpretation. We don't agree—and the differences among us often cut deeply.

Yet public schools systematically teach students to think about the world in secular ways only. They don't even bother to inform them about religious alternatives—apart from distant history. That is, public schooling discriminates against religious ways of making sense of the world. This is no minor problem.

An Economic Argument

To get some sense of what's at issue, let's consider economics.

One can think about the economic domain of life in various ways. Scriptural texts in all religious traditions address questions of justice and morality, poverty and wealth, work and stewardship, for example. A vast body of 20th century literature in moral theology deals with economic issues. Indeed most mainline denominations and ecumenical agencies have official statements on justice and economics. What's common to all of this literature is the claim that the economic domain of life cannot be understood apart from religion.

Needless to say, this claim is not to be found in economics textbooks. Indeed, if we put end to end all the references to religion in the 10 high school economics texts I've reviewed in the past few years, they would add up to about two pages—out of 4,400 pages combined (and all of the references are to premodern times). There is but a single reference to religion—a passing mention in a section on taxation and non-profit organizations—in the 47 pages of the new national content standards in economics. Moreover, the textbooks and the standards say virtually nothing about the problems that are the major concern of theologians—problems relating to poverty, justice, our consumer culture, the Third World, human dignity and the meaningfulness of work.

The problem isn't just that the texts ignore religion and those economic problems of most concern to theologians. A part of the problem is what the texts do teach—that is, neoclassical economic theory. According to the texts, economics is a science, people are essentially self-interested utility-maximizers, the economic realm is one of competition for scarce resources, values are personal preferences and value judgments are matters of cost-benefit analysis. Of course, no religious tradition accepts this understanding of human nature, society, economics and values.

That is, the texts and standards demoralize and secularize economics.

An Appalling Claim

To be sure, they aren't explicitly hostile to religion; rather they ignore it. But in some ways this is worse than explicit hostility, for students remain unaware of the fact that there are tensions and conflicts between their religious traditions and what they are taught about economics.

In fact, the texts and the standards give students no sense that what they are learning is controversial. Indeed, the national economics standards make it a matter of principle that students be kept in the dark about alternatives to neoclassical theory. As the editors put it in their introduction, the standards were developed to convey a single conception of economics, the "majority paradigm" or neoclassical model of economic behavior. For, they argue, to include "strongly held minority views of economic processes [would only risk] confusing and frustrating teachers and students who are then left with the responsibility of sorting the qualifications and alternatives without a sufficient foundation to do so."

This is an appalling statement. It means, in effect, that students should be indoctrinated; they should be given no critical perspective on neoclassical economic theory.

The problem with the economics texts and standards is but one aspect of the much larger problem that cuts across the curriculum, for in every course students are taught to think in secular ways that often (though certainly not always) conflict with religious alternatives. And this is always done uncritically.

Even in history courses, students learn to think about historical meaning and causation in exclusively secular ways in spite of the fact that Judaism, Christianity and Islam all hold that God acts in history, that there is a religious meaning to history. True, they learn a few facts about religion, but they learn to think about history in secular categories.

Nurturing Secularity

Outside of history courses and literature courses that use historical literature, religion is rarely even mentioned, but even on those rare occasions when it is, the intellectual context is secular. As a result, public education nurtures a secular mentality. This marginalizes religion from our cultural and intellectual life and contributes powerfully to the secularization of our culture.

Ignoring religious ways of thinking about the world is a problem for three important reasons.

•   *It is profoundly illiberal.*

Here, of course, I'm not using the term "liberal" to refer to the left wing of the Democratic Party. A liberal education is a broad education, one that provides students with the perspective to think critically about the world and their lives. A good liberal education should introduce students—at least older students—to the major ways humankind has developed for making sense of the world and their lives. Some of those ways of thinking and living are religious and it is illiberal to leave them out of the discussion. Indeed, it may well constitute indoctrination—secular indoctrination.

We indoctrinate students when we uncritically initiate them into one way of thinking and systematically ignore the alternatives. Indeed, if students are to be able to think critically about the secular ways of understanding the world that pervade the curriculum, they must understand something about the religious alternatives.

•   *It is politically unjust.*

Public schools must take the public seriously. But religious parents are now, in effect, educationally disenfranchised. Their ways of thinking and living aren't taken seriously.

Consider an analogy. A generation ago textbooks and curricula said virtually nothing about women, blacks and members of minority subcultures. Hardly anyone would now say that that was fair or just. We now—most of us—realize this was a form of discrimination, of educational disenfranchisement. And so it is with religious subcultures (though, ironically, the multicultural movement has been almost entirely silent about religion).

•   *It is unconstitutional.*

It is, of course, uncontroversial that it is constitutionally permissible to teach about religion in public schools when done properly. No Supreme Court justice has ever held otherwise. But I want to make a stronger argument.

The court has been clear that public schools must be neutral in matters of religion—in two senses. Schools must be neutral among religions (they can't favor Protestants over Catholics or Christians over Jews), and they must be neutral between religion and nonreligion. Schools can't promote religion. They can't proselytize. They can't conduct religious exercises.

Of course, neutrality is a two-edged sword. Just as schools can't favor religion over nonreligion, neither can they favor nonreligion over religion. As Justice Hugo Black put it in the seminal 1947 *Everson* ruling, "State power is no more to be used so as to handicap religions than it is to favor them."

Similarly, in his majority opinion in *Abington* v. *Schempp* in 1963, Justice Tom Clark wrote that schools can't favor "those who believe in no religion over those who do believe." And in a concurring opinion, Justice Arthur Goldberg warned that an "untutored devotion to the concept of neutrality [can lead to a] pervasive devotion to the secular and a passive, or even active, hostility to the religious."

Of course this is just what has happened. An untutored, naïve conception of neutrality has led educators to look for a smoking gun, an explicit hostility to religion, when the hostility has been philosophically rather more subtle—though no less substantial for that.

The only way to be neutral when all ground is contested ground is to be fair to the alternative. That is, given the Supreme Court's longstanding interpretation of the Establishment Clause, public schools must require the study of religion if they require the study of disciplines that cumulatively lead to a pervasive devotion to the secular—as they do.

Classroom Practices

So how can we be fair? What would a good education look like? Here I can only skim the surface—and refer readers to *Taking Religion Seriously Across the Curriculum*, in which Charles Haynes and I chart what needs to be done in some detail.

Obviously a great deal depends on the age of students. In elementary schools students should learn something of the relatively uncontroversial aspects of different religions—their traditions, holidays, symbols and a little about religious histories, for example. As students mature, they should be initiated into the conversation about truth and goodness that constitutes a good liberal education. Here a two-prong approach is required.

First, students should learn something about religious ways of thinking about any subject that is religiously controversial in the relevant courses. So, for example, a biology text should include a chapter in which scientific ways of understanding nature are contrasted with religious alternatives. Students should learn that the relationship of religion and science is controversial, and that while they will learn what most biologists believe to be the truth about nature, not everyone agrees.

Indeed, every text and course should provide students with historical and philosophical perspective on the subject at hand, establishing connections and tensions with other disciplines and domains of the culture, including religion.

This is not a balanced-treatment or equal-time requirement. Biology courses should continue to be biology courses and economics courses should continue to be economics courses. In any case, given their competence and training, biology and economics teachers are not likely to be prepared to deal with a variety of religious ways of approaching their subject. At most, they can provide a minimal fairness.

A robust fairness is possible only if students are required to study religious as well as secular ways of making sense of the world in some depth, in courses devoted to the study of religion.

A good liberal education should require at least one year-long high school course in religious studies (with other courses, I would hope, available as electives). The primary goal of such a course should be to provide students with a sufficiently intensive exposure to religious ways of thinking and living to enable them to actually understand religion (rather than simply know a few facts about religion). It should expose students to scriptural texts, but it also should use more recent primary sources that enable students to understand how contemporary theologians and writers within different traditions think about those subjects in the curriculum—morality, sexuality, history, nature, psychology and the economic world—that they will be taught to interpret in secular categories in their other courses.

Of course, if religion courses are to be offered, there must be teachers competent to teach them. Religious studies must become a certifiable field in public education, and new courses must not be offered or required until competent teachers are available.

Indeed, all teachers must have a much clearer sense of how religion relates to the curriculum and, more particularly, to their respective subjects. Major reforms in teacher education are necessary—as is a new generation of textbooks sensitive to religion.

Some educators will find it unrealistic to expect such reforms. Of course several decades ago textbooks and curricula said little about women and minority cultures. Several decades ago, few universities had departments of religious studies. Now multicultural education is commonplace and most universities have departments of religious studies. Things change.

Stemming an Exodus

No doubt some educators will find these proposals controversial, but they will be shortsighted if they do. Leaving religion out of the curriculum is also controversial. Indeed, because public schools don't take religion seriously many religious parents have deserted them and, if the Supreme Court upholds the legality of vouchers, as they may well do, the exodus will be much greater.

In the long run, the least controversial position is the one that takes everyone seriously. If public schools are to survive our culture wars, they must be built on common ground. But there can be no common ground when religious voices are left out of the curricular conversation.

It is religious conservatives, of course, who are most critical of public schooling—and the most likely to leave. But my argument is that public schooling doesn't take any religion seriously. It marginalizes all religion—liberal as well as conservative, Catholic as well as Protestant, Jewish, Muslim and Buddhist as well as Christian. Indeed, it contributes a great deal to the secularization of American culture—and this should concern any religious person.

But, in the end, this shouldn't concern religious people only. Religion should be included in the curriculum for three very powerful secular reasons. The lack of serious study of religion in public education is illiberal, unjust and unconstitutional.

POSTNOTE

Parents rightfully want to pass on to their children their most deeply held beliefs. Many of these beliefs, like what constitutes a good life and what is a person's true nature, are theological questions that are embedded in their religious convictions. For a variety of reasons, many of which are touched on in this article, the public schools have ignored and marginalized religion. Besides the educational implications of this policy, the impact on the public support of public schools is beginning to show. America is a religious nation, founded on religious principles ("In God we trust" and "All men are created equal"). Also, about 80 percent of American adults describe themselves as belonging to some religion. It would seem, then, that the current condition of the two powerful educational influences on children—the media and the public school system—being areligious or anti-religious is bound to have political consequences. Since parents can do little to punish Hollywood, the temptation is strong to take out their resentments on the local, tax-supported schools.

Discussion Questions

1. Warren Nord ends his essay with the words, "The lack of serious study of religion in public education is illiberal, unjust and unconstitutional." What is your reaction to this statement?
2. Has your previous school experience strengthened, undermined, or had no effect on your religious convictions?
3. What solutions does Nord offer to the problem he has outlined? Do you agree with them? Why? Why not?

RELATED WEBSITE RESOURCES

 Web Resources:

Guidance on Constitutionally Protected Prayer in Public Elementary and Secondary Schools. Available at:

http://www.ed.gov/policy/gen/guid/ religionandschools/prayer_guidance.html.

This website by the U.S. Government provides teachers with guidelines on the state of the law regarding prayer in public schools.

The Core Knowledge Curriculum—What's Behind Its Success?

E. D. Hirsch, Jr.

E. D. Hirsch, Jr. is professor emeritus in education and humanities from the University of Virginia, and he is the founder of the Core Knowledge Foundation. Among his most widely known books are *Cultural Literacy, The Schools We Need and Why We Don't Have Them*, and *The Knowledge Deficit*. Hirsch is an elected member of both the American Academy of Arts and Sciences and the International Academy of Education.

E. D. Hirsch, Jr., "The Core Knowledge Curriculum—What's Behind Its Success?" *Educational Leadership*, Vol. 50, No. 8, May 1993, pp. 23–30.

|F|O|C|U|S| QUESTION

How does the core knowledge curriculum differ from the typical elementary school curriculum?

KEY TERM

Core knowledge curriculum

The Mohegan School, in the South Bronx, is surrounded by the evidence of urban blight: trash, abandoned cars, crack houses. The students, mostly Latino or African-American, all qualify for free lunch. This public elementary school is located in the innermost inner city.

In January 1992, CBS Evening News devoted an "Eye on America" segment to the Mohegan School. Why did CBS focus on Mohegan of several schools that had experienced dramatic improvements after adopting the Core Knowledge guidelines? I think it was in part because this school seemed an unlikely place for a low-cost, academically solid program like Core Knowledge to succeed.

Mohegan's talented principal, Jeffrey Litt, wrote to tell me that "the richness of the curriculum is of particular importance" to his students because their educational experience, like that of "most poverty-stricken and educationally underserved students, was limited to remedial activities." Since adopting the Core Knowledge curriculum, however, Mohegan's students are engaged in the integrated and coherent study of topics like: Ancient Egypt, Greece, and Rome; the Industrial Revolution; limericks, haiku, and poetry; Rembrandt, Monet, and Michelangelo; Beethoven and Mozart; the Underground Railroad; the Trail of Tears; Brown v. Board of Education; the Mexican Revolution; photosynthesis; medieval African empires; the Bill of Rights; ecosystems; women's suffrage; the Harlem Renaissance—and many more.

The Philosophy Behind Core Knowledge

In addition to offering compelling subject matter, the Core Knowledge guidelines for elementary schools are far more specific than those issued by most school districts. Instead of vague outcomes such as "First graders will be introduced to map skills," the geography section of the *Core Knowledge Sequence* specifies that 1st graders will learn the meaning of "east," "west," "north," and "south" and locate on a map the equator, the Atlantic and Pacific Oceans, the seven continents, the United States, Mexico, Canada, and Central America.

Our aim in providing specific grade-by-grade guidelines—developed after several years of research, consultation, consensus-building, and field-testing—is *not* to claim that the content we recommend is better than some other well-thought-out core. No specific guidelines could plausibly claim to be the Platonic ideal. But one must make a start. To get beyond the talking stage, we created the best specific guidelines we could.

Nor is it our aim to specify *everything* that American schoolchildren should learn (the Core Knowledge guidelines are meant to constitute about 50 percent of a school's curriculum, thus leaving the other half to be tailored to a district, school, or classroom). Rather, our point is that a core of shared knowledge, grade by grade, is needed to achieve excellence and fairness in elementary education.

International studies have shown that *any* school that puts into practice a similarly challenging and specific program will provide a more effective and fair education than one that lacks such commonality of content in each grade.[1] High-performing systems such as those in France, Sweden, Japan, and West Germany bear out this principle. It was our intent to test whether in rural, urban, and suburban settings of the United States we would find what other nations have already discovered.

Certainly the finding that a schoolwide core sequence greatly enhances achievement *for all* is supported at the Mohegan School. Disciplinary problems there are down; teacher and student attendance are up, as are scores on standardized tests. Some of the teachers have even transferred their own children to the school, and some parents have taken their children out of private schools to send them to Mohegan. Similar results are being reported at some 65 schools across the nation that are taking steps to integrate the Core Knowledge guidelines into their curriculums.

In the broadcast feature about the Mohegan School, I was especially interested to hear 5th grade teacher Evelyn Hernandez say that Core Knowledge "tremendously increased the students' ability to question." In other words, based on that teacher's classroom experience, *a coherent approach to specific content enhances students' critical thinking and higher-order thinking skills.*

I emphasize this point because a standard objection to teaching specific content is that critical thinking suffers when a teacher emphasizes "mere information." Yet Core Knowledge teachers across the nation report that a coherent focus on content leads to higher-order thinking skills more securely than any other approach they know, including attempts to inculcate such skills directly. As an added benefit, children acquire knowledge that they will find useful not just in next year's classroom but for the rest of their lives.

Why Core Knowledge Works

Here are some of the research findings that explain the correlation between a coherent, specific approach to knowledge and the development of higher-order skills.

Learning can be fun, but is nonetheless cumulative and sometimes arduous. The dream of inventing methods to streamline the time-consuming activity of learning is as old as the hills. In antiquity it was already an old story. Proclus records an anecdote about an encounter between Euclid, the inventor of geometry, and King Ptolemy I of Egypt (276–196 B.C.), who was impatiently trying to follow Euclid's *Elements* step by laborious step. Exasperated, the king demanded a faster, easier way to learn geometry—to which Euclid gave the famous, and still true, reply: "There is no royal road to geometry."

Even with computer technology, it's far from easy to find short-cuts to the basic human activity of learning. The human brain sets limits on the potential for educational innovation. We can't, for instance, put a faster chip in the human brain. The frequency of its central processing unit is timed in thousandths rather than millionths of a second.[2] Nor can we change the fundamental, constructivist psychology of the learning process, which dictates that we humans must acquire new knowledge much as a tree acquires new leaves. The old leaves actively help nourish the new. The more "old growth" (prior knowledge) we have, the faster new growth can occur, making learning an organic process in which knowledge builds upon knowledge.

Because modern classrooms cannot effectively deliver completely individualized instruction, effective education requires grade-by-grade shared knowledge. When an individual child "gets" what is being taught in a classroom, it is like someone understanding a joke. A click occurs. If you have the requisite background knowledge, you will get the joke, but if you don't, you will remain puzzled until somebody explains the knowledge that was taken for granted. Similarly, a classroom of 25 to 35 children can move forward as a group only when *all* the children have the knowledge that is necessary to "getting" the next step in learning.

Studies comparing elementary schools in the United States to schools in countries with core knowledge systems disclose a striking difference in the structure of classroom activities.[3] In the best-performing classrooms constant back-and-forth interaction among groups of students and between students and the teacher consumes more than 80 percent of classroom time. By contrast, in the United States, over 50 percent of student time is spent in silent isolation.[4]

Behind the undue amount of "alone time" in our schools stands a theory that goes as follows: Every child is a unique individual; hence each child should receive instruction paced and tailored to that child. The theory should inform classroom practice as far as feasible: one hopes for teachers sensitive to the individual child's needs and strengths. The theory also reveals why good classroom teaching is difficult, and why a one-on-one tutorial is the most effective form of instruction. But modern education cannot be conducted as a one-on-one tutorial. Even in a country as affluent as the United States, instruction is carried out in classes of 25 to 35 pupils. In Dade County, Florida, the average class size for the early grades is 35. When a teacher gives individual attention to one child, 34 other pupils are left to fend for themselves. This is hardly a good trade-off, even on the premise that each child deserves individual attention.

Consider the significance of these facts in accounting for the slow progress (by international standards) of American elementary schools. If an entire classroom must constantly pause while its lagging members acquire background knowledge that they should have gained in earlier grades, progress is bound to be slow. For effective, fair classroom instruction to take place, all members of the class need to share enough common reference points to enable everyone to understand and learn—though of course at differing rates and in response to varied approaches. When this commonality of knowledge is lacking, progress in learning will be slow compared with systems that use a core curriculum.

Just as learning is cumulative, so are learning deficits. As they begin 1st grade, American students are not far behind beginners in other developed nations. But as they progress, their achievement falls farther and farther behind. This widening gap is the subject of one of the most important recent books on American education, *The Learning Gap* by Stevenson and Stigler.

This progressively widening gap closely parallels what happens *within* American elementary schools between advantaged and disadvantaged children. As the two groups progress from grades 1–6, the achievement gap grows ever larger and is almost never overcome.[5] The reasons for the parallels between the two kinds of gaps—the learning gap and the fairness gap—are similar.

In both cases, the widening gap represents the cumulative effect of learning deficits. Although a few talented and motivated children may overcome this ever-increasing handicap, most do not. The rift grows ever wider in adult life. The basic causes of this permanent deficit, apart from motivational ones, are cognitive. Learning builds upon learning in a cumulative way, and lack of learning in the early grades usually has, in comparative terms, a negatively cumulative effect.

We know from large-scale longitudinal evidence, particularly from France, that this fateful gap between haves and have-nots *can* be closed.[6] But only one way

to close it has been devised: to set forth explicit, year-by-year knowledge standards in early grades, so they are known to all parties—educators, parents, and children. Such standards are requisites for home-school cooperation and for reaching a general level of excellence. But, equally, they are requisites in gaining fairness for the academic have-nots: explicit year-by-year knowledge standards enable schools in nations with strong elementary core curriculums to remedy the knowledge deficits of disadvantaged children.

High academic skill is based upon broad general knowledge. Someone once asked Boris Goldovsky how he could play the piano so brilliantly with such small hands. His memorable reply was: "Where in the world did you get the idea that we play the piano with our hands?"

It's the same with reading: we don't read just with our eyes. By 7th grade, according to the epoch-making research of Thomas Sticht, most children, even those who read badly, have already attained the purely technical proficiency they need. Their reading and their listening show the same rate and level of comprehension; thus the mechanics of reading are not the limiting factor.[7] What is mainly lacking in poor readers is a broad, ready vocabulary. But broad vocabulary means broad knowledge, because to know a lot of words you have to know a lot of things. Thus, broad general knowledge is an *essential* requisite to superior reading skill and indirectly related to the skills that accompany it.

Superior reading skill is known to be highly correlated with most other academic skills, including the ability to write well, learn rapidly, solve problems, and think critically. To concentrate on reading is therefore to focus implicitly on a whole range of educational issues.[8]

It is sometimes claimed (but not backed up with research) that knowledge changes so rapidly in our fast-changing world that we need not get bogged down with "mere information." A corollary to the argument is that because information quickly becomes obsolete, it is more important to learn "accessing" skills (how to look things up or how to use a calculator) than to learn "mere facts."

The evidence in the psychological literature on skill acquisition goes strongly against this widely stated claim.[9] Its fallacy can be summed up in a letter I received from a head reference librarian. A specialist in accessing knowledge, he was distressed because the young people now being trained as *reference specialists* had so little general knowledge that they could not effectively help the public access knowledge. His direct experience (backed up by the research literature) had caused him to reject the theory of education as the gaining of accessing skills.

In fact, the opposite inference should be drawn from our fast-changing world. The fundamentals of science change very slowly; those of elementary math hardly at all. The famous names of geography and history (the "leaves" of that knowledge tree) change faster, but not root and branch from year to year. A wide range of this stable, fundamental knowledge is the key to rapid adaptation and the learning of new skills. It is precisely *because* the needs of a modern economy are so changeable that one needs broad general knowledge in order to flourish. Only high literacy (which implies broad general knowledge) provides the flexibility to learn new things fast. The only known route to broad general knowledge for all is for a nation's schools to provide all students with a substantial, solid core of knowledge.

Common content leads to higher school morale, as well as better teaching and learning. At every Core Knowledge school, a sense of community and common purpose have knit people together. Clear content guidelines have encouraged those who teach at the same grade level to collaborate in creating effective lesson plans and schoolwide activities. Similarly, a clear sense of purpose has encouraged cooperation among grades as well. Because the *Core Knowledge Sequence* makes no requirements about *how* the specified knowledge should be presented, individual schools and teachers have great scope for independence and creativity. Site-based governance is the order of the day at Core Knowledge schools—but with definite aims, and thus a clear sense of communal purpose.

The Myth of the Existing Curriculum

Much of the public currently assumes that each elementary school already follows a schoolwide curriculum. Yet frustrated parents continually write the Core Knowledge Foundation to complain that principals are not able to tell them with any explicitness what their child will be learning during the year. Memorably, a mother of identical twins wrote that because her children had been placed in different classrooms, they were learning completely different things.

Such curricular incoherence, typical of elementary education in the United States today, places enormous burdens on teachers. Because they must cope with such diversity of preparation at each subsequent grade level, teachers find it almost impossible to create learning communities in their classrooms. Stevenson and Stigler rightly conclude that the most significant diversity faced by our schools is *not* cultural diversity but, rather, diversity of academic preparation. To achieve excellence and fairness for all, an elementary school *must* follow a coherent sequence of solid, specific content.

ENDNOTES

1. International Association for the Evaluation of Educational Achievement (IEA), (1988), *Science Achievement in Seventeen Countries: A Preliminary Report,* (Elmsford, N.Y.: Pergamon Press). The table on page 42 shows a consistent correlation between core knowledge systems and equality of opportunity for all students. The subject is discussed at length in E. D. Hirsch, Jr., "Fairness and Core Knowledge," *Occasional Papers 2,* available from the Core Knowledge Foundation, 2012-B Morton Dr., Charlottesville, VA 22901.

2. An absolute limitation of the mind's speed of operation is 50 milliseconds per minimal item. See A. B. Kristofferson, (1967), "Attention and Psychophysical Time," *Acta Psychologica* 27: 93–100.

3. The data in this paragraph come from H. Stevenson and J. Stigler, (1992), *The Learning Gap,* (New York: Summit Books).

4. Stevenson and Stigler, pp. 52–71.

5. W. Loban, (March 1964), *Language Ability: Grades Seven, Eight, and Nine,* (Project No. 1131), University of California, Berkeley; as expanded and interpreted by T. G. Sticht, L. B. Beck, R. N. Hauke, G. M. Kleiman, and J. H. James, (1974), *Auding and Reading: A Developmental Model,* (Alexandria, Va.: Human Resources Research Organization); J. S. Chall, (1982), *Families and Literacy, Final Report to the National Institute of Education;* and especially, J. S. Chall, V. A. Jacobs, and L E. Baldwin, (1990), *The Reading Crisis: Why Poor Children Fall Behind,* (Cambridge, Mass.: Harvard University Press).

6. S. Boulot and D. Boyzon-Fradet, (1988), *Les immigrés et l'école: une course d'obstacles,* Paris, pp. 54–58; Centre for Educational Research and Innovation (CERI), (1987), *Immigrants' Children At School,* Paris, pp. 178–259.

7. T. G. Sticht and H. J. James, (1984), "Listening and Reading," In *Handbook of Reading Research,* edited by P. D. Pearson, (New York: Longman).

8. A. L. Brown, (1980), "Metacognitive Development and Reading," in *Theoretical Issues in Reading Comprehension,* edited by R. J. Spiro, B. C. Bruce, and W. F. Brewer, (Hillsdale, N.J.: L. Earlbaum Associates).

9. J. R. Anderson, ed., (1981), *Cognitive Skills and Their Acquisition,* (Hillsdale, NJ.: L. Earlbaum Associates).

POSTNOTE

In 1987, E. D. Hirsch, Jr., published the enormously successful book, *Cultural Literacy: What Every American Needs to Know.* In that book, Hirsch argues that Americans need to possess cultural literacy—that is, knowledge of the persons, events, literature, and science that forms the basis of shared knowledge in American culture.

Since the publication of *Cultural Literacy,* Hirsch has worked with educators to develop his Core Knowledge curriculum for the elementary grades. It is currently being implemented in over 700 schools. In a series of books, Hirsch and his collaborators have set forth the cultural knowledge that they believe should be taught at each grade level. Hirsch believes that children from advantaged homes have always had access to this knowledge but that children from disadvantaged homes have not. By teaching children a common core of knowledge in school, Hirsch believes that the barriers to adult literacy can be overcome.

In spite of careful attention to including cultural knowledge from many facets of American society in his Core Knowledge curriculum, some people still believe Hirsch promotes Western European culture over other cultures represented in our society. Examine *What Every First Grader Needs to Know,* as well as other similarly titled books for grades 2 through 8, and decide for yourself.

Discussion Questions

1. Why doesn't the United States have a common national curriculum as many other countries do?
2. Do you agree or disagree with Hirsch's contention that cultural literacy is important in sustaining a democracy? Why?
3. Would you like to teach in a school that has implemented the Core Knowledge curriculum? Why or why not?

RELATED WEBSITE RESOURCES

 ### Web Resources:

Core Knowledge Foundation. Available at:

http://coreknowledge.org/CK/index.htm.

This foundation's official website contains many resources and answers to questions about core knowledge.

Teaching Themes of Care

Nel Noddings

Nel Noddings is among the leading figures in the field of educational philosophy. She is Lee L. Jacks Professor of Child Education Emerita at Stanford University, and a past president of the National Academy of Education, the Philosophy of Education Society, and the John Dewey Society. Noddings has written extensively on the culture of care and education.

"Teaching Themes of Care" by Nel Noddings, *Phi Delta Kappan*, May 1995. Reprinted by permission of the author.

F O C U S QUESTION

In your opinion, do our schools need to give more attention to caring as part of the curriculum and, if so, how such themes of caring could be implemented?

Some educators today—and I include myself among them—would like to see a complete reorganization of the school curriculum. We would like to give a central place to the questions and issues that lie at the core of human existence. One possibility would be to organize the curriculum around themes of care—caring for self, for intimate others, for strangers and global others, for the natural world and its nonhuman creatures, for the human-made world, and for ideas.[1]

A realistic assessment of schooling in the present political climate makes it clear that such a plan is not likely to be implemented. However, we can use the rich vocabulary of care in educational planning and introduce themes of care into regular subject-matter classes. In this article, I will first give a brief rationale for teaching themes of care; second, I will suggest ways of choosing and organizing such themes; and, finally, I'll say a bit about the structures required to support such teaching.

Why Teach Caring?

In an age when violence among schoolchildren is at an unprecedented level, when children are bearing children with little knowledge of how to care for them, when the society and even the schools often concentrate on materialistic messages, it may be unnecessary to argue that we should care more genuinely for our children and teach them to care. However, many otherwise reasonable people seem to believe that our educational problems consist largely of low scores on achievement tests. My contention is, first, that we should want more from our educational efforts than adequate academic achievement and, second, that we will not achieve even that meager success unless our children believe that they themselves are cared for and learn to care for others.

There is much to be gained, both academically and humanly, by including themes of care in our curriculum. First, such inclusion may well expand our students' cultural literacy. For example, as we discuss in math classes the attempts of great mathematicians to prove the existence of God or to reconcile a God who is all good with the reality of evil in the world, students will hear names, ideas, and words that are not part of the standard curriculum. Although such incidental learning cannot replace the systematic and sequential learning required by those who plan careers in mathematically oriented fields, it can be powerful in expanding students' cultural horizons and in inspiring further study.

Second, themes of care help us to connect the standard subjects. The use of literature in mathematics classes, of history in science classes, and of art and music in all classes can give students a feeling of the wholeness in their education. After all, why should they seriously study five different subjects if their teachers, who are educated people, only seem to know and appreciate one?

Third, themes of care connect our students and our subjects to great existential questions. What is the meaning of life? Are there gods? How should I live?

Fourth, sharing such themes can connect us person-to-person. When teachers discuss themes of care, they may become real persons to their students and so enable them to construct new knowledge. Martin Buber put it this way:

> Trust, trust in the world, because this human being exists—that is the most inward achievement of the relation in education. Because this human being exists, meaninglessness, however hard pressed you are by it, cannot be the real truth. Because this human being exists, in the darkness the light lies hidden, in fear salvation, and in the callousness of one's fellow-man the great love.[2]

Finally, I should emphasize that caring is not just a warm, fuzzy feeling that makes people kind and likable. Caring implies a continuous search for competence. When we care, we want to do our very best for the objects of our care. To have as our educational goal the production of caring, competent, loving, and lovable people is not anti-intellectual. Rather, it demonstrates respect for the full range of human talents. Not all human beings are good at or interested in mathematics, science, or British literature. But all humans can be helped to lead lives of deep concern for others, for the natural world and its creatures, and for the preservation of the human-made world. They can be led to develop the skills and knowledge necessary to make positive contributions, regardless of the occupation they may choose.

Choosing and Organizing Themes of Care

Care is conveyed in many ways. At the institutional level, schools can be organized to provide continuity and support for relationships of care and trust.[3] At the individual level, parents and teachers show their caring through characteristic forms of attention: by cooperating in children's activities, by sharing their own dreams and doubts, and by providing carefully for the steady growth to the children in their charge. Personal manifestations of care are probably more important in children's lives than any particular curriculum or pattern of pedagogy.

However, curriculum can be selected with caring in mind. That is, educators can manifest their care in the choice of curriculum, and appropriately chosen curriculum can contribute to the growth of children as carers. Within each large domain of care, many topics are suitable for thematic units: in the domain of "caring for self," for example, we might consider life stages, spiritual growth, and what it means to develop an admirable character; in exploring the topic of caring for intimate others, we might include units on love, friendship, and parenting; under the theme of caring for strangers and global others, we might study war, poverty, and tolerance; in addressing the idea of caring for the human-made world, we might encourage competence with the machines that surround us and a real appreciation for the marvels of technology. Many other examples exist. Furthermore, there are at least two different ways to approach the development of such themes: units can be constructed by interdisciplinary teams, or themes can be identified by individual teachers and addressed periodically throughout a year's or semester's work.

The interdisciplinary approach is familiar in core programs, and such programs are becoming more and more popular at the middle school level. One key to a successful interdisciplinary unit is the degree of genuinely enthusiastic support it receives from the teachers involved. Too often, arbitrary or artificial groupings are formed, and teachers are forced to make contributions that they themselves do not value highly. For example, math and science teachers are sometimes automatically lumped together, and rich humanistic possibilities may be lost. If I, as a math teacher, want to include historical, biographical, and literary topics in my math lessons, I might prefer to work with English and social studies teachers. Thus it is important to involve teachers in the initial selection of broad areas for themes, as well as in their implementation.

Such interdisciplinary arrangements also work well at the college level. I recently received a copy of the syllabus for a college course titled "The Search for Meaning," which was co-taught by an economist, a university chaplain, and a psychiatrist.[4] The course is interdisciplinary, intellectually rich, and aimed squarely at the central questions of life.

At the high school level, where students desperately need to engage in the study and practice of caring, it is harder to form interdisciplinary teams. A conflict arises as teachers acknowledge the intensity of the subject-matter preparation their students need for further education. Good teachers often wish there were time in the day to co-teach unconventional topics of great importance, and they even admit that their students are not getting what they need for full personal development. But they feel constrained by the requirements of a highly competitive world and the structures of schooling established by that world.

Is there a way out of this conflict? Imaginative, like-minded teachers might agree to emphasize a particular theme in their separate classes. Such themes as war, poverty, crime, racism, or sexism can be addressed in almost every subject area. The teachers should agree on some core ideas related to caring that will be discussed in all classes, but beyond the central commitment to address themes of care, the topics can be handled in whatever way seems suitable in a given subject.

Consider, for example, what a mathematics class might contribute to a unit on crime. Statistical information might be gathered on the location and number of crimes, on rates for various kinds of crime, on the ages of offenders, and on the cost to society; graphs and charts could be constructed. Data on changes in crime rates could be assembled. Intriguing questions could be asked: Were property crime rates lower when penalties were more severe—when, for example, even children were hanged as thieves? What does an average criminal case cost by way of lawyers' fees, police investigation, and court processing? Does it cost more to house a youth in a detention center or in an elite private school?

None of this would have to occupy a full period every day. The regular sequential work of the math class could go on at a slightly reduced rate (e.g., fewer textbook exercises as homework), and the work on crime could proceed in the form of interdisciplinary projects over a considerable period of time. Most important would be the continual reminder in all classes that the topic is part of a larger theme of caring for strangers and fellow citizens. It takes only a few minutes to talk about what it means to live in safety, to trust one's neighbors, to feel secure in greeting strangers. Students should be told that metal detectors and security guards were not part of their parents' school lives, and they should be encouraged to hope for a safer and more open future. Notice the words I've used in this paragraph: caring, trust, safety, strangers, hope. Each could be used as an organizing theme for another unit of study.

English and social studies teachers would obviously have much to contribute to a unit on crime. For example, students might read *Oliver Twist,* and they might also study and discuss the social conditions that seemed to promote crime in 19th-century England. Do similar conditions exist in our country today? The selection of materials could include both classic works and modern stories and films. Students might even be introduced to some of the mystery stories that adults read so avidly on airplanes and beaches, and teachers should be engaged in lively discussion about the comparative value of the various stories.

Science teachers might find that a unit on crime would enrich their teaching of evolution. They could bring up the topic of social Darwinism, which played such a strong role in social policy during the late 19th and early 20th centuries. To what degree are criminal tendencies inherited? Should children be tested for the genetic defects that are suspected of predisposing some people to crime? Are females less competent than males in moral reasoning? (Why did some scientists and philosophers think this was true?) Why do males commit so many more violent acts than females?

Teachers of the arts can also be involved. A unit on crime might provide a wonderful opportunity to critique "gangsta rap" and other currently popular forms of music. Students might profitably learn how the control of art contributed to national criminality during the Nazi era. These are ideas that pop into my mind. Far more various and far richer ideas will come from teachers who specialize in these subjects.

There are risks, of course, in undertaking any unit of study that focuses on matters of controversy or deep existential concern, and teachers should anticipate these risks. What if students want to compare the incomes of teachers and cocaine dealers? What if they point to contemporary personalities from politics, entertainment, business, or sports who seem to escape the law and profit from what seems to be criminal behavior? My own inclination would be to allow free discussion of these cases and to be prepared to counteract them with powerful stories of honesty, compassion, moderation, and charity.

An even more difficult problem may arise. Suppose a student discloses his or her own criminal activities? Fear of this sort of occurrence may send teachers scurrying for safer topics. But, in fact, any instructional method that uses narrative forms or encourages personal expression runs this risk. For example, students of English as a second language who write proudly about their own hard lives and new hopes may disclose that their parents are illegal immigrants. A girl may write passages that lead her teacher to suspect sexual abuse. A boy may brag about objects that he has "ripped off." Clearly, as we use these powerful methods that encourage students to initiate discussion and share their experiences, we must reflect on the ethical issues involved, consider appropriate responses to such issues, and prepare teachers to handle them responsibly.

Caring teachers must help students make wise decisions about what information they will share about themselves. On the one hand, teachers want their students to express themselves, and they want their students to trust in and consult them. On the other hand, teachers have an obligation to protect immature students from making disclosures that they might later regret. There is a deep ethical problem here. Too often educators assume that only religious fundamentalists and right-wing extremists object to the discussion of emotionally and morally charged issues. In reality, there is a real danger of intrusiveness and lack of respect in methods that fail to recognize the vulnerability of students. Therefore, as teachers plan units and lessons on moral issues, they should anticipate the tough problems that may arise. I am arguing here that it is morally irresponsible to simply ignore existential questions and themes of care; we must attend to them. But it is equally irresponsible to approach these deep concerns without caution and careful preparation.

So far I have discussed two ways of organizing interdisciplinary units on themes of care. In one, teachers actually teach together in teams; in the other, teachers agree on a theme and a central focus on care, but they do what they can, when they can, in their own classrooms. A variation on this second way—which is also open to teachers who have to work alone—is to choose several themes and weave them into regular course material over an entire semester or year. The particular themes will depend on the interests and preparation of each teacher.

For example, if I were teaching high school mathematics today, I would use religious/existential questions as a pervasive theme because the biographies of mathematicians are filled with accounts of their speculations on matters of God, other dimensions, and the infinite—and because these topics fascinate me. There are so many wonderful stories to be told: Descartes's proof of the existence of God, Pascal's famous wager, Plato's world of forms, Newton's attempt to verify Biblical chronology, Leibnitz' detailed theodicy, current attempts to describe a divine domain in terms of metasystems, and mystical speculations on the infinite.[5] Some of these stories can be told as rich "asides" in five minutes or less. Others might occupy the better part of several class periods.

Other mathematics teachers might use an interest in architecture and design, art, music, or machinery as continuing themes in the domain of "caring for the human-made world." Still others might introduce the mathematics of living things. The possibilities are endless. In choosing and pursuing these themes, teachers should be aware that they are both helping their students learn to care and demonstrating their own caring by sharing interests that go well beyond the demands of textbook pedagogy.

Still another way to introduce themes of care into regular classrooms is to be prepared to respond spontaneously to events that occur in the school or in the neighborhood. Older teachers have one advantage in this area: they probably have a greater store of experience and stories on which to draw. However, younger teachers have the advantage of being closer to their students' lives and experiences; they are more likely to be familiar with the music, films, and sports figures that interest their students.

All teachers should be prepared to respond to the needs of students who are suffering from the death of friends, conflicts between groups of students, pressure to use drugs or to engage in sex, and other troubles so rampant in the lives of today's children. Too often schools rely on experts—"grief counselors" and the like—when what children really need is the continuing compassion and presence of adults who represent constancy and care in their lives. Artificially separating the emotional, academic, and moral care of children into tasks for specially designated experts contributes to the fragmentation of life in schools.

Of course, I do not mean to imply that experts are unnecessary, nor do I mean to suggest that some matters should not be reserved for parents or psychologists. But our society has gone too far in compartmentalizing the care of its children. When we ask whose job it is to teach children how to care, an appropriate initial response is "Everyone's." Having accepted universal responsibility, we can then ask about the special contributions and limitations of various individuals and groups.

Supporting Structures

What kinds of schools and teacher preparation are required, if themes of care are to be taught effectively? First, and most important, care must be taken seriously as a major purpose of our schools; that is, educators must recognize that caring for students is fundamental in teaching and that developing people with a strong capacity for care is a major objective of responsible education. Schools properly pursue many other objectives—developing artistic talent, promoting multicultural understanding, diversifying curriculum to meet the academic and vocational needs of all students, forging connections with community agencies and parents, and so on. Schools cannot be single-purpose institutions. Indeed, many of us would argue that it is logically and practically impossible to achieve that single academic purpose if other purposes are not recognized and accepted. This contention is confirmed in the success stories of several inner-city schools.[6]

Once it is recognized that school is a place in which students are cared for and learn to care, that recognition should be powerful in guiding policy. In the late 1950s, schools in the U.S., under the guidance of James Conant and others, placed the curriculum at the top of the educational priority list. Because the nation's leaders wanted schools to provide high-powered courses in mathematics and science, it was recommended that small high schools be replaced by efficient larger structures complete with sophisticated laboratories and specialist teachers. Economies of scale were anticipated, but the main argument for consolidation and regionalization centered on the curriculum. All over the country, small schools were closed, and students were herded into larger facilities with "more offerings." We did not think carefully about schools as communities and about what might be lost as we pursued a curriculum-driven ideal.

Today many educators are calling for smaller schools and more family-like groupings. These are good proposals, but teachers, parents, and students should be engaged in continuing discussion about what they are trying to achieve through the new arrangements. For example, if test scores do not immediately rise, participants should be courageous in explaining that test scores were not the main object of the changes. Most of us who argue for caring in schools are intuitively quite sure that children in such settings will in fact become more competent learners. But, if they cannot prove their academic competence in a prescribed period of time, should we give up on caring and on teaching them to care? That would be foolish. There is more to life and learning than the academic proficiency demonstrated by test scores.

In addition to steadfastness of purpose, schools must consider continuity of people and place. If we are concerned with caring and community, then we must make it possible for students and teachers to stay together for several years so that mutual trust can develop and students can feel a sense of belonging in their "school-home."[7]

More than one scheme of organization can satisfy the need for continuity. Elementary school children can stay with the same teacher for several years, or they can work with a stable team of specialist teachers for several years. In the latter arrangement, there may be program advantages; that is, children taught by subject-matter experts who get to know them well over an extended period of time may learn more about the particular subjects. At the high school level, the same specialist teaching might work with students throughout their years in high school. Or, as Theodore Sizer has suggested, one teacher might teach two subjects to a group of 30 students rather than one subject to 60 students, thereby reducing the number of different adults with whom students interact each day.[8] In all the suggested arrangements, placements should be made by mutual consent whenever possible. Teachers and students who hate or distrust one another should not be forced to stay together.

A policy of keeping students and teachers together for several years supports caring in two essential ways: it provides time for the development of caring relations, and it makes teaching themes of care more feasible. When trust has been established, teachers and students can discuss matters that would be hard for a group of strangers to approach, and classmates learn to support one another in sensitive situations.

The structural changes suggested here are not expensive. If a high school teacher must teach five classes a day, it costs no more for three of these classes to be composed of continuing students than for all five classes to comprise new students—i.e., strangers. The recommended changes come directly out of a clear-headed assessment of our major aims and purposes. We failed to suggest them earlier because we had other, too limited, goals in mind.

I have made one set of structural changes sound easy, and I do believe that they are easily made. But the curricular and pedagogical changes that are required may be more difficult. High school textbooks rarely contain the kinds of supplementary material I have described, and teachers are not formally prepared to incorporate such material. Too often, even the people we regard as strongly prepared in a liberal arts major are unprepared to discuss the history of their subject, its relation to other subjects, the biographies of its great figures, its connections to the great existential questions, and the ethical responsibilities of those who work in that discipline. To teach themes of care in an academically effective way, teachers will have to engage in projects of self-education.

At present, neither liberal arts departments nor schools of education pay much attention to connecting academic subjects with themes of care. For example, biology students may learn something of the anatomy and physiology of mammals but nothing at all about the care of living animals; they may never be asked to consider the moral issues involved in the annual euthanasia of millions of pets. Mathematics students may learn to solve quadratic equations but never study what it means to live in a mathematicized world. In enlightened history classes, students may learn something about the problems of racism and colonialism but never hear anything about the evolution of childhood, the contributions of women in both domestic and public caregiving, or the connection between the feminization of caregiving and public policy. A liberal education that neglects matters that are central to a fully human life hardly warrants the name,[9] and a professional education that confines itself to technique does nothing to close the gaps in liberal education.

The greatest structural obstacle, however, may simply be legitimizing the inclusion of themes of care in the curriculum. Teachers in the early grades have long included such themes as a regular part of their work, and middle school educators are becoming more sensitive to developmental needs involving care. But secondary schools—where violence, apathy, and alienation are most evident—do little to develop the capacity to care. Today, even elementary teachers complain that the pressure to produce high test scores inhibits the work they regard as central to their mission: the development of caring and competent people. Therefore, it would seem that the most fundamental change required is one of attitude. Teachers can be very special people in the lives of children, and it should be legitimate for them to spend time developing relations of trust, talking with students about problems that are central to their lives, and guiding them toward greater sensitivity and competence across all the domains of care.

NOTES

1. For the theoretical argument, see Nel Noddings, *The Challenge to Care in Schools* (New York: Teachers College Press, 1992); for a practical example and rich documentation, see Sharon Quint, *Schooling Homeless Children* (New York: Teachers College Press, 1994).
2. Martin Buber, *Between Man and Man* (New York: Macmillan, 1965), p. 98.
3. Noddings, chap. 12.
4. See Thomas H. Naylor, William H. Willimon, and Magdalena R. Naylor, *The Search for Meaning* (Nashville, Tenn.: Abingdon Press, 1994).
5. For many more examples, see Nel Noddings, *Educating for Intelligent Belief and Unbelief* (New York: Teachers College Press, 1993).
6. See Deborah Meier, "How Our Schools Could Be," *Phi Delta Kappan*, January 1995, pp. 369–73; and Quint, op. cit.
7. See Jane Roland Martin, *The Schoolhome: Rethinking Schools for Changing Families* (Cambridge, Mass.: Harvard University Press, 1992).
8. Theodore Sizer, *Horace's Compromise: The Dilemma of the American High School* (Boston: Houghton Mifflin, 1984).
9. See Bruce Wilshire, *The Moral Collapse of the University* (Albany: State University of New York Press, 1990).

POSTNOTE

Getting over selfishness and self-preoccupation is a major task of one's early years. As Nel Noddings demonstrates in this article, schools have a responsibility to help children develop the habit of caring for others. She makes a strong case for giving this task a more prominent place in our educational planning.

As children grow older, however, they need to develop some sterner virtues to complement caring. They need to acquire self-discipline and self-control. They need to acquire the habit of persistence at hard tasks. They also need to learn how to strive for individual excellence and to compete against others without hostility. We could argue that both a strong individual and a strong nation need a balance of strengths. To pursue one strength, such as caring, without developing the full spectrum of human virtues leaves both the individual and the nation incomplete.

Discussion Questions

1. Do you agree with the primacy given to caring by the author? Why or why not?
2. What obstacles does the author identify and what additional ones can you name that would stand in the way of implementing themes of care in the school curriculum?
3. What practical classroom suggestions to advance caring have you gleaned from this article?

Instruction

"What should we teach?" is a fundamental question teachers ask. But next in importance is: "How do we teach it?" Instructional questions range from the very nature of students as learners to how to organize a third-grade classroom.

In this section, we present a palette of new and old ideas about how to organize classrooms and schools to meet the needs of new students and a new society. A number of the most high-profile topics in education—such as cooperative learning, classroom management, assessment, constructivism, and differentiated instruction—are presented. It is important to realize, however, as you read about an instructional methodology or set of procedures that each represents a view of what the teaching-learning process is and what students are like. So, as you read these articles, we urge you to probe for their foundational ideas.

26

Confronting the Achievement Gap

David Gardner

David Gardner retired from the classroom in 2005 and is now head teacher for Explorations in Math, a nonprofit group working with the Seattle schools.

"Confronting the Achievement Gap" by David Gardner, *Phi Delta Kappan*, March 2007, pp. 542–546. Reprinted by permission of the author.

| F | O | C | U | S | QUESTION |

What causes so many children of color to underachieve throughout school, and what can be done to remedy this problem?

KEY TERM
Achievement gap

Over the course of 33 years, I have taught in schools with high concentrations of low-income families, children of color, and students and families who speak little or no English, and I have taught in schools in mostly affluent, white neighborhoods. The difference in achievement levels will surprise no one: high in the affluent, white schools; much lower in schools where poverty is common.

The question is, Why is this so? Why do so many urban minority students come into fifth grade with low skills in virtually every area? Many cannot add or subtract accurately; they don't know their multiplication and division facts; they can't write a decent paragraph or, in some cases, a decent sentence. Why do they have so much trouble reasoning out problems?

For example, during a discussion in an American history class made up of students from the South End of Seattle, I handed out tables that showed how much money was spent to educate white children in the South in the 1920s as opposed to how much was spent for black children. One of the tables showed a breakdown by county in Mississippi. I asked my students to find the difference in the amount spent for white students and black students in each county. Most of the students had a very difficult time even understanding what I wanted them to do. When they did grasp the concept, they had still more difficulty using the table to determine the answer. And even then most of the answers were wrong because of problems with subtraction. I posed questions about another table, asking students to identify a particular state. Most answered with dollar amounts.

When I ask why this should be so, I'm repeating a question that continues to be asked by educators, schools, parents, and communities across the country. Why is there such a large achievement gap between so many children of color and their white peers?

Of course, this quandary is nothing new. The gap dates back to the first mass-administered achievement tests given by the U.S. Army in World War I. Even as crude as those tests were, they measured an achievement gap between black recruits and white recruits that persists today, in spite of everything we have tried.

The first and most obvious response to my question is almost always unequal funding. Throughout most of our history the funding disparities between white schools and those serving children of color have been enormous. Scott Nearing, in *Black America* (from which I took the tables I used in the history lesson above), first published in 1929, documented these disparities as they existed in the South in the 1920s.[1] For example, in 1927, South Carolina spent $2.74 per "Negro" student and $27.88 per white student. Or even more astoundingly, Mississippi counties in 1926 averaged $3.59 a year per black student as opposed to $68.15 per white student. Nearing cited 162 kindergartens for white children in eight southern cities, but just eight for black children. All eight were in Kentucky: seven of them in Louisville, one in Lexington.

While disparities of that magnitude no longer exist, it's still true that affluent districts outspend their poorer counterparts. Ironically, though, even as funding disparities are reduced, the playing field for students of color remains badly tilted. Spending the same amount of money on each individual student harks back to a time when teachers would say, "I treat every student exactly the same." We know that notion has been discredited: all students are *not* the same, and to treat them as if they were does them a disservice. Funding schools as if all populations faced the same problems and had the same needs is an equally ineffective means of addressing the achievement gap.

My own district of Seattle instituted a weighted student funding formula several years ago. This formula distributes money to schools based on a number of factors, including such things as the number of students on free or reduced-price lunch, the number of special education students, and the number of English-language learners. Schools with greater needs receive more money per student. Has this approach made a difference? There has been some slight, but by no means significant, movement toward closing the achievement gap. But there has been no way to tell how much of that change is the result of the funding formula and how much is the result of other efforts the district has undertaken.

Soon after the funding answer to my question has been proposed, another common response—this one spoken more softly—is that children of color must be inherently less capable, less intelligent. I'm tempted to dismiss this as utter nonsense, except for the tremendous harm such thinking has caused and continues to cause. To believe it is to say we might as well give up on these children. Except for the occasional anomaly, they'll never make it. As a result of an at least tacit belief in this answer, many teachers, schools, and even whole communities *have* given up on children of color. When this belief prevails, teachers can transfer much of the responsibility for the failure to learn from their own shoulders to those of their students. Teachers go through the motions of educating these children, pay

lip service to the ideals, but don't believe, deep down, that these children will ever catch up. And if teachers don't believe in them, how in the world will the children ever believe in themselves?

Let me parse the problem into two separate questions and deal with each one separately: What causes so many children of color to underachieve throughout school? And what are the remedies?

Why the Achievement Gap?

The reasons for the achievement gap are as varied as the students who pass through my classes every year. First, many come from a background of poverty. One of the detrimental effects of growing up in poverty is receiving inadequate nourishment at a time when bodies and brains are rapidly developing. Proper human development requires a steady and healthy diet. Poor children rarely get such a diet. Add to that the fact that poor mothers-to-be are rarely well nourished themselves and don't often receive adequate prenatal care, and you have a recipe for lower achievement among the children.

Poverty also means that there are fewer resources in the home for the child to draw on. Parents (or other caretakers) often work two or more jobs, or they work a night shift, either of which takes away time they might spend with their children. In such circumstances, parents can't be as involved with their children's education as they need to be or would like to be.

Poverty can also make it difficult to develop a child's self-esteem. Poor children have fewer opportunities for enriching experiences. Poor people don't take trips to Europe or Africa; indeed, some rarely leave their neighborhoods. They may have trouble even taking trips to the zoo or art museum or library. This is not to say that poor children have no enriching experiences, for they clearly do. However, their experiences may not be the kind valued by the larger community. When the greater society does not value a child's culture, what is his or her likely response? Anger. Resentment. Loss of trust. Seeing school as an obstacle rather than a way out. These factors drive down motivation, drive down confidence. Many poor children are stuck in this cycle.

Still another factor that can adversely affect a child's learning is the parents' own experiences with school and teachers. For many poor parents, these experiences were negative. These parents will thus be more reluctant to come to school, to participate in school events, to contact teachers, or to place any confidence in the school and the education system. Add to the mix the large and increasing number of people who are new to the country—who do not speak English, are unfamiliar with the culture, and in many cases are themselves minimally educated—and the problems are magnified.

Still another reason for the achievement gap has to do with what in academic circles is called "locus of control." People with an internal locus of control see themselves as primarily responsible for their successes and failures. People with an external locus of control tend to attribute their successes and failures to outside factors: luck, fate, the boss likes me, the teacher doesn't like me, etc. A great example of external locus of control can be seen in a "Peanuts" comic strip in which Peppermint Patty bemoans the F she got on a test. "I think I got an F," she tells Franklin, "because I have a big nose. Sometimes a teacher just doesn't like the way a kid looks. I've got a big nose so I fail. It's as simple as that."

Research shows that many people of color have an external locus of control. And there are some good reasons for that. People of color generally experience success (promotions, raises, upward mobility) at lower and slower rates than do whites. They may work as hard or harder and be just as competent, but their efforts are not routinely rewarded. Does this affect their children? It seems entirely possible. After all, they see their parents struggling, year after year, and they hear their parents talking about the difficulty or impossibility of getting ahead. Then they come to school, work as hard as other students, and see that they, too, fail to achieve at the same rate as their white and Asian peers. They deduce, not unreasonably, that external factors, things beyond their control, must be responsible. This conclusion leads them to reduce their effort and resign themselves to not doing well.

Finally, the long-term effects of racism on the achievement gap should not be underestimated. Schooling for whites in this country extends back for several centuries. Though not equally distributed even among whites, free public education has nonetheless an expectation that education leads to success—at least for those in the majority. For people of color no such centuries-long positive history exists. From the slave codes that forbade educating those who were enslaved, to the Jim Crow laws that followed, to the institutional racism that has only been weakened, not eliminated, all have had a devastatingly negative impact on the education of children of color, an impact that continues to this day.

In all of this, can any blame be assigned to today's schools and teachers? Sadly, the answer is yes, for there's plenty of blame to go around. There are bad schools, and there are incompetent teachers. And, once again, both are all too often found in African American neighborhoods or in the barrios or on the reservations. And in these locales, even the good schools with good teachers are affected by an undercurrent of racism that undermines what we try to do. This is not intentional racism; it is racism that we're not even aware of practicing. It's a colleague who stands, smiles, and shakes hands with white parents at the start of a parent/teacher conference but fails to show the same courtesies to black parents in the next conference. The teacher is doubtless unaware of the differential treatment. But the unconscious stereotypes and expectations we carry around with us can and do affect how we teach. You can hear those stereotypes just beneath the surface of the frequently voiced assumption that minority parents don't care as much about education as white parents.

For all of these reasons, closing the achievement gap presents us with an extremely difficult problem. However, the idea that schools alone are responsible for the existence of this gap and so bear sole responsibility for closing it is disingenuous at best. And attributing blame to the schools, which has been going on for at least a decade, has simply made teachers defensive while failing to improve the situation. Hundreds of millions of dollars are expended on the problem every year. Expensive programs are implemented, attempted for a couple of years, and then tossed out when they fail to produce results, like the long line of failed efforts that preceded them. School staffs attend workshop after workshop in an effort to acquire the skills and the attitudes needed to close the achievement gap, but their efforts are doomed before they start, as long as schools alone are deemed to be responsible for the problem. The achievement gap and the problems that continue to feed it are a reflection of society and its attitudes. And until these change, we will meet with little success.

What Is the Solution?

The solution to the problem of the achievement gap lies within each one of us as citizens and within each of us who teaches. This is not the kind of problem that is going to be eliminated by an institutional response. No school system and no state or federal department of education will ever be able to mandate a solution.

The achievement gap will begin to disappear when attitudes in this country begin to change, when eliminating poverty becomes a national priority. It will begin to disappear when racism is recognized as the pervasive and insidious cancer that it is and when Americans are united in their willingness to do something about it.

The only way this kind of change will happen is for each of us, individually, to want it to happen and to be willing to make it happen. As a teacher, I do many things that are designed to help my students change their attitudes toward themselves and toward school and learning. They, too, need to be a part of a national change of heart. Here are two places to start, places that are within the ability of each individual educator to control.

First, I believe in my kids. I *know* they are capable, and so I'm not reluctant to set high standards for them. But believing in them isn't enough; they need to *know* that I believe in them. I communicate that belief to them every day, and I do it in many ways, both explicitly and implicitly. Explicitly, I tell them they're capable. I tell them I believe in them. I tell them each of them has a good brain and is capable of doing what I ask of them. I tell them I have high expectations of them, that I will not accept poor work, and that I will return slipshod work to them to be redone.

I routinely refuse to answer the standard "I don't get this. How do you do it?" lament when it's about a problem or question that I know a student can figure out. And I let students know that they must do their part. I draw analogies for them: body builders develop their muscles by gradually increasing the weight they lift. Students increase their abilities by accepting the challenges posed by their teachers to do work that steadily increases in difficulty. I also challenge them to take risks. There are no wrong answers, I tell them. If you give me a wrong answer, it tells me two good things about you. One, you're paying attention. And two, you're thinking. If you're doing those two things, you can't help but learn.

I talk to my students explicitly about failure. I tell them that failure is not only okay, it's critical to learning. When you were learning to ride a bike, you fell. And every fall marked a failure in learning to ride a bike. When you were learning to skate, you fell, and every fall marked a failure in learning to skate. But those failures guided your learning, and persistence paid off. The same thing happens when you're learning at school. You're going to fail before you succeed. Long division, writing a decent paragraph, thinking through a difficult problem, success in any of these comes about only after failures. At first, you'll get wrong answers more often than not in long division, but your failures let you see what you need to do differently. You'll write many bad paragraphs before you write a good one. You'll stumble over difficult problems before you're able to solve them. If you're willing to work at it, success will come through these failures. Children need to hear these messages regularly, because they're afraid of failure, which means they're afraid to take risks. And when they don't take risks, of course, they do fail, only they fail in a much more significant and dangerous way: they lose the opportunity to learn a skill, and they reinforce their own feelings of deficiency. To get them out of that self-defeating loop, I do everything in my power to get them to believe in themselves. Once that happens, they will begin to close the achievement gap on their own.

Another critical step in helping students to do well is to make learning fun. Think about it: the things we all do well tend to be the things we enjoy doing. But when I say learning must be fun, that doesn't mean it comes without effort. When learning is fun, it is interesting, challenging, and rewarding. Drill and kill, rote memorization, round-robin reading, dull textbooks, a 100% teacher-centered classroom, all of these are poisonous to learning because they do not engage students. On the contrary, students are turned off and tuned out, the first steps on the road to falling behind and dropping out. Just as bad, they are obstacles to closing and eliminating the achievement gap.

How does a good teacher go about making learning fun? It may sound like an oxymoron, but making learning fun is hard work. You need to be prepared to discard much of the conventional wisdom of teaching and most of the commercially produced texts and worksheets. And you'll have to deal with the dual anxiety that can come from not having a manual to guide you while you do have a principal who insists that you use the prescribed texts.

Then, too, to make learning fun you'll have to be willing to bust your brain thinking up better ways—more interesting, more challenging, more rewarding, more enjoyable ways—of covering the curriculum in each content area. This means scrounging for materials in the stockroom, in vacant classrooms, in garage sales and flea markets, in stores that sell school supplies, and in many other places. This means making many of your own teaching materials, such as graphs, posters, and charts. It means creating your own worksheets for each lesson, tailoring them to fit both the specific objectives you have in mind and the needs of your students. It means being creative and flexible. It means giving students more autonomy and a greater say in how they're going to learn. It means that humor and laughter are integral parts of the classroom environment, an environment that leads to achievement rather than boredom.

Making learning fun means using games and manipulatives. And for me, a key part of making learning fun is interspersing brain games and other short, quick activities throughout the day. For example, after I take attendance and we listen to the opening announcements each day, my class solves some kind of puzzle on the board, or we engage in some brainteasers. We always have time for two or three students chosen randomly to do "Acting in a Can" (like charades), to play Taboo® (using the words from the commercially produced game), or to play categories. Throughout the day, when there are a few minutes to fill, we do mental math or mental spelling and play word games or "Guess My Number." I put a premium on humor, imagination, and creativity. All of these activities engage students and keep them coming back for more.

Believing in my students and letting them know I believe in them and making school a place they find rewarding will not, in and of themselves, eliminate the achievement gap. But these measures are within our control as educators, and they will have a positive effect on our students, both now and in the future.

NOTE

1. Scott Nearing, *Black America* (1929; reprint, New York: Schocken,1969), pp. 61–63, 268–69.

POSTNOTE

Many people see the problem of low academic achievement of students from urban poverty schools as being intractable. Poverty is too great . . . parents don't care . . . drugs and violence take a toll. Gardner argues that the major remedy lies in eliminating both poverty and attitudes that expect less from children of color. With high standards, a challenging curriculum, and good teachers, children from poverty schools can learn—and at surprisingly high levels. As Jaime Escalante demonstrated at Garfield High School in East Los Angeles, poor Latino youths could learn calculus well enough to score at high levels on AP exams. He set high standards and made serious demands on students. His success is celebrated in the Academy Award–nominated movie *Stand and Deliver.* Marva Collins, in Chicago, also demonstrated that poor African American children could learn a classical curriculum at high levels.

Discussion Questions

1. Was there anything in this article that surprised you? If so, what?

2. Do you agree with the author's assertion that poverty and institutional racism are the major deterrents for children of color to achieve comparably with middle class white students? Why or why not?

3. In addition to the author's suggestions, what do you believe can be done to improve the quality of schools serving the urban poor?

RELATED WEBSITE RESOURCES

 ### Web Resources:

Education Trust. Available at:

http://www.edtrust.org.

The Education Trust works to ensure high academic achievement for all students. The website contains many resources toward that end.

Children's Defense Fund. Available at:

http://www.childrensdefense.org.

The Children's Defense Fund provides a voice for all children, paying particular attention to the needs of poor and minority children and those with disabilities. The website contains policy positions, research, and papers on issues related to children.

27

The Key to Classroom Management

Robert J. Marzano and Jana S. Marzano

Robert J. Marzano is a senior scholar at Mid-Continent Research for Education and Learning in Aurora, Colorado, and an associate professor at Cardinal Stritch University in Milwaukee, Wisconsin. **Jana S. Marzano** is a licensed professional counselor in private practice in Greenwood, Colorado.

"The Key to Classroom Management" by Robert J. Marzano and Jana S. Marzano, *Educational Leadership*, September 2001, pp. 6–13. Used with permission. The Association for Supervision and Curriculum Development is a worldwide community of educators advocating sound policies and sharing best practices to achieve the success of each learner. To learn more, visit ASCD at **www.ascd.org.**

F O C U S QUESTION

What teacher behaviors promote effective teacher-student relationships, a key to good classroom management and student achievement?

KEY TERMS

Assertive behavior
Dominance

Today, we know more about teaching than we ever have before. Research has shown us that teachers' actions in their classrooms have twice the impact on student achievement as do school policies regarding curriculum, assessment, staff collegiality, and community involvement (Marzano, 2003a). We also know that one of the classroom teacher's most important jobs is managing the classroom effectively.

A comprehensive literature review by Wang, Haertel, and Walberg (1993) amply demonstrates the importance of effective classroom management. These researchers analyzed 86 chapters from annual research reviews, 44 handbook chapters, 20 government and commissioned reports, and 11 journal articles to produce a list of 228 variables affecting student achievement. They combined the results of these analyses with the findings from 134 separate meta-analyses. Of all the variables, classroom management had the largest effect on student achievement. This makes intuitive sense—students cannot learn in a chaotic, poorly managed classroom.

Research not only supports the importance of classroom management, but it also sheds light on the dynamics of classroom management. Stage and Quiroz's meta-analysis (1997) shows the importance of there being a balance between teacher actions that provide clear consequences for unacceptable behavior and teacher actions that recognize and reward acceptable behavior. Other researchers (Emmer, Evertson, & Worsham, 2003; Evertson, Emmer, & Worsham, 2003) have identified important components of classroom management, including beginning the school year with a positive emphasis on management; arranging the room in a way conducive to effective management; and identifying and implementing rules and operating procedures.

In a recent meta-analysis of more than 100 studies (Marzano, 2003b), we found that the quality of teacher-student relationships is the keystone for all other aspects of classroom management. In fact, our meta-analysis indicates that on average, teachers who had high-quality relationships with their students had 31 percent fewer discipline problems, rule violations, and related problems over a year's time than did teachers who did not have high-quality relationships with their students.

What are the characteristics of effective teacher-student relationships? Let's first consider what they are not. Effective teacher-student relationships have nothing to do with the teacher's personality or even with whether the students view the teacher as a friend. Rather, the most effective teacher-student relationships are characterized by specific teacher behaviors: exhibiting appropriate levels of dominance; exhibiting appropriate levels of cooperation; and being aware of high-needs students.

Appropriate Levels of Dominance

Wubbels and his colleagues (Wubbels, Brekelmans, van Tartwijk, & Admiral, 1999; Wubbels & Levy, 1993) identify appropriate dominance as an important characteristic of effective teacher-student relationships. In contrast to the more negative connotation of the term *dominance* as forceful control or command over others, they define dominance as the teacher's ability to provide clear purpose and strong guidance regarding both academics and student behavior. Studies indicate that when asked about their preferences for teacher behavior, students typically express a desire for this type of teacher-student interaction. For example, in a study that involved interviews with more than 700 students in grades 4–7, students articulated a clear preference for strong teacher guidance and control rather than more permissive types of teacher behavior (Chiu & Tulley, 1997). Teachers can exhibit appropriate dominance by establishing clear behavior expectations and learning goals and by exhibiting assertive behavior.

Establish Clear Expectations and Consequences

Teachers can establish clear expectations for behavior in two ways: by establishing clear rules and procedures, and by providing consequences for student behavior.

The seminal research of the 1980s (Emmer, 1984; Emmer, Sanford, Evertson, Clements, & Martin, 1981; Evertson & Emmer, 1982) points to the importance of establishing rules and procedures for general classroom behavior, group work, seat work, transitions and interruptions, use of materials and equipment, and beginning and ending the period or the day. Ideally, the class should establish these rules and procedures through discussion and mutual consent by teacher and students (Glasser, 1969, 1990).

Along with well-designed and clearly communicated rules and procedures, the teacher must acknowledge students' behavior, reinforcing acceptable behavior and providing negative consequences for unacceptable behavior. Stage and Quiroz's research (1997) is instructive. They found that teachers build effective relationships through such strategies as the following:

- Using a wide variety of verbal and physical reactions to students' misbehavior, such as moving closer to offending students and using a physical cue, such as a finger to the lips, to point out inappropriate behavior.
- Cuing the class about expected behaviors through prearranged signals, such as raising a hand to indicate that all students should take their seats.
- Providing tangible recognition of appropriate behavior—with tokens or chits, for example.
- Employing group contingency policies that hold the entire group responsible for behavioral expectations.
- Employing home contingency techniques that involve rewards and sanctions at home.

Establish Clear Learning Goals

Teachers can also exhibit appropriate levels of dominance by providing clarity about the content and expectations of an upcoming instructional unit. Important teacher actions to achieve this end include

- Establishing and communicating learning goals at the beginning of a unit of instruction.
- Providing feedback on those goals.
- Continually and systematically revisiting the goals.
- Providing summative feedback regarding the goals.

The use of rubrics can help teachers establish clear goals. To illustrate, assume that a teacher has identified the learning goal "understanding and using fractions" as important for a given unit. That teacher might present students with the following rubric:

4 points. You understand the characteristics of fractions along with the different types. You can accurately describe how fractions are related to decimals and percentages. You can convert fractions to decimals and can explain how and why the process works. You can use fractions to understand and solve different types of problems.

3 points. You understand the basic characteristics of fractions. You know how fractions are related to decimals and percentages. You can convert fractions to decimals.

2 points. You have a basic understanding of the following, but have some small misunderstandings about one or more: the characteristics of fractions; the relationships among fractions, decimals, and percentages; how to convert fractions to decimals.

1 point. You have some major problems or misunderstandings with one or more of the following: the characteristics of fractions; the relationships among fractions,

decimals, and percentages; how to convert fractions to decimals.

0 points. You may have heard of the following before, but you do not understand what they mean: the characteristics of fractions; the relationships among fractions, decimals, and percentages; how to convert fractions to decimals.

The clarity of purpose provided by this rubric communicates to students that their teacher can provide proper guidance and direction in academic content.

Exhibit Assertive Behavior

Teachers can also communicate appropriate levels of dominance by exhibiting assertive behavior. According to Emmer and colleagues, assertive behavior is

> the ability to stand up for one's legitimate rights in ways that make it less likely that others will ignore or circumvent them. (2003, p. 146)

Assertive behavior differs significantly from both passive behavior and aggressive behavior. These researchers explain that teachers display assertive behavior in the classroom when they

- Use assertive body language by maintaining an erect posture, facing the offending student but keeping enough distance so as not to appear threatening and matching the facial expression with the content of the message being presented to students.
- Use an appropriate tone of voice, speaking clearly and deliberately in a pitch that is slightly but not greatly elevated from normal classroom speech, avoiding any display of emotions in the voice.
- Persist until students respond with the appropriate behavior. Do not ignore an inappropriate behavior; do not be diverted by a student denying, arguing, or blaming, but listen to legitimate explanations.

Appropriate Levels of Cooperation

Cooperation is characterized by a concern for the needs and opinions of others. Although not the antithesis of dominance, cooperation certainly occupies a different realm. Whereas dominance focuses on the teacher as the driving force in the classroom, cooperation focuses on the students and teacher functioning as a team. The interaction of these two dynamics—dominance and cooperation—is a central force in effective teacher-student relationships. Several strategies can foster appropriate levels of cooperation.

Provide Flexible Learning Goals

Just as teachers can communicate appropriate levels of dominance by providing clear learning goals, they can also convey appropriate levels of cooperation by providing flexible learning goals. Giving students the opportunity to set their own objectives at the beginning of a unit or asking students what they would like to learn conveys a sense of cooperation. Assume, for example, that a teacher has identified the topic of fractions as the focus of a unit of instruction and has provided students with a rubric. The teacher could then ask students to identify some aspect of fractions or a related topic that they would particularly like to study. Giving students this kind of choice, in addition to increasing their understanding of the topic, conveys the message that the teacher cares about and tries to accommodate students' interests.

Take a Personal Interest in Students

Probably the most obvious way to communicate appropriate levels of cooperation is to take a personal interest in each student in the class. As McCombs and Whisler (1997) note, all students appreciate personal attention from the teacher. Although busy teachers—particularly those at the secondary level—do not have the time for extensive interaction with all students, some teacher actions can communicate personal interest and concern without taking up much time. Teachers can

- Talk informally with students before, during, and after class about their interests.
- Greet students outside of school—for instance, at extracurricular events or at the store.
- Single out a few students each day in the lunchroom and talk with them.
- Be aware of and comment on important events in students' lives, such as participation in sports, drama, or other extracurricular activities.
- Compliment students on important achievements in and outside of school.
- Meet students at the door as they come into class; greet each one by name.

Use Equitable and Positive Classroom Behaviors

Programs like Teacher Expectations and Student Achievement emphasize the importance of the subtle ways in which teachers can communicate their interest in students (Kerman, Kimball, & Martin, 1980). This program recommends many practical strategies that emphasize equitable and positive classroom interactions with all students. Teachers should, for example,

- Make eye contact with each student. Teachers can make eye contact by scanning the entire room as they speak and by freely moving about all sections of the room.
- Deliberately move toward and stand close to each student during the class period. Make sure that the seating arrangement allows the teacher and students clear and easy ways to move around the room.
- Attribute the ownership of ideas to the students who initiated them. For instance, in a discussion a teacher might say, "Cecilia just added to Aida's idea by saying that...."
- Allow and encourage all students to participate in class discussions and interactions. Make sure to call on students who do not commonly participate, not just those who respond most frequently.
- Provide appropriate wait time for all students to respond to questions, regardless of their past performance or your perception of their abilities.

Awareness of High-Needs Students

Classroom teachers meet daily with a broad cross-section of students. In general, 12–22 percent of all students in school suffer from mental, emotional, or behavioral disorders, and relatively few receive mental health services (Adelman & Taylor, 2002). The Association of School Counselors notes that 18 percent of students have special needs and require extraordinary interventions and treatments that go beyond the typical resources available to the classroom (Dunn & Baker, 2002).

Although the classroom teacher is certainly not in a position to directly address such severe problems, teachers with effective classroom management skills are aware of high-needs students and have a repertoire of specific techniques for meeting some of their needs (Marzano, 2003b). Table 1 summarizes five categories of high-needs students and suggests classroom strategies for each category and subcategory.

- *Passive* students fall into two subcategories: those who fear *relationships* and those who fear *failure*. Teachers can build strong relationships with these students by refraining from criticism, rewarding small successes, and creating a classroom climate in which students feel safe from aggressive people.
- The category of *aggressive* students comprises three subcategories: *hostile, oppositional,* and *covert.*

Hostile students often have poor anger control, low capacity for empathy, and an inability to see the consequences of their actions. Oppositional students exhibit milder forms of behavior problems, but they consistently resist following rules, argue with adults, use harsh language, and tend to annoy others. Students in the covert subcategory may be quite pleasant at times, but they are often nearby when trouble starts and they never quite do what authority figures ask of them. Strategies for helping aggressive students include creating behavior contracts and providing immediate rewards and consequences. Most of all, teachers must keep in mind that aggressive students, although they may appear highly resistant to behavior change, are still children who are experiencing a significant amount of fear and pain.

- Students with *attention* problems fall into two categories: *hyperactive* and *inattentive.* These students may respond well when teachers contract with them to manage behaviors; teach them basic concentration, study, and thinking skills; help them divide tasks into manageable parts; reward their successes; and assign them a peer tutor.
- Students in the *perfectionist* category are driven to succeed at unattainable levels. They are self-critical, have low self-esteem, and feel inferior. Teachers can often help these students by encouraging them to develop more realistic standards, helping them to accept mistakes, and giving them opportunities to tutor other students.
- *Socially inept* students have difficulty making and keeping friends. They may stand too close and touch others in annoying ways, talk too much, and misread others' comments. Teachers can help these students by counseling them about social behaviors.

School may be the only place where many students who face extreme challenges can get their needs addressed. The reality of today's schools often demands that classroom teachers address these severe issues, even though this task is not always considered a part of their regular job.

In a study of classroom strategies (see Brophy, 1996; Brophy & McCaslin, 1992), researchers examined how effective classroom teachers interacted with specific types of students. The study found that the most effective classroom managers did not treat all students the same; they tended to employ different strategies with different types of students. In contrast, ineffective classroom managers did not appear sensitive to the diverse needs of students. Although Brophy did not

TABLE 1

Categories of High-Needs Students

Category	Definitions & Source	Characteristics	Suggestions
Suggestion	Behavior that avoids the domination of others or the pain of negative experiences. The child attempts to protect self from criticism, ridicule, or rejection, possibly reacting to abuse and neglect. Can have a biochemical basis, such as anxiety.	**Fear of relationships:** Avoids connection with others, is shy, doesn't initiate conversations, attempts to be invisible. **Fear of failure:** Gives up easily, is convinced he or she can't succeed, is easily frustrated, uses negative self-talk.	Provide safe adult and peer interactions and protection from aggressive people. Provide assertiveness and positive self-talk training. Reward small successes quickly. Withhold criticism.
Aggressive	Behavior that overpowers, dominates, harms, or controls others without regard for their well-being. The child has often taken aggressive people as role models. Has had minimal or ineffective limits set on behavior. Is possibly reacting to abuse and neglect. Condition may have a biochemical basis, such as depression.	**Hostile:** Rages, threatens, or intimidates others. Can be verbally or physically abusive to people, animals, or objects. **Oppositional:** Does opposite of what is asked. Demands that others agree or give in. Resists verbally or nonverbally. **Covert:** Appears to agree but then does the opposite of what is asked. Often acts innocent while setting up problems for others.	Describe the student's behavior clearly. Contract with the student to reward corrected behavior and set up consequences for uncorrected behavior. Be consistent and provide immediate rewards and consequences. Encourage and acknowledge extracurricular activities in and out of school. Give student responsibilities to help teacher or other students to foster successful experiences.
Attention problems	Behavior that demonstrates either motor or attentional difficulties resulting from a neurological disorder. The child's symptoms may be exacerbated by family or social stressors or biochemical conditions, such as anxiety, depression, or bipolar disorders.	**Hyperactive:** Has difficulty with motor control, both physically and verbally. Fidgets, leaves seat frequently, interrupts, talks excessively. **Inattentive:** Has difficulty staying focused and following through on projects. Has difficulty with listening, remembering, and organizing.	Contract with the student to manage behaviors. Teach basic concentration, study, and thinking skills. Separate student in a quiet work area. Help the student list each step of a task. Reward successes; assign a peer tutor.
Perfectionist	Behavior that is geared toward avoiding the embarrassment and assumed shame of making mistakes. The child fears what will happen if errors are discovered. Has unrealistically high expectations of self. Has possibly received criticism or lack of acceptance while making mistakes during the process of learning.	Tends to focus too much on the small details of projects. Will avoid projects if unsure of outcome. Focuses on results and not relationships. Is self-critical.	Ask the student to make mistakes on purpose, then show acceptance. Have the student tutor other students.

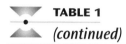

TABLE 1
(continued)

Category	Definitions & Source	Characteristics	Suggestions
Socially inept	Behavior that is based on the misinterpretation of nonverbal signals of others. The child misunderstands facial expressions and body language. Hasn't received adequate training in these areas and has poor role modeling.	Attempts to make friends but is inept and unsuccessful. Is forced to be alone. Is often teased for unusual behavior, appearance, or lack of social skills.	Teach the student to keep the appropriate physical distance from others. Teach the meaning of facial expressions, such as anger and hurt. Make suggestions regarding hygiene, dress, mannerisms, and posture.

Source: Marzano, R. J. (2003). *What works in schools: Translating research into action* (pp. 104–105). Alexandria, VA: ASCD.

couch his findings in terms of teacher-student relationships, the link is clear. An awareness of the five general categories of high-needs students and appropriate actions for each can help teachers build strong relationships with diverse students.

Don't Leave Relationships to Chance

Teacher-student relationships provide an essential foundation for effective classroom management—and classroom management is a key to high student achievement. Teacher-student relationships should not be left to chance or dictated by the personalities of those involved. Instead, by using strategies supported by research, teachers can influence the dynamics of their classrooms and build strong teacher-student relationships that will support student learning.

REFERENCES

Adelman, H. S., & Taylor, L. (2002). School counselors and school reform: New directions. *Professional School Counseling, 5*(4), 235–248.

Brophy, J. E. (1996). *Teaching problem students*. New York: Guilford.

Brophy, J. E., & McCaslin, N. (1992). Teachers' reports of how they perceive and cope with problem students. *Elementary School Journal, 93*, 3–68.

Chiu, L. H., & Tulley, M. (1997). Student preferences of teacher discipline styles. *Journal of Instructional Psychology, 24*(3), 168–175.

Dunn, N. A., & Baker, S. B. (2002). Readiness to serve students with disabilities: A survey of elementary school counselors. *Professional School Counselors, 5*(4), 277–284.

Emmer, E. T. (1984). *Classroom management: Research and implications.* (R & D Report No. 6178). Austin, TX: Research and Development Center for Teacher Education, University of Texas. (ERIC Document Reproduction Service No. ED251448)

Emmer, E. T., Evertson, C. M., & Worsham, M. E. (2003). *Classroom management for secondary teachers* (6th ed.). Boston: Allyn and Bacon.

Emmer, E. T., Sanford, J. P., Evertson, C. M., Clements, B. S., & Martin, J. (1981). *The classroom management improvement study: An experiment in elementary school classrooms. (*R & D Report No. 6050). Austin, TX: Research and Development Center for Teacher Education, University of Texas. (ERIC Document Reproduction Service No. ED226452)

Evertson, C. M., & Emmer, E. T. (1982). Preventive classroom management. In D. Duke (Ed.), *Helping teachers manage classrooms* (pp. 2–31). Alexandria, VA: ASCD.

Evertson, C. M., Emmer, E. T., & Worsham, M. E. (2003). *Classroom management for elementary teachers* (6th ed.). Boston: Allyn and Bacon.

Glasser, W. (1969). *Schools without failure*. New York: Harper and Row.

Glasser, W. (1990). *The quality school: Managing students without coercion*. New York: Harper and Row.

Kerman, S., Kimball, T., & Martin, M. (1980). *Teacher expectations and student achievement*. Bloomington, IN: Phi Delta Kappa.

Marzano, R. J. (2003a). *What works in schools*. Alexandria, VA: ASCD.

Marzano, R. J. (with Marzano, J. S., & Pickering, D. J.). (2003b). *Classroom management that works*. Alexandria, VA: ASCD.

McCombs, B. L., & Whisler, J. S. (1997). *The learner-centered classroom and school*. San Francisco: Jossey-Bass.

Stage, S. A., & Quiroz, D. R. (1997). A meta-analysis of interventions to decrease disruptive classroom behavior in public education settings. *School Psychology Review, 26*(3), 333–368.

Wang, M. C., Haertel, G. D., & Walberg, H. J. (1993). Toward a knowledge base for school learning. *Review of Educational Research, 63*(3), 249–294.

Wubbels, T., Brekelmans, M., van Tartwijk, J., & Admiral, W. (1999). Interpersonal relationships between teachers and students in the classroom. In H. C. Waxman & H. J. Walberg (Eds.), *New directions for teaching practice and research* (pp. 151–170). Berkeley, CA: McCutchan.

Wubbels, T., & Levy, J. (1993). *Do you know what you look like? Interpersonal relationships in education.* London: Falmer Press.

POSTNOTE

No issue is of greater concern to beginning teachers than classroom management. New teachers worry that they may not be effective because of their inability to maintain discipline. The authors point out that being an effective teacher is not a function of your personality or being a friend to students. Rather, establishing effective teacher-student relationships is the key to effective management and instruction. The authors identify specific teacher behaviors that characterize effective relationships: appropriate levels of dominance, appropriate levels of cooperation, and awareness of high-needs students. Work on developing these behaviors, and you will experience greater success and fewer discipline problems. There are a number of excellent books, based on research, to guide you in becoming a good classroom manager, some of which are mentioned in the references of this article.

Discussion Questions

1. Think of some teachers you have had who could not maintain discipline in their classrooms. What made them ineffective in managing the classroom?
2. Conversely, think of some teachers who were very effective in maintaining order and had good relations with students. What made them so effective?
3. Are there any points in the article with which you disagree? Are there other aspects to effective classroom management that you think should have been discussed? If so, what are they?

RELATED WEBSITE RESOURCES AND VIDEO CASES

 Web Resources:

Education World. Available at:

**http://educationworld.com/a_curr/archives/
classmanagement.shtml.**

This website presents a range of information concerning classroom management, including a database of teacher resources.

Learning Network. Available at:

**http://www.teachervision.fen.com/lesson-plans/
lesson-5776.html.**

This section of the website presents advice from experienced teachers and specialists regarding various aspects of behavior management.

⏩ ▶ ⏪ *Video Case:*

Classroom Management: Best Practices

In this video, you will see several teachers share classroom management techniques that have served them well over the years. As you watch the clips and study the artifacts in the case, reflect on the following questions:

1. State three to five classroom rules you would want to establish in your classroom. Why are these rules so important?
2. How would you organize your classroom (seating arrangements, procedures, etc.) to minimize disruptions and to facilitate good instructional practice?

⏩ ▶ ⏪ *Video Case:*

Cardinal Rules of Classroom Management: Perspectives from an Urban Elementary School

In this video case, you will see fourth-grade teacher, Benvinda Timas, demonstrate her approach to classroom management as she teaches a math lesson on mode, median, and mean. As you watch the clips and study the artifacts in the case, reflect upon the following questions:

1. What are two or three examples of Benvinda's positive approach to classroom management?
2. In the bonus feature, Benvinda's eight classroom rules are listed. What do you think of these rules? Are there any rules that you would either add or delete?

28

Students Need Challenge, Not Easy Success

Margaret M. Clifford

At the time this article was written, **Margaret M. Clifford** was professor emeritus of educational psychology, College of Education, University of Iowa, Iowa City. She died in 2003.

"Students Need Challenge, Not Easy Success" by Margaret M. Clifford, *Educational Leadership* 48, no. 1, pp. 32–36. Reprinted with permission of the Association for Supervision and Curriculum Development and the author. The Association for Supervision and Curriculum Development is a worldwide community of educators advocating sound policies and sharing best practices to achieve the success of each learner. To learn more, visit ASCD at **www.ascd.org.**

| F | O | C | U | S | QUESTION

What psychological principles advocated by the author will enhance the likelihood of motivating students to succeed?

KEY TERMS

Formative evaluation

Intrinsic motivation

Summative evaluation

Hundreds of thousands of apathetic students abandon their schools each year to begin lives of unemployment, poverty, crime, and psychological distress. According to Hahn (1987), "Dropout rates ranging from 40 to 60 percent in Boston, Chicago, Los Angeles, Detroit, and other major cities point to a situation of crisis proportions." The term *dropout* may not be adequate to convey the disastrous consequences of the abandonment of school by children and adolescents; *educational suicide* may be a far more appropriate label.

School abandonment is not confined to a small percentage of minority students, or low ability children, or mentally lazy kids. It is a systemic failure affecting the most gifted and knowledgeable as well as the disadvantaged, and it is threatening the social, economic, intellectual, industrial, cultural, moral, and psychological well-being of our country. Equally disturbing are students who sever themselves from the flow of knowledge while they occupy desks, like mummies.

Student apathy, indifference, and under-achievement are typical precursors of school abandonment. But what causes these symptoms? Is there a remedy? What will it take to stop the waste of our intellectual and creative resources?

To address these questions, we must acknowledge that educational suicide is primarily a motivational problem—not a physical, intellectual, financial, technological, cultural, or staffing problem. Thus, we must turn to motivational theories and research as a foundation for examining this problem and for identifying solutions.

Curiously enough, modern theoretical principles of motivation do not support certain widespread practices in education. I will discuss four such discrepancies and offer suggestions for resolving them.

Moderate Success Probability Is Essential to Motivation

The maxim, "Nothing succeeds like success," has driven educational practice for several decades. Absolute success for students has become the means *and* the end of education: It has been given higher priority than learning, and it has obstructed learning.

A major principle of current motivation theory is that tasks associated with a moderate probability of success (50 percent) provide maximum satisfaction (Atkinson 1964). Moderate probability of success is also an essential ingredient of intrinsic motivation (Lepper and Greene 1978, Csikszentmihalyi 1975, 1978). We attribute the success we experience on easy tasks to task ease; we attribute the success we experience on extremely difficult tasks to luck. Neither type of success does much to enhance self-image. It is only success at moderately difficult or truly challenging tasks that we explain in terms of personal effort, well-chosen strategies, and ability; and these explanations give rise to feelings of pride, competence, determination, satisfaction, persistence, and personal control. Even very young children show a preference for tasks that are just a bit beyond their ability (Danner and Lonky 1981).

Consistent with these motivational findings, learning theorists have repeatedly demonstrated that moderately difficult tasks are a prerequisite for maximizing intellectual development (Fischer 1980). But despite the fact that moderate challenge (implying considerable error-making) is essential for maximizing learning and optimizing motivation, many educators attempt to create error-proof learning environments. They set minimum criteria and standards in hopes of ensuring success for all students. They often reduce task difficulty, overlook errors, de-emphasize failed attempts, ignore faulty performances, display "perfect papers," minimize testing, and reward error-free performance.

It is time for educators to replace easy success with challenge. We must encourage students to reach beyond their intellectual grasp and allow them the privilege of learning from mistakes. There must be a tolerance for error-making in every classroom, and gradual success rather than continual success must become the yardstick by which learning is judged. Such transformations in educational practices will not guarantee the elimination of educational suicide, but they are sure to be one giant step in that direction.

External Constraints Erode Motivation and Performance

Intrinsic motivation and performance deteriorate when external constraints such as surveillance, evaluation by others, deadlines, threats, bribes, and rewards are accentuated. Yes, even rewards are a form of constraint! The reward giver is the General who dictates rules and issues orders; rewards are used to keep the troops in line.

Means-end contingencies, as exemplified in the statement, "If you complete your homework, you may watch TV" (with homework being the means and TV the end), are another form of external constraint. Such contingencies decrease interest in the first task (homework, the means) and increase interest in the second task (TV, the end) (Boggiano and Main 1986).

Externally imposed constraints, including material rewards, decrease task interest, reduce creativity, hinder performance, and encourage passivity on the part of students—even preschoolers (Lepper and Hodell 1989)! Imposed constraints also prompt individuals to use the "minimax strategy"—to exert the minimum amount of effort needed to obtain the maximum amount of reward (Kruglanski et al. 1977). Supportive of these findings are studies showing that autonomous behavior—that which is self-determined, freely chosen, and personally controlled—elicits high task interest, creativity, cognitive flexibility, positive emotion, and persistence (Deci and Ryan 1987).

Unfortunately, constraint and lack of student autonomy are trademarks of most schools. Federal and local governments, as well as teachers, legislate academic requirements; impose guidelines; create rewards systems; mandate behavioral contracts; serve warnings of expulsion; and use rules, threats, and punishments as routine problem-solving strategies. We can legislate school attendance and the conditions for obtaining a diploma, but we cannot legislate the development of intelligence, talent, creativity, and intrinsic motivation—resources this country desperately needs.

It is time for educators to replace coercive, constraint-laden techniques with autonomy-supportive techniques. We must redesign instructional and evaluation materials and procedures so that every assignment, quiz, text, project, and discussion activity not only allows for, but routinely *requires,* carefully calculated decision making on the part of students. Instead of minimum criteria, we must define multiple criteria (levels of minimum, marginal, average, good, superior, and excellent achievement), and we must free students to choose criteria that provide optimum challenge. Constraint gives a person the desire to escape; freedom gives a person the desire to explore, expand, and create.

Prompt, Specific Feedback Enhances Learning

A third psychological principle is that specific and prompt feedback enhances learning, performance, and motivation (Ilgen et al. 1979, Larson 1984). Informational feedback (that which reveals correct responses) increases learning (Ilgen and Moore 1987) and also promotes a feeling of increased competency (Sansone

1986). Feedback that can be used to improve future performance has powerful motivational value.

Sadly, however, the proportion of student assignments or activities that are promptly returned with informational feedback tends to be low. Students typically complete an assignment and then wait one, two, or three days (sometimes weeks) for its return. The feedback they do get often consists of a number or letter grade accompanied by ambiguous comments such as "Is this your best?" or "Keep up the good work." Precisely what is good or what needs improving is seldom communicated.

But, even if we could convince teachers of the value of giving students immediate, specific, informational feedback, our feedback problem would still be far from solved. How can one teacher provide 25 or more students immediate feedback on their tasks? Some educators argue that the solution to the feedback problem lies in having a tutor or teacher aide for every couple of students. Others argue that adequate student feedback will require an increased use of computer technology. However, there are less expensive alternatives. First, answer keys for students should be more plentiful. Resource books containing review and study activities should be available in every subject area, and each should be accompanied by a key that is available to students.

Second, quizzes and other instructional activities, especially those that supplement basic textbooks, should be prepared with "latent image" processing. With latent image paper and pens, a student who marks a response to an item can watch a hidden symbol emerge. The symbol signals either a correct or incorrect response, and in some instances a clue or explanation for the response is revealed. Trivia and puzzle books equipped with this latent image, immediate feedback process are currently being marketed at the price of comic books.

Of course, immediate informational feedback is more difficult to provide for composition work, long-term projects, and field assignments. But this does not justify the absence of immediate feedback on the learning activities and practice exercises that are aimed at teaching concepts, relationships, and basic skills. The mere availability of answer keys and latent image materials would probably elicit an amazing amount of self-regulated learning on the part of many students.

Moderate Risk Taking Is a Tonic for Achievement

A fourth motivational research finding is that moderate risk taking increases performance, persistence, perceived competence, self-knowledge, pride, and satisfaction (Deci and Porac 1978, Harter 1978, Trope 1979). Moderate risk taking implies a well-considered choice of an optimally challenging task, willingness to accept a moderate probability of success, and the anticipation of an outcome. It is this combination of events (which includes moderate success, self-regulated learning, and feedback) that captivates the attention, interest, and energy of card players, athletes, financial investors, lottery players, and even juvenile video arcade addicts.

Risk takers continually and freely face the probability of failing to attain the pleasure of succeeding under specified odds. From every risk-taking endeavor—whether it ends in failure or success—risk takers learn something about their skill and choice of strategy, and what they learn usually prompts them to seek another risk-taking opportunity. Risk taking—especially moderate risk taking—is a mind-engaging activity that simultaneously consumes and generates energy. It is a habit that feeds itself and thus requires an unlimited supply of risk-taking opportunities.

Moderate risk taking is likely to occur under the following conditions.

- The success probability for each alternative is clear and unambiguous.
- Imposed external constraints are minimized.
- Variable payoff (the value of success increases as risk increases) in contrast to fixed payoff is available.
- The benefits of risk taking can be anticipated.

My own recent research on academic risk taking with grade school, high school, and college students generally supports these conclusions. Students do, in fact, freely choose more difficult problems (a) when the number of points offered increases with the difficulty level of problems, (b) when the risk-taking task is presented within a game or practice situation (i.e., imposed constraint or threat is minimized), and (c) when additional opportunities for risk taking are anticipated (relatively high risk taking will occur on a practice exercise when students know they will be able to apply the information learned to an upcoming test). In the absence of these conditions we have seen students choose tasks that are as much as one-and-a-half years below their achievement level (Clifford 1988). Finally, students who take moderately high risks express high task interest even though they experience considerable error making.

In summary, risk-taking opportunities for students should be (a) plentiful, (b) readily available, (c) accompanied by explicit information about success probabilities, (d) accompanied by immediate feedback that communicates competency and error information, (e) associated with payoffs that vary with task difficulty, (f) relatively free from externally imposed evaluation, and (g) presented in relaxing and nonthreatening environments.

In today's educational world, however, there are few opportunities for students to engage in academic risk taking and no incentives to do so. Choices are seldom provided within tests or assignments, and rarely are variable payoffs made available. Once again, motivational theory, which identifies risk taking as a powerful source of knowledge, motivation, and skill development, conflicts with educational practice, which seeks to minimize academic risk at all costs.

We must restructure materials and procedures to encourage moderate academic risk taking on the part of students. I predict that if we fill our classrooms with optional academic risk-taking materials and opportunities so that all students have access to moderate risks, we will not only lower our educational suicide rate, but we will raise our level of academic achievement. If we give students the license to take risks and make errors, they will likely experience genuine success and the satisfaction that accompanies it.

Using Risk Can Ensure Success

Both theory and research evidence lead to the prediction that academic risk-taking activities are a powerful means of increasing the success of our educational efforts. But how do we get students to take risks on school-related activities? Students will choose risk over certainty when the consequences of the former are more satisfying and informative. Three basic conditions are needed to ensure such outcomes.

- First, students must be allowed to freely select from materials and activities that vary in difficulty and probability of success.
- Second, as task difficulty increases, so too must the payoffs for success.
- Third, an environment tolerant of error making and supportive of error correction must be guaranteed.

The first two conditions can be met rather easily. For example, on a 10-point quiz, composed of six 1-point items and four 2-point items, students might be asked to select and work only 6 items. The highest possible score for such quizzes is 10 and can be obtained only by correctly answering the four 2-point items and any two 1-point items. Choice and variable payoff are easily built into quizzes and many instructional and evaluation activities.

The third condition, creating an environment tolerant of error making and supportive of error correction, is more difficult to ensure. But here are six specific suggestions.

First, teachers must make a clear distinction between formative evaluation activities (tasks that guide instruction during the learning process) and summative evaluation activities (tasks used to judge one's level of achievement and to determine one's grade at the completion of the learning activity). Practice exercises, quizzes, and skill-building activities aimed at acquiring and strengthening knowledge and skills exemplify formative evaluation. These activities promote learning and skill development. They should be scored in a manner that excludes ability judgments, emphasizes error detection and correction, and encourages a search for better learning strategies. Formative evaluation activities should generally provide immediate feedback and be scored by students. It is on these activities that moderate risk taking is to be encouraged and is likely to prove beneficial.

Major examinations (unit exams and comprehensive final exams) exemplify summative evaluation; these activities are used to determine course grades. Relatively low risk taking is to be expected on such tasks, and immediate feedback may or may not be desirable.

Second, formative evaluation activities should be far more plentiful than summative. If, in fact, learning rather than grading is the primary object of the school, the percentage of time spent on summative evaluation should be small in comparison to that spent on formative evaluation (perhaps about 1:4). There should be enough formative evaluation activities presented as risk-taking opportunities to satisfy the most enthusiastic and adventuresome learner. The more plentiful these activities are, the less anxiety-producing and aversive summative activities are likely to be.

Third, formative evaluation activities should be presented as optional; students should be enticed, not mandated, to complete these activities. Enticement might be achieved by (a) ensuring that these activities are course-relevant and varied (e.g., scrambled outlines, incomplete matrices and graphs, exercises that require error detection and correction, quizzes); (b) giving students the option of working together; (c) presenting risk-taking activities in the context of games to be played individually, with competitors, or with partners; (d) providing immediate, informational, nonthreatening feedback; and (e) defining success primarily in terms of improvement over previous performance or the amount of learning that occurs during the risk-taking activity.

Fourth, for every instructional and evaluation activity there should be at least a modest percentage of content (10 percent to 20 percent) that poses a challenge to even the best students completing the activity. Maximum development of a country's talent requires that *all* individuals (a) find challenge in tasks they attempt, (b) develop tolerance for error making, and (c) learn to adjust strategies when faced with failure. To deprive the most talented students of these opportunities is perhaps the greatest resource-development crime a country can commit.

Fifth, summative evaluation procedures should include "retake exams." Second chances will not only encourage risk taking but will provide good reasons for students to study their incorrect responses made on previous risk-taking tasks. Every error made on an initial exam and subsequently corrected on a second chance represents real learning.

Sixth, we must reinforce moderate academic risk taking instead of error-free performance or excessively high or low risk taking. Improvement scores, voluntary correction of errors, completion of optional risk-taking activities—these are behaviors that teachers should recognize and encourage.

Toward a New Definition of Success

We face the grim reality that our extraordinary efforts to produce "schools without failure" have not yielded the well-adjusted, enthusiastic, self-confident scholars we anticipated. Our efforts to mass-produce success for every individual in every educational situation have left us with cheap reproductions of success that do not even faintly represent the real thing. This overdose of synthetic success is a primary cause of the student apathy and school abandonment plaguing our country.

To turn the trend around, we must emphasize error tolerance, not error-free learning; reward error correction, not error avoidance; ensure challenge, not easy success. Eventual success on challenging tasks, tolerance for error making, and constructive responses to failure are motivational fare that school systems should be serving up to all students. I suggest that we engage the skills of researchers, textbook authors, publishers, and educators across the country to ensure the development and marketing of attractive and effective academic risk-taking materials and procedures. If we convince these experts of the need to employ their creative efforts toward this end, we will not only stem the tide of educational suicide, but we will enhance the quality of educational success. We will witness self-regulated student success and satisfaction that will ensure the intellectual, creative, and motivational well-being of our country.

REFERENCES

Atkinson, J. W. (1964). *An Introduction to Motivation.* Princeton, N.J.: Van Nostrand.

Boggiano, A. K., and D. S. Main. (1986). "Enhancing Children's Interest in Activities Used as Rewards: The Bonus Effect." *Journal of Personality and Social Psychology* 51: 1116–1126.

Clifford, M. M. (1988). "Failure Tolerance and Academic Risk Taking in Ten- to Twelve-Year-Old Students." *British Journal of Educational Psychology* 58: 15–27.

Csikszentmihalyi, M. (1975). *Beyond Boredom and Anxiety.* San Francisco: Jossey-Bass.

Csikszentmihalyi, M. (1978). "Intrinsic Rewards and Emergent Motivation." In *The Hidden Costs of Reward,* edited by M. R. Lepper and D. Greene. Hillsdale, N.J.: Lawrence Erlbaum Associates.

Danner, F. W., and D. Lonky. (1981). "A Cognitive-Developmental Approach to the Effects of Rewards on Intrinsic Motivation." *Child Development* 52: 1043–1052.

Deci, E. L., and J. Porac. (1978). "Cognitive Evaluation Theory and the Study of Human Motivation." In *The Hidden Costs of Reward,* edited by M. R. Lepper and D. Greene. Hillsdale, N.J.: Lawrence Erlbaum Associates.

Deci, E. L., and R. M. Ryan. (1987). "The Support of Autonomy and the Control of Behavior." *Journal of Personality and Social Psychology* 53: 1024–1037.

Fischer, K. W. (1980). "Learning as the Development of Organized Behavior." *Journal of Structural Learning* 3: 253–267.

Hahn, A. (1987). "Reaching Out to America's Dropouts: What to Do?" *Phi Delta Kappan* 69: 256–263.

Harter, S. (1978). "Effective Motivation Reconsidered: Toward a Developmental Model." *Human Development* 1: 34–64.

Ilgen, D. R., and C. F. Moore. (1987). "Types and Choices of Performance Feedback." *Journal of Applied Psychology* 72: 401–406.

Ilgen, D. R., C. D. Fischer, and M. S. Taylor. (1979). "Consequences of Individual Feedback on Behavior in Organizations." *Journal of Applied Psychology* 64: 349–371.

Kruglanski, A., C. Stein, and A. Riter. (1977). "Contingencies of Exogenous Reward and Task Performance: On the 'Minimax' Strategy in Instrumental Behavior." *Journal of Applied Social Psychology* 2: 141–148.

Larson, J. R., Jr. (1984). "The Performance Feedback Process: A Preliminary Model." *Organizational Behavior and Human Performance* 33: 42–76.

Lepper, M. R., and D. Greene. (1978). *The Hidden Costs of Reward.* Hillsdale, N.J.: Lawrence Erlbaum Associates.

Lepper, M. R., and M. Hodell. (1989). "Intrinsic Motivation in the Classroom." In *Motivation in Education, Vol. 3,* edited by C. Ames and R. Ames. New York: Academic Press.

Sansone, C. (1986). "A Question of Competence: The Effects of Competence and Task Feedback on Intrinsic Motivation." *Journal of Personality and Social Psychology* 51: 918–931.

Trope, Y. (1979). "Uncertainty Reducing Properties of Achievement Tasks." *Journal of Personality and Social Psychology* 37: 1505–1518.

POSTNOTE

In the 1980s, educators and their many critics recognized that our schools were failing many of our students and that our students were failing many of our schools. An avalanche of reports, books, television specials, and columns lambasted the schools' performance. In response, standards have been raised, graduation requirements increased, and more rigorous courses of study implemented.

However, as an old adage says, "You can lead a horse to water, but you can't make it drink." Vast numbers of students still commit "educational suicide," and student apathy, indifference, and underachievement are widespread. Margaret Clifford's remedy first takes a realistic look at the mismatch between the student and the school and then suggests quite tangible modifications to match the student's motivational system with the goals of schooling.

Discussion Questions

1. This article pinpoints student motivation as a major source of school problems. Do you agree with this assessment? Why or why not?
2. What are the most important remedies Clifford offers for our schools' ills? In your judgment, will these remedies solve the problem?
3. What is the author's new definition of *success?* Do you agree with it? Why or why not?

RELATED WEBSITE RESOURCES

 Web Resources:

Northwest Regional Educational Laboratory. Available at:

http://www.nwrel.org/request/oct00/index.html.

This paper, "Increasing Student Engagement and Motivation: From Time-on-Task to Homework," provides many useful ideas and strategies to get students engaged in academic tasks.

Center for Research on Learning and Teaching. Available at:

http://www.crlt.umich.edu/tstrategies/tsms.php.

This particular website has links to other websites dealing with teaching strategies for motivating students.

29

Seven Practices for Effective Learning

Jay McTighe and Ken O'Connor

Jay McTighe is an education consultant who has held a variety of positions in Maryland, including director of the Maryland Assessment Consortium. **Ken O'Connor** is an educational consultant who was formerly the curriculum coordinator with the Toronto District School Board in Ontario, Canada.

"Seven Practices for Effective Learning" by Jay McTighe and Ken O'Connor, *Educational Leadership* 63, no. 3, November 2005, pp. 10–17 (including figure, "Student Learning Curves"). Used with permission.

| F | O | C | U | S | QUESTION

When assessing students, what information do you need and what will you do with it?

KEY TERMS

Benchmarks
Diagnostic assessment
Feedback
Formative assessment
Performance assessment
Rubric
Summative assessment

Classroom assessment and grading practices have the potential not only to measure and report learning but also to promote it. Indeed, recent research has documented the benefits of regular use of diagnostic and formative assessments as feedback for learning (Black, Harrison, Lee, Marshall, & Wiliam, 2004). Like successful athletic coaches, the best teachers recognize the importance of ongoing assessments and continual adjustments on the part of both teacher and student as the means to achieve maximum performance. Unlike the external standardized tests that feature so prominently on the school landscape these days, well-designed classroom assessment and grading practices can provide the kind of specific, personalized, and timely information needed to guide both learning and teaching.

Classroom assessments fall into three categories, each serving a different purpose. *Summative* assessments summarize what students have learned at the conclusion of an instructional segment. These assessments tend to be evaluative, and teachers typically encapsulate and report assessment results as a score or a grade. Familiar examples of summative assessments include tests, performance tasks, final exams, culminating projects, and work portfolios. Evaluative assessments command the attention of students and parents because their results typically "count" and appear on report cards and transcripts. But by themselves, summative assessments are insufficient tools for maximizing learning. Waiting until the end of a teaching period to find out how well students have learned is simply too late.

Two other classroom assessment categories—diagnostic and formative—provide fuel for the teaching and learning engine by offering descriptive feedback along the way. *Diagnostic* assessments—sometimes known as *pre-assessments*—typically precede instruction. Teachers use them to check students' prior knowledge and skill levels, identify student misconceptions, profile learners' interests, and reveal learning-style preferences. Diagnostic assessments provide information to assist teacher planning and guide differentiated instruction. Examples of diagnostic assessments include prior knowledge and skill checks and interest or learning preference surveys. Because pre-assessments serve diagnostic purposes, teachers normally don't grade the results.

Formative assessments occur concurrently with instruction. These ongoing assessments provide specific feedback to teachers and students for the purpose of guiding teaching to improve learning. Formative assessments include both formal and informal methods, such as ungraded quizzes, oral questioning, teacher observations, draft work, think-alouds, student-constructed concept maps, learning logs, and portfolio reviews. Although teachers may record the results of formative assessments, we shouldn't factor these results into summative evaluation and grading.

Keeping these three categories of classroom assessment in mind, let us consider seven specific assessment and grading practices that can enhance teaching and learning.

Practice 1: Use Summative Assessments to Frame Meaningful Performance Goals

On the first day of a three-week unit on nutrition, a middle school teacher describes to students the two summative assessments that she will use. One assessment is a multiple-choice test examining student knowledge of various nutrition facts and such basic skills as analyzing nutrition labels. The second assessment is an authentic performance task in which each student designs a menu plan for an upcoming two-day trip to an outdoor education facility. The menu plan must provide well-balanced and nutritious meals and snacks.

The current emphasis on established content standards has focused teaching on designated knowledge and skills. To avoid the danger of viewing the standards and benchmarks as inert content to "cover," educators should frame the standards and benchmarks in terms of desired performances and ensure that the performances are as authentic as possible. Teachers should then present the summative performance assessment tasks to students at the beginning of a new unit or course.

This practice has three virtues. First, the summative assessments clarify the targeted standards and benchmarks for teachers and learners. In standards-based education, the rubber meets the road with assessments because they define the evidence that will determine whether or not students have learned the content standards and benchmarks. The nutrition vignette is illustrative: By knowing what the culminating assessments will be, students are better able to focus on what the teachers expect them to learn (information about healthy eating) and on what they will be expected to do with that knowledge (develop a nutritious meal plan).

Second, the performance assessment tasks yield evidence that reveals understanding. When we call for authentic application, we do not mean recall of basic facts or mechanical plug-ins of a memorized formula. Rather, we want students to transfer knowledge—to use what they know in a new situation. Teachers should set up realistic, authentic contexts for assessment that enable students to apply their learning thoughtfully and flexibly, thereby demonstrating their understanding of the content standards.

Third, presenting the authentic performance tasks at the beginning of a new unit or course provides a meaningful learning goal for students. Consider a sports analogy. Coaches routinely conduct practice drills that both develop basic skills and purposefully point toward performance in the game. Too often, classroom instruction and assessment overemphasize decontextualized drills and provide too few opportunities for students to actually "play the game." How many soccer players would practice corner kicks or run exhausting wind sprints if they weren't preparing for the upcoming game? How many competitive swimmers would log endless laps if there were no future swim meets? Authentic performance tasks provide a worthy goal and help learners see a reason for their learning.

Practice 2: Show Criteria and Models in Advance

A high school language arts teacher distributes a summary of the summative performance task that students will complete during the unit on research, including the rubric for judging the performance's quality. In addition, she shows examples of student work products collected from previous years (with student names removed) to illustrate criteria and performance levels. Throughout the unit, the teacher uses the student examples and the criteria in the rubric to help students better understand the nature of high-quality work and to support her teaching of research skills and report writing.

A second assessment practice that supports learning involves presenting evaluative criteria and models of work that illustrate different levels of quality. Unlike selected-response or short-answer tests, authentic performance assessments are typically open-ended and do not yield a single, correct answer or solution process. Consequently, teachers cannot score student responses using an answer key or a Scantron machine. They need to evaluate products and performances on the basis of explicitly defined performance criteria.

A rubric is a widely used evaluation tool consisting of criteria, a measurement scale (a 4-point scale, for example), and descriptions of the characteristics for each score point. Well-developed rubrics communicate the important dimensions, or elements of quality, in a product or performance and guide educators in evaluating student work. When a department or grade-level team—or better yet, an entire school or district—uses common rubrics, evaluation results are more consistent because the performance criteria don't vary from teacher to teacher or from school to school.

Rubrics also benefit students. When students know the criteria in advance of their performance, they have clear goals for their work. Because well-defined criteria provide a clear description of quality performance, students don't need to guess what is most important or how teachers will judge their work.

Providing a rubric to students in advance of the assessment is a necessary, but often insufficient, condition to support their learning. Although experienced teachers have a clear conception of what they mean by "quality work," students don't necessarily have the same understanding. Learners are more likely to understand feedback and evaluations when teachers show several examples that display both excellent and weak work. These models help translate the rubric's abstract language into more specific, concrete, and understandable terms.

Some teachers express concern that students will simply copy or imitate the example. A related worry is that showing an excellent model (sometimes known as an exemplar) will stultify student creativity. We have found that providing multiple models helps avoid these potential problems. When students see several exemplars showing how different students achieved high-level performance in unique ways, they are less likely to follow a cookie-cutter approach. In addition, when students study and compare examples ranging in quality—from very strong to very weak—they are better able to internalize the differences. The models enable students to more accurately self-assess and improve their work before turning it in to the teacher.

Practice 3: Assess Before Teaching

Before beginning instruction on the five senses, a kindergarten teacher asks each student to draw a picture of the body parts related to the various senses and show what each part does. She models the process by drawing an eye on the chalkboard. "The eye helps us see things around us," she points out. As students draw, the teacher circulates around the room, stopping to ask clarifying questions ("I see you've drawn a nose. What does the nose help us do?"). On the basis of what she learns about her students from this diagnostic pre-test, she divides the class into two groups for differentiated instruction. At the conclusion of the unit, the teacher asks students to do another drawing, which she collects and compares with their original pre-test as evidence of their learning.

Diagnostic assessment is as important to teaching as a physical exam is to prescribing an appropriate medical regimen. At the outset of any unit of study, certain students are likely to have already mastered

some of the skills that the teacher is about to introduce, and others may already understand key concepts. Some students are likely to be deficient in prerequisite skills or harbor misconceptions. Armed with this diagnostic information, a teacher gains greater insight into *what to teach,* by knowing what skill gaps to address or by skipping material previously mastered; into *how to teach,* by using grouping options and initiating activities based on preferred learning styles and interests; and into *how to connect* the content to students' interests and talents.

Teachers can use a variety of practical pre-assessment strategies, including pre-tests of content knowledge, skills checks, concept maps, drawings, and K-W-L (*K*now-*W*ant to learn-*L*earn) charts. Powerful pre-assessment has the potential to address a worrisome phenomenon reported in a growing body of literature (Bransford, Brown, & Cocking, 1999; Gardner, 1991): A sizeable number of students come into school with misconceptions about subject matter (thinking that a heavier object will drop faster than a lighter one, for example) and about themselves as learners (assuming that they can't and never will be able to draw, for example). If teachers don't identify and confront these misconceptions, they will persist even in the face of good teaching. To uncover existing misconceptions, teachers can use a short, nongraded true-false diagnostic quiz that includes several potential misconceptions related to the targeted learning. Student responses will signal any prevailing misconceptions, which the teacher can then address through instruction. In the future, the growing availability of portable, electronic student-response systems will enable educators to obtain this information instantaneously.

Practice 4: Offer Appropriate Choices

As part of a culminating assessment for a major unit on their state's history and geography, a class of 4th graders must contribute to a classroom museum display. The displays are designed to provide answers to the unit's essential question: How do geography, climate, and natural resources influence lifestyle, economy, and culture? Parents and students from other classrooms will view the display. Students have some choice about the specific products they will develop, which enables them to work to their strengths. Regardless of students' chosen products, the teacher uses a common rubric to evaluate every project. The resulting class museum contains a wide variety of unique and informative products that demonstrate learning.

Responsiveness in assessment is as important as it is in teaching. Students differ not only in how they prefer to take in and process information but also in how they best demonstrate their learning. Some students need to "do";

others thrive on oral explanations. Some students excel at creating visual representations; others are adept at writing. To make valid inferences about learning, teachers need to allow students to work to their strengths. A standardized approach to classroom assessment may be efficient, but it is not fair because any chosen format will favor some students and penalize others.

Assessment becomes responsive when students are given appropriate options for demonstrating knowledge, skills, and understanding. Allow choices—but always with the intent of collecting needed and appropriate evidence based on goals. In the example of the 4th grade museum display project, the teacher wants students to demonstrate their understanding of the relationship between geography and economy. This could be accomplished through a newspaper article, a concept web, a PowerPoint presentation, a comparison chart, or a simulated radio interview with an expert. Learners often put forth greater effort and produce higher-quality work when given such a variety of choices. The teacher will judge these products using a three-trait rubric that focuses on accuracy of content, clarity and thoroughness of explanation, and overall product quality.

We offer three cautions. First, teachers need to collect appropriate evidence of learning on the basis of goals rather than simply offer a "cool" menu of assessment choices. If a content standard calls for proficiency in written or oral presentations, it would be Inappropriate to provide performance options other than those involving writing or speaking, except in the case of students for whom such goals are clearly inappropriate (a newly arrived English language learner, for example). Second, the options must be worth the time and energy required. It would be inefficient to have students develop an elaborate three-dimensional display or an animated PowerPoint presentation for content that a multiple-choice quiz could easily assess. In the folksy words of a teacher friend, "With performance assessments, the juice must be worth the squeeze." Third, teachers have only so much time and energy, so they must be judicious in determining when it is important to offer product and performance options. They need to strike a healthy balance between a single assessment path and a plethora of choices.

Practice 5: Provide Feedback Early and Often

Middle school students are learning watercolor painting techniques. The art teacher models proper technique for mixing and applying the colors, and the students begin working. As they paint, the teacher provides feedback both to individual students and to the class as a whole. She targets common mistakes, such as using too much paint and not enough water, a practice that reduces the desired transparency effect. Benefiting from continual feedback from the teacher, students experiment with the medium on small sheets of paper. The next class provides additional opportunities to apply various watercolor techniques to achieve such effects as color blending and soft edges. The class culminates in an informal peer feedback session. Skill development and refinement result from the combined effects of direct instruction, modeling, and opportunities to practice guided by ongoing feedback.

It is often said that feedback is the breakfast of champions. All kinds of learning, whether on the practice field or in the classroom, require feedback based on formative assessments. Ironically, the quality feedback necessary to enhance learning is limited or nonexistent in many classrooms.

To serve learning, feedback must meet four criteria: It must be timely, specific, understandable to the receiver, and formed to allow for self-adjustment on the student's part (Wiggins, 1998). First, feedback on strengths and weaknesses needs to be prompt for the learner to improve. Waiting three weeks to find out how you did on a test will not help your learning.

In addition, specificity is key to helping students understand both their strengths and the areas in which they can improve. Too many educators consider grades and scores as feedback when, in fact, they fail the specificity test. Pinning a letter (*B*-) or a number (82%) on a student's work is no more helpful than such comments as "Nice job" or "You can do better." Although good grades and positive remarks may feel good, they do not advance learning.

Specific feedback sounds different, as in this example:

> Your research paper is generally well organized and contains a great deal of information on your topic. You used multiple sources and documented them correctly. However, your paper lacks a clear conclusion, and you never really answered your basic research question.

Sometimes the language in a rubric is lost on a student. Exactly what does "well organized" or "sophisticated reasoning" mean? "Kid language" rubrics can make feedback clearer and more comprehensible. For instance, instead of saying, "Document your reasoning process," a teacher might say, "Show your work in a step-by-step manner so the reader can see what you were thinking."

Here's a simple, straightforward test for a feedback system: Can learners tell *specifically* from the given feedback what they have done well and what they could do next time to improve? If not, then the feedback is not specific or understandable enough for the learner.

Finally, the learner needs opportunities to act on the feedback—to refine, revise, practice, and retry. Writers rarely compose a perfect manuscript on the first try, which is why the writing process stresses cycles of drafting, feedback, and revision as the route to excellence. Not surprisingly, the best feedback often surfaces in the performance-based subjects—such as art, music, and physical education—and in extracurricular activities, such as band and athletics. Indeed, the essence of coaching involves ongoing assessment and feedback.

Practice 6: Encourage Self-Assessment and Goal Setting

> Before turning in their science lab reports, students review their work against a list of explicit criteria. On the basis of their self-assessments, a number of students make revisions to improve their reports before handing them in. Their teacher observes that the overall quality of the lab reports has improved.

The most effective learners set personal learning goals, employ proven strategies, and self-assess their work. Teachers help cultivate such habits of mind by modeling self-assessment and goal setting and by expecting students to apply these habits regularly.

Rubrics can help students become more effective at honest self-appraisal and productive self-improvement. In the rubric in Figure 1, students verify that they have met a specific criterion—for a title, for example—by placing a check in the lower left-hand square of the applicable box. The teacher then uses the square on the right side for his or her evaluation. Ideally, the two judgments should match. If not, the discrepancy raises an opportunity to discuss the criteria, expectations, and performance standards. Over time, teacher and student judgments tend to align. In fact, it is not

unusual for students to be harder on themselves than the teacher is.

The rubric also includes space for feedback comments and student goals and action steps. Consequently, the rubric moves from being simply an evaluation tool for "pinning a number" on students to a practical and robust vehicle for feedback, self-assessment, and goal setting.

Initially, the teacher models how to self-assess, set goals, and plan improvements by asking such prompting questions as,

- What aspect of your work was most effective?
- What aspect of your work was least effective?
- What specific action or actions will improve your performance?
- What will you do differently next time?

Questions like these help focus student reflection and planning. Over time, students assume greater responsibility for enacting these processes independently.

Educators who provide regular opportunities for learners to self-assess and set goals often report a change in the classroom culture. As one teacher put it,

> My students have shifted from asking, "What did I get?" or "What are you going to give me?" to becoming increasingly capable of knowing how they are doing and what they need to do to improve.

Practice 7: Allow New Evidence of Achievement to Replace Old Evidence

> A driver education student fails his driving test the first time, but he immediately books an appointment to retake the test one week later. He passes on his second attempt be-

FIGURE 1

Analytic Rubric for Graphic Display of Data

	Title	Labels	Accuracy	Neatness
3	The graph contains a title that clearly tells what the data show.	All parts of the graph (units of measurement, rows, etc.) are correctly labeled. ✓	All data are accurately represented on the graph. ✓✓	The graph is very neat and easy to read.
2	The graph contains a title that suggests what the data show.	Some parts of the graph are inaccurately labeled. ✓✓	Data representation contains minor errors.	The graph is generally neat and readable. ✓
1	The title does not reflect what the data show OR the title is missing. ✓	The graph is incorrectly labeled OR labels are missing. ✓	The data are inaccurately represented, contain major errors, OR are missing.	The graph is sloppy and difficult to read.

Comments: _____

Goals/Actions: _____

Source: Richard Ingersoll, cited in "No Dream Denied: A Pledge to America's Children," by the National Commission on Teaching and America's Future and the National Center for Education Statistics.

cause he successfully demonstrates the requisite knowledge and skills. The driving examiner does not average the first performance with the second, nor does the new license indicate that the driver "passed on the second attempt."

This vignette reveals an important principle in classroom assessment, grading, and reporting: New evidence of achievement should replace old evidence. Classroom assessments and grading should focus on *how well*—not on when—the student mastered the designated knowledge and skill.

Consider the learning curves of four students in terms of a specified learning goal (see fig. 2). Bob already possesses the targeted knowledge and skill and doesn't need instruction for this particular goal. Gwen arrives with substantial knowledge and skill but has room to improve. Roger and Pam are true novices who demonstrate a high level of achievement by the *end* of the instructional segment as a result of effective teaching and diligent learning. If their school's grading system truly documented learning, all these students would receive the same grade because they all achieved the desired results over time. Roger and Pam would receive lower grades than Bob and Gwen, however, if the teacher factored their earlier performances into the final evaluation. This practice, which is typical of the grading approach used in many classrooms, would

misrepresent Roger and Pam's ultimate success because it does not give appropriate recognition to the real—or most current—level of achievement.

Two concerns may arise when teachers provide students with multiple opportunities to demonstrate their learning. Students may not take the first attempt seriously once they realize they'll have a second chance. In addition, teachers often become overwhelmed by the logistical challenges of providing multiple opportunities. To make this approach effective, teachers need to require their students to provide some evidence of the corrective action they will take—such as engaging in peer coaching, revising their report, or practicing the needed skill in a given way—before embarking on their "second chance."

As students work to achieve clearly defined learning goals and produce evidence of their achievement, they need to know that teachers will not penalize them for either their lack of knowledge at the beginning of a course of study or their initial attempts at skill mastery. Allowing new evidence to replace old conveys an important message to students—that teachers care about their successful learning, not merely their grades.

Motivated to Learn

The assessment strategies that we have described address three factors that influence student motivation to learn (Marzano, 1992). Students are more likely to put forth the required effort when there is

- *Task clarity*—when they clearly understand the learning goal and know how teachers will evaluate their learning (Practices 1 and 2).
- *Relevance*—when they think the learning goals and assessments are meaningful and worth learning (Practice 1).
- *Potential for success*—when they believe they can successfully learn and meet the evaluative expectations (Practices 3–7).

By using these seven assessment and grading practices, all teachers can enhance learning in their classrooms.

REFERENCES

Black, P., Harrison, C., Lee., C., Marshall, B., & Wiliam, D. (2004). Working inside the black box: Assessment for learning in the classroom. *Phi Delta Kappan, 86*(1), 8–21.

Bransford, J. D., Brown, A. L., & Cocking, R. R. (Eds.). (1999). *How people learn: Brain, mind, experience, and school.* Washington, DC: National Research Council.

Gardner, H. (1991). *The unschooled mind.* New York: BasicBooks.

FIGURE 2

Student Learning Curves

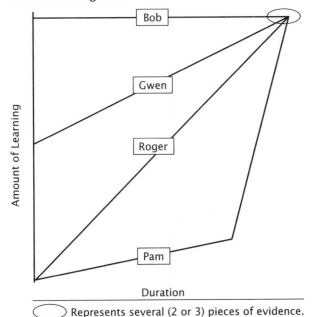

⬭ Represents several (2 or 3) pieces of evidence.

Marzano, R. (1992). *A different kind of classroom: Teaching with dimensions of learning.* Alexandria, VA: ASCD.

Wiggins, G. (1998). *Educative assessment: Designing assessments to inform and improve student performance.* San Francisco: Jossey-Bass.

POSTNOTE

Assessment is a vital part of the instructional process. Finding out what students already know and don't know (diagnostic assessment) is an important step before beginning instruction. Finding out what students are learning during the midst of instruction (formative assessment) provides the teacher with guidance on how to proceed. Finding out what students have learned after instruction is over (summative assessment) lets the teacher know how successful he/she and the students have been.

Unfortunately, policymakers seem much more interested in assessments for accountability purposes; that is, holding educators and students accountable for student learning by offering rewards to those who succeed and punishment to those who don't. The high-stakes testing that accompanies most states' standards of learning are usually worthless as guides to teachers for adjusting instructional decisions to help particular students. The results come months after the students have taken the tests and do not provide enough information to guide students in self-assessments to improve their learning. The authors of this article give the reader practical advice on how to make the diagnostic, formative, and summative forms of assessment vital to improving student learning.

Discussion Questions

1. Thinking back on your own educational experiences, have you ever experienced assessments (e.g., tests, papers, projects) that motivated you to want to learn more? If so, what made them so exceptional?

2. Describe the most creative assessment you ever completed as a student. What made it creative?

3. What questions about assessment do you have? How will you get them answered?

RELATED WEBSITE RESOURCES AND VIDEO CASES

 Web Resources:

The National Center for Research on Evaluation, Standards, and Student Testing. Available at:

http://www.cse.ucla.edu/.

This website contains numerous articles and reports that discuss current assessment and evaluation issues.

Yahoo's Directory of K–12 Lesson Plans. Available at:

http://dir.yahoo.com/Education/Standards_ and_Testing.

This website contains a wide variety of resources for testing, assessment, measurement, and benchmarking.

Video Case:

Assessment in the Elementary Grades: Formal and Informal Literary Assessment

In this video case, you will see how Chris Quinn, a second-grade teacher, administers both a formal assessment (a standardized test on phonics) and an informal literacy assessment (a running record) to her students. As you watch the clips and study the artifacts in the case, reflect on the following questions:

1. How do you anticipate combining formal and informal assessments in your classroom?

2. How does this teacher show that she is using assessment as a key part of instruction?

3. Do you agree that students should help determine the assessment process? Why or why not?

Alternatively, you could watch **Assessment in the Middle Grades: Measurement of Student Learning.**

The Courage to Be Constructivist

Martin G. Brooks and Jacqueline Grennon Brooks

Martin Brooks, Ed.D., is superintendent of schools in the Kings Park Central School District, New York. **Jacqueline Grennon Brooks,** Ed.D., is associate professor in the Department of Curriculum and Teaching at Hofstra University, New York.

"The Courage to Be Constructivist" by Martin G. Brooks and Jacqueline Grennon Brooks, *Educational Leadership* 57, no. 3, November 1999, pp. 18–24. Used with permission.

F O C U S QUESTION

What does it mean to be a constructivist teacher?

KEY TERMS

Constructivism

High-stakes accountability (see high-stakes tests)

Performance-based assessment (see performance assessment)

For years, the term *constructivism* appeared only in journals read primarily by philosophers, epistemologists, and psychologists. Nowadays, *constructivism* regularly appears in the teachers' manuals of textbook series, state education department curriculum frameworks, education reform literature, and education journals. Constructivism now has a face and a name in education.

A theory of learning that describes the central role that learners' ever-transforming mental schemes play in their cognitive growth, constructivism powerfully informs educational practice. Education, however, has deep roots in other theories of learning. This history constrains our capacity to embrace the central role of the learner in his or her own education. We must rethink the very foundations of schooling if we are to base our practice on our understandings of learners' needs.

One such foundational notion is that students will learn on demand. This bedrock belief is manifested in the traditional scope and sequence of a typical course of study and, more recently, in the new educational standards and assessments. This approach to schooling is grounded in the conviction that all students can and will learn the same material at the same time. For some students, this approach does indeed lead to the construction of knowledge. For others, however, it does not.

The people working directly with students are the ones who must adapt and adjust lessons on the basis of evolving needs. Constructivist educational practice cannot be realized without the classroom teacher's autonomous, on-going, professional judgment. State education departments could and should support good educational practice. But too often they do not.

Their major flaw is their focus on high-stakes accountability systems and the ramifications of that focus on teachers and students. Rather than set standards for professional practice and the development of local capacity to enhance student learning, many state education departments have placed even greater weight on the same managerial equation that has failed repeatedly in the past: State Standards = State Tests; State Test Results = Student Achievement; Student Achievement = Rewards and Punishments.

We are not suggesting that educators should not be held accountable for their students' learning. We believe that they should. Unfortunately, we are not holding our profession accountable for learning, only for achievement on high-stakes tests. As we have learned from years of National Assessment of

Educational Progress research, equating lasting student learning with test results is folly.

The Emerging Research from Standards-Driven States

In recent years, many states have initiated comprehensive educational reform efforts. The systemic thinking that frames most standards-based reform efforts is delectably logical: Develop high standards for all students; align curriculum and instruction to these standards; construct assessments to measure whether all students are meeting the standards; equate test results with student learning; and reward schools whose students score well on the assessments and sanction schools whose students don't.

Predictably, this simple and linear approach to educational reform is sinking under the weight of its own flaws. It is too similar to earlier reform approaches, and it misses the point. Educational improvement is not accomplished through administrative or legislative mandate. It is accomplished through attention to the complicated, idiosyncratic, often paradoxical, and difficult to measure nature of learning.

A useful body of research is emerging from the states. With minor variations, the research indicates the following:

- Test scores are generally low on the first assessment relating to new standards. Virginia is an extreme example of this phenomenon: More than 95 percent of schools failed the state's first test. In New York, more than 50 percent of the state's 4th graders were deemed at risk of not graduating in 2007 after taking that state's new English language arts test in 1999.
- Failure, or the fear of failure, breeds success on subsequent tests. After the first administration of most state assessments, schools' scores rise because educators align curriculum closely with the assessments, and they focus classroom instruction directly on test-taking strategies.
- To increase the percentages of students passing the state assessments—and to keep schools off the states' lists of failing schools—local district spending on student remediation, student test-taking skills, and faculty preparation for the new assessments increases.
- Despite rising test scores in subsequent years, there is little or no evidence of increased student learning. A recent study by Kentucky's Office of Educational Accountability (Hambleton et al., 1995) suggests that test-score gains in that state are a function of

students' increasing skills as test takers rather than evidence of increased learning.

When Tests Constrict Learning

Learning is a complex process through which learners constantly change their internally constructed understandings of how their worlds function. New information either transforms their current beliefs—or doesn't. The efficacy of the learning environment is a function of many complex factors, including curriculum, instructional methodology, student motivation, and student developmental readiness. Trying to capture this complexity on paper-and-pencil assessments severely limits knowledge and expression.

Inevitably, schools reduce the curriculum to only that which is covered on tests, and this constriction limits student learning. So, too, does the undeviating, one-size-fits-all approach to teaching and assessment in many states that have crowned accountability king. Requiring all students to take the same courses and pass the same tests may hold political capital for legislators and state-level educational policymakers, but it contravenes what years of painstaking research tells us about student learning. In discussing the inordinate amount of time and energy devoted to preparing students to take and pass high-stakes tests, Angaran (1999) writes

> Ironically, all this activity prepares them for hours of passivity. This extended amount of seat time flies in the face of what we know about how children learn. Unfortunately, it does not seem to matter. It is, after all, the Information Age. The quest for more information drives us forward. (P. 72)

We are not saying that student success on state assessments and classroom practices designed to foster understanding are inherently contradictory. Teaching in ways that nurture students' quests to resolve cognitive conflict and conquer academic challenges fosters the creative problem solving that most states seek. However, classroom practices designed to prepare students for tests clearly do not foster deep learning that students apply to new situations. Instead, these practices train students to mimic learning on tests.

Many school districts question the philosophical underpinnings of the dominant test-teach-test model of education and are searching for broader ways for students to demonstrate their knowledge. However, the accountability component of the standards movement has caused many districts to abandon performance-based assessment practices and refocus instead on preparing students for paper-and-pencil tests. The consequences for districts and their students are too great if they don't.

Constructivism in the Classroom

Learners control their learning. This simple truth lies at the heart of the constructivist approach to education.

As educators, we develop classroom practices and negotiate the curriculum to enhance the likelihood of student learning. But controlling what students learn is virtually impossible. The search for meaning takes a different route for each student. Even when educators structure classroom lessons and curriculums to ensure that all students learn the same concepts at the same time, each student still constructs his or her own unique meaning through his or her own cognitive processes. In other words, as educators we have great control over what we teach, but far less control over what students learn.

Shifting our priorities from ensuring that all students learn the same concepts to ensuring that we carefully analyze students' understandings to customize our teaching approaches is an essential step in educational reform that results in increased learning. Again, we must set standards for our own professional practice and free students from the anti-intellectual training that occurs under the banner of test preparation.

The search for understanding motivates students to learn. When students want to know more about an idea, a topic, or an entire discipline, they put more cognitive energy into classroom investigations and discussions and study more on their own. We have identified five central tenets of constructivism (Grennon Brooks & Brooks, 1993).

- First, constructivist teachers seek and value students' points of view. Knowing what students think about concepts helps teachers formulate classroom lessons and differentiate instruction on the basis of students' needs and interests.
- Second, constructivist teachers structure lessons to challenge students' suppositions. All students, whether they are 6 or 16 or 60, come to the classroom with life experiences that shape their views about how their worlds work. When educators permit students to construct knowledge that challenges their current suppositions, learning occurs. Only through asking students what they think they know and why they think they know it are we and they able to confront their suppositions.
- Third, constructivist teachers recognize that students must attach relevance to the curriculum. As students see relevance in their daily activities, their interest in learning grows.
- Fourth, constructivist teachers structure lessons around big ideas, not small bits of information.

Exposing students to wholes first helps them determine the relevant parts as they refine their understandings of the wholes.
- Finally, constructivist teachers assess student learning in the context of daily classroom investigations, not as separate events. Students demonstrate their knowledge every day in a variety of ways. Defining understanding as only that which is capable of being measured by paper-and-pencil assessments administered under strict security perpetuates false and counterproductive myths about academia, intelligence, creativity, accountability, and knowledge.

Opportunities for Constructing Meaning

Recently, we visited a classroom in which a teacher asked 7th graders to reflect on a poem. The teacher began the lesson by asking the students to interpret the first two lines. One student volunteered that the lines evoked an image of a dream. "No," he was told, "that's not what the author meant." Another student said that the poem reminded her of a voyage at sea. The teacher reminded the student that she was supposed to be thinking about the first two lines of the poem, not the whole poem, and then told her that the poem was not about the sea. Looking out at the class, the teacher asked, "Anyone else?" No other student raised a hand.

In another classroom, a teacher asked 9th graders to ponder the effect of temperature on muscle movement. Students had ice, buckets of water, gauges for measuring finger-grip strength, and other items to help them consider the relationship. The teacher asked a few framing questions, stated rules for handling materials safely, and then gave the students time to design their experiments. He posed different questions to different groups of students, depending on their activities and the conclusions that they seemed to be drawing. He continually asked students to elaborate or posed contradictions to their responses, even when they were correct.

As the end of the period neared, the students shared initial findings about their investigations and offered working hypotheses about the relationship between muscle movement and temperature. Several students asked to return later that day to continue working on their experiments.

Let's consider these two lessons. In one case, the lesson was not conducive to students' constructing deeper meaning. In the other case, it was. The 7th grade teacher communicated to her students that there is one interpretation of the poem's meaning, that she knew it, and that only that interpretation was an acceptable response. The students' primary quest, then, was to figure out what the teacher thought of the poem.

The teacher spoke to her students in respectful tones, acknowledging each one by name and encouraging their responses. However, she politely and calmly rejected their ideas when they failed to conform to her views. She rejected one student's response as a misinterpretation. She dismissed another student's response because of a procedural error: The response focused on the whole poem, not on just the designated two lines.

After the teacher told these two students that they were wrong, none of the other students volunteered interpretations, even though the teacher encouraged more responses. The teacher then proceeded with the lesson by telling the students what the poet really meant. Because only two students offered comments during the lesson, the teacher told us that a separate test would inform her whether the other students understood the poem.

In the second lesson, the teacher withheld his thoughts intentionally to challenge students to develop their own hypotheses. Even when students' initial responses were correct, the teacher challenged their thinking, causing many students to question the correctness of their initial responses and to investigate the issue more deeply.

Very few students had awakened that morning thinking about the relationship between muscle movement and temperature. But, as the teacher helped students focus their emerging, somewhat disjointed musings into a structured investigation, their engagement grew. The teacher provoked the students to search for relevance in a relationship they hadn't yet considered by framing the investigation around one big concept, providing appropriate materials and general questions, and helping the students think through their own questions. Moreover, the teacher sought and valued his students' points of view and used their comments to assess their learning. No separate testing event was required.

What Constructivism Is and Isn't

As constructivism has gained support as an educational approach, two main criticisms have emerged. One critique of constructivism is that it is overly permissive. This critique suggests that constructivist teachers often abandon their curriculums to pursue the whims of their students. If, for example, most of the students in the aforementioned 9th grade science class wished to discuss the relationship between physical exercise and muscle movement rather than pursue the planned

lesson, so be it. In math and science, critics are particularly concerned that teachers jettison basic information to permit students to think in overly broad mathematical and scientific terms.

The other critique of constructivist approaches to education is that they lack rigor. The concern here is that teachers cast aside the information, facts, and basic skills embedded in the curriculum—and necessary to pass high-stakes tests—in the pursuit of more capricious ideas. Critics would be concerned that In the 7th grade English lesson described previously, the importance of having students understand the one true main idea of the poem would fall prey to a discussion of their individual interpretations.

Both of these critiques are silly caricatures of what an evolving body of research tells us about learning. Battista (1999), speaking specifically of mathematics education, writes,

> Many . . . conceive of constructivism as a pedagogical stance that entails a type of nonrigorous, intellectual anarchy that lets students pursue whatever interests them and invent and use any mathematical methods they wish, whether those methods are correct or not. Others take constructivism to be synonymous with "discovery learning" from the era of "new math," and still others see it as a way of teaching that focuses on using manipulatives or cooperative learning. None of these conceptions is correct. (P. 429)

Organizing a constructivist classroom is difficult work for the teacher and requires the rigorous intellectual commitment and perseverance of students. Constructivist teachers recognize that students bring their prior experiences with them to each school activity and that it is crucial to connect lessons to their students' experiential repertoires. Initial relevance and interest are largely a function of the learner's experiences, not of the teacher's planning. Therefore, it is educationally counterproductive to ignore students' suppositions and points of view. The 7th grade English lesson is largely nonintellectual. The 9th grade science lesson, modeled on how scientists make state-of-the-art science advancements, is much more intellectually rigorous.

Moreover, constructivist teachers keep relevant facts, information, and skills at the forefront of their lesson planning. They usually do this within the context of discussions about bigger ideas. For example, the dates, battles, and names associated with the U.S. Civil War have much more meaning for students when introduced within larger investigations of slavery, territorial expansion, and economics than when presented for memorization without a larger context.

State and local curriculums address *what* students learn. Constructivism, as an approach to education, addresses *how* students learn. The constructivist teacher, in mediating students' learning, blends the *what* with the *how*. As a 3rd grader in another classroom we visited wrote to his teacher, "You are like the North Star for the class. You don't tell us where to go, but you help us find our way." Constructivist classrooms demand far more from teachers and students than lockstep obeisance to prepackaged lessons.

The Effects of High-Stakes Accountability

As we stated earlier, the standards movement has a grand flaw at the nexus of standards, accountability, and instructional practice. Instructional practices designed to help students construct meaning are being crowded out of the curriculum by practices designed to prepare students to score well on state assessments. The push for accountability is eclipsing the intent of standards and sound educational practice.

Let's look at the effects of high-stakes accountability systems. Originally, many states identified higher-order thinking as a goal of reform and promoted constructivist teaching practices to achieve this goal. In most states, however, policymakers dropped this goal or subsumed it into other goals because it was deemed too difficult to assess and quantify. Rich evidence relating to higher-order thinking is available daily in classrooms, but this evidence is not necessarily translatable to paper-and-pencil assessments. High-stakes accountability systems, therefore, tend to warp the original visions of reform.

Education is a holistic endeavor. Students' learning encompasses emerging understandings about themselves, their relationships, and their relative places in the world. In addition to academic achievement, students develop these understandings through non-academic aspects of schooling, such as clubs, sports, community service, music, arts, and theater. However, only that which is academic and easily measurable gets assessed, and only that which is assessed is subject to rewards and punishments. Jones and Whitford (1997) point out that Kentucky's original educational renewal initiative included student self-sufficiency and responsible group membership as goals, but these goals were dropped because they were deemed too difficult to assess and not sufficiently academic.

Schools operating in high-stakes accountability systems typically move attention away from principles of learning, student-centered curriculum, and constructivist teaching practices. They focus instead on obtaining higher test scores, despite research showing that higher test scores are not necessarily indicative of increased student learning.

Historically, many educators have considered multiple-choice tests to be the most valid and reliable form of assessment—and also the narrowest form of assessment. Therefore, despite the initial commitment of many states to performance assessment, which was to have been the cornerstone of state assessment efforts aligned with broader curriculum and constructivist instructional practices, multiple-choice questions have instead remained the coin of the realm. As Jones and Whitford (1997) write about Kentucky,

> The logic is clear. The more open and performance based an assessment is, the more variety in the responses; the more variety in the responses, the more judgment is needed in scoring; the more judgment in scoring, the lower the reliability. . . . At this point, multiple-choice items have been reintroduced, performance events discontinued. (P. 278)

Ironically, as state departments of education and local newspapers hold schools increasingly accountable for their test results, local school officials press state education departments for greater guidance about material to be included on the states' tests. This phenomenon emboldens state education departments to take an even greater role in curriculum development, as well as in other decisions typically handled at the local level, such as granting high school diplomas, determining professional development requirements for teachers, making special education placements, and intervening academically for at-risk students. According to Jones and Whitford (1997),

> [In Kentucky] there has been a rebound effect. Pressure generated by the state test for high stakes accountability has led school-based educators to pressure the state to be more explicit about content that will be tested. This in turn constrains local school decision making about curriculum. This dialectical process works to increase the state control of local curriculum. (P. 278)

Toward Educational Reform

Serious educational reform targets cognitive changes in students' thinking. Perceived educational reform targets numerical changes in students' test scores. Our obsession with the perception of reform, what Ohanian (1999) calls "the mirage theory of education," is undermining the possibility of serious reform.

History tells us that it is likely that students' scores on state assessments will rise steadily over the next decade and that meaningful indexes of student learning generally will remain flat. It is also likely that teachers, especially those teaching in the grades in which high-stakes assessments are administered, will continue to narrow their curriculum to match what is covered on the assessments and to use instructional practices designed to place testing information directly in their students' heads.

We counsel advocacy for children. And vision. And courage.

Focus on student learning. When we design instructional practices to help students construct knowledge, students learn. This is our calling as educators.

Keep the curriculum conceptual. Narrowing curriculum to match what is covered on state assessments results in an overemphasis on the rote memorization of discrete bits of information and pushes aside big ideas and intellectual curiosity. Keep essential principles and recurring concepts at the center.

Assess student learning within the context of daily instruction. Use students' daily work, points of view, suppositions, projects, and demonstrations to assess what they know and don't know, and use these assessments to guide teaching.

Initiate discussions among administrators, teachers, parents, school boards, and students about the relationship among the state's standards, the state's assessments, and your district's mission. Ask questions about what the assessments actually assess, the instructional practices advocated by your district, and the ways to teach a conceptual curriculum while preparing students for the assessments. These are discussions worth having.

Understand the purposes of accountability. Who wants it, and why? Who is being held accountable, and for what? How are data being used or misused? What are the consequences of accountability for all students, especially for specific groups, such as special education students and English language learners?

Students must be permitted the freedom to think, to question, to reflect, and to interact with ideas, objects, and others—in other words, to construct meaning. In school, being wrong has always carried negative consequences for students. Sadly, in this climate of increasing accountability, being wrong carries even more severe consequences. But being wrong is often the first step on the path to greater understanding.

We observed a 5th grade teacher return a test from the previous day. Question 3 was, "There are 7 blue chips and 3 green chips in a bag. If you place your hand in the bag and pull out 1 chip, what is the probability that you will get a green chip?" One student wrote, "You probably won't get one." She was "right"—and also "wrong." She received no credit for the question.

REFERENCES

Angaran, J. (1999, March). Reflection in an age of assessment. *Educational Leadership, 56*, 71–72.

Grennon Brooks, J., & Brooks, M. G. (1993). *In search of understanding: The case for constructivist classrooms.* Alexandria, VA: ASCD.

Hambleton, R., Jaeger, R. M., Koretz, D., Linn, R. L, Millman, J., & Phillips, S. E. (1995). *Review of the measurement quality of the Kentucky instructional results information system 1991–1994.* (Report prepared for the Kentucky General Assembly.) Frankfort, KY: Office of Educational Accountability.

Jones, K., & Whitford, B. L. (1997, December). Kentucky's conflicting reform principles: High stakes accountability and student performance assessment. *Phi Delta Kappan, 78* (4), 276–281.

Ohanian, S. (1999). *One size fits few.* Portsmouth, NH: Heinemann.

POSTNOTE

This article was chosen as a Classic because the topic of constructivism has become such a dominant instructional philosophy in American education. Research from cognitive scientists has taught us that when confronted with new learning, human beings "construct" new understandings of relationships and phenomena, rather than simply receiving others' understandings. Learners are always fitting new information into the schemas they carry in their heads, or else they adjust or change the schema to fit the new information. As the authors of this article state, students bring their prior experiences with them. Therefore, teachers need to design lessons that connect to students' experiential repertoires.

The implications for teachers are enormous. Constructivism suggests that educators should invite students to explore the world's complexity, proposing situations for students to think about and observing how students use their prior knowledge to confront the problems. When students make errors, teachers can analyze the errors to understand better just how the students are approaching the matter. Throughout the process, teachers must accept that there is no single "right" way to solve a problem.

Discussion Questions

1. In what ways does constructivism challenge your ideas about how people learn?

2. How do you think constructivism will affect what goes on in classrooms? Describe a scenario in which a teacher conducts a lesson, using constructivist principles similar to those presented by the authors. Choose any subject or grade level you wish.

3. How does constructivism dispute the notion of a fixed world that students need to understand?

RELATED WEBSITE RESOURCES AND VIDEO CASES

 ### Web Resources:

Constructivism. Available at:

http://carbon.cudenver.edu/~mryder/itc_data/ constructivism.html.

This website by Martin Ryder contains multiple links to definitions and readings on constructivism.

Video Case:

Constructivist Teaching in Action: A High School Classroom Debate

In this video case you will see how teacher Sarabinh Levy-Brightman sets the stage for students to become expert on the topic of Jeffersonian democracy, figure out how best to express opposing ideas, and evaluate their own effectiveness. As you watch the clips and study the artifacts in the case, reflect upon the following questions:

1. In what ways is this teacher's approach consistent with constructivist learning philosophy?

2. Describe the process the students use in preparing for the debate. What are some of its advantages and possible drawbacks?

31

Orchestrating Multiple Intelligences

Seana Moran, Mindy Kornhaber, and Howard Gardner

Seana Moran is an advanced doctoral student at the Harvard Graduate School of Education. **Mindy Kornhaber** is an associate professor in the College of Education at The Pennsylvania State University. **Howard Gardner,** the originator of the theory of multiple intelligences, is the John H. and Elisabeth A. Hobbs Professor of Cognition and Education at the Harvard Graduate School of Education and senior director of Harvard Project Zero.

"Orchestrating Multiple Intelligences" by Seana Moran, Mindy Kornhaber, and Howard Gardner, *Educational Leadership* 64, no. 1, September 2006, pp. 22–27. Used with permission.

| F | O | C | U | S | QUESTION

How can the theory of multiple intelligences be implemented in classrooms?

KEY TERM

Multiple intelligences theory

Education policymakers sometimes go astray when they attempt to integrate multiple intelligences theory into schools. They mistakenly believe that teachers must group students for instruction according to eight or nine different intelligence scores. Or they grapple with the unwieldy notion of requiring teachers to prepare eight or nine separate entry points for every lesson.

Multiple intelligences theory was originally developed as an explanation of how the mind works—not as an education policy, let alone an education panacea. Moreover, when we and other colleagues began to consider the implications of the theory for education, the last thing we wanted to do was multiply educators' jobs ninefold. Rather, we sought to demonstrate that because students bring to the classroom diverse intellectual profiles, one "IQ" measure is insufficient to evaluate, label, and plan education programs for all students.

Adopting a multiple intelligences approach can bring about a quiet revolution in the way students see themselves and others. Instead of defining themselves as either "smart" or "dumb," students can perceive themselves as potentially smart in a number of ways.

Profile Students, Don't Score Them

Multiple intelligences theory proposes that it is more fruitful to describe an individual's cognitive ability in terms of several relatively independent but interacting cognitive capacities rather than in terms of a single "general" intelligence. Think of LEGO building blocks. If we have only one kind of block to play with, we can build only a limited range of structures. If we have a number of different block shapes that can interconnect to create a variety of patterns and structures, we can accomplish more nuanced and complex designs. The eight or nine intelligences work the same way.

The greatest potential of a multiple intelligences approach to education grows from the concept of a *profile* of intelligences. Each learner's intelligence profile consists of a combination of relative strengths and weaknesses among the different intelligences: linguistic, logical-mathematical, musical, spatial, bodily-kinesthetic, naturalistic, interpersonal, intrapersonal, and (at least provisionally) existential (Gardner, 2006).

Most people have jagged profiles; they process some types of information better than other types. Students who exhibit vast variation among their intelligences—with one or two intelligences very strong and the others relatively weak—have what we call a *laser* profile. There students often have a strong area of interest and can follow a clear path to success by developing their peak intelligences. Given the ubiquity of high-stakes testing, educators' challenge with laser-profile students is deciding whether to accentuate the students' strengths through advanced opportunities to develop their gifts or to bolster their weak areas through remediation so that they can pass the tests. Policy and funding currently favor the second option unless the student is gifted in the traditional academic areas.

Other students have a *searchlight* profile: They show less pronounced differences among intelligences. The challenge with searchlight-profile students is to help them choose a career and life path. Time and resource limitations often preclude developing all intelligences equally, so we need to consider which intelligences are most likely to pay off for a particular student. Policy and funding currently favor developing primarily linguistic and logical-mathematical intelligences at the expense of the others.

Intelligences are not isolated; they can interact with one another in an individual to yield a variety of outcomes. For example, a successful dancer must combine musical, spatial, and bodily kinesthetic intelligences; a science fiction novelist must use logical-mathematical, linguistic, interpersonal, and some existential intelligences; an effective trial lawyer must combine linguistic and interpersonal intelligences; a skillful waiter uses linguistic, spatial, interpersonal, and bodily-kinesthetic intelligences; and a marine biologist needs strong naturalistic and logical-mathematical intelligences. In the education setting, the different intelligences can interact in two ways: within the student and across students.

An Internal Orchestra

Just as the sounds of string, woodwind, and percussion instruments combine to create a symphony, the different intelligences intermix within a student to yield meaningful scholastic achievement or other accomplishments. And as in an orchestra, one intelligence (instrument) in an individual can interfere with others, compensate for others, or enhance others.

INTERFERENCE

Intelligences may not always work in harmony; sometimes they create discord. For example, even a student who has good social skills (strong interpersonal intelligence), may have trouble making friends if she cannot

talk with others easily because she has weak linguistic intelligence. Another student who loves to read and receives frequent praise in English class may sit in the back row and bury her head in a novel during math class, where she feels less confident. Thus, her linguistic strength is a bottleneck for the development of her logical-mathematical intelligence. A third student's weakness in intrapersonal intelligence, which makes it difficult for him to regulate his moods or thoughts, may prevent him from completing his math homework consistently and thus mask his strong logical-mathematical intelligence.

COMPENSATION

Sometimes one intelligence compensates for another. A student may give great class presentations because he can effectively use his body posture and gestures even though his sentence structure is somewhat convoluted. That is, his bodily-kinesthetic intelligence compensates for his linguistic limitations. (We can think of more than one U.S. president who fits this profile.) Or a student may earn a high mark on a paper for writing with a powerful rhetorical voice, even though her argument is not quite solid: Her linguistic intelligence compensates for her logical-mathematical limitations.

ENHANCEMENT

Finally, one intelligence may jump-start another. Strong spatial intelligence may improve a student's ability to conceptualize a mathematical concept or problem. This was certainly the case with Einstein. Strong musical intelligence may stimulate interest and playfulness in writing poetry. Understanding how intelligences can catalyze one another may help students—and teachers—make decisions about how to deploy the intellectual resources they have at their disposal.

The profile approach to multiple intelligences instruction provides teachers with better diagnostic information to help a particular student who is struggling. Before providing assistance, we need to ask *why* the student is having difficulty. For example, consider three beginning readers who have trouble comprehending a story. The first is struggling because of poor reading comprehension skills (a linguistic intelligence challenge). The second has poor social understanding of the dynamics among the story's characters (an interpersonal intelligence challenge). The third has such strong spatial intelligence that he has trouble seeing beyond the physical pattern of the letter symbols (a challenge that Picasso, for example, faced in his early years). More reading practice, which is often the default intervention, may not help all of these students.

A student's potential is not the sum of his or her intelligence "scores," as some multiple intelligence inventory measures on the market imply. If one intelligence is a bottleneck for others, then the student's overall potential may be lower than the straight sum. If intelligences are compensating for or enhancing one another, the student's overall potential may be higher than the straight sum. Intelligences have multiplicative as well as additive effects.

An Effective Ensemble

Intelligences can also work across students. The information explosion has greatly escalated the amount of information that each person must assimilate and understand—frequently beyond what we can handle by ourselves. Work teams, institutional partnerships, and interdisciplinary projects have increasingly become the norm. These ensembles support individuals as they seek to learn, understand, and perform well.

Multiple intelligences theory encourages collaboration across students. Students with compatible profiles (exhibiting the same patterns of strengths and weaknesses) can work together to solidify and build on strengths. For example, two students highly capable in storytelling can support each other by moving beyond the basics of plot to explore and develop twists in the narrative. A group of students who are skilled in numerical computation might extend a statistics lesson beyond mean, median, mode, and range to understand correlation or regression.

Students with complementary profiles (in which one student's weak areas are another student's strengths) can work together to compensate for one another. Such students can approach material in different but equally valid ways. For example, a student who is strong in logical-mathematical intelligence and sufficient in spatial intelligence might be able to translate abstract math problems into dance choreography or sculpture contexts to make them understandable to a student with strong spatial and bodily-kinesthetic intelligences.

Provide Rich Experiences

The eminent psychologist L. S. Vygotsky (1978) emphasized that *experience*—the idiosyncratic way each individual internalizes the environment's information—is important in both cognitive and personality development. If we give all students the same material, each student will have a different experience according to his or her background, strengths, and challenges. Thus, to promote learning across student intelligence profiles, teachers need to offer students rich experiences—activities in which they can engage with the material personally rather than just absorb it in an abstract, decontextualized way.

Rich experiences enable students to learn along several dimensions at once—socially, spatially, kinesthetically, self-reflectively, and so on. Often, these experiences cross subject-area lines. At Searsport Elementary School in Searsport, Maine, a 5th grade teacher who had strong storytelling abilities and an avid interest in history joined forces with her colleague, an expert in hands-on science, to develop an archaeology unit. Students studied history and geography as well as scientific method and archaeology techniques. They investigated local history, conducted a state-approved archaeological dig, identified and classified objects, and displayed the artifacts in a museum exhibit that met real-world curatorial standards (Kornhaber, Fierros, & Veenema, 2004).

Rich experiences also provide diagnostic information. Teachers can observe student performances to find root causes of misunderstandings and to figure out how students can achieve superior understandings. One small group of 2nd and 3rd graders in Chimene Brandt's class at Pittsburgh's McCleary Elementary School produced a mural depicting a rainy street scene. Their spatial portrayal of material was ambiguous: The connection to the unit's topic of rivers and the lesson's topic of the water cycle laws was not obvious. The students' understanding came through linguistically, however, when they presented in class how the water from the street would evaporate, condense into clouds, and again produce rain. By giving the students multiple ways to express the concepts, Brandt was able to confirm that the students understood the material even though their linguistic skills outstripped their spatial skills (Kornhaber, Fierros, & Veenema, 2004).

Two programs exemplify how rich experiences can serve as venues for developing and assessing multiple intelligences. The first, Project Spectrum, is an interactive assessment process for preschool children developed in the 1980s at Harvard Project Zero (Gardner, Feldman, & Krechevsky, 1998). This process evaluates each intelligence directly, rather than funneling the information through a linguistic paper-and-pencil test. Spatial orientation and manipulation tasks evaluate spatial intelligence; group tasks evaluate interpersonal intelligence; self-assessments paired with the other assessments evaluate intrapersonal intelligence. Project Spectrum environments do not segment tasks strictly into one intelligence or another. Instead, they set up situations in which a student can interact with rich materials—and teachers can observe these interactions—to see which intelligences come to the fore and which are relegated to the background.

A naturalist's corner provides biological specimens for students to touch and move (using bodily-kinesthetic intelligence), arrange (naturalistic), create relationships among (logical-mathematical), tell stories about (linguistic), or even compare themselves with (intra-personal). In a storytelling area, students can tell tales (linguistic), arrange props and character figurines (spatial and possibly bodily-kinesthetic), make characters interact (interpersonal), and design their own storyboards (spatial). Fifteen other activities provide opportunities for evaluating intelligences through reliable scoring rubrics that have been used widely in early childhood education in the United States, Latin America, Europe, and Asia (Gardner, Feldman, & Krechevsky, 1998).

Another environment providing rich experiences using a multiple intelligences approach is the Explorama at Danfoss Universe, a science park in Nordborg, Denmark (see **www.danfossuniverse.com**). Designed according to multiple intelligences theory, this interactive museum is used by people of all ages—from school groups to corporate teams. The designers have devised separate exhibits, games, and challenges for each intelligence and for numerous combinations of intelligences. One experience asks participants to balance themselves (bodily-kinesthetic); another asks them to balance in a group (bodily-kinesthetic and interpersonal). A computer program encourages participants to add, subtract, or combine different musical qualities and see on screen how the tone frequencies change, tapping into musical, spatial, and logical-mathematical intelligences.

Three activities deserve particular attention for their innovativeness in assessing several intelligences concurrently and in emphasizing intelligences that are often neglected in mainstream academic testing. One game involves manipulating a joystick to control a robot that can lift and move a cube to a target space. When played alone, this exhibit primarily assesses bodily-kinesthetic and spatial intelligence. But when two to four people each control a different joystick—one that controls the left wheel of the robot, another that controls the right wheel, another that raises the cube, and another that lowers the cube—they must coordinate their play to accomplish the task, employing linguistic, logical-mathematical, and interpersonal intelligences.

Another game has two players sitting opposite each other at a table, with a ping-pong ball in the center. Each player tries to move the ball toward the opponent by relaxing. Relaxing reduces the player's stress level, creating alpha waves in the brain that sensors pick up to move the ball forward. This task requires self-control, and thus taps into intrapersonal intelligence. However, the players must also employ interpersonal intelligence, paying attention to each other and trying to produce more alpha waves than the opponent does.

A third notable Explorama activity is a computerized questionnaire in which participants assess their own intelligence profiles. Participants take the self-assessment before entering the Explorama and again after they have engaged in the various activities and tasks. Participants thus get an idea of how well they know their own capabilities. They also can compare their self-assessments before and after the Explorama experience to learn whether their self-perceptions stayed constant or changed. This process develops participants' intrapersonal intelligence.

Get Personal

The orientation toward profiles, interactions, and experience emphasizes a need to develop, in particular, the two personal intelligences.

Intrapersonal intelligence involves knowing yourself—your talents, energy level, interests, and so on. Students who strengthen their intrapersonal intelligence gain a better understanding of areas in which they can expect to excel, which helps them plan and govern their own learning.

Interpersonal intelligence involves understanding others through social interaction, emotional reactions, conversation, and so on. An individual's interpersonal intelligence affects his or her ability to work in groups. Group projects can create environments for students to improve their interpersonal intelligence as they develop other skills and knowledge.

Donna Schneider, a 3rd grade teacher at the John F. Kennedy Elementary School in Brewster, New York, developed a real-world publishing company in her classroom: "Schneider's Ink." Each spring when the school puts on performances and events, Schneider's 3rd graders create programs, banners, advertisements, and other publicity materials for their clients, the sponsoring teachers. Each student assumes a different job—editor, sales manager, typist, accountant, customer service representative, or designer. Before taking on a given position, each student writes a resumé and cover letter, obtains letters of recommendation, and is interviewed by the teacher. Students explore their own strengths and become aware of how those strengths can enable them to succeed in various jobs.

Schneider's Ink also engages students' interpersonal intelligence. For example, the quality-control manager, who is responsible for handling customer complaints, has to work with both clients and the editor to review problems. As company employees, the students juggle simultaneous print orders, coordinating the sequencing of tasks among themselves to produce high-quality work on time. They must understand others through social interaction, emotional reactions, and conversation. Through this process, students acquire a better understanding of the interdependence of individual strengths (Kornhaber, Fierros, & Veenema, 2004).

Gardner's Multiple Intelligences

Linguistic. Ability to understand and use spoken and written communication. Ideal vocation: poet*

Logical-mathematical. Ability to understand and use logic and numerical symbols and operations. Ideal vocation: computer programmer.

Musical. Ability to understand and use such concepts as rhythm, pitch, melody, and harmony. Ideal vocation: composer.

Spatial. Ability to orient and manipulate three-dimensional space. Ideal vocation: architect.

Bodily-kinesthetic. Ability to coordinate physical movement. Ideal vocation: athlete.

Naturalistic. Ability to distinguish and categorize objects or phenomena in nature. Ideal vocation: zoologist.

Interpersonal. Ability to understand and interact well with other people. Ideal vocation: politician; salesperson.

Intrapersonal. Ability to understand and use one's thoughts, feelings, preferences, and interests. Ideal vocation: autobiographer; entrepreneur. (Although high intrapersonal intelligence should help in almost any job because of its role in self-regulation, few paid positions reward a person solely for knowing himself or herself well.)

Existential. Ability to contemplate phenomena or questions beyond sensory data, such as the infinite and infinitesimal. Ideal vocation: cosmologist; philosopher.

Building Active Learners

The multiple intelligences approach does not require a teacher to design a lesson in nine different ways so that all students can access the material. Rather, it involves creating rich experiences in which students with different intelligence profiles can interact with the materials and ideas using their particular combinations of strengths and weaknesses.

Often, these experiences are collaborative. As the amount of information that students—and adults—must process continues to increase dramatically, collaboration enables students to learn more by tapping into others' strengths as well as into their own. In ideal multiple intelligences instruction, rich experiences and collaboration provide a context for students to become aware of their own intelligence profiles, to develop self-regulation, and to participate more actively in their own learning.

REFERENCES

Gardner, H. (2006). *Multiple intelligences: New horizons.* New York: BasicBooks.

Gardner, H., Feldman, D. H., & Krechevsky, M. (Eds.). (1998). *Project Zero frameworks for early childhood education: Volume 1. Building on children's strengths: The experience of Project Spectrum.* New York: Teachers College Press.

Kornhaber, M., Fierros, E., & Veenema, S. (2004). *Multiple intelligences: Best ideas from research and practice.* Boston: Pearson.

Vygotsky, L. S. (1978). *Mind in society: The development of higher psychological processes.* Cambridge, MA: Harvard University Press.

ENDNOTE

*Most vocations involve several intelligences.

POSTNOTE

Howard Gardner's theory of multiple intelligences refutes the widely accepted idea that there is a single, general intelligence. The eight or nine intelligences—*linguistic, logical-mathematical, musical, spatial, bodily-kinesthetic, interpersonal, intrapersonal, naturalist,* and perhaps *existentialist*—that he has identified appeal greatly to many educators, who see them as ways that schools can reach more students. In Gardner's theory, abilities in diverse areas would be valued as indicators of intelligence and would be considered worthy of further nurturance and development in school. If teachers provide multiple ways for students to be taught and assessed that recognize and value the kinds of differences that exist among students, then greater numbers of students will succeed and receive recognition. As a result, fewer students are likely to think of themselves as failures. Acknowledging and fostering individual abilities in a variety of areas, as suggested in this article, is a way that teachers can help students succeed.

Teachers of gifted and talented students also see the theory of multiple intelligences as broadening conceptions of who is gifted or talented. The concept of giftedness can embrace dancers, athletes, musicians, artists, or naturalists, and programs can be established to help foster these talents. Gardner raises the issue of whether or not these abilities should be called intelligence or talent. He argues that to call linguistic or logical-mathematical ability intelligence, but spatial or musical ability talent, elevates certain types of ability and devalues others. Gardner's

argument is not generally accepted, as society and most schools seem to value language and mathematical capabilities over other types of abilities. Except, of course, NFL and NBA athletes!

Discussion Questions

1. Do you believe the different types of intelligences identified by Gardner are valued equally in our society? If yes, why? If not, why?

2. Which of the intelligences are strengths of yours? How do you know this?

3. What challenges would you anticipate in trying to orchestrate attention to multiple intelligences in your classroom?

RELATED WEBSITE RESOURCES AND VIDEO CASES

 ### Web Resources:

Association for Supervision and Curriculum Development (ASCD). Available at:

http://www.ascd.org.

ASCD has many resources on multiple intelligences and learning styles. Click on Education Topics, Multiple Intelligences, for more resources on this topic.

Video Case:

Multiple Intelligences: Elementary School Instruction

In this 4th grade classroom, you will see how teacher Frederick Won Park draws upon multiple intelligences theory to help his students improve their writing abilities. As you watch the clips and study the artifacts in the case, reflect upon the following questions:

1. How does this teacher's emphasis on the ability to solve problems compare to general-ability theories of intelligence?

2. How does the writing activity link multiple intelligences with one another?

3. In your opinion, does this teacher use multiple intelligences activities in a way that supports standard learning goals or in a way that detracts from achievement standards? Why do you think so?

CLASSIC

32

Making Cooperative Learning Work

David W. Johnson and Roger T. Johnson

David W. Johnson and **Roger T. Johnson** are professors of education and co-directors of the Cooperative Learning Center at the University of Minnesota. They have been pioneers in the development of—and research on—cooperative learning.

Johnson, D. W., & Johnson, R. T. (1999). "Making Cooperative Learning Work." *Theory into Practice*, 38(2), pp. 67–73. Copyright 1999 by the College of Education, The Ohio State University. All rights reserved.

|F|O|C|U|S| QUESTION

What are the benefits of employing cooperative learning strategies in classrooms?

KEY TERM

Cooperative learning

Sandy Koufax was one of the greatest pitchers in the history of baseball. Although he was naturally talented, he was also unusually well trained and disciplined. He was perhaps the only major-league pitcher whose fastball could be heard to hum. Opposing batters, instead of talking and joking around in the dugout, would sit quietly and listen for Koufax's fastball to hum. When it was their turn to bat, they were already intimidated.

There was, however, a simple way for Koufax's genius to have been negated: by making the first author of this article his catcher. To be great, a pitcher needs an outstanding catcher (his great partner was Johnny Roseboro). David is such an unskilled catcher that Koufax would have had to throw the ball much slower in order for David to catch it. This would have deprived Koufax of his greatest weapon.

Placing Roger at key defensive positions in the infield or outfield, furthermore, would have seriously affected Koufax's success. Sandy Koufax was not a great pitcher on his own. Only as part of a team could Koufax achieve greatness. In baseball and in the classroom, it takes a cooperative effort. Extraordinary achievement comes from a cooperative group, not from the individualistic or competitive efforts of an isolated individual.

In 1966 David began training teachers at the University of Minnesota in how to use small groups for instructional purposes. In 1969 Roger joined David at Minnesota, and the training of teachers in how to use cooperative learning groups was extended into teaching methods courses in science education. The formation of the Cooperative Learning Center soon followed to focus on five areas:

1. Summarizing and extending the theory on cooperation and competition.
2. Reviewing the existing research in order to validate or disconfirm the theory and establish what is known and unknown.
3. Conducting a long-term program of research to validate and extend the theory and to identify (a) the conditions under which cooperative, competitive, and individualistic efforts are effective and (b) the basic elements that make cooperation work.
4. Operationalizing the validated theory into a set of procedures for teachers and administrators to use.
5. Implementing the procedures in classes, schools, school districts, colleges, and training programs.

These five activities result in an understanding of what is and is not a cooperative effort, the different types of cooperative learning, the five basic elements that make cooperation work, and the outcomes that result when cooperation is carefully structured.

What Is and Is Not a Cooperative Effort

Not all groups are cooperative. There is nothing magical about working in a group. Some kinds of learning groups facilitate student learning and increase the quality of life in the classroom. Other types of learning groups hinder student learning and create disharmony and dissatisfaction. To use cooperative learning effectively, one must know what is and is not a cooperative group (Johnson, Johnson, & Holubec, 1998b).

1. *Pseudo learning group:* Students are assigned to work together but they have no interest in doing so and believe they will be evaluated by being ranked from the highest to the lowest performer. Students hide information from each other, attempt to mislead and confuse each other, and distrust each other. The result is that the sum of the whole is less than the potential of the individual members. Students would achieve more if they were working alone.

2. *Traditional classroom learning group:* Students are assigned to work together and accept that they have to do so. Assignments are structured so that students are evaluated and rewarded as individuals, not as members of the group. They seek each other's information but have no motivation to teach what they know to group-mates. Some students seek a free ride on the efforts of group-mates, who feel exploited and do less. The result is that the sum of the whole is more than the potential of some of the members, but the more hard working and conscientious students would perform higher if they worked alone.

3. *Cooperative learning group:* Students work together to accomplish shared goals. Students seek outcomes that are beneficial to all. Students discuss material with each other, help one another understand it, and encourage each other to work hard. Individual performance is checked regularly to ensure that all students are contributing and learning. The result is that the group is more than a sum of its parts, and all students perform higher academically than they would if they worked alone.

4. *High-performance cooperative learning group:* This is a group that meets all the criteria for being a cooperative learning group and outperforms all reasonable expectations, given its membership. The level of commitment members have to each other and the group's success is beyond that of most cooperative groups. Few groups ever achieve this level of development.

How well any small group performs depends on how it is structured. Seating people together and calling them a cooperative group does not make them one. Study groups, project groups, lab groups, homerooms, and reading groups are groups, but they are not necessarily cooperative. Even with the best of intentions, teachers may be using traditional classroom learning groups rather than cooperative learning groups. To ensure that a group is cooperative, educators must understand the different ways cooperative learning may be used and the basic elements that need to be carefully structured within every cooperative activity.

Types of Cooperative Learning

> Two are better than one, because they have a good reward for toil. For if they fall, one will lift up his fellow; but woe to him who is alone when he falls and has not another to lift him up. . . . And though a man might prevail against one who is alone, two will withstand him. A threefold cord is not quickly broken. (Ecclesiastes 4:9–12)

Cooperative learning is a versatile procedure and can be used for a variety of purposes. Cooperative learning groups may be used to teach specific content (formal cooperative learning groups), to ensure active cognitive processing of information during a lecture or demonstration (informal cooperative learning groups), and to provide long-term support and assistance for academic progress (cooperative base groups) (Johnson, Johnson, & Holubec, 1998a, 1998b).

Formal cooperative learning consists of students working together, for one class period or several weeks, to achieve shared learning goals and complete specific tasks and assignments (e.g., problem solving, writing a report, conducting a survey or experiment, learning vocabulary, or answering questions at the end of the chapter) (Johnson, Johnson, & Holubec, 1998b). Any course requirement or assignment may be structured cooperatively. In formal cooperative learning groups, teachers:

1. Make a number of *preinstructional decisions.* Teachers specify the objectives for the lesson (both academic and social skills) and decide on the size of groups, the method of assigning students to groups, the roles students will be assigned, the materials needed to conduct the lesson, and the way the room will be arranged.

2. *Explain* the task and the positive interdependence. A teacher clearly defines the assignment, teaches the required concepts and strategies, specifies the positive interdependence and individual accountability, gives the criteria for success, and explains the social skills to be used.

3. *Monitor* students' learning and *intervene* within the groups to provide task assistance or to increase students' interpersonal and group skills. A teacher systematically observes and collects data on each group as it works. When needed, the teacher intervenes to assist students in completing the task accurately and in working together effectively.

4. *Assess* students' learning and help students process how well their groups functioned. Students' learning is carefully assessed and their performances evaluated. Members of the learning groups then discuss how effectively they worked together and how they can improve in the future.

Informal cooperative learning consists of having students work together to achieve a joint learning goal in temporary, ad-hoc groups that last from a few minutes to one class period (Johnson, Johnson, & Holubec, 1998a; Johnson, Johnson, & Smith, 1998). During a lecture, demonstration, or film, informal cooperative learning can be used to (a) focus student attention on the material to be learned, (b) set a mood conducive to learning, (c) help set expectations as to what will be covered in a class session, (d) ensure that students cognitively process the material being taught, and (e) provide closure to an instructional session.

During direct teaching the instructional challenge for the teacher is to ensure that students do the intellectual work of organizing material, explaining it, summarizing it, and integrating it into existing conceptual structures. Informal cooperative learning groups are often organized so that students engage in 3–5 minute focused discussions before and after a lecture and 2–3 minute turn-to-your-partner discussions interspersed throughout a lecture.

Cooperative base groups are long-term, heterogeneous cooperative learning groups of 3–4 members with stable membership (Johnson, Johnson, & Holubec, 1998a; Johnson, Johnson, & Smith, 1998). Base groups give the support, help, encouragement, and assistance each member needs to make academic progress (attend class, complete all assignments, learn) and develop cognitively and socially in healthy ways. Base groups meet daily in elementary school and twice a week in secondary school (or whenever the class meets). They are permanent (lasting from one to several years) and provide the long-term caring peer relationships

necessary to influence members consistently to work hard in school.

The use of base groups tends to improve attendance, personalize the work required and the school experience, and improve the quality and quantity of learning. School and classroom management is enhanced when base groups are given the responsibility for conducting a year-long service project to improve the school. The larger the class or school and the more complex and difficult the subject matter, the more important it is to have base groups. Base groups are also helpful in structuring homerooms and when a teacher meets with a number of advisees.

Example of Integrated Use of Cooperative Learning

An example of the integrated use of the cooperative learning procedures is as follows. Students arrive at class and meet in their base groups to welcome each other, check each student's homework to make sure all members understand the academic material and are prepared for the class session, and tell each other to have a great day.

The teacher then begins a lesson on the limitations of being human (Billion-Dollar Being, 1974). To help students cognitively organize in advance what they know about the advantages and disadvantages of being human, the teacher uses informal cooperative learning. The teacher asks students to form a triad and ponder, "What are five things you cannot do with your human limitations that a billion-dollar being might be designed to do?" Students have 4 minutes to do so. In the next 10 minutes, the teacher explains that while the human body is a marvelous system, we (like other organisms) have very specific limitations. We cannot see bacteria in a drop of water or the rings of Saturn unaided. We cannot hear as well as a deer or fly like an eagle. Humans have never been satisfied being so limited and, therefore, we have invented microscopes, telescopes, and our own wings. The teacher then instructs students to turn to the person next to them and answer the questions, "What are three limitations of humans, what have we invented to overcome them, and what other human limitations might we be able to overcome?"

Formal cooperative learning is now used in the lesson. The teacher has the 32 students count off from 1 to 8 to form groups of four randomly. Group members sit in a semicircle so they can face each other and still be facing the teacher. Each member is assigned a role: researcher/runner, summarizer/timekeeper, collector/recorder, and technical adviser (role interdependence).

Every group gets one large (2 × 3-feet) piece of paper, a marking pen, a rough draft sheet for designing the being, an assignment sheet explaining the task and cooperative goal structure, and four student self-evaluation checklists (resource interdependence). The task is to design a billion-dollar being that overcomes the human limitations thought of by the class and the group. The group members are to draw a diagram of the being on the scratch paper and, when they have something they like, transfer it to the larger paper.

The teacher establishes positive goal interdependence by asking for one drawing from the group that all group members contribute to and can explain. The criterion for success is to complete the diagram in the 30-minute time limit. The teacher observes each group to ensure that members are fulfilling their roles and that any one member can explain any part of the being at any time. The teacher informs students that the expected social skills to be used by all students are encouraging each other's participation, contributing ideas, and summarizing. She defines the skill of encouraging participation and has each student practice it twice before the lesson begins.

While students work in their groups, the teacher monitors by systematically observing each group and intervening to provide academic assistance and help in using the interpersonal and small group skills required to work together effectively. At the end of the lesson, the groups hand in their diagrams of the billion-dollar being to be assessed and evaluated. Group members then process how well they worked together by identifying actions each member engaged in that helped the group succeed and one thing that could be added to improve their group next time.

The teacher uses informal cooperative learning to provide closure to the lesson by asking students to meet in new triads and write out six conclusions about the limitations of human beings and what we have done to overcome them. At the end of the class session, the cooperative base groups meet to review what students believe is the most important thing they have learned during the day, what homework has been assigned, what help each member needs to complete the homework, and to tell each other to have a fun afternoon and evening.

The Cooperative School

Teachers are not the only ones who need to carefully structure cooperation. Administrators need to create a learning community by structuring cooperation at the school level (Johnson & Johnson, 1994, 1999).

In addition, they have to attend to the cooperation among faculty, between the school and parents, and between the school and the community.

Administrators, for example, may structure three types of cooperative faculty teams. Collegial teaching teams are formed to increase teachers' instructional expertise and success. They consist of 2–5 teachers who meet weekly and discuss how to better implement cooperative learning within their classrooms. Teachers are assigned to task forces to plan and implement solutions to school-wide issues and problems such as curriculum adoptions and lunchroom behavior. Ad hoc decision-making groups are used during faculty meetings to involve all staff members in important school decisions.

The use of cooperative teams at the building level ensures that there is a congruent cooperative team-based organizational structure within both classrooms and the school. Finally, the superintendent uses the same types of cooperative teams to maximize the productivity of district administrators.

Basic Elements of Cooperation

In order for an activity to be cooperative, five basic elements are essential and need to be included (Johnson & Johnson, 1989; Johnson, Johnson, & Holubec, 1998a). The five essential elements are as follows.

1. *Positive interdependence:* Positive interdependence is the perception that we are linked with others in a way so that we cannot succeed unless they do. Their work benefits us and our work benefits them. Within every cooperative lesson, positive goal interdependence must be established through mutual learning goals (learn the assigned material and make sure that all members of your group learn the assigned material). In order to strengthen positive interdependence, joint rewards (if all members of your group score 90 percent correct or better on the test, each will receive 5 bonus points), divided resources (giving each group member a part of the total information required to complete an assignment), and complementary roles (reader, checker, encourager, elaborator) may also be used.

2. *Individual accountability:* Individual accountability exists when the performance of each individual student is assessed and the results are given back to the group and the individual. The purpose of cooperative learning groups is to make each member a stronger individual. Students learn together so that they can subsequently perform higher as individuals. To ensure that each member is strengthened, students are held individually accountable to do their share of the work.

Common ways to structure individual accountability include (a) giving an individual test to each student, (b) randomly selecting one student's product to represent the entire group, or (c) having each student explain what they have learned to a classmate.

3. *Face-to-face promotive interaction:* Individuals promote each other's success by helping, assisting, supporting, encouraging, and praising each other's efforts to achieve. Certain cognitive activities and interpersonal dynamics only occur when students get involved in promoting each other's learning. These include orally explaining how to solve problems, discussing the nature of the concepts being learned, teaching one's knowledge to classmates, and connecting present with past learning. Accountability to peers, ability to influence each other's reasoning and conclusions, social modeling, social support, and interpersonal rewards all increase as the face-to-face interactions among group members increase.

In addition, the verbal and nonverbal responses of other group members provide important information concerning a student's performance. Silent students are uninvolved students who are not contributing to the learning of others as well as themselves. To obtain meaningful face-to-face interaction, the size of groups needs to be small (2–4 members).

4. *Social skills:* Contributing to the success of a cooperative effort requires interpersonal and small group skills. Placing socially unskilled individuals in a group and telling them to cooperate does not guarantee that they will be able to do so effectively. Persons must be taught the leadership, decision-making, trust-building, communication, and conflict-management skills just as purposefully and precisely as academic skills. Procedures and strategies for teaching students social skills may be found in Johnson (1997) and Johnson and F. Johnson (1997).

5. *Group processing:* Group processing exists when group members discuss how well they are achieving their goals and maintaining effective working relationships. Groups need to describe what member actions are helpful and unhelpful and make decisions about what behaviors to continue or change. When difficulties in relating to each other arise, students must engage in group processing and identify, define, and solve the problems they are having working together effectively.

Understanding these five basic elements and developing skills in structuring them allows teachers to (a) adapt cooperative learning to their unique circumstances, needs, and students, (b) fine tune their use of cooperative learning, and (c) prevent and solve problems students have in working together.

What Do We Know About Cooperative Efforts?

Everyone has to work together; if we can't get everybody working toward common goals, nothing is going to happen. (Harold K. Sperlich, president, Chrysler Corporation)

A great deal of research has been conducted comparing the relative effects of cooperative, competitive, and individualistic efforts on instructional outcomes. During the past 100 years, over 550 experimental and 100 correlational studies have been conducted by a wide variety of researchers in different decades with different age subjects, in different subject areas, and in different settings (see Johnson & Johnson, 1989, for a complete listing and review of these studies).

The type of interdependence structured among students determines how they interact with each other, which, in turn, largely determines instructional outcomes. Structuring situations cooperatively results in students interacting in ways that promote each other's success, structuring situations competitively results in students interacting in ways that oppose each other's success, and structuring situations individualistically results in no interaction among students. These interaction patterns affect numerous instructional outcomes, which may be subsumed within the three broad and interrelated categories of effort exerted to achieve, quality of relationships among participants, and participants' psychological adjustment and social competence (see Figure 1) (Johnson & Johnson, 1989).

ACHIEVEMENT

Achievement is a we thing, not a me thing, always the product of many hands and heads. (John Atkinson)

Regarding the question of how successful competitive, individualistic, and cooperative efforts are in promoting productivity and achievement, over 375 studies have been conducted in the past 100 years (Johnson & Johnson, 1989). Working together to achieve a common goal produces higher achievement and greater productivity than does working alone. This is so well confirmed by so much research that it stands as one of the strongest principles of social and organizational psychology.

Cooperative learning, furthermore, results in process gain (i.e., more higher-level reasoning, more frequent generation of new ideas and solutions), greater transfer of what is learned within one situation to another (i.e., group to individual transfer), and more time on task than does competitive or individualistic learning. The more conceptual the task, the more problem solving required; the more higher-level reasoning

FIGURE 1

Outcomes of Cooperative Learning

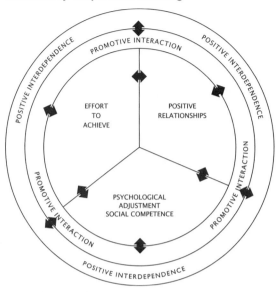

Source: Johnson & Johnson, 1989.

and critical thinking, the more creativity required; and the greater the application required of what is being learned to the real world, the greater the superiority of cooperative over competitive and individualistic efforts.

Cooperative learning ensures that all students are meaningfully and actively involved in learning. Active, involved students do not tend to engage in disruptive, off-task behavior. Cooperative learning also ensures that students are achieving up to their potential and are experiencing psychological success, so they are motivated to continue to invest energy and effort in learning. Those who experience academic failure are at risk for tuning out and acting up, which often leads to physical or verbal aggression.

Interpersonal Relationships

> A faithful friend is a strong defense, and he that hath found him, hath found a treasure. (Ecclesiastes 6:14)

Over 180 studies have been conducted since the 1940s on the relative impact of cooperative, competitive, and individualistic experiences on interpersonal attraction (Johnson & Johnson, 1989). The data indicate that cooperative experiences promote greater interpersonal attraction than do competitive or individualistic ones. Cooperative learning promotes the development of caring and committed relationships for every student. Even when individuals initially dislike each other or are obviously different from each other, cooperative experiences have been found to promote greater liking than is found in competitive and individualistic situations.

Cooperative groups help students establish and maintain friendships with peers. As relationships become more positive, there are corresponding improvements in productivity, morale, feelings of personal commitment and responsibility to do the assigned work, willingness to take on and persist in completing difficult tasks, and commitment to peers' success and growth. Absenteeism and turnover of membership decreases. Students who are isolated or alienated from their peers and who do not have friends are more likely to be at risk for violent and destructive behavior than students who experience social support and a sense of belonging.

Psychological Health and Social Competence

Working cooperatively with peers, and valuing cooperation, results in greater psychological health, higher self-esteem, and greater social competencies than does competing with peers or working independently. When individuals work together to complete assignments, they interact (improving social skills and competencies), promote each other's success (gaining self-worth), and form personal as well as professional relationships (creating the basis for healthy social development).

Cooperative efforts with caring people tend to increase personal ego-strength, self-confidence, independence, and autonomy. They provide the opportunity to share and solve personal problems, which increases an individual's resilience and ability to cope with adversity and stress. The more individuals work cooperatively, the more they see themselves as worthwhile and as having value and the more autonomous and independent they tend to be.

Cooperative groups provide an arena in which individuals develop the interpersonal and small group skills needed to work effectively with diverse schoolmates. Students learn how to communicate effectively, provide leadership, help the group make good decisions, build trust, repair hurt feelings, and understand others' perspectives. Even kindergartners can practice social skills each day in cooperative activities. Cooperative experiences are not a luxury. They are a necessity for the healthy social and psychological development of individuals who can function independently.

Conclusion

Cooperative learning is the instructional use of small groups in which students work together to maximize their own and each other's learning. Cooperative learning may be differentiated from pseudo groups and traditional classroom learning groups. There are three types of cooperative learning: formal cooperative learning, informal cooperative learning, and cooperative base groups. The basic elements that make cooperation work are positive interdependence, individual accountability, promotive interaction, appropriate use of social skills, and periodic processing of how to improve the effectiveness of the group.

When efforts are structured cooperatively, there is considerable evidence that students will exert more effort to achieve (learn more, use higher-level reasoning strategies more frequently, build more complete and complex conceptual structures, and retain information learned more accurately), build more positive and supportive relationships (including relationships with diverse individuals), and develop in more healthy ways (psychological health, self-esteem, ability to manage stress and adversity).

REFERENCES

Billion-Dollar Being. (1974). *Topics in applied science.* Golden, CO: Jefferson County Schools.

Johnson, D. W. (1997). *Reaching out: Interpersonal effectiveness and self-actualization* (6th ed.). Boston: Allyn & Bacon.

Johnson, D. W., & Johnson, F. (1997). *Joining together: Group theory and group skills* (6th ed.). Boston: Allyn & Bacon.

Johnson, D. W., & Johnson, R. (1989). *Cooperation and competition: Theory and research.* Edina, MN: Interaction Book Co.

Johnson, D. W., & Johnson, R. (1994). *Leading the cooperative school* (2nd ed.). Edina, MN: Interaction Book Co.

Johnson, D. W., & Johnson, R. (1999). The three Cs of classroom and school management. In H. Freiberg (Ed.), *Beyond behaviorism: Changing the classroom management paradigm.* Boston: Allyn & Bacon.

Johnson, D. W., Johnson, R., & Holubec, E. (1998a). *Advanced cooperative learning* (3rd ed.). Edina, MN: Interaction Book Co.

Johnson, D. W., Johnson, R., & Holubec, E. (1998b). *Cooperation in the classroom* (7th ed.). Edina, MN: Interaction Book Co.

Johnson, D. W., Johnson, R., & Smith, K. (1998). *Active learning: Cooperation in the college classroom* (2nd ed.). Edina, MN: Interaction Book Co.

POSTNOTE

The authors of this article have been researching and championing cooperative learning for many years, and their efforts have made a major contribution to American education. Cooperative learning has become a staple in both pre-service and in-service teacher education. David and Roger Johnson's contributions in developing and researching cooperative learning strategies have placed them among our Classic selections.

Although most educators applaud the idea of cooperative learning, few use it on a regular basis. Many young teachers read about cooperative learning, become advocates, try it a few times with few of the positive results discussed in this article, then put it away in a mental closet (labeled "Great Ideas from the Ivory Tower That Don't Work in the Trenches") and go on to more traditional "sage on the stage" instructional approaches. The key to a more widespread use of cooperative learning may be captured by the well-known story of the tourist in New York City who stops a native New Yorker and asks: "Sir, how do I get to Carnegie Hall?" The New Yorker doesn't stop, but yells over his shoulder, "Practice! Practice! Practice!" From personal experiences, we know that becoming skillful at cooperative learning takes more than just knowledge of it. Like Sandy Koufax, knowing the mechanics of throwing a fastball is hardly enough. Our advice: Practice! Practice! Practice!

Discussion Questions

1. Describe the experiences you, as a student, have had with cooperative learning.

2. Do you agree or disagree with the common criticism that cooperative learning is unfair because it slows down the progress of the academically gifted?

3. Which aspects of cooperative learning are most appealing? Which are least appealing?

RELATED WEBSITE RESOURCES AND VIDEO CASES

 Web Resources:

The Cooperative Learning Center (CLC) at the University of Minnesota. Available at:

http://www.co-operation.org.

Provided by the CLC, this website contains descriptions of center work; essays and research reports by Johnson and Johnson and others; and book and supply catalogs.

The Jigsaw Classroom. Available at:

http://www.jigsaw.org.

Developed by Eliot Aronson and the Social Psychology Network, this website contains "how-to" explanations, research summaries, implementation tips, and related links.

▶▶ ▶ ◀◀ *Video Case:*

Cooperative Learning in the Elementary Grades: Jigsaw Model

In this fifth-grade class, students use the Jigsaw model of cooperative learning to study the ancient Olympics. As you watch the clips and study the artifacts in the case, reflect upon the following questions:

1. How does this teacher manage the classroom environment during cooperative learning?
2. How are group composition and group-skills training important to the success of these groups?
3. What new things about cooperative learning did you learn from this video case?

▶▶ ▶ ◀◀ *Video Case:*

Cooperative Learning: High School History Lesson

In this high school classroom, the teacher demonstrates great sensitivity to group dynamics as students are assigned to groups to analyze texts and respond to the question of what it means to be a human being. As you watch the clips and study the artifacts in the case, reflect upon the following questions:

1. What do you think of Jake's description of the benefits of cooperative learning? Do his comments ring true to you?
2. What advice about setting up *ad hoc* cooperative groups does the teacher offer in the bonus video, "The Benefits of Ad Hoc Cooperative Learning Groups"? What do you consider to be important criteria for setting up partners and groups?

33

Mapping a Route Toward Differentiated Instruction

Carol Ann Tomlinson

Carol Ann Tomlinson is professor of educational leadership, foundations, and policy at the Curry School of Education, University of Virginia, Charlottesville, Virginia. She is the author of *How to Differentiate Instruction in Mixed-Ability Classrooms* (ASCD, 2001).

"Mapping a Route Toward Differentiated Instruction" by Carol Ann Tomlinson, *Educational Leadership*, September 1999, pp. 12–16.

Used with permission. The Association for Supervision and Curriculum Development is a worldwide community of educators advocating sound policies and sharing best practices to achieve the success of each learner. To learn more, visit ASCD at **www.ascd.org.**

| F | O | C | U | S | QUESTION

How does differentiated instruction address the needs of individual learners?

KEY TERMS
Differentiation
Readiness

Developing academically responsive classrooms is important for a country built on the twin values of equality and excellence. Our schools can achieve both of these competing values only to the degree that they can establish heterogeneous communities of learning (attending to issues of equity) built solidly on high-quality curriculum and instruction that strive to maximize the capacity of each learner (attending to issues of excellence).

A serious pursuit of differentiation, or personalized instruction, causes us to grapple with many of our traditional—if questionable—ways of "doing school." Is it reasonable to expect all 2nd graders to learn the same thing, in the same ways, over the same time span? Do single-textbook adoptions send inaccurate messages about the sameness of all learners? Can students learn to take more responsibility for their own learning? Do report cards drive our instruction? Should the classroom teacher be a solitary specialist on all learner needs, or could we support genuinely effective generalist-specialist teams? Can we reconcile learning standards with learner variance?

The questions resist comfortable answers—and are powerfully important. En route to answering them, we try various roads to differentiation. The concreteness of having something ready to do Monday morning is satisfying—and inescapable. After all, the students will arrive and the day must be planned. So we talk about using reading buddies in varied ways to support a range of readers or perhaps developing a learning contract with several options for practicing math skills. Maybe we could try a tiered lesson or interest centers. Three students who clearly understand the chapter need an independent study project. Perhaps we should begin with a differentiated project assignment, allowing students to choose a project about the Middle Ages. That's often how our journey toward differentiation begins.

The nature of teaching requires doing. There's not much time to sit and ponder the imponderables. To a point, that's fine—and, in any case, inevitable. A reflective teacher can test many principles from everyday interactions in the classroom. In other words, philosophy can derive from action.

We can't skip one step, however. The first step in making differentiation work is the hardest. In fact, the same first step is required to make all teaching and learning effective: We have to know where we want to end up before we start out—and plan to get there. That is, we must have solid curriculum and instruction in place before we differentiate them. That's harder than it seems.

Looking Inside Two Classrooms

Mr. Appleton is teaching about ancient Rome. His students are reading the textbook in class today. He suggests that they take notes of important details as they read. When they finish, they answer the questions at the end of the chapter. Students who don't finish must do so at home. Tomorrow, they will answer the questions together in class. Mr. Appleton likes to lecture and works hard to prepare his lectures. He expects students to take notes. Later, he will give a quiz on both the notes and the text. He will give students a study sheet before the test, clearly spelling out what will be on the test.

Mrs. Baker is also teaching about ancient Rome. She gives her students graphic organizers to use as they read the textbook chapter and goes over the organizers with the class so that anyone who missed details can fill them in. She brings in pictures of the art and the architecture of the period and tells how important the Romans were in shaping our architecture, language, and laws. When she invites some students to dress in togas for a future class, someone suggests bringing in food so that they can have a Roman banquet—and they do. One day, students do a word-search puzzle of vocabulary words about Rome. On another day, they watch a movie clip that shows gladiators and the Colosseum and talk about the favored "entertainment" of the period. Later, Mrs. Baker reads aloud several myths, and students talk about the myths that they remember from 6th grade. When it's time to study for the test, the teacher lets students go over the chapter together, which they like much better than working at home alone, she says.

She also wants students to like studying about Rome, so she offers a choice of 10 projects. Among the options are creating a poster listing important Roman gods and goddesses, their roles, and their symbols; developing a travel brochure for ancient Rome that a Roman of the day might have used; writing a poem about life in Rome; dressing dolls like citizens of Rome or drawing the fashions of the time; building a model of an important ancient Roman building or a Roman villa; and making a map of the Holy Roman Empire. Students can also propose their own topic.

Thinking About the Two Classrooms

Mr. Appleton's class is not differentiated. He does not appear to notice or respond to student differences.

Mrs. Baker's is differentiated—at least by some definitions. Each class has serious flaws in its foundations, however, and for that reason, Mrs. Baker's class may not be any more successful than Mr. Appleton's—and perhaps less so.

Successful teaching requires two elements: student understanding and student engagement. In other words, students must really understand, or make sense of, what they have studied. They should also feel engaged in or "hooked by" the ways that they have learned. The latter can greatly enhance the former and can help young people realize that learning is satisfying.

Mr. Appleton's class appears to lack engagement. There's nothing much to make learning appealing. He may be satisfied by his lecture, but it's doubtful that many of the students are impressed. It is also doubtful that much real student understanding will come from the teaching-learning scenario. Rather, the goal seems to be memorizing data for a test.

Memorizing and understanding are very different. The first has a short life span and little potential to transfer into a broader world. However, at least Mr. Appleton appears clear about what the students should memorize for the test. Mrs. Baker's class lacks even that clarity.

Students in Mrs. Baker's classroom are likely engaged. It is a lively, learner-friendly place with opportunity for student movement, student choice, and peer work. Further, Mrs. Baker's list of project options draws on different student interests or talents—and she is even open to their suggestions.

Although Mrs. Baker succeeds to some degree with engagement, a clear sense of what students should understand as a result of their study is almost totally missing. Thus her careful work to provide choice and to build a comfortable environment for her learners may not net meaningful, long-term learning. Her students are studying "something about ancient Rome." Nothing focuses or ties together the ideas and information that they encounter. Activities are more about being happy than about making meaning. No set of common information, ideas, or skills will stem from completing the various projects. In essence, she has accomplished little for the long haul. Her "differentiation" provides varied avenues to "mush"—multiple versions of fog. Her students work with different tasks, not differentiated ones.

Mr. Appleton's class provides little engagement, little understanding, and scant opportunity for attending to student differences. Mrs. Baker's class provides some engagement, little understanding, and no meaningful differentiation.

An Alternative Approach

To make differentiation work—in fact, to make teaching and learning work—teachers must develop an alternative approach to instructional planning beyond "covering the text" or "creating activities that students will like."

Ms. Cassell has planned her year around a few key concepts that will help students relate to, organize, and retain what they study in history. She has also developed principles or generalizations that govern or uncover how the concepts work. Further, for each unit, she has established a defined set of facts and terms that are essential for students to know to be literate and informed about the topic. She has listed skills for which she and the students are responsible as the year progresses. Finally, she has developed essential questions to intrigue her students and to cause them to engage with her in a quest for understanding.

Ms. Cassell's master list of facts, terms, concepts, principles, and skills stems from her understanding of the discipline of history as well as from the district's learning standards. As the year evolves, Ms. Cassell continually assesses the readiness, interests, and learning profiles of her students and involves them in goal setting and decision making about their learning. As she comes to understand her students and their needs more fully, she modifies her instructional framework and her instruction.

Ms. Cassell is also teaching about ancient Rome. Among the key concepts in this unit, as in many others throughout the year, are culture, change, and interdependence. Students will be responsible for important terms, such as *republic, patrician, plebeian, veto, villa,* and *Romance language;* names of key individuals, for example, Julius Caesar, Cicero, and Virgil; and names of important places, for instance, the Pantheon and the Colosseum.

For this unit, students explore key generalizations or principles: Varied cultures share common elements. Cultures are shaped by beliefs and values, customs, geography, and resources. People are shaped by and shape their cultures. Societies and cultures change for both internal and external reasons. Elements of a society and its cultures are interdependent.

Among important skills that students apply are using resources on history effectively, interpreting information from resources, blending data from several resources, and organizing effective paragraphs. The essential question that Ms. Cassell often poses to her students is, How would your life and culture be different if you lived in a different time and place?

Looking Inside the Third Classroom

Early in the unit, Ms. Cassell's students begin work, both at home and in class, on two sequential tasks that will extend throughout the unit as part of their larger study of ancient Rome. Both tasks are differentiated.

For the first task, students assume the role of someone from ancient Rome, such as a soldier, a teacher, a healer, a farmer, a slave, or a farmer's wife. Students base their choice solely on their own interests. They work both alone and with others who select the same topic and use a wide variety of print, video, computer, and human resources to understand what their life in ancient Rome would have been like.

Ultimately, students create a first-person data sheet that their classmates can use as a resource for their second task. The data sheet calls for the person in the role to provide accurate, interesting, and detailed information about what his or her daily schedule would be like, what he or she would eat and wear, where he or she would live, how he or she would be treated by the law, what sorts of problems or challenges he or she would face, the current events of the time, and so on.

Ms. Cassell works with both the whole class and small groups on evaluating the availability and appropriate use of data sources, writing effective paragraphs, and blending information from several sources into a coherent whole. Students use these skills as they develop the first-person data sheets. The teacher's goal is for each student to increase his or her skill level in each area.

The second task calls on students to compare and contrast their own lives with the lives of children of similar age in ancient Rome. Unlike the first task, which was based on student interest, this one is differentiated primarily on the basis of student readiness. The teacher assigns each student a scenario establishing his or her family context for the task: "You are the eldest son of a lawmaker living during the later years of the period known as Pax Romana," for example. Ms. Cassell bases the complexity of the scenario on the student's skill with researching and thinking about history. Most students work with families unlike those in their first task. Students who need continuity between the tasks, however, can continue in a role familiar from their first investigation.

All students use the previously developed first-person data sheets as well as a range of other resources to gather background information. They must address a common set of specified questions: How is what you eat shaped by the economics of your family and by your location? What is your level of education and how is that affected by your status in society? How is your life interdependent with the lives of others in ancient Rome? How will Rome change during your lifetime? How will those changes affect your life? All students must also meet certain research and writing criteria.

Despite the common elements, the task is differentiated in several ways. It is differentiated by interest because each student adds questions that are directed by personal interests: What games did children play? What was the practice of science like then? What was the purpose and style of art?

Readiness differentiation occurs because each student adds personal research and writing goals, often with the teacher's help, to his or her criteria for success. A wide range of research resources is available, including books with varied readability levels, video and audiotapes, models, and access to informed people. The teacher also addresses readiness through small-group sessions in which she provides different sorts of teacher and peer support, different kinds of modeling, and different kinds of coaching for success, depending on the readiness levels of students.

Finally, the teacher adds to each student's investigation one specific question whose degree of difficulty is based on her most recent assessments of student knowledge, facility with research, and thinking about history. An example of a more complex question is, How will your life differ from that of the previous generation in your family, and how will your grandchildren's lives compare with yours? A less complex, but still challenging question is, How will language change from the generation before you to two generations after you, and why will those changes take place?

Learning-profile differentiation is reflected in the different media that students use to express their findings: journal entries, an oral monologue, or a videotape presentation. Guidelines for each type of product ensure quality and focus on essential understandings and skills established for the unit. Students may work alone or with a "parallel partner" who is working with the same role, although each student must ultimately produce his or her own product.

At other points in the study of ancient Rome, Ms. Cassell differentiates instruction. Sometimes she varies the sorts of graphic organizers that students use when they read, do research, or take notes in class. She may use review groups of mixed readiness and then conduct review games with students of like readiness working together. She works hard to ask a range of questions that move from concrete and familiar to abstract and unfamiliar in all class discussions. She sometimes provides homework options in which students select the tasks that they believe will help them understand important ideas or use important skills best. Of course, the class also plans, works, reviews, and debates as a whole group.

Students find Ms. Cassell's class engaging—and not just because it's fun. It's engaging because it shows the connection between their own lives and life long ago. It helps them see the interconnectedness among times in history and make links with other subjects. It tickles their curiosity. And it provides a challenge that pushes each learner a bit further than is comfortable—and then supports success. Sometimes those things are fun. Often they are knotty and hard. Always they dignify the learner and the subject. Mr. Cassell's class is highly likely to be effective for her varied learners, in part because she continually attempts to reach her students where they are and move them on—she differentiates instruction. The success of the differentiation, however, is not a stand-alone matter. It is successful because it is squarely rooted in student engagement plus student understanding.

This teacher knows where she wants her students to arrive at the end of their shared learning journey and where her students are along that journey at a given time. Because she is clear about the destination and the path of the travelers, she can effectively guide them, and she varies or differentiates her instruction to accomplish this goal. Further, her destination is not merely the amassing of data but rather the constructing of understanding. Her class provides a good example of the close and necessary relationship between effective curriculum and instruction and effective differentiation.

The First Step Is the Compass

Mr. Appleton may have a sense of what he wants his students to know at the end of the road, but not about what his students should understand and be able to do. He teaches facts, but no key concepts, guiding principles, or essential questions. With a fact-based curriculum, differentiating instruction is difficult. Perhaps some students could learn more facts and some, fewer. Perhaps some students could have more time to drill the facts, and some, less. It's difficult to envision a defensible way to differentiate a fact-driven curriculum, probably because the curriculum itself is difficult to defend.

Mrs. Baker also appears to lack a clear vision of the meaning of her subject, of the nature of her discipline and what it adds to human understanding, and of why it should matter to a young learner to study old times.

There is little clarity about facts—let alone concepts, guiding principles, or essential questions. Further, she confuses folly with engagement. She thinks that she is differentiating instruction, but without instructional clarity, her activities and projects are merely different—not differentiated. Because there is no instructional clarity, there is no basis for defensible differentiation.

Ms. Cassell plans for what students should know, understand, and be able to do at the end of a sequence of learning. She dignifies each learner by planning tasks that are interesting, relevant, and powerful. She invites each student to wonder. She determines where each student is in knowledge, skill, and understanding and where he or she needs to move. She differentiates instruction to facilitate that goal. For her, differentiation is one piece of the mosaic of professional expertise. It is not a strategy to be plugged in occasionally or often, but is a way of thinking about the classroom. In her class, there is a platform for differentiation.

Ms. Cassell helps us see that differentiated instruction must dignify each learner with learning that is "whole," important, and meaning making. The core of *what* the students learn remains relatively steady. *How* the student learns—including degree of difficulty, working arrangements, modes of expression, and sorts of scaffolding—may vary considerably. Differentiation is not so much the "stuff" as the "how." If the "stuff" is ill conceived, the "how" is doomed.

The old saw is correct: Every journey *does* begin with a single step. The journey to successfully differentiated or personalized classrooms will succeed only if we carefully take the first step—ensuring a foundation of best-practice curriculum and instruction.

POSTNOTE

The term *differentiated instruction* is relatively new in education circles, but its practice is as old as teachers and classrooms. Teachers know that their classrooms contain students with tremendous diversity—ethnic, cultural, racial, academic, and learning styles, to name but a few of the diverse characteristics. How can teachers plan and deliver instruction and assessment that will respond to these forms of diversity to help students learn better? Differentiated instruction is teaching with student variance in mind and using practical ways to respond to learner needs. Instead of presuming that all of your students are essentially alike, differentiated instruction means starting where the students are and planning varied approaches to what individual students need to learn, how they will learn it, and how they can express what they have learned. The idea of differentiated or personalized instruction has great appeal to teachers and teacher educators, but its implementation may seem overwhelming, particularly for new teachers. In other writings, Carol Ann Tomlinson advises that teachers start the process slowly and gradually expand differentiation as they feel comfortable and have the time. Most important is making a commitment to the process of responding to student differences.

Discussion Questions

1. As you read the three vignettes involving Mr. Appleton, Mrs. Baker, and Ms. Cassell, which approach was more indicative of your elementary and secondary schooling? Which approach did you find more appealing? Why?
2. What concerns or questions do you have regarding differentiated instruction?
3. Did you have a teacher who used differentiated instruction particularly successfully? Describe what he or she did that made the instruction successful.

RELATED WEBSITE RESOURCES AND VIDEO CASES

 Web Resources:

Association for Supervision and Curriculum Development. Available at:

http://www.ascd.org.

This website contains numerous articles on differentiation.

Manteno, Illinois Community Unit School District #5. Available at:

http://www.manteno.k12.il.us/curriculumdiff.

This page on differentiation contains a school district's philosophy and teaching strategies for differentiating instruction.

⏩ ▶ ⏪ *Video Case:*

Academic Diversity: Differentiated Instruction

In this 3rd grade classroom, the teacher tries to design instruction that meets the needs of different types of learners. As you watch the clips and study the artifacts in the case, reflect upon the following questions:

1. How are all students held accountable for mastering the same writing-skills content, even though they approach the task differently?

2. Building on students' strengths when planning instruction is essential, according to the teacher in this video. Can you recall examples of teachers you had who built on your strengths? What were your learning results?

34

Linking Formative Assessment to Scaffolding

Lorrie A. Shepard

Lorrie A. Shepard is dean of the School of Education, University of Colorado at Boulder. Dr. Shepard is a past president of the American Educational Research Association and past president of the National Council on Measurement in Education. She was elected to the National Academy of Education in 1992 and served as vice president of the NAE.

"Linking Formative Assessment to Scaffolding" by Lorrie A. Shepard, *Educational Leadership* 63, no. 3, November 2005, pp. 66–70. Used with permission.

F O C U S QUESTION

How can formative assessment and scaffolding help students learn?

KEY TERMS

Formative assessment

Instructional scaffolding

Metacognition

Reciprocal teaching

Rubric

Zone of proximal development

Some people roll their eyes when ivory tower academics talk theory. But a good theory can be immensely practical. Learning theory provides coherence and big-picture understandings, especially when we're trying to change our teaching practices. Learning theory also helps us decide what to do when we can't rely on past experience. Moreover, it provides a basis for fitting together separate research-based strategies into a pedagogical approach that really works.

Take *formative assessment* and *instructional scaffolding,* for example. When you consider the terms in light of sociocultural learning theory and Vygotsky's (1978) zone of proximal development, they're essentially the same thing. Occurring in the midst of instruction, formative assessment is a dynamic process in which supportive adults or classmates help learners move from what they already know to what they are able to do next, using their zone of proximal development.

Moving Learning Forward

Present-day learning theories and research findings have profound implications for teaching practice because they tell us how intelligence develops. Contemporary learning theories—including constructivism, cognitive theory, and sociocultural theory—share several core principles. Most important are two ideas: that we construct knowledge, and that learning and development are culturally embedded, socially supported processes.

Children develop their abilities to think and reason in the same way that they learn language, gestures, interpersonal behaviors, manners, and tastes—through their social interactions with family and community. According to Vygotsky's (1978) cultural theory of development, any aspect of a child's cognitive development occurs twice: first on the social plane in interaction with others, and then on the psychological or internal plane. Whatever language and logical structures children use in their thinking, they first learned through social interactions.

Vygotsky's zone of proximal development model explains how this development occurs. The zone of proximal development is the space between

the actual developmental level as determined by independent problem solving and the level of potential development as determined through problem solving under adult guidance or in collaboration with more capable peers. (1978, p. 86)

Learning in the zone of proximal development is a joint activity in which the adult simultaneously keeps an eye on the goal of fully proficient performance and on what the learner, with assistance, is currently able to do. In the case of language development, the process is natural and almost invisible as parents encourage and support their children's increasingly competent efforts. Reciprocal teaching (Palincsar & Brown, 1984), which targets reading comprehension, is an example of a formal strategy used to help students develop their language skills.

Terms in Sync

Scaffolding and formative assessment are strategies that teachers use to move learning forward in the zone of proximal development. Scaffolding refers to supports that teachers provide to the learner during problem solving—in the form of reminders, hints, and encouragement—to ensure successful completion of a task. An important feature of scaffolding, especially in authentic, apprenticeship contexts, is keeping the task whole—"controlling those elements that are beyond the learner's capacity" (Wood, Bruner, & Ross, 1976, p. 90).

For example, when a child is first learning to sew or set the table, adults may step in and help with the trickiest or most difficult part—threading the needle or taking the breakable glasses down from the top shelf—but nevertheless, the child completes the real task. In classrooms, teachers help students with their research before sending them to the library on their own. When a student is stuck because he or she can't find information on a given topic, the teacher may suggest a new search term or help the student narrow the topic, but in the end, the student completes the research process on his or her own. Gradually, as competence increases, the teacher cedes more control to the learner. To be successful, the learner must also come to understand and take ownership of the goal.

Formative assessment uses insights about a learner's current understanding to alter the course of instruction and thus support the development of greater competence. From a sociocultural perspective, formative assessment—like scaffolding—is a collaborative process and involves negotiation of meaning between teacher and learner about expectations and how best to improve performance.

When D. Royce Sadler wrote his seminal paper on formative assessment in 1989, he was trying to show why students so often failed to improve, even when teachers provided accurate feedback. He argued that it was insufficient simply to point out right and wrong answers to students. For assessment to be "formative," a student must

- Come to hold a concept of quality roughly similar to that of the teacher.
- Be able to compare the current level of performance with the standard.
- Be able to take action to close the gap.

According to Sadler, the teacher could help the student internalize quality criteria by translating them "from latent to manifest and back to latent again" until these criteria become "so obviously taken for granted that they need no longer be stated explicitly." Sadler wanted to develop evaluative expertise in students so they could become proficient at monitoring their own learning. Like scaffolding, this kind of classroom interaction can foster intrinsic motivation as well as cognitive and metacognitive learning.

The Link Between Assessment and Research

The following four strategies illustrate the strong connection between formative assessment and research on learning. We must keep in mind, however, that educators will not achieve the benefits of formative assessment for learning simply by implementing a string of promising techniques or by using them mechanistically. Research-inspired strategies are not likely to be effective until they are part of a larger cultural shift in which teachers and students jointly take up learning as a worthy endeavor (Shepard, 2000).

Eliciting Prior Knowledge

Students build new understandings—about anything from mathematics to video games—by making sense of new experiences in light of what they already know. In this context, Tharp and Gallimore (1988) offered the metaphor of weaving: We understand new information only when it has been "woven into our *system* of meanings and understandings" (p. 109). Using sociocultural theory, Tharp and Gallimore developed the concepts of responsive teaching and instructional conversations to describe how teachers can assist learning by eliciting students' relevant knowledge.

Teachers should not think of prior-knowledge assessment as a discrete pre-test to use from time to time. Rather, it should be common classroom practice. We should routinely ask ourselves what we already know that will help us solve a problem or learn from a new unit of study. For example, with Ogle's (1986) K-W-L technique, teachers ask students to post on a chart what they already *know* (K) and, through discussion, establish what they *want* (W) to learn. At the end of the activity, students discuss and summarize what they have *learned* (L). Knowledge-activation routines like this help develop students' metacognitive abilities while providing relevant knowledge connections for specific units of study.

Similarly, Moll, Amanti, Neff, and Gonzalez (1992) collaborated with teachers to identify student "funds of knowledge" as another way to draw connections between student learning experiences in and out of school. For example, a teacher who made a home visit observed a child selling Mexican candy to a neighbor and developed a unit using candy as a theme. Students studied the ingredients used to make candy and discovered the differences between the artificial flavors and coloring used in U.S. candies and the vegetable dyes and real fruit used in Mexican ones.

Routinely eliciting and building on prior knowledge can become part of the larger cultural shift required to establish a learning classroom. In a recent study of new formative assessment practices, Black and Wiliam (2004) provided an example of the power of new norms:

> One class, subsequently taught by a teacher not emphasizing assessment for learning, surprised the teacher by complaining, "Look, we've told you we don't understand this. Why are you going on to the next topic?" (p. 35)

Providing Effective Feedback

We think of feedback as essential for learning. Surprisingly, in a comprehensive review of feedback, Kluger and DeNisi (1996) found that one-third of the studies showed negative effects—feedback about performance actually harmed learning outcomes. According to Kluger and DeNisi, positive learning outcomes were more likely when feedback focused on features of the task—such as how the student could improve in relation to the standards—and emphasized learning goals instead of lavishing nonspecific praise or making normative comparisons. In motivational literature, *learning goals* refer to learning for the sake of mastering a skill and becoming competent—intrinsic motivation. In contrast, *performance goals* refer to performing a task to please someone else or to get good grades—external motivation. In classrooms, the kind of task-specific feedback that helps learning might be, "Great, you told us about the most important thing that happened in

the story," or "Try to give more detail about why the puppet looked scary."

Although sustained, one-on-one interactions are not feasible in the regular classroom, detailed studies of one-on-one tutoring can show us how effective feedback works. For example, Lepper, Drake, and O'Donnell-Johnson (1997) observed that expert tutors are highly selective in how they use feedback. They typically ignore errors that are inconsequential to the solution process, such as spelling errors in an early draft. They forestall errors by offering hints when they perceive that a student is likely to repeat a previous error (for example, when a student reads a word problem aloud with a misplaced emphasis, revealing his or her misunderstanding of the problem).

These decisions help maintain student motivation and self-confidence during the feedback process. Consistent with the idea of working in the zone of proximal development and Sadler's point about formative assessment—that students must be able to take action to close the gap between their current and expected performance—feedback is most effective when it helps move the student forward.

In a study that could provide a feasible model for professional development, Elawar and Corno (1985) worked with mathematics teachers to help them learn how to provide more focused feedback to students. Their feedback training emphasized these guiding questions: What is the key error? What is the probable reason the student made this error? How can I guide the student to avoid the error in the future? As a result of this more focused feedback, student achievement dramatically improved compared with several control classes. In addition, students developed more positive attitudes about mathematics.

Teaching for Transfer of Knowledge

A goal of learning is for students to be able to extend their knowledge and apply it in new situations. However, both research findings and practical experience tell us that school learning is often compartmentalized and inert. In contrast, making connections and constructing meaning are integral to teaching for both transfer and robust understanding. Developing this kind of learning requires attention to metacognition. Classroom practices should include a broader discussion of how students can use specific strategies—not just within the narrow perimeters of a given lesson or set of content—and how they can use insights from previous lessons to generate new knowledge. Students might discuss such questions as "What do we already know about fractions that can help us understand decimals?" or "How is learning about ratios and proportions the same as—and different from—learning about fractions?"

One of the many unfortunate influences of popularized behaviorism on education is its narrow conception of learning objectives and test fairness. For behaviorists, a fair test must correspond exactly to what teachers have taught. However, as the teaching-to-the-test literature has shown, repeated practice with familiar formats reduces the likelihood that students will be able to use their knowledge when they encounter problems posed in even slightly different ways (Shepard, 1997). Teachers shouldn't ask students to answer questions on a summative exam that are fundamentally different from the kinds of questions the students experienced during instruction, but they should foster a classroom culture that challenges students to make connections and apply what they have learned to a broad range of problems. For example, as soon as students show me they've "got it," a new question always follows my congratulatory smile: "Now, have you thought about it *this* way?" When this wider range of questioning is the rule in the classroom, it becomes appropriate to expect extensions, applications, reformulations, and connections on summative examinations.

Teaching Students How to Self-Assess

Student self-assessment is not about saving teachers from the work of grading papers. When used in a way that develops student thinking, it can be a deeply principled practice that serves both metacognitive and motivational purposes. In addition to acquiring specific knowledge and skills, becoming competent in a field of study means learning and internalizing the standards by which others will judge our performance. Posting rubrics so that students can see the features of a good essay helps make criteria accessible, but the real metacognitive work takes place as students begin to learn the meaning of rubric components by trying to interpret them and apply them to their own work. High school students learn what it means to support an argument in a history paper in the same way a 3rd grader learns how to write a good summary of a story— first by receiving formative feedback about essential elements and then by being able to self-critique and check for those elements in their own work.

Self-critique increases students' responsibility for their own learning and can make the relationship between teacher and student more collaborative. In case studies of self-evaluation practices in sites in England

and Australia (Klenowski, 1995), students reported that they came to a clearer understanding of the assessment criteria and became more reflective in their judgments because they knew they would have to discuss how they met the criteria. Students also became more interested in teacher comments and feedback than in grades.

A study by White and Frederickson (2000) illustrates the power of self-assessment. In the context of an inquiry-based science curriculum, students learned to evaluate their own and one another's research by applying specific criteria, such as the degree to which the student's work revealed knowledge of the science and a grasp of the processes of inquiry; was systematic; was carefully reasoned; and used the tools of science. Their judgments had a correlation of 0.58 with teacher ratings, whereas the judgments of control students, who saw the criteria only at the end of the curriculum, had a correlation of only 0.23 with teacher ratings. Compared with students in control classrooms, students who learned to self-assess showed greater gains on an inquiry test, earned higher scores on their research projects, and earned higher scores on the conceptual model test. Impressively, the advantages of learning to use the assessment criteria were greatest for previously low-achieving students, raising their performance to the level of high-achieving students in the control classrooms. White and Frederickson's students became successful in science through scaffolding that emphasized the process of self-assessment.

A Learning Culture

Perrenoud (1991) argued that some students will work hard and thrive on formative assessment, whereas others are "imprisoned in the identity of a bad pupil and an opponent" (p. 92). To counteract this, Perrenoud emphasized that teachers who want to practice formative assessment must "reconstruct the teaching contract" (p. 92). Our aim should be to establish classroom practices that encourage peer assessment, regard errors as opportunities for learning, and promote shared thinking. This implies a profound cultural transformation: classrooms in which both students and teachers focus on learning rather than on grades.

REFERENCES

Black, P., & Wiliam, D. (2004). The formative purpose: Assessment must first promote learning. In M. Wilson (Ed.), *Towards coherence between classroom assessment and accountability.* Chicago: University of Chicago Press.

Elawar, M. C., & Corno, L. (1985). A factorial experiment in teachers' written feedback on student homework: Changing teacher behavior a little rather than a lot. *Journal of Educational Psychology, 77*(2), 162–173.

Klenowski, V. (1995). Student self-evaluation process in student-centered teaching and learning contexts of Australia and England. *Assessment in Education, 2,* 145–163.

Kluger, A. N., & DeNisi, A. (1996). Effects of feedback intervention on performance. *Psychological Bulletin, 119*(2), 254–284.

Lepper, M. R., Drake, M. F., & O'Donnell-Johnson, T. (1997). Scaffolding techniques of expert human tutors. In K. Hogan & M. Pressley (Eds.), *Scaffolding student learning: Instructional approaches and issues.* Cambridge, MA: Brookline Books.

Moll, L. C., Amanti, C., Neff, D., & Gonzalez, N. (1992). Funds of knowledge for teaching. *Theory Into Practice, 31*(1), 132–141.

Ogle, D. M. (1986). K-W-L: A teaching model that develops active reading of expository text. *Reading Teacher, 39*(6), 564–570.

Palincsar, A. S., & Brown, A. L. (1984). Reciprocal teaching of comprehension-fostering and comprehension-monitoring activities. *Cognition and Instruction, 1*(2), 117–175.

Perrenoud, P. (1991). Towards a pragmatic approach to formative evaluation. In P. Weston (Ed.), *Assessment of pupils' achievement: Motivation and school success* (pp. 77–101). Amsterdam: Swets & Zeitlinger.

Sadler, D. R. (1989). Formative assessment and the design of instructional systems. *Instructional Science, 18*(2), 119–144.

Shepard, L. A. (1997). *Measuring achievement: What does it mean to test for robust understanding?* William H. Angoff Memorial Lecture Series. Princeton, NJ: Educational Testing Service.

Shepard, L. A. (2000). The role of assessment in a learning culture. *Educational Researcher, 29*(7), 4–14.

Tharp, R. G., & Gallimore, R. (1988). *Rousing minds to life: Teaching, learning, and schooling in social context.* Cambridge, UK: Cambridge University Press.

Vygotsky, L. S. (1978). *Mind in society: The development of higher psychological processes.* (Edited by M. Cole, J. Scribner, V. John-Steiner, & E. Souberman). Cambridge, MA: Harvard University Press.

White, B. Y., & Frederickson, J. R. (2000). Metacognitive facilitation: An approach to making scientific inquiry accessible to all. In J. Minstrell & E. van Zee (Eds.), *Inquiring into inquiry learning and teaching in science* (pp. 331–370). Washington, DC: American Association for the Advancement of Science.

Wood, D., Bruner, J. S., & Ross, G. (1976). The role of tutoring in problem solving. *Journal of Child Psychology and Psychiatry, 17*(2), 89–100.

POSTNOTE

This article by a leading scholar in the field of cognitive theory lives up to her assertion at the beginning of the article that "a good theory can be immensely practical." Lorrie Shepard has provided the theoretical elements of formative assessment, scaffolding, and the zone of proximal development, as well as research-based strategies that work in the classroom. In doing so, she spans the gap between theory and practice. Her main point, stated at the end of the article, argues for a "profound cultural transformation: classrooms in which both students and teachers focus on learning rather than on grades." Although teachers and students in this age of "high-stakes testing" are finding this difficult to do, her point is nevertheless valid.

Discussion Questions

1. According to the article, what characteristics distinguish effective from ineffective feedback about performance?

2. Did any of your teachers effectively employ any of the strategies mentioned in the article? What do you remember about the experiences?

3. The author believes that teaching students to "self-assess" pays great dividends in helping students to think better. Given your subject matter or grade level, what are some ways that you could help your students develop the habit of self-assessment?

RELATED WEBSITE RESOURCES AND VIDEO CASES

 Web Resources:

New York City Teaching Fellows. Available at:

http://condor.admin.ccny.cuny.edu/~group4/.

This website on scaffolding contains several research articles. The site also contains a link to a video of a teacher demonstrating scaffolding in the classroom.

▶▶ ▶ ◀◀ *Video Case:*

Vygotsky's Zone of Proximal Development: Increasing Cognition in an Elementary Literacy Lesson

In this video case, you will see how developmental psychologist Dr. Frances Hurley draws on this theory to support students' abstract thinking in a lesson on poetry. As you watch the clips and study the artifacts in the case, reflect upon the following questions:

1. Which of the Vygotskian instructional techniques is Dr. Hurley describing when she talks about building the children's knowledge in stepwise fashion from day-to-day? How would this step-by-step approach apply to the students and subject you will be teaching?

2. How does this teacher determine the original knowledge level of her students? How can you determine the zone of proximal development for each of your students?

PART

6

Foundations

As a career, education is a practical field like medicine or criminal justice. It is not a discipline or content area, such as anthropology, physics, or English literature. However, education draws on these various disciplines and fields of knowledge to guide teachers in their work.

The term *foundations* as used in *educational foundations* is a metaphor, suggesting that as a house is built upon a foundation, so should the practice of education rest on a solid foundation of basic knowledge. The primary intellectual foundations for the practice of education include philosophy, history, psychology, and sociology. The articles selected for this section demonstrate the contribution of foundational scholarship to the practice of teaching.

My Pedagogic Creed

John Dewey

John Dewey (1859–1952) was a philosopher, educator, and clearly the most influential single figure in the history of American educational thought. He denounced classical approaches to learning and stressed teaching students *how* to use knowledge rather than simply pursue "learning for learning's sake." Although honored as the founder of the Progressive Education movement, his theories receive more lip service than practice.

John Dewey, "My Pedagogic Creed." This article was published originally as a pamphlet by E. L. Kellogg and Co., 1897.

Article I—What Education Is

I BELIEVE THAT

- all education proceeds by the participation of the individual in the social consciousness of the race. This process begins unconsciously almost at birth, and is continually shaping the individual's powers, saturating his consciousness, forming his habits, training his ideas, and arousing his feelings and emotions. Through this unconscious education the individual gradually comes to share in the intellectual and moral resources which humanity has succeeded in getting together. He becomes an inheritor of the funded capital of civilization. The most formal and technical education in the world cannot safely depart from this general process. It can only organize it or differentiate it in some particular direction.
- the only true education comes through the stimulation of the child's powers by the demands of the social situations in which he finds himself. Through these demands he is stimulated to act as a member of a unity, to emerge from his original narrowness of action and feeling, and to conceive of himself from the standpoint of the welfare of the group to which he belongs. Through the responses which others make to his own activities he comes to know what these mean in social terms. The value which they have is reflected back into them. For instance, through the response which is made to the child's instinctive babblings the child comes to know what those babblings mean; they are transformed into articulate language, and thus the child is introduced into the consolidated wealth of ideas and emotions which are now summed up in language.
- this educational process has two sides—one psychological and one sociological—and that neither can be subordinated to the other, or neglected, without evil results following. Of these two sides, the psychological is the basis. The child's own instincts and powers furnish the material and give the starting-point for all education. Save as the efforts of the educator connect with some activity which the child is carrying on of his own initiative independent of the educator, education becomes reduced to a pressure from without. It may, indeed, give certain external results, but cannot truly be called educative. Without insight into

FOCUS QUESTION

What did the "Father of Progressive Education" actually believe?

KEY TERMS

Continuous reconstruction of experience

Social reconstruction

the psychological structure and activities of the individual the educative process will, therefore, be haphazard and arbitrary. If it chances to coincide with the child's activity it will get a leverage; if it does not, it will result in friction, or disintegration, or arrest of the child-nature.

- knowledge of social conditions, of the present state of civilization, is necessary in order properly to interpret the child's powers. The child has his own instincts and tendencies, but we do not know what these mean until we can translate them into their social equivalents. We must be able to carry them back into a social past and see them as the inheritance of previous race activities. We must also be able to project them into the future to see what their outcome and end will be. In the illustration just used, it is the ability to see in the child's babblings the promise and potency of a future social intercourse and conversation which enables one to deal in the proper way with that instinct.
- the psychological and social sides are organically related, and that education cannot be regarded as a compromise between the two, or a superimposition of one upon the other. We are told that the psychological definition of education is barren and formal—that it gives us only the idea of a development of all the mental powers without giving us any idea of the use to which these powers are put. On the other hand, it is urged that the social definition of education, as getting adjusted to civilization, makes of it a forced and external process, and results in subordinating the freedom of the individual to a preconceived social and political status.
- each of these objections is true when urged against one side isolated from the other. In order to know what a power really is we must know what its end, use, or function is, and this we cannot know save as we conceive of the individual as active in social relationships. But, on the other hand, the only possible adjustment which we can give to the child under existing conditions is that which arises through putting him in complete possession of all his powers. With the advent of democracy and modern industrial conditions, it is impossible to foretell definitely just what civilization will be twenty years from now. Hence it is impossible to prepare the child for any precise set of conditions. To prepare him for the future life means to give him command of himself; it means so to train him that he will have the full and ready use of all his capacities; that his eye and ear and hand may be

tools ready to command, that his judgment may be capable of grasping the conditions under which it has to work, and the executive forces be trained to act economically and efficiently. It is impossible to reach this sort of adjustment save as constant regard is had to the individual's own powers, tastes, and interests—that is, as education is continually converted into psychological terms.

In sum, I believe that the individual who is to be educated is a social individual, and that society is an organic union of individuals. If we eliminate the social factor from the child we are left only with an abstraction; if we eliminate the individual factor from society, we are left only with an inert and lifeless mass. Education, therefore, must begin with a psychological insight into the child's capacities, interests, and habits. It must be controlled at every point by reference to these same considerations. These powers, interests, and habits must be continually interpreted—we must know what they mean. They must be translated into terms of their social equivalents—into terms of what they are capable of in the way of social service.

Article II—What the School Is

I BELIEVE THAT

- the school is primarily a social institution. Education being a social process, the school is simply that form of community life in which all those agencies are concentrated that will be most effective in bringing the child to share in the inherited resources of the race, and to use his own powers for social ends.
- education, therefore, is a process of living and not a preparation for future living.
- the school must represent present life—life as real and vital to the child as that which he carries on in the home, in the neighborhood, or on the playground.
- that education which does not occur through forms of life, forms that are worth living for their own sake, is always a poor substitute for the genuine reality, and tends to cramp and to deaden.
- the school, as an institution, should simplify existing social life; should reduce it, as it were, to an embryonic form. Existing life is so complex that the child cannot be brought into contact with it without either confusion or distraction; he is either overwhelmed by the multiplicity of activities which are going on, so that he loses his own power

of orderly reaction, or he is so stimulated by these various activities that his powers are prematurely called into play and he becomes either unduly specialized or else disintegrated.

- as such simplified social life, the school life should grow gradually out of the home life; that it should take up and continue the activities with which the child is already familiar in the home.

- it should exhibit these activities to the child, and reproduce them in such ways that the child will gradually learn the meaning of them, and be capable of playing his own part in relation to them.

- this is a psychological necessity, because it is the only way of securing continuity in the child's growth, the only way of giving a background of past experience to the new ideas given in school.

- it is also a social necessity because the home is the form of social life in which the child has been nurtured and in connection with which he has had his moral training. It is the business of the school to deepen and extend his sense of the values bound up in his home life.

- much of the present education fails because it neglects this fundamental principle of the school as a form of community life. It conceives the school as a place where certain information is to be given, where certain lessons are to be learned, or where certain habits are to be formed. The value of these is conceived as lying largely in the remote future; the child must do these things for the sake of something else he is to do; they are mere preparations. As a result they do not become a part of the life experience of the child and so are not truly educative.

- the moral education centers upon this conception of the school as a mode of social life, that the best and deepest moral training is precisely that which one gets through having to enter into proper relations with others in a unity of work and thought. The present educational systems, so far as they destroy or neglect this unity, render it difficult or impossible to get any genuine, regular moral training.

- the child should be stimulated and controlled in his work through the life of the community.

- under existing conditions far too much of the stimulus and control proceeds from the teacher, because of neglect of the idea of the school as a form of social life.

- the teacher's place and work in the school is to be interpreted from this same basis. The teacher is not in the school to impose certain ideas or to form certain habits in the child, but is there as a member of the community to select the influences which shall affect the child and to assist him in properly responding to these influences.

- the discipline of the school should proceed from the life of the school as a whole and not directly from the teacher.

- the teacher's business is simply to determine, on the basis of larger experience and riper wisdom, how the discipline of life shall come to the child.

- all questions of the grading of the child and his promotion should be determined by reference to the same standard. Examinations are of use only so far as they test the child's fitness for social life and reveal the place in which he can be of the most service and where he can receive the most help.

Article III—The Subject-Matter of Education

I BELIEVE THAT

- the social life of the child is the basis of concentration, or correlation, in all his training or growth. The social life gives the unconscious the unity and the background of all his efforts and of all his attainments.

- the subject-matter of the school curriculum should mark a gradual differentiation out of the primitive unconscious unity of social life.

- we violate the child's nature and render difficult the best ethical results by introducing the child too abruptly to a number of special studies, of reading, writing, geography, etc., out of relation to this social life.

- the true center of correlation on the school subjects is not science, nor literature, nor history, nor geography, but the child's own social activities.

- education cannot be unified in the study of science, or so-called nature study, because apart from human activity, nature itself is not a unity; nature in itself is a number of diverse objects in space and time, and to attempt to make it the center of work by itself is to introduce a principle of radiation rather than one of concentration.

- literature is the reflex expression and interpretation of social experience; that hence it must follow upon and not precede such experience. It, therefore, cannot be made the basis, although it may be made the summary of unification.

- history is of educative value in so far as it presents phases of social life and growth. It must be controlled by reference to social life. When taken simply as history it is thrown into the distant past and becomes dead and inert. Taken as the record of man's social life and progress it becomes full of meaning. I believe, however, that it cannot be so taken excepting as the child is also introduced directly into social life.

- the primary basis of education is in the child's powers at work along the same general constructive lines as those which have brought civilization into being.
- the only way to make the child conscious of his social heritage is to enable him to perform those fundamental types of activity which make civilization what it is.
- the so-called expressive or constructive activities are the center of correlation.
- this gives the standard for the place of cooking, sewing, manual training, etc., in the school.
- they are not special studies which are to be introduced over and above a lot of others in the way of relaxation or relief, or as additional accomplishments. I believe rather that they represent, as types, fundamental forms of social activity, and that it is possible and desirable that the child's introduction into the more formal subjects of the curriculum be through the medium of these activities.
- the study of science is educational in so far as it brings out the materials and processes which make social life what it is.
- one of the greatest difficulties in the present teaching of science is that the material is presented in purely objective form, or is treated as a new peculiar kind of experience which the child can add to that which he has already had. In reality, science is of value because it gives the ability to interpret and control the experience already had. It should be introduced, not as so much new subject-matter, but as showing the factors already involved in previous experience and as furnishing tools by which that experience can be more easily and effectively regulated.
- at present we lose much of the value of literature and language studies because of our elimination of the social element. Language is almost always treated in the books of pedagogy simply as the expression of thought. It is true that language is a logical instrument, but it is fundamentally and primarily a social instrument. Language is the device for communication; it is the tool through which one individual comes to share the ideas and feelings of others. When treated simply as a way of getting individual information, or as a means of showing off what one had learned, it loses its social motive and end.

- there is, therefore, no succession of studies in the ideal school curriculum. If education is life, all life has, from the outset, a scientific aspect, an aspect of art and culture, and an aspect of communication. It cannot, therefore, be true that the proper studies for one grade are mere reading and writing, and that at a later grade, reading, or literature, or science, may be introduced. The progress is not in the succession of studies, but in the development of new attitudes towards, and new interests in, experience.
- education must be conceived as a continuing reconstruction of experience; that the process and the goal of education are one and the same thing.
- to set up any end outside of education, as furnishing its goal and standard, is to deprive the educational process of much of its meaning, and tends to make us rely upon false and external stimuli in dealing with the child.

Article IV—The Nature of Method

I BELIEVE THAT

- the question of method is ultimately reducible to the question of the order of development of the child's powers and interests. The law for presenting and treating material is the law implicit within the child's own nature. Because this is so I believe the following statements are of supreme importance as determining the spirit in which education is carried on:
- the active side precedes the passive in the development of the child-nature; that expression comes before conscious impression; that the muscular development precedes the sensory; that movements come before conscious sensation; I believe that consciousness is essentially motor or impulsive; that conscious states tend to project themselves in action.
- the neglect of this principle is the cause of a large part of the waste of time and strength in school work. The child is thrown into a passive, receptive, or absorbing attitude. The conditions are such that he is not permitted to follow the law of nature; the result is friction and waste.
- ideas (intellectual and rational processes) also result from action and devolve for the sake of the better control of action. What we term reason is primarily the law of orderly and effective action. To attempt to develop the reasoning powers, the powers of judgment, without reference to the selection and arrangement of means in action, is

the fundamental fallacy in our present methods of dealing with this matter. As a result we present the child with arbitrary symbols. Symbols are a necessity in mental development, but they have their place as tools for economizing effort; presented by themselves they are a mass of meaningless and arbitrary ideas imposed from without.

- the image is the great instrument of instruction. What a child gets out of any subject presented to him is simply the images which he himself forms with regard to it.
- if nine-tenths of the energy at present directed towards making the child learn certain things were spent in seeing to it that the child was forming proper images, the work of instruction would be indefinitely facilitated.
- much of the time and attention now given to the preparation and presentation of lessons might be more wisely and profitably expended in training the child's power of imagery and in seeing to it that he was continually forming definite, vivid, and growing images of the various subjects with which he comes in contact in his experience.
- interests are the signs and symptoms of growing power. I believe that they represent dawning capacities. Accordingly the constant and careful observation of interests is of the utmost importance for the educator.
- these interests are to be observed as showing the state of development which the child has reached.
- they prophesy the stage upon which he is about to enter.
- only through the continual and sympathetic observation of childhood's interests can the adult enter into the child's life and see what it is ready for, and upon what material it could work most readily and fruitfully.
- these interests are neither to be humored nor repressed. To repress interest is to substitute the adult for the child, and so to weaken intellectual curiosity and alertness, to suppress initiative, and to deaden interest. To humor the interests is to substitute the transient for the permanent. The interest is always the sign of some power below; the important thing is to discover this power. To humor the interest is to fail to penetrate below the surface, and its sure result is to substitute caprice and whim for genuine interest.
- the emotions are the reflex of actions.
- to endeavor to stimulate or arouse the emotions apart from their corresponding activities is to introduce an unhealthy and morbid state of mind.

- if we can only secure right habits of action and thought, with reference to the good, the true, and the beautiful, the emotions will for the most part take care of themselves.
- next to deadness and dullness, formalism and routine, our education is threatened with no greater evil than sentimentalism.
- this sentimentalism is the necessary result of the attempt to divorce feeling from action.

Article V—The School and Social Progress

I BELIEVE THAT

- education is the fundamental method of social progress and reform.
- all reforms which rest simply upon enactment of law, or the threatening of certain penalties, or upon changes in mechanical or outward arrangements, are transitory and futile.
- education is a regulation of the process of coming to share in the social consciousness; and that the adjustment of individual activity on the basis of this social consciousness is the only sure method of social reconstruction.
- this conception has due regard for both the individualistic and socialistic ideals. It is duly individual because it recognizes the formation of a certain character as the only genuine basis of right living. It is socialistic because it recognizes that this right character is not to be formed by merely individual precept, example, or exhortation, but rather by the influence of a certain form of institutional or community life upon the individual, and that the social organism through the school, as its organ, may determine ethical results.
- in the ideal school we have the reconciliation of the individualistic and the institutional ideals.
- the community's duty to education is, therefore, its paramount moral duty. By law and punishment, by social agitation and discussion, society can regulate and form itself in a more or less haphazard and chance way. But through education society can formulate its own purposes, can organize its own means and resources, and thus shape itself with definiteness and economy in the direction in which it wishes to move.
- when society once recognizes the possibilities in this direction, and the obligations which these possibilities impose, it is impossible to conceive of the resources of time, attention, and money which will be put at the disposal of the educator.

- it is the business of every one interested in education to insist upon the school as the primary and most effective interest of social progress and reform in order that society may be awakened to realize what the school stands for, and aroused to the necessity of endowing the educator with sufficient equipment properly to perform his task.

- education thus conceived marks the most perfect and intimate union of science and art conceivable in human experience.

- the art of thus giving shape to human powers and adapting them to social service is the supreme art; one calling into its service the best of artists; that no insight, sympathy, tact, executive power, is too great for such service.

- with the growth of psychological service, giving added insight into individual structure and laws of growth; and with growth of social science, adding to our knowledge of the right organization of individuals, all scientific resources can be utilized for the purpose of education.

- when science and art thus join hands the most commanding motive for human action will be reached, the most genuine springs of human conduct aroused, and the best service that human nature is capable of guaranteed.

- the teacher is engaged, not simply in the training of individuals, but in the formation of the proper social life.

- every teacher should realize the dignity of his calling; that he is a social servant set apart for the maintenance of proper social order and the securing of the right social growth.

- in this way the teacher always is the prophet of the true God and the usherer in of the true kingdom of God.

POSTNOTE

This article is a Classic because it outlines the core beliefs of John Dewey, the American who has had the most powerful impact on our schools. Dewey, the father of progressivism, was the most influential educational thinker of the last 100-plus years. Many of the beliefs expressed in this article (originally published in 1897) have greatly affected educational practice in America. What we find most curious is how current some of these statements still are. On the other hand, many seem dated and clearly from another era. Those that appeal to altruism and idealism have a particularly old-fashioned ring to them. The question remains, however: Which is "out of sync"—the times or the appeals to idealism and altruism?

Discussion Questions

1. How relevant do you believe Dewey's statements are today? Why?

2. Which of Dewey's beliefs do you personally agree or disagree with? Why?

3. How does Dewey's famous statement that "education . . . is a process of living and not a preparation for future living" square with what your parents, guidance counselors, and teachers have told you over the years? If it is different, how do you explain this?

RELATED WEBSITE RESOURCES AND VIDEO CASES

 Web Resources:

Center for Dewey Studies. Available at:

http://www.siu.edu/~deweyctr/.

This center, located on the campus of the University of Illinois at Carbondale, is a font of valuable insight and information on Dewey and his philosophy of education.

John Dewey: Philosophy of Education. Available at:

**http://wilderdom.com/experiential/
JohnDeweyPhilosophyEducation.html.**

This site, maintained by James Neill, is an outstanding repository of John Dewey's educational thought as well as commentary on his work.

Video Case:

Motivating Adolescent Learners: Curriculum Based on Real Life

In this video clip, sixth-grade math teacher Kelly Franklin breathes new life into her class by having her students start and operate a school store. Her intention is to instill in her students the value of knowing fractions and other math concepts. As you watch the clips and study the artifacts in the case, reflect upon the following questions:

1. What do you see as the benefits and the costs of employing this curricular strategy?

2. How is Kelly Franklin's teaching strategy consistent with the views of John Dewey in the previous article?

CLASSIC

36

Personal Thoughts on Teaching and Learning

Carl Rogers

Carl Rogers [1902–1987] had a powerful influence on American education. As a psychotherapist, he pioneered nondirective, client-centered theory and the actualizing tendency, the built-in motivation present in every lifeform to develop its potentials to the fullest extent possible. When applied to formal education, the theory suggests that each of us already possess the important knowledge. The role of the teacher is to help the student uncover and bring to the surface what he or she already knows. This theory had its profoundest impact on American education in the form of values clarification.

|F|O|C|U|S| QUESTION

One of the twentieth century's most influential psychologists asks the question, "What can teachers really teach us?"

KEY TERMS

Inconsequential learning
Self-discovered learning

I wish to present some very brief remarks, in the hope that if they bring forth any reaction from you, I may get some new light on my own ideas.

I find it a very troubling thing to *think*, particularly when I think about my own experiences and try to extract from those experiences the meaning that seems genuinely inherent in them. At first such thinking is very satisfying, because it seems to discover sense and pattern in a whole host of discrete events. But then it very often becomes dismaying, because I realize how ridiculous these thoughts, which have much value to me, would seem to most people. My impression is that if I try to find the meaning of my own experience it leads me, nearly always, in directions regarded as absurd.

So in the next three or four minutes, I will try to digest some of the meanings which have come to me from my classroom experience and the experience I have had in individual and group therapy. They are in no way intended as conclusions for someone else, or a guide to what others should do or be. They are the very tentative meanings, as of April 1952, which my experience has had for me, and some of the bothersome questions which their absurdity raises. I will put each idea or meaning in a separate lettered paragraph, not because they are in any particular logical order, but because each meaning is separately important to me.

a. I may as well start with this one in view of the purposes of this conference. *My experience has been that I cannot teach another person how to teach.* To attempt it is for me, in the long run, futile.

b. *It seems to me that anything that can be taught to another is relatively inconsequential, and has little or no significant influence on behavior.* That sounds so ridiculous I can't help but question it at the same time that I present it.

c. *I realize increasingly that I am only interested in learnings which significantly influence behavior.* Quite possibly this is simply a personal idiosyncrasy.

d. *I have come to feel that the only learning which significantly influences behavior is self-discovered, self-appropriated learning.*

e. *Such self-discovered learning, truth that has been personally appropriated and assimilated in experience, cannot be directly communicated to another.* As soon as an individual tries to communicate such experience directly, often with a quite natural enthusiasm, it becomes teaching, and its results are inconsequential. It was some relief recently to discover that Søren Kierkegaard, the Danish philosopher, had found this too, in his own experience, and stated it very clearly a century ago. It made it seem less absurd.

f. As a consequence of the above, *I realize that I have lost interest in being a teacher.*

g. When I try to teach, as I do sometimes, I am appalled by the results, which seem a little more than inconsequential, because sometimes the teaching appears to succeed. When this happens I find that the results are damaging. It seems to cause the individual to distrust his own experience, and to stifle significant learning. *Hence I have come to feel that the outcomes of teaching are either unimportant or hurtful.*

h. When I look back at the results of my past teaching, the real results seem the same—either damage was done, or nothing significant occurred. This is frankly troubling.

i. As a consequence, *I realize that I am only interested in being a learner, preferably learning things that matter, that have some significant influence on my own behavior.*

j. *I find it very rewarding to learn,* in groups, in relationship with one person as in therapy, or by myself.

k. *I find that one of the best, but most difficult ways for me to learn is to drop my own defensiveness,* at least temporarily, and try to understand the way in which his experience seems and feels to the other person.

l. *I find that another way of learning for me is to state my own uncertainties, to try to clarify my puzzlements, and thus get closer to the meaning that my experience actually seems to have.*

m. This whole train of experiencing, and the meanings that I have thus far discovered in it, seem to have launched me on a process which is both fascinating and at times a little frightening. *It seems to mean letting my experience carry me on, in a direction which appears to be forward, toward goals that I can but dimly define, as I try to understand at least the current meaning of that experience.* The sensation is that of floating with a complex stream of experience, with the fascinating possibility of trying to comprehend its ever changing complexity.

I am almost afraid I may seem to have gotten away from any discussion of learning, as well as teaching. Let me again introduce a practical note by saying that by themselves these interpretations of my own experience may sound queer and aberrant, but not particularly shocking. It is when I realize the *implications* that I shudder a bit at the distance I have come from the commonsense world that everyone knows is right. I can best illustrate that by saying that if the experiences of others had been the same as mine, and if they had discovered similar meanings in it, many consequences would be implied.

a. Such experience would imply that we would do away with teaching. People would get together if they wished to learn.

b. We would do away with examinations. They measure only the inconsequential type of learning.

c. The implication would be that we would do away with grades and credits for the same reason.

d. We would do away with degrees as a measure of competence partly for the same reason. Another reason is that a degree marks an end or a conclusion of something, and a learner is only interested in the continuing process of learning.

e. It would imply doing away with the exposition of conclusions, for we would realize that no one learns significantly from conclusions.

I think I had better stop there. I do not want to become too fantastic. I want to know primarily whether anything in my inward thinking as I have tried to describe it, speaks to anything in your experience of the classroom as you have lived it, and if so, what the meanings are that exist for you in *your* experience.

POSTNOTE

This article is a Classic because it had a significant influence on educational practice during the 1960s and 1970s, and some of its effects are still with us. Rogers's personal philosophy of teaching and learning, so well expressed in this selection, is of course quite controversial. Give it a little test for yourself. Think of a couple of the most significant things you have learned as a human being. Now think of how you learned them. Did someone teach them to you, or did you discover them yourself through experience? Try a different approach and ask yourself what of significance you have ever been taught. Make your own evaluation. Be specific. What do you think about Rogers's statements now?

Discussion Questions

1. Do you agree or disagree with Rogers's ideas on teaching and learning? Why?

2. Do Rogers's statements have any implications for you as a teacher? Explain your answer.

3. Identify three points in the article with which you agree and three with which you disagree.

RELATED WEBSITE RESOURCES

 Web Resources:

Carl Rogers and Humanistic Education. Available at:

http://www.sageofasheville.com/pub_downloads/ CARL_ROGERS_AND_HUMANISTIC_EDUCATION.pdf.

This site provides a clear explanation of Rogers's views on how education should be reformed.

Nondirective Teaching. Available at:

http://al038.k12.sd.us/Nondirective%20Teaching.ppt.

This PowerPoint presentation provides a clear outline of the key concepts underlying Rogers's educational ideas.

The Educated Person

CLASSIC

37

Ernest L. Boyer

Ernest L. Boyer (1928–1995) was one of the key figures in American education during the last half of the twentieth century. He held numerous positions in education from classroom teacher to president of the Carnegie Foundation for the Advancement of Teaching. Throughout his career he was widely respected for his sound, balanced views. A deeply religious man, he brought what he called his "people-centered" principles to all his work. This essay, published the year of his death, lays out with great clarity his major convictions on what should be taught in our schools.

"The Educated Person" by Ernest L. Boyer, from *Toward a Coherent Curriculum* by James A. Beane, pp. 16–25. Used with permission. The Association for Supervision and Curriculum Development is a worldwide community of educators advocating sound policies and sharing best practices to achieve the success of each learner. To learn more, visit ASCD at **www.ascd.org.**

FOCUS QUESTION

There is no more important question than the one answered here: "What is most worth knowing?"

KEY TERMS
Carnegie unit
Educated person

As we anticipate a new century, I am drawn back to questions that have, for generations, perplexed educators and philosophers and parents. What *is* an educated person? What *should* schools be teaching to students?

In searching for answers to these questions, we must consider first not the curriculum, but the human condition. And we must reflect especially on two essential realities of life. First, each person is unique. In defining goals, it is crucial for educators to affirm the special characteristics of each student. We must create in schools a climate in which students are empowered, and we must find ways in the nation's classrooms to celebrate the potential of each child. But beyond the diversity of individuals, educators also must acknowledge a second reality: the deeply rooted characteristics that bind together the human community. We must show students that people around the world share a great many experiences. Attention to both these aspects of our existence is critical to any discussion of what all children should learn.

What, then, does it mean to be an educated person? It means developing one's own aptitudes and interests and discovering the diversity that makes us each unique. And it means becoming permanently empowered with language proficiency, general knowledge, social confidence, and moral awareness in order to be economically and civically successful. But becoming well educated also means discovering the connectedness of things. Educators must help students see relationships across the disciplines and learn that education is a communal act, one that affirms not only individualism, but community. And for these goals to be accomplished, we need a new curriculum framework that is both comprehensive and coherent, one that can encompass existing subjects and integrate fragmented content while relating the curriculum to the realities of life. This curriculum must address the uniqueness of students' histories and experiences, but it also must guide them to understand the many ways that humans are connected.

Some schools and teachers are aiming to fully educate students, but most of us have a very long way to go in reaching this goal. Today, almost all students in

U.S. schools still complete Carnegie units in exchange for a diploma. The time has come to bury the old Carnegie unit; since the Foundation I now head created this unit of academic measure nearly a century ago, I feel authorized to declare it obsolete. Why? Because it has helped turn schooling into an exercise in trivial pursuit. Students get academic "credit," but they fail to gain a coherent view of what they study. Education is measured by seat time, not time for learning. While curious young children still ask why things are, many older children ask only, "Will this be on the test?" All students should be encouraged to ask "Why?" because "Why?" is the question that leads students to connections.

In abandoning the Carnegie unit, I do not endorse the immediate adoption of national assessment programs; indeed, I think we must postpone such programs until we are much clearer about what students should be learning. The goal, again, is not only to help students become well informed and prepared for lifelong learning, but also to help them put learning into the larger context of discovering the connectedness of things. Barbara McClintock, the 1983 winner of the Nobel Prize for Physiology–Medicine, asserts: "Everything is one. There is no way to draw a line between things." Contrary to McClintock's vision, the average school or college catalog dramatizes the separate academic boxes.

Frank Press, president of the National Academy of Sciences, compares scientists to artists, evoking the magnificent double helix, which broke the genetic code. He said the double helix is not only rational, but beautiful. Similarly, when scientists and technicians watch the countdown to a space launch, they don't say, "Our formulas worked again." They respond, "Beautiful!" instinctively reaching for the aesthetic term to praise a technological achievement. When physicist Victor Weisskopf was asked, "What gives you hope in troubled times?" he replied, "Mozart and quantum mechanics." Most schools, however, separate science and art, discouraging students from seeing the connections between them.

How, then, can we help students see relationships and patterns and gain understanding beyond the separate academic subjects? How can we rethink the curriculum and use the disciplines to illuminate larger, more integrated ends?

Human Commonalities

In the 1981 book *A Quest for Common Learning*, I suggested that we might organize the curriculum not on the basis of disciplines or departments, but on the basis of "core commonalities." By core commonalities, I mean universal experiences that make us human, experiences shared by all cultures on the planet. During the past decade and a half, my thinking about this thematic structure has continued to evolve. I now envision eight commonalities that bind us to one another:

I. THE LIFE CYCLE

As life's most fundamental truth, we share, first, the experience that connects birth, growth, and death. This life cycle binds each of us to others, and I find it sad that so many students go through life without reflecting on the mystery of their own existence. Many complete twelve or sixteen years of formal schooling not considering the sacredness of their own bodies, not learning to sustain wellness, not pondering the imperative of death.

In reshaping the curriculum to help students see connections, I would position study of "The Life Cycle" at the core of common learning. Attention would go to nutrition, health, and all aspects of wellness. For a project, each student would undertake the care of some life form.

My wife is a certified nurse-midwife who delivers babies, including seven grandchildren of our own. Kay feels special pain when delivering the baby of a teenage girl because she knows that she is delivering one child into the arms of another, and that both have all too often lived for nine months on soda and potato chips. Some young mothers first learn about the birth process between the sharp pains of labor.

Too many young women and young men pass through our process of education without learning about their own bodies. Out of ignorance, they suffer poor nutrition, addiction, and violence. "Maintaining children's good health is a shared responsibility of parents, schools, and the community at large," according to former Secretary of Education William Bennett (1986, p. 37). He urges elementary schools "to provide children with the knowledge, habits, and attitudes that will equip them for a fit and healthy life."

Study of the Life Cycle would encourage students to reflect sensitively on the mystery of birth and growth and death, to learn about body functions and thus understand the role of choice in wellness, to carry some of their emotional and intellectual learning into their relations with others, and to observe, understand, and respect a variety of life forms.

II. LANGUAGE

Each life on the planet turns to symbols to express feelings and ideas. After a first breath, we make sounds as a way of reaching out to others, connecting with them. We develop a variety of languages: the language of words (written and spoken), the language of symbols (mathematics, codes, sign systems), and the language of the arts (aesthetic expressions in language, music, painting, sculpture, dance, theater, craft, and so on). A quality education develops proficiency in the written and the spoken word, as well as a useful knowledge of mathematical symbol systems and an understanding that the arts provide countless ways to express ourselves.

Our sophisticated use of language sets human beings apart from all other forms of life. Through the created words and symbols and arts, we connect to one another. Consider the miracle of any moment. One person vibrates his or her vocal cords. Molecules shoot in the direction of listeners. They hit the tympanic membrane; signals go scurrying up the eighth cranial nerve. From that series of events, the listener feels a response deep in the cerebrum that approximates the images in the mind of the speaker. Because of its power and scope, language is the means by which all other subjects are pursued.

The responsible use of language demands both *accuracy* and *honesty*, so students studying "Language" must also learn to consider the ethics of communication. Students live in a world where obscenities abound. They live in a world where politicians use sixty-second sound bites to destroy integrity. They live in a world where clichés substitute for reason. To make their way in this world, students must learn to distinguish between deceit and authenticity in language.

Writers and mathematicians have left a long and distinguished legacy for students to learn from. Through words, each child can express something personal. Through symbols, each child can increase the capacity to calculate and reason. Through the arts, each child can express a thought or a feeling. People need to write with clarity, read with comprehension, speak effectively, listen with understanding, compute accurately, and understand the communicative capabilities of the arts. Education for the next century means helping students understand that language in all its forms is a powerful and sacred trust.

III. THE ARTS

All people on the planet respond to the aesthetic. Dance, music, painting, sculpture, and architecture are languages understood around the world. "Art represents a social necessity that no nation can neglect without endangering its intellectual existence," said John Ruskin (Rand 1993). We all know how art can affect us. Salvador Dali's painting *The Persistence of Memory* communicates its meaning to anyone ever haunted by

time passing. The gospel song "Amazing Grace" stirs people from both Appalachia and Manhattan. "We Shall Overcome," sung in slow and solemn cadence, invokes powerful feelings regardless of the race or economic status of singer or audience.

Archaeologists examine the artifacts of ancient civilization—pottery, cave paintings, and musical instruments—to determine the attainments and quality of a culture. As J. Carter Brown (1983) observes, "The texts of man's achievements are not written exclusively in words. They are written, as well, in architecture, paintings, sculpture, drawing, photography, and in urban, graphic, landscape, and industrial design."

Young children understand that the arts are language. Before they learn to speak, they respond intuitively to dance, music, and color. The arts also help children who are disabled. I once taught deaf children, who couldn't speak because they couldn't hear. But through painting, sculpture, and rhythm, they found new ways to communicate.

Every child has the urge and capacity to be expressive. It is tragic that for most children the universal language of the arts is suppressed, then destroyed, in the early years of learning, because traditional teaching does not favor self-expression and school boards consider art a frill. This is an ironic deprivation when the role of art in developing critical thinking is becoming more widely recognized.

Jacques d'Amboise, former principal dancer with the New York City Ballet, movie star, and founder of the National Dance Institute, offers his view on how art fits into education: "I would take the arts, science and sports, or play, and make all education involve all of them. It would be similar to what kindergarten does, only more sophisticated, right through life. All of the disciplines would be interrelated. You dance to a poem: poetry is meter, meter is time, time is science" (Ames and Peyser 1990).

For our most moving experiences, we turn to the arts to express feelings and ideas that words cannot convey. The arts are, as one poet has put it, "the language of the angels." To be truly educated means being sensitively responsive to the universal language of art.

IV. TIME AND SPACE

While we are all nonuniform and often seem dramatically different from one another, all of us have the capacity to place ourselves in time and space. We explore our place through geography and astronomy. We explore our sense of time through history.

And yet, how often we squander this truly awesome capacity for exploration, neglecting even our personal roots. Looking back in my own life, my most important mentor was Grandpa Boyer, who lived to be one hundred. Sixty years before that, Grandpa moved his little family into the slums of Dayton, Ohio. He then spent the next forty years running a city mission, working for the poor, teaching me more by deed than by word that to be truly human, one must serve. For far too many children, the influence of such intergenerational models has diminished or totally disappeared.

Margaret Mead said that the health of any culture is sustained when three generations are vitally interacting with one another—a "vertical culture" in which the different age groups are connected. Yet in America today we've created a "horizontal culture," with each generation living alone. Infants are in nurseries, toddlers are in day care, older children are in schools organized by age. College students are isolated on campuses. Adults are in the workplace. And older citizens are in retirement villages, living and dying all alone.

For several years, my own parents chose to live in a retirement village where the average age was eighty. But this village had a day-care center, too, and all the three- and four-year-olds had adopted grandparents to meet with every day. The two generations quickly became friends. When I called my father, he didn't talk about his aches and pains, he talked about his little friend. And when I visited, I saw that my father, like any proud grandparent, had the child's drawings taped to the wall. As I watched the two of them together, I was struck by the idea that there is something really special about a four-year-old seeing the difficulty and courage of growing old. And I was struck, too, by watching an eighty-year-old being informed and inspired by the energy and innocence of a child. Exposure to such an age difference surely increases the understanding of time and personal history.

The time has come to break up the age ghettos. It is time to build intergenerational institutions that bring together the old and young. I'm impressed by the "grandteacher" programs in the schools, for example. In the new core curriculum, with a strand called "Time and Space," students should discover their own roots and complete an oral history. But beyond their own extended family, all students should also become well informed about the influence of the culture that surrounds them and learn about the traditions of other cultures.

A truly educated person will see connections by placing his or her life in time and space. In the days ahead, students should study *Western* civilization to understand our past, but they should study *non-Western* cultures to understand our present and our future.

V. GROUPS AND INSTITUTIONS

All people on the planet belong to groups and institutions that shape their lives. Nearly 150 years ago, Ralph Waldo Emerson observed, "We do not make a world of our own, but rather fall into institutions already made and have to accommodate ourselves to them." Every society organizes itself and carries on its work through social interaction that varies from one culture to another.

Students must be asked to think about the groups of which they are members, how they are shaped by those groups, and how they help to shape them. Students need to learn about the social web of our existence, about family life, about how governments function, about the informal social structures that surround us. They also must discover how life in groups varies from one culture to another.

Civic responsibility also must be taught. The school itself can be the starting point for this education, serving as a "working model" of a healthy society in microcosm that bears witness to the ideals of community. Within the school, students should feel "enfranchised." Teachers, administrators, and staff should meet often to find their *own* relationship to the institution of the school. And students should study groups in their own community, finding out about local government.

One of my sons lives in a Mayan village in the jungle of Belize. When my wife and I visit Craig each year, I'm impressed that Mayans and Americans live and work in very similar ways. The jungle of Manhattan and the one of Belize are separated by a thousand miles and a thousand years, and yet the Mayans, just like us, have their family units. They have elected leaders, village councils, law enforcement officers, jails, schools, and places to worship. Life there is both different and very much the same. Students in the United States should be introduced to institutions in our own culture and in other cultures, so they might study, for example, both Santa Cruz, California, and Santa Cruz, Belize.

We all belong to many groups. Exploring their history and functions helps students understand the privileges and the responsibilities that belong to each of us.

VI. WORK

We all participate, for much of our lives, in the commonality of work. As Thoreau reminds us, we both "live" and "get a living." Regardless of differences, all people on the planet produce and consume. A quality education will help students understand and prepare for the world of work. Unfortunately, our own culture has become too preoccupied with *consuming*, too little with the tools for *producing*. Children may see their parents leave the house carrying briefcases or lunch pails in the morning and see them come home again in the evening, but do they know what parents actually do during the day?

Jerome Bruner (1971) asks: "Could it be that in our stratified and segmented society, our students simply do not know about local grocers and their styles, local doctors and their styles, local taxi drivers and theirs, local political activists and theirs? . . . I would urge that we find some way of connecting the diversity of the society to the phenomenon of school" (p. 7). A new, integrative curriculum for the schools needs to give attention to "Producing and Consuming," with each student studying simple economics, different money systems, vocational studies, career planning, how work varies from one culture to another, and with each completing a work project to gain a respect for craftsmanship.

Several years ago when Kay and I were in China, we were told about a student who had defaced the surface of his desk. As punishment, he spent three days in the factory where desks were made, helping the woodworkers, observing the effort involved. Not surprisingly, the student never defaced another desk.

When I was Chancellor of the State University of New York, I took my youngest son, then eight, to a cabin in the Berkshires for the weekend. My goal: to build a dock. All day, instead of playing, Stephen sat by the lake, watching me work. As we drove home, he looked pensive. After several miles, he said, "Daddy, I wish you'd grown up to be a carpenter—instead of you-know-what!"

VII. Natural World

Though all people are different, we are all connected to the earth in many ways. David, my grandson in Belize, lives these connections as he chases birds, bathes in the river, and watches corn being picked, pounded into tortillas, and heated outdoors. But David's cousins in Boston and Princeton spend more time with appliances, asphalt roadways, and precooked food. For them, discovering connectedness to nature does not come so naturally.

When I was United States Commissioner of Education, Joan Cooney, the brilliant creator of *Sesame Street*, told me that she and her colleagues at Children's Television Workshop wanted to start a new program on science and technology for junior high school kids. They wanted young people to learn a little more about

their world and what they must understand as part of living. Funds were raised, and *3–2–1 Contact* went on the air. To prepare scripts, staff surveyed junior high school kids in New York City, asking questions such as "Where does water come from?"—which brought from some students the disturbing reply, "The faucet." They asked, "Where does light come from?" and heard, "The switch." And they asked, "Where does garbage go?" "Down the chute." These students' sense of connectedness stopped at the VCR or refrigerator door.

Canadian geneticist David Suzuki, host of *The Nature of Things*, says: "We ought to be greening the school yard, breaking up the asphalt and concrete. . . . We have to give children hand-held lenses, classroom aquariums and terrariums, lots of field trips, organic garden plots on the school grounds, butterfly gardens, trees. Then insects, squirrels—maybe even raccoons and rabbits—will show up, even in the city. We've got to reconnect those kids, and we've got to do it very early. . . . Our challenge is to reconnect children to their natural curiosity" (Baron Estes 1993).

With all our differences, each of us is inextricably connected to the natural world. During their days of formal learning, students should explore this commonality by studying the principles of science, by discovering the shaping power of technology, and, above all, by learning that survival on this planet means respecting and preserving the earth we share.

VIII. Search for Meaning

Regardless of heritage or tradition, each person searches for some larger purpose. We all seek to give special meaning to our lives. Reinhold Niebuhr said, "Man cannot be whole unless he be committed, he cannot find himself, unless he find a purpose beyond himself." We all need to examine values and beliefs, and develop convictions.

During my study of the American high school, I became convinced ours is less a school problem and more a youth problem. Far too many teenagers feel unwanted, unneeded, and unconnected. Without guidance and direction, they soon lose their sense of purpose—even their sense of wanting purpose.

Great teachers allow their lives to express their values. They are matchless guides as they give the gift of opening truths about themselves to their students. I often think of three or four teachers, out of the many I have worked with, who changed my life. What made them truly great? They were well informed. They could relate their knowledge to students. They created an active, not passive, climate for learning. More than that, they were authentic human beings who taught their subjects and were open enough to teach about themselves.

Service projects instill values. All students should complete a community service project, working in day-care centers and retirement villages or tutoring other students at school. The North Carolina School of Science and Math develops an ethos of responsible citizenship. To be admitted, a child must commit to sixty hours of community service per summer and three hours per week during the school year (Beach 1992, p. 56).

Martin Luther King, Jr., preached: "Everyone can be great because everyone can serve." I'm convinced the young people of this country want inspiration from this kind of larger vision, whether they come across it in a book or in person, or whether they find it inside themselves.

Values, Beliefs, and Connections

What, then, does it mean to be an educated person? It means respecting the miracle of life, being empowered in the use of language, and responding sensitively to the aesthetic. Being truly educated means putting learning in historical perspective, understanding groups and institutions, having reverence for the natural world, and affirming the dignity of work. And, above all, being an educated person means being guided by values and beliefs and connecting the lessons of the classroom to the realities of life. These are the core competencies that I believe replace the old Carnegie units.

And all of this can be accomplished as schools focus not on seat time, but on students involved in true communities of learning. I realize that remarkable changes must occur for this shift in goals to take place, but I hope deeply that in the century ahead students will be judged not by their performance on a single test but by the quality of their lives. It is my hope that students in the classrooms of tomorrow will be encouraged to create more than conform, and to cooperate more than compete. Each student deserves to see the world clearly and in its entirety and to be inspired by both the beauty and the challenges that surround us all.

Above all, I pray that Julie and David, my granddaughter in Princeton and my grandson in Belize, along with all other children on the planet, will grow to understand that they belong to the same human family, the family that connects us all.

Fifty years ago, Mark Van Doren wrote, "The connectedness of things is what the educator contemplates to the limit of his capacity." The student, he says, who can begin early in life to see things as connected has begun the life of learning. This, it seems to me, is what it means to be an educated person.

REFERENCES

Ames, Katrine, and Marc Peyser. (Fall/Winter 1990). "Why Jane Can't Draw (or Sing, or Dance . . .)." *Newsweek* Special Edition: 40–49.

Baron Estes, Yvonne. (May 1993). "Environmental Education: Bringing Children and Nature Together." *Phi Delta Kappan* 74, 9: K2.

Beach, Waldo. (1992). *Ethical Education in American Public Schools*. Washington, D.C.: National Education Association.

Bennett, William J. (1986). *First Lessons*. Washington, D.C.: U.S. Department of Education.

Boyer, Ernest L. (1981). *A Quest for Common Learning: The Aims of General Education*. Washington, D.C.: Carnegie Foundation for the Advancement of Teaching.

Brown, J. Carter. (November/December 1983). "Excellence and the Problem of Visual Literacy." *Design for Arts in Education* 84, 3.

Bruner, Jerome. (November 1971). "Process of Education Reconsidered." An address presented before the 16th Annual Conference of the Association for Supervision and Curriculum Development.

Rand, Paul. (May 2, 1993). "Failure by Design," *The New York Times*, p. E19.

POSTNOTE

In this Classic article, the late Ernest Boyer demonstrates his power as a profound educational thinker. Boyer was widely acknowledged during the last two decades of the twentieth century as America's leading practitioner of education. There is no more important or fundamental question in education than "What is most worth knowing?" Schools have a mission, derived from the society at large, to prepare children to become fully developed people, to prepare them for the demands of adult life in an unknown future. As educators, our mission is to identify what our students need today and will need in the future. But the universe of knowledge, which once inched along at a snail's pace, is currently racing ahead like a sprinter. The child's future, which once we could say would be much like his or her parents' life, now is impossible to predict.

In this essay, Ernest Boyer lays out his answer to the question of what an educated person most needs to know.

Though there is great merit in his educational vision, questions arise: What from civilization's heritage of knowledge and wisdom should be presented to students? And how many of us as teachers have a clear sense of goals, guided by a similar vision of what a person really is and what a person ought to become?

Discussion Questions

1. What feature of Boyer's "educated person" do you believe currently receives the greatest attention in our schools?
2. What feature of his vision do you believe receives the least attention today? Why?
3. Why do you think there is so little discussion of the question, "What is most worth knowing?"

RELATED WEBSITE RESOURCES AND VIDEO CASES

 ## Web Resources:

Ernest Boyer. Available at:

http://www.beckyfiedler.com/boyer/top.htm.

This site, designed by Suzanne Cavanagh and Rebecca L. Fielder, is doing much to keep the work of Ernest Boyer before educators. The site covers his life and his work, and provides many links to other Boyer-related entities.

Award for Innovative Excellence in Teaching, Learning and Technology. Available at:

http://www.teachlearn.org/boyer.html.

This site is attempting to continue the educational legacy of Ernest Boyer through promoting an annual conference and awards program for outstanding teachers.

 ## Video Case:

Education Reform: Teachers Talk About No Child Left Behind

No Child Left Behind (NCLB), the legislative act currently guiding reform in the United States, can be seen as an attempt to help our schools reach Boyer's ideal of an "educated person." Key to NCLB is state-level tests to determine student progress and a new set of guidelines for the determination of what constitutes a "highly qualified teacher." As you watch the clips and study the artifacts in the case, reflect upon the following questions:

1. The educators in this video speak of the importance of understanding individual student data. Why, according to the video, is this so important?
2. The educators on this video offer their opinions as to the advantages and disadvantages of NCLB. List 2 advantages and 2 disadvantages.

For Another Perspective:

Mary Anne Raywid, Accountability: What's Worth Measuring?

www.cengage.com/login

38

A School for the Common Good

Lawrence Baines and Hal Foster

Lawrence Baines is a professor of English education at the University of Toledo and **Hal Foster** is distinguished professor of English education and literacy at the University of Akron.

Lawrence Baines and Hal Foster, "A School for the Common Good," *Educational Horizons*, Vol. 84, No. 4 (Summer 2006), pp. 221–228. Reprinted by permission.

F O C U S QUESTION

What has happened to the public support for the common school?

KEY TERMS

Common school

De-localization

The proponents of the common school were seeking the nurture of a common core of sentiment, of value, and of practice within which pluralism would not become anarchy. They were seeking, in a sense, a means of constant regeneration whereby the inevitable inequities arising out of freedom would not from generation to generation become destructive of its very sources. . . . They were seeking to build and inculcate a sense of community which would function, not at the expense of individualism, but rather as a firm framework within which individuality might be most effectively preserved.

—Lawrence A. Cremin, *The American Common School*

The Common School Movement reformers of the 1850s envisioned schools that would serve as linchpins of the community. They were to be tuition free and open to everyone, places "where the rich and the poor meet together on equal terms, where high and low are taught in the same house, the same class, and out of the same book, and by the same teacher" (Taylor 1837).

In the nineteenth century, it was assumed that good schools were essential to the survival of democracy. After all, a government "of the people, by the people, for the people" meant that the future would be determined by the collective wisdom and character of the citizenry. Although schools have yet to evolve into the kind of Utopian institutions that reformers envisioned, common-school ideals still resonate with many of us today. For example, President Bush was invoking the common-school ideal of learning as a transformative experience when he stated at last year's National Teacher of the Year ceremonies: "When young people become good students with big dreams, they become better citizens. Our country is better off as a result of our teachers instilling passion and hope" (Bush 2005).

Political sound bites notwithstanding, public schools are in actuality becoming less and less places where all citizens meet under one roof, on equal terms, in pursuit of a mutual goal.

De-localized Schooling

Central to the concept of the common school is its symbiotic relationship with the community in which it is located. Common schools were funded and maintained by community residents who, in turn, took great interest in their progress and pride in their accomplishments.

Today, curriculum is controlled by the state and a school's effectiveness is measured according to criteria established by the federal government. Uniform testing and reporting requirements have turned superintendents and boards into little more than intermediaries between schools and enforcement agencies. Local control, once considered an indefeasible right, has suddenly vanished.

Only private schools and selective charter schools maintain any semblance of local control. For example, Dallas charter schools serve the technically inclined who wish to work on computer products made by Cisco Systems; Milwaukee charter schools serve African-American males who wish to study an Afrocentric curriculum; and Southern California online charter schools serve students who would rather complete high school at home than rub elbows with their peers at school. Ironically, charter schools' singular educational visions and enrollments restricted to special populations (U.S. Department of Education 2000) often undercut the "everyone welcome" ideology of the common school.

More than one million students (more than 2 percent of the school-age population) are currently enrolled in K–12 charter schools, and the number is expected to grow as a deluge of new, "pro-charter" bills wends its way through state legislatures. Thus far, forty-seven states, the District of Columbia, and Puerto Rico have enacted laws that encourage continued expansion of charter schools (U.S. Charter Schools 2005).

Much like charter schools, "school choice" allows students to enroll at any number of institutions within a geographic area. In 2004, more than six million students (12 percent of the school-age population) exercised their right of choice.

Additional options are opening up for those wishing to attend private schools. New laws, such as South Carolina's Put Parents in Charge Act, give tuition tax credits directly to parents. Tuition tax credits are already in effect in Minnesota, Iowa, Florida, Pennsylvania, Illinois, and Arizona. Voucher systems of one kind or another are in the works in state legislatures across the country (*Economist* 2005).

If such trends hold, private schools, which have enrolled 10 to 15 percent of the student population for the past several decades (Archer 1996), are likely to experience an abrupt increase in enrollments. A federal study of differences between public and private schools accorded a dozen advantages to private schools, including higher levels of achievement and happier, safer students (National Center for Education Statistics 2004). In another study, two of three parents indicated they would send their children to private schools if they could afford to do so (Golay 1997).

Parents who prefer to keep their children home all day constitute the fastest-growing segment of alternative education providers. More than one million students, or 2 percent of the total K–12 population, are home schooled (Jablonski 2004).

Expressed in mathematical terms, student enrollments can be represented this way:

$$\text{Charter } (2\%) + \text{Home schooled } (2\%) + \text{Choice } (12\%) + \text{Private } (12\%) = 28\% \text{ of the student population}$$

Today, some fifteen million students, more than one in four, no longer attend the neighborhood school. That number is unprecedented in the history of public education. Schools across the country are finding themselves in an unfamiliar role: serving a dwindling proportion of the constituents in their locales. The disengagement comes even after researchers have established how a neighborhood's cohesiveness contributes to lower levels of crime and a higher quality of life (Sampson, Raudenbush, and Earls 1997). However, the evolution of the public school from its communal roots is consistent with the disintegration of community-based social structures described by Putnam (2001) and Skocpol (2003).

The Condition of Neighborhood Schools

Although recent data indicate a dramatic drop in school crime and, in fact, reveal that students are safer in school than out of school (National Center for Education Statistics 2005), 80 percent of Americans still perceive public schools as rife with violence (Horowitz 1997).

Too often, substandard infrastructure makes it difficult to assuage concerns about neighborhood schools' safety. In 1995, the General Accounting Office estimated that $112 billion was needed just to make America's school buildings habitable again. Yet over the past decade, minimal funding has been appropriated for capital improvements. Obviously, buildings must remain in operation, so schools have learned the crude art of deferred maintenance, postponing indefinitely into the future repairs of broken toilets, faulty wiring, and inadequate heating systems (Kozol 2005).

Today, the tab for capital improvements has escalated to $150 billion; 75 percent of all public school buildings have been identified as needing major renovation (Lewis et al. 2000), although the National Education Association places the price tag at $322 billion (*Education Week* 2005). Research confirms that safe, well-lit buildings and grounds can have exponentially positive effects on learning (Crampton, Thompson, and Vesely 2004), but the reverse is also true. A school building in poor condition can be a scourge on local property values and student performance. Yet with no fiscal boon on the horizon, few school buildings are likely to receive attention beyond minimal repairs anytime soon.

Future Revenues

As the U.S. population ages, states have been forced to spend more money on social services. Currently about 12 percent of Americans are sixty-five or older, but by 2025, 20 percent of the population, or seventy million Americans, will be that old (U.S. Census Bureau 2005). More retirees will mean fewer dollars collected from taxes on income and property.

Taxes on business and industry are producing less revenue, too (Berliner 1996; National Education Association 2005; Ohio Department of Taxation 2005; White and Johnston 1997). The multimillion-dollar incentives offered to domestic and foreign automobile manufacturers by various southern locales have set off bidding wars among states for new business. The currency employed usually consists of taxes states and cities are willing to waive. Although new industry may create jobs, tax abatements usually fail to generate new revenues for schools. In 1950, American industry contributed 30 percent to local tax bases; by 1998, the percentage had shrunk to 11 percent. With the relocation of plants and factories to foreign shores, taxes contributed by industry are likely to continue to decline (*USA Today* 1998).

Despite disappointing revenues, many states' expenditures have surged more than 500 percent over the past two decades (U.S. Census Bureau 2005). Proportional funding for education will decline—as it has for the past twenty years—when states are forced to spend more on welfare programs, roads, and prisons (Winters 2003). A predicted 12 percent annual rise in Medicaid costs will create even higher deficits (Madigan 2005).

Recognizing an impending fiscal crisis, forty states have planned significant budget cuts through 2010 (National Association of State Budget Officers 2004). But what impact might budget cuts have on the quality of public education? Perhaps no state illustrates the effects of budget cuts on student performance better than California.

The California tax revolt of 1978, exemplified by Proposition 13, severely limited property tax increases. Shortly after ratification of the proposition, student achievement, teacher quality, and college completion all began to decline (Carroll et al. 2005). Once the envy

of the world, California public schools have become among the worst-performing schools in America. For example, reading and mathematics tests administered by the National Assessment of Educational Progress (NAEP) from 1990 to 2002 ranked California forty-eighth, just behind Alabama and ahead of only Louisiana and Mississippi (Education Watch 2004). Before Proposition 13, though, student performance in California ranked the highest in the nation.

Many states have used profits from lotteries to bridge the gulf between revenues and expenditures. In New York, for example, lotteries pay 5 percent of public education expenditures. With forty-one states now selling lottery tickets and generating $14 billion in profit annually, the "lottery solution" would appear to have "maxed out" (North American Association of State and Provincial Lotteries 2005).

Even the most optimistic economic outlook does not foresee rescuing beleaguered schools with a large infusion of new federal money. Already saddled with the largest deficit in American history, the federal government is grappling with monumental expenditures for the military, homeland security, disaster relief, Medicaid, and Social Security.

Common Schools at the Tipping Point

Public schools stand at the epicenter of four trends: delocalization, disintegration of capital infrastructure, taxpayer angst, and historic governmental deficits. For parents whose children get their education elsewhere than the neighborhood school, it is a confusing time. If a new tax referendum for revitalizing the battered old neighborhood school building comes to a vote, should it be supported or rejected? The dilemma is real—parents placed in the position of financially supporting schools that their children do not attend (Ray 2005). Although the impulse to "escape" a low-performing neighborhood school is understandable, what about the fate of the majority—those thousands of students who cannot transfer because of financial or family difficulties? And what about the prospects for the school, scraping by in a tough neighborhood, facing falling revenues and "bright flight"? What happens to a struggling school when its best students abandon ship? What happens to a community when its neighborhood school is declared low-performing and shuttered?

Undeniably, current legislation and popular sentiment are steering American education toward a social policy predicated upon the fluctuations of unfettered, free-market economics. As the gap between rich and poor widens, the tension between individual and community goals usually escalates (Wessel 2005). According to Galbraith (1998), "A high degree of inequality . . . is leading toward the transformation of the United States from a middle-class democracy into something that more closely resembles an authoritarian quasi-democracy, with an overclass, an underclass, and a hidden politics driven by money."

John F. Kennedy once admonished, "Our progress as a nation can be no swifter than our progress in education." More than 37 percent of the national budget for 2006 is earmarked for individuals over sixty-five, while just over 1 percent has been set aside for children under eighteen. Despite the relatively low percentage of money set aside for public schools, many Americans believe that expenditures on public education are untenably high (DeRugy 2004).

Once upon a time, public schools were supposed to be nonselective, open, tuition-free institutions where all children were welcome to participate in a real-world exercise in democracy. The demise of the ideal of the common school is evident in the proliferation of specialized charter schools; in legislative support for vouchers and private school reimbursements; in the burgeoning businesses ministering to home schoolers; in the empty classrooms and broken windows of neighborhood schools. Common schools once stood for equal opportunity, community, and pluralism, yet American education has become selective, specialized, and caste conscious.

Perhaps a more appropriate model for American education today is not the common school, but the gated community—and the barrios developing just outside its walls.

REFERENCES

Archer, J. 1996. "Today, Private Schools Span Diverse Range." *Education Week* (October 9): 1.

Berliner, D. 1996. "Uninvited Comments from an Uninvited Guest." *Educational Researcher* (November): 47–50.

Bush, G. W. 2005. President Announces 2005 National and State Teachers of the Year. Retrieved January 8, 2005, from **<http://www.whitehouse.gov/news/releases/2005/04/20050420-1.html>**.

Carroll, S., C. Krop, J. Arkes, P. Morrison, and A. Flanagan. 2005. *California's K-12 Public Schools: How Are They Doing?* Santa Monica, Calif.: Rand.

Crampton, F., D. Thompson, and R. Vesely. 2004. "The Forgotten Side of School Finance Equity: The Role of Infrastructure Funding in Student Success." *NASSP Bulletin* (September): 29–51.

Cremin, L. 1951. *The American Common School.* New York: Teachers College.

DeRugy, V. 2004. "Enough Talking about Fiscal Responsibility—Let's Cut Spending." (March 15). Retrieved November 15, 2005, from **<http://www.cato.org/dailys/03-15-04.html>**.

Economist. 2005. "South Carolina's Schools: Shades of the Past Brings Back Unwelcome Memories" (April 2): 30.

Education Watch. 2004. *California: Key Education Facts and Figures, Achievement, Attainment and Opportunity from Elementary School through College.* Washington, D.C.: Education Trust.

Education Week. 2005. "School Construction." Retrieved October 30, 2005, from **<http://www.edweek.org/rc/issues/school-construction/index.html>**.

Galbraith, J. 1998. *Created Unequal.* New York: Free Press, 3–4.

Golay, M. 1997. *Where America Stands.* New York: John Wiley & Sons.

Horowitz, C. 1997. "Controlling School Violence." *Investors Business Daily* (August 19): 1.

Jablonski, A. 2004. *Teachers Who Homeschool Their Children.* Unpublished master's project, University of Toledo.

Kozol, J. 2005. *The Shame of the Nation.* New York: Crown.

Lewis, L., K. Snow, E. Farris, B. Smerdon, S. Cronen, J. Kaplan, and B. Greene. 2000. *Condition of America's Public School Facilities: 1999.* Washington, D.C.: National Center for Education Statistics.

Madigan, E. 2005. "Medicaid Increasingly Heavy State Budget Burden." Retrieved September 4, 2005, from **<http://www.stateline.org/live/ViewPage.action?siteNodeId=136&languageId=1&contentId=15891>**.

National Association of State Budget Officers. 2004. *State Expenditure Report 2003.* Washington, D.C.: NASBO.

National Center for Education Statistics. 2004. *Private School Universe Survey 2004.* Washington, D.C.: U.S. Department of Education.

_____. 2005. Table 1.1: Number of School Associated Violent Deaths and Number of Homicides and Suicides of Youth Ages 5–19 by Location: 1992–2002 and Table 3.1: Percentage of Students Ages 12–18 Who Reported Criminal Victimization at School during the Previous 6 Months, Selected Years 1995–2003. Washington, D.C.: U.S. Department of Education.

National Education Association. 2005. *Estimates: Rankings of the States 2004 and Estimates of School Statistics 2005.* Atlanta, Ga.: NEA.

North American Association of State and Provincial Lotteries. 2005. "Sales and Profits." Available at **<http://www.naspl.org/sales&profits.html>**.

Ohio Department of Taxation. 2005. Available at **<http://www.tax.ohio.gov>**.

Putnam, R. 2001. *Bowling Alone: The Collapse and Revival of American Community.* New York: Simon & Schuster.

Ray, E. 2005. "Board Weighs Options after Tax Issues Go Down." *Toledo Blade* (February 10): Bl.

Sampson, R., S. Raudenbush, and F. Earls. 1997. "Neighborhoods and Violent Crime: A Multilevel Study of Collective Efficacy." *Science* (August 15): 918–924.

Skocpol, T. 2003. *Diminished Democracy: From Membership to Management in American Civic life.* Norman, Okla.: University of Oklahoma Press.

Taylor, O. 1837. *Common School Assistant,* vol. 2:41.

U.S. Census Bureau. 2005. *Statistical Abstract of the United States.* Washington, D.C.: U.S. Government Printing Office.

U.S. Charter Schools. 2005. "Overview." Available at **<http://www.uscharterschools.org>**.

U.S. Department of Education. 2000. *National Study of Charter Schools.* Washington, D.C.: U.S. Government Printing Office.

USA Today. 1998. "Few Real Winners When States Fight for Business." (April 22):A12.

Wessel, D. 2005. "As Rich-Poor Gap Widens in U.S., Class Mobility Stalls." *Wall Street Journal* (May 13): Al.

White, K., and R. Johnston. 1997. "Schools' Taxes Bartered Away to Garner Jobs." *Education Week* (March 12): 1.

Winters, R. 2003. "The Politics of Taxing and Spending in Virginia." In *Politics in the American States: A Comparative Analysis,* V. Gray, R. Hanson, and H. Jacob, eds. Washington, D.C.: CQ Press, 304–348.

POSTNOTE

America has been a pioneer in public education, the free education of all its children. Until recent generations, public schools had wide support within their communities. As the authors point out, that support has eroded dramatically with more than a quarter of the country's children being educated outside the public school system.

The reasons for this are many. One key factor is that as parents become more educated and more affluent, the education of their own children becomes more paramount. They want the best for their children whether it means moving to a new community with a reputedly fine school system, seeking a charter or a private school in their community, or educating them at home. In a society that is built on choice among products and services, those who can afford it desire choice for their children. This condition, plus the strong financial headwinds our nation is encountering, is placing great strains on public education. As a result, community leaders and public educators need both to improve continually the quality of their education and to get their story out to an educationally sophisticated audience.

Discussion Questions

1. What are the major causes for the erosion of the Common School Movement?

2. Can you think of some positive educational or social outcomes from this erosion?

3. Should the Common School Movement be revived? If so, how?

RELATED WEBSITE RESOURCES

 Web Resources:

"*Common School Movement—Colonial and Republican Schooling, Changes in the Antebellum Era, The Rise of the Common School.*" Available at:

http://education.stateuniversity.com/pages/1871/ Common-School-Movement.html.

Go to this website to read an Educational Encyclopedia article about the Common School Movement.

The U.S. Department of State. Available at:

http://www.pbs.org/kcet/publicschool

The U.S. Department of State has a website to promote important American ideas. One of the ideas this agency is projecting to the world is the Common School Movement.

39

Good? Bad? or None of the Above?

William Damon

William Damon is professor of education, director of the Center on Adolescence at Stanford University, and senior fellow at the Hoover Institution.

"Good? Bad? or None of the Above?" by William Damon, *Education Next*, Vol. 4, No. 2, 2005. **http://www.hoover.org/publications/ednext3220576.html.** Reprinted by permission of the Hoover Press.

F | O | C | U | S QUESTION

Is it inevitable that teachers must teach character?

KEY TERMS

Character

Golden rule

It is an odd mark of our time that the first question people ask about character education is whether public schools should be doing it at all. The question is odd because it invites us to imagine that schooling, which occupies about a third of a child's waking time, somehow could be arranged to play no role in the formation of a child's character.

Try to imagine a school that did manage to stay out of the character education business, refraining from promoting virtues such as honesty and respectfulness. Even if the school survived the chaos that would ensue, could we expect that the character of its students wouldn't be affected (adversely, in this case) by the message that such an abdication of responsibility would impart? For better or worse, every school envelops its students in a moral climate. The choices that the school makes—or fails to make—about what sort of moral climate to create inevitably leave lasting marks on the students who live and learn there. Moral education, in the title phrase of one early book on the matter, "comes with the territory."

Still, questions of whether—not how—today's public schools should attempt to educate for character keep popping up. And in their variety, they tell us something about the roundabout journey of public schooling in the United States. For the sake of this narrative, we will consider whether that journey helps to accomplish one of schooling's few totally uncontested aims: teaching kids how to read.

A Perennial Best-Seller

From 1836 to 1922, *McGuffey's Eclectic Readers* were by far the number-one school reading text in most parts of the United States. In their many editions, the readers sold more than 120 million copies. They presented, without hesitation or qualification, the moral and ethical code that their original author, the Reverend William Holmes McGuffey (a Presbyterian minister), believed essential for all children to learn. As exemplified through the dramatic story-problems of these slim volumes, the McGuffey code may be simply stated: A child should be respectful, honest, diligent, kind, fair-minded, temperate in food and drink, and clean.

It may surprise some that the readers still sell about a hundred thousand copies a year, mostly for use in home-school or traditional community settings (such as among the Amish). For the most part, however, the morally centered lessons of McGuffey have been replaced by a different sort of reading text. Some of today's storybooks for students evoke the personal feelings of growing up; some convey the charms of pets; some insightfully delve into problems with friends or family; and some are terrifically funny, with irresistible titles such as *How to Eat Fried Worms* and *Snot Stew*. Yet as well-written, brilliantly illustrated, and personally enlightening as these new books may be, they are not stocked with unambiguous and comprehensive ethical guidance.

This historical change in school reading texts has been neither accidental nor isolated. As a general trend during the 20th century, academic expertise came to prevail over character as public schooling's clear priority. Increasingly, schools became places where children were sent to learn skills first and foremost. The dominant assumption (which had become explicit by the latter part of the 20th century) was that children themselves should figure out—perhaps with some help from family or religious sources, but more likely through their own autonomous rational choices—what to do with the skills they had acquired. Educators wondered—and were pointedly asked—why public schools should presume to muck about with values anyway. And, as public schools increasingly filled with students from diverse backgrounds, determining whose values to teach became more problematic. It all seemed a questionable distraction from the hard and urgent task of skill building.

Where We Lost Our Way

In any historical narrative, events always trump opinion. Although a reborn character-education movement had sprouted in the early 1970s, it was seen as a throwback to a bygone era and thereby marginalized (one of its own leaders wistfully referred to it as "the great lost tradition"). But by the end of the century, in the wake of ceaseless alarming reports from the disheveled, dispirited, and sometimes violent front lines of our nation's schools, the values-free approach to schooling began to seem less progressive, less inevitable, and less wise. Columbine High School was but one data point, albeit an especially vivid one, on the blood-and-graffiti-splattered high school map of the 1990s. When the mayhem invaded tony suburban communities as well as urban centers, mainstream media took notice. A 1993 front-page *New York Times* story reported: "Gang membership grows in middle-class suburbs," showing up in everything from larceny and vandalism in schools to "razors, bats, and bottles, and now to guns." Other forms of scandalous behavior, nonviolent but still terribly disruptive, paralyzed many schools as well. Cheating in particular became epidemic. Among many well-publicized incidents during the early 1990s, students at Taylor Allderdice High School in a prime Pittsburgh suburb collaborated in a systematic cheating ring, buying and selling homework from one another, stealing tests, and smuggling reference books into exams.

The growing perception of violence-racked and cheating-tainted schools in the early 1990s helped spawn a revived and robust character education movement. Organizations and web sites spread the word, and centers—more than 150 by my count—sprang up to produce and distribute curriculum materials for classroom use. The character education movement, given a boost by widespread, continuous reports of youth misbehavior, became an established part of the education landscape in the space of a few years, a surprisingly rapid development in a field that normally adopts changes slowly. It may be that the movement already has had some effect, for as Joel Best pointed out ("Monster Hype," *Education Next*, Summer 2002), evidence shows that school violence has begun to decline in recent years.

I witnessed one facet of the resurgence of the character education movement in the federal government's adoption of it during the Clinton administration. At a 1993 White House conference that I attended, Secretary of Education Richard Riley expressed approval of the movement's aims, but cautioned that such moral uplift was a matter for family and church, not the federal government. By 1996, however, in his State of the Union address, President Clinton proclaimed, "I challenge all our schools to teach character education." That year the Department of Education established the "Partnerships in Character Education" program to support the president's challenge. The Bush administration has continued and expanded the size of the program several fold.

The Inner-Directed Society

Yet the original question—whether, not how, to educate for character—remains essentially unanswered, a condition that creates doubt and debate among educators and the public. Far from worrying about how to preserve children's autonomy, however, skeptics now complain that character education is not forceful enough in presenting children with the stark and incontestable contrast between right and wrong. In a recent book, with the perhaps understandably overwrought title *The Death of Character: Moral Education in an Age without Good or Evil,* James Davison Hunter criticizes character education for its failure to promote morality with sufficient strength and clarity. The problem, according to Hunter, a professor of sociology and religion at the University of Virginia, lies in the psychologically oriented pedagogy that character educators turn to in teaching values to children: "Dominated as it is by perspectives diffused and diluted from professional psychology, this regime is overwhelmingly therapeutic and self-referencing; in character, its defining feature is a moral framework whose center point is the autonomous self." By focusing on the child's everyday behavior and feelings, moral values get watered down and lost.

Indeed, a recent research review by Marvin Berkowitz and Melinda Bier of the University of Missouri (at St. Louis) found that the most common topic in today's character education programs is "social-emotional content"—in particular, what they call "personal improvement/self-management and awareness (self-control, goal setting, relaxation techniques, self-awareness, emotional awareness)." Exactly what part of a child's moral development might be stimulated by relaxation or emotional awareness training is a mystery that neither science nor philosophy has shed much light on. My guess is that such feeling states have little to do with the acquisition of childhood morality and that, as Hunter complains, a pedagogy built primarily around the self's sentiments may distract children from the real challenges of forging character.

The Right, the Wrong, and the Strictly Instrumental

The contemporary character-education movement has thus been misled by the trendy notion that children's positive feelings are the key to all sorts of learning, moral as well as academic. Many educators now engage in silly activities and exercises focused on an obsessive attention to children's self-esteem, a focus that has foisted warehouses' worth of nonsense on students. (One assignment given my youngest daughter in her elementary school days was to write, "I'm terrific," 20 times on a 3×5 card—which she dutifully did, all the while wondering aloud what in fact she was terrific at.) When the drive to boost children's self-esteem interferes with moral instruction, it goes beyond silly to harmful.

Once when I was a guest on a National Public Radio show, a parent of a 5th-grade student called in to discuss an incident that was highly upsetting to her but all too familiar to me. That week her son had been sent home with a note informing her that he had been caught taking money out of fellow students' backpacks. The mother quickly got on the phone to the boy's teacher to tell her she was appalled, that she couldn't bear the thought of her son stealing from his friends. "What can we do about this?" asked the mother. To her astonishment, the teacher responded by asking her to say and do nothing. "We were obliged to inform you of what happened," the teacher said, "but now we wish to handle this in our own professional way. And to start with, we are not calling this incident 'stealing.' That would just give your child a bad self-image. We've decided to call what your son did 'uncooperative behavior'—and we'll point out to him in no uncertain terms that he won't be very popular with his friends if he keeps acting this way!" The parent reported that the boy now ignored her efforts to counsel him about the matter. She worried that he had "blown the whole thing off" without learning anything from it at all.

In its "professional" judgments, the school had translated a wrongful act (stealing) into a strictly instrumental concern (losing popularity). The school did so in order to save the child from feelings (shame, guilt) that it assumed could cause the child discomfort and thereby damage the child's self-image. The school was right on the first count and mistaken on the second. The child probably would have felt embarrassed if forcefully told that he had committed a moral offense—and such an experience in firsthand shame and guilt is precisely what researchers have found to be a primary means of moral learning. There is no credible scientific evidence that supports the idea that a child's self-image can be harmed by reprimands for wrongdoing, as long as the feedback pertains to the behavior rather than to the child's own intrinsic self-worth.

Confusing Ourselves and Our Students

Over the years I have often been asked to help resolve trouble in schools torn apart by cheating scandals. In each case, the resistance of teachers to discussing the moral meaning of the incident with students was palpable. I explain to them that the moral issues are many, but by no means hard to understand. Cheating is wrong for at least four reasons: it gives students who cheat an unfair advantage over those who do not cheat; it is dishonest; it is a violation of trust; and it undermines the academic integrity, the code of conduct, and the social order of the school.

I am still shocked at the number of teachers who say, in front of their students, that it is hard to hold students to a no-cheating standard in a society where people cheat on taxes, on their spouses, and so on. Some teachers sympathize with student cheaters because they think that the tests students take are flawed or unfair. Some pardon students because they believe that sharing schoolwork is motivated by loyalty to friends. In my experience, it can take days of intense discussion, and some arm twisting, to get a school community to develop a no-cheating standard that is solidly supported by expressions of moral concern.

In our time, a hesitancy to use a moral language remains the most stubborn and distracting problem for character education. Teachers worry that words that shame children may wound their self-esteem; that there are no words of moral truth anyway; that it is hypocritical to preach moral codes to the young when so many adults ignore them; or that in a diverse society one person's moral truth is another's moral falsehood. Yet adult expressions of clear moral standards are precisely what guide character formation in the young.

The conviction that moral standards are not arbitrary, that they reflect basic human truths and therefore that they must be passed from generation to generation is a necessary prerequisite of all moral education. This was a point that sociologist Emile Durkheim made in his great 1902–03 lectures, "Moral Education," the foundation for most modern approaches to the subject. Even those who started their moral education work from a different direction, such as Harvard psychologist Lawrence Kohlberg, came around to this view once they tried their hand at the actual practice of teaching children good values.

Back to the Future

The contours of what we must do are clear: Public schools must accept the mandate of educating for character. Since they shape student character no matter what they do, schools may as well try to do a good job at it. Schools must present students with objective standards expressed in a moral language that sharply distinguishes right from wrong and directs students to behave accordingly. Sentiments such as "feeling better" cannot stand as sufficient reason for moral choice. A school must help students understand that they are expected to be honest, fair, compassionate, and respectful whether it makes them feel good or not. The character mandate that adults must pass on to children transcends time, place, or personal feelings.

The cauldron of day-to-day practice, of course, always contains a steamy mixture of disparate elements. What schools actually do with character education cannot be summed up in one easy generalization. At the classroom level, education is a pragmatic, seat-of-the-pants enterprise in which teachers tend to throw whatever they have at students, and character educators are no exception.

For clues about what we can do, let us return for a moment to the James Hunter critique quoted earlier. The complaint was that character education "in a time without good or evil" provides children with the following moral logic: To the question "Why should one not be bad, say, through stealing or cheating?" follows the reply, "How would it make you feel if someone did that to you?" As I suggested earlier, Hunter is correct that the moral logic here is not sufficient, because stealing or cheating is wrong no matter how anyone feels about it. But Hunter's complaint is too sweeping and in its overreach misses a valuable opportunity to educate children about the foundations of moral behavior and belief.

The Heavy Metal of Character

Suppose that the teacher took the response, "How would it make you feel if someone did that to you?" an extra step—backward through the ages of moral tradition—linking what Hunter takes to be a mere touchy-feely sentiment to one of the great moral maxims of all time: the Golden Rule. The version most familiar in Western society—"Do unto others as you would have them do unto you"—is in fact a general precept shared by most of the world's religions (See box, p. 23). While asking the child to take the perspective of another who would be hurt by a harmful act, a teacher could draw the student's attention to the great moral traditions that have proclaimed the importance of doing so, connecting the student's personal sentiments with the earlier wisdom of civilizations. The teacher could introduce students to the glorious panoply of worldwide philosophical thought that has celebrated this principle. A lively classroom discussion could ensue from exploring why so much profound thinking across so many diverse times and places has focused on this classic maxim.

Pointing out the rich religious and historical traditions behind a maxim underlines its deep importance in human life. It informs students of the universal and timeless truths underlying moral strictures. It does not imply proselytizing for a particular religious doctrine, because the universality of core moral principles can be easily demonstrated. This kind of instruction is needed pedagogically not only because it elicits historical interest, but also because it adds a dimension of moral gravity and objectivity to what otherwise would stand only as a simple statement of a child's personal feelings.

If a child's moral education is limited to stimulating self-reflection about his personal feelings, not much has been accomplished. But if the child's moral education begins with a consideration of moral feelings such as empathy and then links these feelings with the enduring elements of morality, the child's character growth will be enhanced by transforming the child's emotions—which do play a key role in behavior—into a lasting set of virtues.

An essential part of moral education is reaffirming the emotional sense of moral regret that young people naturally feel when they harm another person or violate a fundamental societal standard. Every child is born with a capacity to feel empathy for a person who is harmed, with a capacity to feel outrage when a social standard is violated, and with a capacity to feel shame or guilt for doing something wrong. This is a natural, emotional basis for character development, but it quickly atrophies without the right kinds of feedback—in particular, guidance that supports the moral sense and shows how it can be applied to the range of social concerns that one encounters in human affairs. A primary way that schools can provide students with this kind of guidance is to teach them the great traditions that have endowed us with our moral standards.

The Golden Rule is a prototypical moral maxim with both a long historical legacy and widely recognized contemporary usefulness. (It is explicitly taught and practiced in the field of business management, a fact that many high school students would very likely be interested to learn.) There are legions of maxims in the living lore of our common culture, and many, like the Golden Rule, bear a moral message: "Two wrongs don't make a right" (ancient Scots); "You are only as good as your word" (early American); "Honesty is the best policy" (Cervantes, Ben Franklin); "It's better to light a single candle than to curse the darkness" (old Chinese proverb). As education policymaker Arthur Schwartz has written, each of these "wise sayings" encapsulates a store of wisdom that has been handed down to us through countless conversations across the generations.

What these ancient maxims suggest is that societies distant from us in time and place have something important to tell us regarding our efforts to educate young people for character. Among other things, they remind us that neither we nor our children need to invent civilization from scratch. Our journeys in moral learning begin with the aid of our rich cultural traditions and the living wisdom found therein. We are inheritors of a wealth of moral knowledge, a set of universal truths drawn from the forge of human experience over the centuries. In our transient lifestyles and throw-away relationships, in our modernist commitment to the autonomous self, we sometimes forget this. But in our role as guardians of the young, we must share the obligation to pass on to our children that which civilization has given us.

All this, of course, flies in the face of "constructivist" approaches to education favored in recent decades. Supposedly, children learn nothing useful through memorization; and, we have been warned, rote learning leads only to boredom and rejection, going "in one ear and out the other." But as I have written elsewhere, such fears are simplistic as well as unsupported by evidence. The contrast between the "discovery learning" of constructivism and the practice-and-drill of traditional learning is a false opposition. Children benefit from both, they require both, and the two complement rather than fight each other in the actual dynamics of mastering knowledge. The usefulness of memorized bits of wisdom that are stored away and used at later times, when they are better understood in the light of lived experience, has been fully supported by developmental theories ranging from the social-cultural to the biological.

One of the other principles of psychological development is that children learn best when they confront clear and consistent messages in numerous ways and in multiple contexts. In the character arena, young people need to hear moral messages from all the respected people in their lives if they are to take the messages to heart. A student learns honesty in a deep and lasting way when a teacher explains why cheating undermines the academic mission, when a parent demonstrates the importance of telling the truth for family solidarity, when a sports coach discourages deceit because it defeats the purpose of fair competition, and when a friend shows why lies destroy the trust necessary for a close relationship. The student then acquires a sense of why honesty is important to all the human relationships that the student will participate in, now and in the future.

And the past plays a part in moral learning. We do not invent our ethical codes from scratch, nor should we expect that our children could. Our inherited moral traditions are the essential elements of civilized society. When presented to students through a lively pedagogy of received wisdom, such as may be found in common maxims and precepts, these moral traditions can provide a compelling historical dimension to character education. For too long our public schools have hidden away the historical dimension, keeping the traditional foundations of moral instruction out of sight. It is time to remove this unnecessary handicap and build the moral futures of our children on the best wisdom that the past and present can offer.

POSTNOTE

One of the most damaging legacies of the social turmoil of the 1960s and 1970s has been the belief that all morality was relative and private and, in particular, that the schools had no business trying to "indoctrinate" children with moral principles and ideas. Fueled by disagreements over the Vietnam War, recreational drugs, and the then-new sexual and feminist revolutions, many teachers and school districts withdrew from conscious attempts to teach about—and to engage students in—the morality that has been the social glue of our democracy. As the author points out, such a course has had negative consequences. More to the point, one cannot have children in school for sixteen or seventeen years during such a formative period in their lives and not have an impact on their sense of what is right and wrong and how they should conduct themselves in public life.

Whether a teacher is comfortable or uncomfortable with the fact, it is inevitable that he or she is a character educator. It simply "comes with the territory." That said, and given the author's assertion that few teachers have been prepared for this aspect of their work, what are you going to do?

Discussion Questions

1. In what way does "moral education" come with the territory of teaching?
2. In your school experience, was there much attention given to moral and character education?
3. How ready do you feel to assume the responsibilities to be a character educator?

RELATED WEBSITE RESOURCES

 Web Resources:

Character Education Partnership. Available at:

http://www.character.org.

The Character Education Partnership (CEP) is an umbrella organization that has pioneered the revival of character education in schools. Its website offers an array of information and resources for educators.

Practical Guidance Resources Educators Can Trust. Available at:

http://charactered.net/.

This website has many useful lessons for those interested in teaching core values, such as honesty and perseverance.

40

The Ethics of Teaching

Kenneth A. Strike

Kenneth Strike is currently a professor of education at Syracuse University. He is also a professor emeritus at Cornell University and a member of the National Academy of Education.

"The Ethics of Teaching" by Kenneth A. Strike, *Phi Delta Kappan*, October 1988. Reprinted by permission of the author.

F|O|C|U|S QUESTION

What are the ethical principles that underlie teaching?

KEY TERMS
Benefit maximization
Equal respect
Ethics
Values

Mrs. Porter and Mr. Kennedy have divided their third-grade classes into reading groups. In her class, Mrs. Porter tends to spend the most time with students in the slowest reading group because they need the most help. Mr. Kennedy claims that such behavior is unethical. He maintains that each reading group should receive equal time.

Miss Andrews has had several thefts of lunch money in her class. She has been unable to catch the thief, although she is certain that some students in the class know who the culprit is. She decides to keep the entire class inside for recess, until someone tells her who stole the money. Is it unethical to punish the entire class for the acts of a few?

Ms. Phillips grades her fifth-grade students largely on the basis of effort. As a result, less able students who try hard often get better grades than students who are abler but less industrious. Several parents have accused Ms. Phillips of unethical behavior, claiming that their children are not getting what they deserve. These parents also fear that teachers in the middle school won't understand Ms. Phillips' grading practices and will place their children in inappropriate tracks.

The Nature of Ethical Issues

The cases described above are typical of the ethical issues that teachers face. What makes these issues ethical?

First, ethical issues concern questions of right and wrong—our duties and obligations, our rights and responsibilities. Ethical discourse is characterized by a unique vocabulary that commonly includes such words as *ought* and *should, fair* and *unfair.*

Second, ethical questions cannot be settled by an appeal to facts alone. In each of the preceding cases, knowing the consequences of our actions is not sufficient for determining the right thing to do. Perhaps, because Mrs. Porter spends more time with the slow reading group, the reading scores in her class will be more evenly distributed than the scores in Mr. Kennedy's class. But even knowing this does not tell us if it is fair to spend a disproportionate amount of time with the slow readers. Likewise, if Miss Andrews punishes her entire class, she may catch the thief, but this does not tell us whether punishing the entire group was the right thing to do. In ethical reasoning, facts are relevant in deciding what to do. But by themselves they are not enough. We also require ethical principles by which to judge the facts.

Third, ethical questions should be distinguished from values. Our values concern what we like or what we believe to be good. If one enjoys Bach or likes skiing, that says something about one's values. Often there is nothing right or wrong about values, and our values are a matter of our free choice. For example, it would be difficult to argue that someone who preferred canoeing to skiing had done something wrong or had made a mistake. Even if we believe that Bach is better than rock, that is not a reason to make people who prefer rock listen to Bach. Generally, questions of values turn on our choices: what we like, what we deem worth liking. But there is nothing obligatory about values.

On the other hand, because ethics concern what we ought to do, our ethical obligations are often independent of what we want or choose. The fact that we want something that belongs to someone else does not entitle us to take it. Nor does a choice to steal make stealing right or even "right for us." Our ethical obligations continue to be obligations, regardless of what we want or choose.

Ethical Reasoning

The cases sketched above involve ethical dilemmas: situations in which it seems possible to give a reasonable argument for more than one course of action. We must think about our choices, and we must engage in moral reasoning. Teaching is full of such dilemmas. Thus teachers need to know something about ethical reasoning.

Ethical reasoning involves two stages: applying principles to cases and judging the adequacy or applicability of the principles. In the first stage, we are usually called upon to determine the relevant ethical principle or principles that apply to a case, to ascertain the relevant facts of the case, and to judge the facts by the principles.

Consider, for example, the case of Miss Andrews and the stolen lunch money. Some ethical principles concerning punishment seem to apply directly to the case. Generally, we believe that we should punish the guilty, not the innocent; that people should be presumed innocent until proven guilty; and that the punishment should fit the crime. If Miss Andrews punishes her entire class for the behavior of an unknown few, she will violate these common ethical principles about punishment.

Ethical principles are also involved in the other two cases. The first case involves principles of equity and fairness. We need to know what counts as fair or equal treatment for students of different abilities. The third case requires some principles of due process. We need to know what are fair procedures for assigning grades to students.

However, merely identifying applicable principles isn't enough. Since the cases described above involve ethical dilemmas, it should be possible to argue plausibly for more than one course of action.

For example, suppose Miss Andrews decides to punish the entire class. It could be argued that she had behaved unethically because she has punished innocent people. She might defend herself, however, by holding that she had reasons for violating ethical principles that we normally apply to punishment. She might argue that it was important to catch the thief or that it was even more important to impress on her entire class that stealing is wrong. She could not make these points by ignoring the matter. By keeping the entire class inside for recess, Miss Andrews could maintain, she was able to catch the thief and to teach her class a lesson about the importance of honesty. Even if she had to punish some innocent people, everyone was better off as a result. Can't she justify her action by the fact that everyone benefits?

Two General Principles

When we confront genuine ethical dilemmas such as this, we need some general ethical concepts in order to think our way through them. I suggest two: the principle of benefit maximization and the principle of equal respect for persons.

The principle of benefit maximization holds that we should take that course of actions which will maximize the benefit sought. More generally, it requires us to do that which will make everyone, on the average, as well off as possible. One of the traditional formulations of this principle is the social philosophy known as utilitarianism, which holds that our most general moral obligation is to act in a manner that produces the greatest happiness for the greatest number.

We might use the principle of benefit maximization to think about each of these cases. The principle requires that in each case we ask which of the possible courses of action makes people generally better off. Miss Andrews has appealed to the principle of benefit maximization in justifying her punishment of the entire class. Ms. Phillips might likewise appeal to it in justifying her grading system. Perhaps by using grades to reward effort rather than successful performance, the overall achievement of the class will be enhanced. Is that not what is important?

It is particularly interesting to see how the principle of benefit maximization might be applied to the question of apportioning teacher time between groups with different levels of ability. Assuming for the moment that we wish to maximize the overall achievement of the class, the principle of benefit maximization dictates that we allocate time in a manner that will produce the greatest overall learning.

Suppose, however, we discover that the way to produce the greatest overall learning in a given class is for a teacher to spend the most time with the *brightest* children. These are the children who provide the greatest return on our investment of time. Even though the least able children learn less than they would with an equal division of time, the overall learning that takes place in the class is maximized when we concentrate on the ablest.

Here the principle of benefit maximization seems to lead to an undesirable result. Perhaps we should consider other principles as well.

The principle of equal respect requires that our actions respect the equal worth of moral agents. We must regard human beings as intrinsically worthwhile and treat them accordingly. The essence of this idea is perhaps best expressed in the Golden Rule. We have a duty to accord others the same kind of treatment that we expect them to accord us.

The principle of equal respect can be seen as involving three subsidiary ideas. First, it requires us to treat people as ends in themselves, rather than as means to further our own goals. We must respect their goals as well.

Second, when we are considering what it means to treat people as ends rather than as means, we must regard as central the fact that people are free and rational moral agents. This means that, above all, we must respect their freedom of choice. And we must respect the choices that people make even when we do not agree.

Third, no matter how people differ, they are of equal value as moral agents. This does not mean that we must see people as equal in abilities or capacities. Nor does it mean that we cannot take relevant differences between people into account when deciding how to treat them. It is not, for example, a violation of equal respect to give one student a higher grade than another because that student works harder and does better.

That people are of equal value as moral agents does mean, however, that they are entitled to the same basic rights and that their interests are of equal value. Everyone, regardless of native ability, is entitled to equal opportunity. No one is entitled to act as though his or her happiness counted for more than the happiness of others. As persons, everyone has equal worth.

Notice three things about these two moral principles. First, both principles (in some form) are part of the moral concepts of almost everyone who is reading this article. These are the sorts of moral principles that everyone cites in making moral arguments. Even if my formulation is new, the ideas themselves should be familiar. They are part of our common ethical understandings.

Second, both principles seem necessary for moral reflection. Neither is sufficient by itself. For example, the principle of equal respect requires us to value the well-being of others as we value our own well-being. But to value the welfare of ourselves *and* others is to be concerned with maximizing benefits; we want all people to be as well-off as possible.

Conversely, the principle of benefit maximization seems to presuppose the principle of equal respect. Why, after all, must we value the welfare of others? Why not insist that only our own happiness counts or that our happiness is more important than the happiness of others? Answering these questions will quickly lead us to affirm that people are of equal worth and that, as a consequence, everyone's happiness is to be valued equally. Thus our two principles are intertwined.

Third, the principles may nevertheless conflict with one another. One difference between the principle of benefit maximization and the principle of equal respect is their regard for consequences. For the principle of benefit maximization, only consequences matter. The sole relevant factor in choosing between courses of action is which action has the best overall results. But consequences are not decisive in the principle of equal respect; our actions must respect the dignity and worth of the individuals involved, even if we choose a course of action that produces less benefit than some other possible action.

The crucial question that characterizes a conflict between the principle of benefit maximization and the principle of equal respect is this:

When is it permissible to violate a person's rights in order to produce a better outcome? For example, this seems the best way to describe the issue that arises when a teacher decides to punish an entire class for the acts of a few. Students' rights are violated when they are punished for something they haven't done, but the overall consequence of the teacher's action may be desirable. Is it morally permissible, then, to punish everyone?

We can think about the issue of fair allocation of teacher time in the same way. Spending more time with the brightest students may enhance the average learning of the class. But we have, in effect, traded the welfare of the least able students for the welfare of the ablest. Is that not failing to respect the equal worth of the least able students? Is that not treating them as though they were means, not ends?

The principle of equal respect suggests that we should give the least able students at least an equal share of time, even if the average achievement of the class declines. Indeed, we might use the principle of equal respect to argue that we should allocate our time in a manner that produces more equal results—or a more equal share of the benefits of education.

I cannot take the discussion of these issues any further in this short space. But I do want to suggest some conclusions about ethics and teaching.

First, teaching is full of ethical issues. It is the responsibility of teachers, individually and collectively, to consider these issues and to have informed and intelligent opinions about them.

Second, despite the fact that ethical issues are sometimes thorny, they can be thought about. Ethical reflection can help us to understand what is at stake in our choices, to make more responsible choices, and sometimes to make the right choices.

Finally, to a surprising extent, many ethical dilemmas, including those that are common to teaching, can be illuminated by the principles of benefit maximization and equal respect for persons. Understanding these general ethical principles and their implications is crucial for thinking about ethical issues.

POSTNOTE

Ethics seems to be making a comeback. We may not be behaving better, but we are talking about it more. Street crime and white-collar crime, drugs and violence, our inability to keep promises in our personal and professional lives—all these suggest a renewed need for ethics.

Kenneth Strike points out that teaching is full of ethical issues. It is true that teachers make promises to perform certain duties and that they have real power over the lives of children. This article, however, speaks to only one end of the spectrum of ethical issues faced by the teacher: what we call "hard-case" ethics, complex problems, often dilemmas. Certainly, these are important, but there are also everyday teaching ethics—the issues that fill a teacher's day: Should I correct this stack of papers or watch *The Office?* Should I "hear" that vulgar comment or stroll right by? Should I reread this story again this year before I teach it tomorrow or spend some time with my colleagues in the teachers' lounge? Should I bend down and pick up yet another piece of paper in the hall or figure I've done my share for the day?

Like hard-case ethical issues, these questions, in essence, ask: What's the right thing to do? Our answers to these everyday questions often become our habits, good and bad. These, in turn, define much of our ethical behavior as teachers. Finally, it is our behavior that may be our most powerful teacher.

Discussion Questions

1. What three factors or qualities make an issue an ethical one?

2. What two ethical principles are mentioned in the article? Give your own examples of classroom situations that reflect these principles.

3. Do you believe that all one needs to be a moral teacher is to make ethical decisions? Why or why not?

RELATED WEBSITE RESOURCES

 Web Resources:

Professional Ethics Issues and Topics. Available at:

http://www.ethicsweb.ca/resources/professional/ issues.html.

This is part of the Applied Ethics Resources on the World Wide Web which, while dealing with ethics in many fields, has some resources on the teaching profession.

Character Education Partnership. Available at:

http://www.character.org.

The Character Education Partnership (CEP) is an umbrella organization that has pioneered the revival of character education in schools. Its website offers an array of information and resources for educators.

The Teacher's Ten Commandments: School Law in the Classroom

41

Thomas R. McDaniel

Thomas R. McDaniel is senior vice president and professor of education at Converse College in Spartanburg, South Carolina.

"The Teacher's Ten Commandments: School Law in the Classroom" by Thomas R. McDaniel, revised and updated from *Phi Delta Kappan*, June 1979. Reprinted by permission of the author.

|F|O|C|U|S| QUESTION

What are the overarching legal principles that can guide the work of a teacher?

KEY TERMS

Academic freedom

Due process

In recent years public school teachers have been made painfully aware that the law defines, limits, and prescribes many aspects of a teacher's daily life. Schools are no longer protected domains where teachers rule with impunity; ours is an age of litigation. Not only are parents and students ready to use the courts for all manner of grievances against school and teacher, the growing legislation itself regulates more and more of school life. In addition to an unprecedented number of laws at all levels of government, the mind-boggling array of complex case law principles (often vague and contradictory) adds to the confusion for the educator.

The Ten Commandments of School Law described below are designed to provide the concerned and bewildered teacher with some significant general guidelines in the classroom. While statutes and case law principles may vary from state to state or judicial circuit to judicial circuit, these school law principles have wide applicability in the United States today.

Commandment I: Thou Shalt Not Worship in the Classroom

This may seem something of a parody of the Biblical First Commandment—and many teachers hold that indeed their religious freedom and that of the majority of students has been limited by the court cases prohibiting prayer and Bible reading—but the case law principles here have been designed to keep public schools *neutral* in religious matters. The First Amendment to the Constitution, made applicable by the Fourteenth Amendment to state government (and hence to public schools, which are agencies of state government), requires that there be no law "respecting the establishment of religion or prohibiting the free exercise thereof." As the Supreme Court declared in the *Everson* decision of 1947, "Neither [a state nor the federal government] can pass laws that aid one religion, aid all religions, or prefer one religion over another." Such rules, said the Court, would violate the separation of church and state principle of the First Amendment.

In 1971 the Supreme Court ruled in *Lemon* v. *Kurtzman* that separation of church and state required that government action or legislation in education must clear a three-pronged test. It must: 1) not have a religious purpose, 2) not have the primary effect of either enhancing or inhibiting religion, and 3) not create "excessive entanglement" between church and state. This Lemon Test has been attacked by Justice Anton Scalia and others in recent years but continues to be used (at least as a guideline) in court rulings. In a 1992 case, *Lee* v. *Wiseman*, the Supreme Court ruled that an invocation and benediction at commencement by a clergyman was unconstitutional—perhaps because the school principal chose the clergyman and gave him directions for the content of the prayer. In another 1992 case a circuit court of appeals upheld a policy that permitted high school seniors to choose student volunteers to deliver nonsectarian, nonproselytizing invocations at graduation ceremonies. Courts continue to wrestle with questions about "establishment" and "freedom" of religion. However, acts of worship in public schools usually violate the neutrality principle—especially when they appear to be planned and promoted by school officials.

On the other hand, public schools may offer courses in comparative religion, history of religion, or the Bible as literature, because these would be academic experiences rather than religious ones. "Released-time" programs during school hours for outside-of-school religious instruction have been held to be constitutional by the Supreme Court (*Zorach* v. *Clauson*, 1952). Two states, Georgia and South Carolina, had state laws in place by 2008 that granted academic credit for such off-campus released time Bible courses, and several other states are considering requiring Biblical or other religious literacy courses as part of the regular curriculum.

Other religious practices that have been struck down by the Supreme Court include a Kentucky statute requiring that the Ten Commandments be posted in every public school classroom, a Michigan high school's 30-year practice of displaying a 2-foot by 3-foot portrait of Jesus in the hallways, laws in Arkansas and Louisiana requiring that "scientific creationism" (based on Genesis) be taught in science classes to "balance" the teaching of evolution, and the Gideons' distribution of Bibles in the public schools of Indiana.

The Supreme Court has questioned (or struck down) certain practices such as invocations at football games (*Santa Fe Independent School District* v. *Doe*, a 2000 ruling), nativity scenes and other religious displays, and laws requiring a "moment of silence" when the purpose is to promote prayer. On the other hand, most "moment of silence" laws have been found to be legal under the First Amendment. Finding the line that separates church and state has not been easy: The "wall of separation" has often seemed more like a semipermeable membrane.

In 1984, Congress passed the Equal Access Act. This statute made it unlawful for any public secondary school receiving federal funds to discriminate against any students who wanted to conduct a meeting on school premises during "non-instructional time" (before and after regular school hours) if other student groups (such as clubs) were allowed to use school facilities during these times. Religious groups that are voluntary and student initiated (not officially sponsored or led by school personnel) may, under the EAA, meet on school premises. Such meetings may not be conducted or controlled by others not associated with the school nor may they interfere with educational activities of the school. In a 1990 case (*Westside Community Schools* v. *Mergens*) the Supreme Court upheld the constitutionality of the EAA and declared this federal statute did not violate the First Amendment or any of the three prongs of the Lemon Test. However, a 1993 case (*Sease* v. *School District of Philadelphia*) in Pennsylvania disallowed a gospel choir that advertised itself as sponsored by the school district, was directed by the school secretary, had another school employee attending all practices, and had non-school persons regularly attending meetings of the choir. There were several violations of the EAA in this case.

The application of the neutrality principle to education has resulted in some of the following guidelines for public schools:

1. Students may not be required to salute the flag nor to stand for the flag salute, if this conflicts with their religious beliefs.
2. Bible reading, even without comment, may not be practiced in a public school when the intent is to promote worship.
3. Prayer is an act of worship and as such cannot be a regular part of opening exercises or other aspects of the regular school day (including grace at lunch).
4. Worship services (e.g., prayer and Bible reading) are not constitutional even if voluntary rather than compulsory. Not consensus, not majority vote, nor excusing objectors from class or participation makes these practices legal.
5. Prayer and other acts of worship (benedictions, hymns, invocations, etc.) at school-related or school-sponsored events are increasingly under scrutiny by courts and may be disallowed when found to be initiated or controlled by school officials.

Commandment II: Thou Shalt Not Abuse Academic Freedom

Under First Amendment protection, teachers are given the necessary freedom and security to use the classroom as a forum for the examination and discussion of ideas. Freedom of expression is a prerequisite for education in a democracy—and the schools, among other responsibilities, are agents of democracy. Students are citizens too, and they are also entitled to freedom of speech. As Justice Abe Fortas, who delivered the Supreme Court's majority opinion in the famous *Tinker* decision (1969), put it:

> It can hardly be argued that either students or teachers shed their constitutional rights at the schoolhouse gate. . . . In our system state-operated schools may not be enclaves of totalitarianism . . . [and] students may not be regarded as closed-circuit recipients of only that which the state chooses to communicate.

Case law has developed over the years to define the parameters of free expression for both teachers and students.

In one decision, the U.S. Supreme Court upheld a school district that suspended a student for violating the school's no disruption rule prohibiting "obscene, profane language" after the student had delivered a nominating speech on behalf of another student during a student assembly. The speech included several sexual references, and the Supreme Court held that the student's speech may be disciplined when it is proved to be "vulgar, lewd, and plainly offensive" (*Bethel School District # 403 v. Fraser,* 1986). In a more recent case, the U.S. Supreme Court sided with school principal Morse when she disciplined and suspended high school student Frederick for displaying a banner with the words "Bong Hits 4 Jesus" at a school-sanctioned parade during school hours and supervised by teachers and administrators. Frederick was off school grounds, across the street from the school, and caused no disruption. Nonetheless, because of the presumed drug message, the Court said restricting such student speech served an important state interest and it was, therefore, proper (*Morse v. Frederick,* 2007). Consider these guidelines regarding First Amendment freedom of expression in the classroom:

1. Teachers may discuss controversial issues in the classroom if they are relevant to the curriculum, although good judgment is required. Issues that disrupt the educational process, are demonstrably inappropriate to the legitimate objectives of the curriculum, or are unreasonable for the age and maturity of the students may be prohibited by school officials. The routine use of profanity by teachers is not a protected First Amendment right (*Martin v. Parrish,* 1986, Fifth Circuit Court).

2. Teachers may discuss current events, political issues, and candidates so long as neutrality and balanced consideration prevail. When teachers become advocates and partisans, supporters of a single position rather than examiners of all positions, they run the risk of censure.

3. A teacher may use controversial literature containing "rough" language but must "take care not to transcend his legitimate professional purpose" (*Mailoux v. Kiley,* 1971, U.S. District Court, Massachusetts). Again, courts will attempt to determine curriculum relevance, disruption of the educational process, and appropriateness to the age and maturity of the students.

4. Teachers and students are increasingly (but not yet universally) guaranteed symbolic free speech, including hair length and beards, armbands, and buttons. Courts generally determine such issues in terms of the "substantial disruption" that occurs or is clearly threatened. Dress codes for students are generally allowable when they are intended to provide for health, safety, and "decency." When they exist merely to promote the "tastes" of the teacher or administration, they have usually been struck down by the courts.

5. Teachers have some control over school-sponsored publications and plays. In *Hazelwood School District v. Kuhlmeier* (1988) the Supreme Court held that "educators do not offend the First Amendment by exercising editorial control over the style and content of student speech in school-sponsored expressive activities so long as their actions are reasonably related to legitimate pedagogical concerns." This authority, however, does not extend to censorship of student expression. It also does not appear to extend to a school board's banning and regulating textbooks and other "learning materials" (*Virgil v. School Board of Columbia County,* 1989, Eleventh Circuit).

6. Teachers do not have a constitutional right to use any teaching method they want. School district officials and boards may establish course content and teaching methods as matters of policy. Courts will support such policies but will examine the reasonableness of sanctions against teachers. For example, a California court ruled that firing a teacher for unwittingly permitting students to read obscene poetry was too severe (*De Groat v. Newark,* 1976), while a nine-month suspension of a West Virginia teacher for showing cartoons of "Fritz the Cat" undressing was judged appropriate (*DeVito v. Board of Education,* 1984).

Teachers, in short, are free to deal with controversial issues (including politics and sex) and to use controversial methods and materials if these are educationally defensible, appropriate to the students, and not "materially and substantially" disruptive. But school boards also have authority to maintain curricular policies governing what (and even how) teachers should teach. Courts use a balancing test to determine when students' and teachers' rights to academic freedom must give way to the competing need of society to have reasonable school discipline—free of "material and substantial disruption" (*Tinker*, 1969).

Commandment III: Thou Shalt Not Engage in Private Activities That Impair Teaching Effectiveness

Of all the principles of school law, this commandment is probably the most difficult to delineate with precision. The private and professional areas of a teacher's life have been, for the most part, separated by recent court decisions. A mere 75 years ago teachers signed contracts with provisions prohibiting marriage, falling in love, leaving town without permission of the school board, smoking cigarettes, loitering in ice-cream stores, and wearing lipstick. But now a teacher's private life is considered his or her own business. Thus, for example, many court cases have established that teachers have the same citizenship rights outside the classroom that any other person has.

Teachers, however, have always been expected by society to abide by high standards of personal conduct. Whenever a teacher's private life undermines effective instruction in the class, there is a possibility that the courts will uphold his or her dismissal. To guard against this possibility, the teacher should consider some of the following principles:

1. Teachers may belong to any organization or association—but if they participate in illegal activities of that organization they may be dismissed from their job.
2. A teacher may write letters to newspapers criticizing school policies—unless it can be shown that such criticism impairs morale or working relationships. In the landmark *Pickering* decision (1968), the Supreme Court upheld a teacher who had written such a letter but pointed out that there was in this case "no question of maintaining either discipline by immediate supervisors or harmony among co-workers. . . ."
3. Teachers do not have a right to air private grievances or personnel judgments publicly. Free speech on public issues should not lead teachers to criticize superiors or other school employees in public settings. In a 1983 case, *Connick* v. *Myers*,

the Supreme Court ruled against a discharged public employee, saying that he spoke out "not as a citizen upon matters of public concern but instead as an employee on matters of personal interest." A judge in Florida, applying *Connick* to a history teacher discharged for outspoken criticism of his administrators, ruled that the teacher's speech was "nothing more than a set of grievances with school administrators over internal school policies" (*Ferrara* v. *Mills*, 1984). Teachers should distinguish between *public* citizenship issues and *private* personnel issues before making controversial and critical public comments about their schools.

4. A teacher's private affairs do not normally disqualify him or her from teaching except to the extent that it can be shown that such affairs undermine teaching effectiveness. Teachers who are immoral in public, or who voluntarily (or through indiscretion) make known in public private acts of immorality, may indeed be dismissed. Courts are still debating the rights of homosexual teachers, with decisions falling on both sides of this issue.
5. Laws which say that teachers may be dismissed for "unprofessional conduct" or "moral turpitude" are interpreted narrowly, with the burden of proof on the employer to show that the particular circumstances in a case constitute "unfitness to teach." Dismissal must be based on fact, not mere rumor.
6. Whenever a teacher's private affairs include sexual involvement with students, it may be presumed that courts will declare that such conduct constitutes immorality indicating unfitness to teach. Teachers may even be disciplined or dismissed for relationships with students who have already graduated. That was the ruling in a 2004 Michigan case when Laura Flaskamp was denied tenure because she was found to have had a sexual relationship with a student within nine months after the student's graduation.

Commandment IV: Thou Shalt Not Deny Students Due Process

The Fourteenth Amendment guarantees citizens "due process of law" whenever the loss of a right is at stake. Because education has come to be considered such a right (a "property" right), and because students are considered to be citizens, case law in recent years has defined certain procedures to be necessary in providing due process in particular situations:

1. A rule that is patently or demonstrably unfair or a punishment that is excessive may be found by

a court to violate the "substantive" due process of a student (see, for example, the Supreme Court's 1969 *Tinker* decision). At the heart of due process is the concept of fair play, and teachers should examine the substance of their rules and the procedures for enforcing them to see if both are reasonable, nonarbitrary, and equitable.

2. The extent to which due process rights should be observed depends on the gravity of the offense and the severity of punishment that follows. The Supreme Court's *Goss* v. *Lopez* decision (1975) established minimal due process for suspensions of 10 days or less, including oral or written notice of charges and an opportunity for the student to present his or her side of the story.

3. When students are expelled from school, they should be given a statement of the specific charges and the grounds for expulsion, a formal hearing, names of witnesses, and a report of the facts to which each witness testifies (see the leading case, *Dixon* v. *Alabama State Board of Education*, 1961). Furthermore, it is probable that procedural due process for expelled students gives them the right to challenge the evidence, cross-examine witnesses, and be represented by counsel. (See, for example, the New York Supreme Court's 1967 *Goldwyn* v. *Allen* decision.) Finally, such students may appeal the decision to an impartial body for review.

4. Special education students have an added measure of due process protection. In 1990 Congress consolidated earlier special education federal statutes—including the 1975 Education of All Handicapped Children Act (Public Law 94-142)—into the Individuals with Disabilities Education Act (IDEA). These laws stipulate extensive due process rights for *all* children with disabilities (whether or not they have "the ability to benefit") to ensure a free, "appropriate" education. These provisions include prior written notice before any proposed change in a child's educational program; testing that is non-discriminatory in language, race, or culture; parental access to records; fair and impartial hearing by the State Education Agency or local district; and a student's right to remain in a current placement until due process proceedings are completed. These due process guarantees supersede district-level policies relating to placement, suspension, or expulsion of students. As the Supreme Court ruled in *Honig* v. *Doe* (1988), the IDEA does not allow even for a "dangerous exception" to the "stay put" provision. The IDEA was revised in 2004 and—along with the No Child Left Behind Act of 2001 and the Americans with Disabilities Act (ADA),

passed by Congress in 1990—provides strong federal protection for the educational rights of disabled students.

It is advisable for schools to develop written regulations governing procedures for such areas as suspension, expulsion, discipline, publications, and placement of the disabled. The teacher should be aware of these regulations and should provide his or her administration with specific, factual evidence whenever a student faces a serious disciplinary decision. The teacher is also advised to be guided by the spirit of due process—fairness and evenhanded justice—when dealing with less serious incidents in the classroom.

Commandment V: Thou Shalt Not Punish Behavior Through Academic Penalties

It is easy for teachers to lose sight of the distinction between punishing and rewarding academic performance, on the one hand, and disciplinary conduct on the other. Grades, for example, are frequently employed as motivation for both study behavior and paying-attention behavior. There is a great temptation for teachers to use one of the few weapons still in their arsenal (i.e., grades) as an instrument of justice for social infractions in the classroom. While it may indeed be the case that students who misbehave will not perform well academically because of their conduct, courts are requiring schools and teachers to keep those two domains separate.

In particular, teachers are advised to heed the following general applications of this principle:

1. Denial of a diploma to a student who has met all the academic requirements for it but who has broken a rule of discipline is not permitted. Several cases (going back at least as far as the 1921 Iowa *Valentine* case) are on record to support this guideline. It is also probable that exclusion from a graduation ceremony as a punishment for behavior will not be allowed by the courts.

2. Grades should not be reduced to serve disciplinary purposes. In the *Wermuth* case (1965) in New Jersey, the ruling against such practice included this observation by the state's commissioner of education: "Whatever system of marks and grades a school may devise will have serious inherent limitations at best, and it must not be further handicapped by attempting to serve disciplinary purposes too." In a 1984 case in Pennsylvania (*Katzman* v. *Cumberland Valley School District*), the court struck down a policy requiring a reduction

in grades by two percentage points for each day of suspension.

3. Lowering grades—or awarding zeros—for absences is a questionable legal practice. In the Kentucky case of *Dorsey* v. *Bale* (1975), a student had his grades reduced for unexcused absences, and under the school's regulation, was not allowed to make up the work; five points were deducted from his nine-weeks' grade for each unexcused absence. A state circuit court and the Kentucky Court of Appeals declared the regulation to be invalid. The courts are particularly likely to invalidate regulations that constitute "double jeopardy"—e.g., suspending students for disciplinary reasons and giving them zeros while suspended.

In general, teachers who base academic evaluation on academic performance have little to fear in this area. Courts do not presume to challenge a teacher's grades *per se* when the consideration rests only on the teacher's right or ability to make valid academic judgments.

Commandment VI: Thou Shalt Not Misuse Corporal Punishment

Corporal punishment is a controversial method of establishing discipline. The Supreme Court refused to disqualify the practice under a suit (*Ingraham* v. *Wright*, 1977) in which it was argued that corporal punishment was "cruel and unusual punishment" and thus a violation of the Constitution's Eighth Amendment. An increasing number of states—up from only two in 1979 to 27 in 2001—ban corporal punishment in public schools.

In those states not prohibiting corporal punishment, teachers may—as an extension of their *in loco parentis* authority—use "moderate" corporal punishment to establish discipline. There are, however, many potential legal dangers in the practice. *In loco parentis* is a limited, perhaps even a vanishing, concept, and teachers must be careful to avoid these misuses of corporal punishment if they want to stay out of the courtroom:

1. The punishment must never lead to permanent injury. No court will support as "reasonable" or "moderate" that physical punishment which permanently disables or disfigures a student. Many an assault and battery judgment has been handed down in such cases. Unfortunately for teachers, "accidents" that occur during corporal punishment and ignorance of a child's health problems (brittle bones, hemophilia, etc.) do not always excuse a teacher from liability.

2. The punishment must not be unreasonable in terms of the offense, nor may it be used to enforce an unreasonable rule. The court examines all the circumstances in a given case to determine what was or was not "reasonable" or "excessive." In 1980 the Fourth Circuit Court of Appeals ruled that "excessive" corporal punishment might well violate Fourteenth Amendment rights. In 1987 the Tenth Circuit Court of Appeals reached a similar conclusion.

3. The punishment must not be motivated by spite, malice, or revenge. Whenever teachers administer corporal punishment in a state of anger, they run a high risk of losing an assault and battery suit in court. Since corporal punishment is practiced as a method of correcting student behavior, any evidence that physical force resulted from a teacher's bad temper or quest for revenge is damning. On the other hand, in an explosive situation (e.g., a fight) teachers may protect themselves and use that force necessary to restrain a student from harming the teacher, others, or himself.

4. The punishment must not ignore such variables as the student's age, sex, size, and physical condition.

5. The punishment must not be administered with inappropriate instruments or to parts of the body where risk of injury is great. For example, a Texas case ruled that it is not reasonable for a teacher to use his fists in administering punishment. Another teacher lost a suit when he struck a child on the ear, breaking an eardrum. The judge noted, "Nature has provided a part of the anatomy for chastisement, and tradition holds that such chastisement should there be applied." It should be noted that creating mental anguish and emotional stress by demeaning, harassing, or humiliating a child may be construed as illegal punishment too.

6. Teachers must not only take care not to harm children by way of corporal punishment; they also have a responsibility to report suspected child abuse by parents or others. Congress passed the National Child Abuse Prevention and Treatment Act in 1974 and followed with stronger laws in 1988 and 1992. Child abuse is a state (not federal) crime with many variations in definition and reporting procedure. But *all* states require reporting if the neglect or abuse results in physical injury. Teachers need not be absolutely certain of abuse

but must act "in good faith" if they have "reason to believe" a child is being subjected to abuse or neglect. Every state also provides legal protection from suit for such reporting. In most states, failure to report is a misdemeanor.

Courts must exercise a good deal of judgment in corporal punishment cases to determine what is "moderate," "excessive," "reasonable," "cruel," "unusual," "malicious," or "capricious." Suffice it to say that educators should exercise great care in the use of corporal punishment.

Commandment VII: Thou Shalt Not Neglect Students' Safety

One of the major responsibilities of teachers is to keep their students safe from unreasonable risk of harm or danger. The major cases involving teachers grow out of negligence charges relating to the teacher's failure to supervise properly in accordance with *in loco parentis* obligations (to act "in place of the parents"), contractual obligations, and professional responsibility. While the courts do not expect teachers to protect children from "unforeseeable accidents" and "acts of God," they do require teachers to act as a reasonably prudent teacher should in protecting students from possible harm or injury.

Negligence is a tort ("wrong") that exists only when the elements of *duty, violation, cause*, and *injury* are present. Teachers are generally responsible for using good judgment in determining what steps are necessary to provide for adequate supervision of the particular students in their charge, and the given circumstances dictate what is reasonably prudent in each case. A teacher who has a duty to his or her students but who fails to fulfill this duty because of carelessness, lack of discretion, or lack of diligence may violate this duty with a resultant injury to a student. In this instance the teacher may be held liable for negligence as the cause of the injury to the student. The Paul D. Coverdell Teacher Protection Act of 2002, part of the federal No Child Left Behind Act, immunizes teachers from liability if they are "acting within the scope of the teacher's employment or responsibilities."

Several guidelines can help teachers avoid this all-too-common and serious lawsuit:

1. Establish and enforce rules of safety in school activities. This is particularly important for the elementary teacher, since many injuries to elementary students occur on playgrounds, in hallways, and in classroom activity sessions. The prudent teacher anticipates such problems and establishes rules to protect students from such injuries. Generally, rules should be written, posted, and taught.

2. Be aware of school, district, and state rules and regulations as they pertain to student safety. One teacher was held negligent when a child was injured because the teacher did not know that there was a state law requiring safety glasses in a shop activity. It is also important that a teacher's own rules not conflict with regulations at higher levels. *Warn* students of any hazard in a room or in an instructional activity.

3. Enforce safety rules when violations are observed. In countless cases teachers have been found negligent when students repeatedly broke important safety rules, eventually injuring themselves or others, or when a teacher should have foreseen danger but did not act as a "reasonably prudent" teacher would have in the same situation to correct the behavior. One teacher observing a mumblety-peg game at recess was held negligent for not stopping it before the knife bounced up and put out an eye of one of the players.

4. Provide a higher standard of supervision when students are younger, disabled, and/or in a potentially dangerous activity. Playgrounds, physical education classes, science labs, and shop classes require particular care and supervision. Instruction must be provided to insure safety in accordance with the children's maturity, competence, and skill.

5. Learn first aid, because teachers may be liable for negligence if they do not get or give prompt, appropriate medical assistance when necessary. While teachers should not give children medicine, even aspirin, they should, of course, allow any legitimate prescriptions to be taken as prescribed. There should be school policy governing such procedures.

6. Advise substitute teachers (and student teachers) about any unusual medical, psychological, handicapping, or behavioral problem in your class. If there are physical hazards in your class—bare light cords, sharp edges, loose boards, insecure window frames, etc.—warn everyone about these too. Be sure to report such hazards to your administration and janitorial staff—as a "prudent" teacher would do.

7. Be where you are assigned to be. If you have playground, hall, cafeteria, or bus duty, be there. An accident that occurs when you are someplace other than your assigned station may be blamed on your negligence, whereas if you had been there it would

not be so charged. Your responsibility for safety is the same for extracurricular activities you are monitoring as it is for classes.

8. If you have to leave a classroom (particularly a rowdy one), stipulate the kind of conduct you expect and make appropriate arrangements—such as asking another teacher to check in. Even this may not be adequate precaution in terms of your duty to supervise if the students are known to be troublemakers, are quite immature, or are mentally retarded or emotionally disabled. You run a greater risk leaving a science class or a gym class than you do a social studies class.

9. Plan field trips with great care and provide for adequate supervision. Many teachers fail to realize that permission notes from home—no matter how much they disclaim teacher liability for injury—do not excuse a teacher from providing proper supervision. A parent cannot sign away this right of his or her child. Warn children of dangers on the trip and instruct them in rules of conduct and safety.

10. Do not send students on errands off school grounds, because they then become your agents. If they are injured or if they injure someone else, you may well be held liable. Again, the younger and less responsible the child, the greater the danger of a teacher negligence charge. To state the obvious, some children require more supervision than others.

Much of the advice is common sense, but the "reasonably prudent" teacher needs to be alert to the many requirements of "due care" and "proper supervision." The teacher who anticipates potentially dangerous conditions and actions and takes reasonable precautions—through rules, instruction, warnings, communications to superiors, and presence in assigned stations—will do a great deal in minimizing the chances of pupil injury and teacher negligence.

Commandment VIII: Thou Shalt Not Slander or Libel Your Students

This tort is much less common than negligence, but it is an area of school law that can be troublesome. One of the primary reasons for the Family Educational Rights and Privacy Act (1974) was that school records contain so much misinformation and hearsay and so many untrue (or, at least, questionable) statements about children's character, conduct, and morality that access to these records by students or their parents, in order to correct false information, seemed warranted. A

teacher's right to write anything about a student under the protection of confidential files no longer exists. Defamation of character through written communication is "libel" while such defamation in oral communication is "slander." There are ample opportunities for teachers to commit both offenses.

Teachers are advised to be careful about what they say about students (let alone other teachers!) to employers, colleges, parents, and other personnel at the school. Adhere to the following guidelines:

1. Avoid vague, derogatory terms on permanent records and recommendations. Even if you do not intend to be derogatory, value judgments about a student's character, life-style, or home life may be found defamatory in court. In one case, a North Carolina teacher was found guilty of libel when she said on a permanent record card that a student was "ruined by tobacco and whiskey." Avoid characterizing students as "crazy," "immoral," or "delinquent."

2. Say or write only what you know to be true about a student. It is safer to be an objective describer of what you have observed than to draw possibly unwarranted and untrue conclusions and judgments. The truth of a statement is strong evidence that character has not been defamed, but in some cases where the intent has been to malign and destroy the person, truth is not an adequate defense.

3. Communicate judgments of character only to those who have a right to the information. Teachers have "qualified privileged communication," which means that so long as they communicate in good faith information that they believe to be true to a person who has reason to have this information, they are protected. However, the slandering of pupils in a teachers' lounge bull session is another thing altogether.

4. If a student confides a problem to you in confidence, keep that communication confidential. A student who is on drugs, let us say, may bring you to court for defamation of character and/or invasion of privacy if you spread such information about indiscriminately. On the other hand, if a student confides that he or she has participated in a felonious crime or gives you information that makes you aware of a "clear and present" danger, you are obligated to bring such information to the appropriate authorities. Find out the proper limits of communication and the authorized channels in your school and state.

5. As a related issue, be careful about "search and seizure" procedures too. Generally, school lockers

are school property and may be searched by school officials if they have reasonable grounds to suspect that the locker has something dangerous or illegal in it. In its landmark 1985 decision in *New Jersey* v. *T.L.O.*, the Supreme Court rejected the notion that school officials had to have the police standard of "probable cause" before conducting a search; the court approved the lower standard of "reasonable suspicion." So long as both the grounds (i.e., reason) and scope are reasonable, school personnel can search student suspects. The growing concern in society about drugs and weapons in school has led courts to support school officials conducting searches for dangerous or illegal items. For example, the U.S. Supreme Court approved drug testing—requiring the "seizure" of urine samples—for high school athletes (*Vernonia*, 1995) and later for all students involved in extracurricular activities (*Earls*, 2002). Strip searches, however, are often deemed to be too intrusive, and some states prohibit this practice by way of state statutes.

Teachers need to remember that students are citizens and as such enjoy at least a limited degree of the constitutional rights that adult citizens enjoy. Not only "due process," "equal protection," and "freedom of religion" but also protection from teacher torts such as "negligence" and "defamation of character" is provided to students through our system of law. These concepts apply to all students, including those in elementary grades.

Commandment IX: Thou Shalt Not Photocopy in Violation of Copyright Law

In January, 1978, the revised copyright law went into effect and with it strict limitations on what may be photocopied by teachers for their own or classroom use under the broad concept of "fair use." The "fair use" of copyrighted material means that the use should not impair the value of the owner's copyright by diminishing the demand for that work, thereby reducing potential income for the owner.

In general, educators are given greater latitude than most other users. "Spontaneous" copying is more permissible than "systematic" copying. Students have greater latitude than teachers in copying materials.

Teachers may:

1. Make a single copy for their own research or class preparation of a chapter from a book; an article from a periodical or newspaper; a short story, poem, or essay; a chart, graph, diagram, cartoon, or picture from a book, periodical, or newspaper.
2. Make multiple copies for classroom use only (but not to exceed one copy per student) of a complete poem, if it is fewer than 250 words and printed on not more than two pages; an excerpt from a longer poem, if it is fewer than 250 words; a complete article, story, or essay, if it is fewer than 2,500 words; an excerpt from a prose work, if it is fewer than 1,000 words or 10% of the work, whichever is less; one chart, graph, diagram, drawing, cartoon, or picture per book or periodical.

However, teachers may not:

1. Make multiple copies of work for classroom use if another teacher has already copied the work for use in another class in the same school.
2. Make copies of a short poem, article, story, or essay from the same author more than once in the same term.
3. Make multiple copies from the same collective work or periodical issue more than three times a term. (The limitations in Items 1–3 do not apply to current news periodicals or newspapers.)
4. Make a copy of works to take the place of anthologies.
5. Make copies of "consumable" materials such as workbooks, exercises, answer sheets to standardized tests, and the like.

More recent technologies have led to extended applications of the "fair use" doctrine:

1. The "fair use" doctrine does not apply to copyrighted computer software programs; however, teachers may load a copyrighted program onto a classroom terminal or make a "backup" copy for archival purposes. Teachers may not make copies of such programs for student use. In 1991 the Department of Justice and Department of Education called on schools to teach the ethical use of computers to counteract illegal copying of software.
2. Schools may videotape copyrighted television programs but may keep the tape no longer than 45 days without a license. Teachers may use the tapes for instruction during the first 10 consecutive days after taping but may repeat such use only once. Commercial videotapes may not be rented to be played for instruction (or entertainment) in classrooms.
3. Scanning copyrighted material into a computer and distributing it via the Internet is a violation

of copyright law. The Internet should be viewed as a giant photocopying machine. Bills are now in Congress to restrict and punish those who misuse the Internet. We may expect to see other legal complications from this emerging technology: defamation, obscenity, threats of violence, disruption of the academic environment, and sexual harassment—to list but a few.

When teachers make brief, spontaneous, and limited copies of copyrighted materials other than consumables, they are likely to be operating within the bounds of fair use. Whenever multiple copies of copyrighted materials are made (within the guidelines above), each copy should include a notice of the copyright. Teachers should consult media specialists and others in their school about questions relating to "fair use"—whether for print, videotape, or computer materials.

Commandment X: Thou Shalt Not Be Ignorant of the Law

The axiom, "Ignorance of the law is no excuse," holds as true for teachers as anyone else. Indeed, courts are increasingly holding teachers to higher standards of competence and knowledge commensurate with their higher status as professionals. Since education is now considered a right—guaranteed to black and white, rich and poor, "normal" and disabled—the legal parameters have become ever more important to teachers in this litigious era.

How, then, can the teacher become aware of the law and its implications for the classroom? Consider the following possibilities:

1. Sign up for a course in school law. If the local college or university does not offer such a course, attempt to have one developed.
2. Ask your school system administration to focus on this topic in inservice programs.

3. Tap the resources of the local, state, and national professional organizations for pertinent speakers, programs, and materials.
4. Explore state department of education sources, since most states will have personnel and publications that deal with educational statutes and case law in your particular state.
5. Establish school (if not personal) subscriptions to professional journals. *Phi Delta Kappan, Journal of Law and Education*, and *Mental Disability Law Reporter* are only a few of the journals that regularly have columns and/or articles to keep the teacher aware of new developments in school law.
6. Make sure that your school or personal library includes such books as *Teachers and the Law* (Louis Fischer et al., 7th edition, Longman, 2007); *The Law of Schools, Students, and Teachers* (Kern and David Alexander, 7th edition, West, 2007); *Special Education Law* (Peter Latham et al., Pearson Education, Inc., 2008); and *Deskbook Encyclopedia of American School Law* (Data Research, Rosemount, Minnesota, 1996). Monthly newsletters can keep schools up-to-date in the school law area. Consider a subscription to *School Law Bulletin* (Quinlan Publishing Company, Boston) or *Legal Notes for Educators* (Data Research, Rosemount, Minnesota).

The better informed teachers are about their legal rights and responsibilities, the more likely they are to avoid the courtroom—and there are many ways to keep informed.

My Teacher's Ten Commandments are not exhaustive, nor are they etched in stone. School law, like all other law, is constantly evolving and changing so as to reflect the thinking of the times; and decisions by courts are made in the context of particular events and circumstances that are never exactly the same. But prudent professionals will be well served by these commandments if they internalize the spirit of the law as a guide to actions as teachers—in the classroom, the school, and the community.

POSTNOTE

The United States is an increasingly litigious society. Rather than settle disagreements and disputes face to face, we quickly turn over our problems to lawyers. In recent years, business owners and managers, doctors, and even lawyers have been held liable for various consequences of their work. Such situations were almost unknown to their colleagues in an earlier age.

Although relatively few teachers have been prosecuted successfully in the courts, the number of cases has dramatically increased. Therefore, it is important for teachers—both in training and in service—to be aware of areas of legal vulnerability. McDaniel, himself a former teacher, has presented an outstanding summary of the law as it affects teachers.

Discussion Questions

1. Before reading this article, were you aware that school law governed teachers' behavior as much as it does? In which of the areas described by McDaniel do you, personally, feel most vulnerable? Why?
2. As a teacher, what steps can you take to protect yourself from legal liability?
3. Which of these "commandments" has the most negative impact on the effectiveness of the average teacher? Why?

RELATED WEBSITE RESOURCES AND VIDEO CASES

 ### Web Resources:

Acceptable Use Policies: A Handbook. Available at:

http://www.pen.k12.va.us/go/VDOE/Technology/AUP/ home.shtml.

This handbook, available on the Internet, is produced by the Virginia Department of Education. It is a rich source of information on using the Internet in schools and developing acceptable use policies.

The Legal Information Institute's Supreme Court Collection. Available at:

http://supct.law.cornell.edu/supct/index.html

This website gives you access to the most important Supreme Court school-related decisions.

Video Case:

Legal and Ethical Dimensions of Teaching: Reflections from Today's Educators

In this video case, you will witness a discussion among a group of teachers, an administrator, and a lawyer about legal and ethical issues in schools. You will also hear the real concerns of practitioners seeking to do the correct thing. As you watch the clips and study the artifacts in the case, reflect upon the following questions:

1. What is your response to teacher Kate Malinowski's discussion of how she tries to model ethical behavior for both students and fellow teachers?
2. What legal questions are discussed about what students can and cannot legally say in school?

Educational Reform

Since the 1983 publication of *A Nation at Risk,* a report of President Reagan's National Commission on Excellence in Education, American schools have been in what is referred to as an "era of school reform." Both educators and private citizens are worried about our schools' ability to supply an adequately educated workforce. New jobs in the Information Age require workers to solve problems, often as team members; write and speak proficiently; and carry out higher levels of mathematical computations. Dismal research reports on the academic achievement of American students—particularly when compared with students from other countries—have sent a clear message: Something must be done.

In recent years, the primary response has been at the state level, where governors and legislatures across the country have passed laws requiring higher standards for students and teachers alike. Recently their efforts have been reinforced and financially supported by the federal No Child Left Behind Act. In addition, ways of more effectively and efficiently organizing schools have surfaced—some borrowed from industry, some from schools in other nations. Increasingly, parents, politicians, and policymakers are also examining and experimenting with ways to offer students greater educational choice. This section presents a number of ways to consider educational reform and offers an overview of some of the most important developments in reforming education.

Ten Big Effects of the No Child Left Behind Act on Public Schools

42

Jack Jennings and Diane Stark Rentner

Jack Jennings is president of the Center on Education Policy, Washington, DC, where **Diane Stark Rentner** is director of national programs.

"Ten Big Effects of the No Child Left Behind Act on Public Schools" by Jack Jennings and Diane Stark Rentner, *Phi Delta Kappan*, Vol. 88, No. 2, October 2006, pp. 110–113. Reprinted by permission of the authors.

|**F**|**O**|**C**|**U**|**S**| QUESTION

So far, what do we know about the effects of the federal No Child Left Behind program?

KEYTERMS

No Child Left Behind Act
Restructuring
Test-driven accountability

Test-driven accountability is now the norm in public schools, a result of the No Child Left Behind (NCLB) Act, which is the culmination of 15 years of standards-based reform. Many state and local officials believe that this reliance on tests is too narrow a measure of educational achievement, but NCLB has directed greater attention to low-achieving students and intensified efforts to improve persistently low-performing schools.

For the past four years, the Center on Education Policy (CEP), an independent nonprofit research and advocacy organization, has been conducting a comprehensive and continuous review of NCLB, producing the annual reports contained in the series *From the Capital to the Classroom* as well as numerous papers on specific issues related to the law.[1] Each year, the CEP gathers information for this review by surveying officials in all the state departments of education, administering a questionnaire to a nationally representative sample of school districts, conducting case studies of individual school districts and schools, and generally monitoring the implementation of this important national policy.

Ten Effects

Ten major effects of NCLB on American education are evident from this multi-year review and analysis. We describe these effects broadly, because our purpose is to assess the overall influence of this policy on public schools. The effects on particular schools and districts may be different.

1. State and district officials report that student achievement on state tests is rising, which is a cause for optimism. It's not clear, however, that students are really gaining as much as rising percentages of proficient scores would suggest. Scores on state tests in reading and mathematics that are used for NCLB purposes are going up, according to nearly three-fourths of the states and school districts, and the achievement gaps on these same tests are generally narrowing or staying the same. States and districts mostly credit their own policies as important in attaining these results, although they acknowledge that the "adequate yearly progress" (AYP) requirements of NCLB have also contributed. However, under NCLB, student achievement is equated with the proportion of students who are scoring at the proficient level on state tests, and states have adopted various approaches in their testing programs, such as the use of confidence intervals, that result in more test scores being counted as proficient. In addition, some national studies support our survey findings of increased student achievement, while others do not.

2. Schools are spending more time on reading and math, sometimes at the expense of subjects not tested. To find additional time for reading and math, the two subjects that are required to be tested under NCLB and that matter for accountability purposes, 71% of districts are reducing time spent on other subjects in elementary schools—at least to some degree. The subject most affected is social studies, while physical education is least affected. In addition, 60% of districts require a specific amount of time for reading in elementary schools. Ninety-seven percent of high-poverty districts have this requirement, compared to 55%-59% of districts with lower levels of poverty.

3. Schools are paying much more attention to the alignment of curriculum and instruction and are analyzing test score data much more closely. Changes in teaching and learning are occurring in schools that have not made AYP for two years. The most common improvements are greater alignment of curriculum and instruction with standards and assessments, more use of test data to modify instruction, use of research to inform decisions about improvement strategies, improvement in the quality and quantity of professional development for teachers, and the provision of more intensive instruction to low-achieving students.

4. Low-performing schools are undergoing makeovers rather than the most radical kinds of restructuring. More intensive changes are taking place in schools that have not made AYP for five consecutive years and thus must be "restructured" under NCLB. Greater efforts to improve curriculum, staffing, and leadership are the most common changes, but very few of these restructured schools have been taken over by the states, dissolved, or made into charter schools. Though only about 3% of all schools were in restructuring during the 2005-06 school year, the number may increase in the current year. The longer the law is in effect, the more likely it is that some schools will not make AYP for five years.

5. Schools and teachers have made considerable progress in demonstrating that teachers meet the law's academic qualifications—but many educators are skeptical this will really improve the quality of teaching. With regard to teacher quality, 88% of school districts reported that by the end of the 2005-06 school year all their teachers of core academic subjects would have met the NCLB

definition of "highly qualified." Problems persist, however, for special education teachers, high school math and science teachers, and teachers in rural areas who teach multiple subjects. Despite this general compliance with NCLB's provisions, most districts expressed skepticism that this requirement will improve the quality of teaching.

6. Students are taking a lot more tests. Students are taking many more tests as a result of NCLB. In 2002, 19 states had annual reading and mathematics tests in grades 3-8 and once in high school; by 2006, every state had such testing. In the 2007-08 school year, testing in science will be required under NCLB (although the results need not be used for NCLB's accountability requirements), leading to a further increase in the number of assessments.

7. Schools are paying much more attention to achievement gaps and the learning needs of particular groups of students. NCLB's requirement that districts and schools be responsible for improving not only the academic achievement of students as a whole but also the achievement of each subgroup of students is directing additional attention to traditionally under-performing groups of students, such as those who are from low-income families or ethnic and racial minorities, those who are learning English, or those who have a disability. States and school districts have consistently praised NCLB's requirement for the disaggregation of test data by subgroups of students, because it has shone a light on the poor performance of students who would have gone unnoticed if only general test data were considered.

For the past three years, though, states and districts have repeatedly identified as NCLB problem areas the law's testing and accountability provisions for students with disabilities and students learning English. State and district officials have voiced frustration with requirements to administer state exams to students with disabilities because, for disabled students with cognitive impairments, the state test may be inappropriate and serve no instructional purpose. Similarly, officials don't see the merit in administering an English/language arts test to students who speak little or no English. The U.S. Department of Education (ED) has made some administrative changes in those areas, but, in the view of state officials and local educators, these modifications have not been enough.

8. The percentage of schools on state "needs improvement" lists has been steady but is not growing. Schools so designated are subject to NCLB sanctions, such as being required to offer students public school choice or tutoring

services. Over the past several years, there has been a leveling off in the number of schools not making AYP for at least two years. About 10% of all schools have been labeled as "in need of improvement" for not making AYP, though these are not always the same schools every year. Urban districts, however, report greater proportions of their schools in this category than do suburban and rural districts. Earlier predictions had been that by this time there would be a very large number of U.S. schools not making AYP. A major reason for the overall stabilization in numbers of such schools is that, as already noted, test scores are increasing. Another reason is that ED has permitted states to modify their NCLB accountability systems so that it is easier for schools and districts to make AYP.

In the last four years, about 2% of eligible students each year have moved from a school not making AYP for at least two years to another school, using the "public school choice" option. Approximately 20% of eligible students in each of the last two years have taken advantage of additional tutoring (called "supplemental educational services") that must be offered to students from low-income families in schools not making AYP for at least three consecutive years. Although student participation in tutoring has been stable, the number of providers of supplemental services has grown dramatically in the last two years, with more than half of the providers now being for-profit entities. Lower proportions of urban and suburban school districts report that they are providing these services than in the past. School districts are skeptical that the choice option tutoring will lead to increases in academic achievement, though they are somewhat less skeptical about tutoring than they are about choice.

9. The federal government is playing a bigger role in education. Because of NCLB, the federal government is taking a much more active role in public elementary and secondary education than in the past. For example, ED must approve the testing programs states use to carry out NCLB as well as the account ability plans that determine the rules for how schools make AYP. In CEP surveys for the last three years, the states have judged ED's enforcement of many of the key features of the law as being strict or very strict, even while ED was granting some changes in state accountability plans. More states in 2005 than in 2004 reported that ED was strictly or very strictly enforcing the provisions for AYP, supplemental services, public school choice, and highly qualified teachers.

10. NCLB requirements have meant that state governments and school districts also have expanded roles in school operations, but often without adequate federal funds to carry out their duties. State governments are also taking a much more active role in public education, because they must carry out NCLB provisions that affect all their public schools. These state responsibilities include creating or expanding testing programs for grades 3-8 and one year of high school, setting minimum testing goals that all schools must achieve in general and also for their various groups of students, providing assistance to schools in need of improvement, certifying supplemental service providers and then evaluating the quality of their programs, and establishing criteria to determine whether current teachers meet NCLB's teacher-quality requirements. Most state departments of education do not have the capacity to carry out all these duties. Last year, 36 of the 50 states reported to CEP that they lacked sufficient staff to implement NCLB's requirements.

Local school districts must also assume more duties than before because of NCLB. More tests must be administered to students, more attention must be directed to schools in need of improvement, and judgments must be made about whether teachers of core academic subjects are highly qualified. In carrying out these responsibilities, 80% of districts have reported for two years in a row that they are absorbing costs that federal funds are not covering. Overall, federal funding for NCLB has stagnated for several years. Provisions of the law have resulted in a shift of funds so that, in school year 2005-06, two-thirds of school districts in the country received no increases or lost funds compared to the previous year.

NCLB's Future

NCLB is clearly having a major impact on American public education. There is more testing and more accountability. Greater attention is being paid to what is being taught and how it is being taught. Low-performing schools are also receiving greater attention. The qualifications of teachers are coming under greater scrutiny. Concurrently with NCLB, scores on state reading and mathematics tests have risen.

Yet some provisions of the act and of its administration are causing persistent problems. State and local officials have identified the testing and accountability requirements for students with disabilities and for students learning English as troublesome, and other requirements—such as the one to offer a choice of another public school to students in schools needing improvement—have caused administrative burdens with little evidence that they have raised student achievement.

The lack of capacity of state departments of education could undercut the effective administration of NCLB. ED cannot deal with all school districts in the country and so must rely on state agencies to assist in that task. Yet these agencies are under great strain, with little relief in sight. Local school districts must also carry out additional tasks, and they must dig into their own pockets to do so.

The U.S. Congress has begun hearings on the effects of NCLB to prepare for its reauthorization in the new Congress that will assemble in 2007. The key question is whether the strengths of this legislation can be retained while its weaknesses are addressed.

NOTES

1. For more information on NCLB, including the four annual reports and special papers, go to **www.cep-dc.org**, the website for the Center on Education Policy.

POSTNOTE

The No Child Left Behind Act was probably born from increasing frustration over American students' relative poor performance on international achievement tests. The complaints of employers that high school graduates did not possess entry-level skills for many jobs added fuel to the fire. Hearing this chorus of complaints, politicians acted. After much wrangling and compromising, the NCLB Act was created in 2001. The intentions are clear: demand high student achievement in basic skills, give the schools more resources, and evaluate the results. This article, an interim report on NCLB, suggests the jury is still out.

There has been a great deal of criticism leveled at teachers surrounding the entire NCLB effort. "Teachers simply aren't getting the job done!" Perhaps. But teaching involves more than just the teacher. What about the responsibilities of the learner? What about the parents of the learner, who are supposed to be partners in the child's education? And what about the culture—that is, the media that has made a prime goal of capturing the eyes and minds of young Americans? And the makers of videogames, iPods, and cell phones who are dedicated to keeping students' attention on their toys and off their books?

A little acknowledged reason for the poor performance of American students is that they are hooked on pleasure and their appetites for academic work wither early in their lives. "Let's see? I can do math problems or watch cartoons, play videogames, listen to hip-hop, or check out the new Steve Carell movie? Hum-m-m? Let's see?" The elephant in the room of American education is that while 15 or 20 percent of American students have the self-discipline to do their math problems and the rest of the hard work required to get an education, 80 percent [our very rough estimate] do not. We can have NCLB Two or Two Hundred and spend twice what we are presently spending on education, but it will have little impact on academic achievement scores. A key factor in academic achievement is "time on task." Students must learn to stay "on task," which for most of us takes self-discipline and sacrifice. Teachers, of course, can help. So can parents . . . and they must. Ultimately, though, students need to hit the "off" button, close down the screens, and open the books.

Discussion Questions

1. Which three of the ten effects mentioned in this article do you think are most important to improve American education?

2. Which three effects are least important?

3. In your own judgment, what changes in our schools would be most helpful to improve academic achievement? Explain your answer.

RELATED WEBSITE RESOURCES AND VIDEO CASES

 Web Resources:

Reauthorization of No Child Left Behind. Available at:

http://www.ed.gov/nclb/landing.jhtml.

This U.S. Department of Education website is the official website for current information on No Child Left Behind.

What the No Child Left Behind Law Means for Your Child. Available at:

http://www.greatschools.net/cgi-bin/showarticle/205.

Great Schools, an organization advising parents on issues of schooling, has taken a particular interest in the issues surrounding NCLB.

Video Case:

Educational Reform: Teachers Talk About No Child Left Behind

In this video case, you will hear several different teachers discussing the federal reform-oriented legislation and its impact on their school and classroom. As you watch the clips and study the artifacts in the case, reflect upon the following questions:

1. What do you think is the strongest supportive argument in favor of the NCLB legislation?
2. What reservations concerning the impact of NCLB, if any, do they offer?

What Matters Most: A Competent Teacher for Every Child

Linda Darling-Hammond

Linda Darling-Hammond is the Charles Ducommon Professor of Education at Stanford University.

"What Matters Most: A Competent Teacher for Every Child" by Linda Darling-Hammond, *Phi Delta Kappan*, November 1996. Reprinted by permission of the author.

| F | O | C | U | S | QUESTION

How can we fulfill the promise of a competent teacher for every child?

KEY TERMS

Interstate New Teacher
    Assessment and Support
    Consortium (INTASC)
National Board for Professional
    Teaching Standards (NBPTS)
National Commission on Teaching
    and America's Future
National Council for Accreditation
    of Teacher Education (NCATE)
Professional development
Professional development school
Standard

We propose an audacious goal . . . by the year 2006, America will provide all students with what should be their educational birthright: access to competent, caring, and qualified teachers.[1]

With these words, the National Commission on Teaching and America's Future summarized its challenge to the American public. After two years of intense study and discussion, the commission—a 26-member bipartisan blue-ribbon panel supported by the Rockefeller Foundation and the Carnegie Corporation of New York—concluded that the reform of elementary and secondary education depends first and foremost on restructuring its foundation, the teaching profession. The restructuring, the commission made clear, must go in two directions: toward increasing teachers' knowledge to meet the demands they face and toward redesigning schools to support high-quality teaching and learning.

The commission found a profession that has suffered from decades of neglect. By the standards of other professions and other countries, U.S. teacher education has historically been thin, uneven, and poorly financed. Teacher recruitment is distressingly ad hoc, and teacher salaries lag significantly behind those of other professions. This produces chronic shortages of qualified teachers in fields like mathematics and science and the continual hiring of large numbers of "teachers" who are unprepared for their jobs.

Furthermore, in contrast to other countries that invest most of their education dollars in well-prepared and well-supported teachers, half of the education dollars in the United States are spent on personnel and activities outside the classroom. A lack of standards for students and teachers, coupled with schools that are organized for 19th-century learning, leaves educators without an adequate foundation for constructing good teaching. Under these conditions, excellence is hard to achieve.

The commission is clear about what needs to change. No more hiring unqualified teachers on the sly. No more nods and winks at teacher education programs that fail to prepare teachers properly. No more tolerance for incompetence in the classroom. Children are compelled to attend school. Every state guarantees them equal protection under the law, and most promise them a sound education. In the face of these obligations, students have a right to competent, caring teachers who work in schools organized for success.

The commission is also clear about what needs to be done. Like the Flexner report that led to the transformation of the medical profession in 1910, this report, *What Matters Most: Teaching for America's Future,* examines successful practices within and outside the United States to describe what works. The commission concludes that children can reap the benefits of current knowledge about teaching and learning only if schools and schools of education are dramatically redesigned.

The report offers a blueprint for recruiting, preparing, supporting, and rewarding excellent educators in all of America's schools. The plan is aimed at ensuring that all schools have teachers with the knowledge and skills they need to enable all children to learn. If a caring, qualified teacher for every child is the most important ingredient in education reform, then it should no longer be the factor most frequently overlooked.

At the same time, such teachers must have available to them schools and school systems that are well designed to achieve their key academic mission: they must be focused on clear, high standards for students; organized to provide a coherent, high-quality curriculum across the grades; and designed to support teachers' collective work and learning.

We note that this challenge is accompanied by an equally great opportunity: over the next decade we will recruit and hire more than two million teachers for America's schools. More than half of the teachers who will be teaching 10 years from now will be hired during the next decade. If we can focus our energies on providing this generation of teachers with the kinds of knowledge and skills they need to help students succeed, we will have made an enormous contribution to America's future.

The Nature of the Problem

The education challenge facing the U.S. is not that its schools are not as good as they once were. It is that schools must help the vast majority of young people reach levels of skill and competence that were once thought to be within the reach of only a few.

After more than a decade of school reform, America is still a very long way from achieving its educational goals. Instead of all children coming to school ready to learn, more are living in poverty and without health care than a decade ago.[2] Graduation rates and student achievement in most subjects have remained flat or have increased only slightly.[3] Fewer than 10% of high school students can read, write, compute, and manage scientific material at the high levels required for today's "knowledge work" jobs.[4]

This distance between our stated goals and current realities is not due to lack of effort. Many initiatives have been launched in local communities with positive effects. Nonetheless, we have reached an impasse in spreading these promising efforts to the system as a whole. It is now clear that most schools and teachers cannot produce the kind of learning demanded by the new reforms—not because they do not want to, but because they do not know how, and the systems they work in do not support their efforts to do so.

The Challenge for Teaching

A more complex, knowledge-based, and multicultural society creates new expectations for teaching. To help diverse learners master more challenging content, teachers must go far beyond dispensing information, giving a test, and giving a grade. They must themselves know their subject areas deeply, and they must understand how students think, if they are to create experiences that actually work to produce learning.

Developing the kind of teaching that is needed will require much greater clarity about what students need to learn in order to succeed in the world that awaits them and what teachers need to know and do in order to help students learn it. Standards that reflect these imperatives for student learning and for teaching are largely absent in our nation today. States are just now beginning to establish standards for student learning.

Standards for teaching are equally haphazard. Although most parents might assume that teachers, like other professionals, are educated in similar ways so that they acquire common knowledge before they are admitted to practice, this is not the case. Unlike doctors, lawyers, accountants, or architects, all teachers do not have the same training. Some teachers have very high levels of skills—particularly in states that require a bachelor's degree in the discipline to be taught—along with coursework in teaching, learning, curriculum, and child development; extensive practice teaching; and a master's degree in education. Others learn little about their subject matter or about teaching, learning, and child development—particularly in states that have low requirements for licensing.

And while states have recently begun to require some form of testing for a teaching license, most licensing exams are little more than multiple-choice tests of basic skills and general knowledge, widely criticized by educators and experts as woefully inadequate to measure teaching skill.[5] Furthermore, in many states the cutoff scores are so low that there is no effective standard for entry.

These difficulties are barely known to the public. The schools' most closely held secret amounts to a great national shame: roughly one-quarter of newly hired American teachers lack the qualifications for their jobs. More than 12% of new hires enter the classroom without any formal training at all, and another 14% arrive without fully meeting state standards.

Although no state will permit a person to write wills, practice medicine, fix plumbing, or style hair without completing training and passing an examination, more than 40 states allow districts to hire teachers who have not met basic requirements. States pay more attention to the qualifications of the veterinarians treating America's pets than to those of the people educating the nation's youngsters. Consider the following facts:

- In recent years, more than 50,000 people who lack the training required for their jobs have entered teaching annually on emergency or substandard licenses.[6]
- Nearly one-fourth (23%) of all secondary teachers do not have even a minor in their main teaching field. This is true for more than 30% of mathematics teachers.[7]
- Among teachers who teach a second subject, 36% are unlicensed in that field, and 50% lack a minor in it.[8]
- Fifty-six percent of high school students taking physical science are taught by out-of-field teachers, as are 27% of those taking mathematics and 21% of those taking English.[9] The proportions are much greater in high-poverty schools and lower-track classes.
- In schools with the highest minority enrollments, students have less than a 50% chance of getting a science or mathematics teacher who holds a license and a degree in the field in which he or she teaches.[10]

In the nation's poorest schools, where hiring is most lax and teacher turnover is constant, the results are disastrous. Thousands of children are taught throughout their school careers by a parade of teachers without preparation in the fields in which they teach, inexperienced beginners with little training and no mentoring, and short-term substitutes trying to cope with constant staff disruptions.[11] It is more surprising that some of these children manage to learn than that so many fail to do so.

Current Barriers

Unequal resources and inadequate investments in teacher recruitment are major problems. Other industrialized countries fund their schools equally and make sure there are qualified teachers for all of them by underwriting teacher preparation and salaries. However, teachers in the U.S. must go into substantial debt to become prepared for a field that in most states pays less than any other occupation requiring a college degree.

This situation is not necessary or inevitable. The hiring of unprepared teachers was almost eliminated during the 1970s with scholarships and loans for college students preparing to teach, Urban Teacher Corps initiatives, and master of arts in teaching (MAT) programs, coupled with wage increases. However, the cancellation of most of these recruitment incentives in the 1980s led to renewed shortages when student enrollments started to climb once again, especially in cities. Between 1987 and 1991, the proportion of well-qualified new teachers—those entering teaching with a college major or minor and a license in their fields—actually declined from about 74% to 67%.[12]

There is no real system for recruiting, preparing, and developing America's teachers. Major problems include:

Inadequate Teacher Education Because accreditation is not required of teacher education programs, their quality varies widely, with excellent programs standing alongside shoddy ones that are allowed to operate even when they do an utterly inadequate job. Too many American universities still treat their schools of education as "cash cows" whose excess revenues are spent on the training of doctors, lawyers, accountants, and almost any students other than prospective teachers themselves.

Slipshod Recruitment Although the share of academically able young people entering teaching has been increasing, there are still too few in some parts of the country and in critical subjects like mathematics and science. Federal incentives that once existed to induce talented people into high-need fields and locations have largely been eliminated.

Haphazard Hiring and Induction School districts often lose the best candidates because of inefficient and cumbersome hiring practices, barriers to teacher mobility, and inattention to teacher qualifications. Those who do get hired are typically given the most difficult assignments and left to sink or swim, without the kind of help provided by internships and residencies in other professions. Isolated behind classroom doors with little feedback or help, as many as 30% leave in the first few years, while others learn merely to cope rather than to teach well.

Lack of Professional Development and Rewards for Knowledge and Skill In addition to the lack of support for beginning teachers, most school districts invest little in ongoing professional development for experienced teachers and spend much of these limited resources on unproductive "hit-and-run" workshops. Furthermore, most U.S. teachers have only three to five hours each week for planning. This leaves them with almost no regular time to consult together or to learn about new teaching strategies, unlike their peers in many European and Asian countries who spend between 15 and 20 hours per week working jointly on refining lessons and learning about new methods.

The teaching career does not encourage teachers to develop or use growing expertise. Evaluation and tenure decisions often lack a tangible connection to a clear vision of high-quality teaching, important skills are rarely rewarded, and—when budgets must be cut—professional development is often the first item sacrificed. Historically, the only route to advancement in teaching has been to leave the classroom for administration.

In contrast, many European and Asian countries hire a greater number of better-paid teachers, provide them with more extensive preparation, give them time to work together, and structure schools so that teachers can focus on teaching and can come to know their students well. Teachers share decision making and take on a range of professional responsibilities without leaving teaching. This is possible because these other countries invest their resources in many more classroom teachers—typically constituting 60% to 80% of staff, as compared to only 43% in the United States—and many fewer nonteaching employees.[13]

Schools Structured for Failure Today's schools are organized in ways that support neither student learning nor teacher learning well. Teachers are isolated from one another so that they cannot share knowledge or take responsibility for overall student learning. Technologies that could enable alternative uses of personnel and time are not yet readily available in schools, and few staff members are prepared to use them. Moreover, too many people and resources are allocated to jobs and activities outside of classrooms, on the sidelines rather than at the front lines of teaching and learning.

High-performance businesses are abandoning the organizational assumptions that led to this way of managing work. They are flattening hierarchies, creating teams, and training employees to take on wider responsibilities using technologies that allow them to perform their work more efficiently. Schools that have restructured their work in these ways have been able to provide more time for teachers to work together and more time for students to work closely with teachers around more clearly defined standards for learning.[14]

Goals for the Nation

To address these problems, the commission challenges the nation to embrace a set of goals that will put us on the path to serious, long-term improvements in teaching and learning for America. The commission has six goals for the year 2006.

- All children will be taught by teachers who have the knowledge, skills, and commitment to teach children well.
- All teacher education programs will meet professional standards, or they will be closed.
- All teachers will have access to high-quality professional development, and they will have regularly scheduled time for collegial work and planning.
- Both teachers and principals will be hired and retained based on their ability to meet professional standards of practice.
- Teachers' salaries will be based on their knowledge and skills.
- High-quality teaching will be the central investment of schools. Most education dollars will be spent on classroom teaching.

The Commission's Recommendations

The commission's proposals provide a vision and a blueprint for the development of a 21st-century teaching profession that can make good on the nation's educational goals. The recommendations are systemic in scope—not a recipe for more short-lived pilot and demonstration projects. They describe a new infrastructure for professional learning and an accountability system that ensures attention to standards for educators as well as for students at every level: national, state, district, school, and classroom.

The commission urges a complete overhaul in the systems of teacher preparation and professional development to ensure that they reflect current knowledge and practice. This redesign should create a continuum of teacher learning based on compatible standards that operate from recruitment and preservice education through licensing, hiring, and induction into the profession, to advanced certification and ongoing professional development.

The commission also proposes a comprehensive set of changes in school organization and management. And finally, it recommends a set of measures for ensuring that only those who are competent to teach or to lead schools are allowed to enter or to continue in the profession—a starting point for creating professional accountability. The specific recommendations are enumerated below.

1. Get Serious About Standards for Both Students and Teachers

"The Commission recommends that we renew the national promise to bring every American child up to world-class standards in core academic areas and to develop and enforce rigorous standards for teacher preparation, initial licensing, and continuing development."

With respect to student standards, the commission believes that every state should work on incorporating challenging standards for learning—such as those developed by professional bodies like the National Council of Teachers of Mathematics—into curriculum frameworks and new assessments of student performance. Implementation must go beyond the tautology that "all children can learn" to examine what they should learn and how much they need to know.

Standards should be accompanied by benchmarks of performance—from "acceptable" to "highly accomplished"—so that students and teachers know how to direct their efforts toward greater excellence.

Clearly, if students are to achieve high standards, we can expect no less from teachers and other educators. Our highest priority must be to reach agreement on what teachers should know and be able to do in order to help students succeed. Unaddressed for decades, this task has recently been completed by three professional bodies: the National Council for Accreditation of Teacher Education (NCATE), the Interstate New Teacher Assessment and Support Consortium (INTASC), and the National Board for Professional Teaching Standards (the National Board). Their combined efforts to set standards for teacher education, beginning teacher licensing, and advanced certification outline a continuum of teacher development throughout the career and offer the most powerful tools we have for reaching and rejuvenating the soul of the profession.

These standards and the assessments that grow out of them identify what it takes to be an effective teacher: subject-matter expertise coupled with an understanding of how children learn and develop; skill in using a range of teaching strategies and technologies; sensitivity and effectiveness in working with students from diverse backgrounds; the ability to work well with parents and other teachers; and assessment expertise capable of discerning how well children are doing, what they are learning, and what needs to be done next to move them along.

The standards reflect a teaching role in which the teacher is an instructional leader who orchestrates learning experiences in response to curriculum goals and student needs and who coaches students to high levels of independent performance. To advance standards, the commission recommends that states:

- establish their own professional standards boards;
- insist on professional accreditation for all schools of education;
- close inadequate schools of education;
- license teachers based on demonstrated performance, including tests of subject-matter knowledge, teaching knowledge, and teaching skill; and
- use National Board standards as the benchmark for accomplished teaching.

2. Reinvent Teacher Preparation and Professional Development

"The Commission recommends that colleges and schools work with states to redesign teacher education so that the two million teachers to be hired in the next decade are adequately prepared and so that all teachers have access to high-quality learning opportunities."

For this to occur, states, school districts, and education schools should:

- organize teacher education and professional development around standards for students and teachers;
- institute extended, graduate-level teacher preparation programs that provide yearlong internships in a professional development school;
- create and fund mentoring programs for beginning teachers, along with evaluation of teaching skills;
- create stable, high-quality sources of professional development—and then allocate 1% of state and local spending to support them, along with additional matching funds to school districts;
- organize new sources of professional development, such as teacher academies, school/university partnerships, and learning networks that transcend school boundaries; and
- make professional development an ongoing part of teachers' daily work.

If teachers are to be ready to help their students meet the new standards that are now being set for them, teacher preparation and professional development programs must consciously examine the expectations embodied in new curriculum frameworks and assessments and understand what they imply for teaching and for learning to teach. Then they must develop effective strategies for preparing teachers to teach in these much more demanding ways.

Over the past decade, many schools of education have changed their programs to incorporate new knowledge. More than 300 have developed extended programs that add a fifth (and occasionally a sixth) year to undergraduate training. These programs allow beginning teachers to complete a degree in their subject area as well as to acquire a firmer ground in teaching skills. They allow coursework to be connected to extended practice teaching in schools—ideally, in professional development schools that, like teaching hospitals in medicine, have a special mission to support research and training. Recent studies show that graduates of extended programs are rated as better-prepared and more effective teachers and are far more likely to enter and remain in teaching than are their peers from traditional four-year programs.[15]

New teachers should have support from an expert mentor during the first year of teaching. Research shows that such support improves both teacher effectiveness and retention.[16] In the system we propose, teachers will have completed initial tests of subject-matter and basic teaching knowledge before entry and will be ready to undertake the second stage—a performance assessment of teaching skills—during this first year.

Throughout their careers, teachers should have ongoing opportunities to update their skills. In addition to time for joint planning and problem solving with in-school colleagues, teachers should have access to networks, school/university partnerships, and academies where they can connect with other educators to study subject-matter teaching, new pedagogies, and school change. The benefit of these opportunities is that they offer sustained work on problems of practice that are directly connected to teachers' work and student learning.

3. Overhaul Teacher Recruitment and Put Qualified Teachers in Every Classroom

"The Commission recommends that states and school districts pursue aggressive policies to put qualified teachers in every classroom by providing financial incentives to correct shortages, streamlining hiring procedures, and reducing barriers to teacher mobility."

Although each year the U.S. produces more new teachers than it needs, shortages of qualified candidates in particular fields (e.g., mathematics and science) and particular locations (primarily inner city and rural) are chronic.

In large districts, logistics can overwhelm everything else. It is sometimes the case that central offices cannot find out about classroom vacancies, principals are left in the dark about applicants, and candidates cannot get any information at all.

Finally, it should be stressed that large pools of potential mid-career teacher entrants—former employees

of downsizing corporations, military and government retirees, and teacher aides already in the schools—are for the most part untapped.

To remedy these situations, the commission suggests the following actions:

- increase the ability of financially disadvantaged districts to pay for qualified teachers and insist that school districts hire only qualified teachers;
- redesign and streamline hiring at the district level—principally by creating a central "electronic hiring hall" for all qualified candidates and establishing cooperative relationships with universities to encourage early hiring of teachers;
- eliminate barriers to teacher mobility by promoting reciprocal interstate licensing and by working across states to develop portable pensions;
- provide incentives (including scholarships and premium pay) to recruit teachers for high-need subjects and locations; and
- develop high-quality pathways to teaching for recent graduates, mid-career changers, paraprofessionals already in the classroom, and military and government retirees.

4. Encourage and Reward Knowledge and Skill

"The Commission recommends that school districts, states, and professional associations cooperate to make teaching a true profession, with a career continuum that places teaching at the top and rewards teachers for their knowledge and skills."

Schools have few ways of encouraging outstanding teaching, supporting teachers who take on the most challenging work, or rewarding increases in knowledge and skill. Newcomers who enter teaching without adequate preparation are paid at the same levels as those who enter with highly developed skills. Novices take on exactly the same kind of work as 30-year veterans, with little differentiation based on expertise. Mediocre teachers receive the same rewards as outstanding ones. And unlicensed "teachers" are placed on the same salary schedule as licensed teachers in high-demand fields such as mathematics and science or as teachers licensed in two or more subjects.

One testament to the inability of the existing system to understand what it is doing is that it rewards experience with easier work instead of encouraging senior teachers to deal with difficult learning problems and tough learning situations. As teachers gain experience, they can look forward to teaching in more affluent schools, working with easier schedules, dealing with "better" classes, or moving out of the classroom into administration. Teachers are rarely rewarded for applying their expertise to the most challenging learning problems or major needs of the system.

To address these issues, the commission recommends that state and local education agencies:

- develop a career continuum linked to assessments and compensation systems that reward knowledge and skill (e.g., the ability to teach expertly in two or more subjects, as demonstrated by additional licenses, or the ability to pass examinations of teaching skill, such as those offered by INTASC and the National Board);
- remove incompetent teachers through peer review programs that provide necessary assistance and due process; and
- set goals and enact incentives for National Board certification in every district, with the aim of certifying 105,000 teachers during the next 10 years.

If teaching is organized as are other professions that have set consistent licensing requirements, standards of practice, and assessment methods, then advancement can be tied to professional growth and development. A career continuum that places teaching at the top and supports growing expertise should 1) recognize accomplishment, 2) anticipate that teachers will continue to teach while taking on other roles that allow them to share their knowledge, and 3) promote continued skill development related to clear standards.

Some districts, such as Cincinnati and Rochester, New York, have already begun to develop career pathways that tie evaluations to salary increments at key stages as teachers move from their *initial license* to *resident teacher* (under the supervision of a mentor) to the designation of *professional teacher.* The major decision to grant *tenure* is made after rigorous evaluation of performance (including both administrator and peer review) in the first several years of teaching. Advanced certification from the National Board for Professional Teaching Standards may qualify teachers for another salary step and/or for the position of lead teacher—a role that is awarded to those who have demonstrated high levels of competence and want to serve as mentors or consulting teachers.

One other feature of a new compensation system is key. The central importance of teaching to the mission of schools should be acknowledged by having the highest-paid professional in a school system be an experienced, National Board–certified teacher. As in other professions, roles should become less distinct. The jobs of teacher, consultant, supervisor, principal, curriculum developer, researcher, mentor, and professor should be hyphenated roles, allowing many ways

for individuals to use their talents and expertise without abandoning the core work of the profession.

5. Create Schools That Are Organized for Student and Teacher Success

"The Commission recommends that schools be restructured to become genuine learning organizations for both students and teachers: organizations that respect learning, honor teaching, and teach for understanding."

Many experts have observed that the demands of serious teaching and learning bear little relationship to the organization of the typical American school. Nothing more clearly reveals this problem than how we allocate the principal resources of school—time, money, and people. Far too many people sit in offices on the sidelines of the school's core work, managing routines rather than improving learning. Our schools are bureaucratic inheritances from the 19th century, not the kinds of learning organizations required of the 21st century.

Across the United States, the ratio of school staff to students is 1 to 9 (with "staff" including district employees, school administrators, teachers, instructional aides, guidance counselors, librarians, and support staff). However, actual class size averages about 24 and reaches 35 or more in some cities. Teaching loads for high school teachers generally exceed 100 students per day. Yet many schools have proved that it is possible to restructure adults' use of time so that more teachers and administrators actually work in the classroom, face-to-face with students on a daily basis, thus reducing class sizes while creating more time for teacher collaboration. They do this by creating teams of teachers who share students; engaging almost all adults in the school in these teaching teams, where they can share expertise directly with one another; and reducing pullouts and nonteaching jobs.

Schools must be freed from the tyrannies of time and tradition to permit more powerful student and teacher learning. To accomplish this the commission recommends that state and local boards work to:

- flatten hierarchies and reallocate resources to invest more in teachers and technology and less in nonteaching personnel;
- provide venture capital in the form of challenge grants that will promote learning linked to school improvement and will reward effective team efforts; and
- select, prepare, and retain principals who understand teaching and learning and who can lead high-performing schools.

If students have an inalienable right to be taught by a qualified teacher, teachers have a right to be supervised by a highly qualified principal. The job began as that of a "principal teacher," and this conception is ever more relevant as the focus of the school recenters on academic achievement for students. Principals should teach at least part of the time (as do most European, Asian, and private school directors), and they should be well prepared as instructional leaders, with a solid understanding of teaching and learning.

Next Steps

Developing recommendations is easy. Implementing them is hard work. The first step is to recognize that these ideas must be pursued together—as an entire tapestry that is tightly interwoven.

The second step is to build on the substantial work of education reform undertaken in the last decade. All across the country, successful programs for recruiting, educating, and mentoring new teachers have sprung up. Professional networks and teacher academies have been launched, many teacher preparation programs have been redesigned, higher standards for licensing teachers and accrediting education schools have been developed, and, of course, the National Board for Professional Teaching Standards is now fully established and beginning to define and reward accomplished teaching.

While much of what the commission proposes can and should be accomplished by reallocating resources that are currently used unproductively, there will be new costs. The estimated additional annual costs of the commission's key recommendations are as follows: scholarships for teaching recruits, $500 million; teacher education reforms, $875 million; mentoring supports and new licensing assessments, $750 million; and state funds for professional development, $2.75 billion. The total is just under $5 billion annually—less than 1% of the amount spent on the federal savings-and-loan bailout. This is not too much, we believe, to bail out our schools and to secure our future.

A Call to Action

Setting the commission's agenda in motion and carrying it to completion will demand the best of us all. The commission calls on governors and legislators to create state professional boards to govern teacher licensing standards and to issue annual report cards on the status of teaching. It asks state legislators and governors to set aside at least 1% of funds for standards-based teacher training. It urges Congress to put money behind the professional development programs it has already approved but never funded.

Moreover, the commission asks the profession to take seriously its responsibilities to children and the American future. Among other measures, the commission insists that state educators close the loopholes that permit administrators to put unqualified "teachers" in the classroom. It calls on university officials to take up the hard work of improving the preparation and skills of new and practicing teachers. It asks administrators and teachers to take on the difficult task of guaranteeing teaching competence in the classroom. And it asks local school boards and superintendents to play their vital role by streamlining hiring procedures, upgrading quality, and putting more staff and resources into the front lines of teaching.

If all of these things are accomplished, the teaching profession of the 21st century will look much different from the one we have today. Indeed, someone entering the profession might expect to advance along a continuum that unfolds much like this:

> For as long as she could remember, Elena had wanted to teach. As a peer tutor in middle school, she loved the feeling she got whenever her partner learned something new. In high school, she served as a teacher's aide for her community service project. She linked up with other students through an Internet group started by Future Educators of America.
>
> When she arrived at college she knew she wanted to prepare to teach, so she began taking courses in developmental and cognitive psychology early in her sophomore year. She chose mathematics as a major and applied in her junior year for the university's five-year course of study leading to a master of arts in teaching. After a round of interviews and a review of her record thus far, Elena was admitted into the highly selective teacher education program.
>
> The theories Elena studied in her courses came to life before her eyes as she conducted a case study of John, a 7-year-old whom she tutored in a nearby school. She was struck by John's amazing ability to build things, in contrast with his struggles to learn to read. She carried these puzzles back to her seminar and on into her other courses as she tried to understand learning.
>
> Over time, she examined other cases, some of them available on a multimedia computer system that allowed her to see videotapes of children, samples of their work, and documentation from their teachers about their learning strategies, problems, and progress. From these data, Elena and her classmates developed a concrete sense of different learning approaches. She began to think about how she could use John's strengths to create productive pathways into other areas of learning.
>
> Elena's teachers modeled the kinds of strategies she herself would be using as a teacher. Instead of lecturing

from texts, they enabled students to develop and apply knowledge in the context of real teaching situations. These frequently occurred in the professional development school (PDS) where Elena was engaged in a yearlong internship, guided by a faculty of university- and school-based teacher educators.

In the PDS, Elena was placed with a team of student teachers who worked with a team of expert veteran teachers. Her team included teachers of art, language arts, and science, as well as mathematics. They discussed learning within and across these domains in many of their assignments and constructed interdisciplinary curricula together.

Most of the school- and university-based teacher educators who made up the PDS faculty had been certified as accomplished practitioners by the National Board for Professional Teaching Standards, having completed a portfolio of evidence about their teaching along with a set of rigorous performance assessments. The faculty members created courses, internship experiences, and seminars that allowed them to integrate theory and practice, pose fundamental dilemmas of teaching, and address specific aspects of learning to teach.

Elena's classroom work included observing and documenting the learning and behavior of specific children, evaluating lessons that illustrated important concepts and strategies, tutoring and working with small groups, sitting in on family conferences, engaging in school and team planning meetings, visiting homes and community agencies to learn about their resources, planning field trips and curriculum segments, teaching lessons and short units, and ultimately taking major responsibility for the class for a month at the end of the year. This work was supplemented by readings and discussions grounded in case studies of teaching.

A team of PDS teachers videotaped all their classes over the course of the year to serve as the basis for discussions of teaching decisions and outcomes. These teachers' lesson plans, student work, audiotaped planning journals, and reflections on lessons were also available in a multimedia database. This allowed student teachers to look at practice from many angles, examine how classroom situations arose from things that had happened in the past, see how various strategies turned out, and understand a teacher's thinking about students, subjects, and curriculum goals as he or she made decisions. Because the PDS was also wired for video and computer communication with the school of education, master teachers could hold conversations with student teachers by teleconference or e-mail when on-site visits were impossible.

When Elena finished her rich, exhausting internship year, she was ready to try her hand at what she knew would be a demanding first year of teaching. She submitted her portfolio for review by the state professional standards board and sat for the examination of subject-matter and teaching knowledge that was required for an initial teaching license. She was both exhilarated and anxious when she received a job offer, but she felt she was ready to try her hand at teaching.

Elena spent that summer eagerly developing curriculum ideas for her new class. She had the benefit of advice from the district mentor teacher already assigned to work with her in her first year of teaching, and she had access to an on-line database of teaching materials developed by teachers across the country and organized around the curriculum standards of the National Council of Teachers of Mathematics, of which she had become a member.

Elena's mentor teacher worked with her and several other new middle school mathematics and science teachers throughout the year, meeting with them individually and in groups to examine their teaching and provide support. The mentors and their first-year colleagues also met in groups once a month at the PDS to discuss specific problems of practice.

Elena met weekly with the other math and science teachers in the school to discuss curriculum plans and share demonstration lessons. This extended lunch meeting occurred while her students were in a Project Adventure/physical education course that taught them teamwork and cooperation skills. She also met with the four other members of her teaching team for three hours each week while their students were at community-service placements. The team used this time to discuss cross-disciplinary teaching plans and the progress of the 80 students they shared.

In addition to these built-in opportunities for daily learning, Elena and her colleagues benefited from the study groups they had developed at their school and the professional development offerings at the local university and the Teachers Academy.

At the Teachers Academy, school- and university-based faculty members taught extended courses in areas ranging from advances in learning theory to all kinds of teaching methods, from elementary science to advanced calculus. These courses usually featured case studies and teaching demonstrations as well as follow-up work in teachers' own classrooms. The academy provided the technologies needed for multimedia conferencing, which allowed teachers to "meet" with one another across their schools and to see one another's classroom work. They could also connect to courses and study groups at the university, including a popular master's degree program that helped teachers prepare for National Board certification.

With the strength of a preparation that had helped her put theory and practice together and with the support of so many colleagues, Elena felt confident that she could succeed at her life's goal: becoming—and, as she now understood, *always* becoming—a teacher.

NOTES

1. *What Matters Most: Teaching for America's Future* (New York: National Commission on Teaching and America's Future, 1996). Copies of this report can be obtained from the National Commission on Teaching and America's Future, P.O. Box 5239, Woodbridge, VA 22194-5239. Prices, including postage and handling, are $18 for the full report, $5 for the summary report, and $20 for both reports. Orders must be prepaid.

2. *Income, Poverty, and Valuation of Non-Cash Benefits: 1993* (Washington, D.C.: U.S. Bureau of the Census, Current Population Reports, Series P-60, No. 188, 1995), Table D-5, p. D-17. See also *Current Population Survey: March 1988/March 1995* (Washington, D.C.: U.S. Bureau of the Census, 1995).

3. *National Education Goals Report: Executive Summary* (Washington, D.C.: National Education Goals Panel, 1995).

4. National Center for Education Statistics, *Report in Brief: National Assessment of Educational Progress (NAEP) 1992 Trends in Academic Progress* (Washington, D.C.: U.S. Department of Education, 1994).

5. For reviews of teacher licensing tests, see Linda Darling-Hammond, "Teaching Knowledge: How Do We Test It?," *American Educator,* Fall 1986, pp. 18–21, 46; Lee Shulman, "Knowledge and Teaching: Foundations of the New Reform," *Harvard Educational Review,* January 1987, pp. 1–22; C. J. MacMillan and Shirley Pendlebury, "The Florida Performance Measurement System: A Consideration," *Teachers College Record,* Fall 1985, pp. 67–78; Walter Haney, George Madaus, and Amelia Kreitzer, "Charms Talismanic: Testing Teachers for the Improvement of American Education," in Ernest Z. Rothkopf, ed., *Review of Research in Education,* Vol. 14 (Washington, D.C.: American Educational Research Association, 1987), pp. 169–238; and Edward H. Haertel, "New Forms of Teacher Assessment," in Gerald Grant, ed., *Review of Research in Education,* Vol. 17 (Washington, D.C.: American Educational Research Association, 1991), pp. 3–29.

6. C. Emily Feistritzer and David T. Chester, *Alternative Teacher Certification: A State-by-State Analysis* (Washington, D.C.: National Center for Education Information, 1996).

7. Marilyn M. McMillen, Sharon A. Bobbitt, and Hilda F. Lynch, "Teacher Training, Certification, and Assignment in Public Schools: 1990–91," paper presented at the annual meeting of the American Educational Research Association, New Orleans, April 1994.

8. National Center for Education Statistics, *The Condition of Education 1995* (Washington, D.C.: U.S. Department of Education, 1995), p. x.

9. Richard M. Ingersoll, *Schools and Staffing Survey: Teacher Supply, Teacher Qualifications, and Teacher Turnover, 1990–1991* (Washington, D.C.: National Center for Education Statistics, 1995), p. 28.

10. Jeannie Oakes, *Multiplying Inequalities: The Effects of Race, Social Class, and Tracking on Opportunities to Learn Mathematics and Science* (Santa Monica, Calif.: RAND Corporation, 1990).

11. *Who Will Teach Our Children?* (Sacramento: California Commission on Teaching, 1985); and Linda Darling-Hammond, "Inequality and Access to Knowledge," in James Banks, ed., *Handbook of Research on Multicultural Education* (New York: Macmillan, 1995), pp. 465–83.

12. Mary Rollefson, *Teacher Supply in the United States: Sources of Newly Hired Teachers in Public and Private Schools* (Washington, D.C.: National Center for Education Statistics, 1993).

13. *Education Indicators at a Glance* (Paris: Organisation for Economic Cooperation and Development, 1995).

14. Linda Darling-Hammond, "Beyond Bureaucracy: Restructuring Schools for High Performance," in Susan Fuhrman and Jennifer O'Day, eds., *Rewards and Reform* (San Francisco: Jossey-Bass, 1996), pp. 144–94; Linda Darling-Hammond, Jacqueline Ancess, and Beverly Falk, *Authentic Assessment in Action: Studies of Schools and Students at Work* (New York: Teachers College Press, 1995); Fred Newman and Gary Wehlage, *Successful School Restructuring: A Report to the Public and Educators by the Center on Organization and Restructuring of Schools* (Madison: Board of Regents of the University of Wisconsin System, 1995); and Ann Lieberman, ed., *The Work of Restructuring Schools: Building from the Ground Up* (New York: Teachers College Press, 1995).

15. For data on effectiveness and retention, see Michael Andrew, "The Differences Between Graduates of Four-Year and Five-Year Teacher Preparation Programs," *Journal of Teacher Education,* Vol. 41, 1990, pp. 45–51; Thomas Baker, "A Survey of Four-Year and Five-Year Program Graduates and Their Principals," *Southeastern Regional Association of Teacher Educators (SRATE) Journal,* Summer 1993, pp. 28–33; Michael Andrew and Richard L. Schwab, "Has Reform in Teacher Education Influenced Teacher Performance? An Outcome Assessment of Graduates of Eleven Teacher Education Programs," *Action in Teacher Education,* Fall 1995, pp. 43–53; Jon J. Denton and William H. Peters, "Program Assessment Report: Curriculum Evaluation of a Nontraditional Program for Certifying Teachers," unpublished report, Texas A & M University, College Station, 1988; and Hyun-Seok Shin, "Estimating Future Teacher Supply: An Application of Survival Analysis," paper presented at the annual meeting of the American Educational Research Association, New Orleans, April 1994.

16. Leslie Huling-Austin, ed., *Assisting the Beginning Teacher* (Reston, Va.: Association of Teacher Educators, 1989); Mark A. Smylie, "Redesigning Teachers' Work: Connections to the Classroom," in Linda Darling-Hammond, ed., *Review of Research in Education,* Vol. 20 (Washington, D.C.: American Educational Research Association, 1994); and Linda Darling-Hammond, ed., *Professional Development Schools: Schools for Developing a Profession* (New York: Teachers College Press, 1994).

POSTNOTE

The education of teachers has been a long-standing concern both inside and outside the profession. As Linda Darling-Hammond points out, many school reform efforts have been stymied because the teaching force was ill-equipped to put the reforms into effect. Two issues in particular have threatened efforts to reform teacher education. One is underfunding of the preparation of teachers. As a society, we spend few of our social resources on training teachers. While the preparation of most other professions has evolved out of the undergraduate years into concentrated graduate study and practical experience, most teachers still must skimp on their basic liberal education. Until we are ready to support the education of teachers at a much higher level, we will be sending teachers into schools with too much to learn on the job.

The second issue is related to the first: the underestimation of what it takes to be a teacher. If teaching is simply a matter of standing in front of students and transferring information "into them," then perhaps limited teacher education programs are adequate. However, if we want our teachers to help children engage in their own discoveries and become self-starting inquirers, we need a larger vision of the teacher to guide teacher education. The report described by Darling-Hammond offers such a vision.

Linda Darling-Hammond has become the foremost spokesperson for teacher education and the professionalization of teaching in the United States. Her work with the National Commission on Teaching and America's Future places her article among our Classic selections.

Discussion Questions

1. What are some of the developments leading to the call for reform of teacher education?
2. According to Darling-Hammond, what workplace factors are currently affecting the education of teachers?
3. In your own view, what aspect of teacher education is most in need of reform? Why?

RELATED WEBSITE RESOURCES AND VIDEO CASES

 ### Web Resources:

National Board for Professional Teaching Standards. Available at:

http://NBPTS.org.

This organization has been a leader in the reform effort in teacher education. Its website offers a large amount of information on the topic.

American Association of Colleges for Teacher Education. Available at:

http://www.AACTE.org.

This website, maintained by an organization of colleges and universities involved in the education of teachers, is a valuable source of information and provides additional links dealing with the reform of teacher education.

Video Case:

Mentoring First Year Teachers: Keys to Professional Success

In this video case, you will see new high school teacher, Dania Diaz, working with her mentor teacher, Abdi Ali. Throughout the video case, Abdi observes Dania as she interacts with students and colleagues and then helps her reflect on her teaching practice. As you watch the clips and study the artifacts in the case, reflect upon the following questions:

1. What kind of assistance would you want to have from a mentor teacher during your first year of teaching? Does Abdi provide any of that kind of assistance to Dania?
2. Dania tells us in this video case that she keeps a reflective journal. In what ways do you think a reflective journal would be helpful to you?

The Kind of Schools We Need

Elliot W. Eisner

Elliot W. Eisner is Lee Jacks Professor of Education and Art at Stanford University. A trained artist, Eisner has been for several decades the preeminent spokesperson for the arts in education. In addition, he has brought a fresh voice to the core curricular question, "What should we teach our children?" His latest book

is *Re-Imagining Schools: The Selected Works of Elliot Eisner* (World Library of Educationalists Series).

"The Kind of Schools We Need" by Elliot W. Eisner, *Phi Delta Kappan*, April 2002. Reprinted by permission of the author.

As everyone knows, there is both great interest in and great concern about the quality of education in American schools. Solutions to our perceived educational ills are often not very deep. They include mandating uniforms for students to improve their behavior; using vouchers to create a competitive climate to motivate educators to try harder; testing students each year for purposes of accountability; retaining students whose test scores have not reached specified levels; paying teachers and school administrators bonuses in relation to the measured performance of their students; and defining standards for aims, for content, for evaluation practices, and, most important, for student and teacher performance.

Ironically, what seldom gets addressed in our efforts to reform schools is the vision of education that serves as the ideal for both the practice of schooling and its outcomes. We are not clear about what we are after. Aside from literacy and numeracy, what do we want to achieve? What are our aims? What is important? What kind of educational culture do we want our children to experience? In short, what kind of schools do we need?

What we do seem to care a great deal about are standards and monitoring procedures. We want a collection of so-called best methods that will guarantee success. We want a testing program that will display the results of our efforts, often in rank-ordered league standings. We want an assessment program that allows little space for personal judgment, at least when it comes to evaluation. Personal judgment is equated with subjectivity, and we want none of that. We want to boil down teaching and evaluation practices to a scientifically grounded technology.

Whether we can ever have a scientific technology of teaching practice, given the diversity of the students we teach, is problematic. Artistry and professional judgment will, in my opinion, always be required to teach well, to make intelligent education policy, to establish personal relationships with our students, and to appraise their growth. Those of us who work in the field of education are neither bank tellers who have little discretion nor assembly line workers whose actions are largely repetitive. Each child we teach is wonderfully unique, and each requires us to use in our work that most exquisite of human capacities, the ability to make judgments in the absence of rules. Although good teaching uses routines, it is seldom routine. Good teaching

▶ 275 ◀

FOCUS QUESTION

What kind of schools do we want . . . really?

KEY TERMS

Accountability
Intrinsic motivation
Standards
Transfer of learning
Vouchers

depends on sensibility and imagination. It courts surprise. It profits from caring. In short, good teaching is an artistic affair.

But even artistry can profit from a vision of the kind of education we want to provide. The reason I believe it is important to have a vision of education is because without one we have no compass, no way of knowing which way we are headed. As a result, we succumb to the pet ideas that capture the attention of policy makers and those with pseudo-solutions to supposed problems. Is it really the case that more testing will improve teaching and learning or that uniforms will improve student behavior and build character? I have my doubts. We need a conception of what good schools provide and what students and teachers do in them. So let me share with you one man's vision of the kind of schools we need.

The kind of schools we need would provide time during the school day at least once a week for teachers to meet to discuss and share their work, their hopes, and their problems with their colleagues. It is the school, not the university, that is the real center of teacher education.

The idea that the school is the center of teacher education is built on the realization that whatever teachers become professionally, the process is not finished when they complete their teacher education program at age 21. Learning to teach well is a lifetime endeavor. The growth of understanding and skill in teaching terminates only when we do.

This fact means that we need to rethink whom the school serves. The school serves the teachers who work there as well as the students who learn there. The school needs to be designed in a way that affords opportunities to teachers to learn from one another. Such learning is so important that it should not be an addendum, relegated to an after-school time slot. Teachers, like others who do arduous work, are tired at the end of the day. Learning from our colleagues certainly deserves space and attention, and, even more important, it requires a reconceptualization of the sources of teacher development. One thing we can be sure of is that the school will be no better for the students who attend than it is for the teachers who teach there. What we do typically to improve teaching is to send teachers somewhere else to be "inserviced"—every 6,000 miles or so—usually by someone who has never seen them teach. The expectation is that what teachers are exposed to will somehow translate more or less automatically into their classrooms. Again, I have my doubts.

Teaching from a cognitive perspective requires a change in paradigm, what Thomas Kuhn once described as a "paradigm shift." Such shifts are changes in conception. From a behavioral perspective, change requires the development of those sensibilities and pedagogical techniques that make it possible to realize the conceptions and values that one defines for oneself educationally. Of course, the cognitive and the behavioral cannot truly be separated; I make the distinction here for purposes of clarity. What one conceptualizes as appropriate gives direction and guidance to what one does. And what one is able to do culminates in what one achieves. Schools ought to be places in which teachers have access to other teachers so that they have an opportunity to create the kind of supportive and educative community that culminates in higher-quality education than is currently provided.

The kind of schools we need would make teaching a professionally public process. By "professionally public" I mean that teachers would have opportunities to observe other teachers and provide feedback. No longer would isolated teachers be left to themselves to figure out what went on when they were teaching; secondary ignorance is too prevalent and too consequential to depend on one's personal reflection alone. I used the term "secondary ignorance," and I used it intentionally. I like to make a distinction between what I refer to as *primary* ignorance and *secondary* ignorance.

Primary ignorance refers to a condition in which an individual recognizes that he does not know something but also recognizes that, if he wanted to know it, he could find out. He could inquire of others, he could use the library, he could go to school. Primary ignorance is a condition that in some sense is correctable and often easily correctable.

Secondary ignorance, however, is another matter. When an individual suffers from secondary ignorance, not only does she not know something, but she does not know that she does not know. In such a situation, correcting the problem may not be possible. Secondary ignorance is as consequential for the process of parenting and for the sustenance of friendships as it is for the conduct of teaching. The way in which one remedies secondary ignorance is not through self-reflection, but through the assistance of others. Really good friends can help you understand aspects of your behavior that you might not have noticed. These observations need not be negative. It is as important to appreciate one's virtues as to become cognizant of one's weaknesses.

For this process to occur professionally, teachers need access to other teachers' classrooms. Teaching needs to be made a professionally public endeavor. The image of the teacher isolated in a classroom from 8 a.m. to 3 p.m. for five days a week, 44 weeks per year, is not the model of professional teaching practice that we need. If even world-class artists and athletes profit from feedback on their performance from those who know, so too do the rest of us. We need a conception of schooling that makes possible teachers' access to one another in helpful and constructive ways. This will require redefining what the job of teaching entails.

For most individuals who select teaching as a career, the expectation is that they will be with children exclusively, virtually all day long. But teachers also need to interact with other adults so that the secondary ignorance that I described can be ameliorated.

The model of professional life that I am suggesting will not be easy to attain. We are often quite sensitive about what we do in our own classrooms, and many of us value our privacy. Yet privacy ought not to be our highest priority. We ought to hold as our highest priority our students' well-being. And their well-being, in turn, depends on the quality of our pedagogical work. This work, I am arguing, can be enhanced with the assistance of other caring adults.

The kind of schools we need would provide opportunities for members of subject-matter departments to meet to share their work. It would recognize that different fields have different needs and that sharing within fields is a way to promote coherence for students.

Departmentalization in our schools has been a long-standing way of life. It usually begins at the middle school level and proceeds through secondary school. Teachers of mathematics have a field and a body of content that they want to help students understand; so too do teachers of the arts. These commonalities within subject-matter fields can promote a wonderful sense of esprit, a sense built on a common language to describe shared work. The strength of the educational programs in these fields can be promoted when teachers in departmentalized systems have opportunities to meet and share their work, to describe the problems they have encountered, and to discuss the achievements they have made. In short, different fields often have different needs, and these different needs can be met within the school through the colleagueship that teachers within a discipline share. The department in the middle school and in the high school provides a substantial structure for promoting the sense of community I have described.

The kind of schools we need would have principals who spend about a third of their time in classrooms, so that they know firsthand what is going on. We often conceive of the role of the school principal not only as that of a skilled administrator but also as that of an educational leader. At least one of the meanings

of educational leadership is to work with a staff in a way that will make leadership unnecessary. The aim of leadership in an educational institution is to work itself out of a job.

What this approach requires, at a minimum, is an understanding of the conditions of the school and the characteristics of the classrooms in which teachers work. To understand the school and the classroom requires that school administrators leave their offices and spend at least a third of their time in teachers' classrooms. In the business community this is called "supervision by walking around."

The term supervision is a bit too supervisory for my taste. I am not sure that school administrators have "super" vision. But they should have a grasp of what happens in their schools—substantively, as well as administratively. Administrators can be in a position to recognize different kinds of talents among faculty members; they can help initiate activities and support the initiatives of teachers. They can develop an intimacy that will enable them to promote and develop the leadership potential of teachers. Thus, paradoxically, the principal as leader is most successful when he or she no longer leads but promotes the initiative and leadership of others.

The kind of schools we need would use videotaped teaching episodes to refine teachers' ability to take the practice of teaching apart—not in the negative sense, but as a way of enlarging our understanding of a complex and subtle process. No one denies that teaching is a subtle and complex art. At least it is an art when it is done well. To teach really well, it is necessary to reflect on the processes of one's own teaching and on the teaching practices of others. Our ability to perform is related, as I suggested above, to our understanding of the relationship between teaching and learning. This relationship can be illuminated through the analysis of videotaped episodes of teaching practices. Just what is a teacher up to when he or she teaches? What are the consequences? What are the compromises and trade-offs that exist in virtually any context? What institutional or organizational pressures in a school must teachers contend with? How does a teacher insert herself into her teaching? What does his body language express?

Questions such as these can be profitably addressed through the analysis of videotapes. Indeed, the collaborative analysis of a teaching episode can provide a very rich resource that can illuminate differences in perspective, in educational values, and in the meanings being conveyed. This is all to the good. Teaching is not reducible to a single frame. From my perspective, the use of such tapes not only can make our understanding of teaching more appropriately complex, but it can also refine our ability to see and interpret the process of teaching. And the more subtle perspective on teaching that such analysis creates can only enhance the quality of what we have to say to one another about the kind of work we do.

The kind of schools we need would be staffed by teachers who are interested in the questions students ask after a unit of study as they are in the answers students give. On the whole, schools are highly answer-oriented. Teachers have the questions, and students are to have the answers. Even with a problem-solving approach, the focus of attention is on the student's ability to solve a problem that someone else has posed. Yet the most intellectually demanding tasks lie not so much in solving problems as in posing questions. The framing of what we might oxymoronically call the "telling question" is what we ought to care much more about.

Once students come to deal with real situations in life, they will find that few of them provide defined problems. On the contrary, the primary task is often to define a problem so that one can get on with its solution. And to define a problem, one needs to be able to raise a question.

What would it mean to students if they were asked to raise questions coming out of a unit of study? What kinds of questions would they raise? How incisive and imaginative would these questions be? Would the students who do well in formulating questions be the same ones who do well when asked to converge upon a correct answer?

What I am getting at is the importance of developing an intellectual context designed to promote student growth. That context must surely give students an opportunity to pose questions and to entertain alternative perspectives on what they study. The last thing we want in an intellectually liberating environment is a closed set of attitudes and fealty to a single set of correct answers.

The kind of schools we need would not hold as an ideal that all students get to the same destinations at the same time. They would embrace the idea that good schools increase the variance in student performance and at the same time escalate the mean.

To talk about the idea that schools should increase individual differences rather than reduce them may at first seem counterintuitive and perhaps even anti-democratic. Don't we want all students to do the same? If we have a set of goals, don't we want all students to achieve them? To both of those questions I would give a qualified yes and no.

Individuals come into the world with different aptitudes, and, over the course of their lives, they develop different interests and proclivities. In an ideal approach to educational practice—say, one in which teaching practices were ideally designed to suit each youngster—each youngster would learn at an ideal rate. Students whose aptitudes were in math would travel farther and faster in that subject than students who had neither interest nor aptitude in math but who, for example, might have greater aptitude in language or in the visual arts. In those two fields, students would travel faster and farther than those with math aptitudes but with low interests or proclivities in language or the arts. Over time, the cumulative gap between students would grow. Students would travel at their own optimal rates, and some would go faster than others in different areas of work.

What one would have at the end of the school year is wide differences in students' performance. At the same time, since each program is ideally suited to each youngster, the mean for all students in all of the areas in which they worked would be higher than it would be in a more typical program of instruction.

Such a conception of the aims of education would actually be instrumental to the creation of a rich culture. It is through our realized aptitudes that we can contribute to the lives of others and realize our own potential. It is in the symbiotic relationships among us that we come to nurture one another, to provide for others what they cannot provide—at least, not as well—for themselves, and to secure from others the gifts they have to offer that we cannot create—at least, not as well—for ourselves.

The idea that getting everyone to the same place is a virtue really represents a limitation on our aspirations. It does not serve democratic purposes to treat everybody identically or to expect everyone to arrive at the same destination at the same time. Some students need to go farther in one direction and others need to go farther in a different direction because that's where their aptitudes lie, that's where their interests are, and that's where their proclivities lead them.

The British philosopher and humanist Sir Herbert Read once said that there were two principles to guide education.[1] One was to help children become who they are not; the other was to help children become who they are. The former dominates in fascist countries, he believed, where the image defined by the state becomes the model to which children must adapt. The fascist view is to help children become who they are not. Read believed that education was a process of self-actualization and that in a truly educational environment children would come to realize their latent potentials. In this age of high technology and highly monitored systems and standards, I believe that Read's views bear reflection.

The kind of schools we need would take seriously the idea that a child's personal signature, his or her distinctive way of learning and creating, is something to be preserved and developed. We are not in the shoe manufacturing business. By saying that we are not in the shoe manufacturing business, I mean that we are not in the business of producing identical products. On an assembly line, one seeks predictability, even certainty, in the outcomes. What one wants on both assembly lines and airline flights are uneventful events. No surprises.

In education, surprise ought to be seen not as a limitation but as the mark of creative work. Surprise breeds freshness and discovery. We ought to be creating conditions in school that enable students to pursue what is distinctive about themselves; we ought to want them to retain their personal signatures, their particular ways of seeing things.

Of course, their ways of seeing things need to be enhanced and enriched, and the task of teaching is, in part, to transmit the culture while simultaneously cultivating those forms of seeing, thinking, and feeling that make it possible for personal idiosyncrasies to be developed. In the process, we will discover both who children are and what their capabilities are.

The kind of schools we need would recognize that different forms of representation develop different forms of thinking, convey different kinds of meaning, and make possible different qualities of life. Literacy should not be restricted to decoding text and number.

Normally the term literacy refers to the ability to read, and numeracy, the ability to compute. However, I want to recast the meaning of literacy so that it refers to the process of encoding or decoding meaning in whatever forms are used in the culture to express or convey meaning. With this conception in mind and with the realization that humans throughout history have employed a variety of forms to express meaning, literacy becomes a process through which meanings are made. Meanings, of course, are made in the visual arts, in music, in dance, in poetry, in literature, as well as in physics, in mathematics, and in history. The best way to ensure that we will graduate semiliterate students from our schools is to make sure that they have few (or ineffective) opportunities to acquire the multiple forms of literacy that make multiple forms of meaning possible.

That meanings vary with the forms in which they are cast is apparent in the fact that, when we bury and when we marry, we appeal to poetry and music to express what we often cannot express literally. Humans have invented an array of means through which meaning is construed. I use the word *construe* because meaning making is a construal, both with respect to the perception of forms made by others and with respect to the forms that we make ourselves.

We tend to think that the act of reading a story or reading a poem is a process of decoding. And it is. But it is also a process of encoding. The individual reading a story must *make* sense of the story; he or she must produce meanings from the marks on the page. The mind must be constructive, it must be active, and the task of teaching is to facilitate effective mental action so that the work encountered becomes meaningful.

The kind of schools we need would recognize that the most important forms of learning are those that students know how to use outside of school, not just inside school. And the teachers in such schools would consistently try to help students see the connections between the two. The transfer of learning cannot be assumed; it needs to be taught.

The idea that transfer needs to be taught is not a new one. I reiterate an old idea here because it is absolutely fundamental to effective education. If all that students get out of what they learn in history or math or science are ideas they rapidly forget and cannot employ outside of the context of a classroom, then education is a casualty. The point of learning anything in school is not primarily to enable one to do well in school—although most parents and students believe this to be the case—it is to enable one to do well in life. The point of learning something in school is to enrich life outside of school and to acquire the skills and ideas that will enable one to produce the questions and perform the activities that one's outside life will require.

In the field of education, we have yet to begin to conceive of educational evaluation in these terms. But these are precisely the terms that we need to employ if what we do in school is to be more than mere jumping through hoops.

The kind of schools we need would take seriously the idea that, with regard to learning, the joy is in the journey. Intrinsic motivation counts the most because what students do when they can do what they want to do is what really matters. It is here that the educational process most closely exemplifies the lived experience found in the arts. We ought to stop reinforcing our students' lust for "point accumulation."

Point accumulation is *not* an educational aim. Educational aims have to do with matters of enlightenment, matters of developing abilities, matters of aesthetic experience. What we ought to be focusing our attention on is the creation of conditions in our classrooms and in our schools that make the process of education a process that students wish to pursue. The joy must be in the journey. It is the quality of the chase that matters most.

Alfred North Whitehead once commented that most people believe that a scientist inquires in order to know. Just the opposite is true, he said. Scientists know in order to inquire. What Whitehead was getting at was the idea that the vitality, challenge, and engagement that scientists find in their work is what matters most to them. At its best, this kind of satisfaction is an aesthetic experience.

We don't talk much about the aesthetic satisfactions of teaching and learning, but those of us who have taught for more than a few years know full well the feeling we experience when things go really well in our teaching. When things go really well for students, they experience similar feelings.

We ought not to marginalize the aesthetic in our understanding of what learning is about because, in the end, it is the only form of satisfaction that is likely to predict the uses of the knowledge, skills, and perspectives that students acquire in school. There is a huge difference between what a child *can* do and what a child *will* do. A child who learns to read but has no appetite for reading is not really succeeding in school. We want to promote that appetite for learning, and it ought to be built on the satisfactions that students receive in our classrooms. It is the aesthetic that represents the highest forms of intellectual achievement, and it is the aesthetic that provides the natural high and contributes the energy we need to want to pursue an activity again and again and again.

The kind of schools we need would encourage deep conversation in classrooms. They would help students learn how to participate in that complex and subtle art, an art that requires learning how to listen as well as how to speak. Good conversation is an activity for which our voyeuristic interest in talk shows offers no substitute.

It may seem odd recommending that deep conversation be promoted in our classrooms. Conversation has a kind of shallow ring, as if it were something you do when you don't have anything really important to do. Yet conversation, when it goes well, when the participants really listen to each other, is like an acquired taste, an acquired skill. It does not take much in the way of resources, but, ironically, it is among the rarest features of classroom life. It is also, I believe, among the rare features of our personal life, and that is why we often tune in to Oprah Winfrey, Larry King, and other talk show hosts to participate vicariously in conversation. Even when the conversations are not all that deep, they remain interesting.

How do we help students learn to become listeners? How do we enable them to understand that comments and questions need to flow from what preceded and not simply express whatever happens to be on one's mind at the time? How do we enable students to become more like the members of a jazz quartet, whose interplay good conversation sometimes seems to emulate? Conversation is akin to deliberation, a process that searches for possible answers and explores blind alleys as well as open freeways. How do we create in our classrooms a practice that, when done well, can be a model of intellectual activity?

Of course, all of us need to learn to engage in deep conversation. In many ways, we need to model what we expect our students to learn. But I am convinced that conversation about ideas that matter to students and teachers and that occupy a central place in our curriculum can be a powerful means of converting the academic institutions we call schools into intellectual institutions. Such a transformation would represent a paradigmatic shift in the culture of schooling.

The kind of schools we need would help students gradually assume increased responsibility for framing their own goals and learning how to achieve them. We want students eventually to become the architects of their own education. The long-term aim of teaching is to make itself unnecessary.

Saying that the long-term aim of teaching is to render itself unnecessary is simply to make explicit what I hope readers have gleaned from my arguments here. Helping students learn how to formulate their own goals is a way to enable them to secure their freedom. Helping them learn how to plan and execute their lives in relation to those goals is a way of developing their autonomy. Plato once defined a slave as someone who executes the purposes of another. Over the grade levels, we have conceived of teaching as setting problems that students solve. Only rarely have we created the conditions through which students set the problems that they wish to pursue. Yet this is precisely what they will need to be able to do once they leave the protected sphere of the school.

It is interesting to me that, in discourse about school reform and the relation of goals and standards to curriculum reform, the teacher is given the freedom to formulate means but not to decide upon ends.

The prevailing view is that professional judgment pertains to matters of technique, rather than to matters of goals.

I believe this conception of school reform is short-sighted. If our students were simply inert entities, something like copper or plastic, it would be possible in principle to formulate methods of acting on them that would yield uniform responses. A thousand pounds of pressure by a punch press on a steel plate has a given effect. But our students are not uniform, they are not steel, and they do not respond in the same way to pressures of various kinds. Thus teachers will always need the discretionary space to determine not only matters of means but also matters of ends. And we want students, gradually to be sure, to have the opportunity to formulate ends as well. Withholding such opportunities is a form of de-skilling for both teachers and students.

The kind of schools we need would make it possible for students who have particular interests to pursue those interests in depth and, at the same time, to work on public service projects that contribute to something larger than their own immediate interests. This twofold aim—the ability to serve the self through intensive study and the desire and ability to provide a public service—is like the head and tail of a coin. Both elements need to be a part of our educational agenda.

The long-term aim of education may be said to be to learn how to engage in personally satisfying activities that are at the same time socially constructive. Students need to learn that there are people who need services and that they, the students themselves, can contribute to meeting these people's needs. Service learning is a move in the right direction. It affords adolescents an opportunity to do something whose scope is beyond themselves. The result, at least potentially, is the development of an attitude that schools would do well to foster. That, too, should be a part of our curricular agenda.

The kind of schools we need would treat the idea of "public education" as meaning not only the education of the public inside schools, but also the education of the public outside schools. The school's faculty will find it difficult to proceed farther or faster than the community will allow. Our task, in part, is to nurture public conversation in order to create a collective vision of education.

Realistically speaking, our responsibilities as educators extend beyond the confines of our classrooms and even beyond the walls of our schools. We also have responsibilities to our communities. We need desperately to create educational forums for members of the community in which the purposes and processes of education can be discussed, debated, and deliberated and from which consensus can be arrived at with regard to our broad mission as an educational institution. Parents need to know why, for example, inquiry-oriented methods matter, why rote learning may not be in the best long-term interest of their children, why problem-centered activities are important, and why the ability to frame telling questions is crucial.

Most parents and even many teachers have a yellow-school-bus image when it comes to conceiving what teaching, learning, and schooling should look like. The yellow school bus is a metaphor for the model of education that they encountered and that, all too often, they wish to replicate in the 21st century. Our schools, as they are now designed, often tacitly encourage the re-creation of such a model. Yet we know there is a better way. That better way ought to be a part of the agenda the community discusses with teachers and school administrators. Principals and school superintendents ought to perform a leadership role in deepening that community conversation. Without having such a conversation, it will be very difficult to create the kind of schools we need.

I acknowledge that the features of schooling that I have described will not be easy to attain, but they are important. We get so caught up in debating whether or not we should extend the school year that we seem to forget to consider what should go into that year. We seem to forget about our vision of education and the kind of educational practices that will move the school in the direction we value. Too often we find ourselves implementing policies that we do not value. Those of us in education need to take a stand and to serve as public advocates for our students. Who speaks for our students? We need to.

Some of the features I have described—perhaps all of them—may not be ones that you yourself cherish. Fine. That makes conversation possible. And so I invite you to begin that conversation in your school, so that out of the collective wisdom of each of our communities can come a vision of education that our children deserve and, through that vision, the creation of the kind of schools that our children need.

NOTE

1. Herbert Read, *Education Through Art* (New York: Pantheon Books, 1944).

POSTNOTE

Elliot Eisner's contributions to education span many areas, including art education, curriculum development, qualitative research, and educational connoisseurship. His renaissance qualities earn him a place among our Classic authors.

As young graduate students, both editors of *Kaleidoscope* were privileged to have Elliot Eisner (at the time, a young professor) as a teacher. It was at the height of interest in B. F. Skinner's behaviorism and during the applications of programmed instruction and behavioral objectives to American classrooms. There was a heady belief throughout the educational community that this new movement would soon transform our schools. Professor Eisner would have little of it. His was one of the few voices at that time to raise questions and urge caution.

Today we are in the midst of a new national movement that many believe will revolutionize our schools and lead to much higher levels of academic achievement among our students. As he has throughout his career, Eisner is again asking the hard questions, this time about standards and the effects of the tests we use to gauge our successes and failures to reach those standards. Here, he asks us to step back and think hard about what we really desire. "What kind of schools do we *really* need?"

Discussion Questions

1. In what specific ways has Eisner's article challenged you? Or do you agree with everything he seems to suggest?
2. What are the challenges and hurdles to overcome to achieve the kind of schools that Eisner suggests?
3. What are the most positive suggestions for school improvement that the author makes?

RELATED WEBSITE RESOURCES

 ### Web Resources:

Association for Supervision and Curriculum Development. Available at:

http://www.ascd.org.

This extensive website, maintained by the leading curriculum organization in the country, has extensive materials and resources for educators.

Curriculum and Instruction, Thomas B. Fordham Institute. Available at:

http://www.edexcellence.net

This website, sponsored by the reform-minded Fordham Institute, is a leading source of criticism of what is currently taught in our schools.

45

Class and the Classroom

Richard Rothstein

Richard Rothstein is a research associate of the Economic Policy Institute and a visiting lecturer at Teachers College, Columbia University. From 1999 to 2002 he was the national education columnist of *The New York Times*.

|F|O|C|U|S| QUESTION

For over two decades, Americans from the White House to the teachers' lounge have been deeply committed to major improvements in how our schools serve the poor. What is it, then, that keeps real reform from taking place?

KEY TERMS

Conversation gap
Health and housing gap
Reading gap
Role model gap

The achievement gap between poor and middle-class black and white children is widely recognized as our most important educational challenge. But we prevent ourselves from solving it because of a commonplace belief that poverty and race can't "cause" low achievement and that therefore schools must be failing to teach disadvantaged children adequately. After all, we see many highly successful students from lower-class backgrounds. Their success seems to prove that social class cannot be what impedes most disadvantaged students.

Yet the success of some lower-class students proves nothing about the power of schools to close the achievement gap. In every social group, there are low achievers and high achievers alike. On average, the achievement of low-income students is below the average achievement of middle-class students, but there are always some middle-class students who achieve below typical low-income levels. Similarly, some low-income students achieve above typical middle-class levels. Demography is not destiny, but students' family characteristics are a powerful influence on their relative average achievement.

Widely repeated accounts of schools that somehow elicit consistently high achievement from lower-class children almost always turn out, upon examination, to be flawed. In some cases, these "schools that beat the odds" are highly selective, enrolling only the most able or most motivated lower-class children. In other cases, they are not truly lower-class schools—for example, a school enrolling children who qualify for subsidized lunches because their parents are graduate students living on low stipends. In other cases, such schools define high achievement at such a low level that all students can reach it, despite big gaps that remain at more meaningful levels.

It seems plausible that if *some* children can defy the demographic odds, *all* children can, but that belief reflects a reasoning whose naiveté we easily recognize in other policy areas. In human affairs where multiple causation is typical, causes are not disproved by exceptions. Tobacco firms once claimed that smoking does not cause cancer because some people smoke without getting cancer. We now consider such reasoning specious. We do not suggest that alcoholism does not cause child or spousal abuse because not all alcoholics are abusers. We understand that because no single cause is rigidly deterministic, some people can smoke or drink to excess without harm. But we also understand that, on average, these behaviors are dangerous. Yet despite such understanding, quite sophisticated people often proclaim that the success of some poor children proves that social disadvantage does not cause low achievement.

Partly, our confusion stems from failing to examine the concrete ways that social class actually affects learning. Describing these may help to make their influence more obvious—and may make it more obvious why the achievement gap can be substantially narrowed only when school improvement is combined with social and economic reform.

The Reading Gap

Consider how parents of different social classes tend to raise children. Young children of educated parents are read to more consistently and are encouraged to read more to themselves when they are older. Most children whose parents have college degrees are read to daily before they begin kindergarten, but few children whose parents have only a high school diploma or less benefit from daily reading. And, white children are more likely than black children to be read to in their prekindergarten years.

A 5-year-old who enters school recognizing some words and who has turned the pages of many stories will be easier to teach than one who has rarely held a book. The second child can be taught, but with equally high expectations and effective teaching, the first will be more likely to pass an age-appropriate reading test than the second. So the achievement gap begins.

If a society with such differences wants all children, irrespective of social class, to have the same chance to achieve academic goals, it should find ways to help lower-class children enter school having the same familiarity with books as middle-class children have. This requires rethinking the institutional settings in which we provide early childhood care, beginning in infancy.

Some people acknowledge the impact of such differences but find it hard to accept that good schools should have so difficult a time overcoming them. This would be easier to understand if Americans had a broader international perspective on education. Class backgrounds influence *relative* achievement everywhere. The inability of schools to overcome the disadvantage of less-literate homes is not a peculiar American failure but a universal reality. The number of books in students' homes, for example, consistently predicts their test scores in almost every country. Turkish immigrant students suffer from an achievement gap in Germany, as do Algerians in France, as do Caribbean, African, Pakistani, and Bangladeshi pupils in Great Britain, and as do Okinawans and low-caste Buraku in Japan.

An international reading survey of 15-year-olds, conducted in 2000, found a strong relationship in almost every nation between parental occupation and student literacy. The gap between the literacy of children of the highest-status workers (such as doctors, professors, and lawyers) and the lowest-status workers (such as waiters and waitresses, taxi drivers, and mechanics) was even greater in Germany and the United Kingdom than it was in the United States.

After reviewing these results, a U.S. Department of Education summary concluded that "most participating countries do not differ significantly from the United States in terms of the strength of the relationship between socioeconomic status and literacy in any subject." Remarkably, the department published this conclusion at the same time that it was guiding a bill through Congress—the No Child Left Behind Act—that demanded every school in the nation abolish social class differences in achievement within 12 years.

Urging less-educated parents to read to children can't fully compensate for differences in school readiness. Children who see parents read to solve their own problems or for entertainment are more likely to want to read themselves. Parents who bring reading material home from work demonstrate by example to children that reading is not a segmented burden but a seamless activity that bridges work and leisure. Parents who read to children but don't read for themselves send a different message.

How parents read to children is as important as whether they do, and an extensive literature confirms that more educated parents read aloud differently. When working-class parents read aloud, they are more likely to tell children to pay attention without interruptions or to sound out words or name letters. When they ask children about a story, the questions are more likely to be factual, asking for names of objects or memory of events.

Parents who are more literate are more likely to ask questions that are creative, interpretive, or connective, such as "What do you think will happen next?" "Does that remind you of what we did yesterday?" Middle-class parents are more likely to read aloud to have fun, to start conversations, or as an entree to the world outside. Their children learn that reading is enjoyable and are more motivated to read in school.

The Conversation Gap

There are stark class differences not only in how parents read but in how they converse. Explaining events in the broader world to children at the dinner table, for example, may have as much of an influence on test scores as early reading itself. Through such conversations, children develop vocabularies and become familiar with contexts for reading in school. Educated parents are more likely to engage in such talk and to begin it with infants and toddlers, conducting pretend conversations long before infants can understand the language.

Typically, middle-class parents ask infants about their needs, then provide answers for the children. ("Are you ready for a nap now? Yes, you are, aren't you?") Instructions are more likely to be given indirectly: "You don't want to make so much noise, do you?" This kind of instruction is really an invitation for a child to work through the reasoning behind an order and to internalize it. Middle-class parents implicitly begin academic instruction for infants with such indirect guidance.

Yet such instruction is quite different from what policy-makers nowadays consider "academic" for young children: explicit training in letter and number recognition, letter-sound correspondence, and so on. Such drill in basic skills can be helpful but is unlikely to close the social class gap in learning.

Soon after middle-class children become verbal, their parents typically draw them into adult conversations so the children can practice expressing their own opinions. Being included in adult conversations this early develops a sense of entitlement in children; they feel comfortable addressing adults as equals and without deference. Children who ask for reasons, rather than accepting assertions on adult authority, develop intellectual skills upon which later academic success in school will rely. Certainly, some lower-class children have such skills and some middle-class children lack them. But, on average, a sense of entitlement is based on one's social class.

Parents whose professional occupations entail authority and responsibility typically believe more strongly that they can affect their environments and solve problems. At work, they explore alternatives and negotiate compromises. They naturally express these personality traits at home when they design activities in which children figure out solutions for themselves. Even the youngest middle-class children practice traits that make academic success more likely when they negotiate what to wear or to eat. When middle-class parents give orders, the parents are more likely to explain why the rules are reasonable.

But parents whose jobs entail following orders or doing routine tasks show less sense of efficacy. They are less likely to encourage their children to negotiate over clothing or food and more likely to instruct them by giving directions without extended discussion. Following orders, after all, is how they themselves behave at work. Their children are also more likely to be fatalistic about obstacles they face, in and out of school.

Middle-class children's self-assurance is enhanced in after-school activities that sometimes require large fees for enrollment and almost always require parents to have enough free time and resources to provide transportation. Organized sports, music, drama, and dance programs build self-confidence and discipline in middle-class children. Lower-class parents find the fees for such activities more daunting, and transportation may also be more of a problem. Organized athletic and artistic activities may not be available in their neighborhoods, so lower-class children's sports are more informal and less confidence-building, with less opportunity to learn teamwork and self-discipline. For children with greater self-confidence, unfamiliar school challenges can be exciting. These children, who are more likely to be from middle-class homes, are more likely to succeed than those who are less self-confident.

Homework exacerbates academic differences between these two groups of children because middle-class parents are more likely to help with homework. Yet homework would increase the achievement gap even if all parents were able to assist. Parents from different social classes supervise homework differently. Consistent with overall patterns of language use, middle-class parents—especially those whose own occupational habits require problem solving—are more likely to assist by posing questions that break large problems down into smaller ones and that help children figure out correct answers. Lower-class parents are more likely to guide children with direct instructions. Children from both classes may go to school with completed homework, but middle-class children are more likely to gain in intellectual power from the exercise than lower-class children.

Twenty years ago, Betty Hart and Todd Risley, two researchers from the University of Kansas, visited families from different social classes to monitor the conversations between parents and toddlers. Hart and Risley found that, on average, professional parents spoke more than 2,000 words per hour to their children, working-class parents spoke about 1,300, and welfare mothers spoke about 600. So by age 3, the children of professionals had vocabularies that were nearly 50 percent greater than those of working-class children and twice as large as those of welfare children.

Deficits like these cannot be made up by schools alone, no matter how high the teachers' expectations.

For all children to achieve the same goals, the less advantaged would have to enter school with verbal fluency that is similar to the fluency of middle-class children. The Kansas researchers also tracked how often parents verbally encouraged children's behavior and how often they reprimanded their children. Toddlers of professionals got an average of six encouragements per reprimand. Working-class children had two. For welfare children, the ratio was reversed—an average of one encouragement for two reprimands. Children whose initiative was encouraged from a very early age are more likely, on average, to take responsibility for their own learning.

The Role Model Gap

Social class differences in role modeling also make an achievement gap almost inevitable. Not surprisingly, middle-class professional parents tend to associate with, and be friends with, similarly educated professionals. Working-class parents have fewer professional friends. If parents and their friends perform jobs requiring little academic skill, their children's images of their own futures are influenced. On average, these children must struggle harder to motivate themselves to achieve than children who assume, on the basis of their parents' social circle, that the only roles are doctor, lawyer, teacher, social worker, manager, administrator, or businessperson.

Even disadvantaged children usually say they plan to attend college. College has become such a broad rhetorical goal that black eighth-graders tell surveyors they expect to earn college degrees as often as white eighth-graders do. But despite these intentions, fewer black than white eighth-graders actually graduate from high school four years later; fewer enroll in college the following year; and fewer still persist to get bachelor's degrees.

This discrepancy is not due simply to the cost of college. A bigger reason is that while disadvantaged students *say* they plan to go to college, they don't feel as much parental, community, or peer pressure to take the courses or to get the grades they need to become more attractive to college admission offices. Lower-class parents say they expect children to get good grades, but they are less likely to enforce these expectations, for example with rewards or punishments. Teachers and counselors can stress doing well in school to lower-class children, but such lessons compete with children's own self-images, formed early in life and reinforced daily at home.

As John Ogbu and others have noted, a culture of underachievement may help explain why even middle-class black children often don't do as well in school as white children from seemingly similar socioeconomic backgrounds. On average, middle-class black students don't study as hard as white middle-class students and blacks are more disruptive in class than whites from similar income strata.

This culture of underachievement is easier to understand than to cure. Throughout American history, many black students who excelled in school were not rewarded for that effort in the labor market. Many black college graduates could find work only as servants or Pullman car porters or, in white-collar fields, as assistants to less-qualified whites. Many Americans believe that these practices have disappeared and that blacks and whites with similar test scores now have similar earnings and occupational status. But labor market discrimination continues to be a significant obstacle—especially for black males with high school educations.

Evidence for this comes from employment discrimination cases, such as the prominent 1996 case in which Texaco settled for a payment of $176 million to black employees after taped conversations of executives revealed pervasive racist attitudes, presumably not restricted to executives of this corporation alone. Other evidence comes from studies that find black workers with darker complexions have less success in the labor market than those with identical education, age, and criminal records but lighter complexions.

Still more evidence comes from studies in which blacks and whites with similar qualifications are sent to apply for job vacancies; the whites are typically more successful than the blacks. In one recent study where young, well-groomed, and articulate black and white college graduates, posing as high school graduates with identical qualifications, submitted applications for entry-level jobs, the applications of whites with criminal records got positive responses more often than the applications of blacks with no criminal records.

So the expectation of black students that their academic efforts will be less rewarded than the efforts of their white peers is rational for the majority of black students who do not expect to complete college. Some will reduce their academic efforts as a result. We can say that they should not do so and, instead, should redouble their efforts in response to the greater obstacles they face. But as long as racial discrimination persists, the average achievement of black students will be lower than the average achievement of whites, simply because many blacks (especially males) who see that academic effort has less of a payoff will respond rationally by reducing their effort.

The Health and Housing Gaps

Despite these big race and social class differences in child rearing, role modeling, labor market experiences, and cultural characteristics, the lower achievement of lower-class students is not caused by these differences alone. Just as important are differences in the actual social and economic conditions of children.

Overall, lower-income children are in poorer health. They have poorer vision, partly because of prenatal conditions and partly because, even as toddlers, they watch too much television, so their eyes are poorly trained. Trying to read, their eyes may wander or have difficulty tracking print or focusing. A good part of the over-identification of learning disabilities for lower-class children may well be attributable to undiagnosed vision problems that could be easily treated by optometrists and for which special education placement then should be unnecessary.

Lower-class children have poorer oral hygiene, more lead poisoning, more asthma, poorer nutrition, less-adequate pediatric care, more exposure to smoke, and a host of other health problems. Because of less-adequate dental care, for example, they are more likely to have toothaches and resulting discomfort that affects concentration.

Because low-income children live in communities where landlords use high-sulfur home heating oil and where diesel trucks frequently pass en route to industrial and commercial sites, they are more likely to suffer from asthma, leading to more absences from school and, when they do attend, drowsiness from lying awake at night, wheezing. Recent surveys in Chicago and in New York City's Harlem community found one of every four children suffering from asthma, a rate six times as great as that for all children.

In addition, there are fewer primary-care physicians in low-income communities, where the physician-to-population ratio is less than a third the rate in middle-class communities. For that reason, disadvantaged children—even those with health insurance—are more likely to miss school for relatively minor problems, such as common ear infections, for which middle-class children are treated promptly.

Each of these well-documented social class differences in health is likely to have a palpable effect on academic achievement; combined, their influence is probably huge.

The growing unaffordability of adequate housing for low-income families also affects achievement. Children whose families have difficulty finding stable housing are more likely to be mobile, and student mobility is an important cause of failing student performance. A 1994 government report found that 30 percent of the poorest children had attended at least three different schools by third grade, while only 10 percent of middle-class children had done so. Black children were more than twice as likely as white children to change schools this often. It is hard to imagine how teachers, no matter how well trained, can be as effective for children who move in and out of their classrooms as they can be for those who attend regularly.

Differences in wealth are also likely to be important determinants of achievement, but these are usually overlooked because most analysts focus only on annual family income to indicate disadvantage. This makes it hard to understand why black students, on average, score lower than whites whose family incomes are the same. It is easier to understand this pattern when we recognize that children can have similar family incomes but be of different economic classes. In any given year, black families with low income are likely to have been poor for longer than white families with similar income in that year.

White families are also likely to own far more assets that support their children's achievement than are black families at the same income level, partly because black middle-class parents are more likely to be the first generation in their families to have middle-class status. Although the median black family income is about two-thirds the median income of white families, the assets of black families are still only 12 percent those of whites. Among other things, this difference means that, among white and black families with the same middle-class incomes, the whites are more likely to have savings for college. This makes white children's college aspirations more practical, and therefore more commonplace.

Narrowing the Gaps

If we properly identify the actual social class characteristics that produce differences in average achievement, we should be able to design policies that narrow the achievement gap. Certainly, improvement of instructional practices is among these, but a focus on school reform alone is bound to be frustrating and ultimately unsuccessful. To work, school improvement must combine with policies that narrow the social and economic differences between children. Where these differences cannot easily be narrowed, school should be redefined to cover more of the early childhood, after-school, and summer times, when the disparate influences of families and communities are now most powerful.

Because the gap is already huge at age 3, the most important new investment should no doubt be in early childhood programs. Prekindergarten classes for 4-year-olds are needed, but they barely begin to address the problem. The quality of early childhood programs is as important as the existence of such programs themselves. Too many low-income children are parked before television sets in low-quality day-care settings. To narrow the gap, care for infants and toddlers should be provided by adults who can create the kind of intellectual environment that is typically experienced by middle-class infants and toddlers. This requires professional care-givers and low child-adult ratios.

After-school and summer experiences for lower-class children, similar to programs middle-class children take for granted, would also be needed to narrow the gap. This does not mean remedial programs where lower-class children get added drill in math and reading. Certainly, remediation should be part of an adequate after-school and summer program, but only a part. The advantage that middle-class children gain after school and in summer comes from the self-confidence they acquire and the awareness of the world outside that they develop through organized athletics, dance, drama, museum visits, recreational reading, and other activities that develop inquisitiveness, creativity, self-discipline, and organizational skills. After-school and summer programs can be expected to narrow the achievement gap only by attempting to duplicate such experiences.

Provision of health-care services to lower-class children and their families is also required to narrow the achievement gap. Some health services are relatively inexpensive, such as school vision and dental clinics. A full array of health services will cost more, but it cannot be avoided if we truly intend to raise the achievement of lower-class children.

The connection between social and economic disadvantage and an academic achievement gap has long been well known. Most educators, however, have avoided the obvious implication: Improving lower-class children's learning requires ameliorating the social and economic conditions of their lives. School board members—who are often the officials with the closest ties to public opinion—cannot afford to remain silent about the connection between school improvement and social reform. Calling attention to this link is not to make excuses for poor school performance. It is only to be honest about the social support schools require if they are to fulfill the public's expectation that the achievement gap will disappear.

POSTNOTE

It is easy to be discouraged when reading hard-hitting articles such as this one. Richard Rothstein questions the belief of many that America has been a world leader in providing a "social escalator" out of poverty through our public school system. Although that may have been true in the past, the escalator is slowing down and is badly in need of repair.

The solutions offered here for fundamental social and economic change are indeed radical. They are also extraordinarily expensive and represent a quantum jump in educational expenditure. Tallying up the tax implications, public policy analysts will quickly start shaking their heads. Our priorities, such as the burgeoning population of elderly and their sky-rocketing health costs, are making more insistent demands. And, besides, in the real world of American politics, the poor have little political clout.

One answer to this argument is that uneducated and unskilled "graduates" of our schools are potential "social dynamite." The costs to the country of not educating them properly will be far greater than the price tag on the author's proposals. A sounder answer, though, is that we should make these investments in poor children because it is the right—the just—thing to do. If each of us thought about these individual children as our own children— our own flesh, blood, and DNA—this problem would be solved, and we could move on to consider the issue of health care.

Discussion Questions

1. The author mentions several "gaps." What are they, and which one do you believe is most severe?
2. Restate in your own words the relationship between the social and economic disadvantages of poor children and the achievement gap.
3. What do you believe are the key reasons that keep Americans from fundamentally reforming the schools serving poor children?

RELATED WEBSITE RESOURCES AND VIDEO CASES

 Web Resources:

Paulo Freire Institute. Available at:

http://www.paulofreireinstitute.org/.

The PFI, housed at the University of California at Los Angeles, is one of several centers of thought sympathetic to many of the points raised in this article.

Center for Education Reform. Available at:

http://www.edreform.com/

The Center for Education Reform is a major think tank and advocacy institute devoted to school reform through the promoting ideas and research on school choice, advancing the charter school movement, and challenging the education establishment.

Video Case:

Parental Involvement in School Culture: A Literacy Project

In this video case, you will see how literacy specialist, Linda Schwertz, engages parents in a book publishing venture. As you watch the clips and study the artifacts in the case, reflect upon the following questions:

1. What ways can you think of to engage parents in their children's school? What ways are demonstrated in this video case?
2. What are the major obstacles that prevent parents from being involved in their children's school, and how can those obstacles be overcome?

46

Putting Money Where It Matters

Karen Hawley Miles

Karen Hawley Miles is executive director and founder of Education Resource Strategies, a nonprofit organization in Boston, Massachusetts, that specializes in strategic planning, organization, and resource allocation in urban public school districts.

"Putting Money Where It Matters" by Karen Hawley Miles, *Educational Leadership,* September 2001, pp. 53–57. Used with permission.

|F|O|C|U|S| QUESTION

There are only so many dollars to spend on education. How should they be spent?

KEY TERMS

Accountability

Professional development

Standards-based education

Title I

The focus in the United States on creating accountable, standards-based education is pushing districts and schools to more clearly define their goals and priorities for student learning. Districts and states make headlines with bold proclamations about the importance of academic achievement for all students. But the gap between rhetoric and reality threatens hopes for improvement. While teachers scramble to help students meet more ambitious academic targets, school and district spending patterns and organization structures have changed little in the past three decades (Miles, 1997a). No matter what school leaders and communities say is important, the way schools and districts use their dollars, organize their staff, and structure their time dictates the results.

As public institutions, schools and districts try to do everything for everyone—and do it all without making enemies. New dollars come to schools in small increments over time, usually tied to specific purposes. We add new priorities and programs on top of the old. Instead of restructuring and integrating school and district organizations, we create specialities and departments to meet newly defined needs. Schools and districts now spend significantly more to educate each pupil than ever before (Snyder & Hoffman, 1999). Taking advantage of these resources to meet higher academic standards requires a political will and singleness of purpose that is difficult to sustain in public schools. Such action also demands an attention to organizational and budget details that does not come naturally to many educators and policymakers.

If we hope to meet our seemingly unreachable goals, districts and schools must define priorities for student performance, make choices about how to organize to meet them, and then move the dollars and people to match those commitments. If school leaders give priority to improving academic achievement, for example, then the district staff and budget should shift to support that goal. If the district declares that all students will read by 3rd grade, then staff, dollars, and time should support more effective literacy teaching. Districts and schools should expect to give up some long-standing and useful programs to support these choices.

Matching Dollars to Priorities

For the past 10 years, I have helped districts and schools rethink their use of resources to support their reform efforts. In partnership with New American

Schools and with support from Pew Charitable Trusts, I have worked with four large urban districts to analyze their district and school spending and then consider ways to reallocate dollars. My colleagues and I have discovered that, in many cases, the dollars needed for reform efforts are there, but they are tied up in existing staff, programs, and practices. We have found that schools need help shifting their use of resources to take advantage of what they already have and that districts often lag behind schools in changing their own spending and organization structures. To support schools in raising student performance, most districts need to realign spending and staffing in at least five ways.

RESTRUCTURE SALARIES TO ATTRACT AND RETAIN HIGH-QUALITY TEACHERS

It is no secret that U.S. teaching salaries lag behind those of other professions. The discrepancy is especially great for two types of teachers needed in schools: high-performing students from top colleges who have many other career options and teachers trained in math and science (Mohrman, Mohrman, & Odden, 1995). The earnings gap grows wider over a teaching career (Conley & Odden, 1995). Maximum teaching salaries fall well below those in other professions, meaning that the most talented individuals sacrifice much higher potential earnings if they remain in teaching. Districts need to reconsider their practice of paying all teachers the same regardless of subject area. In addition, they must find ways to restructure teacher salaries and responsibilities to provide the most talented, productive teachers with the opportunity to earn more competitive salaries during their careers.

Increasing salaries significantly without bankrupting districts means taking a hard look at the way salary dollars are spent. Since the 1920s, virtually all districts have used a salary structure that applies to every teacher regardless of grade or subject. Teachers can move up the salary ladder either by logging more years of teaching or accumulating education credits. Most districts increase salaries far more for experience than they do for education (Miles, 1997b). Boston Public Schools, for example, spent 36 percent of its 1998–99 salary budget to buy years of experience (29 percent) and education credits (7 percent).

For this investment to make sense for students, both teaching experience and accumulated credits would have to be clearly linked to student achievement. But research shows that after the first five years, the quality of teaching does not automatically improve with either course credits or years of teaching (Hanushek,

1994; Murnane, 1996). Experience and course-work have value, but neither is a fail-safe investment without coaching, hard work, and systems that reward and encourage good teaching. Many districts are currently experimenting with increasing teacher salaries on the basis of more direct measures of teaching quality. Most of these plans give bonuses to teachers who meet certain criteria or student performance targets. These extra dollars are nice symbols, but the plans that have the most promise for significantly raising teacher salary levels redirect existing salary dollars even as they seek to add more.

REDIRECT DISTRICT STAFF AND SPENDING FROM COMPLIANCE EFFORTS TO PROVIDE SCHOOLS WITH INTEGRATED SUPPORT AND ACCOUNTABILITY

Using standards to measure school performance changes the role of the district office. If schools do not have to report student performance, schools and districts are only held accountable for whether they do as they are told and keep children safe. As a result, curriculum offices issue guidebooks and sometimes check whether they are used, and districts create departments to monitor whether dollars from each funding source are spent as stipulated.

When schools become accountable for student learning, the district role must shift to helping schools measure student learning and supporting the changes in teaching and organization that best support improvement. Most districts need to focus more on four purposes: defining standards and targets, supporting schools and teachers, creating accountability, and restructuring school organizations.

Supporting these four goals is often possible by reallocating existing resources. In many large districts, the traditional compliance focus has resulted in a structure that spreads resources thinly across many schools and priorities. For example, one district was surprised to find that it devoted nine experts to supervising services across 30 schools. Each expert was responsible for making sure that schools met program requirements in one specific area, such as special education, Title I, bilingual education, literacy, or technology. Because these nine individuals focused on only one issue in multiple schools, they could conduct only superficial reviews of effectiveness, and they certainly couldn't provide support to underperforming schools. Even though the district devoted $24,000 in salaries and benefits to each school, the schools barely felt an impact. Instead, the schools needed deeper, integrated school support in specific areas where improvement was most needed.

SHIFT MORE RESOURCES TO TEACHING LITERACY IN GRADES K–3

Research consistently shows that smaller group sizes matter most in early grades when students learn to read (Wenglinsky, 2001). It also shows that when students don't learn to read by 3rd grade, they continue to fall farther behind in school and are more likely to be assigned to costly special education programs and to drop out of school. Research suggests concrete ways to improve reading achievement:

- Class size reduction in grades pre-K–2 can make an important, lasting difference in student achievement.
- Small reductions in class size make little difference; only when class sizes get down to 15–17 students does achievement increase predictably.
- Even smaller group sizes, including one-on-one instruction, are critical for developing readers, especially those from disadvantaged homes.
- If teachers don't change their classroom practice to take advantage of class size reductions, they can't expect improved student performance.

To incorporate these lessons, both districts and schools need to shift their use of existing resources. U.S. school districts average one teacher for every 17 students—with the ratio much higher in many urban districts—and one adult for every nine students. Yet, elementary school class size averages in the mid-20s (Miles, 1997a; Snyder & Hoffman, 1999). Most districts allocate more staff and dollars per pupil to high schools than to elementary schools.

To focus resources where they matter most, districts need to look first at how much they spend at the elementary school level compared to the high school level. Next, they need to invest to ensure that teachers have access to powerful professional development in teaching literacy. Third, they must actively support school-level changes that shift resources toward literacy instruction.

This active support of school-level changes in the use of resources creates special challenges for districts. For example, many schools have found ways to create small reading groups for part of the day by making group sizes larger at other times of the day. Others have reconsidered the role of each teacher, support person, and instructional aide to ensure that they support the focus on literacy. In some schools, this may mean changing the role of physical education, art, and music teachers or making these class sizes larger. It may mean hiring a highly trained literacy specialist instead of a traditional librarian. And redirecting resources toward literacy will mean integrating bilingual, Title I, and special education teachers more fully into a school-wide literacy strategy. Schools need help making these shifts, which require changes in district policy, contract language, and staff allocation practices. Districts also need to be prepared to defend school leaders who abandon popular, but outmoded or less important, programs and staff positions to support literacy efforts.

INVEST STRATEGICALLY IN PROFESSIONAL DEVELOPMENT FOR TEACHERS

To take advantage of smaller class sizes and to improve literacy instruction, districts need to offer teachers high-quality professional development. The assertion that districts invest only a small percentage of their budgets in professional development has become a cliché among education reformers. Although some districts may need to invest more money, the priority, for many, will be to refocus existing efforts to create more effective professional development and more useful teacher time. Research shows that professional development that responds to school-level student performance priorities, focuses on instruction, and provides coaching for individual teachers and teams over time can have a powerful impact on teacher practice. But professional development doesn't follow this model in most districts. And providing teachers with more professional time and intensive coaching support can seem expensive to districts that use a few traditional workshops as their "training."

In a detailed analysis of four large urban district budgets, we found that districts spend more than they think on professional development (Miles & Hornbeck, 2000). In these four districts, spending on professional development from all sources ranged 2–4 percent of the district budget. These figures are much larger than those districts traditionally report and manage. For example, one district reported $460,000 spent on strategic professional development, but the district actually spent nearly 20 times this amount when professional development efforts by all departments and sources were included. Worse, our analysis showed that professional development spending is often divided among many fragmented, sometimes conflicting, programs managed by different departments. Spending to support improved academic instruction represented only a fraction of total dollars in these districts, and the amount aimed at literacy instruction was even smaller. Harnessing these dollars requires district and school leaders to challenge the status quo and to abandon worthwhile initiatives in order to support more integrated models of professional development.

REDUCE SPENDING ON NONACADEMIC TEACHING STAFF IN SECONDARY SCHOOLS

The traditional comprehensive high school often employs more teaching staff in nonacademic subjects than it does in English, math, science, and history. Traditional high schools devote only about half of each student's school day to courses covering academic skills, resulting in more than half the high school resources being aimed at goals that are not measured by the state and district standards. This allocation of resources also means that class sizes for the core subjects are usually 30 students or more, with teachers responsible for a total of more than 125 students.

But changing the balance of staff to make a meaningful difference in student loads and academic time would require some high schools to double the number of academic staff. And shifting more resources toward academic subjects means reducing staff in other areas and challenging the structure—or even the existence—of such cherished programs as band and athletics. Given the number of the changes and their sometimes painful nature, it is unreasonable and impractical to expect principals or school-based decision-making groups to make them on their own. Until districts take steps to change the mix of staff, many high schools will make marginal improvements at best.

Making Choices

Organizing resources to act on urgent priorities, such as teaching all students to read in urban schools, requires leaders to take politically difficult stands. Union, district, and school board leaders need courage and strong community support to say:

- Even though all subjects are important, literacy is most important.
- Even though all teachers are important, those who bring deep subject knowledge and can integrate across disciplines or programs are worth more.
- Even though band, sports, and other electives can be a crucial part of a balanced education, the community must find new ways to pay for and provide them.
- Even though student readiness and social health provide a base for student learning, schools cannot be held accountable for providing all services to students, and they aren't staffed to do so.
- Even though investments in teacher professional development and technology may mean an extra student in your class, we can't build and sustain excellent schools without more of such investments.

Ensuring Adequate Funding

Regardless of overall spending levels, district and community leaders need to articulate priorities and direct spending to support them. But they must also ensure that schools have enough money to begin these tasks. There is no one way to define how much money is enough, but a few test questions can help put district spending in perspective: How does spending per pupil in your district compare to spending in other districts with similar student populations? How do teacher salary levels compare? How does the community's tax rate compare to the tax rates in similar districts?

If the community is underinvesting in education, leaders need to make the case for increased spending. But a community may be more likely to support increases in spending if citizens see that leaders have clear priorities and are willing to make difficult choices to ensure that new dollars get to the heart of improving student achievement.

REFERENCES

Conley, S., & Odden, A. (1995). Linking teacher compensation to teacher career development: A strategic examination. *Educational Evaluation and Policy Analysis, 17*, 253–269.

Hanushek, E. A. (1994). *Making schools work: Improving performance and controlling costs.* Washington, DC: Brookings Institute.

Miles, K. H. (1997a). Finding the dollars to pay for 21st century schools: Taking advantage of the times. *School Business Affairs, 63*(6), 38–42.

Miles, K. H. (1997b). *Spending more on the edges: Public school spending from 1967 to 1991.* Ann Arbor, MI: UMI Press.

Miles, K. H., & Hornbeck, M. J. (2000). *Reinvesting in teaching: District spending on professional development.* Arlington, VA: New American Schools.

Mohrman, A., Mohrman, S. A., & Odden, A. (1995). Aligning teacher compensation with systemic school reform: Skill-based pay and group-based performance rewards. *Educational Evaluation and Policy Analysis, 18*, 51–71.

Murnane, R. J. (1996). Staffing the nation's schools with skilled teachers. In E. A. Hanushek & D. W. Jorgenson (Eds.), *Improving America's schools: The role of incentives* (pp. 243–260). Washington, DC: National Academy Press.

Snyder, T. D., & Hoffman, C. M. (1999). *Digest of education statistics 1999.* Washington, DC: National Center for Education Statistics, Office of Educational Research and Improvement, U.S. Department of Education.

Wenglinsky, H. (2001, June). The effect of class size on achievement [Memorandum]. Available: **www.ets.org/search97cgi/s97_cgi**

POSTNOTE

Advocates of school choice, including school vouchers and charter schools, often point fingers at the educational bureaucracies in large school districts as major culprits for student academic failures. These critics argue that these bureaucracies waste money, respond to problems too slowly, and lack accountability.

Rather than just criticizing large school districts, the author works actively with large school systems on how to get "more bang for the buck." The thrust of her recommendations is to invest money in good teachers and their continued professional development. More and more policymakers are coming to the conclusion that high-quality teachers are the essential key to successful educational reform, and school systems must be redesigned to provide the conditions and support that allow teachers to succeed. If school districts make student learning their top priority, then they must surely conclude that teachers need and deserve good working conditions to bring about student academic achievement. Only by investing in good teachers will we achieve the results with students that we seek.

Discussion Questions

1. The author argues that school districts need to reconsider the practice of paying all teachers the same regardless of subject matter. Do you agree with her argument that because highly qualified teachers in certain subject fields (mathematics, special education, for example) are in short supply, their salaries need to be increased in order to attract people to the positions? Why or why not?

2. Do you agree with the author's suggestion that school districts might have to reduce staff—or even abandon programs such as band and athletics—to focus more on academics? Why or why not?

3. What additional recommendations would you make to ensure that educational dollars are spent wisely by school districts on the most important programs?

RELATED WEBSITE RESOURCES

 Web Resources:

Karen Hawley Miles: Audio 1. Available at:

http://www.ncrel.org/sdrs/areas/issues/envrnmnt/go/ hawley3.htm.

The author describes three school-level resources: the use of time, the organization of staff, and the use of funds from external sources.

Consortium for Policy Research in Education (CPRE). Available at:

http://cpre.wceruw.org.

CPRE unites seven of the nation's top research institutions in an effort to improve student learning through research on education reform, policy, and finance. On the home page, click on "School Finance" to access policy papers and research on the topic.

Educational Technology

For much of the past decade, schools have emphasized the acquisition of technology hardware as a major objective. By 2006, it was estimated that there was one instructional computer for every 3.3 students in our public schools. Educators have now reached the point where their goal should not be just to acquire technology. Instead, they should ask how technologies should be used to help students reach the higher standards being developed by states and to prepare students for the professional world they will enter when they leave school.

Although most educators, policymakers, and business leaders believe that technology has the potential to dramatically alter how teachers teach and students learn, some people remain skeptical that technology will have a significant impact on education. These skeptics cite as historical evidence the "hype" that accompanied previous technologies, such as television, that failed to deliver on their promises.

It is clear that if computers and other related technologies are to transform educational practice, much time and effort must go into working with teachers. They need to understand the capabilities of technology and to develop the skills necessary to deliver those capabilities. They need to know how to integrate appropriate technologies into the content they teach. If this teacher development does not occur, then the latest educational technology—like some earlier ones—will prove to be a bust.

47

The Overdominance of Computers

Lowell W. Monke

Lowell W. Monke is assistant professor at Wittenberg University in Springfield, Ohio.

"The Overdominance of Computers" by Lowell W. Monke, *Educational Leadership* 63, no. 4, December 2005/January 2006, pp. 20–23. Used with permission.

| F | O | C | U | S | QUESTION |

When should students receive extensive experience with technology?

The debate churns on over the effectiveness of computers as learning tools. Although there is a growing disillusionment with the promise of computers to revolutionize education, their position in schools is protected by the fear that without them students will not be prepared for the demands of a high-tech 21st century. This fallback argument ultimately trumps every criticism of educational computing, but it is rarely examined closely.

Let's start by accepting the premise of the argument: Schools need to prepare young people for a high-tech society. Does it automatically follow that children of all ages should use high-tech tools? Most people assume that it does, and that's the end of the argument. But we don't prepare children for an automobile-dependent society by finding ways for 10-year-olds to drive cars, or prepare people to use alcohol responsibly by teaching them how to drink when they are 6. My point is that preparation does not necessarily warrant early participation. Indeed, preparing young people quite often involves strengthening their inner resources—like self-discipline, moral judgment, and empathy—before giving them the opportunity to participate.

Great Power and Poor Preparation

The more powerful the tools—and computers are powerful—the more life experience and inner strength students must have to handle that power wisely. On the day my Advanced Computer Technology classroom got wired to the Internet, it struck me that I was about to give my high school students great power to harm a lot of people, and all at a safe distance. They could inflict emotional pain with a few keystrokes and never have to witness the tears shed. They could destroy hours of work accomplished by others who were not their enemies—just poorly protected network users whose files provided convenient bull's-eyes for youth flexing newfound technical muscles.

I also realized that it would take years to instill the ethical discipline needed to say *no* to flexing that technical power. Young people entering my course needed more firsthand experiences guided by adults. They needed more chances to directly connect their own actions with the consequences of those actions, and to reflect on the outcomes, before they started using tools that could trigger serious consequences on the other side of the world.

Students need more than just moral preparation. They also need authentic experiences. As more students grow up spending much of their time in environments dominated by computers, TV, and video games, their diminished experience with real, concrete things prevents them from developing a rich understanding of what they study on computers. The computer is a purely symbolic environment; users are always working with abstract representations of things, never with the things themselves. In a few months my students could learn to build complex relational databases and slick multimedia presentations. But unless they also had a deep knowledge of the physical world and community relationships, they would be unable to infuse depth and meaning into the information they were depicting and discussing.

Do Computers Help Achievement?

Educational technology researchers, who tend to suffer from a severe inability to see the forest for the trees, typically ignore the impact that saturating society with computers and other screen environments is having on children. University of Munich economists Thomas Fuchs and Ludger Woessmann recently examined data from a study of 174,000 15-year-olds in 31 nations who took the Programme for International Student Assessment tests. They found, after controlling for other possible influences, that the more access students had to computers in school and at home, the *lower* their overall test scores were (2004). The authors suggest that rather than inherently motivating young people or helping them learn, computers more likely distract them from their studies. But there may be other problems behind this phenomenon that point to inherent contradictions in the use of educational technology.

For example, although we know that computer programs can help small children learn to read, we also know that face-to-face interaction is one of the most important ingredients in reading readiness (Dodici, Draper, & Peterson, 2003). As a result of increased time spent with computers, video games, and TV, the current generation of elementary students will experience an estimated 30 percent fewer face-to-face encounters than the previous generation (Hammel, 1999). Thus, teachers may be employing the very devices for remediating reading problems that helped cause the problems in the first place.

The issue is not just balancing computer time with other activities in schools. Both inside and outside school, children's lives are dominated by technology. Nearly everything a child does today—from chatting with friends to listening to music to playing games—tends to involve the use of technologies that distance children from direct contact with the living world. If

the task of schools is to produce men and women who live responsible, fulfilling lives—not just human cogs for the high-tech machinery of commerce—then we should not be intensifying children's high-tech existence but compensating for it. Indeed, as advanced technology increasingly draws us toward a mechanical way of thinking and acting, it becomes crucial that schools help students develop their distinctly human capacities. What we need from schools is not balance in using high technology, but an effort to balance children's machine-dominated lives.

To prepare children to challenge the cold logic of the spreadsheet-generated bottom line, we need to teach them to value what that spreadsheet cannot factor in: commitment, loyalty, and tradition. To prepare them to find meaning in the abstract text and images encountered through screens, we need to first engage them in physical realities that screen images can only symbolize. To fit students to live in an environment filled with human-made products, we need to first help them know and respect what cannot be manufactured: the natural, the living, the wild. To prepare students to live well-grounded lives in a world of constant technological change, we need to concentrate their early education on things that endure.

The Cost of Failing to Compensate

Anyone who has spent time in schools knows that what is keeping today's youth from succeeding academically has nothing to do with a lack of technical skills or access to computers. Rather, it is the lack of qualities like hope, compassion, trust, respect, a sense of belonging, moral judgment, stability, community support, parental care, and teacher competence and enthusiasm that keeps so many students imprisoned in ignorance.

Ironically, what students will most need to meet the serious demands of the 21st century is the wisdom that grows out of these inner human capacities and that is developed by community involvement. If the 20th century taught us anything at all, it should have been that technology can be a very mixed blessing. Children entering elementary schools today will eventually have to wrestle with the mess that their elders have left them because of our own lack of wisdom about technology's downside: global warming, increasingly lethal weapons, nuclear waste, overdependence on automobiles, overuse of pesticides and antibiotics, and the general despoiling of our planet. They will also have to take on ethical conundrums posed by advanced technology, such as what to do about cloning, which decisions are off-limits to artificial intelligence devices, and whether or not parents should be allowed to "enhance" the genetic makeup of their offspring (only the wealthy need apply).

Those decisions should not be left to technicians in labs, CEOs in boardrooms, or politicians in debt to those who stand to profit from the technology. Our children should be at the decision tables as adults, and we want them to be able to stand apart from high technology and soberly judge its benefits and detriments to the entire human race.

How can young people develop the wisdom to judge high technology if they are told from the moment they enter school, implicitly if not explicitly, that they need high-tech tools to learn, to communicate, to think? Having been indoctrinated early with the message that their capacity to deal with the world depends not on their own internal resources but on their use of powerful external machines, how can students even imagine a world in which human beings impose limits on technological development or use?

Where to Go from Here

KEEP TO ESSENTIALS IN THE EARLY YEARS

So how, specifically, should educators make decisions and policies about the appropriateness of digital technologies for students of different ages?

One approach to tackling this dilemma comes from the Alliance for Childhood. During the last eight years, the Alliance (whose board of directors I serve on) has engaged educators, children's health professionals, researchers, and technology experts in developing guidelines for structuring a healthy learning environment for children, and has developed a list of essential conditions. Educators should ask themselves to what extent heavy use of computers and the Internet provides children in the lower grades with these essential school experiences:

- Close, loving relationships with responsible adults.
- Outdoor activity, nature exploration, gardening, and other encounters with nature.
- Time for unstructured play as part of the core curriculum.
- Music, drama, puppetry, dance, painting, and the other arts, both as separate classes and as a catalyst to bring other academic subjects to life.
- Hands-on lessons, handicrafts, and other physically engaging activities that provide effective first lessons for young children in the sciences, mathematics, and technology.
- Conversation with important adults, as well as poetry, storytelling, and hearing books read aloud.

This vision places a high priority on a child's direct encounters with the world and with other living beings, but it does not reject technology. On the contrary, tools are an important part of the vision. But at the elementary level, the tools should be simple, putting less distance between the student and the world and calling forth the student's own internal resources.

Schools must also be patient with children's development. It would strike anyone as silly to give the smallest student in a 2nd grade class a scooter so that the child could get around the track as fast as the other kids his or her age. But our society shows decreasing willingness to wait for the natural emergence of students' varying mental and emotional capacities. We label students quickly and display an almost pathological eagerness to apply external technical fixes (including medications) to students who often simply aren't ready for the abstract, academic, and sedentary environment of today's early elementary classrooms. Our tendency to turn to external tools to help children cope with demands that are out of line with their tactile and physically energetic nature reflects the impact that decades of placing faith in technical solutions has had on how we treat children.

STUDY TECHNOLOGY IN DEPTH AFTER ELEMENTARY SCHOOL

After children have had years to engage in direct, firsthand experiences, and as their abstract thinking capacities emerge more fully, it makes sense to gradually introduce computers and other complex, symbolic environments. Computer hardware and software should also become the focus of classroom investigation. A student in a technological society surrounded by black boxes whose fundamental principles he or she does not understand is as functionally illiterate as a student in a world filled with books that he or she can't read. The only thing worse would be to make technology "invisible," preventing children from even being aware of their ignorance.

By high school, digital technologies should take a prominent place in students' studies, both as tools of learning and as tools to learn about. During the last two years of high school, teachers should spend considerable time outfitting students with the high-tech skills they will need when they graduate. This "just-in-time" approach to teaching technical skills is far more efficient—instructionally and financially—than continually retraining younger students in technical skills soon to be obsolete. In addition, students at all education levels should consciously examine technology's role in human affairs.

I am not suggesting that we indiscriminately throw computers out of classrooms. But I do believe it's time to rethink the past decision to indiscriminately throw them in. The result of that rethinking would be, I hope, some much-needed technological modesty, both in school and eventually in society in general. By compensating for the dominance of technology in students' everyday lives, schools might help restore the balance we need to create a more humane society.

The irony of postmodern education is that preparing children for a high-tech future requires us to focus our attention more than ever before on the task of understanding what it means to be human, to be alive, to be part of both social and biological communities—a quest for which technology is increasingly becoming not the solution but the problem.

REFERENCES

Dodici, B. J., Draper, D. C., & Peterson, C. A. (2003). Early parent-child interactions and early literacy development. *Topics in Early Childhood Special Education, 23*(3), 124–136.

Fuchs, T., & Woessmann, L. (2004, November). *Computers and student learning: Bivariate and multivariate evidence on the availability and use of computers at home and at school.* CESifo Working Paper Series (#1321). Available: **www.cesifo.de/~DocCIDL/1321.pdf**

Hammel, S. (1999, Nov. 29). Generation of loners? Living their lives online. *U.S. News and World Report*, p. 79.

POSTNOTE

The author of this article believes strongly that young children need authentic experiences with life before becoming immersed in technology use. Children need to interact with the physical environment to establish a base of understandings, moral fiber, and trust before spending much time in abstract text and images encountered through computer screens. Children should not think that the only way they can experience the world is through technological mediums. Introduction to technology should come gradually, after considerable hands-on experiences with the arts and outdoor activity. Only then will students be sufficiently grounded to deal with technology responsibly.

Discussion Questions

1. Do you agree or disagree with the author's major argument? Why?
2. When do you think children should first have extensive experience with computer technology? Should they have any prerequisite knowledge or experiences?
3. How would you go about introducing children to computer use? When did you first experience computers?

RELATED WEBSITE RESOURCES AND VIDEO CASES

 Web Resources:

International Society for Technology in Education (ISTE), ISTE's Electronic Resources. Available at:

http://www.iste.org/resources.

This website features a superb list of links that cover a wide range of issues, including standards, the "digital divide," professional development, and technology integration.

Alliance for Childhood: Computers and Children. Available at:

http://www.allianceforchildhood.net/projects/ computers/computers_reports.htm.

This website includes a series of reports on children and their use of technology.

⏭ ▶ ⏮ *Video Case:*

Teaching Technology Skills: An Elementary School Lesson on PowerPoint

In this video case, you will meet two teachers who teach students how to create their own PowerPoint slide shows in order to present what they have learned about the Civil Rights movement. As you watch the clips and study the artifacts in the case, reflect upon the following questions:

1. Would the author of this article agree or disagree with the way technology is being used in this video case? Support your position.
2. How else might you teach this lesson without the use of technology?

Video Case:

Using Technology to Promote Discovery Learning: High School Geometry Lesson

In this video case, you will see how high school geometry teacher Gary Simons uses a technological tool that allows students to investigate problems and create their own "conjectures." As you watch the clips and study the artifacts in the case, reflect upon the following questions:

1. Mr. Simons maintains that technology is an essential tool for promoting discovery learning. Is his statement consistent with your experiences? Why or why not?
2. What aspect of using technology tools to support discovery learning do you think will be most challenging to you as a new teacher? How will you approach this challenge?
3. Does this video case support the major argument that Lowell Monke makes in this article? Why or why not?

Technology and the Culture of Learning

Paul Gow

Paul Gow is the academic dean at Beaver Country Day School in Chestnut Hill, Massachusetts.

"Technology and the Culture of Learning" by Paul Gow, *Independent School*, Summer 2004, pp. 18–26. Reprinted by permission.

48

F O C U S QUESTION

Do the benefits of technology outweigh the drawbacks in the educational process?

KEY TERMS
Acceptable use policy
Blogs
Chatrooms

Ruminating on recent conversations with leading technology developers *M.I.T. Technology Review* editor Robert Buderi came to a stark conclusion: "[D]espite being at the forefront of technology, nobody cites technology as a tool for thinking better." Considering the source, this observation should have been enough to vaporize educational technology initiatives from Maine to Hawaii. Whatever else technology was supposed to do in schools, wasn't it supposed to make students think better?

Well, maybe.

Anyone who has followed educational technology knows that many educators, inventors, journalists, and even sci-fi writers have been touting the latest classroom gadget as the gateway to greater student knowledge and/or deeper understanding since at least the era of silent films. But as Larry Cuban has shown in *Teachers and Machines* (1986), educational history in the last hundred years is also littered with the wreckage of "cool tools" designed to make learning and teaching easier and better.

Indeed, it is not hard to find prominent voices expressing caution or even outright dismay about the impact of technology's latest evolution—the digital computer, the Internet, and a raft of chip-based gadgets for communicating, gathering and processing information more readily, and (it is supposed) increasing our output of work. The subtitles of two recent books tell all: Jane M. Healy's *Endangered Minds* (1999) informs us that technology is "Why Our Children Don't Think," and Todd Oppenheimer's *The Flickering Mind* (2003) reveals "The False Promise of Technology in the Classroom and How Learning Can Be Saved." William Pflaum in *The Technology Fix* (2004) and Larry Cuban in *Oversold and Underused* (2001) sum up the least aggressive of the critiques by suggesting that the problem with technology in schools is not that there is too much of it, but rather that students spend too little time using it.

The message from all these worriers is clear. Whatever is wrong with education technology, it is very wrong indeed. It comes down to deciding between extremes—demagoguery, or just negligence? Too much, or too little? And what, exactly, was the "promise" of technology in the first place?

Anecdotal evidence suggests that technology-heavy instruction can lead to important improvements in student performance and understanding. "Research" backs up these claims (although the Jeremiahs can cite anecdotes and studies that demonstrate the opposite). For their part, schools generally put faith in the promise of technology. Since the early 1980s, few schools have failed to sink vast quantities of capital into developing technological infrastructure and large amounts of staff time into technology training.

But the question remains: What has been the total impact of technology on the landscape of education and the culture of schools? The answer, it seems to me, flows from three premises. Each premise invites analysis not simply from a practical point of view but from a moral one as well. In all events, we can agree that technology has profoundly changed the way in which "school" happens.

Premise #1. In Spite of Our Best Efforts, Technology Has Succeeded in Breaching All Barriers Between Schools and the World

Schools, especially independent schools, tend to see themselves as intentional communities, little utopias if you will, that thrive when they have a great amount of control over the influences on their members. The fewer the variables, the more limited the inputs, the more the school's intent can be realized. While this concept does not preclude a school from establishing rich and varied contacts with the world beyond, it does speak to the desirability of being able to manage their extent and nature.

For this reason, it has been a significant issue for schools in the past decade or so that the Internet, while a useful tool for research and learning, is also a playground for those who would exploit, distract, or even physically harm children and adolescents. These are facts of life, and so schools and the vendors who serve them—the educational defense industry—have developed many versions of Hadrian's Wall to keep the electronic barbarians at bay. Firewalls, air-tight acceptable use policies (AUPs), content filters, and a world of tracking and monitoring systems give schools the illusion that they have the capacity to exclude moral threats that travel by wire, or at least to track down and punish incursions.

But technology renders the supposedly secure world of the school simply one more dimension of the external environment, and the internal life of the institution is, regardless of AUPs or filters, open to forces without. We can prohibit instant messaging at school, but firestorms will still break out when malignant home IM-ing inflames the world of children, drawing parents, counselors, and teachers into the blaze. Blogging teenagers, or teachers, can find their anonymity blown and themselves held morally responsible not just for what they might have written but also for how others responded. And even the best filtering software, like the most iron-clad AUP, has loopholes. Risk management in such a world either demands the continual updating of Byzantine (or Machiavellian) preventive

stratagems or simply invites schools to give up. The "prudent person" of legal mythology would unplug, turn off, and drop out, but schools cannot do this; instead, we become more vigilant, and more nervous.

In the same vein, 24/7 cell-phone contact between children and families penetrates a time-honored barrier between home and school. Despite the rules at most schools limiting such communication during school hours, students relay information on their school experience to parents in real time, and parents can respond—to the child or to the teacher—just as swiftly. Even as many independent schools are embracing the notion of parents as partners, instant communication based on immediate reaction, rather than dialogue, can stress that relationship. With some schools making assignments and even grade-books available to parents online, the boundaries between the child working on independence and the parent or guardian learning to let go are at risk. In *Family Matters* (2004), Robert Evans describes a crisis of confidence in American families, and it is at least worth considering that technology might be furthering this crisis by giving insecure parents new and better means for playing out or fueling anxieties about their children's academic experience.

Last but not least, technology has made identity itself a variable rather than a constant. Chatrooms, blogs, and the instant message make it possible for anyone to hide behind an electronic curtain and to manufacture a persona, or personas, suited to the moment. Qualities once thought to be essential to one's being can now be elided, hidden, or changed; age, sex, race, class, ethnicity—all are in play when one chooses to become an e-person. For schools, this means that students—and it must be said, teachers—can experiment with different selves in environments beyond institutional control. Educators strive to develop students' capacities to consider issues from multiple perspectives, and the anonymity granted by technology can free students to find unusual and exciting vantage points. By the same token, however, the masking of identity can enable both the denial of responsibility and the abrogation of empathy.

Although this permeability of the membrane between school and the outside world seems to be all threat, it is not. The downsides discussed above are merely some unintended consequences of the expansion of opportunities for research, for students to connect with resources outside their school, for parents and teachers to engage in communication about children, or even for schools to seek—in a circumspect, protective manner—wider audiences for student work. That school cultures have been evolving in response to concerns does not minimize the degree to which they have also rightly embraced the phenomenal potential of technology.

Premise #2. By Making Many Tasks Much Easier, Technology Has Moved Us Toward Taking on More of Them

Who among us would trade in our word processors and photocopiers for carbon paper, Corrasable bond, or a Selectric typewriter? Technology's greatest gift has been our enhanced ability to generate, process, and disseminate ideas swiftly and efficiently. Modern-day Luddites will say that more ideas don't necessarily make for better ideas, but fewer ideas don't either. The fact is that word processing, to take the most obvious example, allows students and teachers to produce and polish work with an ease that certainly invites continuous improvement, even if such improvement is not always made. In every aspect of school life, chip-based digital technology has transformed the way we work, and it has reduced many of our essential tasks to automatic functions. This, in turn, frees educators and students to think up more tasks for themselves—an effect that makes some people sputter but which actually results, often enough, in our raising the bar of learning and performance.

In the early 1970s, the digital calculator represented a quantum leap over the slide rule in generating precise numerical answers. In the past few years, Google has become to fact-gathering what the calculator is to arithmetic. PowerPoint, even if it has become the whipping boy of the moment, is a pretty good tool for organizing and displaying certain kinds of information. And no business officer reading this would really want to give up the spreadsheet, no development officer the database. Productivity software even more than operating systems has made Bill Gates the world's richest man.

Automation in schools has had truly amazing effects. As a teacher, I am enabled to write more detailed reports to parents than I could (or at least did) with a ballpoint pen and carbonless paper forms. Ten years ago, we mapped our curriculum using notecards pinned to a bulletin board; software now allows us to generate a comprehensive, linkable, searchable document. My ability to create and then improve teaching materials is a hundred times greater than when I had to rely on cleaning up after my own poor typing before cranking out copies on a spirit duplicator (although I miss the smell). Sitting at my desk, I can easily search out the title of that book that I vaguely remember, track my professional development budget, or paste my school's mission statement into a document for teaching candidates. I am able to communicate with colleagues, parents, and students quickly and reliably using voicemail or e-mail. If I used a Smartboard, or if I worked in an environment where all my students had laptop computers or PDAs (Palms and their ilk), my ability to get things done would be even greater, I am sure.

Some among you are now wondering whether all these things are "worth it." I sometimes wonder myself. As teachers, we have a long and proud tradition of making students perform tasks that we have deemed worthy of sweat, many of which are now (some would say, Alas!) history. Long division, spelling exercises past the fourth grade, drawing graphs, calculating chemical equilibria on paper, and writing high school English essays in longhand come to mind. While we may still make students learn to do these things "by hand," as soon as they have mastered the skill, or the basic idea, we permit them to use technology to apply these skills in the service of learning how to solve more complex problems. Any secondary science teacher will tell you that improved instruments of measurement and calculation allow the teaching of concepts that would not have been covered in the Eisenhower era. And anyone teaching in the humanities knows that the Internet and online subscription databases, even as a supplement to the printed works in the library, allow students to see, and force them to consider or reject, points of view that they might never have encountered in decades past. As teachers, we believe we know what are the fundamentals of our work, and we ought to trust ourselves to know when we are doing this work better with technology and when we are simply doing it, or doing more of it, because technology makes it possible to do so.

It is worth noting, however, that the automation of educational tasks, even when it leads clearly to better experiences for students and teachers, is in itself the most obvious and ubiquitous form of change that educators and schools have experienced in recent years. Elizabeth Sky-McIlvain makes this point emphatically in her online essay, "The Flickering Teacher" (2004), and she suggests that having to make technology-based changes in practice can be a primary factor in driving teachers toward feelings of disorientation and inadequacy—and, ultimately, burnout. Often enough, such changes are thrust upon teachers with little or no evidence that improvement will follow, and, as any number of commentators have pointed out, schools have a tendency to provide too little time or too little support and, in the end, too little follow-through to properly implement such changes. The road to hell, it seems, just may be paved with interesting technology initiatives. If my school decreed that each week I should turn in a spreadsheet of my grades, complete with distribution graphs, I would first wonder why and then I probably would say, like Melville's Bartleby (who was, after all, a human office machine, a copyist), that I would prefer not to. Most of us can identify a Bartleby or two in our schools, and it makes sense to consider the role technological change may have played in creating them. But if I could be shown some clear value in making this change, and if my experience were soon to confirm this, I could perhaps be convinced to comply.

In the end, one is forced to wonder whether the net effect of technology has been to relieve humankind of any burdens at all. But "labor saving devices" have always been about reducing one kind of labor to permit the performance of another that is deemed more valuable. As we gain more complex understandings of how children learn and of the subtleties of good teaching, it should not surprise us that we respond by setting higher standards of productivity and quality in our students' work and in our own.

Premise #3. Technology Inevitably Carries Us Along Unseen Pathways, and Its Protean Nature Makes It Difficult to Predict or Control

Thus far, I have considered mainly the uses of technology in school or in relation to school-work, but it is also entertaining and even a bit intoxicating to imagine how these things might change even more. Laptops will evolve to tablets, cell phones will turn to wrist or badge communicators (Dick Tracy or Star Trek; take your pick), textbooks will become e-books, and e-mail and Internet communication will take place in a totally wireless world. We can anticipate next year's fads by checking out *Wired* magazine's "Japanese Schoolgirl Watch"—a monthly feature on how technology is transforming teenage culture—and we can follow the serious science press as it considers the possibilities of nanotechnology, a field so new that its educational potential lies largely unconsidered. We need to consider that technologies far outside the realm of education have been known to intrude on the culture of learning, sometimes to a horrifying degree. At the same time that Walt Disney was producing "Our Friend the Atom," for instance, school buildings were being designed to serve as fallout shelters and classroom documentaries whirring on 16-millimeter projectors were showing us how to duck and cover.

More sobering is the thought that technology's next effects on the culture of schools may come as a result of the technological modification of children themselves. The first babies from the era of advertisements in Ivy League college papers calling for brainy, physically perfect egg donors should be entering kindergarten about now, and it is not unlikely that their affluent and ambitious families will consider independent schools. The next step may be genetically engineered superkids, whatever the legal and moral objections to the idea. If such children do appear, they will require, or at least their parents will think they require, some very special educational experiences. How will schools cope with a cohort of genetically modified "gifted" children? Who will teach them? Nancy Kress explores these questions in her dystopic short stories, but it is more than possible that our schools may have to respond in real life.

New technologies have seldom settled upon society in predictable ways, and the computer chip is no exception. As recently as 1978, the promise of technology involved programming classes and whiz kids performing wondrous mathematical feats. Few of us then would have predicted the prevalence of classroom word-processing or foreseen that translation sites in Denmark would facilitate cheating on Spanish homework. Fewer of us would have imagined the degree to which our worlds have been transformed by e-mail, mobile telephones, or the Internet, but we also have to consider the idea that our students can photograph tests with cell phones or hack into our school's administrative software. Our ability to create teaching materials and to give our students access to information is greater than it has ever been, and technology, though it has also led to a proliferation of standardized testing of uncertain value, can also be used to help us measure student learning.

Technology has changed, and will continue to change, the culture of our schools. By far the greatest lesson of the Digital Age so far has been its very unpredictability. Our attempts to control the direction of technological change, with the best will in the world, almost never succeed on our own terms. Equally unavailing are calls simply to declare the whole thing a bust; technology is with us even if we want it to go away. Whether, as M.I.T. author Robert Buderi suggested, technology fails at being "a tool for thinking better" may not actually matter. If it has not made us think better, it has surely done something else. That we do not yet know with clarity what it is does not diminish the effect.

POSTNOTE

Paul Gow seems to be a realist in his thinking about the effects of technology on the culture of schools. Rather than arguing that technology is good or bad, he identifies some of the important ways that it has changed and affected schooling, including both benefits and drawbacks. There is no doubt, as the author states, that technology's greatest gift has been its ability to generate, process, and disseminate ideas quickly and efficiently. With this ability, however, comes the need or temptation to take on more and more tasks and responsibilities, which often complicate rather than simplify our lives.

One of Gow's most important observations is his third premise: "Technology inevitably carries us along unseen pathways, and its protean nature makes it difficult to predict or control." Ten years ago, who would have thought that one could have mobile telephones that would take and transmit pictures? Furthermore, who would have thought that this capability might be used to take and transmit compromising pictures of classmates as they dressed—and undressed—in locker rooms? And who would have anticipated the dangers of Internet predators? The unintended consequences of technological innovations force educators to respond and react to both the good and bad features of these outcomes, and it will forever do so.

Discussion Questions

1. What unanticipated consequences of technology development and use have you observed?

2. In what ways do some schools still have to take advantage of some of the newer technologies with which you are familiar?

3. What technology skills do you possess that you think will be useful to you as a teacher? What skills do you need to develop?

RELATED WEBSITE RESOURCES

 Web Resources:

Education World. Available at:

http://www.education-world.com/a_tech/.

Education World has a whole section devoted to technology integration, including columnists, specific technology websites, and much more.

49

Listen to the Natives

Marc Prensky

Marc Prensky is a speaker, writer, consultant, and game designer in education and learning.

"Listening to the Natives" by Marc Prensky, *Educational Leadership* 63, no. 4, December 2005/January 2006, pp. 8–13. Reprinted by permission of the author.

F|O|C|U|S QUESTION

How can schools provide tech-savvy students with a relevant education?

KEY TERMS

Blogs

Wikis

School didn't teach me to read—I learned from my games.

—A student

Educators have slid into the 21st century—and into the digital age—still doing a great many things the old way. It's time for education leaders to raise their heads above the daily grind and observe the new landscape that's emerging. Recognizing and analyzing its characteristics will help define the education leadership with which we should be providing our students, both now and in the coming decades.

Times have changed. So, too, have the students, the tools, and the requisite skills and knowledge. Let's take a look at some of the features of our 21st century landscape that will be of utmost importance to those entrusted with the stewardship of our children's 21st century education.

Digital Natives

Our students are no longer "little versions of us," as they may have been in the past. In fact, they are *so* different from us that we can no longer use either our 20th century knowledge or our training as a guide to what is best for them educationally.

I've coined the term *digital native* to refer to today's students (2001). They are native speakers of technology, fluent in the digital language of computers, video games, and the Internet. I refer to those of us who were not born into the digital world as *digital immigrants*. We have adopted many aspects of the technology, but just like those who learn another language later in life, we retain an "accent" because we still have one foot in the past. We will read a manual, for example, to understand a program before we think to let the program teach itself. Our accent from the predigital world often makes it difficult for us to effectively communicate with our students.

Our students, as digital natives, will continue to evolve and change so rapidly that we won't be able to keep up. This phenomenon renders traditional catch-up methods, such as inservice training, essentially useless. We need more radical solutions. For example, students could learn algebra far more quickly and effectively if instruction were available in game format. Students would need to beat the game to pass the course. They would be invested and engaged in the process.

We also need to select our teachers for their empathy and guidance abilities rather than exclusively for their subject-matter knowledge. We all remember best those teachers who cared about us as individuals and who cut us some slack when necessary. In today's rush to find teachers qualified in the curriculum, we rarely make empathy a priority.

Shifting Gears

As educators, we must take our cues from our students' 21st century innovations and behaviors, abandoning, in many cases, our own predigital instincts and comfort zones. Teachers must practice putting engagement before content when teaching. They need to laugh at their own digital immigrant accents, pay attention to how their students learn, and value and honor what their students know. They must remember that they are teaching in the 21st century. This means encouraging decision making among students, involving students in designing instruction, and getting input from students about how *they* would teach. Teachers needn't master all the new technologies. They should continue doing what they do best: leading discussion in the classroom. But they must find ways to incorporate into those discussions the information and knowledge that their students acquire outside class in their digital lives.

Our young people generally have a much better idea of what the future is bringing than we do. They're already busy adopting new systems for communicating (instant messaging), sharing (blogs), buying and selling (eBay), exchanging (peer-to-peer technology), creating (Flash), meeting (3D worlds), collecting (downloads), coordinating (wikis), evaluating (reputation systems), searching (Google), analyzing (SETI), reporting (camera phones), programming (modding), socializing (chat rooms), and even learning (Web surfing).

We need to help all our students take advantage of these new tools and systems to educate themselves. I know this is especially hard when we're the ones floundering, but teachers can certainly ask students, "Does anyone do anything on the Web that is relevant to what we're discussing?" or "Can you think of any examples of this problem in your computer games?" Teachers can also help students figure out who has the best access to technology outside school and encourage students to form study groups so that more students benefit from this access. Teachers can learn what technological equipment they need in their classrooms simply by asking students, and they can lobby to get these items installed in school computer labs and libraries.

Student Engagement

More and more of our students lack the true prerequisites for learning—engagement and motivation—at least in terms of what we offer them in our schools. Our kids *do* know what engagement is: Outside school, they are fully engaged by their 21st century digital lives.

If educators want to have relevance in this century, it is crucial that we find ways to engage students in school. Because common sense tells us that we will never have enough truly great teachers to engage these students in the old ways—through compelling lectures from those rare, charismatic teachers, for example—we must engage them in the 21st century way: electronically. Not through expensive graphics or multimedia, but through what the kids call "gameplay." We need to incorporate into our classrooms the same combination of desirable goals, interesting choices, immediate and useful feedback, and opportunities to "level up" (that is, to see yourself improve) that engage kids in their favorite complex computer games. One elementary school in Colorado, for example, takes its students on a virtual journey to a distant planet in a spaceship powered by knowledge. If the students don't have enough knowledge to move the ship, they need to find it—in one another.

Collaborating with Students

As 21st century educators, we can no longer decide *for* our students; we must decide *with* them, as strange as that may feel to many of us. We need to include our students in everything we do in the classroom, involving them in discussions about curriculum development, teaching methods, school organization, discipline, and assignments. Faculty or administration meetings can no longer be effective without student representation in equal numbers. Our brightest students, trusted with responsibility, will surprise us all with their contributions.

This may sound like the inmates are running the asylum. But it's only by listening to and valuing the ideas of our 21st century students that we will find solutions to many of our thorniest education problems. For example, putting a Webcam in every classroom is a digital native way to show administrators and parents what really goes on. Teachers could also volunteer for this activity to document and share best practices.

Students could quite feasibly invent technological solutions to streamline homework submission and correction, freeing up teachers for more meaningful work. Encouraged to share their expertise, students can be a teacher's best resource for suggesting better access to technology, defining the kinds of technology that teachers should be using in the classroom, and showing teachers how they can use specific hardware and software tools to teach more effectively.

Flexible Organization

In this century, we *must* find alternatives to our primary method of education organization—what I call *herding*. Herding is students' involuntary assignment to specific classes or groups, not for their benefit but for ours. Nobody likes to be herded, and nobody learns best in that environment. As educators become "teacherds" rather than teachers, we all lose. And creating smaller schools or classrooms is no solution if the result is simply moving around smaller herds.

There are two effective 21st century alternatives to herding. The first is one-to-one personalized instruction, continually adapted to each student as he or she learns. This practice has become next to impossible with growing class sizes, but it is still doable. Modern computer and video games have already figured out how to adapt every moment of an experience to a player's precise capabilities and skills. So has computerized adaptive testing. Classrooms need to capitalize on students' individual capabilities and skills in the same way.

How can we make our instruction more adaptive and, as a result, far more effective? Just ask the students; they'll know. Adaptivity, along with connectivity, is where digital technology will have its greatest impact on education.

The second alternative to herding is having all learning groups self-select. Kids love working with their friends, especially virtually. I'm not saying, of course, that students should join *any* group in this context, but that they should be able to choose their own learning partners rather than having teachers assign them. Optimally and under proper supervision, a 4th grader in one school could choose a learning partner in any 4th grade class in the world. Teachers could also guide students in selecting an approved adult expert to partner with.

If we let our students choose all the groups they want to be part of—without forcing them into any one group—we will all be better off. One great advantage of virtual groups over herds is that nobody gets left out. Everybody can find *someone* in the world to work with. Teachers and administrators must be willing to set this up, provide the necessary vetting, and let it happen.

Digital Tools

Today's students have mastered a large variety of tools that we will never master with the same level of skill.

From computers to calculators to MP3 players to camera phones, these tools are like extensions of their brains. Educating or evaluating students without these tools makes no more sense to them than educating or evaluating a plumber without his or her wrench.

One of the most important tools for 21st century students is not the computer that we educators are trying so hard to integrate, but the cell phone that so many of our schools currently ban. "Cell Phones Catapult Rural Africa to 21st Century," blared a recent front-page *New York Times* headline (LaFraniere, 2005). They can catapult our students into the future as well.

Cell phones have enormous capabilities these days: voice, short messaging service (SMS), graphics, user-controlled operating systems, downloadables, browsers, camera functions (still and video), and geopositioning. Some have sensors, fingerprint readers, and voice recognition. Thumb keyboards and styluses as well as plug-in screens and headphones turn cell phones into both input and output mechanisms.

The voice capabilities of the cell phone can help users access language or vocabulary training or narrate a guided tour. Teachers could deliver interactive lessons over a cell phone and use short messaging service to quiz or tutor students. Students could access animations in such subjects as anatomy and forensics. Students will soon be able to download programs into their cell phones, opening up new worlds of learning.

In Europe, China, Japan, and the Philippines, the public is already using mobile phones as learning tools. We in the United States need to join them and overcome objections that students are "using them for cheating" (so make the tests open book!) or for "inappropriate picture taking" (so instill some responsibility!). In the United Kingdom, teachers are evaluating student projects over mobile phones. The student describes the project, and the teacher analyzes the student's voiceprint for authentication.

Let's admit that the *real* reason we ban cell phones is that, given the opportunity to use them, students would "vote with their attention," just as adults "vote with their feet" by leaving the room when a presentation is not compelling. Why shouldn't our students have the same option with their education when educators fail to deliver compelling content?

Programming

The single most important differentiator between 20th century analog and 21st century digital technology is programmability. Programming is perhaps *the* key skill necessary for 21st century literacy. In this arena, teachers and schools are stuck in ancient times.

If you wanted to get something written back then, you had to find a scribe; today, you need a programmer.

All 21st century kids are programmers to some degree. Every time they download a song or ring tone, conduct a Google search, or use any software, they are, in fact, programming. To prepare kids for their 21st century lives, we must help them maximize their tools by extending their programming abilities. Many students are already proficient enough in programs like Flash to submit their assignments in this medium. Schools should actively teach students this technology and encourage them to use it.

Of course, extending this literacy with our current teaching corps is problematic. A number of teachers I know have taken matters into their own hands, creating programming courses—especially in popular game programming—for students during the summer months, after school, and even in class. We need to capture these approaches and curriculums and make them available over the Web for all to use. Teachers can also arrange for certain students to teach these classes to their peers. In addition, outside experts are often willing to volunteer their services.

Legacy versus Future Learning

Currently, the curriculums of the past—the "legacy" part of our kids' learning—are interfering with and cutting into the "future" curriculum—the skills and knowledge that students need for the 21st century. We need to consolidate and concentrate important legacy knowledge and make room in school for 21st century learning. Our schools should be teaching kids how to program, filter knowledge, and maximize the features and connectivity of their tools. Students should be learning 21st century subject matter, such as nanotechnology, bioethics, genetic medicine, and neuroscience.

This is a great place for involving guest teachers from professions doing cutting-edge work in these emerging fields. If every district or school found just one expert willing to contribute his or her expertise; set up and videotaped a meaningful series of Q&A exchanges with students; and put those videos on the Web, enhancing them with additional relevant materials, we'd soon have a 21st century curriculum.

Students want and deserve to receive this content through 21st century tools that are powerful, programmable, and customizable—through tools that belong to them. We could offer this content to them on their cell phones, for example. A big part of our problem is figuring out how to provide this before the end of the 21st century.

School versus After School

Pragmatically, our 21st century kids' education is quickly bifurcating. The formal half, "school," is becoming an increasingly moribund and irrelevant institution. Its only function for many students is to provide them with a credential that their parents say they need. The informal, exciting half of kids' education occurs "after school." This is the place where 21st century students learn about their world and prepare themselves for their 21st century lives. It is revealing that one of the most prevalent student demands regarding technology is to keep their schools' computer labs open until midnight (and for us to stay out of their way while they are there). It is equally telling that so many software and Web programs aimed at enhancing kids' education are designed for after-school rather than in-school use.

If our schools in the 21st century are to be anything more than holding pens for students while their parents work, we desperately need to find ways to help teachers integrate kids' technology-rich after-school lives with their lives in school. It doesn't help if, in the words of Henry Kelly, president of the Federation of American Scientists, "the cookies on my daughter's computer know more about her interests than her teachers do." It helps even less that a great many of our teachers and administrators have no idea what a *cookie* or a *blog* or a *wiki* even is.

Student Voice

Our students, who are empowered in so many ways outside their schools today, have no meaningful voice at all in their own education. Their parents' voices, which up until now have been their proxies, are no longer any more closely aligned with students' real education needs than their teachers' voices are. In the 21st century, this lack of any voice on the part of the customer will soon be unacceptable.

Some organizations are trying to change this. For example, NetDay (**www.netday.org**) conducts an annual online student survey of technology use through its Speak Up Days. All school districts should participate in this survey. Then, instead of hearing from just the 200,000 students who responded in the last survey, we would know what 50 million of them are thinking. Districts would receive valuable input from their students that they could apply to improving instruction.

As we educators stick our heads up and get the lay of the 21st century land, we would be wise to remember this: If we don't stop and listen to the kids we serve, value their opinions, and make major changes on the basis of the valid suggestions they offer, we will be left in the 21st century with school buildings to administer—but with students who are physically or mentally somewhere else.

REFERENCES

LaFraniere, S. (2005, Aug. 25). Cell phones catapult rural Africa to 21st century. *New York Times on the Web.*

Available: **http://msn-cnet.com.com/ Cell+phones+catapult+rural+Africa+to+21st +century/2100-1039_3-5842901.html**

Prensky, M. (2001). Digital natives, digital immigrants. *On the Horizon, 9*(5), 1–2. Available: **www.marcprensky .com/writing/Prenskey%20-%20Digital%20 Natives,%20Digital%20Immigrants%20-%20 Part1.pdf**

POSTNOTE

One reason some teachers do not use much technology in their classrooms is because they believe their technological knowledge and skills is inferior to that of their students and they do not want to appear ignorant before them. In truth, chances are some students do have superior technological knowledge and skills than their teachers. These "digital natives," as the author refers to them, have grown up with—and are very comfortable using—all sorts of technological devices. He argues that schools should recognize this fact and try to create learning environments that engage students using some of these technologies. Teachers do not have to master these technologies themselves, but they do need to use the knowledge that students acquire outside of school through the use of digital technology. By using computers, calculators, MP3 players, and camera phones, to name a few, schools can engage students in learning.

Discussion Questions

1. Do you agree or disagree with the author's main argument? Why?
2. Which technologies do you believe offer the most promise for active student engagement? Why?
3. If you could ask this author one question, what would it be?

RELATED WEBSITE RESOURCES AND VIDEO CASES

 ### Web Resources:

The Cool Cat Teacher Blog—Wiki Wiki Teaching. Available at:

http://coolcatteacher.blogspot.com/2005/12/wiki- wiki-teaching-art-of-using-wiki.html.

This website contains suggestions and examples of using wiki wikis in teaching.

Video Case:

Using Blogs to Enhance Student Learning: An Interdisciplinary High School Unit

In this video case, three teachers offer an interdisciplinary unit on the topic of genocide, and have students respond to what they are learning through the interactive medium of a blog. As you watch the clips and study the artifacts in the case, reflect upon the following questions:

1. According to this video, what is a blog?
2. According to the teachers in this video, what are the advantages of this medium for high school students?
3. How might you use blogs in your teaching?

PART

9

Diversity and Social Issues

The United States is a nation of great diversity—in races, cultures, religions, languages, and lifestyles. Although these forms of diversity are part of what makes the United States strong, they nevertheless create challenges. The major challenge is how to recognize and respect these forms of diversity while still maintaining a common culture to which each subgroup can feel welcomed and valued. Early in the 20th century, American schools tried to create a "melting pot," where group differences were boiled away so that only "Americans" survived. Today, the notion of cultural pluralism has replaced the assimilationist perspective, with the metaphor of a "mosaic" or "quilt" replacing that of the melting pot.

The readings in this section of the book address diversity issues such as multicultural education, immigration and languages, gender issues, and inclusion of children with disabilities. Many of these topics are controversial. The viewpoints of both strong proponents and opponents of the various positions are articulated in the articles. As you read the selections, try to sort out your own positions on the issues.

▶ 311 ◀

CLASSIC

50

A Considered Opinion: Diversity, Tragedy, and the Schools

Diane Ravitch

Diane Ravitch is a historian of education, an educational policy analyst, and former United States Assistant Secretary of Education. She is a nonresident senior fellow in the Brookings Institution governmental studies program and a research professor at New York University's Steinhardt School of Education.

"A Considered Opinion: Diversity, Tragedy, and the Schools" by Diane Ravitch, *Brookings Review*, Winter 2002. Reprinted by permission of The Brookings Institution.

F O C U S QUESTION

What is the appropriate balance between teaching an American culture, on the one hand, and teaching about the contributions of various ethnic and racial minorities, on the other hand? Is it an either-or situation?

KEY TERMS

Assimilation

Melting pot

Multicultural education

As U.S. immigration has surged over the past quarter-century, educators have been developing a new response to demographic diversity in the classroom. The public schools have turned away from their traditional emphasis on assimilating newcomers into the national "melting pot." Instead, they have put a new emphasis on multicultural education, deemphasizing the common American culture and teaching children to take pride in their racial, ethnic, and national origins. In the wake of the terrorist attacks on New York City and Washington last September 11, however, the tide may be turning away from multiculturalism. Americans' remarkable display of national unity in the aftermath of the attacks could change the climate in the nation's schools as much as it has the political climate in Washington.

Immigration is central to the American experience. Though it is on the rise today, immigration is proportionately smaller now than it was in the first three decades of the 20th century. The census of 2000 found that about 10 percent of the population was foreign-born. In the censuses of 1900, 1910, and 1920, that share was some 14 percent. (Then as now, the nation's black population was about 12 percent.) In those early years of the last century, American society was not certain of its ability to absorb millions of newcomers. The public schools took on the job of educating and preparing them for social, civic, and economic participation in the life of the nation.

What did the public schools in those early years do about their new clientele? First, they taught them to speak, read, and write English—a vital necessity for a successful transition into American society. Because many children served as translators for their parents, these skills were valuable to the entire family in negotiating with employers, shops, and government agencies. The schools also taught habits of good hygiene (a matter of public health), as well as appropriate self-discipline and behavior. More than the three "Rs," schools taught children how to speak correctly, how to behave in a group, how to meet deadlines, and how to dress for different situations (skills needed as much by native-born rural youth as by immigrant children). Certainly, the schools taught foreign-born children about American history (especially about national holidays, the Constitution, the Revolutionary War, and the Civil War), with a strong emphasis on the positive aspects of the American drama.

They also taught children about the "American way of life," the habits, ideals, values, and attitudes (such as the American spirit of individualism) that made their new country special. If one could sum up this education policy, it was one that celebrated America and invited newcomers to become full members of American society.

During the late 1960s and early 1970s, assimilation came to be viewed as an illegitimate, coercive imposition of American ways on unwitting children, both foreign-born and nonwhite. With the rise of the black separatist movement in 1966, black nationalists such as Stokely Carmichael began inveighing against racial integration and advocating community control of public schools in black neighborhoods. In response, many black educators demanded African-American history, African-American heroes, African-American literature, and African-American celebrations in the public schools. In the 1970s, the white ethnic revival followed the black model, and soon government was funding celebrations of ethnic heritage in the schools. By the mid-1970s, just as immigration was beginning to increase rapidly, the public schools no longer focused on acculturating the children of newcomers to American society. Instead, they encouraged children to appreciate and retain their ethnic and racial origins.

The expectation that the public schools will teach children about their racial and ethnic heritage has created enormous practical problems. First, it has promoted the belief that what is taught in school will vary in response to the particular ethnic makeup of the school. Thus, a predominantly African-American school will learn one set of lessons, while a predominantly Hispanic school will learn yet another, and an ethnically mixed school will learn—what? Second, schools have begun to lose a sense of a distinctive American culture, a culture forged by people from many different backgrounds that is nonetheless a coherent national culture. No state in the nation requires students to read any particular book, poem, or play. Today schools are uncertain about how to teach American history, what to teach as "American" literature, and how to teach world history without omitting any corner of the world (many children learn no world history). Third, the teaching of racial and ethnic pride is itself problematic, as it appears to be a continuation in a new guise of one of the worst aspects of American history.

From our public schools' experiences over the past century, we have learned much about the relative advantages and disadvantages of assimilationism and multiculturalism in the public schools.

Assimilation surely has its strengths. A democratic society must seek to give every young person, whether native-born or newcomer, the knowledge and skills to succeed as an adult. In a political system that relies on the participation of informed citizens, everyone should, at a minimum, learn to speak, read, and write a common language. Those who would sustain our democratic life must understand its history. To maximize their ability to succeed in the future, young people must also learn mathematics and science. Tailoring children's education to the color of their skin, their national origins, or their presumed ethnicity is in some fundamental sense contrary to our nation's founding ideals of democracy, equality, and opportunity.

And yet we know that assimilationism by itself is an inadequate strategy for American public education, for two reasons. First, it ignores the strengths that immigrants have to offer; and second, it presumes that American culture is static, which is surely not true. When immigrants arrive in America, they tend to bring with them, often after an emotionally costly journey, a sense of optimism, a strong family and religious tradition, and a willingness to work hard—values and attitudes that our society respects, but that affluence and media cynicism have eroded among many of our own citizens.

But neither is "celebrating diversity" an adequate strategy for a multiracial, multi-ethnic society like ours. The public schools exist to build an American community, to help both newcomers and native-born children prepare for adulthood as fellow citizens. Strategies that divide children along racial and ethnic lines encourage resentment and alienation rather than mutual respect. The ultimate democratic lesson is human equality, and the schools must teach our children that we are all in the same boat, all members of one society, regardless of race, ethnicity, or place of origin.

We learned that lesson the hardest way possible on September 11, when thousands of people from many countries died together in a single tragedy.

How will America's schools respond in the days ahead? It seems clear that they must make a pact with the children in their care. They must honor the strong and positive values that the children's families bring to America, and in return they must be prepared to give the children access to the best of America's heritage.

America's newcomers did not come to our shores merely to become consumers. They came to share in our democratic heritage and to become possessors of the grand ideas that created and sustained the democratic experiment in this country for more than two centuries. They too have a contribution to make to the evolving story of our nation. Whether they do so will depend in large part on whether our educational system respects them enough to help them become Americans.

The terrible events of this past fall have shown that Americans of all races and ethnic groups share a tremendous sense of national spirit and civic unity. They recognize that, whatever their origins, they share a common destiny as Americans. America's schools should honor that reality.

POSTNOTE

Diane Ravitch is one of the leading educational thinkers in the United States. Her training as a historian makes her a keen observer of educational trends and an advocate of strengthening student learning in core content subjects. As such, her article is one of our Classic picks.

The tensions Ravitch discusses—between multiculturalism and monoculturalism, between diversity and acculturation—are old and deep in the American schools. Emphasis has shifted back and forth toward one or the other extreme over the years, depending on historical events and, often, the energies of advocates. Currently, because of a huge influx of immigrants into the United States during the 1990s, and fueled by the 9/11 attacks on our country, the emphasis is shifting toward acculturation and a rebirth of patriotism. Nevertheless, this strikes us as an unnecessary distinction. Our national motto is "E pluribus unum"—from the many comes the one. A good school can honor the varied backgrounds of its students and at the same time teach all the requirements and expectations of good citizens. To do less is to miseducate.

Discussion Questions

1. How was multiculturalism taught or exhibited in your schooling, and how did students respond to the school's efforts?
2. Have you seen a change in emphasis on either multiculturalism or national acculturation since 9/11?
3. What ideas do you have for dealing with these issues in your classroom?

Diversity within Unity: Essential Principles for Teaching and Learning in a Multicultural Society

James A. Banks, Peter Cookson, Geneva Gay, Willis D. Hawley, Jacqueline Jordan Irvine, Sonia Nieto, Janet Ward Schofield, and Walter G. Stephan

51

James A. Banks is Russell F. Stark University Professor and director of the Center for Multicultural Education, University of Washington. **Peter Cookson** is a faculty member at Teachers College, Columbia University. **Geneva Gay** is a professor of education and faculty associate at the Center for Multicultural Education, University of Washington. **Willis D. Hawley** is a professor of education and public affairs, University of Maryland. **Jacqueline Jordan Irvine** is the Charles Howard Candler Professor Emerita of Urban Education, Emory University. **Sonia Nieto** is a professor of language, literacy, and culture, University of Massachusetts, Amherst. **Janet Ward Schofield** is a professor of psychology and a senior scientist at the Learning Research and Development Center, University of Pittsburgh. **Walter G. Stephan** is a professor of psychology, New Mexico State University.

"Diversity Within Unity: Essential Principles for Teaching and Learning in a Multicultural Society" by James A. Banks, Peter Cookson, Geneva Gay, Willis D. Hawley, Jacqueline Jordan Irvine, Sonia Nieto, Janet Ward Schofield, and Walter G. Stephan, *Phi Delta Kappan* Vol. 83, No. 3, November 2001, pp. 196–203. Reprinted with the permission of James A. Banks.

F | O | C | U | S | QUESTION

What do we know about education and diversity, and how do we know it?

KEY TERMS
Achievement gap
Conflict resolution
Culturally responsive teaching
Formative assessment
Multicultural education
Summative assessment

What do we know about education and diversity, and how do we know it? This two-part question guided the work of the Multicultural Education Consensus Panel, sponsored by the Center for Multicultural Education at the University of Washington and the Common Destiny Alliance at the University of Maryland. This article is the product of a four-year project during which the panel, with support from the Carnegie Corporation of New York, reviewed and synthesized the research related to diversity.

The panel members are an interdisciplinary group consisting of two psychologists, a political scientist, a sociologist, and four specialists in multicultural education. The panel was modeled after the consensus panels that develop and write reports for the National Academy of Sciences. In such panels, an expert group studies research and practice and arrives at a conclusion about what is known about a particular problem and the most effective actions that can be taken to solve it.

The findings of the Multicultural Education Consensus Panel, which we call *essential principles* in this article, describe ways in which education policy and practice related to diversity can be improved. These principles are derived from both research and practice. They are designed to help practitioners in all types of schools increase student academic achievement and improve intergroup skills. Another aim is to help schools successfully meet the challenges of and benefit from the diversity that characterizes the United States.

Schools can make a significant difference in the lives of students, and they are a key to maintaining a free and democratic society. Democratic societies are fragile and are works in progress. Their existence depends on a thoughtful citizenry that believes in democratic ideals and is willing and able to participate in the civic life of the nation. We realize that the public schools are experiencing a great deal of criticism. However, we believe that they are essential to ensuring the survival of our democracy.

We have organized the 12 essential principles into five categories: 1) teacher learning; 2) student learning; 3) intergroup relations; 4) school governance, organization, and equity; and 5) assessment. Although these categories overlap to some extent, we think readers will find this organization helpful.

Teacher Learning

Principle 1. Professional development programs should help teachers understand the complex characteristics of ethnic groups within U.S. society and the ways in which race, ethnicity, language, and social class interact to influence student behavior. Continuing education about diversity is especially important for teachers because of the increasing cultural and ethnic gap that exists between the nation's teachers and students. Effective professional development programs should help educators to 1) uncover and identify their personal attitudes toward racial, ethnic, language, and cultural groups; 2) acquire knowledge about the histories and cultures of the diverse racial, ethnic, cultural, and language groups within the nation and within their schools; 3) become acquainted with the diverse perspectives that exist within different ethnic and cultural communities; 4) understand the ways in which institutionalized knowledge within schools, universities, and the popular culture can perpetuate stereotypes about racial and ethnic groups; and 5) acquire the knowledge and skills needed to develop and implement an equity pedagogy, defined by James Banks as instruction that provides all students with an equal opportunity to attain academic and social success in school.[1]

Professional development programs should help teachers understand the complex characteristics of ethnic groups and how such variables as social class, religion, region, generation, extent of urbanization, and gender strongly influence ethnic and cultural behavior. These variables influence the behavior of groups both singly and interactively. Indeed, social class is one of the most important variables that mediate and influence behavior. In his widely discussed book, *The Declining Significance of Race,* William Julius Wilson argues that class is becoming increasingly important in the lives of African Americans.[2] The increasing significance of class rather than the declining significance of race might be a more accurate description of the phenomenon that Wilson describes. Racism continues to affect African Americans of every social class, but it does so in complex ways that to some extent—though by no means always—reflect social-class status.

If teachers are to increase learning opportunities for all students, they must be knowledgeable about the social and cultural contexts of teaching and learning. Although students are not solely products of their cultures and vary in the degree to which they identify with them, there are some distinctive cultural behaviors that are associated with ethnic groups.[3] Thus teachers should become knowledgeable about the cultural backgrounds of their students. They should also acquire the skills needed to translate that knowledge into effective instruction and an enriched curriculum.[4] Teaching should be culturally responsive to students from diverse racial, ethnic, cultural, and language groups.

Making teaching culturally responsive involves strategies such as constructing and designing relevant cultural metaphors and multicultural representations to help bridge the gap between what students already know and appreciate and what they are to be taught. Culturally responsive instructional strategies transform information about the home and community into effective classroom practice. Rather than rely on generalized notions of ethnic groups that can be misleading, effective teachers use knowledge of their students' culture and ethnicity as a framework for inquiry. They also use culturally responsive activities, resources, and strategies to organize and implement instruction.

Student Learning

Principle 2. Schools should ensure that all students have equitable opportunities to learn and to meet high standards. Schools can be thought of as collections of opportunities to learn.[5] A good school maximizes the learning experiences of its students. One might judge the fairness of educational opportunity by comparing the learning opportunities students have within and across schools. The most important of these opportunities to learn are 1) teacher quality (indicators include experience, preparation to teach the content, participation in high-quality professional development, verbal ability, and opportunity to receive teacher rewards and incentives); 2) a safe and orderly learning environment; 3) time actively engaged in learning; 4) low student/teacher ratio; 5) rigor of the curriculum; 6) grouping practices that avoid tracking and rigid forms of student assignment based on past performance; 7) sophistication and currency of learning resources and information technology used by students; and 8) access to extracurricular activities.

Although the consequences of these different characteristics of schools vary with particular conditions, the available research suggests that, when two or more cohorts of students differ significantly in their access to opportunities to learn, differences in the quality of education also exist.[6] Such differences affect student achievement and can undermine the prospects for positive intergroup relations.

The content that makes up the lessons students are taught influences the level of student achievement. This is hardly surprising, but the curriculum students experience and the expectations of teachers and others about how much of the material they will learn vary from school to school. In general, students who are taught curricula that are more rigorous learn more than their peers with similar prior knowledge and backgrounds who are taught less-demanding curricula. For example, earlier access to algebra leads to greater participation in higher-level math courses and to increased academic achievement.

Principle 3. The curriculum should help students understand that knowledge is socially constructed and reflects researchers' personal experiences as well as the social, political, and economic contexts in which they live and work. In curriculum and teaching units and in textbooks, students often study historical events, concepts, and issues only or primarily from the points of view of the victors.[7] The perspectives of the vanquished are frequently silenced, ignored, or marginalized. This kind of teaching privileges mainstream students—those who most often identify with the victors or dominant groups—and causes many students of color to feel left out of the American story.

Concepts such as the "discovery" of America, the westward movement, and the role of the pioneers are often taught primarily from the points of view of the European Americans who constructed them. The curriculum should help students to understand how these concepts reflect the values and perspectives of European Americans and describe their experiences in the United States. Teachers should help students learn how these concepts have very different meanings for groups indigenous to America and for those who were brought to America in chains.

Teaching students the different—and often conflicting—meanings of concepts and issues for the diverse groups that make up the U.S. population will help them to better understand the complex factors that contributed to the birth, growth, and development of the nation. Such teaching will also help students develop empathy for the points of view and perspectives of various groups and will increase their ability to think critically.

Principle 4. Schools should provide all students with opportunities to participate in extracurricular and cocurricular activities that develop knowledge, skills, and attitudes that increase academic achievement and foster positive interracial relationships. Research evidence that links student achievement to participation in extracurricular and cocurricular activities is increasing in quantity and consistency.[8] There is significant research that supports the proposition that participation in after-school programs, sports activities, academic clubs, and school-sponsored social activities contributes to academic performance, reduces dropout rates and discipline problems, and enhances interpersonal skills among students from different ethnic backgrounds. Kris Gutiérrez and her colleagues, for example, found that "nonformal learning contexts," such as after-school programs, are useful in bridging home and school cultures for students from diverse groups.[9] Jomills Braddock concluded that involvement in sports activities was particularly beneficial for male African American high school students.[10] When designing extracurricular activities, educators should give special attention to recruitment, selection of leaders and teams, the cost of participating, allocation of school resources, and opportunities for cooperative intergroup contact.

Intergroup Relations

Principle 5. Schools should create or make salient superordinate or cross-cutting groups in order to improve intergroup relations. Creating superordinate groups—groups with which members of other groups in a given situation identify—improves intergroup relations.[11] When membership in superordinate groups is salient, other group differences become less important. Creating superordinate groups stimulates fellowship and cohesion and so can mitigate preexisting animosities.

In school settings many superordinate groups can be created or made salient. For example, it is possible to create superordinate groups through extracurricular activities. And many existing superordinate groups can be made more salient: the classroom, the grade level, the school, the community, the state, and even the nation. The most immediate superordinate groups (e.g., the school chorus rather than the state of California) are likely to be the most influential, but identification with any superordinate group can reduce prejudice.

Principle 6. Students should learn about stereotyping and other related biases that have negative effects on racial and ethnic relations. We use categories in perceiving our environment because categorization is a natural part of human information processing. But the mere act of categorizing people as members of an "in group" and an "out group" can result in stereotyping, prejudice, and discrimination.[12] Specifically, making distinctions between groups can lead to the perception that the "other group" is more homogeneous than one's own group, and this, in turn, can lead to an exaggeration of the extent of the group differences. Thus categorizing leads to stereotyping and to behaviors influenced by those stereotypes.

Intergroup contact can counteract stereotypes if the situation allows members of each group to behave in a variety of ways across different contexts, so that their full humanity and diversity are displayed. Negative stereotypes can also be modified in noncontact situations by providing members of the "in group" with information about members of the "out group" who disconfirm a stereotype across a variety of situations.[13]

Principle 7. Students should learn about the values shared by virtually all cultural groups (e.g., justice, equality, freedom, peace, compassion, and charity). Teaching students about the values that virtually all groups share, such as those described in the UN Universal Bill of Rights, can provide a basis for perceived similarity that can promote favorable intergroup relations.[14] In addition, the values themselves serve to undercut negative intergroup relations by discouraging injustice, inequality, unfairness, conflict, and a lack of compassion. The value of egalitarianism deserves special emphasis since a number of theories suggest that it can help to undermine stereotyping and prejudiced thinking and can help restrict the direct expression of racism.[15]

Principle 8. Teachers should help students acquire the social skills needed to interact effectively with students from other racial, ethnic, cultural, and language groups. One of the most effective techniques for improving intercultural relations is to teach members of the cultural groups the social skills necessary to interact effectively with members of another culture.[16] Students need to learn how to perceive, understand, and respond to group differences. They need to learn not to give offense and not to take offense. They also need to be helped to realize that, when members of other groups behave in ways that are inconsistent with the norms of the students' own group, these individuals are not necessarily behaving antagonistically.

One intergroup relations trainer asks members of the minority and majority groups to discuss what it feels like to be the target of stereotyping, prejudice, and discrimination.[17] Sharing such information informs the majority group of the pain and suffering their intentional or thoughtless acts of discrimination cause. It also allows the members of minority groups to share their experiences with one another. Other techniques that involve sharing experiences through carefully managed dialogue have also been found to improve intergroup relations.[18]

One skill that can be taught in schools in order to improve intergroup relations is conflict resolution.[19] A number of school districts throughout the U.S. are teaching students to act as mediators in disputes between other students.

Principle 9. Schools should provide opportunities for students from different racial, ethnic, cultural, and language groups to interact socially under conditions designed to reduce fear and anxiety. One of the primary causes of prejudice is fear.[20] Fear leads members of social groups to avoid interacting with members of other groups and causes them discomfort when they do. Fears about members of other groups often stem from concern about threats—both realistic and symbolic—to the "in group." Many such fears have little basis in reality or are greatly exaggerated.

To reduce uncertainty and anxiety concerning interaction with members of other groups, the contexts in which interactions between groups take place should be relatively structured, the balance of members of the different groups should be as equal as possible, the likelihood of failure should be low, and opportunities for hostility and aggression should be minimized. Providing factual information that contradicts misperceptions can also counteract prejudice that is based on a false sense of threat. Stressing the similarities in the values of the groups should also reduce the degree of symbolic threat posed by "out groups" and thus reduce fear and prejudice.

School Governance, Organization, and Equity

Principle 10. A school's organizational strategies should ensure that decision making is widely shared and that members of the school community learn collaborative skills and dispositions in order to create a caring learning environment for students. School policies and practices are the living embodiment of a society's underlying values and educational philosophy. They also reflect the values of those who work within schools. Whether in the form of curriculum, teaching strategies, assessment procedures, disciplinary policies, or grouping practices, school policies embody a school's beliefs, attitudes, and expectations of its students.[21] This is true whether the school is one with extensive or limited financial resources, whether its student body is relatively monocultural or richly diverse, or whether it is located in a crowded central city or an isolated rural county.

School organization and leadership can either enhance or detract from the development of learning communities that prepare students for a multicultural and democratic society. Schools that are administered from the top down are unlikely to create collaborative, caring cultures. Too often schools talk about democracy but fail to practice shared decision making.

Powerful multicultural schools are organizational hubs that include a wide variety of stakeholders, ranging from students, teachers, and administrators to parents and members of the community. Indeed, there is convincing research evidence that parent involvement, in particular, is critical in enhancing student learning.[22] And a just multicultural school is receptive to working with all members of the students' communities.

Principle 11. Leaders should ensure that all public schools, regardless of their locations, are funded equitably. Equity in school funding is a critical condition for creating just multicultural schools. The current inequities in the funding of public education are startling.[23] Two communities that are adjacent to one another can provide wholly different support to their public schools, based on property values and tax rates. Students who live in poor communities are punished because they must attend schools that are underfunded by comparison to the schools in more affluent communities.

The relationship between increased school expenditures and school improvement is complex.[24] But when investments are made in ways that significantly improve students' opportunities to learn—such as increasing teacher quality, reducing class size in targeted ways, and engaging parents in their children's education—the result is likely to be improved student knowledge and skills.

The failure of schools and school systems to provide all students with equitable resources for learning will, of course, work to the disadvantage of those receiving inadequate resources and will usually widen the achievement gap between schools. Since achievement correlates highly with students' family income and since people of color are disproportionately represented in the low-income sector, inequity in opportunities to learn contributes to the achievement gap between students of color and white students.

Assessment

Principle 12. Teachers should use multiple culturally sensitive techniques to assess complex cognitive and social skills. Evaluating the progress of students from diverse racial and ethnic groups and social classes is complicated by differences in language, learning styles, and cultures. Hence the use of a single method of assessment will probably further disadvantage students from particular social classes and ethnic groups.

Teachers should adopt a range of formative and summative assessment strategies that give students an opportunity to demonstrate mastery. These strategies should include observations, oral examinations, performances, and teacher-made as well as standardized assessments. Students learn and demonstrate their competencies in different ways. The preferred mode of demonstrating task mastery for some is writing, while others do better speaking, visualizing, or performing; some are stimulated by competition and others by cooperation; some prefer to work alone, while others would rather work in groups. Consequently, a variety of assessment procedures and outcomes that are compatible with different learning, performance, work, and presentation styles should be used to determine whether students are mastering the skills they need to function effectively in a multicultural society.

Assessment should go beyond traditional measures of subject-matter knowledge and include consideration of complex cognitive and social skills. Effective citizenship in a multicultural society requires individuals who have the values and abilities to promote equality and justice among culturally diverse groups.

Conclusion

Powerful multicultural schools help students from diverse racial, cultural, ethnic, and language groups to experience academic success. Academic knowledge and skills are essential in today's global society. However, they are not sufficient to guarantee full and active participation in that society. Students must also develop the knowledge, attitudes, and skills needed to interact positively with people from diverse groups and to participate in the civic life of the nation. Students must be competent in intergroup and civic skills if they are to function effectively in today's complex and ethnically polarized nation and world.

Diversity in the nation's schools is both an opportunity and a challenge. The nation is enriched by the ethnic, cultural, and language diversity of its citizens. However, whenever diverse groups interact, intergroup tension, stereotypes, and institutionalized discrimination develop. Schools must find ways to respect the diversity of their students and to help create a unified nation to which all citizens have allegiance. Structural inclusion in the public life of the nation together with power sharing will engender feelings of allegiance among diverse groups. Diversity within unity is the delicate goal toward which our nation and its schools should strive. We offer these design principles in the hope that they will help education policy makers and practitioners realize the elusive but essential goals of a democratic and pluralistic society.

NOTES

1. James A. Banks, "Multicultural Education: Historical Development, Dimensions, and Practice," in James A. Banks and Cherry A. McGee Banks, eds., *Handbook of Research on Multicultural Education* (San Francisco: Jossey-Bass, 2001), pp. 1–24.
2. William Julius Wilson, *The Declining Significance of Race: Blacks and Changing American Institutions* (Chicago: University of Chicago Press, 1978).
3. A. Wade Boykin, "The Triple Quandary and the Schooling of Afro-American Children," in Ulric Neisser, ed., *The School Achievement of Minority Children: New Perspectives* (Hillsdale, N.J.: Erlbaum, 1986), pp. 57–92.
4. Geneva Gay, *Culturally Responsive Teaching: Theory, Research, and Practice* (New York: Teachers College Press, 2000).
5. Linda Darling-Hammond, *The Right to Learn* (San Francisco: Jossey-Bass, 1997).
6. Robert Dreeben and Adam Gamoran, "Race, Instruction, and Learning," *American Sociological Review,* vol. 51, 1986, pp. 660–69.
7. James A. Banks, *Cultural Diversity and Education: Foundations, Curriculum, and Teaching,* 4th ed. (Boston: Allyn and Bacon, 2001).
8. Jomills Braddock, "Bouncing Back: Sports and Academic Resilience Among African-American Males," *Education and Urban Society,* vol. 24, 1991, pp. 113–31; Jacquelynne S. Eccles and Bonnie L. Barber, "Student Council, Volunteering, Basketball, or Marching Band: What Kind of Extracurricular Involvement Matters?," *Journal of Adolescence Research,* January 1999, pp. 10–43; and Jennifer A. Goorman, ed., *After-School Programs to Promote Child and Adolescent Development: Summary of a Workshop* (Washington, D.C.: National Academy Press, 2000).
9. Kris D. Gutiérrez et al., "Building a Culture of Collaboration Through Hybrid Language Practices," *Theory into Practice,* vol. 38, 1999, pp. 87–93.
10. Braddock, op. cit.
11. Samuel Gaertner et al., "The Contact Hypothesis: The Role of a Common Ingroup Identity on Reducing Intergroup Bias," *Small Group Research,* vol. 25, 1994, pp. 224–49.
12. Henri Tajfel and John C. Turner, "The Social Identity Theory of Intergroup Behavior," in Stephen Worchel and William G. Austin, eds., *Psychology of Intergroup Relations,* 2nd ed. (Chicago: Nelson-Hall, 1986), pp. 7–24.
13. Lucy Johnston and Miles Hewstone, "Cognitive Models of Stereotype Change," *Journal of Experimental Social Psychology,* vol. 28, 1992, pp. 360–86.
14. Lawrence Kohlberg, *Essays on Moral Development* (New York: Harper & Row, 1981).
15. Samuel L. Gaertner and John F. Dovidio, "The Aversive Form of Racism," in John F. Dovidio and Samuel L. Gaertner, eds., *Prejudice, Discrimination, and Racism* (Orlando, Fla.: Academic Press, 1986), pp. 61–90; and Irwin Katz, David C. Glass, and Joyce Wackenhut, "An Ambivalence-Amplification Theory of Behavior Toward the Stigmatized," in Worchel and Austin, pp. 103–17.
16. Stephen Bochner, "Culture Shock," in Walter Lonner and Roy Malpass, eds., *Psychology and Culture* (Boston: Allyn and Bacon, 1994), pp. 245–52.
17. Louis Kamfer and David J. L. Venter, "First Evaluation of a Stereotype Reduction Workshop," *South African Journal of Psychology,* vol. 24, 1994, pp. 13–20.
18. Ximena Zúñiga and Biren Nagda, "Dialogue Groups: An Innovative Approach to Multicultural Learning," in David Schoem et al., eds., *Multicultural Teaching in the University* (Westport, Conn.: Praeger, 1993), pp. 233–48.
19. Morton Deutsch, "Cooperative Learning and Conflict Resolution in an Alternative High School," *Cooperative Learning,* vol. 13, 1993, pp. 2–5.
20. Gaertner and Dovidio, op. cit.; and Walter G. Stephan, *Reducing Prejudice and Stereotyping in Schools* (New York: Teachers College Press, 1999).
21. Sonia Nieto, *The Light in Their Eyes: Creating Multicultural Learning Communities* (New York: Teachers College Press, 1999).
22. Joyce L. Epstein, "School and Family Partnerships," in Marvin C. Alkin, ed., *Encyclopedia of Educational Research,* 6th ed. (New York: Macmillan, 1992), pp. 1139–51.
23. Jonathan Kozol, *Savage Inequalities: Children in America's Schools* (New York: Crown Publishers, 1991).
24. Eric A. Hanushek, "School Resources and Student Performance," in Gary Burtless, ed., *Does Money Matter? The Effect of School Resources on Student Achievement and Adult Success* (Washington, D.C.: Brookings Institution Press, 1996), pp. 43–73.

POSTNOTE

Multicultural education is a controversial issue, partly because there is no generally accepted definition. Some people see multicultural education as being divisive, creating separate pockets of different cultures, rather than helping to create a common culture. Others see multicultural education as valuing cultural pluralism, and recognizing that cultural diversity is a valuable resource that should be preserved and extended. The committee that wrote this article rejects both assimilation and separatism as ultimate goals. They recognize that each subculture exists as part of an interrelated whole. Multicultural education reaches beyond awareness and understanding of cultural differences to recognize the right of these different cultures to exist and to value that existence.

In addition to valuing cultural diversity, multicultural education is also based on the concept of *social justice*, which seeks to do away with social and economic inequalities for those who have been denied these benefits in our democratic society.

African Americans, Native Americans, Asian Americans, Hispanic Americans, women, individuals with special needs, people with limited English proficiency, persons with low incomes, members of particular religious groups, and homosexuals are among those groups that have at one time or another been denied social justice. Educators who support multicultural education see establishing social justice for all groups of people who have experienced discrimination as a moral and ethical responsibility. Extending the concept of multicultural education to include a broader population has also contributed to its controversy.

Discussion Questions

1. In your own words, what does multicultural education mean?
2. In your opinion, should cultural pluralism be a goal of our society and its schools? Why or why not?
3. What examples of multicultural education can you describe from your own education?

RELATED WEBSITE RESOURCES AND VIDEO CASES

 ### Web Resources:

Multicultural Pavilion. Available at:

http://www.edchange.org/multicultural/index.html.

> *This website provides excellent resources for teachers, research, and articles on multicultural education.*

 ### Video Case:

Culturally Responsive Teaching: A Multicultural Lesson for Elementary Students

In this video case, you will see how a literacy specialist weaves a lesson on multiculturalism into a traditional lesson on the five-paragraph essay. As you watch the clips and study the artifacts in the case, reflect upon the following questions:

1. How does this project reflect the principles of culturally responsive teaching?
2. How can you go about acquiring more knowledge of the world and its people?

52

The Challenge of Diversity and Choice

Charles Glenn

Charles Glenn is a professor of education at Boston University, and served for two decades as the Massachusetts state education official responsible for urban education.

"The Challenge of Diversity and Choice" by Charles Glenn, *Educational Horizons*, Vol. 83, No. 2, Winter 2005, pp. 101–109. Reprinted by permission of the author.

|F|O|C|U|S| QUESTION

Does school choice and diversity make schooling more equitable for all students?

KEY TERMS

Equal educational opportunity

School choice

More than twenty years ago, an urban superintendent in Massachusetts lamented to me that he was being asked to encourage differences among the schools in his district. For decades he had sought to ensure that all the schools in his district were as similar as possible, that it wouldn't matter where a student was assigned. Now, to help parents choose out-of-neighborhood schools and thus facilitate voluntary racial integration, he was being asked in the name of "educational equity" to undo what he had devoted his career to doing—also in the name of educational equity. Wouldn't helping schools become distinctive create new inequalities and injustices? he asked.

It was a good question—one that I found myself answering frequently in twenty-one years of directing the state's educational-equity efforts. On the one hand, I told administrators, educators should work to eliminate differences in educational quality, as measured both by inputs of schooling (the training and experience of teachers, for example, and the quality of facilities and other resources) and by outputs of instruction (performance on standardized tests, persistence in education). Those battles are far from won, even after the past thirty or forty years of massive spending and other efforts in the name of equal educational opportunity. In particular, the gap in educational effectiveness among schools in different communities is inexcusably large—in fact, larger than in other Western democracies with diverse populations.

On the other hand, schools of equal educational quality need not be identical, and the recent trend toward increased choice and diversity in American schooling has if anything made the system more equitable for children who previously had no choice but to attend poorly performing schools. That is not to say that all forms of school choice are good public policy: as I will suggest, choice can have positive or negative effects, depending upon the policy framework that guides it.

First, though, a quick overview of what I mean by choice and diversity: In 1970, when I began my career as a state education official, American public schools varied widely in both quality and curricula, but it was essentially an unacknowledged variation, the guilty secret behind what I would later call "the myth of the common school." In most cases, local officials assigned students to public schools according to where they lived. Parents dissatisfied with assignments often enrolled their children in tuition-charging private schools (if they lived in a city, usually Roman Catholic schools) or moved to different districts; in a few cases local policies allowed them to transfer their children on a space-available basis. (In fact, when my division of the Massachusetts Department of Education set out to achieve racial desegregation of the Boston public schools, it found that some 7,000 white students had taken advantage of open enrollment to flee their neighborhood schools in racially changing parts of the city.)

By contrast, parents and students in Boston today can access a bewildering menu of educational opportunities. There are now numerous moderately priced private schools, either non-Roman Catholic or non-sectarian and nonreligious (although fewer Roman Catholic schools are available). More significant, there is a choice process for public school enrollment. Parents indicate their school preferences through parent information centers, and school assignments seek to fulfill those preferences, with random selection for oversubscribed schools.

The first such methods of "controlled choice," pioneered in Cambridge and then adopted in a dozen other Massachusetts cities, were intended not only to increase racial and social class integration but also to allow the staff of each school to develop distinctive educational identities that would satisfy some parents very much rather than barely satisfy many. Nonetheless, policymakers and parents soon discovered that the inflexibility of the school systems limited the schools' distinctiveness. Thus Massachusetts (like two-thirds of all states) adopted charter school legislation that has fostered dozens of new public schools, each approved by the state for its distinctive approach. In response, the Boston Public Schools adopted its own program of distinctive pilot schools freed from some local requirements and went on to break up high schools into smaller units, each with its own flavor and mission.

My oldest grandson, whose family lives in Boston, entered first grade this fall; his parents spent months considering all the alternatives available. Elsewhere, many parents have even more alternatives, including cyberschools, whose students never meet their teachers or one another, and in three states voucher programs, with others on the way.

Americans have good reason to welcome this evolution, though there are dangers. Those who urge expanded parental choice in U.S. schools advance four primary arguments; most advocates employ all four, though generally one or another is emphasized:

1. The liberty to shape the education of one's children through school choice is a fundamental matter guaranteed by international human rights covenants.

2. Publicly funded school choice is especially a matter of justice for poor parents because more-affluent parents already have their choice of schools.
3. Market pressures, freedom from bureaucracy, and the opportunity to focus on a clearly defined mission will make schools more effective educationally.
4. Variety in the forms of schooling is inherently a good thing, given that pupils have differing strengths and needs and respond well to different approaches—the implication, after all, of Howard Gardner's theory of multiple intelligences.

Correspondingly, four primary arguments are raised against school choice—usually without mentioning the ways in which choice threatens the educational status quo.

1. School choice may lead to increased racial and social class segregation.
2. Choice will lead to (further) degradation of the public educational system (or, in the case of choice limited to public schools, to the schools that are already least successful), and thus to inferior education for those who do not participate.
3. Choice will lead to new injustices since the poor will not be able to participate on equal terms.
4. Choice will lead to Balkanization of American society and further conflict by exposing various groups to divisive influences, rather than the socialization provided by the common public school.

Most thoughtful advocates of expanded school choice concede—certainly I do—that all those possibilities are real and serious unless choice is organized effectively, and some thoughtful opponents concede that it is possible to organize choice to prevent negative effects. The dispute often, therefore, comes down to whether the positive effects of choice can be enjoyed and the negative ones prevented once choice is widely available.

Several years ago Joe Nathan of the University of Minnesota and I, longtime allies in working for school reform, spent a day together identifying our agreements and disagreements about parental choice of schools. Dr. Nathan opposes supporting religious schools with public funds (either directly or with vouchers), funding single-sex schools, and allowing schools to set admissions requirements related to their educational mission; I support all three under some circumstances. The result was agreement on the principles any acceptable school choice policy must reflect (see accompanying table).

A Model School Choice Policy

School choice must:

a. Provide better education for poor children and more effective involvement for their parents (the bottom-line criterion for judging whether a school choice policy is acceptable)

b. Provide for more accountability for validly measurable educational outcomes than now provided by public schooling based upon a local monopoly

c. Be based upon clear standards for the educational outcomes that every pupil should achieve at every level in order to participate effectively in our society, political order, and economy

d. Forbid discrimination in admission to schools, or in employment at those schools, on the basis of race

e. Make effective provision for outreach to parents, especially low-income and language-minority parents, to ensure that they are well informed about the choices available and how those can be matched with the strengths, needs, and interests of their children, and with their own hopes and beliefs about education

f. Ensure that geography and the availability of affordable housing do not prevent low-income families from having access to the full range of opportunities, including help with transportation

g. Ensure that no participating school lacks adequate safeguards for treating pupils and teachers fairly and respectfully

h. Ensure that the interests of pupils with special needs, limited proficiency in English, or other conditions requiring additional assistance are met adequately and, so far as possible, while safeguarding their parents' opportunity to make choices about their education

i. Ensure that the resources available to pupils in different schools—teachers and other staff as well as facilities and materials—are adequate and are not based upon their parents' wealth

j. Bar the participation of schools that teach hatred or disrespect for any racial, religious, ethnic, or sexual group

k. Ensure that there are real choices available and that meeting the criteria listed above does not impose a drab uniformity of curriculum, school life, or teaching style

l. Ensure autonomy to make staffing and budgetary decisions at the school level (in order to protect the distinctive character of schools among which parents can choose, based upon clarity of mission and a shared understanding of education)

m. Ensure that reform efforts are applied in a context in which any school that receives public funding, including a "regular" public school, bears the same responsibility as charter schools either to improve its educational results (as measured by standardized tests and other valid indicators over a three- to five-year period) or to be closed

It will be obvious from this extensive list that neither of us is a libertarian, willing to "let the market rip" or "let the devil take the hindmost." Instead, though we differ on whether some forms of educational diversity, such as schools with a religious character, should be eligible for public support, we agree that school choice should operate within a solid framework of policies and public accountability to ensure that all children benefit.

* * *

This article could go on at length about what form policies friendly to parental choice should take: just last year I published, with a European colleague, a two-volume study of how twenty-six different countries have regulated the provision of schooling in order to balance school autonomy and public accountability.

Here, however, I'd like to warn of a danger that can be addressed effectively only by educators, not by government. A painstakingly designed system of public school diversity and choice might allow teachers and other educators to design the schools of their dreams and allow parents to choose among those schools based on solid information about each, all within a framework of protection and accountability—yet the resulting schools might largely prove uninspired carbon copies produced by educators lacking the foggiest idea of how to do anything differently.

I first contemplated that possibility in the late 1980s, when the Boston Public Schools' new "controlled choice" policy required schools to attract pupils without relying on attendance zones to provide a guaranteed clientele. Each school had unprecedented flexibility to redesign its programs and to use external funding to support its distinctive mission. Any school that was not attracting enough applications received generous paid planning time after school and over the summer, as well as a budget for outside consultants of its choosing, to develop attractive programs. A state-federal task force I headed scoured the country for alternative models of effective urban education that schools could adopt.

In some cases, the response from individual teachers or from whole groups of teachers was gratifying, and many schools underwent significant changes. In most cases, though, teachers were reluctant to identify meaningful aspects of the school that required change: "more parking for the teachers" was the only result of one school's planning process! In some cases, the action plans were concerned more with improving the image of the schools than with improving their instructional programs.

There is probably a more basic issue, too: public schools have long practiced a sort of defensive teaching designed not to offend any parent—in effect, "the bland leading the bland." As my book *The Myth of the Common School* shows, urban public schools with large immigrant enrollments came under pressure in the 1850s to remove textbooks that offended Roman Catholics; in the 1970s, my office required every school district in Massachusetts to review all its materials for "sex-role stereotyping" and any failure to reflect the diversity of American society. The courts are frequently the first resort of parents offended by this or that their children experience in school.

Such concerns are often legitimate, and a system of mandatory schooling must be extremely careful not to indoctrinate children or offend their consciences. But the cumulative impact upon public schools has too often led to lowest-common-denominator education, so apprehensive of offending anyone that it fails to engage students in their own education or to expose them to the strongly held and well-argued positions that could provide them with models as they develop their own—often very different—convictions.

That, I suggest, is an additional reason we should do everything possible to develop schools that are truly distinctive—not simply different in some superficial way, but distinctive because the individuals who work in them share a clear set of educational ideas that will ordinarily be based upon a common understanding of human nature and the goals of human development.[1] That characteristic, more than any organizational arrangement, is surely the reason for the repeatedly documented effectiveness of Roman Catholic schools in educating African-American youth and, in other

countries, for the similar effectiveness of schools with a clearly defined educational mission.

By the same token, educators are free to create such distinctive schools only if well-informed parents are free to choose or reject them. The more that such schools come into existence, the more that prospective parents will need accurate, reliable information about each school's educational criteria. Yet even the best-designed system of parental choice, with all the bells and whistles of accountability, parent information, and protections against discrimination, will prove ineffective not only if it lacks significant choices but also if they are made (as happens all too often) according to socioeconomics or to minority enrollments. School choice promotes equity only if it provides parents with better reasons than those to choose a particular school.

It is by no means necessary that the distinctive school's mission be religious, though I suppose that every coherent way of understanding the world is in some sense religious, but its mission must be more than a bag of tricks picked up here and there and lacking any common theme. Kieran Egan has written,

> It's not the lack of a research base of knowledge about development and learning that is hindering educators' wider success; rather, our main problem is our poverty in conceptions of education.... It is always easier and more attractive to engage in technical work under an accepted paradigm than do hard thinking about the value-saturated idea of education.[2]

* * *

I want to challenge those who would improve American public education to "hard thinking about the value-saturated idea of education." If we are to have schools that are distinctively excellent, we must have schools that are different because of hard thinking, thinking that grapples with complicated and delicate questions.

Too much discussion among educators is about how to do things; not nearly enough is about what is worth doing. We are afraid that we will discover basic disagreements, and that it will be impossible for us to work together. But it is precisely around those basic disagreements that—always courteously, always respectfully—we can build a diverse educational system.

Am I proposing that we abandon the goal of a common school that can meet the needs of every student and that teaches them to appreciate one another? Yes and no. Certainly it is past time that we recognize that no one school can be good for every student or satisfy every parent, and we can no longer assume that involuntary assignments, which thirty years of experience have proved ineffective, are the only means of achieving racial and other forms of integration in schools. Instead, we should be seeking what, in one of my annual reports to the Massachusetts Board of Education, I called the "new common school": the school freely chosen by parents and by teachers and, as a result, free to translate a shared vision of education into the thousand details of classroom and school life. Such a policy allows schools to function within a policy framework that stresses outcomes and leaves the ways and means up to those most directly engaged with the process of education and the lives of individual children and youth. As noted earlier, Massachusetts and other states have begun to implement such a framework, with accountability for results and increased autonomy at the school level.

The recent evidence shows that there is still a long way to go. Around the country, constraints—all sorts of limits upon the freedom of charter schools and others to organize instruction, staffing, and accountability—are creeping back. My challenge to those who would improve American public education, though, involves more than technical adjustments at the margins of school choice, however important that task may be. The true challenge is in undertaking what policymakers can only permit and encourage: developing models of educational effectiveness that embrace Egan's "hard thinking about the value-saturated idea of education." Real education will always involve helping to form the person; it will always be "value-saturated" and rest upon consequential choices no research design can make. Parents, educators, and policymakers alike need to rediscover the distinction, so much more emphasized in other languages, between "instruction" and "education": consider the resonance of the words *Bildung* in German,

or *éducation* in French, describing the lifelong enterprise of becoming a fully realized human being. Those called "educators" should recognize the moral weight of that description; Horace Mann said that the teacher at his desk has a calling more sacred than the minister in his pulpit. Do we dare think of ourselves in that way? Do we dare take our calling any less seriously?

It will require imagination and a willingness to think through the implications of different means of teaching and of organizing schools and curricula—thinking based, though, not on mere technical efficiency, but on how such means correspond to and advance a coherent vision of education.

Doing so will lead us—will lead you—along different paths, often parallel, sometimes crossing, at other times diverging widely. It is essential that you not lose nerve because of those differences simply because someone you respect reaches different conclusions about how, and why, education should be provided. It is the richness and the promise of the present moment in education that we are free to create distinctive schools—each a "common school" for those who choose it—without fear that we are somehow betraying the mission of schooling in a democracy.

Free and distinctive schools, created by the hard thinking and hard work of imaginative educators, will not betray the mission of democratic education, but will rather fulfill it as never before in American life.

NOTES

1. See Gary R. Galluzzo, "Moving to the Margins," *Educational Horizons* 82:4 (Summer 2004), for a discussion of the school as "a school of thought."
2. Kieran Egan, *Getting It Wrong from the Beginning* (New Haven, Conn.: Yale University Press, 2002): 180f.

POSTNOTE

This thoughtful article examines how school choice can create more equitable learning opportunities for children attending poorly performing schools. Few people object to choice within the public schools through such programs as magnet schools and intradistrict enrollment plans. Charter schools, although more controversial, are generally supported by both Democrats and Republicans as a way to encourage school reform, respond to parental demand, and still stay within the public school domain. School voucher plans generate the greatest controversy, primarily

by allowing public money to be spent sending children to private and religious schools.

Interestingly, public tax monies going to religious schools is hardly new in this country. During the colonial era and the early years of this nation, taxes regularly went to support religious schools. Even in the 19th and early 20th centuries, our public schools were, de facto, religious schools. There was regular prayer in school. The Christian Bible and the Ten Commandments were mainstays of a child's education. References to God permeated the school day and school functions, such as assemblies and graduation exercises. In addition, in recent years public tax monies, such as Pell Grants, have regularly gone to religious colleges and universities.

Nevertheless, the issue of school vouchers touches sensitivities among the American public that create much debate and argument. The controversy will not likely be solved soon.

Discussion Questions

1. Considering the various forms of school choice that you may know of, which would you support and why?
2. What concerns, if any, do you have regarding the issue of school choice?
3. Which of the four arguments for expanded parental choice and the four arguments against parental choice are the strongest, in your opinion? Why do you think so?

RELATED WEBSITE RESOURCES

 ### Web Resources:

Building Choice.org. Available at:

**http://www.buildingchoice.org/cs/bc/print/
bc_docs/home.htm.**

This website, developed under the auspices of the U.S. Department of Education, contains information, links, tools, and other resources designed to help parents make public school choices.

53

Enabling or Disabling? Observations on Changes in Special Education

James M. Kauffman, Kathleen McGee, and Michele Brigham

James M. Kauffman is professor emeritus, Curry School of Education, University of Virginia. **Kathleen McGee** is a special education teacher at the high school level. **Michele Brigham** teaches high school special education and music.

"Enabling or Disabling? Observations on Changes in Special Education" by James M. Kauffman, Kathleen McGee, and Michele Brigham, *Phi Delta Kappan*, April 2004, pp. 613–620.

|F|O|C|U|S| QUESTION

As you read this article, are you persuaded that the pendulum toward full inclusion has swung too far, thus reducing special education services for youngsters who might need them?

KEY TERMS

Inclusion

Individualized education program (IEP)

Mainstreaming

Schools need demanding and distinctive special education that is clearly focused on instruction and habilitation.[1] Abandoning such a conception of special education is a prescription for disaster. But special education has increasingly been losing its way in the single-minded pursuit of full inclusion.

Once, special education's purpose was to bring the performance of students with disabilities closer to that of their nondisabled peers in regular classrooms, to move as many students as possible into the mainstream with appropriate support.[2] For students not in regular education, the goal was to move them toward a more typical setting in a cascade of placement options.[3] But as any good thing can be overdone and ruined by the pursuit of extremes, we see special education suffering from the extremes of inclusion and accommodation.

Aiming for as much normalization as possible gave special education a clear purpose. Some disabilities were seen as easier to remediate than others. Most speech and language disorders, for example, were considered eminently remediable. Other disabilities, such as mental retardation and many physical disabilities, were assumed to be permanent or long-term and so less remediable, but movement *toward* the mainstream and increasing independence from special educators were clear goals.

The emphasis in special education has shifted away from normalization, independence, and competence. The result has been students' dependence on whatever special programs, modifications, and accommodations are possible, particularly in general education settings. The goal seems to have become the *appearance* of normalization without the *expectation* of competence.

Many parents and students seem to want more services as they learn what is available. Some have lost sight of the goal of limiting accommodations in order to challenge students to achieve more independence. At the same time, many special education advocates want all services to be available in mainstream settings, with little or no acknowledgment that the services are atypical. Although teachers, administrators, and guidance counselors are often willing and able to make accommodations, doing so is not always in students' best long-term interests. It gives students with disabilities what anthropologist Robert Edgerton called a cloak—a pretense, a cover, which actually fools no one—rather than actual competence.[4]

In this article, we discuss how changes in attitudes toward disability and special education, placement, and accommodations can perpetuate disability.

We also explore the problems of ignoring or perpetuating disability rather than helping students lead fuller, more independent lives. Two examples illustrate how we believe good intentions can go awry—how attempts to accommodate students with disabilities can undermine achievement.

"But he needs resource . . . ." Thomas, a high school sophomore identified as emotionally disturbed, was assigned to a resource class created to help students who had problems with organization or needed extra help with academic skills. One of the requirements in the class was for students to keep a daily planner in which they entered all assignments; they shared their planner with the resource teacher at the beginning of class and discussed what academic subjects would be worked on during that period.

Thomas consistently refused to keep a planner or do any work in resource (he slept instead). So a meeting was set up with the assistant principal, the guidance counselor, Thomas, and the resource teacher. As the meeting was about to begin, the principal announced that he would not stay because Thomas felt intimidated by so many adults. After listening to Thomas' complaints, the guidance counselor decided that Thomas would not have to keep a planner or show it to the resource teacher and that the resource teacher should not talk to him unless Thomas addressed her first. In short, Thomas would not be required to do any work in the class! When the resource teacher suggested that under those circumstances, Thomas should perhaps be placed in a study hall, because telling the parents that he was in a resource class would be a misrepresentation, the counselor replied, "But he *needs* the resource class."

"He's too bright. . . ." Bob, a high school freshman with Asperger's Syndrome, was scheduled for three honors classes and two Advanced Placement classes. Bob's IEP (individualized education program) included a two-page list of accommodations. In spite of his having achieved A's and B's, with just a single C in math, his mother did not feel that his teachers were accommodating him appropriately. Almost every evening, she e-mailed his teachers and his case manager to request more information or more help for Bob, and she angrily phoned his guidance counselor if she didn't receive a reply by the end of the first hour of the next school day.

A meeting was scheduled with the IEP team, including five of Bob's seven teachers, the county special education supervisor, the guidance counselor, the case manager, the principal, and the county autism specialist. When the accommodations were reviewed, Bob's mother agreed that all of them were being made. However, she explained that Bob had been removed from all outside social activities because he spent all night, every night, working on homework. The accommodation she demanded was that Bob have *no* homework assignments. The autism specialist agreed that this was a reasonable accommodation for a child with Asperger's Syndrome.

The teachers of the honors classes explained that the homework in their classes, which involved elaboration and extension of concepts, was even more essential than the homework assigned in AP classes. In AP classes, by contrast, homework consisted primarily of practice of concepts learned in class. The honors teachers explained that they had carefully broken their long assignments into segments, each having a separate due date before the final project, and they gave illustrations of their expectations. The director of special education explained the legal definition of accommodations (the mother said she'd never before heard that accommodations could not change the nature of the curriculum). The director also suggested that, instead of Bob's sacrificing his social life, perhaps it would be more appropriate for him to take standard classes. What Bob's mother was asking, he concluded, was not legal. She grew angry, but she did agree to give the team a "little more time" to serve Bob appropriately. She said she would "be back with her claws and broomstick" if anyone ever suggested that he be moved from honors classes without being given the no-homework accommodation. "He's too bright to take anything less than honors classes, and if you people would provide this simple accommodation, he would do just fine," she argued. In the end, she got her way.

Attitudes Toward Disability and Special Education

Not that many decades ago, a disability was considered a misfortune—not something to be ashamed of but a generally undesirable, unwelcome condition to be overcome to the greatest extent possible. Ability was considered more desirable than disability, and anything—whether a device or a service—that helped people with disabilities to do what those without disabilities could do was considered generally valuable, desirable, and worth the effort, cost, and possible stigma associated with using it.

The disability rights movement arose in response to the widespread negative attitudes toward disabilities, and it had a number of desirable outcomes. It helped overcome some of the discrimination against people with disabilities. And overcoming such bias and unfairness in everyday life is a great accomplishment. But the movement has also had some unintended negative consequences. One of these is the outright denial of disability in some cases, illustrated by the contention that disability exists only in attitudes or as a function of the social power to coerce.[5] The argument that disability is merely a "social construction" is particularly vicious in its effects on social justice. Even if we assume that disabilities are socially constructed, what should that mean? Should we assume that socially constructed phenomena are not "real," are not important, or should be discredited? If so, then consider that dignity, civil rights, childhood, social justice, and nearly every other phenomenon that we hold dear are social constructions. Many social constructions are not merely near and dear to us, they are real and useful in benevolent societies. The important question is whether the idea of disability is useful in helping people attain dignity or whether it is more useful to assume that disabilities are not real (i.e., that, like social justice, civil rights, and other social constructions, they are fabrications that can be ignored when convenient). The denial of disability is sometimes expressed as an aversion to labels, so that we are cautioned not to communicate openly and clearly about disabilities but to rely on euphemisms. But this approach is counterproductive. When we are able only to whisper or mime the undesirable difference called disability, then we inadvertently increase its stigma and thwart prevention efforts.[6]

The specious argument that "normal" does not exist—because abilities of every kind are varied and because the point at which normal becomes abnormal is arbitrary—leads to the conclusion that no one actually has a disability or, alternatively, that everyone has a disability. Then, some argue, either no one or everyone is due an accommodation so that no one or everyone is identified as disabled. This unwillingness to draw a line defining something (such as disability, poverty, or childhood) is based either on ignorance regarding the nature of continuous distributions or on a rejection of the unavoidably arbitrary decisions necessary to provide special services to those who need them and, in so doing, to foster social justice.[7]

Another unintended negative consequence of the disability rights movement is that, for some people, disability has become either something that does not matter or something to love, to take pride in, to flaunt, to adopt as a positive aspect of one's identity, or to cherish as something desirable or as a badge of honor. When disability makes no difference to us one way or the other, then we are not going to work to attenuate it, much less prevent it. At best, we will try to accommodate it. When we view disability as a desirable difference, then we are very likely to try to make it more pronounced, not to ameliorate it.

Several decades ago, special education was seen as a good thing—a helpful way of responding to disability, not something everyone needed or should have, but a useful and necessary response to the atypical needs of students with disabilities. This is why the Education for All Handicapped Children Act (now the Individuals with Disabilities Education Act) was written. But in the minds of many people, special education has been transformed from something helpful to something awful.[8]

The full-inclusion movement did have some desirable outcomes. It helped overcome some of the unnecessary removal of students with disabilities from general education. However, the movement also has had some unintended negative consequences. One of these is that special education has come to be viewed in very negative terms, to be seen as a second-class and discriminatory system that does more harm than good. Rather than being seen as helpful, as a way of creating opportunity, special education is often portrayed as a means of shunting students into dead-end programs and killing opportunity.[9]

Another unintended negative consequence of full inclusion is that general education is now seen by many as the *only* place where fair and equitable treatment is possible and where the opportunity to learn is extended to all equally.[10] The argument has become that special education is good only as long as it is invisible (or nearly so), an indistinguishable part of a general education system that accommodates all students, regardless of their abilities or disabilities. Usually, this is described as a "unified" (as opposed to "separate") system of education.[11] Special education is thus something to be avoided altogether or attenuated to the greatest extent possible, regardless of a student's inability to perform in a general setting. When special education is seen as discriminatory, unfair, an opportunity-killing system, or, as one writer put it, "the gold-plated garbage can of American schooling,"[12] then it is understandable that people will loathe it. But this way of looking at special education is like seeing the recognition and treatment of cancer as the cause of the problem.

The reversal in attitudes toward disability and special education—disability from undesirable to inconsequential, special education from desirable to awful—has clouded the picture of what special education is and what it should do for students with disabilities. Little wonder that special education stands accused of failure, that calls for its demise have become vociferous, and that contemporary practices are often more disabling than enabling. An unfortunate outcome of the changing attitudes toward disability and special education is that the benefit of special education is now sometimes seen as freedom from expectations of performance. It is as if we believed that, if a student has to endure the stigma of special education, then the compensation should include an exemption from work.

Placement Issues

Placing all students, regardless of their abilities, in regular classes has exacerbated the tendency to see disability as something existing only in people's minds. It fosters the impression that students are fitting in when they are not able to perform at anywhere near the normal level. It perpetuates disabilities; it does not compensate for them.

Administrators and guidance counselors sometimes place students in programs for which they do not qualify, even as graduation requirements are increasing and tests are mandated. Often, these students' *testing* is modified although their *curriculum* is not. The students may then feel that they have beaten the system. They are taught that the system is unfair and that the only way to win is by gaming it. Hard work and individual responsibility for one's education are often overlooked—or at least undervalued.

Students who consistently fail in a particular curriculum must be given the opportunity to deal with the natural consequences of that fact as a means of learning individual responsibility. For example, social promotion in elementary and middle school teaches students that they really don't have to be able to do the work to pass. Students who have been conditioned to rely on social promotion do not believe that the cycle will end until it does so—usually very abruptly in high school. Suddenly, no one passes them on, and no one gives them undeserved credit. Many of these students do not graduate in four years. Some never recover, while others find themselves forced to deal with a very distasteful situation.

No one wants to see a student fail, but to alter any standard without good reason is to set that same student up for failure later in life. Passing along a student with disabilities in regular classes, pretending that he or she is performing at the same level as most of the class or that it doesn't really matter (arguing that the student has a legal "right" to be in the class) is another prescription for disappointment and failure in later life. Indeed, this failure often comes in college or on the job.

Some people with disabilities do need assistance. Others do not. Consider Deborah Groeber, who struggled through degenerative deafness and blindness. The Office of Affirmative Action at the University of Pennsylvania offered to intercede at the Wharton School, but Groeber knew that she had more influence if she spoke for herself. Today, she is a lawyer with three Ivy League degrees.[13] But not every student with disabilities can do or should be expected to do what Groeber did. Our concern is that too many students with disabilities are given encouragement based on pretense when they could do much more with appropriate special education.

Types of Accommodations

Two popular modifications in IEPs are allowing for the use of calculators and granting extended time on tests and assignments. Calculators can be a great asset, but they should be used when calculating complex problems or when doing word problems. Indiscriminate use of a calculator renders many math tests invalid, as they become a contest to see if buttons can be pushed successfully and in the correct order, rather than an evaluation of ability to do arithmetic or use mathematical knowledge.

Extended time on assignments and tests can also be a useful modification, but it can easily be misused or abused. Extended time on tests should mean *continuous* time so that a test is not studied for first and taken later. Sometimes a test must be broken into smaller segments that can be completed independently. However, this could put students with disabilities at a disadvantage, as one part of a test might help with remembering another part. Extensions on assignments need to be evaluated each time they are given, not simply handed out automatically because they are written into an IEP. If a student is clearly working hard, then extensions may be appropriate. If a student has not even been attempting assignments, then more time might be an avoidance tactic. Sometimes extended time means that assignments pile up and the student gets further and further behind. The result can then be overwhelming stress and the inability to comprehend discussions because many concepts must be acquired in sequence (e.g., in math, science, history, and foreign languages).

Reading tests and quizzes aloud to students can be beneficial for many, but great caution is required. Some students and teachers want to do more than simply read a test. Reading a test aloud means simply reading the printed words on the page *without* inflections that can reveal correct answers and without explaining vocabulary. Changing a test to open-notes or open-book, without the knowledge and consent of the classroom teacher, breaches good-faith test proctoring. It also teaches students dependence rather than independence and accomplishment. Similarly, scribing for a student can be beneficial for those who truly need it, but the teacher must be careful not to add details and to write only what the student dictates, including any run-on sentences or fragments. After scribing, if the assignment is not a test, the teacher should edit and correct the paper with the student, as she might do with any written work. But this must take place *after* the scribing.

How Misguided Accommodations Can Be Disabling

"Saving" a child from his or her own negative behavior reinforces that behavior and makes it a self-fulfilling prophecy. Well-intentioned guidance counselors often feel more responsibility for their students' success or failure than the students themselves feel. Sometimes students are not held accountable for their effort or work. They seem not to understand that true independence comes from *what* you know, not *whom* you know. Students who are consistently enabled and not challenged are never given the opportunity to become independent. Ann Bancroft, the polar explorer and dyslexic, claims that, although school was a torment, it was disability that forged her iron will.[14] Stephen Cannell's fear for other dyslexics is that they will quit trying rather than struggle and learn to compensate for their disability.[15]

Most parents want to help their children. However, some parents confuse making life *easier* with making life *better* for their children. Too often, parents feel that protecting their child from the rigors of academic demands is in his or her best interest. They may protect their child by insisting on curricular modifications and accommodations in assignments, time, and testing. But children learn by doing, and not allowing them to do something because they might fail is denying them the opportunity to succeed. These students eventually believe that they are not capable of doing what typical students can do, even if they are. Sometimes it is difficult for teachers to discern what a student actually can do and what a parent has done until an in-class assignment is given or a test is taken. At that point, it is often too late for the teacher to do much remediation. The teacher may erroneously conclude that the student is simply a poor test-taker.

In reality, the student may have been "protected" from learning, which will eventually catch up with him or her. Unfortunately, students may not face reality until they take a college entrance exam, go away to college, or apply for a job. Students who "get through" high school in programs of this type often go on to

flunk out of college. Unfortunately, the parents of these students frequently blame the college for the student's failure, criticizing the post-secondary institution for not doing enough to help. Instead, they should be upset both with the secondary institution for not preparing the child adequately for the tasks to come and with themselves for their own overprotection.

The Benefits of Demands

Many successful adults with disabilities sound common themes when asked about their ability to succeed in the face of a disability. Tom Gray, a Rhodes Scholar who has a severe learning disability, claims that having to deal with the hardest experiences gave him the greatest strength.[16] Stephen Cannell believes that, if he had known there was a reason beyond his control to explain his low achievement, he might not have worked as hard as he did. Today, he knows he has a learning disability, but he is also an Emmy Award–winning television writer and producer.[17] Paul Orlalea, the dyslexic founder of Kinko's, believes God gave him an advantage in the challenge presented by his disability and that others should work with their strengths. Charles Schwab, the learning-disabled founder of Charles Schwab, Inc., cites his ability to think differently and to make creative leaps that more sequential thinkers don't make as chief reasons for his success. Fannie Flagg, the learning-disabled author, concurs and insists that learning disabilities become a blessing *only if you can overcome them.*[18] Not every student with a disability can be a star performer, of course, but all should be expected to achieve all that they can.

Two decades ago, special educators thought it was their job to assess a student's achievement, to understand what the student wanted to do and what an average peer could do, and then to develop plans to bridge the gap, if possible. Most special educators wanted to see that each student had the tools and knowledge to succeed as independently as possible. Helping students enter the typical world was the mark of success for special educators.

The full-inclusion movement now insists that *every* student will benefit from placement in the mainstream. However, some of the modifications and accommodations now being demanded are so radical that we are doing an injustice to the entire education system.[19] Special education must not be associated in any way with "dumbing down" the curriculum for students presumed to be at a given grade level, whether disabled or not.

Counselors and administrators who want to enable students must focus the discussion on realistic goals and plans for each student. An objective, in-depth discussion and evaluation must take place to determine how far along the continuum of successfully completing these goals the student has moved. If the student is making adequate progress independently, or with minimal help, special education services might not be necessary. If assistance is required to make adequate progress on realistic goals, then special education may be needed. Every modification and every accommodation should be held to the same standard: whether it will help the student attain these goals—*not* whether it will make life easier for the student. Knowing where a student is aiming can help a team guide that student toward success.

And the student must be part of this planning. A student who claims to want to be a brain surgeon but refuses to take science courses needs a reality check. If a student is unwilling to attempt to reach intermediate goals or does not succeed in meeting them, then special education cannot "save" that student. At that point, the team must help the student revisit his or her goals. Goals should be explained in terms of the amount of work required to complete them, not whether or not the teacher or parent feels they are attainable. When goals are presented in this way, students can often make informed decisions regarding their attainability and desirability. Troy Brown, a university dean and politician who has both a doctorate and a learning disability, studied at home with his mother. He estimates that it took him more than twice as long as the average person to complete assignments. Every night, he would go to bed with stacks of books and read until he fell asleep, because he had a dream of attending college.[20]

General educators and special educators need to encourage all students to be responsible and independent and to set realistic expectations for themselves. Then teachers must help students to meet these expectations in a more and more independent manner. Special educators do not serve students well when they enable students with disabilities to become increasingly dependent on their parents, counselors, administrators, or teachers—or even when they fail to increase students' independence and competence.

Where We Stand

We want to make it clear that we think disabilities are real and that they make doing certain things either impossible or very difficult for the people who have them. We cannot expect people with disabilities to be "just like everyone else" in what they can do. The views of other writers differ:

The human service practices that cause providers to believe that clients [students] have inadequacies, shortcomings, failures, or faults that must be corrected or controlled by specially trained professionals must be replaced by conceptions that people with disabilities are capable of setting their own goals and achieving or not. Watered-down curricula, alternative grading practices, special competency standards, and other "treat them differently" practices used with "special" students must be replaced with school experiences exactly like those used with "regular" students.[21]

We disagree. In our view, students with disabilities *do* have specific shortcomings and *do* need the services of specially trained professionals to achieve their potential. They *do* sometimes need altered curricula or adaptations to make their learning possible. If students with disabilities were just like "regular" students, then there would be no need whatever for special education. But the school experiences of students with disabilities obviously will not be—*cannot* be—just like those of students without disabilities. We sell students with disabilities short when we pretend that they are no different from typical students. We make the same error when we pretend that they must *not* be expected to put forth extra effort if they are to learn to do some things—or learn to do something in a different way. We sell them short when we pretend that they have competencies that they do not have or pretend that the competencies we expect of most students are not important for them.

Like general education, special education must push students to become all they can be. Special education must countenance neither the pretense of learning nor the avoidance of reasonable demands.

NOTES

1. James M. Kauffman and Daniel P. Hallahan, *Special Education: What It Is and Why We Need It* (Boston: Allyn & Bacon, forthcoming).
2. Doug Fuchs et al., "Toward a Responsible Reintegration of Behaviorally Disordered Students," *Behavioral Disorders,* February 1991, pp. 133–47.
3. Evelyn Deno, "Special Education as Development Capital," *Exceptional Children,* November 1970, pp. 229–37; and Dixie Snow Huefner, "The Mainstreaming Cases: Tensions and Trends for School Administrators," *Educational Administration Quarterly,* February 1994, pp. 27–55.
4. Robert B. Edgerton, *The Cloak of Competence: Stigma in the Lives of the Mentally Retarded* (Berkeley, Calif.: University of California Press, 1967); idem, *The Cloak of Competence,* rev. ed. (Berkeley, Calif.: University of California Press, 1993); and James M. Kauffman,

"Appearances, Stigma, and Prevention," *Remedial and Special Education,* vol. 24, 2003, pp. 195–98.

5. See, for example, Scot Danforth and William C. Rhodes, "Deconstructing Disability: A Philosophy for Education," *Remedial and Special Education,* November/December 1997, pp. 357–66; and Phil Smith, "Drawing New Maps: A Radical Cartography of Developmental Disabilities," *Review of Educational Research,* Summer 1999, pp. 117–44.

6. James M. Kauffman, *Education Deform: Bright People Sometimes Say Stupid Things About Education* (Lanham, Md.: Scarecrow Education, 2002).

7. Ibid.

8. James M. Kauffman, "Reflections on the Field," *Behavioral Disorders,* vol. 28, 2003, pp. 205–8.

9. See, for example, Clint Bolick, "A Bad IDEA Is Disabling Public Schools," *Education Week,* 5 September 2001, pp. 56, 63; and Michelle Cottle, "Jeffords Kills Special Ed. Reform School," *New Republic,* 18 June 2001, pp. 14–15.

10. See, for example, Dorothy K. Lipsky and Alan Gartner, "Equity Requires Inclusion: The Future for All Students with Disabilities," in Carol Christensen and Fazal Rizvi, eds., *Disability and the Dilemmas of Education and Justice* (Philadelphia: Open University Press, 1996), pp. 144–55; and William Stainback and Susan Stainback, "A Rationale for Integration and Restructuring: A Synopsis," in John W. Lloyd, Nirbhay N. Singh, and Alan C. Repp, eds., *The Regular Education Initiative: Alternative Perspectives on Concepts, Issues, and Models* (Sycamore, Ill.: Sycamore, 1991), pp. 225–39.

11. See, for example, Alan Gartner and Dorothy K. Lipsky, *The Yoke of Special Education: How to Break It* (Rochester, N.Y.: National Center on Education and the Economy, 1989). For an alternative view, see James M. Kauffman and Daniel P. Hallahan, "Toward a Comprehensive Delivery System for Special Education," in John I. Goodlad and Thomas C. Lovitt, eds., *Integrating General and Special Education* (Columbus, Ohio: Merrill, 1993), pp. 73–102.

12. Marc Fisher, "Students Still Taking the Fall for D.C. Schools," *Washington Post,* 13 December 2001, p. B-1.

13. Elizabeth Tener, "Blind, Deaf, and Very Successful," *McCall's,* December 1995, pp. 42–46.

14. Christina Cheakalos et al., "Heavy Mettle: They May Have Trouble Reading and Spelling, but Those with the Grit to Overcome Learning Disabilities Like Dyslexia Emerge Fortified for Life," *People,* 30 October 2001, pp. 18, 58.

15. Ibid.

16. Ibid.

17. Stephen Cannell, "How to Spell Success," *Reader's Digest,* August 2000, pp. 63–66.

18. Cheakalos et al., op cit.

19. Anne Proffit Dupre, "Disability, Deference, and the Integrity of the Academic Enterprise," *Georgia Law Review,* Winter 1998, pp. 393–473.

20. Cheakalos et al., op cit.

21. James E. Ysseldyke, Bob Algozzine, and Martha L. Thurlow, *Critical Issues in Special Education,* 3rd ed. (Boston: Houghton-Mifflin, 2000), p. 67.

POSTNOTE

The movement toward full inclusion of children with disabilities into the regular education classroom has gained considerable support and momentum in the last ten years. Many supporters of full inclusion contend that disabled youngsters have a civil right to be educated with their nondisabled peers. The authors of this article, while supportive of inclusion, believe the movement has gone too far by not always serving the students' long-term interests. The authors believe that many parents, by insisting on the full inclusion of their child in the regular classroom, are denying the child the full range of services that are available in special education settings, particularly for those students whose disabilities are more severe.

Discussion Questions

1. What aspects of inclusion seem to cause controversy, and why is this so?

2. Have you had any experiences working with children with disabilities? If so, describe the circumstances and your successes or failures. If you have not worked with children with disabilities, are you planning to get this experience? If so, how?

3. What do you think are the strongest arguments made by the authors of this article? If you could ask them a question, what would it be?

RELATED WEBSITE RESOURCES AND VIDEO CASES

 Web Resources:

University of Virginia, Office of Special Education: A Web Resource for Special Education. Available at:

http://curry.edschool.virginia.edu/go/specialed.

This website contains much information about special education, including discussion groups.

Video Case:

Including Students with High Incidence Disabilities: Strategies for Success

In this video case, you will see how a veteran teacher accommodates the learning needs of all her students in her elementary inclusion classroom. As you watch the clips and study the artifacts in the case, reflect upon the following questions:

1. This teacher uses several strategies to help all of her students develop as writers. What are the strengths of each of these strategies and which ones might you want to include in your own teaching repertoire?
2. What technologies can be used to help address various learning challenges experienced by these and similar students?

54

Making Inclusive Education Work

Richard A. Villa and Jacqueline S. Thousand

Richard A. Villa is president of Bayridge Consortium, San Diego, California. **Jacqueline S. Thousand** is professor in the College of Education at California State University-San Marcos.

"Making Inclusive Education Work" by Richard A. Villa and Jacqueline S. Thousand, *Educational Leadership*, October 2003, pp. 19–23. Used with permission. The Association for Supervision and Curriculum Development is a worldwide community of educators advocating sound policies and sharing best practices to achieve the success of each learner. To learn more, visit ASCD at **www.ascd.org.**

F O C U S QUESTION

What are the various benefits and challenges that inclusion presents to both the classroom teacher and the disabled child?

KEY TERMS

Complementary teaching
Consultation
Coteaching
Differentiated instruction
Inclusion
Least restrictive environment (LRE)
Parallel teaching
Supportive teaching

As an educator, you are philosophically committed to student diversity. You appreciate that learning differences are natural and positive. You focus on identifying and capitalizing on individual students' interests and strengths. But making inclusive education work requires something more: It takes both systems-level support and classroom-level strategies.

Since the 1975 implementation of the Individuals with Disabilities Education Act (IDEA), federal law has stated that children with disabilities have the right to an education in the least restrictive environment (LRE). According to the act, removal from general education environments should occur only when a student has failed to achieve satisfactorily despite documented use of supplemental supports, aids, and services.

During the past 28 years, the interpretation of what constitutes the least restrictive environment has evolved, along with schools' and educators' abilities to provide effective supports. As a result, increased numbers of students with disabilities are now served in both regular schools and general education classes within those schools.

When IDEA was first promulgated in 1975, schools generally interpreted the law to mean that they should mainstream students with mild disabilities—for example, those with learning disabilities and those eligible for speech and language services—into classes where these students could keep up with other learners, supposedly with minimal support and few or no modifications to either curriculum or instruction. In the early 1980s, however, the interpretation of least restrictive environment evolved to include the concept of integrating students with more intensive needs—those with moderate and severe disabilities—into regular classrooms. By the late 1980s and early 1990s, the interpretation evolved into the approach now known as *inclusion:* the principle and practice of considering general education as the placement of first choice for all learners. This approach encourages educators to bring necessary supplemental supports, aids, and services into the classroom instead of removing students from the classroom for those services.

As the interpretation of least restrictive environment has changed, the proportion of students with disabilities included in general education has increased dramatically. By 1999, 47.4 percent of students with disabilities spent 80 percent or more of their day in general education classrooms, compared with 25 percent of students with disabilities in 1985 (U.S. Department of Education, 2003).

Although the 1997 reauthorization of IDEA did not actually use the term *inclusion,* it effectively codified the principle and practice of inclusion by requiring that students' Individualized Education Programs (IEPs) ensure access to the general education curriculum. This landmark re-authorization broadened the concept of inclusion to include academic as well as physical and social access to general education instruction and experiences (Kluth, Villa, & Thousand, 2002).

Despite the continued evolution toward inclusive education, however, tremendous disparities exist among schools, districts, and states. For example, the U.S. Department of Education (2003) found that the percentage of students with disabilities ages 6–21 who were taught for 80 percent or more of the school day in general education classrooms ranged from a low of 18 percent in Hawaii to a high of 82 percent in Vermont. Further, the nature of inclusion varies. In some schools, inclusion means the mere physical presence or social inclusion of students with disabilities in regular classrooms; in other schools, it means active modification of content, instruction, and assessment practices so that students can successfully engage in core academic experiences and learning.

Why can some schools and districts implement inclusion smoothly and effectively, whereas others cannot? Three sources give guidance in providing high-quality inclusive practice. First, research findings of the past decade have documented effective inclusive schooling practices (McGregor & Vogelsberg, 1998; National Center on Educational Restructuring and Inclusion, 1995; Villa, Thousand, Meyers, & Nevin, 1996). Second, our own experiences as educators suggest several variables. Third, we interviewed 20 nationally recognized leaders in the field of inclusive education who, like ourselves, provide regular consultation and training throughout the United States regarding inclusive practice.

A Systems Approach

Successful promotion and implementation of inclusive education require the five following systems-level practices: connection with other organizational best practices; visionary leadership and administrative support; redefined roles and relationships among adults and students; collaboration; and additional adult support when needed.

CONNECTION WITH BEST PRACTICES
Inclusive education is most easily introduced in school communities that have already restructured to meet the needs of their increasingly diverse student populations in regular education. Initiatives and organizational best practices to accomplish this aim include trans-disciplinary teaming, block scheduling, multi-age student grouping and looping, schoolwide positive behavior support and discipline approaches, detracking, and school-within-a-school family configurations of students and teachers. These initiatives facilitate the inclusion and development of students with disabilities within general education.

School leaders should clearly communicate to educators and families that best practices to facilitate inclusion are identical to best practices for educating all students. This message will help members of the school community understand that inclusion is not an add-on, but a natural extension of promising research-based education practices that positively affect the teaching and learning of all students.

VISIONARY LEADERSHIP
A national study on the implementation of IDEA's least restrictive environment requirement emphasized the importance of leadership—in both vision and practice—to the installation of inclusive education. The researchers concluded,

> How leadership at each school site chose to look at LRE was critical to how, or even whether, much would be accomplished beyond the status quo. (Hasazi, Johnston, Liggett, & Schattman, 1994, p. 506)

In addition, a study of 32 inclusive school sites in five states and one Canadian province found that the degree of administrative support and vision was the most powerful predictor of general educators' attitudes toward inclusion (Villa et al., 1996).

For inclusive education to succeed, administrators must take action to publicly articulate the new vision, build consensus for the vision, and lead all stakeholders to active involvement. Administrators can provide four types of support identified as important by frontline general and special educators: personal and emotional (for example, being willing to listen to concerns); informational (for example, providing training and technical assistance); instrumental (for example, creating time for teachers to meet); and appraisal (for example, giving constructive feedback related to implementation of new practices) (Littrell, Billingsley, & Cross, 1994).

Visionary leaders recognize that changing any organization, including a school, is a complex act. They know that organizational transformation requires ongoing attention to consensus building for the inclusive vision. It also requires skill development on the part of educators and everyone involved in the change; the provision of extra common planning time and fiscal, human, technological, and organizational resources to motivate experimentation with new practices; and the collaborative development and communication of a well-formulated plan of action for transforming the culture and practice of a school (Ambrose, 1987; Villa & Thousand, in press).

REDEFINED ROLES

For school personnel to meet diverse student needs, they must stop thinking and acting in isolated ways: "These are my students, and those are your students." They must relinquish traditional roles, drop distinct professional labels, and redistribute their job functions across the system. To facilitate this role redefinition, some schools have developed a single job description for all professional educators that clearly articulates as expected job functions collaboration and shared responsibility for educating all of a community's children and youth.

To help school personnel make this shift, schools must clarify the new roles—for example, by making general education personnel aware of their legal responsibilities for meeting the needs of learners with disabilities in the least restrictive environment. In addition, schools must provide necessary training through a variety of vehicles, including in-service opportunities, coursework, co-teaching, professional support groups, and other coaching and mentoring activities. After clarifying teachers' new responsibilities and providing training, schools should encourage staff members to reflect on how they will differentiate instruction and design accommodations and modifications to meet the needs of all students. School administrators should monitor the degree of collaboration between general and special educators. They should also include implementation of IEP-mandated activities as part of ongoing district evaluation procedures.

COLLABORATION

Reports from school districts throughout the United States identify collaboration as a key variable in the successful implementation of inclusive education. Creating planning teams, scheduling time for teachers to work and teach together, recognizing teachers as problem solvers, conceptualizing teachers as frontline researchers, and effectively collaborating with parents are all dimensions reported as crucial to successful collaboration (National Center on Educational Restructuring and Inclusion, 1995).

Achievement of inclusive education presumes that no one person could have all the expertise required to meet the needs of all the students in a classroom. For inclusive education to work, educators must become effective and efficient collaborative team members. They must develop skills in creativity, collaborative teaming processes, co-teaching, and interpersonal communication that will enable them to work together to craft diversified learning opportunities for learners who have a wide range of interests, learning styles, and intelligences (Thousand & Villa, 2000; Villa, 2000a; Villa, Thousand, & Nevin, in preparation). In a study of more than 600 educators, collaboration emerged as the only variable that predicted positive attitudes toward inclusion among general and special educators as well as administrators (Villa et al., 1996).

ADULT SUPPORT

An "only as much as needed" principle dictates best practices in providing adult support to students. This approach avoids inflicting help on those who do not necessarily need or want it. Thus, when paraprofessionals are assigned to classrooms, they should be presented to students as members of a teaching team rather than as people "velcroed" to individual students.

Teaching models in which general and specialized personnel work together as a team are effective and efficient ways of arranging adult support to meet diverse student needs (National Center on Educational Restructuring and Inclusion, 1995; Villa, 2002b). Such models include

- *Consultation.* Support personnel provide assistance to the general educator, enabling him or her to teach all the students in the inclusive class.
- *Parallel teaching.* Support personnel—for example, a special educator, a Title I teacher, a psychologist, or a speech language therapist—and the classroom teacher rotate among heterogeneous groups of students in different sections of the general education classroom.
- *Supportive teaching.* The classroom teacher takes the lead role, and support personnel rotate among the students.
- *Complementary teaching.* The support person does something to complement the instruction provided by the classroom teacher (for example, takes notes on a transparency or paraphrases the teacher's statements).
- *Coteaching.* Support personnel coteach alongside the general education teacher.

Promoting Inclusion in the Classroom

Several curricular, instructional, and assessment practices benefit all the students in the classroom and help ensure successful inclusion. For instance, in a study conducted by the National Center on Educational Restructuring and Inclusion (1995), the majority of the districts implementing inclusive education reported cooperative learning as the most important instructional strategy supporting inclusive education. Some other general education theories and practices that also effectively support inclusion are

- Current theories of learning (such as multiple intelligences and constructivist learning).
- Teaching practices that make subject matter more relevant and meaningful (for example, partner learning, project- and activity-based learning, and service learning).
- Authentic alternatives to paper-and-pencil assessment (such as portfolio artifact collection, role playing, and demonstrations).
- A balanced approach to literacy development that combines whole-language and phonics instruction.
- Thematic/interdisciplinary curriculum approaches.
- Use of technology for communication and access to the general education curriculum.
- Differentiated instruction.

Responding to Diversity

Building on the notion of differentiated instruction (Tomlinson, 1999), universal design provides a contemporary approach to facilitate successful inclusion (Udvari-Solner, Villa, & Thousand, 2002).

In the traditional retrofit model, educators determine both content and instructional and assessment strategies without taking into consideration the special characteristics of the actual learners in the classroom. Then, if a mismatch exists between what students can do and what they are asked to do, educators make adjustments. In contrast, educators using the universal design framework consider the students and their various learning styles first. Then they differentiate curriculum *content, processes,* and *products* before delivering instruction.

For example, in a unit on the history of relations between the United States and Cuba, students might access *content* about the Cuban Missile Crisis by listening to a lecture, interviewing people who were alive at that time, conducting Internet research, reading the history text and other books written at a variety of reading levels, or viewing films or videos. The teacher can differentiate the *process* by allowing students to work independently, in pairs, or in cooperative groups. Additional processes that allow learners of differing abilities and learning styles to master standards include

a combination of whole-class instruction, learning centers, reflective journal writing, technology, and field trips. Finally, students may demonstrate their learning through various *products,* including written reports, debates, role-plays, PowerPoint presentations, and songs.

Thus, students can use a variety of approaches to gain access to the curriculum, make sense of their learning, and show what they have learned. A universal design approach benefits every student, not just those identified as having disabilities.

Differentiating to enable a student with disabilities to access the general education curriculum requires creative thinking. Four options suggest varying degrees of student participation (Giangreco, Cloninger, & Iverson, 1998).

- First, a student can simply join in with the rest of the class.
- Second, multilevel curriculum and instruction can occur when all students involved in a lesson in the same curriculum area pursue varying levels of complexity.
- Curriculum overlapping is a third option, in which students working on the same lesson pursue objectives from different curricular areas. A student with severe disabilities, for example, could practice using a new communication device during a hands-on science lesson while others focus primarily on science objectives.
- The fourth option, and the last resort, involves arranging alternative activities when a general education activity is inappropriate. For example, a student may need to participate in an activity within his Individualized Education Program, such as employment training in the community, that falls outside the scope of the general education curriculum.

Bridging the Gap

Systems-level and classroom-level variables such as these facilitate the creation and maintenance of inclusive education. Systemic support, collaboration, effective classroom practices, and a universal design approach can make inclusive education work so that students with disabilities have the same access to the general education curriculum and to classmates as any other student and the same opportunity for academic, social, and emotional success.

Inclusive education is a general education initiative, not another add-on school reform unrelated to other general education initiatives. It incorporates demonstrated general education best practices, and it redefines educators' and students' roles and responsibilities as creative and collaborative partners. The strategies described here can bridge the gap between what schools are doing well and what they can do better to make inclusion part and parcel of a general education program.

REFERENCES

Ambrose, D. (1987). *Managing complex change*. Pittsburgh, PA: The Enterprise Group.

Giangreco, M. F., Cloninger, C. J., & Iverson, V. S. (1998). *Choosing outcomes and accommodations for children (COACH): A guide to educational planning for students with disabilities* (2nd ed.). Baltimore: Paul H. Brookes.

Hasazi, S., Johnston, A. P., Liggett, A. M., & Schattman, R. A. (1994). A qualitative policy study of the least restrictive environment provision of the Individuals with Disabilities Education Act. *Exceptional Children, 60,* 491–507.

Kluth, P., Villa, R. A., & Thousand, J. S. (2002). "Our school doesn't offer inclusion" and other legal blunders. *Educational Leadership, 59* (4), 24–27.

Littrell, P. C., Billingsley, B. S., & Cross, L. H. (1994). The effects of principal support on special and general educators' stress, job satisfaction, school commitment, health, and intent to stay in teaching. *Remedial and Special Education, 15,* 297–310.

McGregor, G., & Vogelsberg, T. (1998). *Inclusive schooling practices: Pedagogical and research foundations*. Baltimore: Paul H. Brookes.

National Center on Educational Restructuring and Inclusion. (1995). *National study on inclusive education*. New York: City University of New York.

Thousand, J. S., & Villa, R. A. (2000). Collaborative teaming: A powerful tool in school restructuring. In R. A. Villa & J. S. Thousand (Eds.), *Restructuring for caring and effective education: Piecing the puzzle together* (2nd ed., pp. 254–291). Baltimore: Paul H. Brookes.

Tomlinson, C. A. (1999). *The differentiated classroom*. Alexandria, VA: ASCD.

Udvari-Solner, A., Villa, R. A., & Thousand, J. S. (2002). Access to the general education curriculum for all: The universal design process. In J. S. Thousand, R. A. Villa, & A. I. Nevin (Eds.), *Creativity and collaborative learning* (2nd ed., pp. 85–103). Baltimore: Paul H. Brookes.

U.S. Department of Education. (2003). *Twenty-third annual report to Congress on the implementation of the Individuals with Disabilities Education Act*. Washington, DC: Author.

Villa, R. A. (2002a). *Collaborative planning: Transforming theory into practice* [Videotape]. Port Chester, NY: National Professional Resources.

Villa, R. A. (2002b). *Collaborative teaching: The coteaching model* [Videotape]. Port Chester, NY: National Professional Resources.

Villa, R. A., & Thousand, J. S. (in press). *Creating an inclusive school* (2nd ed.). Alexandria, VA: ASCD.

Villa, R. A., Thousand, J. S., Meyers, H., & Nevin, A. (1996). Teacher and administrator perceptions of heterogeneous education. *Exceptional Children, 63,* 29–45.

Villa, R. A., Thousand, J. S., & Nevin, A. (in preparation). *The many faces of co-teaching*. Thousand Oaks, CA: Corwin Press.

POSTNOTE

Working successfully with children with disabilities is one of the most challenging tasks facing beginning teachers. About 5.8 million students, 12 percent of the total school population, receive federal aid for their disabilities. As it is likely that you will have students with disabilities in your classroom, it is important that you approach instruction for these children as you would for other students: expect diversity, expect a range of abilities, and look for the particular strengths and learning profiles of each student. If you are a regular education teacher, work with the special education teachers in your school to coordinate instruction and services for your students with disabilities. If you are a special education teacher, you will be expected to work closely with regular education teachers to provide the least restrictive environment and best instruction possible

for these children. Only by working closely together can regular and special education teachers ensure that "no child is left behind."

Discussion Questions

1. What concerns, if any, do you have about teaching children with disabilities? What can you do to address those concerns?

2. Is full inclusion a good idea? What limitations, if any, do you see in its implementation?

3. How would you go about ensuring that your regular education students are accepting of and helpful to any students with disabilities who might be in your class?

RELATED WEBSITE RESOURCES AND VIDEO CASES

 Web Resources:

Council for Exceptional Children. Available at:

http://www.cec.sped.org.

This website of the national professional organization for special education contains many helpful resources.

▶▶ ▶ ◀◀ **Video Case:**

Inclusion: Grouping Strategies for Inclusive Classrooms

In this video case, you will see how a classroom teacher works with an inclusive specialist and additional support staff to ensure that each child in her fourth- and fifth-grade inclusion classroom succeeds in a unit on the Caribbean. As you watch the clips and study the artifacts in the case, reflect upon the following questions:

1. What did you notice about the collaborations that took place between the students with individual needs and typical learners? How would you characterize these interactions?
2. In structuring the groups of students for this unit, what aspects do the teacher and the inclusion specialist consider?

▶▶ ▶ ◀◀ **Video Case:**

Managing an Inclusive Classroom: High School Math Instruction

In this video case, you will see how a general education math teacher and a special education teacher who specializes in math-related learning problems work together to secure the best mathematics education for all of their students. As you watch the clips and study the artifacts in the case, reflect upon the following questions:

1. Have you observed an inclusive classroom? If so, compare and contrast your classroom with the classroom in the video case.
2. The teachers in the video speak of the importance of setting behavioral norms at the beginning of the year. What might a teacher do to encourage student discussion which would lead to a similar code of classroom conduct?
3. What, in your opinion, might be the benefits and challenges of the model shown in the video case?

55

With Boys and Girls in Mind

Michael Gurian and Kathy Stevens

Michael Gurian is cofounder of the Gurian Institute, and **Kathy Stevens** is director of the Gurian Institute, located in Colorado Springs, Colorado.

"With Boys and Girls in Mind" by Michael Gurian and Kathy Stevens, *Educational Leadership,* November 2004, pp. 40–44. Used with permission. The Association for Supervision and Curriculum Development is a worldwide community of educators advocating sound policies and sharing best practices to achieve the success of each learner. To learn more, visit ASCD at **www.ascd.org.**

F O C U S QUESTION

In what ways will schools and teaching practices need to change to address the differences in how boys and girls learn?

KEY TERM

Nature-based approach

Something is awry in the way our culture handles the education needs of boys and girls. A smart 11-year-old boy gets low grades in school, fidgets and drifts off in class, and doesn't do his homework. A girl in middle school only uses the computer to instant-message her friends; when it comes to mastering more essential computer skills, she defers to the boys in the class.

Is contemporary education maliciously set against either males or females? We don't think so. But structurally and functionally, our schools fail to recognize and fulfill gender-specific needs. As one teacher wrote,

> For years I sensed that the girls and boys in my classrooms learn in gender-specific ways, but I didn't know enough to help each student reach full potential. I was trained in the idea that each student is an individual. But when I saw the PET scans of boys' and girls' brains, I saw how differently those brains are set up to learn. This gave me the missing component. I trained in male/female brain differences and was able to teach each individual child. Now, looking back, I'm amazed that teachers were never taught the differences between how girls and boys learn.

New positron emission tomography (PET) and MRI technologies enable us to look inside the brains of boys and girls, where we find structural and functional differences that profoundly affect human learning. These gender differences in the brain are corroborated in males and females throughout the world and do not differ significantly across cultures.

It's true that culture affects gender role, gender costume, and gender nuances—in Italy, for example, men cry more than they do in England—but role, costume, and nuance only affect some aspects of the learning brain of a child. New brain imaging technologies confirm that genetically templated brain patterning by gender plays a far larger role than we realized. Research into gender and education reveals a mismatch between many of our boys' and girls' learning brains and the institutions empowered to teach our children. We will briefly explore some of the differences, because recognizing these differences can help us find solutions to many of the challenges that we experience in the classroom. Of course, generalized gender differences may not apply in every case.

The Minds of Girls

The following are some of the characteristics of girls' brains:

- A girl's corpus callosum (the connecting bundle of tissues between hemispheres) is, on average, larger than a boy's—up to 25 percent larger by adolescence. This enables more "cross talk" between hemispheres in the female brain.
- Girls have, in general, stronger neural connectors in their temporal lobes than boys have. These connectors lead to more sensually detailed memory storage, better listening skills, and better discrimination among the various tones of voice. This leads, among other things, to greater use of detail in writing assignments.
- The hippocampus (another memory storage area in the brain) is larger in girls than in boys, increasing girls' learning advantage, especially in the language arts.
- Girls' prefrontal cortex is generally more active than boys' and develops at earlier ages. For this reason, girls tend to make fewer impulsive decisions than boys do. Further, girls have more serotonin in the bloodstream and the brain, which makes them biochemically less impulsive.
- Girls generally use more cortical areas of their brains for verbal and emotive functioning. Boys tend to use more cortical areas of the brain for spatial and mechanical functioning (Moir & Jessel, 1989; Rich, 2000).

These "girl" brain qualities are the tip of the iceberg, yet they can immediately help teachers and parents understand why girls generally outperform boys in reading and writing from early childhood throughout life (Conlin, 2003). With more cortical areas devoted to verbal functioning, sensual memory, sitting still, listening, tonality, and mental cross talk, the complexities of reading and writing come easier, on the whole, to the female brain. In addition, the female brain experiences approximately 15 percent more blood flow, with this flow located in more centers of the brain at any given time (Marano, 2003). The female brain tends to drive itself toward stimulants—like reading and writing—that involve complex texture, tonality, and mental activity.

On the other hand, because so many cortical areas are used for verbal-emotive functioning, the female brain does not activate as many cortical areas as the male's does for abstract and physical-spatial functions, such as watching and manipulating objects that move through physical space and understanding abstract

mechanical concepts (Moir & Jessel, 1989; Rich, 2000). This is one reason for many girls' discomfort with deep computer design language. Although some girls excel in these areas, more males than females gravitate toward physics, industrial engineering, and architecture. Children naturally gravitate toward activities that their brains experience as pleasurable—"pleasure" meaning in neural terms the richest personal stimulation. Girls and boys, within each neural web, tend to experience the richest personal stimulation somewhat differently.

The biological tendency toward female verbal-emotive functioning does not mean that girls or women should be left out of classes or careers that use spatial-mechanical skills. On the contrary: We raise these issues to call on our civilization to realize the differing natures of girls and boys and to teach each subject according to how the child's brain needs to learn it. On average, educators will need to provide girls with extra encouragement and gender-specific strategies to successfully engage them in spatial abstracts, including computer design.

The Minds of Boys

What, then, are some of the qualities that are generally more characteristic of boys' brains?

- Because boys' brains have more cortical areas dedicated to spatial-mechanical functioning, males use, on average, half the brain space that females use for verbal-emotive functioning. The cortical trend toward spatial-mechanical functioning makes many boys want to move objects through space, like balls, model airplanes, or just their arms and legs. Most boys, although not all of them, will experience words and feelings differently than girls do (Blum, 1997; Moir & Jessel, 1989).
- Boys not only have less serotonin than girls have, but they also have less oxytocin, the primary human bonding chemical. This makes it more likely that they will be physically impulsive and less likely that they will neurally combat their natural impulsiveness to sit still and emphatically chat with a friend (Moir & Jessel, 1989; Taylor, 2002).
- Boys lateralize brain activity. Their brains not only operate with less blood flow than girls' brains, but they are also structured to compartmentalize learning. Thus, girls tend to multitask better than boys do, with fewer attention span problems and greater ability to make quick transitions between lessons (Havers, 1995).

• The male brain is set to renew, recharge, and reorient itself by entering what neurologists call a *rest state*. The boy in the back of the classroom whose eyes are drifting toward sleep has entered a neural rest state. It is predominantly boys who drift off without completing assignments, who stop taking notes and fall asleep during a lecture, or who tap pencils or otherwise fidget in hopes of keeping themselves awake and learning. Females tend to recharge and reorient neural focus without rest states. Thus, a girl can be bored with a lesson, but she will nonetheless keep her eyes open, take notes, and perform relatively well. This is especially true when the teacher uses more words to teach a lesson instead of being spatial and diagrammatic. The more words a teacher uses, the more likely boys are to "zone out," or go into rest state. The male brain is better suited for symbols, abstractions, diagrams, pictures, and objects moving through space than for the monotony of words (Gurian, 2001).

These typical "boy" qualities in the brain help illustrate why boys generally learn higher math and physics more easily than most girls do when those subjects are taught abstractly on the chalkboard; why more boys than girls play video games that involve physical movement and even physical destruction; and why more boys than girls tend to get in trouble for impulsiveness, shows of boredom, and fidgeting as well as for their more generalized inability to listen, fulfill assignments, and learn in the verbal-emotive world of the contemporary classroom.

Who's Failing?

For a number of decades, most of our cultural sensitivity to issues of gender and learning came from advocacy groups that pointed out ways in which girls struggled in school. When David and Myra Sadker teamed with the American Association of University Women in the early 1990s, they found that girls were not called on as much as boys were, especially in middle school; that girls generally lagged in math/science testing; that boys dominated athletics; and that girls suffered drops in self-esteem as they entered middle and high school (AAUW, 1992). In large part because of this advocacy, our culture is attending to the issues that girls face in education.

At the same time, most teachers, parents, and other professionals involved in education know that it is mainly our boys who underperform in school. Since 1981, when the U.S. Department of Education began keeping complete statistics, we have seen that boys lag behind girls in most categories. The 2000 National Assessment of Educational Progress finds boys one and one-half years behind girls in reading/writing (National Center for Education Statistics, 2000). Girls are now only negligibly behind boys in math and science, areas in which boys have historically outperformed girls (Conlin, 2003). Our boys are now losing frightening ground in school, and we must come to terms with it—not in a way that robs girls, but in a way that sustains our civilization and is as powerful as the lobby we have created to help girls. The following statistics for the United States illustrate these concerns:

• Boys earn 70 percent of *D*s and *F*s and fewer than half of the *A*s.
• Boys account for two-thirds of learning disability diagnoses.
• Boys represent 90 percent of discipline referrals.
• Boys dominate such brain-related learning disorders as ADD/ADHD, with millions now medicated in schools.
• 80 percent of high school dropouts are male.
• Males make up fewer than 40 percent of college students (Gurian, 2001).

These statistics hold true around the world. The Organisation for Economic Co-operation and Development (OECD) recently released its three-year study of knowledge and skills of males and females in 35 industrialized countries (including the United States, Canada, the European countries, Australia, and Japan). Girls outperformed boys in every country. The statistics that brought the male scores down most significantly were their reading/writing scores.

We have nearly closed the math/science gender gap in education for girls by using more verbal functioning—reading and written analysis—to teach such spatial-mechanical subjects as math, science, and computer science (Rubin, 2004; Sommers, 2000). We now need a new movement to alter classrooms to better suit boys' learning patterns if we are to deal with the gaps in grades, discipline, and reading/writing that threaten to close many boys out of college and out of success in life.

The Nature-Based Approach

In 1996, the Gurian Institute, an organization that administers training in child development, education, and male/female brain differences, coined the phrase *nature-based approach* to call attention to the importance of basing human attachment and education strategies on research-driven biological understanding of human learning. We argued that to broadly base education and other social processes on anything other than human nature was to set up both girls and boys for unnecessary failure. The institute became especially interested in nature-based approaches to education when PET scans and MRIs of boys and girls revealed brains that were trying to learn similar lessons but in widely different ways and with varying success depending on the teaching method used. It became apparent that if teachers were trained in the differences in learning styles between boys and girls, they could profoundly improve education for all students. Between 1998 and 2000, a pilot program at the University of Missouri–Kansas City involving gender training in six school districts elicited significant results. One school involved in the training, Edison Elementary, had previously tested at the bottom of 18 district elementary schools. Following gender training, it tested in the top five slots, sometimes coming in first or second. Statewide, Edison outscored schools in every subject area, sometimes doubling and tripling the number of students in top achievement levels. Instead of the usual large number of students at the bottom end of achievement testing, Edison now had only two students requiring state-mandated retesting. The school also experienced a drastic reduction in discipline problems.

Statewide training in Alabama has resulted in improved performance for boys in both academic and behavioral areas. Beaumont Middle School in Lexington, Kentucky, trains its teachers in male/female brain differences and teaches reading/writing, math, and science in separate-sex classrooms. After one year of this gender-specific experiment, girls' math and science scores and boys' Scholastic Reading Inventory (SRI) scores rose significantly.

The Nature-Based Classroom

Ultimately, teacher training in how the brain learns and how boys and girls tend to learn differently creates the will and intuition in teachers and schools to create nature-based classrooms (see "Teaching Boys, Teaching Girls" for specific strategies). In an elementary classroom designed to help boys learn, tables and chairs are arranged to provide ample space for each child to spread out and claim learning space. Boys tend to need more physical learning space than girls do. At a table, a boy's materials will be less organized and more widely dispersed. Best practice would suggest having a variety of seating options—some desks, some tables, an easy chair, and a rug area for sitting or lying on the floor. Such a classroom would allow for more movement and noise than a traditional classroom would. Even small amounts of movement can help some boys stay focused.

The teacher can use the blocks area to help boys expand their verbal skills. As the boys are building, a teacher might ask them to describe their buildings. Because of greater blood flow in the cerebellum—the "doing" center of the human brain—boys more easily verbalize what they are doing than what they are feeling. Their language will be richer in vocabulary and more expansive when they are engaged in a task.

An elementary classroom designed to help girls learn will provide lots of opportunities for girls to manipulate objects, build, design, and calculate, thus preparing them for the more rigorous spatial challenges that they will face in higher-level math and science courses. These classrooms will set up spatial lessons in groups that encourage discussion among learners.

Boys and Feelings

An assistant principal at a Tampa, Florida, elementary school shared a story of a boy she called "the bolter." The little boy would regularly blow up in class, then bolt out of the room and out of the school. The assistant principal would chase him and get him back into the building. The boy lacked the verbal-emotive abilities to help him cope with his feelings.

After attending male/female brain difference training, the assistant principal decided to try a new tactic. The next time the boy bolted, she took a ball with her when she went after him. When she found the boy outside, she asked him to bounce the ball back and forth with her. Reluctant at first, the boy started bouncing the ball. Before long, he was talking, then sharing the anger and frustration that he was experiencing at school and at home. He calmed down and went back to class. Within a week, the boy was able to self-regulate his behavior enough to tell his teacher that he needed to go to the office, where he and the assistant principal would do their "ball routine" and talk. Because he was doing something spatial-mechanical, the boy was more able to access hidden feelings.

Girls and Computers

The InterCept program in Colorado Springs, Colorado, is a female-specific teen mentor-training program that works with girls in grades 8–12 who have been identified as at risk for school failure, juvenile delinquency, and teen pregnancy. InterCept staff members use their knowledge of female brain functioning to implement

Teaching Boys, Teaching Girls

For Elementary Boys

- Use beadwork and other manipulatives to promote fine motor development. Boys are behind girls in this area when they start school.
- Place books on shelves all around the room so boys get used to their omnipresence.
- Make lessons experiential and kinesthetic.
- Keep verbal instructions to no more than one minute.
- Personalize the student's desk, coat rack, and cubby to increase his sense of attachment.
- Use male mentors and role models, such as fathers, grandfathers, or other male volunteers.
- Let boys nurture one another through healthy aggression and direct empathy.

For Elementary Girls

- Play physical games to promote gross motor skills. Girls are behind boys in this area when they start school.
- Have portable/digital cameras around and take pictures of girls being successful at tasks.
- Use water and sand tables to promote science in a spatial venue.
- Use lots of puzzles to foster perceptual learning.
- Form working groups and teams to promote leadership roles and negotiation skills.
- Use manipulatives to teach math.
- Verbally encourage the hidden high energy of the quieter girls.

program curriculum. Brittany, 17, came to the InterCept program with a multitude of issues, many of them involving at-risk behavior and school failure.

One of the key components of InterCept is showing teenage girls the importance of becoming "tech-savvy." Girls use a computer-based program to consider future occupations: They can choose a career, determine a salary, decide how much education or training their chosen career will require, and even use income projections to design their future lifestyles. Brittany

quite literally found a future: She is entering a career in computer technology.

The Task Ahead

As educators, we've been somewhat intimidated in recent years by the complex nature of gender. Fortunately, we now have the PET and MRI technologies to view the brains of boys and girls. We now have the science to prove our intuition that tells us that boys and girls do indeed learn differently. And, even more powerful, we have a number of years of successful data that can help us effectively teach both boys and girls.

The task before us is to more deeply understand the gendered brains of our children. Then comes the practical application, with its sense of purpose and productivity, as we help each child learn from within his or her own mind.

REFERENCES

American Association of University Women. (1992). *AAUW Report: How schools shortchange girls*. American Association of University Women Foundation.

Baron-Cohen, S. (2003). *The essential difference: The truth about the male and female brain*. New York: Basic Books.

Blum, D. (1997). *Sex on the brain: The biological differences between men and women*. New York: Viking.

Conlin, M. (2003, May 26). The new gender gap. *Business Week Online*. Available: **www. businessweek.com/ magazine/content/03_21/b3834001_mz001.htm**

Gurian, M., Henley, P., & Trueman, T. (2001). *Boys and girls learn differently! A guide for teachers and parents*. San Francisco: Jossey-Bass/John Wiley.

Havers, F. (1995). Rhyming tasks male and female brains differently. *The Yale Herald, Inc*. New Haven, CT: Yale University.

Marano, H. E. (2003, July/August). The new sex scorecard. *Psychology Today*, 38–50.

Moir, A., & Jessel, D. (1989). *Brain sex: The real difference between men and women*. New York: Dell Publishing.

National Center for Education Statistics. (2000). *National Assessment of Educational Progress: The nation's report card*. Washington, DC: U.S. Department of Education.

Organisation for Economic Co-operation and Development. (2003). *The PISA 2003 assessment framework*. Author.

Rich, B. (Ed.). (2000). *The Dana brain daybook*. New York: The Charles A. Dana Foundation. Rubin, R. (2004, Aug. 23). How to survive the new SAT. *Newsweek*, p. 52.

Sommers, C. (2000). *The war against boys*. Simon and Schuster.

Taylor, S. (2002). *The tending instinct*. Times Books.

POSTNOTE

The authors of this article argue that for true gender equity to occur in our schools, teaching practices need to address the different needs of male and female brains. They also argue that these brain differences help to explain why girls generally outperform boys in reading and writing, while boys generally learn higher mathematics and physics more easily than girls when those subjects are taught abstractly. This is a highly controversial position, as Lawrence Summers, the president of Harvard University, discovered in 2005. Addressing a group of faculty members, he made comments suggesting that women do not perform as well as men in higher mathematics and that the reason is at least partly because of innate differences in men and women. His remarks provoked a maelstrom of protests from many faculty members.

The position taken by the authors of this article raises another interesting question. Will both girls and boys perform better academically in a single-sex setting?

Can teachers better address the particular needs of boys and girls when only one gender is present in class? Research on single-sex schools by Anthony Bryk and his colleagues demonstrates rather conclusively that girls are more likely to flourish academically in a girls-only setting. Anecdotal evidence suggests that many young boys also do better when taught by male teachers in a single-sex setting.

Discussion Questions

1. Which group, girls or boys, do you believe is shortchanged the most in schools today? Why do you think so?
2. What are your views on the value of single-sex education?
3. What problems or obstacles can you identify in trying to implement teaching practices that address the differences in boys' and girls' brains?

RELATED WEBSITE RESOURCES AND VIDEO CASES

 ### Web Resources:

The Gurian Institute. Available at:

http://www.gurianinstitute.com.

This website contains educational materials and provides workshops on how boys and girls learn differently.

⏩ ▶ ⏪ Video Case:

Gender Equity in the Classroom: Girls and Science

In this video case, you will see how a middle school science teacher promotes science learning for all his students: boys and girls. As you watch the clips and study the artifacts in the case, reflect upon the following questions:

1. Do you agree that it is important for students to have gender or ethnic-minority role models in different academic and career areas, as the teachers in the video case suggest? Why or why not?
2. This video focuses on girls and science. How can a teacher ensure equity in mixed-gender classrooms?

Classroom Observation

This appendix is designed to help you develop skills in observing classrooms and schools. You will probably benefit most by reading the rest of this section rather quickly now and rereading it carefully before you observe schools and classrooms. Since the material on the following pages is somewhat technical, you can probably assimilate it best when you know that you will be making use of it soon.

Issues Related to Observation

Virtually all teacher education programs provide opportunities for the prospective teacher to observe experienced teachers. Observation may take place "live," or it may involve viewing digital recordings of classroom sessions. Either alternative can be extremely valuable if it offers an opportunity for insight into how a classroom is organized, how the teacher relates to different students, or how different forms of instruction can be used. However, observation of a classroom can be boring, tedious, and educationally irrelevant. What is it that makes observation valuable or worthless? The difference is a matter of knowing specifically what you are attempting to observe and why, being able to gather information accurately, and interpreting your information in order to learn from it. Thus, to really benefit from observing an actual classroom, you must have some training in observational techniques.

Need for training

It is physically and mechanically impossible to record *everything* that occurs in a classroom, let alone in an entire school. Thus, any technique used to gather data about the classroom environment must of necessity be selective. This is a built-in and unavoidable limitation of all recording instruments and techniques of observation.

Be selective

Furthermore, the observer's background and training influence the classroom phenomena he or she chooses to focus on and the ways in which he or she interprets them. If the variable in question is aggressive behavior among students, for example, an educational psychologist may interpret a classroom outbreak as a result of the teacher's inconsistent reward pattern. An anthropologist might view it as a normal event within the youth subculture. A student teacher, because of personal needs and anxieties, might assume that the students are misbehaving because they do not really like him or her. For this reason, objective interpretation is as impossible as comprehensive observation. However, knowing the limitations of observational techniques will help observers interpret the data better, and being aware of their own particular perceptual habits will help them exert caution in interpretation.

Observer bias

Observer's impact on classroom

Another problem is that anytime someone or something new and different enters a classroom, that person or thing affects the dynamics of the group in some way. Your presence may cause the teacher to be somewhat more nervous, thus affecting his or her behavior. The students, aware of your presence, may turn their heads to see what you are doing. If you are collecting data using some mechanical equipment, such as a camcorder, the teacher's and students' behavior will be affected. Therefore, you can never observe or collect information completely free from the effects of your presence. What you can do, however, is to become a frequent enough visitor to the classroom that your presence will not produce unusual or severe reactions from the regular classroom participants. You can also locate yourself physically in the room to reduce your obtrusiveness and to stay out of the students' direct line of sight.

Behaving professionally

As an observer in someone else's classroom, you are a guest and, as such, need to behave accordingly. This means that you should:

- make your dress and appearance consistent with what the school expects its teachers to wear. If you are uncertain about this, ask your college instructor.
- refrain from judging the school or teachers too quickly if you see things happening with which you disagree. Remember, you probably do not have all the information you need to make such judgments, and you need to accord the teachers some respect for their judgments and decisions. As the old Native American proverb states, "Don't judge another until you've walked a mile in his moccasins."
- not assume that what you see one day is typical of what occurs often. That may or may not be the case. Frequent observations are necessary before one can speak with confidence about patterns or typical behavior.

Confidentiality

- maintain confidentiality. Although you may need to report your observations in some format to your college instructor, it is unprofessional to tattle or gossip to your peers about a particular teacher or classroom. If you feel the need to discuss some incident or events that occurred in a particular school or classroom, try to maintain confidentiality regarding the identities of the particular persons involved. The classroom participants should not suffer embarrassment or harm as a result of your field experience.

Data-Gathering Techniques

The observational methods used in education were developed by the behavioral and social sciences to gather data about and interpret complex environments; they were later found to be appropriate for use in schools as well. This section will introduce you to some of these tools and approaches, as well as the kinds of preliminary decisions and subsequent interpretation that give meaning to observation. The scrupulous observer must ask certain questions: What specifically will be observed? Which method of gathering data will be most effective? What do these data mean? To learn from observation, then, the observer needs (1) objectives, (2) a way to record observations, and (3) a way to interpret observations with respect to objectives.

Purposeful observation

Observation should not be aimless. If you are to find out what life in the classroom is like, you must decide which aspects you wish to focus on. Your objective may be very broad, such as: "What does the teacher do and say during a class period?" Or it may be as narrow as: "How many times does a particular student speak to another student?"

Form hypotheses

From the data that you collect you can form a hypothesis about why certain things occur, and you can test this hypothesis by making predictions about what should happen if it is correct. If your prediction is not validated, you can reexamine your data and try to develop another explanation. If your prediction is validated repeatedly, you will know that you are moving in the direction of understanding what is happening in the classroom and, possibly, why. For example, suppose your objective is to examine the teacher's verbal interaction with each individual student. After performing frequency counts—recording how many times the teacher calls on each student, or how many times each student volunteers information or asks the teacher a question—over a period of a week, you might hypothesize about the frequency distribution for the following week. If your predictions are validated, you should then try to interpret your findings. Was the teacher displaying a bias against certain students? Did the teacher systematically ignore the students seated in a particular part of the room? Were certain groups of students—for example, girls or certain socioeconomic groups—treated in particular ways? Caution must be exercised in drawing conclusions, however, because rival hypotheses may explain the same phenomena.

The point to be emphasized is that to understand the happenings in a classroom, you must select objectives that provide you with a focus. Since you cannot see, hear, and interpret everything, you must be selective. To be selective, you must establish the purpose of your observation.

You may find one of the following techniques of data gathering particularly appropriate, given your objectives, the equipment available, and the degree of access you have to a school. All have been used profitably by classroom observers.

NOTE TAKING

Probably the most common means of gathering data in the school is note taking. The method is borrowed from cultural anthropologists, who take copious notes of their observations while living with the natives of an unfamiliar culture. You can use the same approach to accumulate information about the interpersonal relationships, values, or social status of individuals in a class.

If you choose the note-taking approach, certain preliminary decisions will have to be made. First, how comprehensive should your notes be? You will be attempting to record everything you see that relates to your objective. Thus, the broader your objective, the more you will have to record. In many instances it will be difficult for you to decide quickly on the relevance of a specific event. A handy rule of thumb: When in doubt, write it down. Too much information is better than not enough, for insufficient data can lead to frustration and to erroneous conclusions.

Second, you must decide whether to write a description of what you see and hear, or simply record what is said verbatim. Should you write down your impressions of incidents, or should you be as objective as possible? We recommend that, whenever possible, data be recorded verbatim. In trying to summarize or describe what takes place, you are likely to substitute your own perceptions for what was actually happening. If you wish also to record your impressions, insights, inferences, and comments, keep them in the margin or draw brackets around them to distinguish them from the raw data. This distinction is crucial because of the tendency to make inferences based on selected perceptions or personal biases. If we are happy, we tend to see happy people; if tired, we see the teacher's and students' behavior through the filter of fatigue and interpret it accordingly. We may see relationships that do not actually exist and miss ones that do. Therefore, recognizing that complete objectivity is impossible, we should still aim to achieve it rather than rely on our own interpretations of events.

Techniques of Data Gathering

- Note taking
- Observation systems
- Seating charts
- Analysis of artifacts
- Interviews
- Video and digital recordings

Note taking

Record verbatim

Record verbal behavior

You will find that recording nonverbal behavior tends to be much more impressionistic than recording verbal behavior. If we observe a student fidgeting in her seat, picking her nose, and looking out the window, it is tempting to assert that she is bored; yet that is an inference. Keep checking on yourself to make sure you are distinguishing between actual behavior and inferences drawn from behavior.

**Standard format
and abbreviations**

It is much easier to be comprehensive in your note taking if you establish a standard format and abbreviations. For example, indenting student comments will help you distinguish them from teacher comments and will save you from repeatedly having to indicate who is talking. Abbreviating words by omitting vowels, employing homonyms, and using phonetic representations will also allow you to record more efficiently and quickly. If you have experience at text messaging, those skills should come in handy!

Advantages and disadvantages

Note taking has a number of advantages as a means of gathering data about classroom actions. It is relatively simple and very economical. You can flip back and forth in your notes easily when you begin to interpret the data. The notes can be cut up and juxtaposed in whatever fashion you want to help you discern patterns or repeated themes. You can assimilate ideas and events rapidly by scanning written notes. And notes constitute a permanent record, which you can keep to compare with other observations and to develop, support, or reject hypotheses.

A major disadvantage of note taking is the difficulty of recording everything you can see and hear. Even though you have selected limited objectives to guide your observations, action often develops so fast that you fall behind and miss some of what is said or done. Taking notes forces you to keep your eyes on the paper in front of you and prevents you from observing the class without interruption. In other words, your observation system tends to become overloaded with stimuli. Nevertheless, note taking is probably the most frequently used method of gathering data in the classroom.

SYSTEMATIC OBSERVATION SYSTEMS

Observation systems make use of lists of categories—as minuscule as sneezes or smiles or as broad as teacher-student rapport—to record verbal or nonverbal interaction in the classroom according to predefined rules and definitions. Prior to the observation, decisions are made concerning what is to be observed, the method of observation and recording data, and how the data will be analyzed and used.

Although many observation systems have been developed, only a few are in general use. Probably the best-known category system for observing teachers and pupils is Flanders's Interaction Analysis (see Figure A-1). Flanders identified ten different categories of verbal behavior; the first seven apply to teacher talk, the next two to student talk, and the final category records silence or confusion. The categories are: (1) accepting student feelings; (2) giving praise; (3) accepting, clarifying, or making use of a student's ideas; (4) asking a question; (5) lecturing, giving facts or opinions; (6) giving directions; (7) giving criticism; (8) student response; (9) student initiation; and (10) confusion or silence. Categories 1-4 represent indirect teacher influence, and categories 5-7 represent direct teacher influence. An observer using Flanders's system will record, every three seconds, the category of verbal behavior occurring at that instant; then an analysis is made of verbal interaction during the entire class period. Thus, a profile of the teacher's direct or indirect influence can be obtained.

FIGURE A-1

Categories for Interaction Analysis

TEACHER TALK

Indirect Influence

1. ACCEPTS FEELING: accepts and clarifies the tone of feeling of the students in an unthreatening manner. Feelings may be positive or negative. Predicting or recalling feelings are included.
2. PRAISES or ENCOURAGES: praises or encourages student action or behavior. Jokes that release tension, but not at the expense of another individual; nodding head; or saying "um hm" or "go on" are included.
3. ACCEPTS or USES IDEAS of STUDENT: clarifying, building, or developing ideas suggested by a student. As teacher brings more of his own ideas into play, shift to category 5.
4. ASKS QUESTIONS: asking a question about content or procedure with the intent that a student provides an answer.

Direct Influence

5. LECTURING: giving facts or opinions about content or procedure; expressing his own ideas, asking rhetorical questions.
6. GIVING DIRECTIONS: giving directions, commands, or orders which students are expected to comply with.
7. CRITICIZING or JUSTIFYING AUTHORITY: statements intended to change student behavior from unacceptable to acceptable pattern; bawling out someone; stating why the teacher is doing what he is doing; extreme self-reference.

STUDENT TALK

8. STUDENT TALK—RESPONSE: talk by students in response to teacher. Teacher initiates the contact or solicits student statement.
9. STUDENT TALK—INITIATION: talk initiated by student. If "calling on" student is only to indicate who may talk next, observer must decide whether student wanted to talk.

SILENCE

10. SILENCE or CONFUSION: pauses, short periods of silence, and periods of confusion in which communication cannot be understood by the observer.

There is NO scale implied by these numbers. Each number is for classification, designating a particular kind of communication event. To write these numbers down during observation is merely to identify and enumerate.

Advantages and disadvantages of Flanders's system

Flanders's system has limitations, but it can be a helpful and informative tool in analyzing a certain kind of verbal behavior in the classroom. It has been used extensively, and considerable research data have been collected. Instructional booklets and audiotapes are available to students interested in learning to use the system and to interpret data. Many universities and colleges, as well as public schools, have used Interaction Analysis to help teachers analyze their teaching.

SEATING CHARTS

Using seating charts as an observational tool provides a familiar way of looking at classrooms. Seating charts are useful for collecting important aspects of classroom behavior, such as pupil attentiveness, and they are easy to use. Figure A-2 illustrates how a seating chart can be used to collect data on student on-task and off-task behavior. Each box represents a student, and the boxes are located on the paper to reflect each student's physical location in the classroom. Within each box is a sequence of numbers, each representing one observation of the student. Depending on the length of the observation time period, there may be fewer or more than the eleven observations represented in this instrument. A list of categories with their code symbols, a legend, is also given. The on-task and off-task behaviors are symbolized by letters that represent shorthand reminders of the behavior categories. (Figure A-2 has the coded observations already recorded.) This instrument and others like it are flexible and can be adapted to fit the observer's and the teacher's needs. Many of the on-task and off-task behaviors can be anticipated in advance of the actual observation. However, if one occurs that was not anticipated, just add it to the legend.

Record time

When you are ready to begin the observation, identify the time you begin and then observe the first student. What is he or she doing? Code the behavior appropriately and place the code in the box next to the number 1. Then move quickly to the next student and repeat the process, again placing the code next to the number 1. Continue until you have observed all the students (or at least the ones that you are planning to observe), and then start your second round of observations with the first student and repeat the sequence. Each time you get ready to begin a new observation cycle, record the time you start. The times that you see listed on the instrument in Figure A-2 are not placed there in advance of the actual observation. They are there simply to remind you to record the time so you will know how much time was required for each observation cycle.

Sampling students' behavior

With some practice and familiarity with the instrument, you will soon be able to move quickly from student to student while coding the student's behavior. Remember, you are sampling the student's behavior. The more observations you make, the greater the confidence you can have that your sample validly and reliably represents the full set of behaviors the students demonstrated.

Matrix of types of behavior

Whereas you can analyze each student's pattern of behavior by looking at each box, it is much more difficult to grasp the broader picture of the total class's on-task and off-task behavior. However, you can do this by developing a matrix with the types of behavior listed along one dimension and the time intervals along the other dimension; in this way you can obtain an overall view of the class (Figure A-3). To interpret these data with some accuracy, it is necessary to know what activities are supposed to be occurring throughout the lesson. Do not try to interpret too much from data unless you know what happened in the class.

There are several things worth noting about the data presented in Figure A-3. First, note the percentage of pupils on task throughout the lesson. At the beginning of the lesson the figure is 50 percent, and it climbs to 85 percent after ten minutes. Is there some explanation for why it took ten minutes to reach an 85 percent on-task rate? Similarly, why was there a sharp decline in the on-task percentage rate during the last six minutes?

FIGURE A-2

Pupil On-Task/Off-Task Behavior

Purpose: To determine which students are on or off task during a lesson, and what specific behaviors they are engaged in.

Lesson Type: Teacher-led discussion in eighth-grade social studies.

Note:

On Task
L = listening
TN = taking notes
H = hand raised
T+ = talking (discussion related)

Off Task
R− = reading (non-class related)
T− = talking (non-class related)
WS = working on another subject
OS = out of seat
0 = other

	1	2	3	4	5	6	7	8	9	10	11
Time	9:15	9:17	9:20	9:22	9:25	9:27	9:29	9:32	9:34	9:37	9:40
Corrine	L	L	TN	TN	H	T+	L	L	TN	TN	OS
Mike	T−	T−	WS	WS	WS	WS	OS	T−	H	OS	OS
Jim	T−	T−	L	L	L	TN	H	TN	T+	T+	0
Nancy	R−	R−	R−	L	L	L	TN	T+	OS	OS	OS
Jo	WS	WS	L	L	TN	TN	L	L	H	T+	T+
Mary Kay	L	L	TN	TN	TN	T+	T−	L	L	H	H
Will	OS	0	0	0	T−	R−	R−	R−	R−	H	OS
Mildred	L	L	L	TN	T+	T+	H	L	L	L	H
Carlos	L	L	L	L	L	TN	TN	TN	TN	TN	TN
James	OS	T−	T−	T−	L	L	L	TN	TN	TN	L
Frank	H	H	TN	TN	TN	L	L	L	L	L	T+
Betty	L	L	L	L	L	TN	L	L	L	L	L
Marilyn	R−	R−	R−	WS	WS	WS	WS	WS	WS	H	H
Fran	H	L	L	T+	T+	L	H	TN	TN	TN	TN
Howie	OS	L	L	TN	TN	T+	T−	T−	T−	OS	OS
Jack	T+	TN	TN	TN	L	L	L	WS	WS	WS	WS
Bob	T+	TN	L	L	L	TN	H	H	0	0	0
Maria	L	L	L	L	H	L	L	L	L	L	L
Vince	T−	T−	T−	L	L	L	H	T+	OS	OS	OS
Chet	R−	R−	R−	R−	L	TN	TN	TN	TN	R−	R−

Source: Adapted from James M. Cooper, "Observation Skills," in *Developing Skills for Instructional Supervision*, ed. James M. Cooper (New York: Longman, 1984), p. 96.

FIGURE A-3

On-Task/Off-Task Matrix

	BEHAVIOR CATEGORIES										
	1	2	3	4	5	6	7	8	9	10	11
	9:15	9:17	9:20	9:22	9:25	9:27	9:29	9:32	9:34	9:37	9:40
On Task											
Listening	6	8	9	8	9	7	7	7	5	4	3
Taking notes	0	2	4	6	4	6	3	5	5	4	2
Hand raised	2	1	0	0	2	0	5	1	2	3	3
Talking (discussion related)	2	0	0	0	2	4	0	2		2	2
Off Task											
Reading (non-class related)	3	3	3		0						
Talking (non-class related)	3	4	2	1		0	2	2		0	0
Working on another subject	1	1	1	2	2	2	1	2	2	1	1
Out of seat	3	0	0	0	0	0	1	0	2	4	6
Other	0	1	1	1	0	0	0	0	1	1	2
Percentage of students on task	50	55	65	70	85	85	75	75	65	65	50

Second, during the beginning of the lesson there were as many as four students engaged in non-class-related talking. Why?

Third, why were so many students out of their seats during the last six minutes of the class? Was the teacher aware of them? The data do not provide us with answers to these questions, but they do provoke us to ask the questions.

If you are interested in learning more about other observation systems, the following books and articles will be helpful:

Sources of observation instruments

- Acheson, Keith A., and Meredith Damien Gall. *Techniques in the Clinical Supervision of Teachers,* 4th ed. New York: Longman, 1997.
- Borich, Gary D. *Observation Skills for Effective Teaching,* 5th ed. Columbus, OH: Merrill, 2008.
- Good, Thomas L., and Jere E. Brophy. *Looking in Classrooms.* 10th ed. Columbus, OH: Allyn & Bacon/Merrill Education 2007.

ANALYSIS OF ARTIFACTS

Much can be learned about life in the classroom without directly observing teachers and students. The textbooks and supplementary materials in use can reveal a *lot* to the careful observer. Similarly, the tests given, the placement of chairs and desks, the materials displayed on the bulletin board, and the audio-visual equipment used (or neglected) are clues about what activities take place and what kind of learning is valued.

Tests Given   What kinds of questions are on the examinations? Do they emphasize the acquisition of facts to the exclusion of solving problems, analyzing or synthesizing ideas, making evaluations, comparing or contrasting different points of view, drawing inferences from limited data, or forming generalizations?

Placement of Chairs and Desks   Do the chairs and desks always face the teacher, the dominant person in the classroom? Or are they frequently grouped in small circles, indicating opportunities for pupil-pupil interaction?

Materials Displayed on the Bulletin Board   Is the bulletin board primarily a construct of the teacher, or does it display student work? What student works are displayed?

Audiovisual Equipment   Is a multimedia approach used so that students may learn from a variety of sources?

You probably have the idea by now: clues about what a teacher thinks is important, whether students are involved in instruction as well as learning, and how the teacher views his or her role can be garnered by a careful analysis of materials used and produced in the classroom. Valuable inferences may be made from data available to the naked eye, but it is crucial to remember that such inferences are only hypotheses and that additional data must be gathered to confirm or invalidate them.

INTERVIEWS

Interviewing teachers, students, administrators, counselors, librarians, and other school personnel is an excellent way to gather data about life in school. People who play different roles in the school, and thus see it from different vantage points, often have highly disparate views of it. The cook in the school kitchen may have a very different opinion of the food's quality than the students or the teachers, and the administrator's view of detention hall is probably very unlike the students'. Questioning the students about what occupies most of their time in the classroom, what they think the school's purpose is, why they go to school or, in general, how their good teachers differ from the poor ones can produce fascinating and highly valuable data. Some sample questions follow. The answers to them should help you better understand life in a particular school.

1. Where is the school located in the community?
2. How old is the school?
3. Is it a parent-, teacher-, administration-, or student-centered school? What evidence leads you to your conclusion?
4. Is there a school media center or library? Where is it? How does a student gain access to it? What are the library procedures?
5. Where is the nurse's office? What are the major concerns of the health administrator in this school? What are the major complaints (types of illnesses)? What are the procedures for being sent home or remaining in the health office?
6. Where does physical education take place? What are the usual activities? Who participates? What do students do if they are not participating?
7. What is the procedure for tardy students?
8. Who administers this procedure?

9. Do students move from one classroom to another during the school day? How is this accomplished?
10. Is there a formal dress code? Or an informal one? How would you describe the school's dress code?
11. What are some frequent causes of disciplinary action against students?
12. Is there a teachers' lounge? How is it used?
13. Is there a student council and does it have any real power to promote change in the school? If the answer is "yes," ask for some examples. Does the student council represent the entire student body, or is it a select group?
14. Do parents come to the school? If so, when and for what reasons?
15. Do students congregate in identifiable patterns in the lunch room?
16. Are there extracurricular activities, such as music, sports, clubs, and meetings?
17. Does the school empty quickly at the end of the day?
18. If you are investigating a secondary school, does it have a newspaper? Ask the editor or a staffer what its function is and how much freedom students have to print what they wish.
19. Are students bused to school? If you can, ride a school bus one day to see what it is like. Is it different in the morning than in the afternoon?
20. Listen to the students' language, in class and out. Is there any difference?
21. Ask an administrator, secretary, custodian, teacher, librarian, and nurse to describe the student population.
22. Are students trusted? What evidence can you find one way or the other?
23. What is unusual about this school?
24. What do the school's administrators do? What are their major areas of responsibility? What are the major pressures on them?*

Answers to these questions will help you to gain an understanding of the culture of the school, the "hidden curriculum" of the school, and what life in the school is like for students.

VIDEO AND DIGITAL RECORDINGS

Public schools and colleges are making increasing use of mechanical recording devices as analytical and training tools. Both audio and video recorders have been available for quite a while, and now DVDs and digital video clips are also available. All these devices have enabled teachers and researchers to analyze what happens in the classroom more completely and objectively. Recording devices can register both the image and the sound of classroom interaction, and the resulting record is more accurate and comprehensive than either notes or an observation schedule. Such devices have many other advantages: The recordings can be replayed without limit, the available features make it possible to locate or repeat a particular passage quickly, and the data can be stored almost indefinitely.

Many advantages

The same criteria or objectives may be applied to recorded data as to live observation. The advantage, of course, is that something that is missed in the first viewing can be repeated until the viewer has absorbed it, a luxury unavailable in live observation. You might wish to analyze verbal interactions using Flanders's Interaction Analysis, or to watch the behavior of a particular child,

---

*The authors are indebted to Professor Emma Cappelluzzo of the University of Massachusetts for many of these questions. Used by permission.

or to count the number of encouraging gestures the teacher makes toward students. The possibilities are endless.

Many teacher education programs are collecting digital recordings to demonstrate particular classroom phenomena to prospective teachers; some show only a single "critical incident." The video can be stopped to allow speculation about how the teacher will or should respond, started again to view the teacher's actual actions, and stopped for further discussion. The video cases produced by Cengage Learning that have been cited at the end of many of the articles, along with many support articles noted throughout this book, are excellent examples of the power of video recordings to reveal classroom interactions.

We have not attempted to train you in the techniques, methods, and tools of classroom observation, believing that to be better and more appropriately accomplished as part of your teacher education program. Instead, we have tried to acquaint you with methods that have been—and are currently being—used by educators to better understand school environments.

Study Tips

Teachers play many roles from communicator to character educator. One of a teacher's most central tasks is to be a learning specialist, someone skilled at helping others gain new information, organize it, and make it available for recall later.

Many college students (pre-service teachers included) come to higher education well equipped to handle the new and more demanding study requirements. They can study effectively. However, they do not know how they do it nor are they able to pass on their skills to others. Many more college students falter under the new academic demands they encounter on campus. The methods that worked for them in high school are not adequate in college. Frequently, these students become frustrated and discouraged. They drop out or fatalistically settle for being a "C student" or worse. They convince themselves that they "just don't have it."

What they fail to realize (or were never told) is that the "it" that they do not have is quite learnable. The "it" is a group of acquirable skills and techniques. The "it" can make the difference between a successful and happy college educated person and a failure.

The Internet is filled with excellent study skill websites which address problems such as time management, test taking, writing research papers for particular subjects, note taking, and many other specific skills. Two sites, in particular, are:

http://www.stthomas.edu/academicsupport/helpful_study_skills_links.htm and http://www.how-to-study.com/

We urge you to make a small investment in sharpening your study skills for two reasons: first, to get the very most return on your substantial investment of time and money; and second, to equip yourself to be the learning specialist expected of every teacher.

Finally, we believe that study skills are part of a large set of skills and competencies that people need to participate effectively in the world today. In our textbook, *Those Who Can, Teach,* we call these "the New Basics," the intellectual equipment everyone who wishes to function in a globalized society should possess.

Sample of the Tools for Learning

Here is a list of some of the skills, which we call *tools for learning,* that we believe ought to be taught to all students:

- *Various methods for remembering important information.* This largely involves teaching people how not to forget: how to move information from the fleeting short-term memory to the more enduring long-term memory.

- *Two or three methods of taking notes and saving important information.* Definite skills are associated with capturing what another person is saying, and students should systematically learn these skills.

- *Study reading.* A person practices "study reading" when the material is complex and contains information he or she wants to remember later. This technique is quite different from reading a novel or reading a telephone book. This set of skills lies at the heart of academic success, as well as success in many jobs.

- *Preparing for different kinds of tests.* Schools should show students how to study for different types of tests, such as objective and essay tests, and how to deal with test anxiety in various situations. Because examinations and tests do not end with graduation, schools should teach students how to cope with and master these challenges.

- *Doing research.* Students need to learn how to get answers to questions by using libraries, the Internet, expert sources, and data-gathering resources of all kinds. In essence, these skills focus on finding and accessing different data sources and using the information to solve a problem.

- *Thinking through a problem in a systematic way.* Instead of jumping to conclusions or relying on how they feel about an issue, students should learn how to think critically.

- *Generating creative ideas.* Much of life in and out of school requires new solutions or imaginative resolutions. Students need to learn techniques for generating novel and creative ideas individually, as well as group-oriented techniques such as brainstorming.

- *Getting the academic job done.* Students need to know how to set goals, develop a work plan, monitor their own behavior, bring a task to successful closure, and gradually become more successful at academic learning. This is important not simply to succeed in school, but because the modern workplace demands these same skills.

How to Participate in Discussions

An important part of one's education is learning how to speak in a group setting and participate in organized discussion. While some students acquire these skills in high school, many do not. Whether through shyness, reticence, or just a lack of skill, these students are cut off from one of the major benefits of a college education: the ability to participate in the give-and-take exchange so necessary in a democratic society and so many occupations and professions.

Being able to speak in a group setting, listening, and responding to others is crucial in the teaching profession. Whether in your own classroom, faculty meetings, or as a member of a professional association, educators must be able to actively engage in deliberations. They must be able to debate positions, engage in the formulation of plans, and perform a variety of other activities which require discussion skills.

Your college years are the ideal setting to overcome your reticence and gain the skills to actively engage in group discussions. The following are a few valuable websites which can guide you toward becoming comfortable and proficient in discussions.

http://www.lc.unsw.edu.au/onlib/pdf/disc.pdf
http://www.yorku.ca/srowley/critdiscuss.htm
http://www.ac.wwu.edu/~gmyers/ehe/discpart.html
http://www.swccd.edu/~asc/lrnglinks/oldiscbd.html
http://www.abacon.com/commstudies/groups/roles.html

Web Resources for Teachers

The following are the primary educational organizations of interest to educators and their websites.

National Education Association (**http://www.nea.org**)
American Federation of Teachers (**http://www.aft.org**)
United States Department of Education (**http://ed.gov**)
Council for Exceptional Children (**http://www.cec.sped.org**)
National Science Teachers Association (**http://www.nsta.org**)
National Council of Teachers of English (**http://www.ncte.org**)
National Council for the Social Studies (**http://www.ncss.org**)
National Association for Music Education (**http://www.menc.org**)
National Association for the Education of Young Children (**http://www.naeyc.org**)
Association of Career and Technical Education (**http://www.acteonline.org**)
International Reading Association (**http://www.reading.org**)
National Council of Teachers of Mathematics (**http://www.nctm.org**)
American Council on the Teaching of Foreign Language (**http://www.actfl.org**)
National Art Education Association (**http://www.naea-reston.org**)
American Alliance for Health, Physical Education, Recreation and Dance (**http://www.aahperd.org**)
Association for Education Communications and Technology (**http://www.aect.org**)

Nationwide Special-Interest Groups in Education

National School Boards Association (**http://www.nsba.org**)
American Association of School Administrators (**http://www.aasa.org**)
Association for Supervision and Curriculum Development (**http://www.ascd.org**)
American Educational Research Association (**http://www.aera.net**)
Council of Chief State School Officers (**http://www.ccsso.org**)
Association of Teacher Educators (**http://www.ate1.org/pubs/home.cfm**)
American Association of Colleges for Teacher Education (**http://www.aacte.org**)

Note: Boldfaced terms that appear within definitions can be found elsewhere in the glossary.

Academic freedom   The ability of teachers to teach about an issue or to use a source without fear of penalty, reprisal, or harassment.

Academic learning time   Time spent by students performing academic tasks with a high success rate.

Acceptable use policy (AUP)   A statement of rules governing student use of school computers, especially regarding access to the Internet.

Accountability   The effort to hold a party responsible for the results of an activity.

Achievement gap   Differences in educational achievement between students of different socioeconomic or racial and ethnic groups.

Adaptation   Changes in instruction or materials made to meet the needs of learners with special needs.

Aesthetic   Appreciative of or responsive to that which is beautiful.

American Federation of Teachers (AFT)   The nation's second-largest teacher's association/union. Founded in 1916, it is affiliated with the AFL-CIO, the nation's largest union.

Assertive behavior   The ability to stand up for one's legitimate rights in ways that make it less likely that others will ignore or circumvent them.

Assessment   The process of determining students' learning progress.

Assimilation   The absorption of an individual or a group into the cultural tradition of a population or another group.

Assistive technology   The array of devices and services that help people with special needs to perform better in their daily lives. Such devices include motorized chairs, remote control units that turn appliances on and off, computers, and speech synthesizers.

At-homeness   A sense of awareness of and equanimity with the world in which one lives.

At risk   A term used to describe conditions—for example, poverty, poor health, or learning disabilities—that put children in danger of not succeeding in school.

Behavioral indicators of child abuse   Changes or signals in a child's behavior that suggest the child is being abused or neglected.

Benchmarks   Standards by which something can be measured or judged.

Benefit maximization   An ethical principle suggesting that individuals should choose the course of action that will make people generally better off.

Bilingual education   A variety of approaches to educating students who speak a primary language other than English.

Block scheduling   An approach to class scheduling in which students take fewer classes each school day, but spend more time in each class.

Blogs   A blog is short for web log. Blogs are personal websites consisting of regularly updated entries displayed in reverse chronological order. It is essentially an online diary or journal.

Carnegie unit   A measure of clock time used to award high school credits toward graduation.

Charter school   School in which the educators, often joined by members of the local community, have made a special contract, or charter, with the school district. Usually the charter allows the school a great deal of independence in its operation.

Chatrooms   A chatroom is a place on the Internet where people with similar interests can communicate in real time by typing messages on their computers.

Child abuse   Physical, emotional, or sexual maltreatment or neglect of a child.

Coalesced content standard   A modest repacking or reworking of a state's existing curricular standards.

Common school   Public elementary schools that are open to children of all races, nationalities, and classes. During the 19th century, the common school became the embodiment of universal education.

Complementary teaching   A term used in special education when a support person does something to complement the instruction provided by the classroom teacher, such as taking notes or paraphrasing the teacher's statements.

Comprehensive high school   The predominant form of secondary education in the United States in the 20th century. It provides both a preparation for college and a vocational education for students not going to college.

Conflict resolution   A process for resolving a dispute or disagreement.

Constructivism A theory, based on research from cognitive psychology, that people learn by constructing their own knowledge through an active learning process, rather than by simply absorbing knowledge directly from another source.

Consultation When support personnel in special education provide assistance to general educators, enabling them to teach all the students in an inclusive class.

Content standards Statements outlining the knowledge and skills that students are expected to learn.

Continuous reconstruction of experience A curricular principle in which the student's daily experience serves as the focus of learning.

Conversation gap The disparity between poor and middle classes in the frequency and quality of child-adult verbal interaction.

Cooperative learning An educational strategy, composed of a set of instructional methods, in which students work in small, mixed-ability groups to master the material and to ensure that all group members reach the learning goals.

Core knowledge curriculum A curriculum based on a strong, specific elementary core of studies, including literature, history, mathematics, science, art, and music.

Coteaching A situation in which two teachers, often a special education teacher and a general education teacher, teach the same class together.

Council for Exceptional Children A national organization of individuals concerned about the education of children with special needs or gifts. The organization promotes research, public policies, and programs that champion the rights of exceptional individuals.

Culturally responsive teaching A method of embracing students' cultural backgrounds by modifying classroom conditions or activities to include elements that relate to the students' culture.

Curriculum All the organized and intended experiences of the student for which the school accepts responsibility.

Cyberbullying Bullying through information and communication technologies, such as mobile phone text messages, e-mail messages, Internet chatrooms, and social networking websites such as MySpace, Facebook, and Bebo.

De-localization The erosion of local control over school affairs, such as curricular decisions and standards.

Derivative assessment framework A framework gleaned from a state's curricular standards that focuses on a small number of reconceptualized, eligible-to-be-taught curricular targets.

Deskilled teachers Teachers who no longer possess the processes of deliberation and reflection.

Developmentally responsive Being alert and sensitive to the mental, emotional, and physical changes of students and being respectful of their needs and interests.

Dewey, John American philosopher, educator, and author (1859–1952) who taught that learning by doing should form the basis of educational practice.

Diagnostic assessment Assessments given to students prior to instruction to determine what they already know and do not know.

Didactic instruction A lecture approach to teaching that emphasizes compliant behavior on the part of the student while the teacher dispenses information.

Differentiation (differentiated instruction) A variety of techniques used to adapt instruction to the individual ability levels and learning styles of each student in the classroom.

Discipline problems Violations of, or students who violate, classroom rules.

Disempowerment The condition of persons who have been separated from what is rightly their own.

Distance learning The use of technology to link students and teachers who are separated in terms of location.

Dominance The teacher's ability to provide clear purpose and strong guidance regarding both academics and student behavior.

Due process The deliberative process that protects a person's constitutional right to receive fair and equal protection under the law.

Early childhood education Programs that concentrate on educating young children (usually up to age eight). Early childhood education has become an important priority in helping children from disadvantaged backgrounds achieve educational parity with other children.

Educated person An individual who is able to see the connectedness of all things.

Empathetic listening Attending to another by participating in his or her feelings or ideas.

Equal educational opportunity The legal principle that all children should have equal chances to develop their abilities and aptitudes to the fullest extent regardless of family background, social class, or individual differences.

Equal respect An ethical principle suggesting that our actions acknowledge the equal worth of humans (i.e., the Golden Rule).

Ethics A branch of philosophy that emphasizes values that relate to "good" and "bad" behavior; examining morality; and rules of conduct. Proponents believe that an educated person must have these values and that all children should be taught them.

Extrinsic motivation Rewards or motivation that are external to an activity itself, such as grades, gold stars, and prizes.

Feedback The return of information about the result of a process or activity.

Fight-or-flight response A psychological term referring to a behavioral pattern of either immediate conflict or fleeing when difficulties are encountered.

Fixed mind-set An attitude whereby students care whether they are judged smart or not smart.

Formative assessment *See* **Formative evaluation.**

Formative evaluation Evaluation used as a means of identifying a particular point of difficulty and prescribing areas in need of further work or development. It is applied in developmental or implementation stages.

Full-service schools Schools where the educational, health, psychological, and social requirements of students and their families are addressed by coordinating the services of professionals from these various disciplines at the school site.

Golden Rule The universal maxim that in our culture is stated as, "do unto others as you would have others do unto you."

"Good" school A favorable judgment made about a school based on variable criteria, such as student achievement, test scores, low delinquency, and/or school climate.

Growth mind-set An attitude whereby students care about learning and believe intellectual ability can be developed through effort and education.

Guided reflection protocol Method developed to aid teachers, alone or with colleagues, to think about their teaching practice.

Health and housing gap The disparity between poor and middle children in the quality of health care and comfortable housing available.

High performing school A place where adults and children live, grow, and learn well.

High-stakes tests The use of standardized test scores as a major determinant of significant educational outcomes, such as graduation, admission, or promotion.

Home schooling A movement that allows parents to keep their children out of regular public or private school and to educate them in the home.

Human perfectibility The view that the human species is capable of reaching heights of achievement.

Inclusion The commitment to educate each child, to the maximum extent appropriate, in the regular school and classroom, rather than moving children with disabilities to separate classes or institutions.

Inconsequential learning Information taught by another, rather than self-discovered, which has little or no importance to the learner.

Individualized education program/plan (IEP) A management tool required for every student covered by the provisions of the **Individuals with Disabilities Education Act.** It must indicate a student's current level of performance, short- and long-term instructional objectives, services to be provided, and criteria and schedules for evaluation of progress.

Individuals with Disabilities Education Act (IDEA) Federal law passed in 1990, extending and expanding the provisions of the Education for All Handicapped Children Act of 1975.

Inservice training Training provided by a school or school district to improve the skills and competencies of its professional staff, particularly teachers.

Institutional perspective The point of view or policy position of a social entity such as a school.

Instructional scaffolding Refers to supports that teachers provide to the learner during problem solving—in the form of reminders, hints, and encouragement—to ensure successful completion of a task.

Interstate New Teacher Assessment and Support Consortium (INTASC) A project sponsored by the Council of Chief State School Officers that is identifying standards for what beginning teachers should know and be able to do.

Intrinsic motivation Motivation that comes from the satisfaction of doing something, in contrast to **extrinsic motivation,** which comes from the reward received for doing something.

Least restrictive environment (LRE) A requirement of the **Individuals with Disabilities Education Act** that students with special needs should participate in regular education programs to the extent appropriate.

Liberal democracy A form of popular government dependent on the self-maintained values of its citizenry.

Mainstreaming The practice of placing special education students in general education classes for at least part of the school day, while also providing additional services, programs, or classes as needed.

Melting pot A metaphor and historical theory that suggests that although America takes in a wide variety of peoples (races, creeds, nationalities, and classes), the process of living in this country and being an American melts away differences so that all peoples blend together.

Merit pay The system of paying teachers according to the quality of their performance, usually by means of a bonus given for meeting specific goals.

Metacognition Knowledge of your own thoughts and factors that influence your thinking.

Moral ecology The ethical balance or pattern needed to maintain a society.

Multicultural education An approach to education intended to recognize cultural diversity and foster the cultural enrichment of all children and youth.

Multiple intelligences theory A theory of human intelligence advanced by Howard Gardner, which suggests that humans have the psychobiological potential to solve problems or to fashion products that are valued in at least one cultural context. Gardner's research indicates at least eight and maybe nine separate faculties.

A Nation at Risk: The Imperative for Educational Reform A highly influential 1983 national commission report calling for extensive education reform, including more academic course requirements, more stringent college entrance requirements, upgraded and updated textbooks, and longer school days and years.

National Board for Professional Teaching Standards (NBPTS) A professional agency that is setting voluntary standards for what experienced teachers should know and be able to do in more than thirty different teaching areas.

National Commission on Teaching and America's Future Blue-ribbon panel that in 1996 released the report *What Matters Most: Teaching for America's Future.* The report emphasized the importance of high-quality teaching and recommended the National Board certification of 105,000 teachers by the year 2006.

National Council for Accreditation of Teacher Education (NCATE) Nationally recognized organization awarding voluntary accreditation to college-level teacher education programs. Approximately 600 colleges and universities in the United States are accredited through NCATE.

National Education Association (NEA) The nation's largest teachers' association, founded in 1857 and having a membership of over 2.2 million educators.

Nature-based approach Basing education strategies upon a research-driven, biological understanding of human learning.

No Child Left Behind Act The most recent reauthorization, in 2001, of the Elementary and Secondary Education Act, the federal government's single largest investment in elementary and secondary education, including Title I.

Parallel teaching A situation in which support personnel (such as a special educator or Title I teacher) and the classroom teacher rotate among heterogeneous groups of students in different sections of the general education classroom.

Paraprofessional A trained aide who assists a professional, such as a teacher's aide.

Pedagogy The art or profession of teaching.

Pedagogic caring Instruction with a strong component of consideration for the total world of the learner.

Peer coaching A method by which teachers help one another learn new teaching strategies and material. It often involves release time to allow teachers to visit one another's classes as they start to use new programs, such as **cooperative learning.**

Performance assessment A form of assessment that requires students to actually perform, such as writing or drawing, to demonstrate the knowledge or skill being measured.

Physical indicators of child abuse Physical symptoms that suggest a child is being abused.

Plagiarism An act or instance of passing off the ideas or words of another as one's own without crediting the source.

Professional development Continuous advances in teacher's knowledge and skills; lifelong learning.

Progressive school A school that focuses on students' personal and social development. *See* **progressivism.**

Progressivism (progressive ideals) An educational philosophy that embraces largely unstructured educational programs, focusing on implicit teaching and individualized instruction.

Readiness A judgment that a student is capable of learning a specific topic or skill.

Reading gap The difference between the amount of time spent reading and the quality of reading material to which poor and middle-class children are exposed; disparities in performance on reading assessments between poor and middle-class children.

Reciprocal teaching An instructional technique in which the teacher and students take turns leading small-group discussions. First, the teacher models questioning strategies, and then the students gradually assume the teaching role, following the model of the teacher.

Reflective practitioner An individual who has established the habit of reviewing his or her performance in order to continually improve practice.

Restructuring The process of change demanded of schools which consistently fail to meet state standards for students' achievement.

Role model gap The disparity between poor and middle-class children in availability of successful, achieving adults.

Rubric A set of rules for scoring student products or student performance. Typically takes the form of a checklist or a rating scale.

School choice Allowing parents to select alternative educational programs for their children, either within a given school or among different schools.

Self-discovered learning Private truths that each individual has personally uncovered and assimilated into his or her consciousness.

Social justice The concept of doing away with social and economic inequalities for those in our society who have been denied these benefits of a democratic society.

Social reconstruction Desired goal of progressive education's focus on teaching the child to function in the community.

Socially equitable An environment which is democratic and fair, and which provides every student with high-quality teachers, resources, and learning opportunities.

Standard Exemplary performance that serves as a benchmark.

Standards-based education *See* **Standard** and **Standards movement.**

Standards-based reform *See* **Standards movement.**

Standards movement Efforts at the local, state, and federal level to make clear exactly what students need to know and be able to do and, therefore, what schools need to teach. Implicit in the standards movement is an attempt to increase the academic achievement of students.

Summative assessment *See* **Summative evaluation.**

Summative evaluation Evaluation used to assess the adequacy or outcome of a program after the program has been fully developed and implemented.

Supportive teaching A situation in an inclusive classroom in which the classroom teacher takes the lead role, and support personnel rotate among the students.

Teacher competencies The characteristics that make a teacher qualified to do the job, including various areas of subject-matter expertise and a wide range of personality variables. Some school reform proposals urge that teachers undergo periodic assessment of their competencies to maintain licensure or earn incentives.

Teacher expectations A teacher's preconceptions about how a given student will behave or perform.

Teacher-proof curriculum A pejorative term for educational materials which stand on their own, needing little or no mediation from a teacher.

Teaching portfolio Collection of such items as research papers, pupil evaluations, teaching units, and videocassettes of lessons to reflect the quality of a teacher's teaching. Portfolios can be used to illustrate to employers the teacher's expertise or to obtain national board certification.

Test-driven accountability The national movement to ensure that schools are meeting state-set standards through regular testing for students' achievement of academic goals.

Title I (Chapter 1) Part of the 1965 Elementary and Secondary Education Act that delivers federal funds to local school districts and schools for the education of students from low-income families. It also supplements the educational services provided to low-achieving students in those districts.

Traditional school A school that seeks to transmit to its students the best knowledge, skills, and values in society.

Transfer of learning Connection or application of learned material to future knowledge or skill acquisition.

Transformative intellectual An individual with the capacity and habit of mind to rise above the social and intellectual constraints of one's society and critically analyze his or her situation.

Values Principles or qualities we like or believe to be good or desirable. Certain concepts, such as responsibility, justice, fairness, and caring, are frequently mentioned as values that form the basis of civil life and morality.

Voucher programs A type of **school choice** plan that gives parents a receipt or written statement that they can exchange for the schooling they feel is most desirable for their child. The school, in turn, can cash in its received vouchers for the money to pay teachers and buy resources.

Whole language   A progressive approach to the teaching of reading that emphasizes the integration of language arts skills and knowledge across the curriculum.

Wikis   A website that allows visitors to add, remove, edit, and change content, typically without the need for registration.

Zero-tolerance policies   School policies calling for automatic suspension or expulsion of students who bring forbidden items, such as drugs or weapons, to school, or who engage in forbidden behavior while at school.

Zone of proximal development   A range of tasks that a person cannot do alone yet but can accomplish when assisted by a more skilled partner. This zone is the point at which instruction can succeed and real learning is possible.

How We Treat One Another in School

The Association for Supervision and Curriculum Development is a worldwide community of educators advocating sound policies and sharing best practices to achieve the success of each learner. To learn more, visit ASCD at **www.ascd.org.**

The Perils and Promises of Praise

The Association for Supervision and Curriculum Development is a worldwide community of educators advocating sound policies and sharing best practices to achieve the success of each learner. To learn more, visit ASCD at **www.ascd.org.**

The Core Knowledge Curriculum—What's Behind Its Success?

E.D. Hirsch, Jr. is Chairman of the Board of the Core Knowledge Foundation, 810 East High Street, Charlottesville, VA 22902; **www.coreknowledge.org.** From E.D. Hirsch, Jr., "Seeking Breadth and Depth in the Curriculum," Educational Leadership, October 2001, pp. 22-25. Reprinted with permission of The Core Knowledge Foundation.

Seven Practices for Effective Learning

The Association for Supervision and Curriculum Development is a worldwide community of educators advocating sound policies and sharing best practices to achieve the success of each learner. To learn more, visit ASCD at **www.ascd.org.**

The Courage to Be Constructivist

The Association for Supervision and Curriculum Development is a worldwide community of educators advocating sound policies and sharing best practices to achieve the success of each learner. To learn more, visit ASCD at **www.ascd.org.**

Orchestrating Multiple Intelligences

The Association for Supervision and Curriculum Development is a worldwide community of educators advocating sound policies and sharing best practices to achieve the success of each learner. To learn more, visit ASCD at **www.ascd.org.**

Linking Formative Assessment to Scaffolding

The Association for Supervision and Curriculum Development is a worldwide community of educators advocating sound policies and sharing best practices to achieve the success of each learner. To learn more, visit ASCD at **www.ascd.org.**

Putting Money Where It Matters

The Association for Supervision and Curriculum Development is a worldwide community of educators advocating sound policies and sharing best practices to achieve the success of each learner. To learn more, visit ASCD at **www.ascd.org.**

The Overdominance of Computers

The Association for Supervision and Curriculum Development is a worldwide community of educators advocating sound policies and sharing best practices to achieve the success of each learner. To learn more, visit ASCD at **www.ascd.org.**